Educational
Psychology

Educational
Psychology

Readings for the Canadian Context

edited by
Shelagh Towson

broadview press

Cataloguing in Publication Data

Main entry under title:
 Educational psychology

ISBN   0-921149-21-2

1.   Educational psychology.
I.   Towson, Shelagh M.J.

       LB1051.E38   1992   370.15   C92-093420-X

broadview press   OR   broadview press
P.O. Box 1243   269 Portage Rd.
Peterborough, Ontario   Lewiston, NY
K9J 7H5   Canada   14092   USA

printed in Canada

Table of Contents

Introduction

A traditional function of the introduction to a book of readings is an attempt to justify the book's existence. Why a book of educational psychology readings when there are many excellent textbooks available? And why a book of Canadian readings? Aren't principles of learning and teaching the same regardless of geographical location? The answer to the first question has to do with my notion of what makes a good educational psychology course. In addition to their mastery of facts, I want my students to grapple with some of the issues that have influenced educational psychology theory and research over the past several decades. Why do educators advocate mainstreaming some students and segregating others? To what extent is our approach to education guided by an underlying conviction that heredity—or environment—can explain most of the differences that exist among students? Does multiculturalism mean teaching everyone in their first language or should we use English (or French) as the medium of instruction and find other ways to celebrate cultural diversity? Textbooks can summarize current concerns in educational psychology, but my students seem able to understand and discuss these concerns more easily if they start with a concrete example, the kind provided through the reading of a particular study about a particular group of students in a clearly defined context. I also believe students should have some understanding of the process involved in reaching the conclusions reported in their textbooks. Although my students are not expected to become intimately involved with research methods and statistical analyses, reading the articles in this book should give them at least a nodding acquaintance with these components of psychology. Finally, textbooks tend to underemphasize the indeterminacy of research findings. Reading actual studies can give students a better sense that science, including educational psychology, involves the posing of questions as much as the provision of answers.

As for the justification for a book of Canadian readings, I have little doubt that laboratory rats in the United States behave much the same as Canadian rats—or rats in France or England or Zimbabwe. But students and teachers are a different matter. Although we share a common border, Canada differs from the United States, in obvious and more subtle ways. Just for example, there are fewer of us, our ethnic, cultural, language and religious mix is different, and we have different political and health care systems and different attitudes and laws regarding capital punishment and gun control. As compared to the United States, our educational systems are characterized by relatively more provincial and relatively less federal authority and by more complex and diverse relationships with religious denominations. And of course, Canada has two official languages. What difference do these differences make for educational psychology? There is no simple answer to that question, and this book does not attempt to provide one. Rather, it is hoped that students reading this book will get a sense of what learning and teaching look like in the Canadian context, as opposed to the more abstract and general picture provided by books in which most of the research has been conducted somewhere else. I am also enough of a nationalist that I would like Canadian university students to realize that researchers working in Canada are making significant contributions to educational psychology research.

In fact, until I began to look for suitable articles for this book, I had no idea of just how productive Canadian researchers have been. Although my literature search was limited to articles published since 1986, Canadian authors had contributed several hundred articles to relevant journals. The 32 articles included in this book were chosen on the basis of several criteria. First, some excellent articles were eliminated because their theoretical and/or methodological complexity would have made them very difficult for undergraduates to read and understand. Second, given the desire for concrete examples of research, most of the articles are reports of field studies and field and laboratory experiments rather than literature reviews or theoretical papers. Finally, I tried to select articles that would give students a sense of the diversity of educational experience and the breadth of research talent in Canada. The subjects of the articles included in this book are students from all regions of Canada, ranging in age from 3 to 49 and attending every kind of school from day care to university. The authors of these articles come from everywhere in Canada except the Northwest Territories, the Yukon and Prince Edward Island. (And one of the articles includes Prince Edward Island in its title!)

I learned a great deal compiling these articles and gained new respect for my colleagues. I do hope that you enjoy reading this book as much as I enjoyed putting it together.

Teacher Characteristics

The three articles in this section summarize the "life cycle" of a teacher. In their study, Violato and Travis explored the first stage of that cycle, the decision to enter the teaching profession, with a survey of students enroled in education programmes at ten Canadian universities. Their results suggest that Canadian, American and British teachers are similar in some ways. For example, teaching in all three countries is an avenue of upward social mobility, especially for men. On the other hand, more Canadian than American prospective teachers chose teaching as a career for its material benefits, and Canadian students probably differed from their American counterparts in terms of the percentage who classified themselves as socialist in political orientation. Perhaps most interesting, a significant proportion of the education students in the Violato and Travis study had found reading difficult as children, still didn't like reading very much and, in fact, did not read very often.

After receiving some sort of training, teachers then begin to teach and, as we all know from personal experience, some teachers are good and some are not. Murray, Rushton and Paunonen examined the relationship between colleague ratings of personality characteristics, and student ratings of effectiveness for 46 university psychology teachers. The results indicated that personality traits and teaching effectiveness are related, but that the personality traits that make a good teacher in one kind of class are not the same as those which make a good teacher in another kind of class. The university teachers in this study had somewhat more freedom than secondary or elementary school teachers to choose the kind of classes they would teach. Perhaps some of the bad elementary and secondary school teachers we remember would have been better at a different grade level, with a different subject or with different kinds of students.

A third career stage experienced by an increasing number of teachers is burnout, the inability to function effectively as a result of job-related stress. Burnout encompasses feelings of emotional exhaustion, the depersonalization of other people and an increased sense of dissatisfaction with one's accomplishments. In her study of elementary, intermediate, secondary, and university teachers, Byrne found that the background factors of teacher gender and age and type of student taught contributed significantly to various aspects of burnout. For example, female elementary and university teachers reported more emotional exhaustion than men, but male secondary school teachers had higher levels of depersonalization than women. Different factors produced different levels of burnout at different levels in the educational system. However, all teachers reported that organizational factors related to the administration of their respective educational institutions contributed significantly to the levels of stress they experienced.

A National Study of Education Students: Some Data on Background, Habits, and Reasons for Entering Education

Claudio Violato
University of Calgary
LeRoy D. Travis
University of British Columbia

A sample of 583 education students from ten Canadian universities responded anonymously to a questionnaire on their backgrounds, habits and outlooks. Their reports of family background; religiosity and political identification; reading history, habits and orientation; coursework and education status; and their expressed reasons for pursuing a teaching career showed: (1) their socio-economic backgrounds were representative of the broader Canadian society, although slightly advantaged; (2) women were more privileged than men; (3) most students were offspring of parents who had not attended university, and their expectations of social interaction and material benefits led the list of reasons for entering education; (4) persons in the sample had a conventional political and religious orientation; (5) their patterns of reading and mass media use indicated that few were interested in or attached to "high" cultural pursuits and preferred mass commercial culture; (6) many in this sample of education students (especially men) recalled protracted difficulties with reading, and the sample as a whole was noticeably non-bookish.

*   *   *

LORTIE'S OPINION THAT "WE KNOW NEXT TO NOTHING ABOUT THE FLOW OF people into teaching" (1973, p. 486) is nearly as true today as it was 15 years ago (Feiman-Nemser & Floden, 1986). Empirical evidence about the background, habits, and outlook of entrants to teaching is very limited and narrow (Lortie, 1986; Schalock, 1979). In Canada little has been added to our first papers on this topic (Travis, 1979b, 1983; Travis & Violato, 1981; 1985).

Teaching has become what Jacoby (1983) calls "a decultured trade" (p. 160). A renewed and urgent interest in teacher quality (Gallup, 1986; Lortie, 1986) has led government bodies, foundations, and universities to

The authors wish to acknowledge grants from the Social Sciences and Humanities Research Council and the British Columbia Department of Labour in aid of this research.

examine the quality of teachers and teacher preparation programs (Berliner, 1983; McQuaid, 1984). We should thus anticipate changes in teacher education (Cogan, 1975; Zumwalt, 1982). Knowledge about the nature and circumstances of those who would be teachers may be critical to ensure these changes are rational and sensible.

Researchers' interest in teacher quality is not new (Barzun, 1954; Conant, 1963; Waller, 1932). By 1963, however, Getzels and Jackson concluded that despite massive research on teacher personality since the 1930s, virtually nothing had been discovered about what personal qualities make a "good" teacher. Getzels and Jackson's evaluation effected a moratorium on this line of research. Potential predictors of teaching success that were studied include intelligence, academic achievement, previous experience with children; knowledge of principles and procedures to be used in conveying knowledge to others; skills of teaching as assessed in micro-teaching, physical characteristics; letters of recommendation, photographs, professional course marks, ratings on student teaching, and more. This research has been fruitless (Schalock, 1979)—no crucial variables have been linked to teacher "effectiveness." Considering the variety and complexity of endeavours denoted by "teaching" (Collini, 1987; Hearne, 1987; Norris, 1987; Stokes, 1987); the superficiality (Bruner, 1983, p. 183) and insistent credulity (Sharpe, 1978, p. 191) that conventionally attend "applications" of "theory" (Murray, 1984, pp. 6-17); and the conceptual and methodological muddles typical of so-called "effectiveness" research, this failure is unsurprising (Travis, 1987). We require a better understanding of the social structure of schools and of their culture, and of the culture and characteristics of teachers. Unfortunately, as Lortie (1973) observed, "the social structure, social psychology and culture of schools and teachers remain largely unknown" (p. 493). This still rings true.

Even so, some important studies of teachers and prospective teachers have been published. These include the National Education Association's (NEA) national surveys of American teachers (1961, 1967, 1972). In Britain, Lomax (1972), Crocker (1974) and Wilson et al. (1984) made contributions. However, this foreign work is of limited use to Canadians, and is somewhat dated and narrow in scope.

Even Lortie's (1975) fine study is limited in several ways (Pedersen & Fleming, 1979). Its data, collected during 1963 and 1964, are stale. Further, Lortie did not distinguish between elementary and secondary school teachers on important characteristics such as their reasons for becoming teachers. His own data are based on a small sample ($N=94$); he usually presents them in a statistical form that prevents the reader from making an independent interpretation. And like the NEA surveys, Lortie's work is in any case American.

The value of these other studies arises from what they suggest for research. "Basic demographic and personal characteristic variables have proved time and again in survey research to account for large proportions of attitudinal variance; we have yet to 'map' the general outlines of teacher viewpoints and relate them to basic social variables" (Lortie, 1975, p. 490). The search for a few crucial variables to predict success at teaching is therefore unrealistic; "it is as if we were trying to chart a particular acreage without a map of the general terrain" (Lortie, 1975, p. 493). The present paper pertains to the Canadian landscape but is not as limited in focus as the earlier works.

An earlier Canadian study (Bulcock, Mercer, Quinlan, & Sullivan, 1973) focused solely on women teachers in Newfoundland. A second by the Canadian Teachers' Federation (1981) provided no data on teacher qualities although it dealt with class size, salaries, and teaching load. Even the CSSE Yearbook on *The Education of Teachers in Canada* (MacIver, 1978) contained no information about who was being described. Accordingly, Canadians studying teacher characteristics often use the scanty American data.

Our study aims to enhance understanding of the background, habits, and outlooks of Canadian education students and of their expressed reasons for entry into teaching. It contributes to a "map of the general terrain" in Canada.

Method

Subjects

We drew a non-probability (volunteer) sample of subjects from students enrolled in teacher preparation programs at ten Canadian universities (Victoria, British Columbia, Alberta, Saskatchewan, Regina, Lakehead, Western Ontario, McGill, Dalhousie, and Mount Allison). The total sample of 583 included 217 men (37.2%) and 366 women (62.8%) enrolled in both pre-baccalaureate programs (B.Ed.) and post-baccalaureate programs. Three hundred and fifty-two subjects (60.4%) were studying for their first degree while 231 (39.6%) held at least one degree (see Table 1).

Subjects ranged in age from 18 to 49 years with a mean age of 23.4 years ($SD=5.04$; mode$=20$). One hundred and seventy-four (29.8%) were 20 or younger; 284 (48.7%) were between 21 and 25; and 125 (21.4%) were 26 or older. Four hundred and forty-seven, or more than three-fourths of the sample (76.7%) were single; 120 (20.6%) were married; and 2.3% ($n=16$) were "other" (divorced, widowed). Other characteristics of this sample have been reported previously (Travis, 1979b, 1983; Travis & Violato, 1981, 1985).

TABLE 1

Educational Status, Types of Degrees Held, and Field of Specialization

Part A: Educational Status of Subjects (N=583)

	Male		Female		Total	
	N	percent	N	percent	N	percent
Junior (years 1 and 2)	37	23.6	120	76.4	157	26.9
Senior (years 3, 4, and 5)	54	27.7	141	72.3	195	33.4
Post-Baccalaureate	126	54.5	105	45.5	231	39.6

Part B: Types of Degrees Held (n=231)

Bachelors	N	Percent	Advanced	N	Percent
B.A.	140	60.6	M.A.	4	57.1
B.Sc.	36	15.6	Ph.D.	3	42.9
B.P.E.	47	20.3			
Other	8	4.5			
Total	231	39.6	Total	7	1.2

Part C: Fields of Specialization of Degree Holders

Field	N	Percent
Humanities	96	39.8
Life Sciences	56	23.2
Physical Education	47	19.5
Physics, Math, Chemistry	19	7.9
Fine Arts	9	3.7
Other	14	5.9
Total	241*	100

*Some of the 231 degree holders had credentials for more than one subject.

Procedures

Questionnaires were mailed to university contacts (faculty members) who administered them to the subjects during the 1977-1978, 1978-1979, and 1979-1980 academic sessions according to standardized procedures that included guarantees of anonymity.

The Questionnaire

The questionnaire had a variety of item types (open-ended, multiple choice, yes-no, rank order, and checklists) designed to gather data on respondents' background, habits, and outlooks. We considered especially subjects' educational background, political orientation and religiosity, family of origin, and stated reasons for entering education.

Results

Subjects' Status and Educational Background

More than one third of our sample (39.6%; $n=231$) held at least one degree; a greater proportion of men (58.1%) than women (28.7%) held degrees. Subjects' educational status, types of degrees held, and field of specialization appear in Table 1.

COURSES

The respondents indicated the number of courses they had taken in various subject areas. The number and percentages of respondents who had taken at least one course in each of the following areas were: psychology ($n=525$; 90.1%); history ($n=403$; 69.1%); sociology ($n=339$; 58.1%); economics ($n=126$; 21.6%); and political science ($n=121$; 20.8%). Psychology was the most widely taken subject; least frequent were economics and political science. Nearly half of the sample ($n=265$; 45.4%) had taken at least one course in the teaching of reading, and nearly all of these students were prospective elementary school teachers.

READING PROBLEMS AND ENJOYMENT

Subjects were asked to report their memories of reading in their early years at school. Nearly a quarter of the sample reported either vivid (11.7%; $n=65$) or vague (12.5%; $n=73$) memories of difficulties with reading, and only 41.5% ($n=242$) indicated that reading was easy and enjoyable. From these data, subjects were classified into one of two groups: those with early reading difficulties ($n=138$; 23.7%) and those without difficulties ($n=324$; 55.6%). Significantly more men than women reported reading difficulties ($X^2=6.56$; $df=1$; $p<.05$).

CURRENT ORIENTATION TO LEISURE READING

Nearly 83% ($n=484$; 82.6%) of the sample reported that they read infrequently; 37.2% ($n=187$) reported that they never read during leisure time, and more men (51.2%) than women (32.7%) indicated that they did no reading. One hundred and seventeen (20.1%) indicated that they were indifferent to or disliked reading. Over 80% of those who read in leisure time chose material that is culturally and intellectually unsubstantial (for example, *T.V. Guide, People*). Further analysis showed that 58.3% of the sample considered television their main source, or one of their two main sources, of "adequate and reliable information" about what happens in the world—though it has been demonstrated that television paints an inaccurate picture of world affairs (Lapham, 1981).

TABLE 2
Parental Occupation, Educational Background, and Reading Habits

	Mother		Father		Socio-economic class based on father's occupation
	N	%	N	%	
Occupational Category					
Physicians, lawyers, dentists	1	0.2	17	2.9	
Teachers, professors	56	9.6	38	6.5	Professional/
Social workers, nurses	41	7.0	6	1.0	managerial
Professional (not specified)	16	2.8	73	12.5	n=213 (36.5%)
Managerial	6	1.0	79	13.6	
Private business	15	2.6	51	8.7	Entrepreneurial
Farmers, fishermen	3	0.5	70	12.0	n=121 (20.7%)
Skilled work	20	3.4	115	19.8	Skilled labour
Police, military, jail guards	2	0.3	24	4.1	n=139 (23.9%)
Non-skilled work	29	5.0	71	12.2	Unskilled labour
Clerical workers	106	18.2	21	3.6	n=92 (15.8%)
Homemakers	263	45.1	—	—	
Attended University					
Yes	83	14.2	125	21.4	
No	489	83.8	448	76.8	
Frequency of Reading					
Every day	271	46.5	297	50.9	High (Father)
Several times per week	146	25.0	126	21.6	n=423 (72.5%)
Occasional/irregular	92	15.8	79	13.6	
Rarely	39	6.7	43	8.1	Low (Father)
Never	8	1.4	11	1.9	n=133 (23.6%)

Nature of the Family of Origin

Subjects' reports about their parents' occupation, education, and reading
habits are summarized in Table 2. These data show that nearly half of
the mothers were not employed outside the home (homemakers), while
the largest maternal occupation group was clerical. Most fathers were in
the skilled work category (licensed workers such as plumbers or electri-
cians). On the basis of father's occupation, subjects were classified into
one of four socio-economic classes (see Table 2): (1) professional/mana-
gerial, (2) entrepreneurial, (3) skilled labour, and (4) unskilled labour.

Some 39.7% of our sample came from lower socio-economic strata
(skilled and unskilled labour). This is remarkably similar to the situation in
Britain (Lomax, 1972) and in the United States: the 1961 national survey
of American teachers showed that 37.6% came from families where the
father was employed in skilled or unskilled labour occupations, and in 1971
the same group represented 39.6% of American teachers (NEA, 1972).
Lortie (1975, p. 35) wrote that "teaching is clearly white-collar, middle

class work, and as such offers upward mobility for people who grew up in blue-collar or lower-class families." Our respondents from the two lowest socio-economic strata may therefore change their social status by becoming teachers. This is not to say that cultural elevation accompanies status elevation.

In our sample, just as was seen in the United States and Britain (Lortie, 1975; NEA, 1967, 1972; Lomax, 1972), teaching is a more important medium of upward mobility for men than for women. There are notable differences in the socio-economic class of men and women ($X^2 = 12.02$; $df = 3$; $p < .01$; see Table 3). Of the women, 64.1% belonged to either the professional/managerial or entrepreneurial classes while only 52.2% of the men did so; 35.9% of women were in the skilled or unskilled labour designations while 47.9% of the men were also in this group. Moreover, disproportionate numbers of women, compared to men, had fathers who had attended university ($X^2 = 6.80$; $df = 1$; $p < .01$). These findings suggest that the social rank of teaching recruits differentially among men and women.

TABLE 3

Sample Proportions (%) for Each Bifurcated Variable in Each Occupational Class

Variable		Father's occupation[a]				X^{2b}
		Prof/man	Ent	Skl	Uskl	
1. Sex	Male	31.7	20.5	25.9	22.0	12.02**
	Female	37.0	27.1	24.0	11.9	
2. Income-producing property	Yes	24.3	51.4	16.7	7.6	77.73**
	No	38.1	14.8	28.3	18.8	
3. Father's birth origin	Canadian	38.1	25.6	24.4	11.9	14.82**
	Non-Canadian	27.8	22.8	25.3	24.1	
4. Mother's birth origin	Canadian	37.7	27.4	22.5	12.4	17.16**
	Non-Canadian	29.9	18.8	26.0	25.3	
5. Father's university attendance	Yes	76.0	16.5	4.1	3.4	120.63**
	No	23.4	27.1	30.4	19.2	
6. Mother's university attendance	Yes	55.1	15.4	23.1	6.4	18.81**
	No	31.6	26.1	25.0	17.3	
7. Father's reading frequency	High	37.1	26.3	23.8	12.8	10.15*
	Low	27.4	22.2	28.2	22.2	
8. Mother's reading frequency	High	38.0	25.6	23.1	13.4	9.68*
	Low	25.8	25.0	27.3	22.0	
9. Subject's reading difficulty	No	36.2	25.6	24.1	14.1	10.06*
	Yes	27.1	21.5	29.1	22.3	

[a] Prof/man = professional/managerial; Ent = Entrepreneurial; Skl = Skilled labour; Uskl = Unskilled labour

More than three fourths of the fathers (76.8%) and mothers (83.8%) had not attended university (see Table 2). Only 28 respondents (4.8%) had parents who both attended university. Since for 70.5% neither parent had attended university, the large majority of our sample are first-generation university attenders. The educational and cultural implications of this deserve close attention and reflection. Nearly all parents who *had* attended university were in the professional, managerial, or entrepreneurial classes, and they tended to have similar educational backgrounds.

Respondents were asked to report their parents' reading habits (Table 2). Some 423 subjects (72.5%) indicated that their fathers read every day or several times per week ("High") while 133 subjects (23.6%) indicated that their fathers read irregularly, rarely, or never ("Low"). University-educated fathers read more frequently than non-university-educated fathers ($X^2=25.78$; $df=2$; $p<.001$) as did university-educated mothers compared with mothers who did not attend ($X^2=15.46$; $df=2$; $p<.001$). Reading habits of parents tended to be similar within families.

Data on the number of children and subjects' ordinal position in the family were also collected. The number of children per family ranged from 1 to 13 with a mean of 3.8 ($SD=1.88$; mode$=4$), which is almost identical to the national Canadian mean (3.9) for the time period 1955-1960, when most of the present subjects were born (Urquhart & Buckley, 1965, p. 38). Nearly one third of our sample (32.6%, $n=190$) were eldest children.

Of the total sample, 25.7% ($n=150$) reported that their parents owned "income-producing property" while 74.3% ($n=433$) said they did not. As might be expected, there was a correlation between ownership of such property and father's occupation, with most property-owners being entrepreneurs ($X^2=77.73$; $df=3$; $p<.001$; see Table 3).

Finally, we collected data on the citizenship and ethnicity of the subjects and their parents. The vast majority (92.6%; $n=561$) of the subjects were Canadian citizens. Most of the fathers ($n=410$; 70.3%) and mothers ($n=407$; 60.8%) were Canadian-born. Of the foreign-born parents, 67 fathers (38.7%) were born in Britain or the United States, as were 54 mothers (33.1%); 82 fathers (47.2%) and 83 mothers (50.9%) were born in continental Europe; 21 fathers (12.1%) and 24 mothers (14.7%) were born in Asia, Latin America, or Africa; and 3 fathers (1.7%) and 2 mothers (1.2%) were born elsewhere. Foreign-born fathers were overrepresented in skilled or non-skilled labour occupations, while they were underrepresented in professional, managerial, or entrepreneurial occupations ($X^2=14.82$; $df=3$; $p<.01$; see Table 3).

Table 3 summarizes the notable socio-economic differences in the sample. General patterns are apparent. Lower socio-economic subjects tend to be male, with foreign-born parents who did not attend university and who read little. Subjects' memories of reading difficulties are also associated with socio-economic class; less privileged men most frequently reported difficulties ($X^2 = 10.06$; $df = 3$; $p < .05$; Table 3). Multivariate discriminant analyses also showed that lower class men (who were predominantly in elementary programs) were a distinct group as described above (Wilks' lambda = .69; approximate $F = 12.17$; $p < .001$), although these characteristics were not, of course, unique to this group.

Political Orientation and Religiosity

Subjects indicated their generic political orientation. The number and percentages in each category were as follows: 114 (19.6%) conservative; 172 (28.5%) liberal; 122 (20.9%) socialist; 14 (2.4%) radical socialist; 20 (3.4%) anarchist; 45 (7.7%) apolitical or non-political; and 96 (16.4%) "other." More than half—317 (55.7%)—considered themselves religious, and 309 (53.7%) said they had formal religious affiliations. There were no sex differences in religiosity or political orientation.

For further analyses, subjects were classified as Conventionals (conservatives, liberals) or Socialists (socialists, radical socialists) based on self-reported political orientation. Slightly less than half (49.1%) were classified as Conventionals. Several differences by political orientation emerged. First, self-proclaimed religiosity showed Conventionals were more religious than Socialists ($X^2 = 5.51$; $df = 1$; $p < .05$). Second, older (aged 24 or more) more than younger (23 years or less) subjects tended to be Socialist ($X^2 = 9.52$; $df = 1$; $p < .01$). Third, subjects with foreign-born fathers were more often Socialist than those who had Canadian-born fathers ($X^2 = 5.04$; $df = 1$; $p < .05$). And, fourth, subjects from families that had income-producing property were more often Conventional than those whose families did not ($X^2 = 4.98$; $df = 1$; $p < .05$). Thus younger more privileged subjects tended to be more Conventional (and religious) than older less privileged subjects.

Reasons for Entering Education

Subjects were asked, "Why do you want to be a teacher?" Responses fell into 15 categories, and these were subsequently classified as belonging to one of five themes: interpersonal, service, continuation, material benefits, and time flexibility. Both Lortie (1975) and the NEA surveys (1967, 1972) found that these are the general attractors to teaching.

The interpersonal theme is a consequence of teachers' opportunity to work with people. Lortie (1975) pointed out that the highest-ranked occupations (high government office, learned professions) involve social exchanges; thus for some people, an occupation where one "works with people" has an aura of prestige and dignity. The service theme posits teaching as a valuable service of special moral worth. "Continuation" refers to a desire to remain in a school setting or to an interest in a subject (for example, literature) by which it is difficult to earn a living. Material benefits include money, prestige or status, and employment security. Finally, time flexibility (for instance, summer and holiday breaks) attracts some people to teaching.

Table 4 shows respondents' thematic reasons for entering teaching, along with sex and program differences associated with particular reasons. The following reasons, given by small proportions of the sample, could not be classified under one of the five themes: "didn't know what else to do" (2.1%), "not sure I want to be a teacher" (0.7%), "always wanted to be a teacher" (2.3%), and "it is a route to self-improvement" (2.1%).

TABLE 4

Percentages Nominating Each Theme as Attracting Subjects to Teaching, and Chi-Square Statistics for Sex and Program Differences for Each Theme

Themes	Total sample (N=583)	Elementary			Secondary			Program differences		
		Male	Female	X^2	Male	Female	X^2	Male X^2	Female X^2	Total X^2
Interpersonal	43.6	45.2	47.5	0.07**	32.7	47.3	3.85*	2.75	0.00	2.50
Material benefits	32.4	47.3	28.8	9.67**	29.9	30.1	0.00	5.68*	0.01	0.64
Continuation	23.2	10.8	20.6	3.86*	31.8	33.3	0.01	11.62**	5.37*	14.18**
Service	22.5	18.3	17.9	0.00	31.8	25.8	0.60	4.09*	2.20	8.34**
Time flexibility	9.8	6.5	6.6	0.00	13.1	16.1	0.17	1.75	6.34*	8.44**

[a]Yates corrected Chi-Square for 2 x 2 contingency tables.
*$p<.05$
**$p<.01$

The interpersonal theme was nominated by the largest proportion of the sample, with material benefits second, continuation third, service fourth, and time flexibility fifth. (The total exceeds 100% because subjects could, and some did, give more than one reason.) Clearly, both teaching's social nature and its perceived material benefits attract many (76% of our sample). However, there are notable sex and program differences in expressed motives. Although the interpersonal theme is not linked to sex differences in the elementary program nor to overall program differences, secondary women stressed the interpersonal theme more than did secondary men. Moreover, men in the elementary program favoured material benefits more than did females in the elementary program and more than both men and women in the secondary program. This greater concern for material rewards comes from the large proportion of men among prospective elementary school teachers, men from homes characterized by economic insecurity and low social status (Lortie, 1975; NEA, 1967, 1972). Our study further supports this interpretation in that men tended to come from comparatively less privileged circumstances than did women (see Table 3).

Men in elementary education programs placed significantly less emphasis on the continuation theme ("pass on knowledge" and "interest in the subject matter") than did other respondents. Not surprisingly, there were also overall program differences: both men and women in secondary programs emphasized continuation more than did people in elementary education. The significance of subject matter is less appreciated by people bound for elementary work.

In the service theme ("important work," "influence others"), there are no within-program sex differences, but there are overall program differences: secondary men emphasize this theme more than do elementary men (women do not differ across programs). Finally, the overall program differences show secondary women students value time flexibility more than do other students.

In sum, the interpersonal theme figures prominently in all groups but appeals slightly less to secondary men. The attraction of material benefits was strongest for elementary men, who were also relatively less attracted to the continuation theme. Both men and women in secondary programs found continuation more attractive than did their elementary counterparts. Service was more attractive to secondary men, while secondary women put more emphasis on time flexibility.

These interpretations were supported by multivariate discriminant analyses that revealed that continuation provided the greatest discrimination between gender and program (Wilks' lambda$= .97$; approximate $F = 6.39$; $p < .001$), and the interpersonal theme provided minimal discrimination.

Discussion

In our study of the backgrounds, habits, and outlooks of Canadian education students, we emphasized two basic categories of variables: first, salient background features of social status, ethnicity, and parental educational example and reading; second, students' political attachments, religiosity, reading habits, and motives for choosing teaching as an occupation.

In exploring the "culture of teaching" (Feiman-Nemser & Floden, 1986) in the tradition of Waller (1932) and Lortie (1975), we looked for important characteristics of prospective teachers. Except for its slight upward bias, our sample resembles a social cross-section of the general Canadian population. In the 1978 Canadian census (Statistics Canada, 1981, p. 271), for example, 23% of the population belonged to the professional or managerial group, 29% to the entrepreneurial group, 20% to the skilled labour group, and 28% to the unskilled labour group. In our sample, there was a slight overrepresentation from the professional and managerial groups and a similar underrepresentation from the unskilled labour group (see Table 2). American teachers also come close to representing a cross-section of the American public but with a slight upward bias (NEA, 1963, 1972).

The sexes differed in socio-economic background. Considered alone, men were 31.7% from the professional and managerial groups, 20.5% from the entrepreneurial group, 25.9% from the skilled labour group, and 22.0% from the unskilled labour group. This distribution resembles the Canadian population more than does the total sample. Fewer men than women from relatively privileged socio-economic circumstances see teaching as an attractive option (Lortie, 1975); the social mobility factor in teaching is more important to men than to women. This interpretation is supported by the fact that men were more attracted by the material benefits of teaching than were women (see Table 4).

Perhaps marriage has been a more viable mechanism of social mobility for women than for men—women typically marry within their social class or above it, while men typically marry within their social class or below it. As Lortie (1975) said, within the usual possibilities for women, teaching has ranked high for relatively advantaged women, allowing them to maintain their social class and leaving open the possibility of social mobility through marriage. For men, this option is less obvious. Teaching offers little or no social mobility if they already have socio-economic advantages.

The data for reading difficulties and leisure time reading habits of our sample indicate reading is a low-frequency activity. Most subjects (83%) do not read in their leisure time, and those who do, read "entertainment" material. Moreover, large proportions of the sample (58.3%) said that television is their main source or one of their main sources of information about world affairs. These general patterns of television use and reading are also exhibited by veteran teachers. Travis and Violato (1981, 1985) reported that veteran teachers were more discriminating in their use of mass media than education undergraduates, but that both groups preferred entertainment fare, whether televised or published. Moreover, both groups trusted commercial mass media as reliable sources of information and ideas.

These patterns of reading and mass media use strongly resemble those of the general Canadian population (Statistics Canada, 1981, p. 638). This should give us pause, considering what we know of common taste. We have no reason to suppose that the poet Blake was wrong when he said that without the commingling of contraries there is no progression. Accordingly, one might suppose we want to recruit people whose "reflection-in-action" (Schon, 1983) is the reflection of the "educated imagination" (Frye, 1963), not the musings of mass man (Ortega y Gasset, 1961). If a taste for mass commercial culture predominates in education faculties, we can thank those who are not offended by spray-on sentiment, and faddish notions floating on velleity, and short-term "tool thinking" (Bettelheim, 1980, pp. 144-150; Travis, 1989).

About half of our sample of would-be teachers have conventional political orientations and more than half (approximately 56%) consider themselves religious, with no sex differences on these factors. The absence of a Newfoundland complement may affect these results since Bulcock et al. (1973) reported that 85.7% of women teachers in Newfoundland were religious.

Nearly one third of our sample (32.6%; $n=90$) consisted of people who were first born (eldest) children. Lortie (1975, p. 45) has suggested that birth order might influence children to behave in ways which might elicit labelling as a future teacher; older children nurture and "teach" younger siblings. The large number of eldest children in our sample suggests that this matter warrants further study.

As in previous studies (Lortie, 1975; NEA, 1967, 1972), the interpersonal theme figures most prominently in our subjects' stated reasons for pursuing a career in teaching. High-prestige occupations in our society often entail sociability; the social character of teaching apparently attracts gregarious people. Although in our study the perceived material benefits of a teaching career also figured prominently as an attractor, especially among men, they figured only minimally in American teachers' stated reasons for becoming teachers (Lortie, 1975). (It may be significant that in the past American teachers have enjoyed fewer material benefits than Canadian teachers.)

Lortie (1975) found that teaching was the first occupational choice of only about one third of teachers; most settled on teaching because their original aspirations had been blocked. (For example, many would have preferred to be lawyers or physicians.) By contrast, only a small proportion of our sample said they chose education because of "blocked aspirations"; that is, few said teaching was not their preferred occupational choice. Perhaps the cynics who say that the world (of education at least) "is run by 'C' students" are wrong. However, we should discover how much the heart is at home in school—how many teachers choose this career because of blocked aspirations. To this end, future research might profitably include interviews of subjects.

Finally, the reader should note several limitations in our sample. First, it is difficult to judge its representativeness: although respondents came from all major regions, an ideal random stratified sample should not be assumed. Given the current requirement that all human subjects be volunteers, and given what is known about the non-representative character of volunteer samples, we adopted a strategy of describing the sample in detail. Feasible alternatives are not obvious. Nonetheless, several characteristics of our sample (for example, gender and program proportions) suggest that it was not markedly biased or skewed.

Second, since some of the data were collected as long ago as 1977, some information may now be dated. Although this may be so, there are few reasons to suppose conditions have changed so much that our sample differs markedly from current education students. Indeed, historical studies have shown that some characteristics of classrooms and teachers have been remarkably stable over time (for example, Cuban, 1984). Even so, generalizations from our sample must be made very cautiously.

As we have noted, this kind of research is both scarce and difficult to do. Nevertheless, such work enhances our understanding of teachers and of the "culture of teaching," both at the centre of education. Moreover, effective change and improvement in education must take into account the pivotal people, the teachers whose limitations can in no way be transcended. If we aim to study reflection-in-action, we will be wise to determine whose reflection is under study, and what stocks the imagination of the actor.

References

Anderson, C.C., & Travis, L.D. (1983). *Psychology and the liberal consensus*. Waterloo, ON: Wilfrid Laurier University Press.

Barzun, J. (1954). *Teacher in America*. Garden City, NJ: Doubleday.

Berliner, W. (1983, December 30). Closer scrutiny of teacher training planned. *The Guardian*, p. 5.

Bettelheim, B. (1980). The decision to fail. In B. Bettelheim, *Surviving and other essays* (pp. 142-168), New York, NY: Vintage.

Bruner, J.S. (1983). *In search of mind*. New York, NY: Harper and Row.

Bulcock, J.W., Mercer, W., Quinlan, B.B., & Sullivan, M. (1973). *Women teachers in Newfoundland and Labrador 1972: A Statistical description*. St. John's, NF: Memorial University, Faculty of Education.

Canadian Teachers' Federation. (1981). *Key characteristics of teachers in public elementary and secondary schools: 1972-73 to 1979-80*. Ottawa, ON: Canadian Teachers' Federation.

Cogan, M. (1975). Current issues in the education of teachers. In K. Ryan (Ed.), *Teacher education* (pp. 204-229). Chicago, IL: University of Chicago Press.

Collini, S. (1987, April 3). Research in the humanities. *Times Literary Supplement*, p. 349.

Conant, J.B. (1963). *The education of American teachers*. New York, NY: McGraw-Hill.

Crocker, A.C. (1974). *Predicting teacher success*. London, UK: National Foundation for Educational Research.

Cuban, L. (1984). *How teachers taught: Constancy and change in American classrooms, 1890-1980* . New York, NY: Longman.

Feiman-Nemser, S., & Floden, R.E. (1986). The cultures of teaching. In M.C. Wittrock (Ed.), *Handbook of research on teaching* (3rd ed.) (pp. 505-526). New York, NY: Macmillan.

Frye, N. (1963). *The educated imagination*. Toronto, ON: CBC (Massey Lectures).

Gallup, G.H. (1986). The 18th Annual Gallup Poll of the public's attitudes toward the public schools. *Phi Delta Kappan, 68,* 43-59.

Getzels, J.W., & Jackson, P.W. (1963). The teacher's personality and characteristics. In N.L. Gage (Ed.), *The handbook of research on teaching* (pp. 506-582). Chicago, IL: Rand McNally.

Hearne, V. (1987). What teaching dogs teaches us. *New Scientist, 113* (1551), 38-40.

Jacoby, R. (1983). *The repression of psychoanalysis.* New York, NY: Basic Books.

Lapham, L. (1981, July). Gilding the news. *Harper's,* 31-39.

Lomax, D.E. (1972). Review of British research in teacher education. *Review of Educational Research, 42,* 289-326.

Lortie, D.C. (1973). Observations on teaching as work. In R.M. Travers (Ed.), *Second handbook of research on teaching* (pp. 474-497). Chicago, IL: American Educational Research Association.

Lortie, D.C. (1975). *School teacher: A sociological study.* Chicago, IL: University of Chicago Press.

Lortie, D.C. (1986). Teacher status in Dade County: A case of structural strain? *Phi Delta Kappan, 67,* 568-575.

MacIver, D.A. (Ed.). (1978). *The education of teachers in Canada.* Edmonton, AB: Canadian Society for the Study of Education.

McQuaid, E.P. (1984, January 13). U.S. concern over slipping standards. *Times Higher Education Supplement,* p. 9.

Murray, F. (1984). The application of theories of cognitive development. In B. Gholson & T.L. Rosenthal (Eds.), *Applications of cognitive-developmental theory* (pp. 3-18), New York, NY: Academic Press.

National Education Association. (1963). *The American public-school teacher.* Washington, DC: National Education Association.

National Education Association. (1967). *The American public-school teacher, 1965-66.* Washington, DC: National Education Association.

National Education Association. (1972). *Status of the American public-school teacher, 1970-71.* Washington, DC: National Education Association.

Norris, W. (1987, April 10). Sex school discovers demand for Ph.D. in striptease. *Times Higher Education Supplement,* p. 7.

Ortega y Gasset, J. (1961). *The revolt of the masses.* London, UK: Unwin Books.

Pedersen, K.L., & Fleming, T. (1979). Review of *School teacher: A sociological study,* by D.C. Lortie. *Canadian Journal of Education, 4* (4), 103-110.

Schalock, D.R. (1979). Research on teacher selection. In D.C. Berliner (Ed.), *Review of research in education* (pp. 364-416). Chicago, IL: American Educational Research Association.

Schon, D. (1983). *The reflective practitioner: How professionals think in action.* New York, NY: Basic Books.

Sharpe, T. (1978). *Wilt.* London, UK: Pan/Secker & Warburg.

Statistics Canada. (1981). *Canada Year Book: 1980-81.* Ottawa, ON: Minister of Supply and Services.

Stokes, J. (1987, February 20). Jokers and wingers. *Times Literary Supplement,* p. 194.

Travis, L.D. (1979a). Hinterland schooling and branch-plant psychology: Educational psychology in Canada today. *Canadian Journal of Education, 4* (4), 24-42.

Travis, L.D. (1979b, June). *Canada's would-be teachers: A national survey of background habits and outlook.* Paper presented to the CAEP/CSSE Conference, Saskatoon, SK.

Travis, L.D. (1983). Teacher as content and the metaphor problem: Teacher selection and preparation revisited. In *Higher Education by the Year 2000: Proceedings of the*

Fourth International Congress of EARDHE (pp. 52-99). Frankfurt, Germany: European Association for Research and Development in Higher Education.

Travis, L.D. (1987). Secondary pupils and teacher qualities: Contrasts in appraisals. *Canadian Journal of Education, 12,* 152-176.

Travis, L.D. (1989). Noisy communications and imagination in education. In R. Firdo (Ed.), *Communication in education* (pp. 385-396). Calgary, AB: Detselig.

Travis, L.D., & Violato, C. (1981). Mass media use, credulity and beliefs about youth: A survey of Canadian education students. *Alberta Journal of Educational Research, 27,* 16-34.

Travis, L.D., & Violato, C. (1985). Experience, mass media use and beliefs about youth: A comparative study. *Alberta Journal of Educational Research, 31,* 99-112.

Urquhart, M.C., & Buckley, K.A. (Eds.). (1965). *Historical statistics of Canada.* Toronto, ON: Macmillan.

Waller, W. (1932). *Sociology of teaching.* New York, NY: Russell & Russell.

Wilson, J., Mitchell, L., Barclay, A., Jenkins, D., Mackay, B., Turner, B., & Young, J. (1984). Selecting "the best": Entry to initial teacher training in Scotland. *Scottish Educational Review, 16* (2), 88-103.

Zumwalt, K. (1982). Research on teaching: Policy implications for teacher education. In A. Lieberman & M. McLaughlin (Eds.), *Policy making in education* (pp. 215-248), Chicago, IL: University of Chicago Press.

Teacher Personality Traits and Student Instructional Ratings in Six Types of University Courses

Harry G. Murray, J. Philippe Rushton, and Sampo V. Paunonen
University of Western Ontario

Colleague ratings of 29 personality traits were studied in relation to student ratings of teaching effectiveness in a sample of 46 psychology teachers. Instructors were evaluated in six different types of university courses, ranging from freshman lecture classes to graduate research seminars. Major findings were as follows: (1) Rated teaching effectiveness varied substantially across different types of courses for a given instructor; (2) teaching effectiveness in each type of course could be predicted with considerable accuracy from colleague ratings of personality; and (3) the specific personality traits contributing to effective teaching differed markedly for different course types. It was concluded that psychology instructors tend to be differentially suited to different types of courses and furthermore that the compatibility of instructors to courses is determined in part by personality characteristics.

*   *   *

STUDENT RATINGS HAVE GAINED WIDESPREAD ACCEPTANCE OVER THE PAST 20 years as a measure of teaching effectiveness in North American colleges and universities. This trend has resulted in part from political factors and in part from research showing that student ratings can provide reliable and valid information on certain aspects of university teaching. Although findings are sometimes contradictory, the weight of evidence suggests that student ratings of a given instructor are reasonably stable across items, raters, and time periods; are affected to only a minor extent by extraneous factors such as class size and severity of grading; are consistent with comparable ratings made by alumni, colleagues, and trained classroom observers; and most important of all, are significantly correlated with more objective measures of teaching effectiveness, such as student performance on standardized examinations (Marsh, 1984; H.G. Murray, 1980). On the basis of

This research was supported by a grant from Imperial Oil Limited of Canada to Harry G. Murray and by Social Sciences and Humanities Research Council Grant 410-78-0108 to J. Phillipe Rushton. We gratefully acknowledge the assistance of departmental colleagues who served as subjects or raters in this study.

these data, most writers have concluded that the use of student instructional ratings is justifiable both as a source of diagnostic feedback to instructors and as one of several measures of teaching effectiveness in administrative decisions on faculty salary, retention, tenure, and promotion.

Despite the abundance of research on the reliability, validity, and utility of student ratings, relatively little is known about characteristics of instructors that contribute to positive or negative evaluations from students. Given that teaching is in part a social or interpersonal process, it seems reasonable to expect that teacher personality traits might correlate significantly with rated teaching effectiveness. Although early investigations using self-report personality inventories failed to support this hypothesis (e.g., Bendig, 1955; Sorey, 1968), more recent studies in which teacher personality was measured by colleague ratings, student ratings, or both, have yielded positive results (see review by Feldman, 1986). For example, H.G. Murray (1975) found that colleague ratings of instructor extraversion, leadership, objectivity, and (lack of) anxiety accounted for approximately 67% of between-teacher variance in student instructional ratings. In a study contrasting the personality profiles of "teachers" and "researchers," Rushton, Murray, and Paunonen (1983) reported correlations of .40 or higher between colleague ratings of extraversion, leadership, liberalism, supportingness, exhibitionism, objectivity, and lightheartedness and student rartings of teaching. Sherman and Blackburn (1975), using students rather than colleagues as judges of teacher personality, found that instructional effectiveness ratings were predictable from teacher potency, pragmatism, amicability, and intellectual competence. Tomasco (1980) reported that teacher affiliation, achievement, endurance, nurturance, definitiveness, changeability, and exhibitionism were significant correlates of global effectiveness ratings. In summary, previous research suggests a reasonably consistent pattern of personality characteristics contributing to effective college teaching, in which successful teachers are viewed both by colleagues and by students as showing leadership, objectivity, and high intellect on the one hand, and extraversion, liberalism, and nurturance on the other.

The present study investigated relations between peer ratings of teacher personality traits and student ratings of teaching effectiveness in six types of university psychology courses. Previous research on student instructional ratings suggests that although evaluations of a given instructor are reasonably stable across different years for the same course, they are much less consistent across different courses (or course types) taught in the same year. H.G. Murray (1980) reported reliability coefficients ranging from .62 to .89 ($M = .74$) for the same course taught by the same instructor in successive years, as compared with reliability coefficients ranging from .33 to .55 ($M = .42$) for different courses taught by the same instructor in the same year. Similarly, Marsh (1981) found an average correlation of .71 in same course/different year comparisons, as compared with an average correlation of .52 in different course/same year comparisons. The relatively low correlation of student ratings across different courses taught in the same year suggests that college teaching effectiveness may be to some extent context-dependent. In other words, instructors may be differentially suited to different types of courses rather than uniformly effective or ineffective in all types of courses. Another possibility, given previous research on teacher personality, is that differences in teaching effectiveness in different types of courses are predictable from teacher personality traits. For example, it may be that instructors with personality traits A, B, and C perform well in large lecture classes but poorly in small discussion groups, whereas instructors with personality traits X, Y, and Z tend to be good discussion leaders but poor lecturers. Consistent with this view, Sherman and Blackburn (1975) found that instructor pragmatism was related to student ratings in natural science courses but not in humanities or social science courses, whereas instructor amicability was related to teaching effectiveness in humanities courses but not in natural or social science courses.

The types of courses investigated in the present study ranged from freshman lecture classes to required methodology courses to graduate research seminars. Teacher personality traits were measured by peer ratings, whereas teaching effectiveness was assessed independently through archival student ratings. These procedures minimize the possibility of spurious correlations between personality and teaching because of "halo effect" or "implicit personality theory," a situation that can arise when all variables are rated by the same judges. On the basis of previous research, it was expected that instructors would differ in their relative standing in different types of courses, and, furthermore, that these differences would be related to instructor personality traits.

Method

Teachers

The sample of teachers consisted of 46 faculty members in the Department of Psychology at the University of Western Ontario. Each instructor had held a full-time appointment in the Department for at least 5 years. The breakdown of the sample in terms of gender and academic rank was as follows: 40 men and 6 women; 19 assistant professors, 17 associate professors, and 10 full professors. Each of the participating instructors had taught and received student ratings in at least 10 previous courses, including at least two courses from each of three or more of the categories defined below. Each instructor signed a consent form agreeing to participate in the study.

Courses

The Department of Psychology at the University of Western Ontario offers approximately 110 different courses (140 class sections) in a given year. Total student enrolment in the department is approximately 7,000. Undergraduate majors may complete either a 3-year "area of concentration" or a 4-year "honors" degree. Both MA and PhD programs are offered at the graduate level.

For purposes of the present research, psychology courses were divided into the six categories defined in Table 1. It may be noted that the six course types differed substantially in class size, student composition, and method of instruction. For example, class size ranged from 3 to 450, and method of teaching ranged from straight lecture to lecture-discussion to seminar.

Measures of Personality

Peer ratings of the 29 personality traits defined in Table 2 were obtained for each participating instructor. A full range of personality variables was included to represent the diversity of characteristics that might contribute to teaching effectiveness in six different types of courses. The first 20 personality traits in the table were derived from Jackson's (1984) Personality Research Form, an omnibus personality inventory based on H.A. Murray's (1938) need definitions. The last 2 traits, namely extraversion and neuroticism, were adapted from the Eysenck Personality Questionnaire (Eysenck & Eysenck, 1975), whereas the remaining 7 traits were selected because of their predictive validities in H.G. Murray's (1975) study of personality and college teaching. Peer ratings of personality were solicited from a rater group consisting of 48 full-time faculty members in the Department of Psychology. Included in this group were 36 of the 46

Table 1
Characteristics of Six Types of Courses

Course type	Definition	Class size	Student composition	Method of instruction
Introductory	Multiple-section, freshman survey course	200–250	Nonmajors. Year 1	Lecture-laboratory
General	Elective survey courses for non-psychology students	150–450	Nonmajors. Years 2 & 3	Lecture
Required honors	Mandatory core courses in research methodology and experimental psychology	30–60	Psychology majors. Years 2, 3, & 4	Lecture-laboratory
Optional junior honors	Elective survey courses in basic content areas (e.g., social, developmental)	20–60	Psychology majors. Year 2	Lecture-discussion
Optional senior honors	Senior elective courses in specialized topics	5–25	Psychology honors students only. Years 3 & 4	Seminar
Graduate	Advanced seminars for MA and PhD candidates	3–15	Graduate students	Seminar

instructors serving as subjects in the present study. Each faculty rater was provided with a list of trait names and trait definitions, as in Table 2, and was asked to rate a random sample of 12 to 18 colleagues on each trait, using a 9-point rating scale. Instructions emphasized that ratings were to be based solely on personal observation and were to be made relative to other university professors rather than the population at large. The number of peer raters per instructor ranged from 9 to 15; the mean was 12.2. This corresponds to an overall return rate of 77.9%. Ratings were averaged across raters to obtain mean ratings of 29 personality traits for each of 46 instructors.

Measure of Teaching Effectiveness

Teaching effectiveness was measured from archival student rating data collected since 1969. The University of Western Ontario requires that student instructional ratings be solicited annually in all courses, with results to be considered in salary, promotion, and tenure decisions. The Department of Psychology uses two standardized student evaluation forms for this purpose, one for undergraduate courses and one for graduate courses. The undergraduate form consists of 9 items focusing on expositional skills of the instructor (e.g., clarity, use of examples), plus a final item assessing instructor "overall effectiveness." All 10 items are rated on 5-point scales. The graduate evaluation form consists of only two items, one dealing with course quality and the other with overall effectiveness of the instructor. Both items are rated on 7-point scales. In both undergraduate and graduate courses, student instructional ratings are obtained in a regular class period during the last 2 weeks of the academic term. Students respond anonymously to the questionnaire, the instructor is absent during the evaluation period, and the results are released to the instructor only after final grades have been submitted. The criterion of teaching effectiveness used in the present study was the item assessing overall effectiveness of the instructor, which was common to both undergraduate and graduate evaluation forms. Thus, students in all types of courses rated the same global characteristic, namely overall teaching effectiveness, although sometimes on a 5-point and sometimes on a 7-point rating scale. The latter anomaly caused no difficulties in statistical analyses because ratings were standardized separately for each course type in the computation of correlation coefficients.

Student instructional ratings were averaged across courses for each instructor (unweighted by class size) to obtain a cumulative mean effectiveness rating for each eligible course type. No data were computed in cases where an instructor had taught fewer than two courses in a given category. As noted previously, all 46 instructors had taught the requisite number of courses in at least three different course categories. However, only 6 instructors had taught at least two courses in all six categories, and only 21 instructors had taught at least two courses in five or more categories.

Table 2
Grand Mean, Standard Deviation, and Reliability of Mean Peer Ratings of Instructor Personality (N = 46)

Personality trait	Abbreviated trait definition	M	SD	Rater reliability
Meek	Mild-mannered, accepts blame or criticism, subservient	4.07	1.24	.86
Ambitious	Aspires to accomplish difficult tasks, maintains high standards	5.87	1.60	.94
Sociable	Friendly, outgoing, enjoys being with people	5.42	1.26	.87
Aggressive	Argumentative, quarrelsome, gets angry easily	4.79	1.46	.89
Independent	Avoids restraints and confinement, enjoys being free	5.43	1.04	.77
Changeable	Flexible, restless, likes new and different experiences	4.68	1.11	.79
Seeks definiteness	Does not like ambiguity or uncertainty, seeks structure	5.78	1.12	.87
Defensive	Suspicious, guarded, takes offense easily	4.70	1.23	.85
Dominant	Forceful, decisive, attempts to control environment	5.20	1.61	.90
Enduring	Persevering, steadfast, does not give up quickly	6.03	1.60	.87
Attention-seeking	Dramatic, colorful, wants to be center of attention	4.76	1.51	.89
Harm-avoiding	Careful, cautious, avoids excitement or danger	4.82	1.19	.78
Impulsive	Spontaneous, impetuous, acts on spur of moment	4.76	1.39	.85
Supporting	Gives sympathy and comfort, helpful, indulgent	5.15	1.35	.85
Orderly	Neat and organized, dislikes clutter and confusion	5.43	1.33	.88
Fun-loving	Easygoing, playful, does things just for fun	5.02	1.38	.89
Aesthetically sensitive	Sensitive to sights, sounds, tastes, and other experiences	5.21	1.14	.89
Approval-seeking	Works for approval and recognition of others, agreeable	5.28	1.07	.75
Seeks help and advice	Desires and needs support, sympathy, and advice from others	4.29	1.33	.82
Intellectually curious	Reflective, seeks understanding and synthesis of ideas	5.85	1.26	.85
Anxious	Tense, nervous, uneasy	4.82	1.10	.78
Intelligent	Bright, quick, clever, excels in general cognitive ability	5.93	1.38	.88
Liberal	Progressive, modern, adaptable, seeks change	5.24	1.14	.81
Shows leadership	Takes initiative and responsibility for getting things done	5.20	1.53	.91
Objective	Just, fair, free of bias	5.42	1.21	.76
Compulsive	Meticulous, perfectionistic, concerned with details	5.65	1.20	.76
Authoritarian	Rigid, inflexible, obedient to authority, opinionated	4.77	1.11	.80
Extraverted	Has many friends, likes parties, craves excitement, optimistic	4.94	1.48	.89
Neurotic	Emotional, moody, constantly worried things will go wrong	4.76	1.00	.69

Results

Reliability of Personality Ratings

Table 2 shows the grand mean, standard deviation, and reliability of mean peer ratings of 29 personality traits for 46 instructors. It may be noted that the grand mean fell within 1 point of the midpoint of the 9-point rating scale (i.e., between 4.00 and 6.00) for 28 of 29 traits. Also, the standard deviation of mean peer ratings equalled or exceeded 1.00 for all 29 traits. These results suggest that peer ratings of instructor personality were distributed throughout the full range of the 9-point rating scale.

The reliability of peer ratings of personality was estimated using intraclass correlation procedures advocated by Shrout and Fleiss (1979). Each personality trait was subjected to a one-way analysis of variance (ANOVA) in which teachers served as "treatments" and raters as "subjects." Within- and between-teacher mean squares from the ANOVA were then used to estimate the reliability of the mean rating of k raters (mean $k = 12.2$). Reliability coefficients computed in this way ranged from .69 to .94 and averaged .83, indicating that peer assessments of personality showed substantial interrater reliability, or generalizability across potential sets of raters.

Reliability of Teacher Effectiveness Ratings

Table 3 indicates the number of instructors teaching at least two courses within each of the six course categories, as well as the grand mean, standard deviation, and retest reliability of mean student instructional ratings for the sample of instructors teaching each course type. For example, it may be noted that for the 29 of 46 instructors who taught introductory psychology at least twice, the grand mean and standard deviation of cumulative mean student ratings for this type of course were 3.27 and .67, respectively. Student ratings were higher for graduate than for undergrad-

Table 3
Grand Mean, Standard Deviation, and Reliability of Mean Student Ratings of Instructor Effectiveness in Six Types of Courses

Course type	N	M	SD	Retest reliability
Introductory	29	3.27	0.67	.91
General	30	3.27	0.57	.80
Required honors	29	3.20	0.63	.87
Optional junior honors	35	3.54	0.59	.93
Optional senior honors	38	3.66	0.62	.88
Graduate	40	5.66	0.66	.78

uate courses, reflecting the use of a 7-point rating scale in the former case. Also, consistent with previous research, ratings were higher in senior than in junior courses and higher in optional than in required courses (Feldman, 1978).

The reliability of teacher effectiveness ratings was estimated by intraclass correlation procedures as described above, with the exception that within-teacher mean squares were computed across k years per instructor (minimum $k=2$, $M=4.66$), rather than across raters. Retest reliabilities ranged from .78 to .93 and averaged .86, indicating that student instructional ratings were highly stable across years for a given teacher and a given type of course.

Consistency of Teacher Ratings Across Course Types

Table 4 shows correlations between instructor effectiveness ratings in different types of courses (entries above the diagonal), as well as the number

Table 4
Intercorrelation of Instructor Mean Teaching Effectiveness Ratings in Six Types of Courses

Course type	1	2	3	4	5	6
1. Introductory	—	.78	.78	.52	.66	.12
2. General	20	—	.60	.53	.62	.06
3. Required honors	21	15	—	.76	.68	.11
4. Optional junior honors	23	24	17	—	.71	.13
5. Optional senior honors	24	27	20	31	—	.33
6. Graduate	26	27	22	31	36	—

Note. Below-diagonal entries are cell *n*s.

of instructors teaching each combination of course types (entries below the diagonal). For example, 23 instructors taught two or more courses in both introductory and optional junior honors categories, and the correlation between instructor effectiveness ratings in these two types of courses was .52. Although all instructors did not teach all types of courses or all combinations of course types, a chi-square analysis showed that there was no significant tendency for instructors teaching one type of course to be either more or less likely to teach another type of course than would be expected on the basis of marginal frequencies, $X^2(14, N=46)=4.32$, $p>.05$. It would appear, then, that correlations between course types were not appreciably distorted by overrepresentation or underrepresentation of certain groups of instuctors in certain combinations of course types.

It may be noted in Table 4 that correlations between instructor mean ratings in different types of courses were positive in all cases. Correlation coefficients ranged from .06 to .78, and averaged .49. This result suggests that, although there appears to be a general or *g* factor in college teaching performance, instructor effectiveness can vary substantially across different types of courses. In other words, receiving high or low instructional ratings in one type of course is no guarantee that ratings will be similarly high or low in another type of course. Teacher ratings showed much higher consistency across undergraduate course types (mean $r = .66$) than for undergraduate versus graduate course types (mean $r = .15$). Furthermore, for each type of course, the retest reliability coefficient shown in Table 3 was higher than any of the between-category correlations shown in Table 4. This result is consistent with previous evidence that instructor ratings correlate higher across years for the same course than across different courses taught in the same year (e.g., Marsh, 1981). It should be noted that for undergraduate courses, both between-year and between-course correlations (mean values = .88 and .66, respectively) were higher in absolute terms in the present study than in previous studies, presumably because of aggregation of teacher ratings across several courses in this study.

Further information on the cross-situational consistency of teaching performance was obtained by transforming each instructor's mean rating for each applicable course type to a standard (z) score computed in relation to the overall mean and standard deviation of ratings for that type of course. The average range of z scores *within* instructors was 1.48. This result implies that an instructor who scores at the 32nd percentile of the ratings distribution ($z = -0.48$), in his or her worst course type would, on average, score at the 84th percentile ($z = 1.00$) in his or her best course type. Although there is no denying the between-course consistency that exists in these data, it would appear that teaching effectiveness can nonetheless vary markedly for a given instructor as a function of course type. An even more dramatic demonstration of this point is the fact that only 3 of the 46 instructors participating in this study scored in the top third of the department ($z > 0.45$) in all course types taught, and only 3 scored in the bottom third of the department ($z < -0.45$) in all course types taught. These results show that it is rare indeed for an instructor to be either uniformly "good" or uniformly "poor" in all types of teaching.

Zero-Order Correlations Between Personality and Teaching

Given that instructor ratings show less than perfect consistency across different types of courses, the next question is whether between-course differences in teaching effectiveness are related to instructor personality characteristics. In other words, do teachers who perform well in certain types of courses share certain personality traits that differ from those of teachers who excel in other types of courses? Table 5 shows zero-order correlations between peer ratings of personality and student ratings of teaching effectiveness in different types of courses. The first noteworthy finding is that, consistent with previous research (e.g., Rushton et al., 1983), there was a substantial overall or main effect relationship between personality and teaching. Seventy-two of 174 correlations between personality traits and teacher ratings were statistically significant, whereas only 8.7 (0.5×174) significant correlations would be expected under the null hypothesis. The mean absolute value of the 174 correlations was .295. Secondly, it is apparent that teaching effectiveness in each of the six types of courses was separately predictable from ratings of instructor personality. Each course type showed at least 10 significant correlations with individual personality traits, and the mean absolute correlation with personality variables ranged from .23 (for graduate courses) to .34 (for introductory courses). Stepwise multiple regression analysis yielded significant multiple Rs ranging from .695 to .877 between the best five personality predictor variables for a given type of course and cumulative mean teacher ratings. With correction for shrinkage, corresponding estimates of variance accounted for (adjusted R^2) ranged from 41.5% to 73.2%, indicating that teaching effectiveness in each type of course could be predicted with considerable accuracy from peer ratings of as few as five personality traits. A similar analysis of mean standard scores for all types of courses taught by a given instructor yielded a multiple R of .754 and an adjusted R^2 of .521, indicating that composite or global teaching effectiveness is also highly predictable from personality variables. The five best predictors of the composite effectiveness measure were leadership, liberalism, seeks definiteness, supportingness, and extraversion.

Table 5
Correlations Between Peer Ratings of Personality and Student Ratings of Teaching in Six Types of Courses (decimals omitted)

Personality trait	Introductory	General	Required honors	Optional junior honors	Optional senior honors	Graduate
				Course type		
Meek	02	-30	-11	06	21	02
Ambitious	24	19	31	14*	03	43*
Sociable	64**	33	37*	55*	57*	-04
Aggressive	07	20	12	-03	-21*	-08
Independent	-09	13	22	09	-03	12
Changeable	46*	37**	49*	50*	44*	-08
Seeks definiteness	06	12	34	02	-16	32*
Defensive	-35	-16	-19	-34*	-56*	-24
Dominant	30	36*	40*	30	01	08
Enduring	29	26	38**	25	18	52**
Attention-seeking	56*	50**	42*	51*	29	-18
Harm-avoiding	-16	-28	-26	-45**	-48**	-06
Impulsive	36*	39*	01	37*	12	-31*
Supporting	53*	11*	43*	58**	64*	11
Orderly	34*	25*	37**	07	25*	29*
Fun-loving	56**	32	35	49*	48*	-22
Aesthetically sensitive	27	40*	18	40*	52**	-22
Approval-seeking	48*	29	16	24	12	11*
Seeks help and advice	46*	15	14*	32	34*	-34**
Intellectually curious	29	38*	42*	23	24	46*
Anxious	-22	-16	-35*	-24	-41*	-19
Intelligent	28	37*	42*	19	11	35*
Liberal	60*	52**	35*	55*	65**	-06
Shows leadership	51*	40*	56**	54*	43*	44**
Objective	40*	20	31	34**	59*	40**
Compulsive	32	20	39*	12*	11	46*
Authoritarian	-34*	-24	-12	-30	-42*	05
Extraverted	64**	41*	50*	54*	45*	-12
Neurotic	01	03	-15	-08	-25	-27
Mean r	34	28	30	30	32	23
Stepwise R ($k = 5$)	.801*	.786*	.737*	.771*	.877*	.695*
Variance explained (adjusted R^2)	56.3%	53.7%	43.0%	52.6%	73.2%	41.5%

*One of five variables used to obtain stepwise R for each course type.
* $p < .05$.

The third and most important finding in Table 5 is that the pattern of relations between personality and teaching differed markedly for different types of courses. In other words, personality traits that contributed to effective teaching in one type of course did not necessarily contribute similarly in other types of courses. For example, the traits of sociability, changeableness, attention-seeking, liberalism, and extraversion correlated positively and significantly with teacher ratings in undergraduate courses, whereas the same traits tended to show nonsignificant negative correlations with teacher ratings in graduate courses. On the other hand, ambitiousness, endurance, orderliness, and compulsiveness were positively related to performance in graduate courses and in required honors courses, but did not correlate significantly with performance in other types of courses. Two other traits, impulsiveness and seeking help and advice, correlated significantly but in opposite directions with instructional ratings in different types of courses. In general, it appears that different and sometimes incompatible combinations of personality traits are necessary for effective performance in different types of courses, which of course would explain why very few teachers are outstanding in all types of courses taught. It is interesting to note that only 1 of the 29 personality traits, namely leadership, correlated significantly and in the same direction with instructor ratings in all six

Table 6
Factor Loadings From Principal-Components Factor Analysis of Peer-Rated Personality Traits (decimals omitted)

	Factor				
Personality trait	I Extraversion	II Achievement	III Negative affect	IV Liberalism	V Neuroticism
Extraverted	93	−04	15	23	−16
Sociable	91	00	−23	20	−07
Attention-seeking	82	12	45	20	−05
Fun-loving	74	−21	−02	48	−24
Approval seeking	74	23	−18	−10	38
Shows leadership	71	58	−01	−22	−18
Seeks help and advice	65	−36	−32	28	48
Enduring	06	92	−01	−13	−09
Intelligent	04	92	14	18	−09
Intellectually curious	03	91	00	25	−14
Ambitious	11	91	16	−06	−09
Seeks definiteness	−13	81	23	−21	09
Compulsive	00	70	−10	−49	33
Dominant	44	60	58	−15	−06
Aggressive	18	36	86	03	06
Objective	25	24	−84	11	−20
Meek	−14	−45	−79	04	16
Defensive	−15	−07	75	−29	44
Supporting	53	−04	−74	−23	−07
Independent	−15	47	65	35	−30
Impulsive	56	−04	64	41	04
Aesthetically sensitive	35	−07	−15	76	08
Liberal	59	17	−25	75	−13
Authoritarian	−22	06	52	−70	17
Changeable	55	22	09	70	−17
Orderly	07	44	−15	−63	19
Neurotic	05	−10	15	−06	93
Anxious	−19	−03	19	−12	89
Harm-avoiding	−37	−09	−40	−38	54
Eigenvalue	8.41	7.63	4.29	3.27	1.52
Cumulative variance	29.0	55.3	70.1	81.4	86.6
Alpha reliability	.90	.93	.88	.84	.79

Note. Boxes indicate traits that loaded highest on a given factor.

types of courses. It may be that teachers with leadership ability are sufficiently flexible to adapt or modify their teaching style to the demands of different types of courses.

Factor Analysis

To derive a smaller set of uncorrelated personality variables for use in further analyses, instructor mean ratings on the 29 personality scales were subjected to a principal-components, varimax-rotation factor analysis. As indicated in Table 6, the analysis yielded five factors with eigenvalues greater than 1.0 that collectively accounted for 86.6% of the total variance in mean personality ratings. The orthogonal, 5-factor solution provided good approximation to simple structure. Most traits loaded highly on only one factor, and each factor was defined by at least three high-loading traits. Factor 1, interpreted as Extraversion, accounted for 29.0% of ratings variance. High scorers on this factor were perceived by peers as friendly, lighthearted, colorful, and charismatic. Factor 2, Achievement, accounted for 26.3% of variance. High scorers were rated as dominant, intelligent, and hardworking. Factor 3, Negative Affect, which accounted for 14.8% of variance, was a bipolar factor on which high scorers were perceived as aggressive, defensive, and impulsive, and low scorers as objective, mild-mannered, and supporting. Factor 4, Liberalism, accounted for 11.3% of variance and was defined by traits such as aesthetic sensitivity, flexibility, and nonauthoritarianism. Factor 5, interpreted as Neuroticism, accounted for 5.2% of variance and included traits such as fearfulness and cautiousness.

Instructors were assigned factor scores on each of the above dimensions according to the SPSS factor score procedure (Nie, Hull, Jenkins, Steinbrenner, & Bent, 1975). Factor scores computed in this way had means of 0, standard deviations of 1.0, and intercorrelations of 0. Alpha reliabilities of factor scores (based solely on the marker variables designated in Table 6) ranged from .79 to .93.

Analysis of Factor Scores

A preliminary analysis of personality factor scores was undertaken to determine whether instructors who had taught a particular type of course at least twice differed significantly in mean scores on any of the five personality factors from instructors who had not taught that type of course. Of 30 such comparisons (6 course types×5 personality factors), only 1 was statistically significant. Given that approximately 1.5 significant contrasts would be expected by chance alone under these circumstances, it seems reasonable to attribute the obtained result to Type I error and to conclude that assignment of instructors to course types was not systematically related to instructor personality. A direct implication of this conclusion is that the occurrence of missing data for particular instructor/course type combinations was unrelated to instructor personality. Results presented earlier indicated that the presence or absence of data for a given instructor/course type combination was unrelated to the presence or absence of data for other types of courses. Thus, it would appear that the occurrence of missing data in the present study was random with respect to both of the independent variables under investigation (i.e., personality factors and course types) and that, for this reason, the results obtained are representative of what would have been found with a complete data set (Cohen & Cohen, 1975).

Factor scores were next analyzed to determine personality profiles of highly successful instructors in different types of courses. Figure 1 shows mean factor score profiles for instructors whose cumulative mean ratings

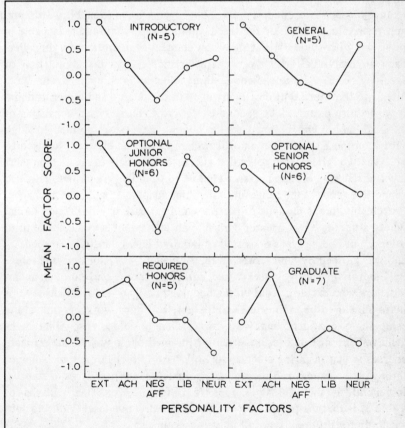

Figure 1. Mean personality factor score profiles for top-ranking instructors in six types of college courses. (EXT = extraversion; ACH = achievement; NEG AFF = negative affect; LIB = liberalism; NEUR = neuroticism.)

ranked in the top 16% ($z > 1.0$) among those teaching each type of course. The number of "top teachers" varied slightly for different course types as a function of the total number of instructors teaching each type of course (see Table 3). A two-way ANOVA, in which course type was treated as a between-subjects variable (despite some overlap in membership among high-ranking groups) and personality factor was a within-subjects variable, yielded a significant interaction effect, $F(20, 112) = 3.03$, $MS_e = .294$, $p < .001$, reflecting the fact that personality profiles differed substantially across course types. Inspection of Figure 1 suggests that the six course types can be divided into three subcategories with respect to profile shape, or in other words, with respect to the relative contribution of different personality factors to teaching effectiveness. The first category, consisting of introductory and general courses, is characterized by elevated scores on the Extraversion and Neurosis factors and by relatively low scores on Negative Affect. Apparently the instructor who excels in large, lower-level, lecture classes is a "neurotic extravert" type who is friendly, warm, and approachable, has a flair for the dramatic, and is fair and reasonable in relations with students, but shows an element of neurotic worrying. Perhaps an individual with these characteristics enjoys the stimulation of speaking before a large audience, but nonetheless is compulsive enough to attend to the myriad of details involved in organizing and orchestrating a large lecture course. The second category of course types, consisting of optional junior and optional senior honors courses, is defined by high scores on the Extraversion and Liberalism factors and by very low scores on Negative Affect. It appears that successful teachers in smaller, higher-level, discussion-oriented classes tend to be friendly, gregarious, fair, and supportive, and, at the same time, flexible, adaptable, and open to change. Presumably this is the type of person who is at ease in a discussion format where students exert greater control over classroom activities. The third category of course types consisted of required honors and graduate courses and was defined by high scores on the Achievement factor, average scores on Liberalism and Negative Affect, and low scores on Neuroticism. Instructors who excel in required methodology courses and in graduate seminars appear to be ambitious, competent, and hard working and, at the same time, confident and worry free. One possible reason that high-achievement instructors are effective in methodology and in graduate courses is that inspiring students to work hard (either through modeling or through exhortation) is a prerequisite for success in these types of courses. In general, the picture that emerges from Figure 1, consistent with that of Table 5, is that the personality profile of the effective teacher differs substantially for different types of university courses.

Another factor score analysis was performed to identify personality characteristics of instructors who, contrary to the general rule, were uniformly effective or uniformly ineffective in all types of courses taught. Mean personality profiles were computed for 8 teachers who taught four or more course types with below-average ratings in all cases. These data are plotted in Figure 2. The most distinguishing characteristics of uniformly "good" teachers were high scores on the Extraversion and Liberalism factors. On the other hand, uniformly "poor" teachers were characterized by very low scores on Extraversion and somewhat elevated levels of Neuroticism.

A two-way ANOVA of the data in Figure 2 yielded a significant Groups×Factors interaction effect. $F(1,52)=4.21$, $MS_e=.201$, $p<.05$. Follow-up Tukey Honestly Significant Difference tests showed that group differences were significant only for the Extraversion and Liberalism factors, suggesting that these two personality dimensions are critical in determining breadth of teaching effectiveness. Comparison of uniformly good and uniformly poor teachers on the 12 individual personality traits loading highest on Extraversion and Liberalism in the factor analysis reported in Table 6 revealed that the trait contributing most to the differentiation of these two groups was leadership. This result is consistent with the fact that

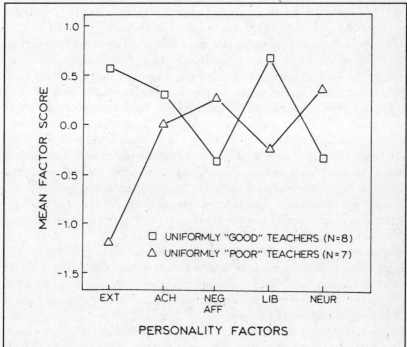

Figure 2. Mean personality factor score profiles for instructors receiving uniformly high or uniformly low student ratings in all types of courses taught. (EXT = extraversion: ACH = achievement: NEG AFF = negative affect: LIB = liberalism: NEUR = neuroticism.)

leadership was the only personality trait to correlate significantly with instructor ratings in all six types of courses (see Table 5). As elaborated further below, leadership qualities appear to play a pivotal role in university teaching effectiveness.

Discussion

In summary, the results of this research suggest three major conclusions concerning teacher personality traits in relation to instructional effectiveness in different types of university-level psychology courses. First, clear evidence was found that perceived teaching effectiveness does in fact vary substantially across different types of courses for the same instructor. Correlations between cumulative instructor ratings in different types of courses ranged from .06 to .78, and averaged .49, indicating that even with aggregated and reliable measures, college teaching effectiveness shows only moderate cross-situational consistency. In other words, it is the exception rather than the rule for an instructor to perform exceptionally well or exceptionally poorly in all types of courses. The second major conclusion is that, for any given type of course or for all types combined, student instructional ratings were strongly related to peer ratings of instructor personality traits. Consistent with previous research (e.g., Rushton et al., 1983), multiple regression analyses showed that 40 to 70% of between-teacher variance in student instructor ratings was predictable from peer ratings of as few as five personality traits. Personality traits correlating highest with composite teacher effectiveness ratings included leadership, extraversion, liberalism, supportingness, intellectual curiosity, and changeableness. The third and most important finding of this study is that the specific personality traits contributing to effective teaching varied substantially for different types of courses. For example, instructor extraversion and liberalism correlated positively and significantly with student ratings in undergraduate courses, whereas these same traits showed zero or negative correlations with ratings in graduate courses. Conversely, instructor achievement and endurance contributed significantly to teaching effectiveness in graduate and required honors courses, but were unrelated to performance in other types of courses.

The results of this study provide evidence that, at least in the field of psychology, university teachers tend to be differentially suited to different types of courses rather than uniformly effective or ineffective in all types of courses. Furthermore, the compatibility of teachers to courses appears to be determined in part by personality characteristics. According to this interpretation, very few teachers will have the necessary range of personality traits to excel in all types of courses. One of the secrets of effective teaching, therefore, is to discover the conditions under which one teaches most effectively. Gage and Berliner (1984) stated this principle as follows:

Just as plays and movies require casting, and not every actor is suitable for every role, so teaching methods require matching with the strengths and weaknesses of the teacher. If a teacher's personality is unsuited for lecturing, it will be much more worthwhile for that instructor to choose a method other than lecturing than to try to learn to use the method effectively. (p. 482)

The present findings also have important implications for the validity and utility of student instructor ratings, and more generally, for the improvement of university teaching. Some writers (e.g., Small, Hollenbeck, & Haley, 1982) have argued that a strong relationship between teacher personality and student instructional ratings implies that student ratings are invalid, in that they reduce to nothing more than a "personality contest." Ware and Williams (1980) reached a similar conclusion in their analysis of the Dr. Fox effect, defined as a prepotent influence of instructor charisma or expressiveness on student ratings. An alternative interpretation, favored by the present authors, is that personality traits of the instructor (e.g., orderliness) are translated into specific classroom teaching behaviors (e.g., putting an outline on blackboard), which in turn are validly reflected in student ratings. In support of this view, Erdle, Murray, and Rushton (1985) showed by path analytical procedures that more than 50% of the relationship between teacher personality and student ratings was mediated by specific classroom behaviors. It is not unreasonable to conclude, therefore, that a correlation between teacher personality and student ratings provides positive (rather than negative) evidence with respect to the validity of student ratings, in that ratings are shown to be systematically related to pedagogically relevant instructor characteristics.

The low to moderate correlations found in the present research between student ratings in different types of courses suggest that when instructional ratings are used in administrative decisions on faculty retention, tenure, and promotion, data should be available from as many types of courses as possible. Otherwise, an instructor denied tenure or promotion on the basis of poor teaching evaluations in a limited range of course types could rightfully argue that more favorable evaluations might have been obtained in other types of courses. A further implication of the modest correlation of ratings across different course types is that the overall quality of teaching in an academic department could be significantly improved simply by assigning teachers to the types of courses in which they have received their highest ratings. Ideally this should be a posttenure arrangement, instituted only after the instructor has had the opportunity to teach several different types of courses. As a case in point, if each of the 46 instructors participating in the present study was in the future assigned only to the two types of courses in which he or she had performed best, the department mean teacher rating for undergraduate courses would be expected to increase from 3.41 to 3.75 (on a 5-point scale), whereas the department mean for graduate courses would increase from 5.66 to 6.06 (on a 7-point scale).

Assuming that peer ratings provide a valid index of stable, enduring personality characteristics, the present findings suggest that a faculty member's effectiveness as a teacher is determined, at least in part, before he or she sets foot in the classroom. In other words, preexisting personality traits (among other factors) are assumed to determine the instructor's classroom teaching behaviors, which in turn determine student ratings and student achievement. Given that current selection and training procedures virtually guarantee that college teachers will be more heterogeneous with respect to personality characteristics than with respect to cognitive or intellectual variables, it is perhaps not too surprising that personality should account for such a large proportion of variance in college teaching effectiveness. Whatever the reasons, the existence of strong correlations between personality and teaching suggests that personality measures (e.g. peer ratings) might be used in selecting new faculty members who are likely to be effective teachers. Alternatively, such measures might be used to assign instructors to the types of courses in which they are likely to be most successful. According to the present research, faculty who are extraverted, dramatic, and perhaps a bit neurotic would be expected to excel in lower-level, lecture courses; whereas those who are extraverted, liberal, and fair-minded might be predicted to do well in higher-level discussion or seminar courses; and those who are ambitious, hard-working, and organized would perhaps be the most successful in graduate seminars and undergraduate methodology courses. Finally, faculty who are liberal, flexible, and high in leadership ability would be expected to excel in a wide range of different types of courses.

It is noteworthy that the personality traits of leadership and flexibility (liberalism) were found to be associated with generalized or wide-ranging teaching effectiveness in the present study. Previous writers have suggested, on the one hand, that teaching and leadership are similar in many ways (e.g., Norr & Crittenden, 1975) and, on the other hand, that a good teacher is, above all else, flexible and adaptable in approach (e.g., Berliner, 1976). Possibly the superordinate trait of "role flexibility" is part of what defines both an effective leader and a master teacher—that is, a teacher who excels in all types of courses. A master teacher, like an effective leader, presumably has the ability to modify his or her approach so as to adapt successfully to the requirements of different situations. Teachers who excel in all types of courses are capable of being either friendly and supportive or strict and demanding, either student-centered or teacher-centered, either a "therapist" or a "drillmaster," depending on what will accomplish the task most effectively. Lowman (1984) offers a similar analysis in his characterization of "complete master" teachers. These rare individuals excel both in expository and in interpersonal skills, and are able to modify their approach so as to motivate both brilliant and mediocre students and to perform well in both the lecture hall and the seminar room.

An obvious limitation of the present approach is that the correlational design used does not allow direct, unambiguous interpretation of cause-effect relationships. Whereas the preceding discussion has assumed that personality traits determine teaching behaviors, which in turn determine perceived teaching effectiveness, it is conceivable that causality operates in the opposite direction, such that prior successes or failures in teaching lead to systematic changes in instructor personality characteristics. Alternatively, it is possible that actual or hearsay knowledge of instructors' prior student ratings influenced colleague assessments of personality traits. Although neither of these alternative causal models can be unambiguously eliminated with the data at hand, their plausibility is reduced both by the normal temporal precedence of personality traits to classroom teaching behaviors and by H.G. Murray's (1975) finding that student ratings of new, previously unrated college instructors could be accurately predicted from peer ratings of personality traits obtained at least 5 months prior to student assessment of teaching.

A final comment should be added concerning possible implications of the present study for the controversial issue of whether teaching effectiveness and research productivity are positively related in university faculty members. Although many faculty are steadfastly confident that these factors are (or should be) positively associated, empirical studies have consistently reported a correlation of close to zero between measures of teaching quality and measures of research productivity (e.g., Feldman, 1987; Rushton et al., 1983). It appears, however, that no previous study has investigated research productivity in relation to rated teaching effectiveness in different types of courses. The present finding that instructor ambitiousness, endurance, compulsiveness, and intelligence correlated significantly with student ratings in graduate seminars and undergraduate methodology courses, in combination with Rushton et al's (1983) finding that these same personality traits correlated significantly with faculty publication rates and citation counts, implies that research productivity may in fact be positively related to teaching effectiveness, but only for certain very research-oriented or "work-oriented" types of courses.

References

Bendig, A.W. (1955). Ability and personality characteristics of introductory psychology instructors rated competent and empathetic by their students. *Journal of Educational Research, 48,* 705-709.

Berliner, D.C. (1976). Impediments to the study of teacher effectiveness. *Journal of Teacher Education, 27,* 5-13.

Cohen, J., & Cohen, P. (1975). *Applied multiple regression/correlation analysis of the behavioral sciences.* Hillsdale, NJ: Erlbaum.

Erdle, S., Murray, H.G., & Rushton, J.P. (1985). Personality, classroom behavior, and college teaching effectiveness: A path analysis. *Journal of Educational Psychology, 77,* 394-407.

Eysenck, H.J., & Eysenck, S.B.G. (1975). *Manual of Eysenck Personality Questionnaire.* San Diego, CA: Educational and Industrial Testing Service.

Feldman, K.A. (1978). Course characteristics and college students' ratings of their teachers: What we know and what we don't. *Research in Higher Education, 9,* 199-242.

Feldman, K.A. (1986). The perceived instructional effectiveness of college teachers as related to their personality and attitudinal characteristics: A review and synthesis. *Research in Higher Education, 24,* 139-213.

Feldman, K.A. (1987). Research productivity and scholarly accomplishment of college teachers as related to their instructional effectiveness: A review and exploration. *Research in Higher Education, 26,* 227-298.

Gage, N.L., & Berliner, D.C. (1984). *Educational Psychology* (3rd ed.). Boston, MA: Houghton-Mifflin.

Jackson, D.N. (1984). *Personality Research Form Manual.* Port Huron, MI: Research Psychologists Press.

Lowman, J. (1984). *Mastering the techniques of teaching.* San Francisco, CA: Jossey-Bass.

Marsh, H.W. (1981). The use of path analysis to estimate teacher and course effects in student ratings of instructional effectiveness. *Applied Psychological Measurement, 6,* 47-60.

Marsh, H.W. (1984). Students' evaluations of university teaching: Dimensionality, reliability, validity, potential biases, and utility. *Journal of Educational Psychology, 76,* 707-754.

Murray, H.A. (1938). *Explorations in personality.* Cambridge, MA: Harvard University Press.

Murray, H.G. (1975). Predicting student ratings of college teaching from peer ratings of personality type. *Teaching of Psychology, 2,* 66-70.

Murray, H.G. (1980). *Evaluating university teaching: A review of research.* Toronto, ON: Ontario Confederation of University Faculty Associations.

Nie, N.H., Hull, C.H., Jenkins, J.G., Steinbrenner, K., & Bent, D.H. (1975). *Statistical package for the social sciences.* New York, NY: McGraw-Hill.

Norr, J.L., & Crittenden, K.S. (1975). Evaluating college teaching as leadership. *Higher Education, 4,* 335-350.

Rushton, J.P., Murray, H.G., & Paunonen, S.V. (1983). Personality, research creativity, and teaching effectiveness in university professors, *Scientometrics, 5,* 93-116.

Sherman, B.R., & Blackburn, R.T. (1975). Personal characteristics and teaching effectiveness of college faculty. *Journal of Educational Psychology, 67,* 124-131.

Shrout, P.E., & Fleiss, J.L. (1979). Intraclass correlations: Uses in assessing rater reliability. *Psychological Bulletin, 86,* 420-428.

Small, A.C., Hollenbeck, A.R., & Haley, R.L. (1982). The effect of the emotional state on student ratings of instructors. *Teaching of Psychology, 9,* 205-211.

Sorey, K.E. (1968). A study of the distinguishing personality characteristics of college faculty who are superior in regard to the teaching function. *Dissertational Abstracts International, 28,* 4916A. (University Microfilms No. 68-8502).

Tomasco, A.T. (1980). Student perceptions of instructional and personality characteristics of faculty: A canonical analysis. *Teaching of Psychology, 7,* 79-82.

Ware, J.E., & Williams, R.G. (1980). A reanalysis of the Dr. Fox experiments. *Instructional Evaluation, 4,* 15-18.

Burnout: Investigating the Impact of Background Variables for Elementary, Intermediate, Secondary, and University Educators

Barbara M. Byrne
University of Ottawa

The primary intent of the study was to investigate the impact of particular background variables on three dimensions of burnout (Emotional Exhaustion, Depersonalization, Personal Accomplishment) for elementary (n=98), intermediate (n=163), secondary (n=162), and university (n=219) educators. Using setwise multiple regression procedures, these variables (gender, age, marital/family status, type of student taught) were effects-coded and interpreted within an analysis of variance framework. A secondary purpose of the study was to delineate factors which educators perceive as contributing most to feelings of work-related stress. While findings revealed gender, age, and type of student taught to be the most salient, their influence varied with teaching level and specific burnout facet under study. Organizational factors related to the administration of educational institutions ranked high as a substantial contributor to feelings of stress by educators at all levels of the academic system.

*   *   *

Bᴜʀɴᴏᴜᴛ, ᴀ ᴛᴇʀᴍ ꜰɪʀꜱᴛ ɪɴᴛʀᴏᴅᴜᴄᴇᴅ ʙʏ Fʀᴇᴜᴅᴇɴʙᴇʀɢᴇʀ (1974), ᴅᴇɴᴏᴛᴇꜱ the inability to function effectively in one's job as a consequence of prolonged and extensive job-related stress. Over this past decade, the escalation and pervasiveness of burnout among members of the teaching profession has drawn the attention of educational administrators, clinicians, and academicians alike; indeed, their concern has precipitated a plethora of research on the topic.

Educator burnout is purportedly a function of stressors engendered at both the organizational and individual levels (Cooper & Marshall, 1976; Farber, 1983; Ianni & Reuss-Ianni, 1983; Iwanicki, 1983; Perlman & Hartman, 1982). However, there is growing evidence that moderating fac-

The author wishes to extend her gratitude to teachers of the Carleton Board of Education and Professors at the University of Ottawa, who gave freely of their valuable time to participate in this study. Special thanks are due also to Lisa M. Hall for her assistance in categorizing the qualitative data.

tors such as background variables play an important role in its generation among educators (e.g., Anderson & Iwanicki, 1984; Beck & Gargiulo, 1983; Feitler & Tokar, 1982; Schwab, 1983; Schwab & Iwanicki, 1982; Schwab, Jackson, & Schuler, 1986); these factors involve personal (gender, age, years of experience, marital/family status), as well as environmental (grade taught, type of student taught) factors. Although the literature suggests their importance in explaining individual differences in particular dimensions of the syndrome, reported findings have been inconsistent. The primary purpose of the present paper, in broad terms, was to reexamine the impact of these background variables on burnout among educators at the elementary, intermediate, secondary, and university levels. A secondary purpose of the study was to identify factors perceived by teachers as contributing most to feelings of work-related stress.

The Concept of Educator Burnout

The seminal research of Maslach and colleagues was the first of an empirical nature to investigate the phenomenon of burnout (for an historical summary, see Maslach and Jackson, 1981, 1984). Their findings were consistent in supporting a multidimensional construct comprising three related, yet independent components: (a) emotional exhaustion—feelings of fatigue that develop as one's emotional energies become drained, (b) depersonalization—the development of negative and uncaring attitudes toward others, and (c) reduced personal accomplishment—a deterioration of self-competence, and dissatisfaction with one's achievements.

These three elements of burnout have been empirically validated for elementary, intermediate, and secondary school teachers (Belcastro, Gold, & Hays, 1983; Gold, 1984; Iwanicki & Schwab, 1981), and for university professors (Meier, 1984). Teachers are purported to exhibit signs of emotional exhaustion when they perceive themselves as unable to give of themselves to students, as they did earlier in their careers; depersonalization, when teachers develop negative, cynical, and sometimes callous attitudes towards students, parents, and colleagues; and feelings of reduced personal accomplishment, when they perceive themselves as ineffective in helping students to learn, and in fulfilling other school responsibilities. Overall, educators who fall victim to burnout are likely to be less sympathetic toward students, have a lower tolerance for classroom disruption, be less apt to prepare adequately for class, and feel less committed and dedicated to their work which ultimately leads to increased absenteeism and impetus to leave the profession (Farber & Miller, 1981; Schwab et. al., 1986).

Background Variables Bearing on Educator Burnout

Research investigating the importance of particular background variables on educator burnout have shown the following to be worthy of further study: gender, age, years of experience, marital/family status, grade(s) taught, and type of student taught.

Gender. Except for the depersonalization facet, investigations of gender differences in educator burnout have yielded inconsistent findings. Depersonalization, however, has been shown to be significantly higher for males than for females across elementary and high school teachers (Anderson & Iwanicki, 1984; Schwab & Iwanicki, 1982; Schwab et. al., 1986). Whereas Maslach and Jackson (1981) reported significantly higher levels of emotional exhaustion for females than males among a wide variety of human service professionals, Anderson and Iwanicki (1984) found the reverse to be true for teachers; Maslach and Jackson (1985) and Schwab and Iwanicki (1982) found no significant differences. Finally, while Maslach and Jackson (1981) and Anderson and Iwanicki (1984) found significantly greater feelings of reduced personal accomplishment for females than for males, Maslach and Jackson (1985), and Schwab and Iwanicki (1982) reported no significant differences; in all cases, the absolute gender differences were small.

Age. Age appears to be a very salient differentiating variable with respect to the emotional exhaustion component of burnout. Young teachers have shown significantly higher levels of emotional exhaustion than their older colleagues (Anderson & Iwanicki, 1984; Maslach & Jackson, 1981; Schwab & Iwanicki, 1982; Schwab et. al., 1986). Findings are less consistent for the other two facets of the syndrome. While Maslach and Jackson (1981) found their young respondents to score significantly higher on the depersonalization, and lower on the personal accomplishment scales, Iwanicki and associates found no significant age differences in these dimensions for teachers.

Years of experience. Although years on the job would appear to be an important variable in terms of burnout, research findings do not support this notion. In their studies of teachers, Anderson and Iwanicki (1984), and Schwab and Iwanicki (1982) found no significant findings with respect to the emotional exhaustion and depersonalization dimensions. Anderson and Iwanicki reported significantly lower levels of personal accomplishment for teachers in the 13-24 year group than for any other group.

Marital/family status. The literature is quite consistent in reporting no significant effect of marital status, albeit a significant effect of family status on the incidence of burnout among other human service professionals (Maslach & Jackson, 1981, 1985; Schwab & Iwanicki, 1982). Individuals with children experience less burnout than those with no children, on all three aspects of the syndrome.

Grade level. There is some evidence in the literature to suggest that educator burnout is more prevalent among high school, than among elementary school teachers (Anderson & Iwanicki, 1984; Feitler & Tokar, 1982; Schwab & Iwanicki, 1982; Schwab et. al. ,1986). Furthermore, investigations of specific aspects of burnout have yielded findings indicating that intermediate and high school teachers exhibit higher levels of depersonalization than their elementary school counterparts. Moreover, Anderson and Iwanicki (1984) found significant differences in feelings of reduced personal accomplishment; high school teachers suffered the most from this aspect of the syndrome.

Type of student taught. Anecdotal studies of teacher burnout have suggested that, based on intensity of direct contact with children, special education teachers are probably more vulnerable to burnout than regular teachers. Research findings, however, have been inconsistent. For example, Beck and Gargiulo (1983) and Bensky, Shaw, Gouse, Bates, Dixon, and Beane (1980) found teachers of regular students to experience higher levels of burnout than teachers of children with learning disabilities; Olson and Matuskey (1982) found no significant differences between the two groups of educators.

From the literature reviewed, it seems evident that more work is needed to further identify the primary background variables contributing to educator burnout. Our present knowledge is limited for several reasons. First, while the teacher burnout literature is vast there is a paucity of systematic empirical research on the topic; most studies have been of an anecdotal or descriptive nature. Second, many studies have not considered the multidimensional structure of burnout and have reported findings based on global scores only. Third, no study has yet examined the impact of background variables for teacher populations that span four levels of the educative process. Finally, although a number of descriptive studies have sought to delineate sources of educator stress (see, e.g., Friesen, Prokop, & Sarros, 1988; Friesen & Williams, 1985; Hiebert, 1985; Kuzsman & Schnall, 1987; Makinen & Kinnunen, 1986; Schwab et. al., 1986), none has yet examined the university population, or compared perceived stressors across elementary, intermediate, secondary, or university educators. The present study was designed to address these issues.

Method

Sample and Procedure

Participants in the study were 642 teachers from six elementary (males=82; females=16), six intermediate (males=75; females=87), and four secondary (males=101; females=61) schools, and one university (males = 104; females = 115) in a large central Canadian city. By necessity, data collection procedures differed for the non-university and university samples. For the former, schools, rather than teachers, were randomly selected from one school district; administrative policy determined the number of participating schools and method of data collection. Moreover, the principal of each selected school was free to veto the collection of data from teachers under his/her jurisdiction. Subsamples of approximately 200 teachers were targeted for each of the elementary, intermediate, and secondary school levels. For the university sample, 200 male and 200 female professors were randomly selected from a master list of full-time faculty; a larger target number was used for this population in an attempt to maximize the number of return-mail responses.

Questionnaires, together with a cover letter, detailed instructions, and a return envelope, were mailed to each subject in the case of the university sample, and were delivered to the principal of each participating school, in the case of the non-university sample; these administrators were fully supportive of the study and encouraged all their teachers to complete the questionnaire.

Instrumentation

The instrument developed to gather data for the present study was titled "The Teacher Stress Survey" (see also Schwab & Iwanicki, 1982) and consisted of three sections. Part A comprised eight items related to selected background variables. Part B constituted the Educator's Survey version of the Maslach Burnout Inventory (MBI; Maslach & Jackson, 1986); based on a point Likert scale (0 to 6), it is composed of 22 items measuring three components of burnout—emotional exhaustion, depersonalization, and reduced personal accomplishment. Finally, Part C comprised an open-ended question that asked respondents to list phenomena related to their work which they believed contributed most to feelings of stress.

Exploratory factor analyses of the MBI have yielded three well-defined factors representing emotional exhaustion, depersonalization, and personal accomplishment for helping professions in general (Firth, McIntee, McKeown, & Britton, 1985; Maslach & Jackson, 1981), and for teachers in particular (Beck & Gargiulo, 1983; Belcastro et. al., 1983; Gold, 1984; Iwanicki & Schwab, 1981). Reported reliability findings have yielded internal consistency coefficients ranging from .76 to .90 (mean $\alpha = .81$) (Beck & Gargiulo, 1981; Belcastro et. al., 1983; Iwanicki & Schwab, 1981; Maslach & Jackson, 1981), and subscale test–retest coefficients (Emotional Exhaustion .82; Depersonalization .60; Personal Accomplishment .80), based on a 2-4 week interval (Maslach & Jackson, 1981).

Finally, strong evidence of convergent validity has been reported for educators (Jackson, Schwab, & Schuler, 1986; Meier, 1984), as well as for other human service professionals (Maslach & Jackson, 1981). Discriminant validity, on the other hand, is less clear. While evidence in support of discriminant validity has been illustrated by low and nonsignificant correlations between MBI scores and job dissatisfaction, and social desirability (Jackson et. al., 1986; Maslach & Jackson, 1981), Meier (1984) reported substantially high correlations with factors of depression. These latter findings notwithstanding, the literature generally provides adequately strong support for the MBI as a potentially reliable and valid measure of educator burnout.

Analyses of the Data

The quantitative data (Parts A & B of the Teacher Stress Survey) were analyzed in two stages. First, background variables were effects-coded and then entered setwise (i.e., sets of membership categories for each background variable) into a multiple regression analysis (MRA). (Membership categories for each background variable are listed in the Appendix.) Quantifying group membership in this way provided the means for equating the regression model with an analysis of variance (ANOVA) model. As such, it became possible to interpret findings within an ANOVA framework (i.e., 1-way ANOVA), with the added bonus of gaining important correlational information (Cohen & Cohen, 1983; Pedazur, 1982). In the same way that effects associated with the ANOVA model are interpreted as explaining variance in some dependent variable, effects associated with the MRA model reflect the amount of variance attributable to group membership.

Given (a) relatively low intercorrelations among Emotional Exhaustion, Depersonalization, and Personal Accomplishment ($Md = .17$, .21, .28, and .02 for elementary, intermediate, secondary, and university educators, respectively), and (b) the exploratory nature of the study, it was considered appropriate to examine relations between background variables and burnout for each of its factors separately (see Huberty & Morris, 1989). Possible experimentwise error (i.e., Type I error) was controlled through use of the improved Bonferroni correction procedure recently proposed by Holland and Copenhaver (1988). Additionally. Fisher's "protected t" procedure guided the interpretation of significant partial regression coefficients. That is, any significant contribution of a background variable to the variance of a particular facet of burnout, as indicated by the t-statistic, was interpreted only if the F-value for R was itself statistically significant. Likewise. this contingency held for the interpretation of significant membership effects, as reflected by the unstandardized regression coefficients (see Cohen & Cohen, 1983; Pedhazur, 1982).

As with ANOVA, the MRA coded effects derived in Stage 1 were able only to demonstrate the extent to which the mean of one particular membership group differed from the grand mean of all groups in combination. Additional *post hoc* analyses were therefore needed to test for differences among membership groups comprising each background variable; effects-coded nominal variables are particularly suited to such analyses (Cohen & Cohen, 1983; Pedhazur, 1982). The second stage of the analyses, then, involved the conduct of multiple comparisons based on procedures designed specifically for use with effects-coded variables (see Cohen & Cohen, 1983). Again analyses were carried out only if the overall F-ratio related to R^2 was significant.

The qualitative data (Part C) were first reviewed for overall content and then categorized into factors considered plausible in representing work-related stressors associated with teaching at each of the four institutional levels; the 10 most salient factors were subsequently rank ordered for each group. The intent in formulating these factors was to provide a base for future research that investigates substantive issues related to stress as a determinant of burnout.

Results

Means, standard deviations, and alpha internal consistency reliability coefficients for each burnout factor by educator group are presented in Table 1. Except for the Depersonalization and Personal Accomplishment factors, as they relate to elementary school teachers, reliability coefficients for all MBI subscales were substantial and relatively consistent across groups.

Background variables

Initial multiple regression analyses revealed that, for intermediate teachers, group membership related to selected background variables failed to explain significant amounts of variance in each of the three factors of burnout. Significant findings for elementary, secondary, and university

Table 1

Means, Standard Deviations, and Cronbach Alpha Reliability Coefficients for Factors of Teacher Burnout

	Emotional Exhaustion			Depersonalization			Personal Accomplishment		
	M	*SD*	α	*M*	*SD*	α	*M*	*SD*	α
Elementary (n = 98)	21.59	11.71	.90	5.24	3.63	.64	40.28	6.00	.69
Intermediate (n = 163)	23.24	11.78	.92	7.41	6.41	.83	38.19	6.29	.77
Secondary (n = 162)	21.27	10.71	.89	6.64	5.15	.71	35.88	8.19	.84
University (n = 219)	17.80	10.46	.89	7.01	6.51	.74	36.90	7.64	.83

α = Cronbach alpha reliability coefficient.

educators are summarized in Table 2.[1] We turn now to an elaboration of these results.

Table 2

Setwise Multiple Regression Results for Significant Membership Effects on Factors of Burnout

Variable	R	R^2	$F(df)$[a]	Group	Effects B[b]	Y[c]	$t(df)$
			Elementary teachers ($n = 98$)				
Emotional Exhaustion							
Gender	.22	.05	5.06* (1,96)	Males	−3.53	19.22	−2.25*(94)
Personal Accomplishment							
Age	.30	.09	3.16* (3,94)	40–49 years	1.79	39.95	1.94*(94)
			Secondary teachers ($n = 162$)				
Emotional Exhaustion							
Type[d]	.20	.04	3.43* (2,159)	Vocational	−3.13	20.97	−2.43* (159)
				combinations	2.27	20.97	2.14* (159)[e]
Depersonalization							
Gender	.23	.05	9.03** (1,160)	Males	1.22	6.35	3.01** (160)
Personal Accomplishment							
Type	.21	.05	3.99** (2,159)	Regular	−2.46	56.25	−2.81** (159)
			University professors ($n = 219$)				
Emotional Exhaustion							
Gender	.23	.06	12.99***(1,217)	Males	2.48	17.67	−3.60***(217)
Age	.23	.05	4.07** (3,215)	Over 50 years	−3.69	18.79	−2.79** (215)[d]
Personal Accomplishment							
Gender	.21	.04	9.58** (1,217)	Males	1.57	36.98	3.10** (217)
Age	.23	.05	4.14** (3,215)	Over 50 years	3.16	36.29	3.26** (215)[d]
Type[e]	.26	.07	7.72***(2,216)	Undergraduates	−2.32	37.80	−3.28** (216)
				Graduates	3.43	37.80	3.76***(216)

* $p < .05$; ** $p < .01$; *** $p < .001$.
[a] Degrees of freedom.
[b] Unstandardized regression coefficient, which reflects the treatment effect.
[c] Grand mean of burnout factor as represented by the intercept.
[d] Type of student taught.
[e] See note 2.

Elementary School Educators

For elementary teachers, only the factors of Emotional Exhaustion and Personal Accomplishment were significantly influenced by particular background variables; gender accounted for 5% of the variance in Emotional Exhaustion, while age accounted for 9% of the variance in Personal Accomplishment; the significant age effect, however, was attributed to the 40-49 year group only. Examination of the unstandardized regression coefficients (Bs), which represent the effects, reveals males to exhibit a lower level of emotional exhaustion than females, and the 40-49 age group to have a slightly higher, albeit significant, level of personal accomplishment relative to the overall group mean.

Multiple comparison results, as shown in Table 3, revealed males to exhibit a significantly lower level of emotional exhaustion than females. With respect to membership categories related to age, a significant difference was found between teachers in the 30-39 year age bracket and those in the 40-49 year range; the latter exhibited a higher level of personal accomplishment than their younger colleagues.

Table 3

Multiple Comparison Results for Significant Membership Effects on Factors of Burnout

Variable	Comparison groups	M	SD	$t(df)$[a]
		Elementary teachers ($n = 98$)		
Emotional Exhaustion				
Gender	Males vs.	15.69	7.68	−2.31* (96)
	females	22.74	12.04	
Personal Accomplishment				
Age	30–39 yrs vs.	38.45	6.83	−2.47* (94)
	40–49 yrs	41.74	5.26	
		Secondary teachers ($n = 162$)		
Emotional Exhaustion				
Type[b]	Vocational vs.	17.84		−2.28* (159)
	combination	23.24		
Depersonalization				
Gender	Males vs.	7.57	5.69	2.79** (160)
	females	5.13	3.69	
		University professors ($n = 219$)		
Emotional Exhaustion				
Gender	Males vs.	15.19	9.48	−3.44*** (217)
	females	20.16	10.77	
Age	30–39 yrs vs.	20.95	10.39	3.29** (215)
	50 yrs and over	15.10	9.96	
Personal Accomplishment				
Gender	Males vs.	38.55	6.98	2.96** (217)
	females	35.40	7.94	
Age	30–39 yrs vs.	35.28	8.48	−3.21** (215)
	50 yrs and over	39.45	6.88	
Type	Undergraduate vs.	35.48	7.35	3.95*** (216)
	graduate	41.23	5.07	

* $p < .05$; ** $p < .01$; *** $p < .001$.
[a]Degrees of freedom.
[b]Type of student taught.

Secondary School Educators

Type of student taught was found to have an important effect on both the Emotional Exhaustion and Personal Accomplishment aspects of burnout for secondary school teachers, accounting for 4% and 5% of the variance, respectively. This variable was found to have a significant effect on Emotional Exhaustion for both teachers of vocational students, and those of classes comprising a composite of regular academic and special education students. Relative to the overall mean for the three teaching categories, vocational teachers demonstrated lower levels of emotional exhaustion, while teachers of combination classes yielded levels that were higher.[2] Rather surprisingly, teachers of regular academic students exhibited a lower level of personal accomplishment than the overall mean of the three groups.

Also of importance for secondary school teachers was the finding of a highly significant gender effect for the factor of Depersonalization, accounting for 5% of the variance. Interestingly, this was the only group of educators for whom depersonalization seemed influenced by background effects. As such, males yielded higher levels of depersonalization than females.

Examination of the multiple comparison results reveals a significant difference in level of emotional exhaustion between teachers of vocational students, and those who teach combination classes, the latter demonstrating the higher level. With respect to gender differences, males exhibited a significantly higher level of depersonalization than females. No significant differences in personal accomplishment were found for membership categories related to type of student taught.

University Educators

Somewhat surprisingly, the impact of background variables on facets of burnout for university professors was found to be profound and comparatively stronger than for either of the other two levels of teaching. This finding is especially interesting in light of the sparseness of burnout research bearing on the university population. Once again, gender was found to be a particularly salient variable, having a highly significant effect on both Emotional Exhaustion and Personal Accomplishment; 6% of the variance in Emotional Exhaustion, and 4% of the variance in Personal Accomplishment was attributable to the effect of gender. Whereas males demonstrated lower levels of emotional exhaustion than females, their levels of personal accomplishment were higher.

Age, as well, was found to have a remarkably strong impact on both Emotional Exhaustion and Personal Accomplishment, accounting for 5% of the variance in both factors. Not unexpectedly, this effect was associated with the over-50 age group for both Emotional Exhaustion and Personal Accomplishment. Relative to the overall mean for age, the over-50 group exhibited lower levels of emotional exhaustion albeit higher levels of personal accomplishment.

Finally, type of student taught yielded a highly significant effect on Personal Accomplishment, accounting for 7% of the variance. Professors whose teaching was limited primarily to undergraduate students, and those teaching mainly graduate students were the sole contributors to the type-of-student effect. Compared with the overall mean, professors of mainly undergraduates demonstrated lower levels of personal accomplishment, while those teaching mainly graduate students demonstrated levels that were higher.

Results of the multiple comparison analyses revealed highly significant differences between males and females with respect to both emotional exhaustion and personal accomplishment; as with elementary school teachers, male professors exhibited lower levels of emotional exhaustion than their female colleagues. In contrast, levels of personal accomplishment were higher for male, than for female professors. With respect to comparisons among the age categories, significant differences were found between the 40-49, and the over-50 age groups. Finally, professors who teach mainly undergraduate students demonstrated lower levels of personal accomplishment than those whose teaching was limited largely to graduate students.

Stress factors

Rank-ordered factors of work-related stress revealed some interesting findings for educators in each of the four teaching panels; these are presented in Table 4. First, it is clear that, irrespective of educational level, teachers share many similar frustrations: imposed time constraints, large class sizes, excessive administrative demands and paperwork, perceived lack of ad-

Table 4

Rank Order of Factors Perceived by Teachers as Contributing Most to Feelings of Work-related Stress

Elementary (n = 82)	Secondary (n = 138)
1. Excessive administrative paperwork	1. Time constraints
2. Time constraints	2. Student attitudes and behavior
3. Number of students	3. External personal factors
4. Parents' expectations	4. Lack of administrative/parental support and recognition
6. Extracurricular and supervisory duties	5. Apathy and increasing burnout of many colleagues
7. Classes with students of varying abilities and need	6. Sense of powerlessness
8. Lack of administrative/parental support and recognition	7. Number of students
9. Excessive course loads; ever-changing curriculum	8. Excessive administrative paperwork
10. Multiplicity of roles expected to play	9. Student discipline problems
	10. Multiplicity of roles expected to play

Intermediate (n = 148)	University (n = 172)
1. Number of students	1. Time constraints
2. Time constraints	2. Publish/perish syndrome
3. Parents' expectations	3. Excessive administrative paperwork
4. Excessive administrative paperwork and interference	4. Lack of administrative support and recognition
5. Student attitudes and behavior	5. Multiplicity of roles expected to play
6. Multiplicity of roles expected to play	6. Budgetary constraints; limited resources
7. Extracurricular and supervisory duties	7. Number of students
8. Lack of administrative/parental support and recognition	8. External personal factors
9. Student discipline problems	9. Poor academic training of undergraduate students
10. Apathy and increasing burnout of many colleagues	10. Student attitudes and behavior

ministrative support, and the need to "wear many different hats." Second, a common theme repeatedly expressed by teachers at the elementary and intermediate levels was the intense pressure they experienced from trying to meet the demands of many masters—principal, parents, students, school board officials; they felt drained from the pull in many directions, with little reward in the form of support or recognition. Finally, while student-related problems were relatively high on the list of stress-inducing factors for intermediate and secondary school teachers, they were well down the list for university professors. For the latter, it seems evident that pressures associated with the conduct of research and the need to publish ranked higher on their agenda. Overall, these findings for non-university educators are consistent with those reported in the literature (see Friesen & Williams, 1985; Friesen et. al., 1988; Hiebert 1985; Kuzsman & Schnall, 1987; Makinen & Kinnunen, 1986; Schwab et. al., 1986).

Discussion

Background Variables

No background variable was found to bear importantly on burnout for teachers at the intermediate school level. This finding, however, may be a consequence of confusion related to the operational definition of "intermediate." While the related questionnaire item identified grades 6-8 as those defining the intermediate level, in practice, the existence of a few intermediate schools as physically independent entities may have confounded the term; in Ontario, grades taught in these schools can be some variant of 6-8, 6-9, 7-8, or 7-9. The ensuing discussion, therefore, is limited to those teaching at the elementary, secondary, and university levels.

Gender. For each of these groups of educators, gender was found to have an important effect on at least one facet of burnout. Consistent with Maslach and Jackson's (1981, 1985) extensive study of human service professionals in general, female educators at both the elementary and university levels demonstrated significantly higher levels of emotional exhaustion than their male colleagues. Socialization factors related to sex-role expectations may possibly explain these findings in at least two ways. First, despite the incidence of working wives and mothers in present North American society, old traditions die hard; women more than men still tend to be responsible for satisfying both the emotional and physical needs of the family. Thus, for women teachers, the fulfillment of family needs, along with those of students, parents, and administrators, assigns them a double dose of caring for others which may subsequently lead to extensive emotional exhaustion. Although the influence of marital/family status on emotional exhaustion is implied here, findings were not significant in this regard. Nonetheless, this proposition remains intuitively plausible particularly for elementary teachers, only 17% of whom were single with no dependants; small sample size probably bore importantly on these findings. In contrast, the impact of marital/family status for women professors appeared to be less salient, with 27% of them being single with no dependants. A second factor contributing to the import of gender on emotional exhaustion may be that women are more likely than men to become emotionally involved with the problems of their students, this added strain again leading to increased emotional exhaustion.

The fact that female professors exhibited reduced feelings of personal accomplishment, compared with their male colleagues, again supports the work of Maslach and Jackson (1981, 1985); the results, nonetheless, are difficult to explain. Maslach and Jackson (1985) have suggested that, as a consequence of feeling emotionally drained from their work, women may feel that they have not accomplished a lot in that work. For women professors, however, this link between emotional exhaustion and personal accomplishment did not hold in the present sample ($r = .02$); the association was similarly weak for males ($r = -.10$).[3] Given comparable findings relative to depersonalization ($r = -.08$), it would appear that feelings of reduced personal accomplishment, for women professors, derive from external factors that may or may not be related to academia.

Finally, results were consistent with past research related to human service professionals in general, and to teachers in particular, in showing male high school teachers to exhibit higher levels of depersonalization than female teachers.

Age. Although consistent with the literature in showing younger teachers to experience more emotional exhaustion than older teachers, results were pertinent to university professors only. Not unexpectedly, professors at the beginning of their careers (30-39 years), confronted with the hurdles of rank and tenure, demonstrated significantly higher levels of emotional exhaustion than their older, presumably more well-established colleagues (50 years and over).

Age also contributed meaningfully to perceptions of personal accomplishment for both elementary and university educators; in both cases, younger educators exhibited significantly lower levels of perceived personal accomplishment than their older colleagues. While the major difference lay between the 30-39 and 40-49 age groups for elementary teachers, the gap was much wider at the university level; professors in their 30s again differed from their colleagues who were 50 years and over. Once again, the stage of one's career appears to have an important bearing on educators' perceptions of personal accomplishment. Typically, elementary teachers in their 30s are busy attaining the necessary certification for the administrative positions of principal, superintendent, and the like; by the time they reach their 40s, such goals have probably been achieved, with the result that they perceive their accomplishments in a more favorable light. The same argument can be made for university professors, albeit the goals are somewhat different (i.e., rank, tenure, international recognition), and the time span somewhat more extensive.

Type of student taught. It seems reasonable to expect that certain types of students generate high levels of stress and frustration for teachers; typically, these students require extra attention, discipline, and/or special care (e.g., vocational, learning disabled). Although the anecdotal literature generally supports this notion, little quantitative empirical research has investigated the impact of this variable on burnout among educators. Indeed, the present study revealed type of student taught to have an important impact on emotional exhaustion for high school teachers, and on perceptions of personal accomplishment for both high school teachers and university professors.

That feelings of emotional exhaustion for high school teachers of vocational students tended to be lower than those exhibited by teachers of other classes may be a function of two factors: (a) class sizes for vocational students are usually smaller than those of regular students, and (b) society's expectations for these children are less demanding than they are for regular academic students; this, in turn may impose less pressure on their teachers. Relatedly, it seems perfectly reasonable that teachers of classes composed of a mix of regular academic and special education students should experience higher levels of emotional exhaustion. Indeed, one of the most frequently expressed concerns by secondary school teachers in both the United States and Canada is the legislated mandate that students of widely diverse intellectual abilities share the same classroom learning climate; the ultimate consequence of such legislation on the well-being of its teachers, however, appears to be rapidly taking its toll.

Although high school teachers of regular academic students, on the average, demonstrated feelings of reduced personal accomplishment compared with teachers of other types of students, no significant differences related to group membership were found. These negative perceptions by teachers are possibly explained by the fact that the fruits of their efforts are not as readily discernible, for example, as those of their colleagues who teach vocational students; for teachers of regular students, the skill-transfer process is necessarily more complex and extends over a substantially longer period of time.

Finally, findings that university professors teaching graduate students experienced a greater sense of personal accomplishment than those teaching undergraduate students cannot be considered surprising. Undoubtedly, substantially smaller class sizes provide the means for important teacher/student dialogue; this, together with the commonality of academic purpose, probably leads to a more positive sense of personal accomplishment.

Stress Factors

In general, although certain common stress-inducing factors were found across educators, (e.g., time constraints, number of students, multiplicity of expected roles, lack of administrative/parental support), these results indicate, not unexpectedly, that educators at the university level march to a different drummer than do their public school colleagues. Whereas the major contributors to stress for the latter tend to be largely student and parent-related, those for university educators are linked to research and administrative tasks. Overall, results for the elementary, intermediate, and secondary school samples appear consistent with findings reported in the many anecdotal studies for these school levels in general, and within the North American milieu, in particular. Given their saliency across educational panels, these factors appear to be potentially valuable links to advancing our current knowledge of stress as a determinant of educator burnout.

In summary, based on this study and other research, four facts seem abundantly clear: (a) burnout is a multidimensional construct, the facets of which are differentially affected by particular background variables, (b) gender, age, and type of student taught are highly salient background variables associated with educator burnout, (c) the grade level at which an educator is teaching bears importantly on the impact of these variables on aspects of burnout, and (d) organizational factors related to the administration of educational institutions contribute weightily to teacher stress at all levels of the educative system.

It is evident that current educational policy bearing on teachers' work environments must change. But first, it remains the task of researchers to delineate the stress points in the educational structure. Future research should address the problem by investigating the nomological network of teacher burnout as it relates to the organizational (e.g., role conflict, decision making power) and personal variables (locus of control, personality type) shown to bear importantly upon it.

Notes

1   Although years of experience was initially intended for inclusion in the analyses, preliminary investigation showed it to be a potential suppressor variable; it was subsequently deleted from the multiple regression analyses.

2   Because in effects coding the last of a set of membership groups is coded as -1, there is no test of its partial coefficients reported on the usual MRA computer output. These values were therefore calculated manually (see Cohen & Cohen, 1983).

3   In contrast, this correlation for non-university educators was as follows: elementary (males, $r=-.31$; females, $r=-.25$), intermediate (males, $r=-.22$; females, $r=-.30$), secondary (males, $r=-.30$; females, $r=-.22$).

References

Anderson, M.B., & Iwanicki, E.F. (1984). Teacher motivation and its relationship to burnout. *Educational Admistration Quarterly, 20*, 109-132.

Beck, C.L. & Gargiulo, R.M. (1983). Burnout in teachers of retarded and nonretarded children. *Journal of Educational Research, 76*, 169-173.

Belcastro, P.A., Gold, R.S., & Hays, L.C. (1983). Maslach Burnout Inventory: Factor structures for samples of teachers. *Psychological Reports, 53*, 364-366.

Bensky, J.M., Shaw, S.F., Gouse, A.S., Bates, H., Dixon, B., & Beane, W.E. (1980). Public Law 94-142 and stress: A problem for educators, *Exceptional Children, 47*, 24-29.

Cohen, J., & Cohen, P. (1983). *Applied multiple regression/correlation analysis for the behavioral sciences.* Hillsdale, NJ: Erlbaum.

Cooper, C.L., & Marshall, J. (1976). Occupational sources of stress: A review of the literature relating to coronary heart disease and mental ill health. *Journal of Occupational Psychology, 49*, 11-28.

Farber, B.A. (1983). A critical perspective on burnout. In B.A. Farber (Ed.). *Stress and burnout in the human service professions* (pp. 1-20). New York: Pergamon Press.

Farber, B.A., & Miller, J. (1981). Teacher burnout: A psychoeducational educational perspective. *Teachers College Record, 83*, 235-243.

Feitler, F.C., & Tokar, E. (1982). Getting a handle on teacher stress: How bad is the problem? *Educational Leadership, 39*, 456-458.

Firth, H., McIntee, J., McKeown, & Britton, P.G. (1985). Maslach Burnout Inventory: Factor structure and norms for British nursing staff. *Psychological Reports, 57*, 147-150.

Friesen, D., Prokop, C.M., & Sarros, J.C. (1988). Why teachers burn out. *Educational Research Quarterly, 12*, 9-19.

Friesen, D., & Williams, M.J. (1985). Organizational stress among teachers. *Canadian Journal of Education, 10*, 13-34.

Freudenberger, H.J. (1974). Staff burn-out. *Journal of Social Issues, 30*, 159-165.

Gold, Y. (1984). The factorial validity of the Maslach Burnout Inventory in a sample of California elementary and junior high school classroom teachers. *Educational and Psychological Measurement, 44*, 1009-1016.

Hiebert, B. (1985). *Stress and teachers: The Canadian scene.* Toronto: Canadian Educational Association.

Holland, B.S., & Copenhaver, M.D. (1988). Improved Bonferroni-type multiple testing procedures. *Psychological Bulletin, 104*, 145-149.

Huberty, C.J., & Morris, J.D. (1989). Multivariate analysis versus multiple univariate analyses. *Psychological Bulletin, 105*, 302-308.

Ianni, F.A., & Reuss-Ianni, E. (1983). "Take this job and shove it!" A comparison of organizational stress and burnout among teachers and police. In B.A. Farber (Ed.), *Stress and burnout in the human service profession* (pp.. 82-96). New York: Pergamon Press.

Iwanicki, E.F. (1983). Toward understanding and alleviating teacher burnout. *Theory into Practice, 12*, 27-32.

Iwanicki, E.F., & Schwab, R.L. (1981). A cross validation study of the Maslach Burnout Inventory. *Educational and Psychological Measurement, 41*, 1167-1174.

Jackson, S.E., Schwab, R.L., & Schuler, R.S. (1986). Toward an understanding of the burnout phenomenon. *Journal of Applied Psychology, 71*, 630-640.

Kuzsman, F.J., & Schnall, H. (1987). Managing teachers' stress: Improving discipline. *The Canadian School Executive, 6*, 3-10.

Makinen, R., & Kinnunen, U. (1986). Teacher stress over a school year. *Scandinavian Journal of Educational Research, 30*, 55-70.

Maslach, C., & Jackson, S.E. (1981). The measurement of experienced burnout. *Journal of Occupational Behaviour, 2*, 99-113.

Maslach, C., & Jackson, S.E. (1984). Burnout in organizational settings. In S. Oskamp (Ed.), *Applied social psychology annual vol. 6: Applications in organizational settings* (pp. 133-153). Beverly Hills, CA: Sage.

Maslach, C., & Jackson, S.E. (1985). The role of sex and family variables in burnout. *Sex Roles, 12*, 837-851.

Maslach, C., & Jackson, S.E. (1986). *Maslach Burnout Inventory Manual* (2nd. ed.). Palo Alto, CA: Consulting Psychologists Press.

Meier, S.T. (1984). The construct validity of burnout. *Journal of Occupational Psychology, 57*, 211-219.

Olson, J., & Matuskey, P.V. (1982). Causes of burnout in SLD teachers. *Journal of Learning Disabilities, 15*, 97-99.

Pedhazur, E.J. (1982). *Multiple regression in behavioral research.* New York: Holt, Rinehart & Winston.

Perlman, B., & Hartman, E.A. (1982). Burnout: Summary and future research. *Human Relations, 35*, 283-305.

Schwab, R.L., Jackson, S.E., & Schuler, R.S. (1986). Educator burnout: Sources and consequences. *Educational Research Quarterly, 10*, 14-30.

Schwab, R.L. (1983). Teacher burnout: Moving beyond "psychobabble." *Theory into Practice, 12*, 21-26.

Schwab, R.L., & Iwanicki, E.F. (1982). Who are our burned out teachers? *Educational Research Quarterly, 7*, 5-16.

Appendix

Membership categories for each background variable (except gender) were as follows:

Age:
>   1. 20-29 years
>   2. 30-39 years
>   3. 40-49 years
>   4. 50 years and over

Marital/Family status:
>   1. Married with no children
>   2. Married with children
>   3. Single with no children
>   4. Single with children

Teacher Experience
>   1. 0-4 years

2. 5-12 years
3. 13-20 years
4. 21 years and over

Type of student taught
(a) Public school[a]
    1. Regular academic
    2. General
    3. Basic
    4. Gifted
    5. Learning disabled
    6. Combination of regular academic and one or more of categories 2-5

(b) University
    1. Undergraduate
    2. Graduate
    3. Both graduate and undergraduate

a   Given the presence of cells that were either empty or had n values <5, the original six categories were collapsed to two categories (regular academic, combined regular and special education) for elementary and intermediate teachers, and to three categories (regular academic, vocational, combination of regular and special education) for secondary teachers; for the latter, general and basic level classes were combined to form the vocational category.

Learner Characteristics

Every Zobole is yellow.
All red things have a nose.
Do Zoboles have a nose?

If you're not sure of the answer, pay particular attention to the study in which Markovits, Schleifer, and Fortier analyzed the ability of 6-, 8-, and 11-year-olds to use deductive reasoning to solve syllogisms like this one. Their results indicated that, although the youngest children quite often solved syllogisms correctly, they were relying on syntactic cues rather than on a genuine understanding of the relationship between the premises. The above syllogism is *illogical*. You cannot tell from the information given whether Zoboles have noses or not. However, the youngest children in the Markovits et al. study would answer that Zoboles do have a nose because the second premise is worded positively: *all* red things have a nose. If the second premise was worded negatively—*no* red things have a nose—the children would give a "no" response. By using this technique on *logical* syllogisms (e.g. Every Zobole is yellow, All yellow things have a nose, Do Zoboles have a nose?), the children looked as if they were using deductive reasoning.

The relationship between language and cognition is explored in the study by Moore, Bryant, and Furrow. Past research indicates that children start to talk about intangible mental states like *knowing* and *remembering* as early as two or three, but the age at which they actually understand what these words mean is still not clear. The authors used monkey puppets and hidden candy to determine the age at which children understood that the word *know* implies more certainty than the word *think*, which in turn implies more certainty than the word *guess*. Their results suggest that children differentiate clearly between know and the other two words by five. However, even the oldest children tested did not seem to recognize any difference between *think* and *guess*. Of course, as the authors mention, the problem may be that think and guess do not represent different degrees of certainty for many adults!

What do Piaget and cognitive development have to do with art? According to Gebotys and Cupchik, the move from the "artistic flair" of the preschool child to the "restrained art" of middle childhood is related to the movement from the preoperational to the concrete operational stage, as the child sacrifices spontaneity in order to master specific artistic techniques like perspective. Once these techniques are part of their repertoire, children can let themselves go again. So, as in many other domains, the cognitive aspect of art appreciation and production improves with age. With regard to affective responses to art, however, Gebotys and Cupchik contend that younger children, not yet concerned with the rules governing "good art," should have a stronger emotional response to aesthetic efforts. They may not know how it's done, but they know what they like. The results of their study tended to support these hypotheses, with 6-year-olds responding more emotionally to other people's artwork and producing more expressive artwork than 9- or 12-year-olds, while the older children demonstrated a greater understanding of what they were seeing and produced more technically proficient drawings.

Pancer and Weinstein investigated the development of a number of affective skills (e.g., the ability to infer another person's feelings), the relationship between these skills and cognitive skills, and the relationship between affective skills and emotional adjustment. As expected, four of the five affective skills examined improved with age from Grade 3 to Grade 6, and cognitive and affective skills were correlated. However, affective skills and emotional adjustment seemed to be related only for Grade 4 students. In other words, at some ages, not being very good at interpersonal relationships did not seem to be particularly bothersome. Perhaps it is only as children get older that a lack of such skills becomes a liability.

Serbin and Sprafkin's article on the salience of gender and the process of sex-typing in 3- to 7-year-old children is challenging to read but worth the effort. The authors' contention, supported by the results of their study, is that all children initially categorize people on the basis of gender because, like colour, it is a readily available basis for classification. As they grow older, children learn about sex roles, the characteristics associated with the gender category in our society, just as they learn about characteristics (shade, intensity) associated with the colour category. In terms of cognitive development, once they have mastered all aspects of the sex-role classification scheme, children move on to other classification schemata. Children's affectively based responses to gender differences are more variable, reflecting individual environmental differences in sex-typing. The results of Serbin and Sprafkin's study provide support for this explanation. Classification on the basis of gender declined steadily between ages 3 and 7, while knowledge of sex roles increased over the same age span. However, boys increasingly used gender as the basis of affiliation with adults as they got older, while girls' use of gender as a basis for affiliation preference remained fairly constant over age.

Development of Elementary Deductive Reasoning in Young Children

Henry Markovits, Michael Schleifer, and Lorraine Fortier
Université du Québec à Montréal

This study examined the claim (Hawkins, Pea, Glick, & Scribner, 1984), that young children can reason deductively with content for which "practical knowledge is irrelevant." Ss 6, 8, and 11 years of age were given a set of standard logical syllogisms and a matching set of illogical ones. Six-year-olds gave similar responses to and used similar types of justifications for both logical and illogical forms, indicating that correct performance on the former might be accounted for by a low-level matching strategy, not necessarily by deductive reasoning. A clear developmental pattern emerged, showing that the ability of children to differentiate responses to the two forms improves over this age period. However, the number of children able to explicitly describe illogicality remained small, even among 11-year-olds.

*   *   *

A RECENT STUDY (HAWKINS, PEA, GLICK, & SCRIBNER, 1984) CLAIMED TO show that children as young as 4 years old can reason deductively with content for which "practical knowledge is irrelevant." The authors called into question Inhelder and Piaget's (1958) view that young children cannot reason syllogistically. In the Hawkins et al. study, a form of syllogism was used for which subjects were asked to answer *yes* or *no* to a conclusion. They were also evaluated as to whether they referred only to the premises to justify their response. Both the high rate of correct conclusions for specific content using "fantasy" terms and the presence of referral to premises were taken to be evidence of deductive (syllogistic) reasoning.

The results obtained by Hawkins et al. (1984) are convincing, but, nevertheless, somewhat limited in scope. They indicate that when very young children do not use empirical knowledge, they appear capable of using syntactic information in a consistent manner for a limited number of syllo-

Preparation of this article was supported by grants from the Quebec Ministry of Education (FCAR) and the Natural Sciences and Engineering Research Council of Canada to Henry Markovits. We would like to thank Kim Surette for help in data collection. We would also like to thank Dave Moshman and two anonymous reviewers for their very helpful comments.

gistic forms (those with determinate answers). There are many possible ways that this might be done. One such strategy is the "atmosphere effect." Studies have shown that adult subjects tend to use the presence or absence of positive and negative components in presented syllogisms to give their responses (Evans & Lynch, 1973; Woodworth & Sells, 1935). In the context of the syllogisms used by Hawkins et al., use of such a strategy would imply that a *yes* response would be generated by syllogisms with positive premises, whereas those with a negative premise would receive *no* responses. This would result in a high level of "correct" responses solely on the basis of information contained in the premises and is clearly a possible explanation for the level of correct responding found with young children. There may, of course, be other such strategies that would permit children to generate correct responses to verbal syllogisms on the basis of syntactic information. The problem remains of the extent to which the ability of young children to respond correctly in a consistent manner in this context may be a sufficient criterion for ascribing a deductive reasoning capacity.

There is, however, no clear consensus as to what might be considered a sufficient criterion in this context. Nonetheless, it might be argued that any discussion of deductive reasoning competence should include the recognition of situations of undecidability (Piaget, 1981/1987; Piéraut-Le Bonniec, 1980; Scholnick & Wing, 1988). In this perspective, if subjects are able to reason deductively with syllogisms, they should be able to distinguish between premises that are logically connected and those that are not. This would not necessarily be the case if subjects were using a strategy that was based on the atmosphere effect, because this, although using only information contained in the premises, does not require analysis of the logical structure of the syllogism.

One major purpose in the present study was to examine the hypothesis that very young children are able to provide correct responses to the forms of syllogism used by Hawkins et al. (1984) without necessarily being able to understand logical relations sufficiently to distinguish consistently between connected and unconnected premises. The basic method used here involved the construction of a series of six syllogisms that were based on those used by Hawkins et al., each with a logical structure of the basic form A-B, B-C. A second set of six corresponding syllogisms with the same content was constructed. This set was altered so as to have the form A-B, C-D (i.e., so that the two premises had no logical links). Specifically, we hypothesized that the youngest (6-year-old) children that we examined would give similar responses to both the logical and illogical syllogisms. In addition, we wished to examine developmental patterns in the logical reasoning abilities of children from 6 to 11 years on these elementary forms of abstract or fantasy syllogisms.

Method

Subjects

The subjects were 85 French-speaking children from a public elementary school on the outskirts of Montreal. Of these, 33 were in kindergarten, ($M=6.12$ years, $SD=0.32$), 23 were in second grade ($M=8.15$ years, $SD=0.45$), and 29 were in fifth grade ($M=11.26$ years, $SD=0.43$).

Materials

Six syllogisms were constructed along the same pattern as those used by Hawkins et al. (1984). The syllogisms included two each of the universal, particular, and action-functional forms, in accordance with the Hawkins et al. design. Two of the six were in the negative mood. Henceforth, we will refer to these six syllogisms as *logical* syllogisms. (See the Appendix for the specific examples.)

A modified version of the six logical syllogisms was made by changing the third term of the syllogism and breaking the link between the two premises but preserving the content of the syllogism. Henceforth, we will refer to these syllogisms as *illogical* syllogisms. (See the Appendix for the specific examples.)

Procedure

Subjects received all 12 (logical and illogical) syllogisms in one of the following orders:

Sequence A. The six logical syllogisms followed by the six illogical syllogisms (in the order given in the Appendix). This sequence will be referred to as the *logical* sequence.

Sequence B. The six illogical syllogisms followed by the six logical syllogisms (in the order given in the Appendix). This sequence will be referred to as the *illogical* sequence.

Sequence C. The 12 syllogisms were presented in a random order with the first syllogism alternating systematically between the logical and the illogical form. This sequence will be referred to as the *random* sequence.

At each age level an approximately equal number of subjects received the logical and illogical sequences. Among the 6-year-olds, there were 11 children in each group that received the logical, illogical, and random sequences. Among the 8-year-olds, 8, 7, and 8 children received these sequences, respectively, and, among the 11-year-olds, the comparative numbers were 10, 9, and 10.

All the materials were presented in French. In what follows, an English translation is used. All the syllogisms were individually presented to each subject. Following the procedure used by Hawkins et al. (1984), a set of short instructions preceded the syllogism presentation. The instructions were as follows:

> I am going to read you some short stories. These stories are about make-believe characters who live on a make-believe planet. After each story, I will ask you a question. I want you to be attentive and pretend that everything the stories say is true.

After the child answered the question, the experimenter asked the child, "How do you know that?" All the answers and justifications were recorded.

Scoring

Subjects responded *yes, no, I don't know,* or *there's no answer* to the initial question. For logical syllogisms, the correct response was *yes* or *no* (depending on the mood of the syllogism). For illogical syllogisms, the theoretically correct response was *there is no way to know* and never *yes* or *no*. For the logical problems, the responses were labeled as *correct, incorrect,* and *don't know.* The incorrect responses included only *yes* or *no* responses that were logically incorrect. To facilitiate comparison between the logical and illogical problems, responses to the latter were

Table 1
Mean Number of Response Types for the Six Logical and Illogical Problems by Age

	Logical problems			Illogical problems		
Age (years)	Correct	Incorrect	Don't know	Equiv-alent	Not equiv-alent	Don't know
6	4.58	1.15	.28	3.91	1.52	0.58
8	4.79	1.10	.10	2.43	3.30	0.26
11	5.31	.54	.12	1.45	3.38	1.17

Note. The logically correct response to the Illogical problems is *don't know.*

labeled *equivalent, nonequivalent,* and *don't know.* An equivalent response was the one that would be correct for the corresponding logical form. A nonequivalent response was one that would be incorrect for the corresponding logical form.

The justifications to the responses were grouped in categories using the following criteria:

None. Express declaration of incapacity to justify the response; no verbal expression at all (e.g., "I don't understand"; "I don't know").

Premises. Reference to one or both premises (e.g., "Yes, because Plouques are tall"; "Yes, because Plouques are tall, and tall things are green").

Conclusion. Repetition of conclusion (e.g., "Yes, because Plouques are green").

Empirical. Reference to empirical knowledge (e.g., "Yes, because Zoboles should have a nose to smell with"; "I don't know, because I've never seen a Plouque").

Authority. Reference to own or other's authority (e.g., "Yes, because I've seen a Plouque"; "Yes, because my father told me").

Invention. Creation of a link between premises by adding invented details (e.g., "Plouques are not green because they are tall, and tall people don't cry").

Illogical. Explicit recognition of lack of relation between premises (e.g., "I can't answer because you didn't tell me if Plouques cry"; "They could be green or not.... If they can cry, then they are not green").

Results

Analysis of Responses to Logical and Illogical Problems

In initial analysis we examined children's responses to the logical and illogical problems. Table 1 indicates the average number of possible responses to the six logical problems and to the six illogical problems, and, as can be seen, there is a clear developmental pattern. All the children produced a very high level of correct responses to the logical problems, in line with the Hawkins et al. (1984) results. However, the 6-year-olds and, to a certain extent, the 8-year-olds produced similar patterns of results to the illogical problems. In the initial analysis, we also examined the extent to which children responded in the same way to the equivalent logical and illogical problems (irrespective of the specific response produced). Children were scored for the number of problems for which they gave an identical response on a logical problem and on the corresponding illogical problem. (Thus, this score varied between 0 and 6.) This indicated that there was a mean of 4.27 matching problems for the 6-year-olds. The corresponding means for the 8- and 11-year-olds were 3.00 and 1.72, respectively. An analysis of variance (ANOVA), with number of matching responses as the dependent variable and age as the independent variable, indicated that there was a significant decrease in matching responses with age, $F(2,117)=27.94$, $p<.001$. Post hoc analyses showed that 6-year-olds produced more matches than did 8-year-olds, who in turn produced more matches than did 11-year-olds.

In a subsequent analysis, we specifically examined the extent to which correct responding on the logical problems could be attributed to an atmosphere effect. To do this, we examined the relation between the number of correct responses on the logical problems and the number of equivalent responses on the illogical problems. We performed a two-way ANOVA, with age level and type of problem (logical and illogical) as independent variables with repeated measures on the latter. This indicated main effects for age, $F(2,117)=6.47$, $p<.01$, and for problem type, $F(1,117)=253.2$, $p<.001$. The Age×Problem Type interaction was also significant, $F(2,117)=44.71$, $p<.001$. Post hoc analyses indicated that there were fewer equivalent responses than correct responses for the 6-year-olds. The difference between the number of correct and equivalent responses increased with age, mainly because of decreasing numbers of equivalent responses.

Thus, these global results indicate that there is a developmental pattern in the ability of children to respond differently to the illogical problems. Although the 6-year-olds did have some ability to do this, they showed a clear tendency to respond to these problems in the same way as to the logical problems. The difference between performance on the logical and illogical problems increased with age, primarily because of the decreasing tendency to respond to the illogical problems in the same way as the logical ones.

Given the number of problems, it is useful to examine performance by individual problem in order to determine the extent to which the overall statistics may be unbalanced by individual variation. Table 2 gives the proportion of correct and equivalent responses to each of the 6 logical and illogical problems by age level. This table indicates that, on the whole, performance on individual problems reflects the overall pattern. We were particularly interested in verifying that the similarity between logical and illogical problems observed among the 6-year-olds was not concentrated in a subset of the 6 problems. In an initial analysis, therefore, we examined the proportion of correct or equivalent responses (for the logical and illogical problems, respectively) over the 12 problems for the youngest group. Cochran's Q test indicated that there was no significant difference among

Table 2
Percentage of Correct Responses to Each of the Six Logical Problems and Percentage of Equivalent Responses to Each of the Six Illogical Problems by Age Level

Age (years)	Logical problems						Illogical problems					
	1	2[a]	3	4[a]	5	6	1	2[a]	3	4[a]	5	6
6	72	81	78	75	83	75	64	81	64	56	58	64
8	91	87	87	87	74	70	43	61	30	48	35	26
11	93	99	93	93	83	86	17	62	10	24	21	10

[a] Indicates problems with negative forms.

the 12 problems, $Q(11) = 1.23$. In a second analysis, we looked at transitions between individual problems. The sign test was used to examine whether there was any significant change in the proportion of correct responses on each of the 6 logical problems and the proportion of equivalent responses for the corresponding illogical problem. This also indicated that, for the youngest children, there was no significant difference between correct and equivalent responses for each of the 6 problems.

Analysis of Response Justifications

Another important aspect that must also be considered concerns the kinds of justifications that subjects gave. Table 3 gives the mean numbers of types of justification for logical and illogical problems as a function of age. Inspection of this table indicates that the pattern of justifications was similar across logical and illogical problems for the 6-year-olds and increasingly differed for the 8- and 11-year-olds. We used repeated measures ANOVAS, with the overall frequency of production of justification types on logical and on illogical problems as the dependent variables and age as the independent variable, to examine differences for the major categories—premises, empirical, and authority. For the premises category, there were significant main effects for type of problem, $F(1,82) = 153.11$, $p < .001$, and for age, $F(2,82) = 29.77$, $p < .001$. In addition, there was a significant Type×Age interaction, $F(2,82) = 29.77$, $p < .001$. Post hoc analyses indicated that, for the youngest subjects, the degree of use of premises was similar for both logical and illogical problems. It was only among the 8- and 11-year-olds that there was a significant difference, because of an increase in the use of the premises category for the logical problems. For both the empirical and authority categories, the analyses indicated no effect of problem type but did reveal an overall decrease in production

Table 3
Mean Numbers of Categories of Justification Produced for Logical and Illogical Problems by Age

Justification category	6-year-olds		8-year-olds		11-year-olds	
	Logic	Illogic	Logic	Illogic	Logic	Illogic
None	1.36	1.82	0.39	0.43	0.07	0.55
Premises	1.24	0.82	3.91	1.61	5.55	1.59
Conclusion	0.73	0.45	0.43	0.52	0.17	0.10
Empirical	1.58	1.18	1.00	1.13	0.14	0.34
Authority	1.09	1.33	0.26	0.09	0.03	0.00
Invention	0.00	0.39	0.00	2.09	0.00	2.34
Illogical	0.00	0.00	0.00	0.13	0.00	1.03

Note. None = no verbal justification, Premises = reference only to one or both premises, Conclusion = repetition of conclusion, Empirical = reference to empirical knowledge, Authority = argument of authority, Invention = creation of a link between premises by adding invented details, and Illogical = overt acceptance of lack of relation between premises.

of these categories over the age range examined. The overall developmental pattern can be summarized as (a) an increase in the level of referral to premises on the logical problems, although not on the illogical ones, (b) a decrease in the use of authority and empirical arguments on both sorts of problems, and (c) an increase in the *invention* of nonexistent links between premises for the illogical problems. This last element is particularly interesting and will be examined subsequently.

One of the arguments that Hawkins et al. (1984) used to support their thesis was that children who referred to premises almost always gave the correct answer, whereas those who used empirical justifications had much lower success rates. This argument assumes that when children are not using extraneous information they are attending to the logical form of the propositions. If this is the case, then children who use the premises justification on the illogical problems should detect the logical inconsistency if they are indeed able to do so. For the youngest children, 37 of 41 logical problems for which subjects referred to premises were correctly resolved (90%). For the 8- and 11-year-olds, the corresponding totals were 76 of 90 (86%) and 150 of 161 (93%), respectively. Thus, the basic finding of Hawkins et al. was replicated. However, for the youngest children, 21 of 27 illogical problems with referral to premises received an equivalent response (78%). Although this proportion was lower than for the logical problems, a chi-square procedure indicated that there was no significant difference between the logical and illogical problems in this respect, $X^2(1, N=68)=1.15$, *ns*. Thus, for the 6-year-olds, use of the premises category was not associated with a major improvement in the detection of the inconsistencies characterizing the illogical problems. This was less the case for the 8- and 11-year-olds, because the percentages of equivalent responses associated with the premises category were 40% and 37%, respectively. For the older children, referral to premises was associated with significantly lower levels of equivalent responses. In fact, both the 8- and 11-year-olds produced a majority of nonequivalent responses when they referred only to the premises, clearly differentiating their responses from those of the youngest children.

One further point must be made here. Hawkins et al. (1984) found that the proportion of correct responses was higher when subjects referred only to premises than when they used empirical justifications. The performance on the logical problems of the 6-year-olds in this study duplicated this result, because the proportion of correct responses after use of the empirical category was 67%, compared with 90% for the premises category. However, the percentages of correct responses associated with the conclusion and authority categories were 88% and 81%, respectively. Thus, although the inclusion of extraneous empirical information does affect children's responses, justifications that could only with difficulty be construed as indicating attention to logical structure, such as the two above, are also associated with high levels of correct responding.

Order of Presentation

Finally, we examined the effect of the sequence of presentation of the logical and illogical problems. Table 4 indicates the mean numbers of responses for the logical and illogical problems by age and presentation sequence. We performed 2 two-way ANOVAs, with age and sequence as the independent variables and number of equivalent responses to the illogical problems as the dependent variable. There was no significant effect of sequence type for the number of correct responses. There was, however, a main effect of sequence type for the number of equivalent responses, $F(2,76)=3.28$, $p<.05$. Post hoc comparisons indicated that this was due to a smaller number of equivalent responses when the illogical problems were presented first. However, although there was an effect of sequence presentation on the production of equivalent responses, this was not the case when the relation between correct responses on the logical problems and equivalent responses on the illogical problems was considered. This indicated that the lower number of equivalent responses produced on the illogical problems when these were presented first was accompanied by lower numbers of correct responses on the logical problems.

These results nonetheless indicated that all of the children had less of a tendency to respond to the illogical problems with equivalent responses when these were presented first. To examine to what extent the different

Table 4
Mean Number of Responses to Logical and Illogical Problems by Form of Presentation and Age

Presentation	Logical problems			Illogical problems		
	Correct	Incorrect	Don't know	Equivalent	Not equivalent	Don't know
6-year-olds						
Logical ($n = 11$)	4.64	1.00	0.36	3.91	1.45	0.64
Illogical ($n = 11$)	4.36	1.36	0.27	3.27	1.73	1.00
Random ($n = 11$)	4.73	1.09	0.18	4.55	1.36	0.09
8-year-olds						
Logical ($n = 8$)	5.63	0.38	0.00	3.25	2.62	0.12
Illogical ($n = 7$)	4.43	1.29	0.29	1.57	4.00	0.43
Random ($n = 8$)	4.75	1.25	0.00	2.38	3.38	0.25
11-year-olds						
Logical ($n = 10$)	5.20	0.60	0.20	1.30	3.60	1.10
Illogical ($n = 9$)	5.56	0.44	0.00	1.33	2.89	1.78
Random ($n = 10$)	5.70	0.30	0.00	1.70	3.60	0.70

forms of presentation affected the (possible) use of a strategy on the basis of the atmosphere effect, we used the binomial test to examine the relative ratio of equivalent and nonequivalent responses. This indicated that, for the 6-year-olds, there were significantly more equivalent than nonequivalent responses when the illogical problems were presented first, whereas there was no significant difference for the logical-first and random presentations. Finally, for the 11-year-olds, there were significantly more nonequivalent than equivalent responses for all three forms of presentation. Thus, these results basically reinforced the previous ones. They indicated that even the youngest children could distinguish logical and illogical premises to a certain extent, and that this distinction was facilitated by receiving the illogical problems first. When these children responded to these problems, however, there was still a clear tendency to generate a response using a strategy associated with the atmosphere effect (or another similar strategy), irrespective of order of presentation. For the 8-year-olds, the overall tendency to produce responses associated with an atmosphere effect disappeared, but it was only when the illogical problems were presented first that these children responded consistently with nonequivalent responses, something that the 11-year-olds did irrespective of presentation.

Discussion

A major problem in understanding the implication of these results concerns the theoretical context in which they might be inserted. The lack of any clear consensus as to the nature of deductive reasoning makes categorical statements about what children can do or cannot do problematic. For example, if deductive reasoning is seen as simply requiring the use of coherent rules that result in the correct answer to specific kinds of reasoning problems, then both our results and those of Hawkins et al. (1984) lead to the clear conclusion that kindergarten-level children do have access to deductive reasoning. If, on the other hand, deductive reasoning is considered to imply a full understanding of the relations of necessity that govern classes of propositions, then almost none of the children examined here (except for the small minority who were simultaneously aware of the indeterminacy of the illogical forms and the necessity of the logical ones) could be said to have access to deductive reasoning. Thus, it is more prudent to attempt to describe what young children appear to be able to do in reasoning situations and leave attributions of logical competence aside.

These results confirm those obtained by Hawkins et al. (1984) and show that children as young as 5 or 6 years can respond to a limited class of propositional reasoning problems correctly when they do not use their empirical knowledge in doing so. These results indicate that in certain circumstances young children are able to consider syntactic cues in responding to such problems. However, the results are also consistent with the notion that much of the correct responding observed at this age may be due to the use of a strategy that relies on the "atmosphere effect," in which the response is chosen as a function of the positive or negative mood of the premises (or some similar strategy that does not involve understanding the relations of necessity between premises and conclusions). Finally, the 6-year-olds do show some signs of differentiating logically consistent and logically inconsistent premises, primarily in terms of their responses to the latter (although not in terms of their justifications).

These results also provide a developmental picture of how children change in their approach to these problems. It is clear that children's ability to detect the lack of a logical link between two premises undergoes a clear developmental improvement. Although even 6-year-olds show some limited ability to do this, it is not until 11 years of age that children make clear distinctions in their responses to logical and illogical syllogisms. Even the 8-year-olds responded identically to logical and illogical problems 50% of the time, whereas the 11-year-olds only did so for 29% of the problems.

Once again, the pattern of justifications that are used by the children on the logical and illogical problems also reveals a similar developmental pattern. The proportion of problems for which subjects referred to premises increases consistently with age for the logical problems; by 11 years of age almost all justifications are of this type. The proportion of referral to premises for the illogical problems, however, does not undergo a similar increase. Moreover, for the 6-year-olds, referral to premises on the illogical problem is associated with a matching response, but this is not the case for the 8- or 11-year-olds. Once again, the difference between referral to premises on the logical and illogical problems reveals the same basic developmental pattern, indicating that 6-year-olds do not consistently differentiate between logical and illogical syllogisms and that the ability to do so increases with age. An interesting phenomenon in this respect involves the form of justification that we have called *invention* of an imaginary link between premises. This form of justification appears almost exclusively with respect to illogical premises, and only in 8- and 11-year-olds. The invention of a link between premises is clearly associated with the recognition that two premises do not go together and indicates the beginnings of an explicit understanding of the distinction between logical and illogical forms of argument. Such a justification involves using extraneous information in order to "fill in the hole" between two unrelated premises. As such, it requires use of the child's empirical knowledge. It is interesting that the percentages of nonequivalent responses associated with use of the invention justification were 69% and 82%, for the 8- and 11-year-olds, respectively. Thus, in the case of these children, use of empirical knowledge was clearly subordinated to their understanding of the relations between the premises.

Once again, this is the inverse of the situation with the 6-year-olds, for whom empirical knowledge is generally at odds with their appreciation of the premises. Thus, for the older children, there appears to be the beginning of the inversion between real-world knowledge and structural knowledge that characterizes the Piagetian description of formal thought.

It must also be remarked that there is a very low level of explicit justifications, indicating that the premises on the illogical problems were unconnected (0%, 2%, and 17% of 6-, 8-, and 11-year-olds' responses, respectively, were of this sort). This indicates that even the older children find it difficult to account explicitly for indeterminacy. Note that this must be distinguished from the low level of *don't know* responses obtained on the illogical problems, which might have been due to the children's reluctance to use such a response (Rumain, Connell, & Braine, 1983).

Finally, the presence of effects that were due to the order of presentation of the problems must be mentioned. The results indicate that for both the 6- and 8-year-olds, receiving the illogical problems first improved their performance on these problems and somewhat lowered their performance on the logical problems. The youngest children still retained the overall tendency to respond similarly to illogical and logical problems, whereas the 8-year-olds showed a definite ability to differentiate the two when presented with the illogical problems first. These results indicate the presence of a response set to the logical forms for both 6- and 8-year-olds (although not for the 11-year-olds). This is particularly striking among the 8-year-olds, since they show a clear developing ability to distinguish logical and illogical forms. However, the status of such a response set remains an open question. The fact that the influence of order of presentation of logical and illogical problems follows closely the overall developmental pattern in the ability to distinguish logical and illogical problems may suggest that this effect is not simply a "performance" factor but may be tied to reasoning competence. The lack of any order effect among the 11-year-olds is particularly striking in this respect.

Conclusion

The results of the present study, taken in their totality, present a more differentiated picture of the development of elementary syllogistic reasoning abilities than has previously been found. They suggest that children as young as 5 or 6 years are able to use syntactic cues to respond to limited kinds of reasoning problems, but that the strategies that these children use do not allow them to differentiate reliably between premises that are logically related and those that are not. This latter ability develops with age, and, by 11 years, the strategies that children use to process verbal syllogisms permit a clear distinction between these two forms. In addition, there is evidence that older children can begin to subordinate empirical knowledge to their understanding of structural relations. These results are thus consistent with a variety of others that indicate that there are important developmental steps in the understanding of elementary inferential principles that cover roughly the same age-period (6 to 11 years) that we have examined here (Byrnes & Overton, 1986; Piéraut-Le Bonniec, 1980; Scholnick & Wing, 1988). However, these results also suggest that children's explicit ability to recognize and account for lack of a logical relation between premises continues to develop subsequently. That is, children can distinguish between logical and illogical syllogisms in terms of differential responses and justifications before they appear able to describe explicitly the nature of the distinction. This kind of metalogical understanding appears to develop after 11 years, in line with results obtained by Moshman and Franks (1986) on the development of the notion of logical necessity.

References

Byrnes, J.P., & Overton, W.F. (1986). Reasoning about certainty and uncertainty in concrete, causal, and propositional contexts. *Developmental Psychology, 22,* 793-799.

Evans, J.St B.T., & Lynch, J.S. (1973). Matching bias in the selection task. *British Journal of Psychology, 64*(3), 391-397.

Hawkins, J., Pea, R.D., Glick, J., & Scribner, S. (1984). "Merds that laugh don't like mushrooms": Evidence for deductive reasoning by preschoolers. *Developmental Psychology, 20,* 584-594.

Inhelder, B., & Piaget, J. (1958). *The growth of logical thinking from childhood to adolescence.* New York, NY: Basic Books.

Moshman, D., & Franks, B.A. (1986). Development of the concept of inferential validity. *Child Development, 57*(1), 153-165.

Piaget, J. (1987). *Possibility and necessity: 1. The role of possibility in cognitive development* (H. Feider, Trans.). Minneapolis, MN: University of Minnesota Press. (Original work published 1981)

Piéraut-Le Bonniec, G. (1980). *The development of modal reasoning: Genesis of necessity and possibility notions.* New York, NY: Academic Press.

Rumain, B., Connell, J., & Braine, M.D.S. (1983). Conversational comprehension processes are responsible for reasoning fallacies in children as well as adults. *Developmental Psychology, 19,* 471-481.

Scholnick, E.K., & Wing, C.S. (1988). Knowing when you don't know: Developmental and situational considerations. *Developmental Psychology, 24,* 190-196.

Woodworth, R.S., & Sells, S.B. (1935). An atmosphere effect in syllogistic reasoning. *Journal of Experimental Psychology, 18,* 451-460.

Appendix

Logical syllogisms

1. Every Zobole is yellow.
   All yellow things have a nose.

Do Zoboles have a nose?

2. Every Plouque is tall.
   No tall thing is green.
   Are Plouques green?

3. Plitosores have legs.
   Nounou is a plitosore.
   Does Nounou have legs?

4. Risomes cannot sing.
   Zapp is a Risome.
   Can Zapp sing?

5. Mibules cough when they are touched.
   All things that cough are smooth.
   Are Mibules smooth?

6. Pliks sleep when they are cold.
   All sleeping things are blue.
   Are Pliks blue?

Illogical syllogisms

1. Every Zobole is yellow.
   All red things have a nose.
   Do Zoboles have a nose?

2. Every Plouque is tall.
   No crying thing is green.
   Are Plouques green?

3. Plitosores have legs.
   Nounou is a Fiola.
   Does Nounou have legs?

4. Risomes cannot sing.
   Zapp is a Touki.
   Can Zapp sing?

5. Mibules cough when they are touched.
   All things that cry are smooth.
   Are Mibules smooth?

6. Pliks sleep when they are cold.
   All jumping things are blue.
   Are Pliks blue?

Mental Terms and the Development of Certainty

Chris Moore, Dana Bryant, and David Furrow
Mount Saint Vincent University

*In the present study, we examined children's understanding of the prag-
matic function of mental terms to express relative certainty. 69 children
between the ages of 3-1 [three years, one month] and 8-11 [eight years,
eleven months] were presented with contrasting pairs of statements by 2
puppets. Different trials contained all the possible pairwise combinations
of the terms* know, think, *and* guess. *On the basis of what they heard,
children were required to find an object hidden in 1 of 2 places. Results
showed a significant improvement with age for the* know-think *and* know-
guess *contrasts, but no improvement with age for the* think-guess *contrast.
By 4 years of age,* know *was differentiated from* think *and from* guess.
In both cases, know *was chosen as a more reliable indicator of the
location of the object. Further improvement occurred for both contrasts
involving the word* know *between 4 and 5 years of age, so that by 5
years, performance had reached asymptote. These results demonstrate the
development of pragmatic competence with mental terms over the preschool period and may also indicate the appearance of the mental state
concept of certainty.*

*   *   *

THE YOUNG CHILD'S ACQUISITION OF MENTAL TERMS, OR WORDS THAT
refer to mental processes or states, has attracted interest for a variety of
reasons. First, as part of the early lexicons of children, mental terms are
of interest in their own right. Second, the acquisition of mental terms may
be taken as indicating an understanding of mental state and therefore reflects the development of the concept of mind in children (Johnson, 1982).
Understanding of mental terms has also been studied for insight into the
young child's reasoning (Macnamara, Baker, & Olson, 1976).

To date, research on mental terms has been conducted in two main
ways: observational studies of the appearance of these terms in the lexicons
of young children (e.g., Bretherton & Beeghly, 1982; Bretherton, McNew,

This research was supported by grant 410-87-1315 from the Social
Sciences and Humanities Research Council of Canada to the first and
third authors. The authors would like to thank the staff and children of
the schools that participated in the study. Thanks also to Tom Barrett
for assistance with the analysis.

& Beeghly-Smith, 1981; Shatz, Wellman, & Silber, 1983) and experimental studies of the understanding of the semantic differences between various mental terms (e.g., Abbeduto & Rosenberg, 1985; Bassano, 1985; Johnson & Maratsos, 1977; Johnson & Wellman, 1980; Macnamara et al., 1976; Miscione, Marvin, O'Brien, & Greenberg, 1978; Wellman & Johnson, 1979). Observational studies of mental terms have shown that some mental terms, such as *know, think* and *remember*, start to appear in children's lexicons in the second and third years of life (Bretherton & Beeghly, 1982; Shatz et al., 1983). Initially, however, these terms are used rarely and are not used to refer to mental states, but play the role of conversational devices (Shatz et al., 1983). For example, *know what?* serves to introduce information, rather than to make reference to the listener's knowledge. By the end of the third year, there is evidence of true mental state references. The changing use of such terms likely reflects the appearance of a primitive "theory of mind" (Bretherton et al., 1981; Shatz et al., 1983).

At the same time, experimental work on children's comprehension of mental terms has revealed that the subtleties of these lexical items are not understood until somewhat later. The research strategy has generally been to request children to select the mental term that best describes a person's mental orientation (either their own or that of a story character) toward a statement or event. The aspect of the comprehension of mental terms that has attracted most attention is that of presupposition. Certain verbs, such as *know* and *remember*, presuppose the truth of the complement, whereas others, such as *think* and *guess*, do not. For example, "John knows that it's raining" presupposes that it is in fact raining, whereas "John thinks that it's raining" implies that it may or may not be raining. Verbs that presuppose the truth of the complement are often called *factives*, whereas those that do not presuppose the truth of the complement are called *nonfactives* (Abbeduto & Rosenberg, 1985). Work on the child's understanding of the presuppositions of mental verbs (Abbeduto & Rosenberg, 1985; Bassano, 1985; Johnson & Maratsos, 1977; Johnson & Wellman, 1980; Miscione et al., 1978; Wellman & Johnson, 1979) has shown that children do not start to differentiate the verbs on the basis of their presuppositions until 4-5 years of age.

These experimental studies have uniformly attempted to assess the young child's understanding of the semantics of the various mental terms. However, an understanding of semantics is only one aspect of the acquisition of these, or any, terms. In addition, it is important for children to recognize how they are used pragmatically. This issue has been addressed in the literature (e.g., Johnson & Wellman, 1980) but has not been studied experimentally. A common use of mental verbs is to signal the reliability or relative certainty with which a statement is made (Bassano, 1985; Johnson & Wellman, 1980; Richards, 1982; Shatz et al., 1983). A speaker will select a particular mental term depending on his or her subjective certainty about the proposition. Thus the statement "I know that John went to the store" would be used to indicate a high degree of certainty on the part of the speaker that John did go to the store, whereas "I think that John went to the store" would be used to indicate less certainty. This function of mental terms has also been called "modulation of assertion" (Shatz et al., 1983).

Here we report an experiment designed to test children's understanding of the use of mental terms to indicate relative certainty or reliability. The question is, do young children recognize that speakers use mental terms to indicate differential degrees of certainty, and can they respond appropriately on the basis of this information? In an attempt to answer this question, we designed a task in which the child is required to determine the location of a hidden object. The object is in one of two possible places, and the only clues that the child has are two conflicting statements involving contrasting mental terms. These statements are presented by the experimenter using two puppets, so that one puppet indicates that the object is hidden in one location, while the other puppet indicates the other location. Thus the child has to make a choice between two locations on the basis of one or other mental term. The particular mental terms used in this experiment were, *know*, *think*, and *guess*. In terms of semantic analysis, *know* would be considered a factive, presupposing the truth of the complement, whereas *think* and *guess* would be considered nonfactives. Pragmatically, *know* would probably be used to indicate a high degree of certainty, but *think* and *guess* would be used to indicate less certainty. The difference between *guess* and *think* is less obvious. On the basis of an informal survey of adult opinion, we decided to order the various terms on a continuum of certainty, with *know* indicating most certainty and *guess* indicating least certainty. The three possible binary combinations of these verbs were presented to children in five age groups in an attempt to see whether children would use them as indicators of relative certainty, and, if so, how they would be treated.

Method

Subjects

Subjects were 69 children, divided into five age groups, from Halifax, Nova Scotia. There were 14 3-year-olds (mean age, 3-6 and range 3-1 to 3-11), 14 4-year-olds (mean 4-4, range 4-0 to 4-11), 14 5-year-olds (mean 5-6, range 5-0 to 5-11), 13 6-year-olds (mean 6-7, range 6-3 to 7-0), and 14 8-year-olds (mean 8-5, range 8-0 to 8-11).

Design

Each child received 12 test trials in four sets of three. Each set contained one of each of the possible pairwise contrasts between the mental terms *know*, *think*, and *guess*, with the order of the contrasts in each set determined randomly. The four sets were presented in four different orders according to a Latin square.

Procedure

Before the trials began, the child was told that she would play a hiding game, in which she had to find a hidden candy. She would have help from two monkeys, which were puppets, manipulated by the female experimenter. In addition to the 12 test trials, each child was presented with three practice trials. In each trial the child was presented with two small boxes, one blue and one red, and told that candy was hidden in one of the boxes. She was told that she should listen to the monkeys, who would help her find the candy. Then the two puppets would each make a statement in turn indicating one of the boxes. For the three practice trials, one puppet would say, "it's really in the red/blue box," and the other would say "I'm pretending it's in the blue/red box." The experimenter would then ask the child to find the candy and the child would search. These practice trials were used because the distinction between pretense and reality is acquired very early (Leslie, 1987), and, therefore, it was felt that this distinction would serve as the best introduction to the nature of the task. If children failed any of the three pretest trials, these trials were continued until the child was correct on three consecutive trials. If this criterion was not reached in six trials, the session was discontinued. Only two children, both from the youngest age group, took more than three trials to reach criterion, and all reached criterion in six trials.

For the 12 test trials, the two puppets each made a statement involving one of the mental terms, *know*, *think*, or *guess* as follows, "I know/think/guess it's in the blue/red box." In these trials, the child was not allowed to search after each trial but was told to choose one of the boxes, and her choices would be put aside, so that she could see how many candies she had won at the end. In this way, the child was prevented from getting feedback as to the correctness of her choices through the session. The particular puppet that made each statement, the order in which the puppets made the statement, and the box to which each referred were randomly varied throughout all the trials. The candy was always hidden in the box that was indicated by the statement implying more certainty. In the case of the think-guess contrast, the candy was always hidden in the box indicated by the think statement.

Results

For the purposes of analysis, a response was scored as correct if the child chose the box indicated by the statement including *know* over that indicated by the statement including *think* or *guess*, and the box indicated by the statement including *think* over that indicated by the statement including *guess*. To detect changes in performance through the testing session, responses were divided into two blocks, with scores summed over the first two sets of three trials, and over the second two sets of three trials. For each of the three contrasts in each block, therefore, there was a possible score of 0-2.

A three-way, repeated-measures analysis of variance was performed on the data, with age as a between-subjects variable and contrast and block as within-subjects variables. The only significant differences were a main effect of age, $F(4,64)=7.55$, $p<.0001$, a main effect of contrast, $F(2,128)=71.85$, $p<.0001$, and a contrast$\times$age interaction, $F(8,128)=6.30$, $p<.0001$. Univariate tests of the contrast main effect revealed that the *think-guess* contrast was significantly more difficult than the *know-think* contrast and the *know-guess* contrast, which did not differ: single degree of freedom contrasts, $F(1,64)=81.21$, $p<.0001$; $F(1,64)=85.06$, $p<.0001$, respectively.

To investigate the contrast$\times$age interaction further, scores were pooled across blocks, giving a total possible score of 0-4 for each contrast. One-way analyses of variance were performed for each contrast, with age as the independent variable. Results showed that there was a main effect for age for both the *know-think*, $F(4,68)=13.55$, $p<.0001$, and the *know-guess*, $F(4,68)=11.66$, $p<.0001$, contrasts, but not for the *think-guess* contrast. The means for each contrast at each age are shown in Table 1. For the *know-think* contrast, comparisons of least-square means revealed that the 3-year-olds performed significantly worse than all of the other age groups (all p's $<.001$), and that the 4-year-olds performed significantly worse than

TABLE 1

MEAN NUMBER OF CORRECT RESPONSES FOR EACH CONTRAST AT EACH AGE
(Maximum = 4)

AGE GROUP	N	CONTRAST		
		Know-Think	Know-Guess	Think-Guess
3-year-olds	14	2.07	2.21	2.14
4-year-olds	14	3.14	2.93	1.86
5-year-olds	14	3.64	3.79	1.43
6-year-olds	13	3.92	3.85	1.38
8-year-olds	14	3.93	3.79	2.21

the 6-year-olds and the 8-year-olds (p's $< .05$). For the *know-guess* contrast, comparisons of least-square means revealed that the 3-year-olds performed significantly worse than all other groups (p's $< .05$), and that the 4-year-olds performed significantly worse than all of the older groups (p's $< .001$). No other differences were significant.

Discussion

These results provide evidence that comprehension of the use of mental terms to express certainty or uncertainty develops over the preschool years. By 4 years of age, children have some understanding of the distinction between *know* and *think*, and between *know* and *guess*, and they appreciate that *know* gives a better index of the reliability of a statement than *think* or *guess*. This understanding appears complete by 5 years of age. The distinction between *think* and *guess*, however, was not well understood at any age studied in this experiment.

These results supplement and extend the knowledge of children's understanding of mental verbs derived from previous experimental studies on the semantics of these verbs. These studies have generally placed the acquisition of the understanding of the semantic difference between *think* and *know* at between 4 and 5 years of age (e.g., Abbeduto & Rosenberg, 1985; Johnson & Maratsos, 1977). These authors have argued that before age 4 *think*, like *know*, is treated as a factive. Therefore, in this case, semantic and pragmatic understanding seem to develop together. However, it should be noted that there is some observational evidence on mental term production, that the use of these terms, including *think*, to mark relative certainty develops toward the end of the third year (Shatz et al., 1983).

The finding of a differentiation between *know* and *guess* by 4 years of age in the present study indicates that this distinction starts to be acquired at an earlier age than was previously believed. Research on children's semantic understanding of the distinction between *know* and *guess* (e.g., Johnson & Wellman, 1980; Miscione et al., 1978) has placed the acquisition of the distinction at about 5 years. Previously, as far as we are aware, no studies have examined the understanding of *think* and *guess* together. The present study indicates that children up to 8 years of age do not recognize a difference between these two terms with respect to marking speaker certainty. Of course, a significant difference between *think* and *guess* might not exist even for an adult sample in a similar context.

It should also be pointed out that, although the children in this study did show evidence of pragmatically differentiating the mental terms employed, it remains unclear whether the children consider speaker certainty to be continuous or dichotomous. Because there was no difference between *think* and *guess*, whereas both were differentiated from *know*, certainty may be believed by young children to be dichotomous with no shades of reliability.

In other words, they interpret *know* to mean *true* and *think* and *guess* to mean *untrue*. A firm conclusion on these questions, however, must await further research.

In sum, this study has provided evidence that preschool children have some understanding of the pragmatic implications of certain mental terms. By 4 years, children understand *know* to be an indicator of speaker certainty, and *think* and *guess* to be indicators of speaker uncertainty. These findings complement the picture that has emerged from experimental studies of children's understanding of the semantics of mental terms (e.g., Abbeduto & Rosenberg, 1985; Johnson & Maratsos, 1977; Johnson & Wellman, 1980), which have traced this development in the late preschool and early grade school years, and from observational studies of children's productive use of mental terms (Shatz et al., 1983), which have identified the earliest functions of these words. At present, the relation between the pragmatics and the semantics of mental terms remains obscure, a condition which is, of course, true for the case of language in general. Children's understanding of the pragmatic function of marking relative certainty might be based on the semantic understanding of the properties of factive and nonfactive mental verbs. However, the opposite is equally possible. Nevertheless, we believe that we have a useful experimental technique for investigation into the neglected area of the pragmatics of mental term use.

Finally, if it is allowed that the present study reveals the development of the pragmatic understanding of mental terms, then this work may also provide evidence of aspects of the emerging concept of mind. Children's ability to understand statements involving mental terms as being more or less reliable sources of information may well presuppose an ability to represent the speaker as being more or less certain. This interpretation must remain tentative, given the nature of the present task, in which it is difficult to know the extent to which the child is willing to enter into the role-playing context and treat the puppets as animate individuals. Perhaps, however, we can count certainty as another mental state, along with pretense (e.g., Leslie, 1987), false belief (Perner, Leekam, & Wimmer, 1987), and intention (e.g., Poulin-Dubois & Shultz, 1988), that is, understood by children in the preschool period.

References

Abbeduto, L., & Rosenberg, S. (1985). Children's knowledge of the presuppositions of know and other cognitive verbs. *Journal of Child Language, 12*, 621-641.

Bassano, D. (1985). Five-year-olds' understanding of "savoir" and "croire." *Journal of Child Language, 12*, 417-432.

Bretherton, I., & Beeghly, M. (1982). Talking about internal states: The acquisition of an explicit theory of mind. *Developmental Psychology, 18*, 906-921.

Bretherton, I., McNew, S., & Beeghly-Smith, M. (1981). Early person knowledge as expressed in gestural and verbal communication: When do infants acquire a "theory of mind"? In M. Lamb & L. Sherrod (Eds.), *Infant social cognition* (pp. 333-373). Hillsdale, NJ: Erlbaum.

Johnson, C.N. (1982). Acquisition of mental verbs and the concept of mind. In S. Kuczaj (Ed.), *Language development: Vol. 1. Syntax and semantics* (pp. 455-478). Hillsdale, NJ: Erlbaum.

Johnson, C.N., & Maratsos, M.P. (1977). Early comprehension of mental verbs: Think and know. *Child Development, 48*, 1743-1747.

Johnson, C.N., & Wellman, H.M. (1980). Children's developing understanding of mental verbs: Remember, know, and guess. *Child Development, 51*, 1095-1102.

Leslie, A.M. (1987). Pretense and representation: The origins of "theory of mind." *Psychological Review, 94*, 412-426.

Macnamara, J., Baker, E., & Olson, C.L. (1976). Four-year-olds' understanding of pretend, forget, and know: Evidence for propositional operations. *Child Development, 47*, 62-70.

Miscione, J.L., Marvin, R.S., O'Brien, R.G., & Greenberg, M.T. (1978). A developmental study of preschool children's understanding of the words "know" and "guess." *Child Development, 49*, 1107-1113.

Perner, J., Leekam, S.R., & Wimmer, H. (1987). Three year olds' difficulty with false belief: The case for a conceptual deficit. *British Journal of Developmental Psychology, 5*, 125-137.

Poulin-Dubois, D., & Shultz, T.R. (1988). The development of the understanding of human behavior: From agency to intentionality. In J. Astington, P. Harris, & D. Olson (Eds.), *Developing theories of mind*. Cambridge, UK: Cambridge University Press.

Richards, M.M. (1982). Empiricism and learning to mean. In S. Kuczaj (Ed.), *Language development: Vol. 1. Syntax and semantics* (pp. 365-396). Hillsdale, NJ: Erlbaum.

Shatz, M., Wellman, H.M., & Silber, S. (1983). The acquisition of mental verbs: A systematic investigation of the first reference to a mental state. *Cognition, 14*, 301-321.

Wellman, H.M., & Johnson, C.N. (1979). Understanding mental processes: A developmental study of "remember" and "forget." *Child Development, 50*, 79-88.

Perception and Production
in Children's Art

Robert J. Gebotys
Wilfrid Laurier University
Gerald C. Cupchik
University of Toronto

This study examined cognitive and affective aspects of aesthetic perception and production in children. The subjects comprised 120 children with equal numbers of males and females in each of three age groups: 6, 9, and 12. The perception task involved arranging three stimuli in a meaningful order within two sets of adult paintings, two sets of adult sculpture, and two sets of artworks produced by children. A literal-visual effects dimension underlay the adult artworks, while a global-differentiated dimension underlay the children's artworks. Dependent measures included accuracy, time, certainty, and affective response. The reasons that children gave for their orders were scored for emphasis on dramatic or replete qualities of the artworks. Results showed that 6 year olds had a stronger affective response to the artworks than did the 9 and 12 year olds. However, cognitive responses, such as the accuracy and speed of judgment, improved with age. Half of the children (60) also performed a production task that required them to make a drawing of "home and family." A monotonic increase was found in the use of techniques such as projection. However, u-shaped curves were found for adult judgments of expression and quality in the drawings. Overall, these data suggest the relative independence of emotionality and cognition in the aesthetic responses of children.

*   *   *

Psychologists and philosophers have acknowledged "two faces of artistry," the Apollonian and the Dionysian (Gardner & Winner, 1982). According to them, the Apollonian pole involves an application of the rules and conventions of symbolic systems, while the Dionysian pole reflects an energetic, playful, and experimental approach to artistic creativity.

The research reported here was accomplished with the support of the Wilfrid Laurier Research Office and the Waterloo County Board of Education. The authors would like to thank the staff and students of Suddaby and Wilson Avenue Schools for their cooperation. The authors would also like to thank Andrew Winston for his helpful comments on the manuscript.

Sparshott (1982, p. 204) treats the distinction as a "contrast between the detached and the involved. Contemplating something as an object in a calm and steady way differs from being involved in it as a process." Thus, both the rational and the emotional sides of human experience and action are explored in aesthetic perception and production.

Gardner and Winner (1982) have used the Apollonian-Dionysian distinction to characterize stages of artistic development. The original artistic productions of preschool children suggest a Dionysian attitude. During this "golden age," the child is pleasurably involved in an exploration of the medium. This brief flowering of artistry is replaced during middle childhood with an Apollonian concern for literal representation. Learning artistic techniques, such as perspective and foreshortening, takes precedence over the generation of images. However, these conventionalized works lack the individuality and spontaneity prized in the drawings of younger children. Only when children have mastered the rules of artistry can they "break them with full effectiveness" (Winner, 1982) and produce original artworks. Thus a u-shaped curve (Gardner & Winner, 1982) describes the shift in aesthetic quality from the artistic flair of the preschool child to the restrained art of middle childhood and the reappearance of quality in the art of older children and adults.

Gardner and Winner have adopted a cognitively oriented approach to this seemingly enigmatic problem. It is enigmatic because younger children appear to produce artworks while "unaware of the norms that are violated" (Winner, 1982, p. 76) and although "they display little sensitivity to aesthetic properties of pictorial art" (p. 173). The former conclusion is logically assumed and the latter is supported in studies conducted by Carothers and Garner (1979) and Winner et al. (1986) on the aesthetic comprehension skills of children. In both studies the authors did not observe sensitivity on the part of preschool children to "replete" (Goodman, 1976) qualities of line in artificial drawings. The quality of children's drawings is therefore tied to "originality," which in turn is treated as a violation of aesthetic "conventions," presumably unintentional on the part of the young child.

Another approach to the problem of quality, which may resolve the problem of preschool artistry, is founded on the work of the Gestalt psychologists (Arnheim, 1971; Werner & Kaplan, 1963). They argue that visual precepts and the scenes to which they refer, both pictorial and natural, can be ordered in two distinct ways. We are familiar with the "geometric-technical" organizing principles that lie at the heart of architectural and design renderings. "Geometric-technical" properties reduce objects to static and conventionalized structure of planes, masses, and directions. The elimination of non-essential visual information makes identifying isolated objects as volumes in space easier.

A conventionalized approach to art is founded on "geometric-technical" principles that create the illusion of space and form in two-dimensional surfaces. The technical refinements of art build upon this foundation, extending to qualities of line, color, texture, composition, and so forth. Clearly, this kind of knowledge and skill develops over time, and that a "jump" in competence might take place during the early school years, when children are less egocentric and more observationally sensitive is understandable. The concrete operational skills (Piaget, 1951) associated with this period are ideally suited to a rational organization of visual space. These include decentering, attention to transformation, cognitive reversibility, and coherent systems of action.

A second notion, that of "dynamic-physiognomic" properties, can help to account for the intuitive artistry of the preschool child. Physiognomic properties are expressed, for example, in pictorial images of "weeping willows" and "moody skies." Gestaltists treat them as "forces" that permeate an image and are spontaneously experienced. These qualities are not restricted to individual objects and so they serve to unify the image in an expressive manner. Arnheim (1971, p. 443) has argued that the dynamic qualities of pictorial space are founded on contrasts such as "expansion and contraction, conflict and concordance, rising and falling, approach and withdrawal." These qualities evoke moods much as "geometric-technical" qualities produce knowledge about the image.

Werner and Kaplan (1963) have urged that physiognomic perception develops before geometric-technical perception. It emerges from early forms of motor expression practiced by very young children and anticipates later symbolic sophistication. Thus, preschool children should be able to respond to expressive qualities that spontaneously emerge in their own artworks and are present in those of others. This implies that the artistry of preschool children is not founded on a departure from conventions about which they are minimally informed. Rather, it reflects a holistic and emotional response to the artwork that compensates for a limited repertoire of artistic skills.

School-age children focus on geometric-technical qualities of objects and art-works. This emphasis on technique narrows their attention to local and isolated qualities of particular objects that unify an image. Further, their detached viewpoint reduces the potential for disruption and variation in the act of production, which lends an artwork the mark of individuality. However, after mastering stylistic conventions, older children appear more readily able to shift from detached to involved attitudes and from local to global perception, thereby producing coherent and appealing images.

This argument is not meant to imply that preoperational children cannot discern formal stylistic properties of artworks. They should be able to discern qualities that are globally present in artworks. However, researchers have had varied success in assessing the aesthetic comprehension skills of preoperational children. For example, Carothers and Gardner (1979) and Winner et al. (1986) did not find sensitivity on the part of preschool children to the "replete" (Goodman, 1976) qualities of line in artificial stimuli. However, their experimental paradigms required children to attend to local properties of the test stimulus and, according to our argument, this may not have suited the more holistic sensibilities of preschool children. Hardiman and Zernich (1985), using genuine paintings, found that preschool children were able to perceive similarities across realistic, semiabstract, and nonobjective styles. Genuine artworks may be more appropriate for testing the discrimination skills of preoperational children.

In this study aesthetic perception and production were examined in three groups of children aged 6, 9, and 12. These ages roughly correspond to Piaget's preoperational, concrete operational, and formal operational stages. The perception task was developed to maximize the chance that preoperational children could demonstrate their aesthetic perception skills. Children were presented with triads of paintings and sculptures and instructed to place them in a meaningful order. A single theme (e.g., landscape) was chosen for each triad to eliminate "centration" (Piaget, 1969) as an explanation for limited aesthetic discrimination in preoperational children (i.e., distraction by salient narrative elements). The choice of this procedure was based on Piaget and Inhelder's (1970, p. 247) distinction between classification and seriation: "...first a relation can be perceived while a class as such cannot, and...second...a serial configuration constitutes a 'good form' perceptually." The added information provided by the transitive relations among the three items in each series should make it easier to perceive a meaningful relationship, even if the child could not classify the underlying transformation.

Two painting triads and two sculpture triads were chosen from a larger set developed for a study on adult aesthetic sensitivity (Cupchik & Gebotys, 1988). The items from the triads map onto the dimension *literal-visual effects*. Items at the literal effects end include more representational or denotative information, while those at the visual effects end explore properties of style such as color, texture, composition, and so forth. This dimension is comparable with the representational-abstract dimension that has consistently emerged in multidimensional scaling studies of adult perception of stylistic similarities among works of art (Berlyne & Ogilvie, 1974; Cupchik, 1974; O'Hare, 1976). In addition, two triads (one sculpture and one painting) were chosen to reflect the development in children's art from simple to more differentiated forms (Arnheim, 1971).

A variety of measures were used to maximize the amount of information obtained from the perception task. The children's judgments were scored for accuracy, time required to order the triad, certainty, perceived complexity of the stimuli, and emotional response to the stimuli (happy-sad). In addition, children were asked to account for their orders and these responses were scored for emphasis on replete (i.e., line and composition) and narrative (i.e., storytelling) elements.

The production task required children to draw a picture of "home and family" and these drawings were analyzed in terms of objective and subjective rating schemes. The objective ratings were based on established measures of drawing properties: area covered, number of colors used, kind of outlining, complexity of the major figure, and use of spatial projection. Subjective ratings were made by two art teachers on eight dimensions deemed appropriate for judging children's drawings: realism, color, composition, quality, originality, harmony, happiness, and expressiveness.

This research strategy made possible the comparison of comprehension and production in different age groups. Monotonic increases in development were expected for cognitively oriented dimensions of aesthetic activity. Thus, children should be progressively more skilled at performing the perception task, although six-year-old children should also be able to perform the task, albeit at a lower level. A monotonic increase was also expected for objective qualities of drawing performance such as use of outline, selection of color, complexity of the dominant figures, and spatial projection. U-shaped curves were expected for measures that pertain to affective processes. Thus, affective responses to the triads and expressive qualities in the drawings were expected to be lowest among the nine year olds, who are absorbed in geometric-technical aspects of drawing. Consistent with past literature, the quality of drawing should also diminish during this period.

Method

Subjects

Letters were sent to 200 parents soliciting the participation of their children in a study on art. One hundred and twenty volunteers performed the perception task. They were students at two elementary schools in Waterloo, Ontario, Canada, with a predominantly middle-class population. Three groups of 40 children were selected, representing the ages 6, 9, and 12 years—plus or minus 6 months. Equal numbers of males and females were included in each group. Sixty of these children also performed the drawing task—20 children in each age group with equal numbers of males and females.

Materials

WISC-R. The WISC-R (Wechsler, 1974) picture arrangement subtest was used to compare this sample of subjects with standardized scores as a population normality check. A child can complete 10 sets in accordance with the WISC-R manual (Wechsler, 1974, pp. 76-79). The format of this test requires the child to place three to five cards in an order to form a story.

Perception Task. The materials consisted of 18 photographic prints (3.5 in. ×5 in. format) organized in 6 sets of 3. Two painting and two sculpture triads (see Table 1) were selected from materials developed in an earlier study of adult aesthetic perception (Cupchik & Gebotys, 1988). Within each triad the works were produced by a single artist and addressed a common theme (e.g., landscape or torso). The works were carefully chosen to map onto the dimension *literal-visual effects*. Works located toward the *literal* end embody more denotative or representational information in relation to the other two. Works located toward the *visual effects* end reflect an exploration of stylistic qualities such as color, composition, brushwork (in paintings), and shape (in sculpture).

Two triads incorporating children's artistic treatment of animals could be mapped onto the dimension *gross-differentiated*. The *gross* work afforded a crude treatment of the theme, while the more *differentiated* works addressed aesthetic qualities of line and shape. One triad comprised three drawings of a horse by the same child (Fein, 1976) at the ages 6, 9, and 12. The second triad included three clay sculptures of a "bunny" done by children of different ages with progressively greater sensitivity to aesthetic properties. Pilot work indicated that six triads were a reasonable number for children to place in sequence without attention lapses.

Drawing Task. Children were provided with 8.5 in. ×11 in. sheets of brown Manila paper and 8 new standard Crayola™ crayons.

Procedure

Perception Task. Testing took place individually in a quiet room of the school. Half of the children performed the picture arrangement subtest of the WISC-R before doing the perception task and the rest completed it afterward. For the perception task the subject was presented with a set of three photographs of paintings, drawings, or sculptures and instructed to arrange them in a *meaningful* order. The triads were presented in a randomized order. After each triad the subject was asked for reasons why the particular order was chosen. This response was tape recorded and transcribed for later analysis.

The following additional questions were then asked concerning the pictures and the chosen sequence: (1) How sure was the subject of the chosen order? (*certainty*); (2) How difficult would it be to create the pictures or sculptures? (*difficulty*); (3) How do the pictures make the subject feel...happy or sad? (*affect*). A drawing of a ladder with seven rungs, representing a seven-point scale, was provided for each of the questions. Key words for each question were placed at the top and the bottom of the ladder. The child pointed to the rung that best indicated the degree of his or her answer.

Drawing Task. Sixty of the children performed the drawing task individually in a testing room. They were given materials and asked to produce a drawing of their "home and family."

Table 1
Stimulus Materials

Set No. and Artist	Type	Title or Description
1. Heidi	Children's Art	A drawing of a horse by a 6 year old. A drawing of a horse by a 9 year old. A drawing of a horse by a 12 year old.
2.	Children's Art	A child's crude sculpture of a bunny, clay. A child's sculpture of a bunny, clay. A child's sculpture of a detailed imaginary animal, clay.
3. Pollock	Adult Painting	Eyes in the Heat. Gothic. Birth.
4. Pollock	Adult Painting	The Flame. Going West. Camp with Oil Rig.
5. Brancusi	Adult Sculpture	Prometheus, marble. Sleeping Child, marble. Sleeping Child, bronze.
6. Lipchitz	Adult Sculpture	Reclining Woman, bronze. Reclining Figure, bronze. Reclining Figure, bronze.

Scoring

Perception Task. The children's tape-recorded responses to the question, "Why did you put the pictures in that order?" were independently transcribed and classified into the categories listed below by two judges. The classification was based on the presence (coded 1) or absence (coded 0) of the listed category. The percentage of agreement between the two judges is given in brackets.

1. COLOR: reference to color as a reason for the sequence. [99%]
2. STORYTELLING: refers to storytelling involving the description of a single picture or the entire set of pictures as long as it is a creative unit

within itself and also includes creative descriptions that have fantasy elements (e.g., "This is them going over the hill and then they camped out and left again.") [95%]

3. COMPOSITION, STYLE, and LINE: refers to descriptors of the artworks that include reference to form, shape, and details of the artworks (e.g., this one has more details than that one or that one). [81%]

Drawing Task

Objective Scoring. One of the judges scored the drawings in randomized order on the following measures:

1. *area covered*—number of squares with any markings in them on a 60-square grid;

2. *number of colors*—used out of a possible 8;

3. *outlining*—(i) *pure*: majority of characters outlined in a color different from the interior coloring (not including black, brown, or orange, which are considered by most children as "pencil" outlining);

4. *draw-a-person test*—the most complex figure in the drawing was given a score out of 73 based on the Harris (1963) scale;

5. *projection*—(0) none: no overlap of figures or objects implying distance, no attempt at perspective using lines, (1) overlap: some overlap of objects or figures in which part of the farther object or figure is occluded to imply distance, no attempt at linear perspective, (2) perspective: some attempt at perspective using lines that may be vertical or diverge, may also show overlapping technique.

Subjective Scoring. Two art teachers, who are also professional artists, scored the drawings on eight 25-point scales. The drawings were randomized and all were scored on one scale at a time. The scales included: realism, use of color, composition, overall quality, originality, harmony, happiness, and expressiveness.

Design and Analysis

Perception Task. The experimental design was a $3 \times 2 \times (6)$ repeated measures design. The independent variables were age (6, 9, 12 years old), sex, and picture (a total of 6 sets: 2 sets of adult paintings, 2 sets of adult sculpture, and 2 sets of children's art). The between-subjects factors were age and sex and the within-subject factor was picture set.

The following dependent variables were analyzed using an ANOVA procedure:

1. *Accuracy.* A triad correctly ordered on the literal-visual effects dimension (without regard to direction) received a score of 1 and an incorrect order was scored 0.

2. *Time*. This measured time in seconds that was taken to complete the ordering task of a triad. Because the distribution of this measure was somewhat skewed, the natural logarithm of time was used in the analysis.

3. *Certainty*. This measured how sure the child was of the order expressed on a seven-point scale.

4. *Difficulty*. This measured the degree of difficulty involved in producing the artworks as expressed on a seven-point scale.

5. *Affect*. The degree of positive (happy) or negative (sad) affect produced by the pictures (neutral point of 4) was expressed on a seven-point scale.

6. *Color*

7. *Storytelling*

8. *Composition, Style, and Line*

Drawing Task. A correlation was obtained between the ratings of the two art teachers on the eight 25-point scales and ANOVAs were done comparing the 6-, 9-, and 12-year-old groups on the eight scales.

Results

The mean WISC-R test ages for each group confirmed that they were representative of a normal population (M: 6 yr=6.9, 9 yr=10.6, 12 yr=13.2). No differences were found between male and female scores, $F(1,114)=1.5, p>.05$.

Perception Task

Age Effects. The results of the study (see Figure 1) are informative regarding developmental changes in emotional and cognitive responses to artworks. From an affective standpoint, younger children were significantly more responsive to the artworks than were the older children, $F(2,114)=8.99, p<.01$. Results in Figure 1 reveal that 6-year-olds felt happier in response to the artworks compared with the 9- and 12-year-olds, whose means were closer to the neutral point.

While emotional response diminished with increasing age, perceptual/cognitive skills increased. Older children were more accurate at discriminating the transformation embedded in the triads $F(2,114)=5.96$, $p<.01$. Note, however, that even six-year-old children were more accurate (45%) than would be expected by chance (33%) according to a test of proportion, $z=3.2, p<.001$. The time needed to place the triads in a meaningful sequence decreased for older children, $F(2,114)=3.40, p<.04$. This increased speed of processing implies the automization of cognitive skills. Older children also judged the artworks as more difficult to create, indicating an increasing appreciation of the complexity of aesthetic properties of

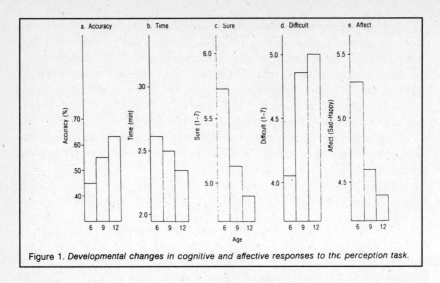

Figure 1. *Developmental changes in cognitive and affective responses to the perception task.*

artworks $F(2,114)=4.31$, $p<.01$. Not surprisingly, older children were less certain or sure of their orders, $F(2,114)=4.10$, $p<.02$.

Note that while males and females did not differ in accuracy, males ordered the triads in less time ($M=2.39$ sec) than did the females ($M=2.59$ sec), $F(1,114)=6.38$, $p<.01$.

Picture Effects. This analysis compares the effects of the "adult" and "child" art forms on the subjects (see Figure 2). The adult materials included two painting and two sculpture triads, while the children's materials comprised one triad of drawings and one triad of clay animal figures. No

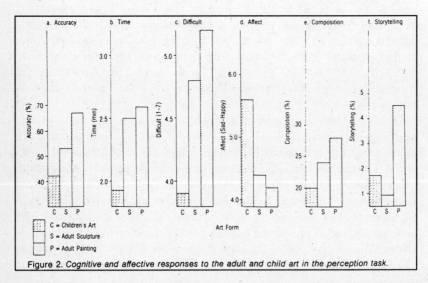

Figure 2. *Cognitive and affective responses to the adult and child art in the perception task.*

interactions were found between age and stimulus materials for the various dependent measures. "Child" and "adult" art generally affected the children in different ways. Child art evoked more affect (i.e., happiness) than did adult art, $F(5,570) = 12.15$, $p < .001$. Children generally ordered the child art in less time than the adult art, $F(5,570) = 7.55$, $p < .001$, and acknowledged that it was less difficult to create than the adult art, $F(5,570) = 8.52$, $p < .001$.

Correspondingly, they made less reference to composition and style when describing the child art compared with the adult art, $F(5,570) = 3.89$, $p < .001$. The complex structure of the adult paintings had the greatest potential for evoking imaginative storytelling responses, $F(5,570) = 50.00$, $p < .001$. Adult art was also more accurately ordered than child art, $F(5,570) = 11.14$, $p < .001$, although at 45% it was still above chance level.

Correlations

Partial correlations were computed between the dependent variables, controlling for the independent variables age, sex, and picture, to clearly define their interrelations without the independent variables confounding effects. The following partial correlations were small (in part because of the crudeness of the scale, 1 through 7 or 0-1), but significant ($p < .01$).

Consistent with the ANOVA findings, certainty decreased as ratings of difficulty increased ($r = -.18$). The difficulty ratings were negatively correlated with affect ratings ($r = -.20$). This is consistent with the traditional finding (Berlyne, 1974) that more complex stimuli diminish the adult viewer's experience of pleasure. Storytelling was negatively correlated with composition, style, and line ($r = -.26$), and color ($r = -.13$) variables. Children who used storytelling as a criterion paid less attention to the replete aspects of the triads. This supports Gardner's (1980) distiction between "dramatists," who are interested in events, and "patterners," who analyze their works in terms of physical attributes.

Drawing Task

Objective Measures. Half of the children were asked to produce a picture on the theme of "home and family" after performing the perception task. Several features of the data reveal developmental changes in the artworks across the three age groups (see Figure 3). The most complex figure in each drawing was scored according to the Harris (1963) Draw-a-Person scheme. As would be expected, a significant main effect, $F(2,54) = 41.00$, $p < .001$, demonstrates increasing complexity in the treatment of the figure as a function of age of the child. A comparable linear increase was found in projection as a function of age, $F(2,54) = 11.34$, $p < .001$. Older children were progressively more skilled at the use of overlap and perspective to produce visual effects.

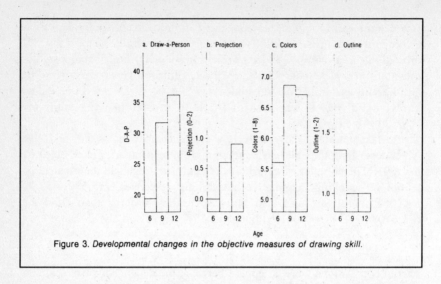

Figure 3. *Developmental changes in the objective measures of drawing skill.*

A discontinuity was found for the two color variables, juxtaposing the youngest age group (6) against the other two (9 and 12). The 6-year-olds used fewer colors than the other two groups, $F(2,54)=4.51, p<.02$. They also adopted a different approach to the use of color for outlining compared with the 9- and 12-year-olds. The 6-year-olds tended toward differential outlining, using a different color to outline than was used to color the interior of a majority of figures (other than black, brown, or orange), $F(2,54)=10.76, p<.001$. In contrast 9-and 12-year olds purely outlined figures with the same color as they were colored inside or outlined with no interior coloring.

Finally, two interesting sex differences were found. Females ($M=6.75$) generally used more colors than males ($M=5.9$), $F(1,54)=5.04, p<.03$, whereas males ($M=.68$) used more overlap and perspective in projection than did the females ($M=.31$), $F(1,54)=4.50, p<.04$.

Subjective Measures. Two teacher/artists independently judged the artworks in a random order on eight 25-point scales. The scales are rank-ordered below in terms of the degree of correlation (shown in parentheses) between their two ratings and all correlations are significant at $p<.001$. The eight scales include: realism ($r=.753$), quality ($r=.597$), composition ($r=.523$), expressiveness ($r=.413$), originality ($r=.368$), happiness ($r=.368$), color ($r=.312$), and harmony ($r=.310$). An arbitrary cutoff of .40 was used to determine which scales would be used for additional analyses.

A series of 3×2 ANOVAs (see Figure 4) were done comparing the three age groups and two sexes on each dimension using the ratings of one of the judges (randomly selected). Significant main effects were found on three

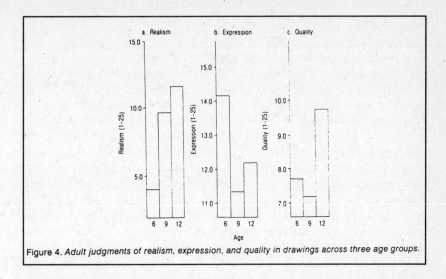

Figure 4. *Adult judgments of realism, expression, and quality in drawings across three age groups.*

dependent measures: realism, $F(2,54)=22.50$, $p<.001$; expressiveness, $F(2,54)=8.61$, $p<.001$; and quality, $F(2,54)=3.54$, $p<.03$. The results in Figure 4 show a linear increase in realism as a function of age group with the greatest increase occurring between 6- and 9-year-olds. A significant quadratic curve was obtained for expressiveness, $t(54)=3.09$, $p<.001$. Ratings of expressiveness drop markedly from the 6- to 9-year old groups, recovering somewhat for the 12-year-old group. The quadratic effect for quality was marginally significant, $t(54)=1.76$, $p<.10$. Ratings of quality drop between the 6- and 9-year-old groups and increase dramatically between the 9- and 12-year-old groups.

Correlations Between Subjective Measures and Perception Measures Including WISC-R

The strongest correlations ($p<.001$) were between scores on the WISC-R and realism ($r=.45$) and expressiveness ($r=-.35$). Children who provided the kind of detail that leads to higher WISC-R scores produced more realistic but less emotionally expressive pictures. Weak but significant ($p<.001$) correlations were obtained between the subjective rating of realism and the accuracy ($r=.10$), time ($r=.14$), and certainty ($r=-.17$) measures in the perception task. Thus, children who produced more realistic pictures were more sensitive to the literal-visual effects dimension, spent more time examining and ordering the artworks, but were less sure of their orders. Finally, judgments of quality were positively correlated ($r=.18$) with amount of time spent ordering the artworks, and negatively correlated ($r=-.11$) with certainty regarding the orders.

Discussion

The results of the study are informative about cognitive and affective processes in the development of aesthetic perception and production in children. The perception task provided a means of examining different facets of aesthetic processing. Internally consistent linear results were obtained for the four cognitively related measures. Older children were more accurate at perceiving a meaningful relationship among the items in the triads and accomplished this with greater speed than did the younger children. At the same time, older children appreciated the difficulty involved in creating the artworks and were correspondingly less certain of their judgments.

While cognitive variables favored older children, affective response to the artworks was greatest among the younger children. The six year olds reported stronger feelings of happiness, while the older children offered more neutral reactions. Of course, these responses occurred in the context of instructions to place the stimuli in a meaningful order. The ordering task itself may have been rewarding to the children. Nonetheless, we have clear evidence of the emotional involvement of preoperational children in an aesthetic perception task. The use of the ladder to measure emotional and cognitive responses was fruitful with the younger group, who may not be comfortable with abstract scales of one through seven.

A difference between the procedure used in this study and the one reported in a recent study of adult aesthetic perception (Cupchik & Gebotys, 1988) should be noted. The triad perception task was first developed for use with adults who were instructed to place the three items in an order of *increasing* meaningfulness. The children in this study were not instructed to place the "most meaningful" artwork at the end of the sequence. The simpler procedure was used so the task would not appear too complex to the children. They did not display a significant tendency to place the most meaningful stimulus either at the beginning or end of the chosen order. Ideally, in an extension of the current study, this directional instruction would be implemented.

Comparisons among the three classes of stimulus materials—adult painting, adult sculpture, and child art (combining painting and sculpture)—are interesting but should only be considered suggestive because of the small sample of stimuli. Children were more accurate and spent more time ordering the adult artworks compared with the children's artworks. They also correctly judged the adult artworks to be more difficult to produce than the children's artworks. The two adult painting triads elicited the greatest use of composition and storytelling accounts for the chosen order. Thus, the more complex materials, which required the greatest amount of processing, were also the most accurately placed in a meaningful order. However, cognitive processing did not predict affective response. Children experienced the greatest amount of happiness when viewing art produced by other children. This is a second piece of evidence that demonstrates the relative independence of cognitive and affective processing.

The production task also revealed basic differences in cognitive and affective processing. Monotonic increases were generally found for objective measures of performance, with the most dramatic shift occurring between the six year olds and the two older groups. Thus, complexity of the central figure (Draw-a-Person measure) increased as a function of age. Older children also used more colors than did the 6-year-olds, implying a more differentiated drawing technique.

The boundary between preoperational and concrete operational stages also marked a radical shift in important drawing skills. None of the 6-year-olds in the study demonstrated a skillful use of projection. The use of projection increased from the 9- to the 12-year-old groups. Similarly, the tendency to outline figures in a different color from that used internally disappeared with the onset of concrete operations. The use of differential outlining by preoperational children may reflect their past experience with outline (e.g., in coloring books) as a means of denoting objects and narrative elements in their artworks. Indeed, Smith and Fucigna (1988) have found that children develop skills of contour drawing well before they can adequately represent form. Concrete operational children are also less egocentric and their new sense of observation may reduce the need for the visual symbols of their earlier childhood.

The subjective rating of realism in the drawings follows a pattern similar to that of the objective measures. The degree of realism in the drawings monotonically increases as a function of age. However, suggestions of two u-shaped curves imply that a second process may underlie aesthetic development. In particular, judgments of expression in the drawings were very high for the 6-year-olds, dropped markedly for the 9-year-olds, and increased again for the 12-year-olds. A tendency was found for expert judgments of quality to diminish from 6 to 9 years of age and increase dramatically with the onset of formal operations. The clearest effects for the 6-year-old group therefore pertain to the expression of emotion in art.

The drawing results for the six year olds are consistent with those obtained for the perception data. Preoperational children appear to be more emotionally responsive to the drawings of others and to invest more expression in their own artworks. This supports the ideas of Werner and Kaplan (1963) regarding the onset of physiognomic perception before that of geometric-technical perception. However, after children have an opportunity to develop their geometric-technical skills, they can attend again to their expressive reactions to art. This yields the kind of controlled expression associated with more mature artworks. In a sense, adult art may reflect a preservation of imaginative involvement associated with the preoperational art combined with the detached analysis and planning developed in later childhood.

In conclusion, this study has shown that cognitive and affective aspects of aesthetics are relatively independent for perception and production. While preoperational children can discern stylistic properties of artworks, older children are still more skilled at this kind of interpretive activity. In a similar manner, preoperational children use some artistic devices in their own drawings that express their imaginative world views. But older children have a more sophisticated repertoire of techniques for observing and representing objects in the external world. When it comes to emotion, preoperational children are more emotionally involved in the art of others and more expressive in their own art. Thus, emotional response and cognitive sophistication appear to be relatively independent in aesthetic processing.

References

Arnheim, R. (1971). *Art and visual perception*. Berkeley, CA: University of California Press.

Berlyne, D. (1971). *Aesthetics and psychobiology*. New York, NY: Appleton-Century-Crofts.

Berlyne, D.E. (1974). *Studies in the new aesthetics*. Washington, DC: Hemisphere.

Cupchik, G.C. (1980). An experimental investigation of perceptual and stylistic dimensions of paintings suggested by art history. In D.E. Berlyne (Ed.), *Studies in the new experimental aesthetics*. Washington, DC: Hemisphere.

Cupchik, G.C., & Gebotys, R.J. (1988). The search for meaning in art: Interpretive styles and judgments of quality. *Visual Arts Research, 14*(2), 38-50.

Carothers, T., & Gardner, H. (1979). The emergence of aesthetic production and perception. *Developmental Psychology, 15*, 570-580.

Fein, S. (1976). *Heidi's horse*. Pleasant Hill, CA: Exelrod Press.

Gardner, H. (1980). *Artful scribbles: The significance of children's drawings*. New York, NY: Basic Books.

Gardner, H., & Winner, E. (1982). First intimations of artistry. In S. Strauss (Ed.), *U-shaped behavioral growth*. New York, NY: Academic Press.

Goodman, N. (1976). *Languages of Art*. Indianapolis, IN: Hackett.

Hardiman, G., & Zernich, T. (1985). Discrimination of style in painting. A developmental study. *Studies in Art Education, 26*(3), 157-162.

Harris, D. (1963). *Children's drawings as measures of intellectual maturity*. New York, NY: Harcourt, Brace, & Jovanovich.

Inhelder, B., & Piaget, J. (1970). *The early growth of logic in the child*. London, UK: Routledge and Kegan Paul.

O'Hare, D. (1976). Individual differences in perceived similarity and preferences for art: A multidimensional scaling analysis. *Perception and Psychophysics, 20*, 445-452.

Piaget, J. (1951). *Judgment and reasoning in the child*. London, UK: Routledge and Kegan Paul.

Piaget, J. (1969). *The mechanisms of perception*. New York, NY: Basic Books.

Smith, N.R., & Fucigna, C. (1988). Drawing systems in children's pictures: Contour and form. *Visual Arts Research, 14*(1), 66-76.

Sparshott, F. (1982). *The theory of the arts*. Princeton, NJ: Princeton University Press.

Wechsler, D. (1974). *Manual for the Wechsler intelligence scale for children* (Revised). New York, NY: The Psychological Corporation.

Werner, H., & Kaplan, B. (1963). *Symbol formation*. New York, NY: Wiley.

Winner, E. *Invented worlds: The psychology of the arts*. Cambridge, MA: Harvard University Press.

Winner, E. et al. (1986). Children's perception of "aesthetic" properties of the arts: Domain-specific or pan-artistic? *British Journal of Developmental Psychology, 4*, 149-160.

The Development of Affective Skills in School-Aged Children

S. Mark Pancer
Wilfrid Laurier University
Sue M. Weinstein
Thistletown Regional Centre for Children and Adolescents
Rexdale, Ontario

Over the last several years, a number of programs have been developed to teach children social and affective skills that will presumably enhance their social and emotional adjustment. One component of many of these programs involves training in skills relating to the understanding and expression of affect. The major objectives of this study were to determine the extent to which a number of affective skills are present at different age levels, to examine the relationship between children's affective and cognitive skills, and to identify those affective skills that are most highly related to emotional adjustment. One hundred twenty children in Grades 3, 4, 5, and 6 were administered measures of affective and cognitive skills and emotional adjustment. The results indicated that 4 of the 5 affective skills assessed increase with age, with the greatest change occurring between Grades 4 and 5. Moreover, children's affective skills were significantly correlated with their cognitive skills. While affective skills did not relate to emotional adjustment across all grade levels, there was some indication that affective skills are related to emotional adjustment at the Grade 4 level. Results are discussed in terms of their implications for programming in the affective domain.

*   *   *

THERE HAS BEEN INCREASING RECOGNITION AMONG EDUCATORS THAT IT IS not sufficient to attend to students' intellectual needs alone. In addition to being a place where children acquire academic skills, school is also a place where many of the social and affective skills they will need in later life are also acquired (Carkhuff, 1982; Cooper, Munger, & Ravlin, 1980; Elias &

This research was funded under contract by the Ministry of Education, Ontario. The authors would like to thank Andrew Pakula and Robert Gebotys for their assistance with the statistical analyses, Karen Pancer and Bob Hallman for their editorial assistance; and the Dellcrest Children's Centre, under whose auspices this research was conducted. Thanks are also due to an anonymous reviewer for his or her helpful comments on the manuscript.

Maher, 1983). In recognition of this, a great number of programs have been developed to teach positive interpersonal skills such as cooperation and sharing (cf.. Gottman, Gonso, & Schuler, 1975; Oden & Asher, 1977), to help children solve interpersonal problems (cf.. Shure & Spivack, 1978; Spivack, Platt, & Shure, 1976; Spivack & Shure, 1974), and to foster feelings of competence and self-worth (cf.. Canfield & Wells, 1976; Coopersmith, 1976).

One component of many programs in the affective domain involves training in skills relating to the understanding and expression of emotion. Children are taught to recognize feelings in themselves and others, to express their own emotions, and to understand how their behavior might affect the feelings of others. For example, Project Aware (Elardo & Cooper, 1977), a popular program designed to teach children to be more aware of their own and others' feelings, involves children in a number of discussions and role-playing exercises. In one such exercise, children are provided with a story about a boy who has worked hard to make some extra money to buy something for himself, but decides to buy a present for his brother instead. Children are asked to discuss the feelings that each of the characters in the story might have had, and how the characters might have acted. They are then asked to act out the situation themselves.

The Development of Affective Skills

A review of the psychological research literature on emotional development reveals that many of the skills taught in affective programs show changes with age. A number of studies, for example, have examined children's ability to anticipate the effects of various situations on their emotional responses. In one study (Borke, 1971), children as young as 3 years of age were able to correctly identify the emotions likely to be produced by situations such as losing a toy or getting lost in the woods, and demonstrated an increasing capacity to identify such emotions with age. A later study by Gove and Keating (1979) found that older children (mean age = 5 years 2 months) were better able to identify the likely emotions experienced by story characters than were younger children (mean age = 3 years 10 months). In addition, younger children in this and other studies (Urberg & Docherty, 1976) showed greater difficulty in understanding the fact that different individuals might respond with different emotions to the same event.

Young children appear to have even greater difficulty in assessing or understanding emotional reactions when some form of inference is required. They tend to base their judgments and explanations of emotional states on situational cues and publicly observable behavior rather than on inferences about covert psychological states. Flapan (1968), for example, found that older children who had viewed films of social interactions gave fewer literal reports and gave more explanations for the social interactions when asked what had happened in the films. In addition, older children embellished their explanations of what happened in the episodes with inferences about the thoughts, feelings, and intentions of others. Later studies (Gove & Keating, 1979; Harris, Olthof, & Terwogt, 1981; Hughes, Tingle, & Sawin, 1981) support the notion that younger children are unable to infer emotions to the same extent as older children.

Other studies suggest developmental changes in children's understanding that a person's verbalizations are not necessarily an accurate reflection of what that individual is feeling. In other words, younger children may have difficulty in understanding that individuals may often mask the emotions they feel (Harris, Olthof, & Terwogt, 1981; Saarni, 1979).

One of the most widely used programs in the affective and social domains is the Interpersonal Cognitive Problem Solving (ICPS) program developed by Spivack and Shure (Shure & Spivack, 1978; Spivack, Platt, & Shure, 1976). Their program consists of a series of lessons, activities, and games designed to teach specific skills presumed to relate to social adjustment in children. One such skill is "alternative thinking," the ability to generate multiple potential alternative solutions to a given interpersonal problem situation. A study by McGillicuddy-DeLisi (1980) suggested that this alternative thinking skill is also one that changes with age, and, indeed, she found that older children were able to generate more unique solutions to interpersonal conflict situations than were younger children.

In summary, it appears that many important affective and social skills undergo marked changes with age. Older children are more able to anticipate the effects of various situations and events on emotions, they understand that the same event can produce different emotional reactions in different individuals, they are better at making inferences about how a person might be feeling, they show more cognizance of the fact that a person's overt expression may not be an accurate reflection of his or her true feelings, and they can generate more alternative solutions to interpersonal conflicts. This has important implications for the development of programs in the affective domain. It is conceivable, for example, that many current programs may be attempting to teach children skills that they already have. For example, several studies (Hamilton, 1973; Izard, 1971; Makarenko, Simonov, Sidrova, & Karpovitch, 1977; Odom & Lemond, 1972) indicated that children are able to identify many emotions from photographs well before reaching the Grade 1 age level. Programs that use such techniques to teach children at higher grade levels how to recognize emotions in others may well be unnecessary. Conversely, some programs may attempt to teach skills that children may have a great deal of difficulty in acquiring until they are older. Programs designed to teach affective skills would likely be most effective if they are provided to children at an age when they are just beginning to develop these skills, rather than at an age when few or most children have already acquired the skills. This necessitates research that would identify when such skills are acquired.

The Relationship Between Affective and Cognitive Development

A number of the studies of affective skills in children have found a relationship between the development of affective skills and cognitive or intellectual development. Rothenberg (1970), for example, assessed children's "social sensitivity"—their ability to accurately perceive the feelings and motives of other individuals—by asking children to describe the feelings of characters portrayed in tape-recorded stories. Intellectual level was measured by means of the Peabody Picture Vocabulary Test (PPVT), and the Block Design sub test of the Wechsler Intelligence Scale for Children. Social sensitivity was significantly correlated with both verbal (PPVT) and nonverbal (Block Design) measures of intelligence.

Other studies have noted a relationship between affective skills and the development of certain cognitive abilities, particularly role-taking (Flavell, Botkin, Fry, Wright, & Jarvis, 1968)—the ability to perceive and understand events from another's perspective. A number of investigators (Borke, 1971, 1973; Deutsch, 1974; Gove & Keating, 1979; Greenspan, Barenboim, & Chandler, 1976) claimed that the ability to understand different roles and perspectives is essential for an individual to understand the emotional reactions that others might have to various events and situations.

The relationship between cognitive skills, such as role-taking, and affective skills involving the recognition and understanding of emotions in others may have important implications for the development of sound programs in the affective domain. It suggests that programs aimed at enhancing such affective skills would benefit from the inclusion of program elements designed to improve related cognitive skills. Before incorporating such elements into affective programs, however, it is necessary to determine which cognitive skills are most importantly related to relevant affective skills.

Affective Skills and Socio-Emotional Functioning

The basic assumption underlying the concept of affective education is that such training will enhance learning, increase feelings of competence and self-esteem, improve peer relations, and reduce the incidence of social and emotional problems. In consequence of this, bodies such as the Joint Commission on Mental Health of Children have endorsed the need for affective education (Joint Commission on Mental Health of Children, 1969). Cooper et al. (1980) emphasized the role of affective education in the prevention of social and emotional problems in children.

A number of studies indicated that there is indeed a relationship between the level of various affective skills and characteristics related to mental health. Rothenberg's (1970) study of social sensitivity in children found that children's ability to perceive and comprehend the feelings of others was significantly correlated with peer relations, feelings of self-esteem and self-worth, and teachers' ratings on dimensions such as leadership and gregariousness. Light (1979) found a significant relationship between role-taking ability and social adjustment in children, as measured by the Bristol Social Adjustment Guide. Studies by Richard and Dodge (1982) and Asarnow and Callan (1985) indicated that the ability to generate solutions to interpersonal problems is related to social adjustment problems in boys. However, decisions about specific affective skills to be included in affective programs should be preceded by research that identifies those skills that are most importantly related to good social and emotional adjustment.

Objectives of the Study

Our review of the psychological literature indicates that many important affective and social skills undergo pronounced changes with age. Such skills include:

(1) The ability to anticipate the effects of situations and events on emotions.

(2) The ability to understand that the same event can produce different emotional reactions in different individuals.

(3) The ability to infer a person's emotions.

(4) The ability to generate alternative ways of dealing with interpersonal problems.

(5) The ability to understand that overt expression may not be an accurate reflection of one's true feelings.

The major objectives of this study were to determine the extent to which each of these skills is present at varying age levels, from Grades 3 to 6, to examine the relationship between children's affective skills and the level of cognitive skill they demonstrate, and to identify those affective skills that are related to emotional adjustment.

Method

Subjects

A total of 120 children in Grades 3, 4, 5, and 6 with approximately equal numbers of boys and girls from each grade participated in this study. Mean ages of subjects were 8.79 years (Grade 3), 9.95 years (Grade 4), 11.00 years (Grade 5), and 11.85 years (Grade 6). Participants were drawn from four public schools in the North York and Etobicoke boroughs of Toronto. The schools were located in districts ranging from lower to middle socioeconomic status, serving students of mixed ethnic backgrounds.

Measures

The measures employed in this study assessed children's functioning in three areas: (a) understanding emotions, (b) cognitive skills, and (c) social adjustment.

Understanding Emotions—The Affective Skill Questionnaire (ASQ). The Affective Skill Questionnaire was a measure developed by the authors to assess the extent to which children demonstrated each of the five affective skills described earlier. Ten stories representing the five affective skill areas (2 stories per area) were constructed. Each story was followed by a series of open-ended questions. A pilot test was conducted to ensure that children in Grades 3, 4, 5, and 6 understood the stories and questions. Following pilot work, the final version of the ASQ was compiled.

The first pair of stories was designed to assess children's ability to realize that the same event can affect different people in different ways. In these vignettes, two children displayed different behavioral reactions to the same situation.

David has just been given a dog for Christmas. He's really excited about his new dog, so he decides to take him over to some of his friends' houses. When his friend Jamie saw the dog, he started to pat him. When Michael saw the dog, he just stood in a corner.

The open-ended question following the stories determined whether children saw that the reactions were different, and how they characterized the different reactions.

The second pair of stories was designed to assess children's skills in anticipating the effects of events on emotions, based upon knowledge of the situation. In these stories two friends were portrayed in situations that would likely lead to different emotional reactions from each character.

Jennifer and Sarah are good friends. Their teacher asked them to draw a picture. The teacher says that she will pick the best of the two to put up on the wall for Parent-Teacher Night. Jennifer and Sarah both worked very hard on their pictures. In the end, the teacher picks Sarah's picture and puts it up on the wall.

Open-ended questions following these vignettes asked how each character would feel and why they would experience the stated emotion.

The third affective skill addressed by the questionnaire was the ability to anticipate the effects of events on emotions, based upon information about a person. Here stories portrayed a protagonist's reaction in two different situations. The character's response was the same in each situation. A third situation involving the same character was described and subjects were asked to predict how the protagonist would react and why he or she would react in that particular manner.

> This is a story about a girl named Ann. Ann was coming out of her school one day, when one of the boys in her class jumped out from around the corner and shouted, "Boo!" Ann got very scared and started to cry.
> Another time, Ann was late getting home from school and it had started getting dark. By the time she got home she was very frightened and started to cry.
> Another time, Ann's friend had gotten a new dog and brought the dog over to Ann's house to show it to her. The dog started barking. How do you think Ann reacted? Why?

The fourth affective skill tapped by the questionnaire was the ability to generate a number of different ways to change a person's affective state. Vignettes in this area presented situations in which a character was experiencing a negative emotion, for example, "Suppose your friend's bicycle has just been stolen from the school yard and he or she is very unhappy." Subjects were asked what they could do to cheer up their friend. Prompts, in the form of: "Yes, that's one thing you could do, what else could you do?" were administered until the child indicated that he or she had run out of ideas.

The final section of the affective questionnaire addressed children's understanding of controlling displays of emotion. Protagonists were presented in situations where a display of their true emotions could lead to embarrassing or negative reactions from others.

> Imagine that you're with friends at the fair and your friends want to go on one of those rides that swings you upside down way up in the air. You're so afraid that you don't dare go on it, but you don't want your friends to laugh at you.

The subsequent open-ended question asked what the character could do in his or her predicament.

Cognitive Skills—Inventory of Piaget's Developmental Tasks (IPDT) (Furth, 1970). The IPDT is an untimed, multiple-choice, paper-and-pencil test designed to measure children's cognitive development in terms of Piagetian concepts. It translates some of Piaget's concrete and formal operational tasks into an objective, quickly administered instrument, requiring minimal reading and language skills. The IPDT can be administered to children ranging from 8 years of age to mid-adolescence, either in groups or individually. The full inventory consists of 72 items covering five problem areas: conservation (4 subtests), images (4 subtests), relations (3 subtests), classification (4 subtests), and laws (3 subtests). The 18 subtests (comprised of 4 items each), are presented in the form of pictorial illustrations in a test booklet. Each sub test is introduced with an example that is correctly answered in the test booklet. For each item children mark down or point to the correct answer chosen from a set of four alternatives.

For the purposes of this study, five subtests were selected that assessed children's reasoning in the areas of conservation of quantity, conservation of weight, perspective-taking, conservation of volume, and inferential thinking.

Reliability and validity data are available on the IPDT (Patterson & Milakofsky, 1980). Test-retest reliability coefficients range from .62 to .95 across a variety of age groups. Internal consistency split-half reliability coefficients range from .63 to .84. IPDT construct validity has been demonstrated in terms of significant differences in scores across grades and in terms of its correlations with IQ and achievement test scores.

Social Adjustment—The Child and Adolescent Adjustment Profile Scale (CAAP Scale) (Ellsworth, 1979). The CAAP Scale is a standardized scale for measuring adjustment of children and adolescents aged 3-18 years. It consists of 20 items divided into five subscales of four items each. The subscales assess: (a) peer relations, (b) dependency, (c) hostility, (d) productivity, and (e) withdrawal. Two additional subscales measuring rule following and frustration tolerance were added to the original 20-item scale.

The CAAP is completed by parents, teachers, counselors, or other staff who work with children. For the purposes of this study, teachers completed the CAAP rating scales.

Reliability scores for the five subscales of the CAAP range from .80 to .90 (as indicated by coefficient Alpha) and from .78 to .89 (as indicated by test-retest reliability) (Ellsworth, 1979). Validity data have indicated that CAAP scales discriminate groups of normal, clinic, and probationer youths. In addition, some of the scales discriminate between groups of older and younger normal children.

Procedure

All testing was conducted by one female experimenter who met with each child individually in a quiet room located in the school. Each interview lasted approximately 25 minutes. Children were first given a brief explanation of the purpose of the study. They were told that the experimenter was interested in seeing how children in different grades think about feelings and emotions (i.e., affective skills) and how they think about problems that are not related to emotions (i.e., cognitive skills).

Following this introduction, subjects were read each of the 10 affective stories and associated questions (half of the subjects heard Story 1 from each skill area first; half heard Story 2 first). To ensure that responses were not hampered by failure to remember story content, subjects were asked to reiterate the first two stories. They seemed to have no difficulty recalling important aspects of these stories. All of the responses were tape-recorded. Subjects were then presented with the IPDT items, where the experimenter read each problem aloud, while the child read along in the test booklet. Subjects pointed out the correct response alternative.

Teachers completed the adjustment profile (CAAP Scale) within one week of their students' participation in the project.

Scoring

Affective Questionnaire. Tape recordings of children's responses on the ASQ were transcribed. Two female judges who were blind with respect to the purposes of this study scored each protocol according to a predetermined rating scheme. In general, lower scores were given to responses that demonstrated a lesser degree of the skill involved, and higher scores were awarded to responses that demonstrated a greater degree of skill. For example, the first story described a situation in which two children displayed different behavioral reactions to the same situation, and was designed to assess the ability to understand that the same event can produce different emotions in different individuals. Subjects were given lower scores for responses that indicated no perception of differences in the story characters' feelings, and higher scores for inferring differences in the affective responses of the characters. In general, higher scores were given to responses that described emotions in more specific, differentiated terms and attributed reactions to inner feelings and thoughts about self and others.

The fourth affective skill (the ability to generate alternatives designed to change someone's affective state) was scored somewhat differently. One point was given for each relevant and different class of alternatives suggested by the subject, for each of the two stories. For example, in the first story (breaking Mother's plate), responses such as fix the plate, buy a new one, and clean the house, each received 1 point. However, responses such as wash the dishes, clean your room, and vacuum the house were only given a total of 1 point, since they all refer to the same class of alternative, that is, doing housework.

Interrater reliability (percentage of agreements) in scoring the ASQ protocols was 92% across the 5 skill areas.

IPDT Scoring. The number of correct responses on each of the 5 subscales of the IPDT were used in the data analysis. The maximum number of correct responses for each subscale was 4.

CAAP Scale Scoring. Teacher ratings (ranging from 1, rarely; to 4, always) on each item of the CAAP Scale were totaled separately for each of the 7 subscales. These subscale scores were employed in the data analyses. Maximum score per subscale was 16 (rating of 4×4 items).

Results

Development of Affective Skills

Means and standard deviations of the five affective skills, organized by grade and sex, are presented in Table 1. Results were analyzed by means of a 2-way multivariate analysis of variance with Sex (boys, girls) and Grade (3, 4, 5, and 6) as the independent variables, and the five affective skill scores as the dependent variables. This analysis revealed a significant Grade effect, $F(15,301)=3.58, p<.001$), indicating that affective skills undergo significant changes across grade levels. Univariate analysis of variance for each of the affective skills in turn was used to further examine differences across grade levels. These univariate analyses indicated significant differences among grade levels on four of the five affective skills, $F(3,113)=2.41, 5.64, 7.87, 3.91,$ and $1.89; p<.07, .001, .001, .01,$ and .15 for Skills 1 to 5, respectively). Only the fifth affective skill, the ability to understand that overt expression may not reflect one's true feelings, did not show any change across grade levels. Multivariate orthogonal contrasts of Grade 3 versus Grade 4, Grades 3 and 4 versus Grades 5 and 6, and Grade 5 versus Grade 6, indicate that these changes were primarily due to shifts in affective skills from Grades 3 and 4 to Grades 5 and 6, $F(5,113)=7.58, p<.001$). Univariate contrasts of individual affective skills show a significant increase from Grades 3 and 4 to Grades 5 and 6 on four of the five affective skills, $F(1,117)=6.63, 15.10, 22.84, 3.25,$ and $0.03; p<.01, .001, .001, .08,$ and .87; for Skills 1 to 5, respectively). Once again, only Skill 5 did not show a significant increase from Grades 3 and 4 to Grades 5 and 6. The multivariate contrast of Grade 3 versus Grade 4 was also significant, $F(5,113)=2.79, p<.025$). Univariate contrasts of the individual skill measures indicate that this was primarily due to a decrease in scores for Skills 4 and 5 from Grades 3 to 4, $F(1,117)=8.20, 4.61; p<.005, .05;$ for Skills 4 and 5, respectively).

Multivariate analysis also revealed a significant Sex effect, $F(5,109)=2.59, p<.05$). Univariate analyses indicate that this was primarily due to the fact that boys had significantly higher scores than girls on the first affective skill (understanding that the same event can affect different people in different ways), $F(1,113)=6.54, p<.025$). The remaining four affective skills showed no difference between boys and girls. Multivariate analysis of variance revealed no Sex $\times$ Grade interaction, $F(15,301)=0.41, p=ns$).

In summary, then, children in different grades show significant differences in their level of affective skill. The greatest difference in affective

TABLE 1
Mean Affective Skill Levels by Grade and Sex

Grade	Males		Females	
	M	SD	M	SD
Skill 1—same event, different effects				
3	4.60	0.91	4.07	1.10
4	4.87	0.92	4.06	1.29
5	5.14	1.03	4.63	0.81
6	4.93	1.10	4.87	0.99
Skill 2—anticipation based on situation				
3	11.33	2.74	11.00	2.78
4	12.20	2.27	9.56	2.56
5	14.07	3.29	11.94	3.75
6	13.00	3.84	14.33	3.72
Skill 3—anticipation based on person				
3	6.13	1.73	5.80	1.52
4	6.00	1.65	5.94	1.73
5	7.21	1.48	7.00	1.75
6	7.87	1.41	7.20	1.15
Skill 4—changing another's affect				
3	6.80	2.21	6.67	2.19
4	5.53	1.51	5.25	1.57
5	7.07	1.77	6.44	1.71
6	5.87	1.36	7.33	2.16
Skill 5—control of emotional display				
3	4.40	1.35	4.47	1.41
4	4.13	1.41	3.19	1.33
5	4.64	1.45	3.94	1.48
6	3.87	1.36	3.93	1.62

skills appears to occur between Grades 4 and 5, when four of the five affective skills undergo a significant increase.

Relationship Between Affective and Cognitive Skills

The relationship between affective and cognitive skills was examined by determining the canonical correlation between the five affective skill measures and the five subscale scores on the IPDT (cf. Pedhazur, 1982). In canonical analysis, a linear combination of variables from each set is derived such that the highest possible correlation between the two linear combinations is obtained. Canonical analysis results in a number of pairs of linear combinations (or variate pairs), the total number being equal to the number of variables in the smaller data set. In this case, canonical analysis produced 5 variate pairs. However, analysis of the variate pairs yielded only 1 significant canonical correlation, $F(25,413) = 1.90, p < .006$. The canonical correlation between affective skills and IPDT scores for this variate pair was $R = .455$. The squared canonical correlation (R-squared = .207) indicates a moderate degree of overlap between the two sets of variables. The correlations between the constituent measures of each set of measures and their corresponding linear combination are presented in Table 2.

Using a loading cutoff of .40 (Wood & Erskine, 1977), the skills most important in defining the set of affective skills are the ability to understand that the same event can affect people in different ways, the ability to anticipate the effects of events on emotions, and the ability to anticipate emotional reactions based on a knowledge of a person's past behavior. Skills most important in defining the cognitive domain are conservation of quantity, perspective taking, and inferential thinking.

In summary, canonical analysis indicates a significant correlation between affective and cognitive skills. Moreover, the specific affective skills that contribute the most to this relationship are the same skills that show changes from one grade level to the next, namely, the ability to anticipate the effects of events on emotions, and the ability to infer a person's emotions from a knowledge of the person's past behavior.

Affective Skill and Social/Emotional Adjustment

The third objective of this study was to identify those affective skills that are most important in producing optimal social and emotional development. Separate multiple regression analyses, with the five affective skill scores

TABLE 2
Correlations Between Original Variables and Weighted Sums

Affective Skills	Canonical Loading
1. Understanding that same event can affect different people in different ways	.495
2. Ability to anticipate effects on emotion based on knowledge of situation	.717
3. Ability to anticipate effects on emotion based on knowledge of person	.706
4. Ability to generate ways of changing another's emotional state	.352
5. Ability to control display of emotion	−.097
IPDT Subscales	
1. Conservation of quantity	.802
2. Conservation of weight	.146
3. Perspective taking	.439
4. Conservation of volume	.375
5. Inferential thinking	.685

as the independent variables, and each of the CAAP subscales (in turn) as the dependent variables, revealed no significant relationships between levels of affective skills and any of the dimensions of social/emotional adjustment. This is not surprising, however, given that the affective skill measures increase across grade levels, while CAAP ratings, which are made relative to other children of the same age, do not change with grade level. Multiple regression analyses, with the residuals of the affective skill scores (after grade level had been removed) as the independent variables, and each of the CAAP subscales as the dependent variables, did not reveal any significant relationship between affective skill and social/emotional adjustment, either.

The lack of any significant overall relationship between scores on the ASQ and CAAP scales may not necessarily indicate that affective skills are unrelated to social and emotional adjustment. It may be that level of affective skill relates to emotional adjustment only at certain age levels. One might suspect that the strongest relationship between affective skill and emotional adjustment might be at those age and grade levels in which affective skills undergo the greatest amount of change. The earlier analyses, which indicate the greatest changes in affective skills occurring between Grades 4 and 5, suggest that the relationship between affective skills and emotional adjustment would be greatest at the Grade 4 or 5 level.

In order to explore this possibility further, Pearson product-moment correlations were calculated between ASQ scores and CAAP subscale scores at each grade level. These are presented in Table 3.

Examination of the correlations across grade levels reveals very few significant correlations between affective skill and emotional adjustment in Grades 3, 5, and 6. A number of significant correlations do occur in Grade 4, however. Affective Skills 1 (same event producing different effects) and 4 (changing another's affect) correlate significantly with a number of CAAP subscales, as well as correlating significantly with the CAAP scale total, a number indicating the overall level of emotional adjustment, $r(29) = .35$ and .39 between total CAAP score and Skills 1 and 4, respectively ($p < .025$ for both). This suggests that certain affective skills, namely, the ability to understand that the same event can produce different emotional reactions in different individuals, and the ability to generate alternative strategies designed to change a person's affective state, may be related to emotional adjustment, but only at particular age and grade levels.

Discussion

The results of this study indicated that four of the five affective skills assessed by the ASQ undergo significant changes from one grade level to the next. Older children were better able to understand that the same event can produce different emotional reactions in different individuals, they

TABLE 3
Correlations Between ASQ and CAAP Subscale Scores by Grade Level

ASQ	Peers	Dependency	Hostility	Productivity	Withdrawal	Rules	Frustration	Total
Grade 3								
Same event, different effects	.08	.08	-.26	.05	.01	-.22	-.21	-.14
Anticipation based on situation	.03	-.17	.00	-.03	-.01	.09	.08	.00
Anticipation based on person	.11	.05	-.24	.17	-.04	-.23	-.17	-.17
Changing another's affect	-.17	-.04	-.01	-.06	.03	.04	.05	.04
Control of emotional display	.01	-.12	.05	-.03	-.14	.19	.06	.02
Grade 4								
Same event, different effects	.20	-.45**	-.04	.39**	-.38*	-.16	-.08	-.35*
Anticipation based on situation	.08	-.13	-.09	.05	-.07	-.05	-.23	-.14
Anticipation based on person	.26	.18	-.04	-.21	.03	.15	-.08	.05
Changing another's affect	.24	-.24	-.21	.36*	-.23	-.32*	-.30*	-.39*
Control of emotional display	.30	-.22	-.05	.31*	-.28	-.20	.13	-.25
Grade 5								
Same event, different effects	-.26	.28	.21	-.22	.34*	.16	.24	.29
Anticipation based on situation	.01	.20	.32*	-.13	.20	.27	.25	.23
Anticipation based on person	.27	-.13	-.08	.10	-.02	-.05	-.06	-.12
Changing another's affect	.26	.29	-.01	.00	.15	.06	.03	.04
Control of emotional display	-.06	-.20	.26	.02	.33*	.22	.23	.15
Grade 6								
Same event, different effects	-.17	-.13	.06	.00	-.09	.08	-.09	-.01
Anticipation based on situation	.28	-.17	-.07	.18	-.24	-.09	-.13	-.21
Anticipation based on person	.05	.08	.14	-.36*	.31*	.22	.07	.22
Changing another's affect	-.29	-.01	-.04	.04	.09	-.14	.02	.03
Control of emotional display	.06	-.15	-.14	.13	-.20	-.01	-.25	-.17

*$p < .05$.
**$p < .01$.

were more able to anticipate the emotions that different situations were likely to produce, they showed a greater capacity to predict a child's emotional reaction to an event from the child's reaction to similar events in the past, and there was some indication that they were more proficient at thinking of ways of changing another person's affective state. Moreover, it appears that the greatest overall change in these skills occurs between Grades 4 and 5.

These findings support the notion that affective skills similar to those taught in a variety of programs undergo regular developmental changes. The fact that the greatest amount of change occurs between Grades 4 and 5 may indicate that this is a critical time in the development of many of these skills.

The conclusion that Grades 4 and 5 represent a critical period in the acquisition of affective skills is further supported by the evidence that certain affective skills are significantly correlated with emotional adjustment only at the Grade 4 level, and not at other grade levels. The skills most highly related to emotional adjustment at this grade level were the ability to understand that the same event can produce different emotional reactions in different individuals, and the ability to think of different ways of changing a person's affective state. This suggests that training in these skills might be more beneficial in enhancing a child's overall emotional adjustment than training in other skills that are less highly correlated with adjustment. The research literature (see Shantz, 1975; Spivack & Shure, 1982) provides many examples of affect-related skills that seem to be important in the development of positive peer relations and enhanced emotional adjustment. This research, however, indicated that future research should identify not only which skills are related to adjustment, but at what age they are most likely to affect the child's social and emotional well-being. It is conceivable that measures such as the ASQ might eventually be useful in assessing children's skills in affective expression and judgment and in determining when and how a child could benefit from training. Before making definitive statements about which skills should be taught to a particular group, however, it would be advisable to assess both affective skills, and their relationship to emotional adjustment, in the children who are to receive training.

The results of this study also indicated that there is a relationship between affective skill and the level of Piagetian cognitive skills. The cognitive skills that contributed the most to this relationship were the conservation of quantity, inferential thinking, and the ability to see things from another's perspective. This finding supports the notion that certain basic cognitive skills may be necessary in order for a child to acquire related affective skills. For example, a child might need to be able to understand another's perspective of physical arrangements before being able to acquire the more difficult skill of understanding that another's emotional reaction to a certain situation might be different from one's own. This suggests that programs aimed at enhancing affective skills might benefit from the inclusion of program elements aimed at improving related cognitive skills. Indeed, many of the skills that we have described as being "affective" have often been described as cognitive skills in the research literature. Skills such as role-taking and solution-generating, as assessed in our study, are affective to the extent that they are involved in the understanding, expression, and alteration of affect, and may be described more appropriately as having a combination of affective and cognitive elements.

With few exceptions, currently available programs in the affective domain are rarely based on systematic research designed to identify program elements that would be most likely to produce the desired result of enhanced social and emotional adjustment. The results of this study indicate that a more systematic approach is required in the design of such programs. They suggest that such programs should teach specific skills (identified by prior research) to children at a specific age and grade level, if they are to be of maximum effectiveness. The relationship between affective and cognitive skills indicates, furthermore, that such programs might attempt to integrate training in affective skills with training in cognitive skills to which they relate.

References

Asarnow, J.R., & Callan, J.W. (1985). Boys with peer adjustment problems: Social cognitive processes. *Journal of Consulting and Clinical Psychology, 53,* 80-87.

Borke, H. (1971). Interpersonal problem perception for young children: Egocentrism or empathy? *Developmental Psychology, 5,* 263-269.

Borke, H. (1973). The development of empathy in Chinese and American children between the ages of three and six years: A cross-culture study. *Developmental Psychology, 9.* 102-108.

Canfield, I., & Wells, H. (1976). *100 ways to enhance self-concept.* Englewood Cliffs, NJ: Prentice-Hall.

Carkhuff, R.R. (1982). Affective education in the age of productivity. *Educational Leadership, 39,* 484-487.

Cooper, S., Munger, R., & Ravlin, M.M. (1980). Mental health prevention through affective education in the schools. *Journal of Prevention, 1,* 24-34.

Coopersmith, S. (Ed.). (1976). *Developing motivation in children.* San Francisco: Albion.

Deutsch, F. (1974). Female preschoolers' perceptions of affective responses and interpersonal behavior in videotaped episodes. *Developmental Psychology, 10,* 733-740.

Elardo, P.T., & Cooper, M. (1977). *Project aware: A handbook for teachers.* Reading, MA: Addison-Wesley.

Elias, M.J., & Maher, C.A. (1983). Social and affective development of children: A programmatic perspective. *Exceptional Children, 49,* 336-349.

Ellsworth, R.B. (1979). CAAP Scale: *The measurement of child and adolescent adjustment.* Roanoke, VA: Institute for Program Evaluation.

Flapan, D. (1968). *Children's understanding of social interaction.* New York: Teacher's College, Columbia University.

Flavell, J.H., Botkin, P.T., Fry, C.L., Wright, I.C., & Jarvis, P.E. (1968). *The development of role-taking and communication skills in children*. New York: Wiley.

Furth, H. (1970). *An inventory of Piaget's developmental tasks*. Washington, DC: Catholic University, Department of Psychology, Centre for Research in Thinking and Language.

Gottman, I., Gonso, J., & Schuler, B. (1975). Social competence, social interaction, and friendship in children. *Child Development, 46*, 709-718.

Gove, L.F., & Keating, D.P. (1979). Empathic role-taking precursors. *Developmental Psychology, 15*, 594-600.

Greenspan, S., Barenboim, C., & Chandler, M. (1976). Empathy and pseudo-empathy: The affective judgements of first and third graders. *Journal of Genetic Psychology, 129*, 77-88.

Hamilton, M. (1973). Imitative behavior and expressive ability in facial expression of emotion. *Developmental Psychology, 8*, 138.

Harris, P.L., Olthof, T., & Terwogt, M. (1981). Children's knowledge of emotion. *Journal of Child Psychology and Psychiatry, 22*, 247-261.

Hughes, R., Tingle, B., & Sawin, D.B . (1981). Development of empathic understanding in children. *Child Development, 52*, 122-128.

Izard, C.E. (1971). *The face of emotion*. New York: Appleton-Century-Crofts.

Joint Commission on Mental Health of Children (1969). *Crisis in child mental health*. New York: Harper & Row.

Light, P. (1979). *The development of social sensitivity*. Cambridge, England: Cambridge University Press.

Makarenko, J., Simonov, P.V., Sidrova, O.A., & Karpovitch, E.A. (1977). Development of recognition and reproduction of facial expressions in children. *Activitas Nervosa Superior, 19*, 270-271.

McGillicuddy-DeLisi, A.V. (1980). Predicted strategies and success in children's resolution of interpersonal problems. *Journal of Applied Developmental Psychology, 1*, 175-187.

Oden, S., & Asher, S.R. (1977). Coaching children in social skills for friendship making. *Child Development, 48*, 495-506.

Odom, R.D., & Lemond, C.M. (1972). Developmental differences in the perception and production of facial expressions. *Child Development, 43*, 359-369.

Patterson, H.O., & Milakofsky, L. (1980). A paper and pencil inventory for the assessment of Piaget's tasks. *Applied Psychological Measurement, 4*, 341-353.

Pedhazur, E. (1982). *Multiple regression in behavioral research*. New York: CBS College Publishing.

Richard, B.A., & Dodge, K.A. (1982). Social maladjustment and problem solving in school-aged children. *Journal of Consulting and Clinical Psychology, 50*, 226-233.

Rothenberg, B. (1970). Children's social sensitivity and relationship to interpersonal competence, intrapersonal comfort and intellectual level. *Developmental Psychology, 2*, 335-350.

Saarni, C. (1979). Children's understanding of display rules of expressive behavior. *Developmental Psychology, 15*, 424-429.

Shantz, C.U. (1975). The development of social cognition. In E.M. Hetherington (Ed.). *Review of Child Development Research: Vol 5* (pp. 257-324). Chicago: University of Chicago Press.

Shure, M.B., & Spivack, G. (1978). *Problem solving techniques in child-rearing*. San Francisco: Jossey-Bass.

Spivack, G., Plan, J.J., & Shure, M.B. (1976). *Problem solving approaches to adjustment*. San Francisco: Jossey-Bass.

Spivack, G., & Shure, M.B. (1974). *Social adjustment of young children.* San Francisco: Jossey-Bass.

Spivack, G., & Shure, M.B. (1982). The cognition of social adjustment: Interpersonal cognitive problem-solving thinking. In B.B. Lahey & A.E. Kazdin (Eds.), *Advances in Clinical Child Psychology: Vol 5.* (pp. 323-372). New York: Plenum.

Urberg, K.A., & Docherty, E.M. (1976). Development of role-taking skills in young children. *Developmental Psychology, 12,* 198-203.

Wood, D.A., & Erskine. J.A. (1977). Strategies in canonical correlation with application to behavioral data. *Educational and Psychological Measurement, 36,* 861-878.

The Salience of Gender and the Process of Sex Typing in Three- to Seven-Year-Old Children

Lisa A. Serbin and Carol Sprafkin
Concordia University

Two measures of children's use of gender as a schematic dimension were developed, 1 using gender-based categorization, the other reflecting the degree to which children use the gender dimension to make personal affiliation choices when other schematic bases for responding are available. Two samples, totaling 147 boys and girls aged 3-7, were tested on the 2 measures of gender salience to establish developmental patterns of gender-based categorization and affiliation. Relations with sex-role knowledge and gender concepts, and with measures of sex-role adoption, were also examined. A Guttman Scale analysis confirmed the developmental sequence in which a decline in gender-based categorization occurred after sex-role knowledge regarding activities and occupations was acquired. Further, once the decline in gender-based categorization occurred, children began to show more cognitive flexibility on a measure of sex-role attitudes. In contrast, use of the gender dimension to make personal affiliation choices did not decline with age but seemed to reflect individual differences in degree of sex typing. Because of these distinct underlying cognitive processes, there seems to be little relation between what a child knows about sex roles and how sex typed the child's attitudes and behavior will be during this period.

*   *   *

OVER THE PAST 20 YEARS, THERE HAS BEEN MUCH DISCUSSION OF THE RELA-tive merits of cognitive-developmental and social learning approaches to the explanation of sex typing. Empirical studies suggest that there may be

This research was partially supported by a grant from the FCAR of the Ministry of Education of Quebec. The authors would like to thank Drs. Eleanor E. Maccoby, S. Shirley Feldman, and Ellen M. Markman for their helpful comments on an earlier draft of this manuscript. They would also like to thank the staff and the children of St. George's School, the day-care centre of the Davis YWHA, Garderie Terre des Enfants, and the Concordia University Child Care Centre in Montreal, and the Butternut Hill School of SUNY—Binghamton, Binghamton, NY, for their participation in this project. Finally, many thanks go to our colleagues Drs. Anna-Beth Doyle, Donna White, and Frances Aboud, who have given us continuing encouragement, advice, and feedback.

a distinction between the "cognitive" and "affective" aspects of the sex-typing process. That is, learning about sex roles may be a distinct process from developing sex-typed preferences or behavior patterns (Huston, 1983; Perry, White, & Perry, 1984). Potentially, the two theoretical perspectives—cognitive-developmental and social learning—may each be useful in understanding distinct aspects of the sex-typing process.

A cognitive-developmental model for the acquisition of sex roles was initially proposed by Kohlberg (1966). This approach suggests that young children have a natural tendency to classify people on the basis of gender, as it is an obvious and concrete dimension. They learn about the properties of male and female sex roles by observing the association of physical attributes, activities, and traits with either the male or the female category. Eventually, an associative network is established, corresponding to the sex-role norms of the child's culture. Children then assume that all individuals labeled as male or female possess the characteristics associated with these categories. One limitation of this approach is that it does not account for individual differences in sex typing, that is, in the degree to which children adopt or conform to sex-role norms (Huston, 1983; Mischel, 1966). Mischel and others have argued that the degree of sex typing of an individual's attitudes and behavior is extensively influenced by external social learning factors, such as modeling and reinforcement.

Whereas Kohlberg's cognitive-developmental approach explains how children acquire sex-role knowledge but does not explain satisfactorily why there are individual differences in sex-role adoption or sex-typed behavior, Bem's (1981) schematic approach focuses on individual differences in tendency to use a gender scheme, once acquired. Consistent with Kohlberg's original model, Bem suggests that a vast associative network, based on gender, is learned in childhood and is then applied in processing information about the self and others. She suggests that all individuals in our society come to possess an extensive gender schema as a result of the dichotomy drawn between male and female attributes that is part of our culture, but that there are strong individual differences in tendencies to use or apply this schema. A "sex-typed" individual would be one who thinks extensively in terms of the gender dimension, as opposed to using other available social dimensions to process information about the self and others. Concerning the origins of individual differences in "sex typing, " or tendency to use the gender schema, Bem suggests that "individual differences presumably derive from the extent to which one's particular socialization history has stressed the functional importance of the gender dichotomy" (1981, p. 392).

This approach suggests the possibility of examining cognitive-developmental and environmental contributions to the sex-typing process within a single model. In our view, a schematic approach suggests that the process underlying sex typing is cognitive, in that the individual processes information according to a dichotomous gender dimension that acquires an extensive associative network including personal attributes, behaviors, and even inanimate objects. In this way, an early tendency to sort or classify incoming information on the basis of gender would lead to the development of sex-role concepts. However, while all children would acquire this associative network, the extent to which it is used, or is dominant over other available dimensions in organizing information, might depend on environmental factors, such as reinforcement, modeling, or other circumstances that increase the salience of the gender dimension. Further, while the process of forming gender categories may be cognitively based and universal, the specific content of these categories and their extensiveness would depend on the child's individual experiences.

Indeed, there is evidence that school-aged and preschool children process information according to the gender dimension (Cordua, McGraw, & Drabman, 1979; Kail & Levine, 1976; Koblinsky, Cruse, & Sugawara, 1978; Martin & Halverson, 1981), and that there are individual differences in the tendency to use or apply a gender schema (Cordua et al., 1979; Kail & Levine, 1976; Liben & Signorella, 1980). However, the origins and developmental course of gender-based schematic processing have not yet been studied empirically. Further, few attempts have been made to differentiate the cognitive processes related to the acquisition of sex-role knowledge from those involved in the "affective" aspects of the phenomenon: the adoption of sex-typed values, preferences, and behavior.

Our research focuses on the salience or predominance of gender as a "cognitive schema," or dimension along which incoming information is processed and classified. We have hypothesized that classification using a particular dimension enables the child to learn about the properties of its categories. In the case of gender, these "properties" are the things associated with male and female gender in our culture, or, in other words, sex roles. As the characteristics of the male and female categories are mastered, gender should decline as a salient or dominant classification dimension in favor of more challenging, not yet learned or mastered social dimensions. Thus, we would predict that the salience of gender as a dimension for classification should be greatest just before sex roles are learned and should decline as they are mastered conceptually.

Even though classification on the basis of a particular dimension may decline after the inclusion rules of that dimension are mastered, the schema itself remains readily available. Thus, although 5-year-olds do not typically sort by color when other dimensions such as size or shape are available for classification, they remain readily able to apply color labels. Further, they are likely to continue to use the color dimension in a variety of ways, particularly with reference to their own color preferences. There may also be large individual differences in children's tendency to use or apply a particular dimension once the inclusion rules for the relevant category system are mastered.

With regard to social dimensions, such as gender, it seems particularly important to distinguish between the predominance of the dimension for classification while the category system is being learned and the salience of gender once the system is mastered. The "mastery" of the gender dimension may be a fairly universal phenomenon, at least in a highly dichotomized culture. However, the degree to which the gender schema is used to make personal choices and decisions after the associative system of sex-role categorization is mastered (which occurs as early as age 5 or 6) may vary among individuals.

Thus, in addition to examining children's tendency to classify by gender, we needed a measure of the tendency to use or apply the gender schema as opposed to other available associative networks in making personal choices and preferences. For this "affective" measure we decided to examine children's use of gender when making affiliation choices. We reasoned that a preference task of this type might reveal individual differences in the salience or tendency to apply the gender dimension, in contrast to the classification task, which would show primarily a developmental pattern. Thus, a major focus of our research was to contrast the use of gender as a dimension for classification with its use as a dimension for preference.

In contrast to the predictions concerning classification by gender, we did not expect the use of gender as a basis for preference decisions to decline over the preschool years. We did expect children's use of the gender dimension on this affiliation preference task to reflect individual differences in children's degree of sex typing. That is, we expected this measure of gender-based affiliation preference to correlate with measures of sex-role adoption and preference for sex-typed activities.

The present article describes two measures of gender salience, one assessing the use of the gender dimension in classifying new information and the other assessing its use in making affiliation choices. The developmental course of gender salience from age 3 to 7, and the relation between salience and sex-role development, were examined.

Method

Subjects

To obtain a sample of girls and boys across the age span from 3-7, children were recruited from two settings in urban Montreal: a day-care centre (3-6-year-olds) and a private elementary school (4-8-year-olds). Both programs operated in English, although a few of the children spoke French or another language at home. The day-care centre families were primarily lower middle class, with Jewish religious affiliations. The elementary school group was primarily upper middle class, with varied religious and ethnic backgrounds. To avoid confounding age with sample, siblings and family friends were recruited from each sample as necessary to obtain samples of approximately equal size from each population at each age level.

One hundred and forty-seven children participated in the study, 14 or 15 girls and boys in each of five age groups, aged 3-7. This included 42 children from the day-care centre and 24 of their siblings and friends, and 50 children fom the elementary school plus 31 of their siblings and friends. In order to obtain this final sample, three children had to be eliminated due to random responding, 23 for inability to match on the basis of nongender cues (see below), and nine were lost due to withdrawal from school or prolonged absence.

Measures of Gender Salience

Gender-based classification.—The tests of gender salience for classification and affiliation preference were comprised of similar stimuli. Both tests involved photographs of adults, allowing the child to base his or her response on either the sex of the person in the photo or some other characteristic, such as the person's activity (as determined by the objects they are holding), their body stance, or facial expression. In the classification section, the child is handed a photo of, for example, a man stirring a pot. The child is then shown three other photos: a man reading, a woman rolling dough, and a woman sweeping. The child is asked, "Which one of these pictures goes with the one you are holding?" The child then matches the original stimulus to the one that seems to be most congruent. The choice of the man reading would be a gender-based match, the choice of the woman rolling dough would be an activity or "prop" match, and the choice of the woman sweeping would be a "random" or nonschematically based match. There are 12 matching items of this type. Any child making one-third or more nonschematic ("random") responses in the classification section of the test was dropped from further analyses, assuming that these children were responding randomly to the items.

Items were selected that yielded approximately 50% gender-based responding in pilot testing of 3-year-olds. This ensured that the items were not too difficult for these young children. This 50% could then be used as a "benchmark" in examining developmental changes.

To obtain a meaningful measure of children's tendency to classify by gender when other schematic dimensions are available, it is important to demonstrate that the children are aware of and capable of matching according to the alternative dimensions (prop, body posture, facial expression, or activity) used in the test. A series of six items was developed to ensure that all children were aware of the alternative dimension provided and were capable of classifying on this basis when gender was not available as a basis for matching. The four photographs within each of these items all show adults of the same sex, and thus the only schematic match available was based on prop, facial expression, or body posture. Thus the child was asked to match a photo of, for example, a man sweeping to one of the three alternatives: a man vacuuming, a man stirring a pot, or a man rolling dough. Children who matched correctly on fewer than three of these items were assumed to be unable to match on the basis of the nongender cues used in these pictures. Because gender responses made by such children on the classification items could merely reflect this inability to match by non-gender cues rather than the actual salience of the gender dimension, these children were excluded from the analyses.

Gender-based affiliation preference.—First, to assess whether a child preferred to affiliate with same- or opposite-sex adults, the child was presented with a series of eight pairs of photos, each containing a picture of a man or a woman. For each pair, the child was asked which person they would most like to play with. Most children at all ages tested indicated a preference for same-sex affiliations on these items.

Then, based on the child's preference for same- or opposite-sex adults, a series of five items was presented in which a choice had to be made among an adult of the preferred gender who had a blank facial expression and was not involved in any activity, an adult of the nonpreferred gender who was holding an attractive prop, doing something interesting, or smiling warmly, and a third picture of an uninteresting adult of the nonpreferred sex, as a random or nonschematically based choice. In cases where the child did not display a clear preference for female or male companions, the own-sex form of the test was administered. The child was asked questions such as, "Who would you like to go to the zoo with?" or "Who would you like to invite to your birthday party?" Here the child needed to choose between her or his preferred gender and an alternative, attractive cue.

Scoring of the gender salience measures.—The child was given one score for the classification test and one score for the affiliation preference test, based on the number of gender-based choices made on each. These scores could range from 0 to 12 for the classification test and from 0 to 5 for the affiliation preference measure.

Reliability.—In pilot work with three samples, totaling 79 3-6-year-olds, the average internal consistency coefficient was .80 for the classification measure (standardized alpha; SPSS version 8.3) and .66 for the affiliation preference items. Test-retest reliability over a 3-week period was measured in a sample of 21 3-5-year-olds and was found to be .88 for the classification section and .68 for the affiliation preference measure.

Measures of Sex-Role Knowledge, Sex Typing, Level of Gender Comprehension, and General Intellectual Functioning

In addition to the measures of gender salience described above, the children were also given a series of tests designed to measure certain correlates of gender-based processing. Two major sets of correlates were examined: measures of "sex-role knowledge" and measures of "sex typing." Based on our initial hypotheses, we expected the first set of measures to be related developmentally to the classification test and the second set to relate to individual differences on the affiliation preference test. In addition, measures of gender constancy and IQ were included to examine the relation between general and specific (gender-related) measures of level of cognitive functioning and the gender salience tests. These tests were administered in a fixed order, following the gender salience measures. Children attending the elementary school or the day-care centre had two testing sessions at their school, approximately 3 weeks apart. The remaining children were tested at home in a single session. Testing was done by one of four female examiners.

Measures of sex-role knowledge and flexibility.—To examine the relation between gender salience and sex-role knowledge and attitudes, a portion of the Sex Role Learning Index (Edelbrock & Sugawara, 1978) was used. This portion of the SERLI contains 20 drawings of objects, 10 traditionally associated with the male sex role (e.g., hammer, shovel, baseball, etc.) and 10 with the female sex role (e.g., iron, needles and thread, broom, baby bottle, etc.). We wished to make a distinction between children's *knowledge* of traditional sex roles and the degree of the *flexibility* of their attitudes regarding these roles. In order to obtain a measure of flexibility of sex-role concept, the child was handed each picture and asked, "Who do you think would use this [name of item]..., a boy, a girl, or both boys or girls?" with the order of the words "boy" and "girl" alternating during testing. "Flexibility" scores were computed from the number of "both" responses given and could range from 0 to 20.

In order to obtain a measure of the child's knowledge of traditional sex roles, the child was then asked in a forced-choice format to identify the items previously labeled as used by both boys and girls (i.e., "I know you said both boys and girls might use this, but who do you think would use it more, boys or girls?"). Knowledge scores were computed by adding the number of traditional responses on the 10 male and 10 female sex-typed items, including both initial choices and subsequent forced choices. These scores could also range from 0 to 20.

Measures of sex typing.—Three measures of sex typing or sex-role adoption were given. The first was a section of the SERLI test (the "Sex Role Preference" section) in which the child was asked to rank order two series of 10 pictures each. The first series consisted of drawings of a child of the subject's sex engaged in five male stereotyped and five female stereotyped activities. The second set consisted of 10 drawings of an adult of the child's sex engaged in five male stereotyped and five female stereotyped adult occupations and activities. For the adult and child sets of pictures, the subject chose the activity she or he would most like to do, then the next favorite activity, and so forth, until nine of the 10 pictures were chosen. A score was then computed based on the order in which own-sex and opposite-sex activities were chosen in each set of pictures. Scores on the combined adult and child pictures range from 20 to 80, following the scoring system developed by Edelbrock and Sugawara (1978). A second measure of sex typing was a modification of the DeLucia Toy Choice procedure (DeLucia, 1963) in which the child is shown 22 pairs of photos of "masculine" and "feminine" toys. For each pair, the child is asked to point to the toy she or he would prefer to play with. A score from 0 to 22 is computed based on the number of same-sex toys chosen.

A third measure of sex typing was derived from a peer-nomination procedure. Children were shown photos of the members of their class and asked to identify the three children they would most like to play outdoors with, to sit next to, and to "do something" with. Next, the children were asked to name three children they would not like to choose for each of these activities. The number of own- and opposite-sex children nominated in response to each question was recorded. A sex-typing score was derived by adding the number of same-sex nominations made in response to the "positive" questions to the number of opposite-sex nominations made to the "negative" questions. Scores could range from 0 to 18.

Gender constancy.—A test of gender constancy developed by Slaby and Frey (1975) was given to assess children's comprehension of gender. This test classifies children according to their level of comprehension, with Level I indicating the child cannot identify gender, Level II indicating the child can identify own and others' gender, Level III indicating that the child is aware that gender does not vary over time, and Level IV indicating an awareness that gender cannot be changed through modifications of behavior, hair, style of dress, or desire to be the opposite sex. Scores on this measure reflect this categorization system and range from I to IV.

Intellectual functioning.—As a measure of general level of intellectual functioning, the children were given the Peabody Picture Vocabulary Test (PPVT, 1981 revision) to determine relations between the two gender salience measures and IQ.

Results

Since similar developmental patterns and correlations between measures were found for the two samples, the results presented below are based on the samples combined. Sex differences are discussed only when statistically significant. Since a few children missed or failed to cooperate on particular tests, and since one measure, the peer sociometric, could only be given to the children attending day-care or school, the sample sizes for each analysis vary slightly, as indicated in the degrees of freedom for each analysis.

Reliability of the Classification and Affiliation Preference Measures

As in the previous three samples used in the development of the measures, the two measures of gender salience each showed satisfactory internal consistency. The standardized alpha coefficients for each measure were .92 for the classification section and .64 for the affiliation preference measure.

IQ and Gender Salience

There were low negative correlations between the two measures of gender salience and scores on the Peabody Picture Vocabulary Test, $r(140)=-.14$, $p<.09$, and $r(140)=-.19$, $p<.03$, respectively, for the classification and affiliation sections. There was a negative relation between age and IQ, with the youngest group marginally higher on IQ ($M=111$) than the other four groups ($M=105$). Since there were also significant correlations between age and the two gender salience measures, it was necessary to partial out the effects of age to examine clearly the relations between the two gender salience measures and IQ. The first-order correlations, partialing out age effects, confirmed the low negative relations between gender-based processing on the classification and affiliation preference measures, and PPVT IQ, with $r(139)=-.19$, $p<.03$, and $r(139)=-.16$, $p<.06$, respectively. This indicates that, within each age group, brighter children tended to make fewer gender-based responses on either measure than less bright children.

Developmental Patterns of Gender-based Processing

The mean scores for gender-based responding on the classification and affiliation preference measures are shown in Table 1 and Figure 1. Since there was no correlation between the two measures of gender-based processing, $r(146) = .03$, the data for each measure were analyzed separately in two, two-way (age×sex) analyses of variance.

TABLE 1

GENDER CLASSIFICATION AND AFFILIATION BY AGE AND SEX

AGE	CLASSIFICATION[a]			AFFILIATION[b]		
	Girls	Boys	Total	Girls	Boys	Total
3 years:						
Mean ...	60	53	57	40	31	35
SD	20	21	20	22	21	22
N	14	15	29	14	15	29
4 years:						
Mean ...	43	36	40	56	25	41
SD	26	22	24	28	28	32
N	15	15	30	15	15	30
5 years:						
Mean ...	40	43	42	39	51	45
SD	39	38	38	31	33	32
N	14	15	29	14	15	29
6 years:						
Mean ...	29	35	33	53	63	58
SD	40	45	42	34	28	31
N	15	15	30	15	15	30
7 years:						
Mean ...	10	31	20	44	75	60
SD	27	38	34	34	31	35
N	14	15	29	14	15	29
Total:						
Mean ...	36	40	38	47	49	48
SD	35	34	34	30	33	32
N	72	75	147	72	75	147

[a] Percentage of gender responses given to the 12 items of the section.
[b] Percentage of gender responses given to the five items of the section.

For the 12 items on the classification measure, a main effect of age, $F(4,137) = 4.64, p < .002$, can be clearly seen in Figure 1. The youngest group averaged 56% gender-based responding, while this declined gradually over ages 4, 5, and 6, with a sharp decline to 20% in the oldest group. Post-hoc Scheffé tests revealed a significant difference between the youngest and oldest groups, $p < .05$. There was no sex difference in gender-based classification and no interaction between age and sex.

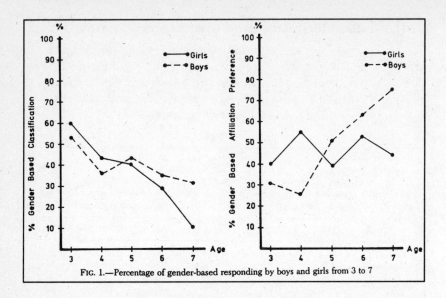

FIG. 1.—Percentage of gender-based responding by boys and girls from 3 to 7

The measure of gender-based affiliation preference showed a very different pattern. On these five items, there was a significant main effect of age, $F(4,137)=4.03, p < .005$. There was also a significant interaction of age and sex, $F(4,137)=4.63, p < .002$. Examining the means (see Table 1), it appears that boys increased their gender-based affiliation choices in a linear fashion from 31% at age 3 to 74% at age 7. Girls, in contrast, responded fairly consistently in the different age groups.

The two measures differed not only in these developmental patterns but also in the patterns of response distribution within age groups. In using gender as the basis for classification, the 3- and 4-year-old groups showed a normally distributed pattern of response, with all but one child in the 3-year-old group making some gender-based choices. The percentage of children making no gender-based responses at all increased to 40% at age 6 and to 60% in the oldest group. In the three oldest groups, gender-based responding was bimodally distributed. That is, children in these older groups tended to classify either by gender or by the competing "prop" dimension, rather than making some responses based on each dimension, as did the majority of 3- and 4-year-olds. Only two of the 90 children in these three oldest groups made equal numbers (i.e., scores between 5 and 7, out of 12) of gender and prop responses, while 50% of the 3-year-olds and 40% of the 4-year-olds scored in this middle range. Thus, in the oldest groups there seemed to be two distinct styles of response to the classification task: children either classified by gender or by the alternative prop/activity dimension.

In contrast, the distribution of responses on the affiliation items was essentially normal at each age level, with most children in each age group making some gender-based responses. In other words, while many children had a preference for making affiliation choices based on either the gender or prop dimension, most made some of their five selections based on gender and some based on the alternate available cue. This suggests that the tendency to affiliate by gender may be a matter of degree, whereas, at least for 5-7-year-olds, classification is either done by gender or by an alternative dimension.

Classification by Gender and Sex-Role Knowledge and Flexibility

One of our initial hypotheses was that classification by gender would precede knowledge of traditional sex roles and would decline after sex-role knowledge was achieved. As can be seen from the standard scores in Figure 2, gender-based classification was highest at age 3, when sex-role knowledge, measured by SERLI test, was at its lowest point. Gender-based classification declined as sex-role knowledge increased, dropping off

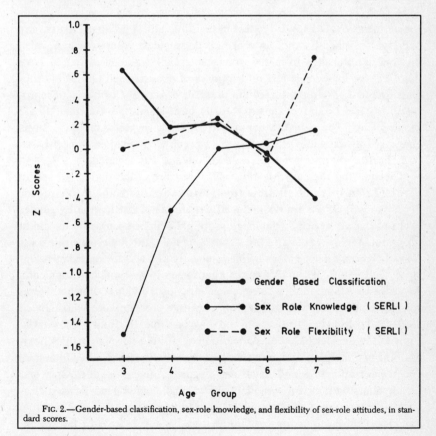

FIG. 2.—Gender-based classification, sex-role knowledge, and flexibility of sex-role attitudes, in standard scores.

sharply after knowledge of traditional roles was established. The mean scores for sex-role ranged from 76% correct (where 50% would be a random or chance level) for the youngest group, to 97% correct for the oldest group.

Our hypothesis regarding the developmental sequence of these two measures—that sex-role knowledge would be acquired before gender-based classification declined—was tested by examining the response patterns of individual subjects. That is, we expected that subjects' responses would fall into one of three categories: either showing high gender-based responding and low sex-role knowledge (the earliest pattern), or showing high sex-role knowledge and low gender-based responding (the final stage). Children were not expected, however, to switch away from gender-based responding before mastering the knowledge of sex typing (i.e., the pattern of low sex-role knowledge and low gender-based responding should not occur).

The existence of this sequence was tested using a Guttman Scale analysis. Cutoff points for this analysis were 25% gender responding or less on the classification task and 95% or greater on the SERLI Sex Role Knowledge Test. This cutoff was selected to reflect the average level of responding on the sex-role knowledge test in the three oldest groups. That is, any child who reached the median score for these oldest groups (each of which differed significantly from the youngest group) was considered to have "passed" the knowledge test for purposes of this analysis. Out of 144 subjects, only 12 children violated the prescribed pattern. Coefficient of reproducibility (.92) and scalability (.80) confirmed the Guttman Scale requirements. Thus, the developmental sequence suggested in Figure 2 was confirmed by examining the responses of individual children: gender-based classification declined after sex-role knowledge was acquired.

Considering the sex-role flexibility measure of the SERLI, we see in Figure 2 that it is initially low (the mean score of "both" responses for 3-year-olds is 25% of a possible 20), rising as classification by gender declines sharply at age 7 (the mean score of "both" responses for the oldest group is 38% of a possible 20). Thus, cognitive flexibility regarding sex roles increases after gender declines radically as a classification dimension.

A Guttman Scale analysis was again used to test this developmental sequence by examining the response patterns of individual subjects. Here, we expected children to fall into one of three groups: those who showed high gender-based classification and low sex-role flexibility, those who showed low gender-based classification but still did not give many "flexible" answers on the SERLI, and finally those who switched away from gender-based responding and have also begun to give "flexible" answers. Children should not, if this model is valid, make many gender-based classification responses once they have started to display "flexible" sex-role attitudes. Cutoff points for this Guttman analysis were 25% or fewer gender responses on the classification test and flexibility scores of 40% or greater on the SERLI. This cutoff on the flexibility score was selected to reflect the average level of responding in the oldest group, the only group that differed significantly from any of the others on this measure. Satisfactory coefficients of reproducibility (.90) and scalability (.71) confirmed this sequence. Only 16 children violated the prescribed sequence in this analysis. Thus the children appeared to increase their flexibility regarding sex roles only after gender-based categorization declined.

The acquisition of sex-role knowledge and the achievement of flexibility regarding sex roles seem to be separate processes, although they both increase with age. Sex-role knowledge on the SERLI seems to be virtually mastered by age 5, where the average score is 95.5% correct, whereas flexibility only reaches an average level of 38% by age 7. The average standard deviations of the two measures in the three oldest groups are 5.56 for the knowledge measure, contrasted with 15.88 for flexibility. Thus, there is much greater uniformity in sex-role knowledge in these older groups than in sex-role flexibility.

Classification by Gender and Sex Typing

The gender salience classification measure was not significantly correlated with any of the three measures of sex-role adoption: the SERLI Sex Role Preference Scale, the DeLucia Toy Choice, or the peer sociometric. This confirms that gender-based classification primarily reflects a developmental cognitive stage rather than an individual response tendency toward sex typing. Guttman Scale analyses of the relation between classification and these sex-typing measures also failed to show any clear sequences.

Classification by Gender and Gender Constancy

Correlational and Guttman Scale analyses were performed to examine the relation between the measure of gender constancy and the measures of gender salience and sex typing. Gender constancy did not predict differences in tendency to classify or affiliate by gender and was also unrelated to sex-role knowledge, to flexibility, or to any of the three sex-typing measures.

Gender-based Affiliation Preference and Sex Typing

As predicted, the measure of gender-based affiliation was positively related to the three measures of sex typing: the SERLI Sex Role Preference measure, the DeLucia Toy Choice, and the peer sociometric (see Table 2). All of these measures increased with age, however. To determine whether gender salience in affiliation preference simply increased developmentally with measures of sex typing, or actually predicted individual differences in sex typing within age groupings, we computed a series of partial cor-

TABLE 2

CORRELATIONS BETWEEN GENDER-BASED AFFILIATION PREFERENCE AND SEX-TYPING MEASURES

	Zero Order ($df = 126$)	Controlling for Age ($df = 125$)
Gender-based affiliation preference and SERLI sex-role preference	.37 ($p < .001$)	.27 ($p < .002$)
Gender-based affiliation preference and DeLucia toy choice	.40 ($p < .001$)	.30 ($p < .001$)
Gender-based affiliation preference and peer sociometric	.36 ($p < .001$)	.28 ($p < .001$)

relations controlling for variance contributed by age to these measures (partial correlations controlling for IQ were also completed but were identical to the zero-order correlations). Table 1 shows that the affiliation preference measure is significantly related to all of the sex-typing measures, even when controlling for age.

Discussion

The results indicate that it is possible to measure and to differentiate between children's use of the gender dimension for classification and for expression of affiliation preference. These two measures seem to reflect different processes. Gender-based classification is apparently a developmental phenomenon that virtually disappears in most children by age 7, at least when alternative dimensions for classification of the type used in the measure are available. Gender-based affiliation, in contrast, does not diminish with age and seems to reflect individual differences in children's tendencies to use the gender dimension in expressing preferences.

These individual differences in "gender salience" seem related to sex typing and sex-role adoption. In this study, sex typing of activity and occupational preferences, sex typing of toy choices, and preference for same-sex peers were all found to relate to the use of gender in our affiliation preference measure. Unlike the traditional measures of sex typing, our gender salience measure gives the child the choice of using either gender or an alternative schematic dimension as the basis of choice and measures the relative degree to which the gender dimension is selected. If sex typing is, as Bem (1981) suggests, the individual's tendency to make use of the gender dimension when other schematic bases for processing information or making choices are available, we may have developed a more direct measure of the process underlying the sex-typing phenomenon than had been previously available.

In contrast to the affiliation preference measure, our measure of classification by gender did not correlate significantly with the sex-typing measures. Rather, it declined with age as sex-role knowledge was acquired. This suggests that the tendency to classify by gender may be the early basis for learning the sex-role category system. Classification by gender diminishes as mastery of this system is achieved, presumably to be replaced by the use of other, not yet mastered dimensions. The sequence with which various social dimensions become salient or dominant for classification remains to be explored.

A number of theorists have speculated about the reasons for the early salience of the gender dimension. Bem (1981) and Martin and Halverson (1981) have suggested that gender is an important aspect of the self-concept emerging at age 2-3, which is why children are motivated to attend to and learn about gender categories. Constantinople (1979) has suggested an alternative model: that gender-based categorization and category building occur independently of the development of the self-concept, and that the two are merged only later, after the sex-role categories are mastered. In this case, the motive for gender-based classification remains obscure. Possibly, the early salience of gender results from an innate tendency to categorize, combined with societal cultural and linguistic emphasis on the gender dimension. Children learn of the existence of this dimension quite early, in the second or third year of life, making gender a readily available dimension to use to express the tendency to categorize. Certainly, there is a wealth of information on the nature of sex-role categories available for "category building" in most children's environments!

The decline of gender-based categorization at ages 6 and 7 would seem to signal that the child has mastered the sex-role category system. Certainly, on the SERLI, which measures knowledge of sex typing of occupations and activities, most children approach the ceiling of the test by this age. Other aspects of sex typing, such as knowledge of masculine and feminine traits, may not be fully mastered by this age, however (Williams, Bennett, & Best, 1975). The decline of gender-based categorization may occur because certain basic aspects of sex-role knowledge are mastered, or possibly because gender is pushed aside by other schematic bases for categorization. Alternatively, the gender match may be made first mentally, and then discarded as an answer as "too obvious" by the sophisticated 7-year-old. Such automatization of categorization appears to occur for other labeling and matching schema when they have been "overlearned." Potentially, a reaction time paradigm might be used to assess whether gender matches become more automatic (i.e., rapid) at the point when gender-based classification declines.

Another aspect of the decline in gender-based matching at age 7 is the concomitant increase in "flexible" responses on the SERLI. Children began at this point to increase the number of activities and occupations they identify as appropriate for both sexes. It seems likely that underlying both the decline in gender-based classification and the increase in sex-role flexibility may be some broader aspect of cognitive maturation. The preconserving child, under age 6 or 7, may have a strong motive to match and classify by gender. Since gender is defined for most young children primarily by "superficial" aspects of appearance and behavior rather than by anatomy or biological reproductive function, it may be important for the preconserving child to know all about sex roles and to focus on this classification dimension in order to understand the "defining" characteristics of each sex.

Finally, our results seem to support the suggestion that everyone develops a gender schema in early childhood, but that there are individual differences in individual tendencies to apply this schema. Gender-based classification does not seem to reflect individual differences but rather to be a developmental process whereby most individuals match by gender in the early preschool years and gradually switch over to using other available dimensions for classification after the "gender schema," including basic aspects of sex-role knowledge, is acquired. Subsequently, children differ in the extent to which they use the gender dimension as the basis for individual choices, and these differences are related to the extent to which the child is "sex typed" on measures of sex-role adoption.

The reasons that individuals do or do not make use of their gender schema remain to be explored. Possibly they relate to the reinforcement history and modeling to which the individual has been exposed or to situational factors in the immediate environment. We would predict that family patterns, such as extent of sex-role differentiation by parents, might predict children's use of gender and its related associative network in processing information and making personal choices. The role of such environmental influences in determining individual differences in children's use of the gender dimension in expressing preference may be especially strong after about age 7, when the child has matured cognitively to the point where classification by gender has declined and cognitive flexibility regarding sex-role attitudes has begun to develop.

In sum, it appears that learning about sex roles may be a universal phenomenon based on the early tendency to classify according to the gender dimension. Using the gender dimension to make personal choices and decisions, however, seems to differ among individuals and may be related to learning history and environmental factors. This possibility remains to be explored directly in further research.

References

Bem, S. (1981). Gender schema theory: A cognitive account of sex typing. *Psychology Review, 88,* 354-364.

Constantinople, A. (1979). Sex-role acquisition: In search of the elephant. *Sex Roles, 5,* 121-133.

Cordua, G.D., McGraw, K.O., & Drabman, R.S. (1979). Doctor or nurse: Children's perception of sex-typed occupations. *Child Development, 50,* 590-593.

DeLucia, L.A. (1963). The toy preference test: A measure of sex-role identification. *Child Development, 34,* 107-117.

Edelbrock, C., & Sugawara, A.I. (1978). Acquisition of sex-typed preferences in preschool aged children. *Developmental Psychology, 14,* 614-623.

Huston, A.C. (1983). Sex-typing. In E.M. Hetherington (Ed.), P.H. Mussen (Series Ed.), *Handbook of child psychology: Vol. 4. Socialization, personality, and social development* (pp. 387-467). New York, NY: Wiley.

Kail, R.V., & Levine, L.E. (1976). Encoding processes and sex-role preferences. *Journal of Experimental Child Psychology, 21,* 256-263.

Koblinsky, S., Cruse, D.F., & Sugawara, A.I. (1978). Sex-role stereotypes and children's memory for story content. *Child Development, 49,* 452-458.

Kohlberg, L. (1966). A cognitive-developmental analysis of children's sex-role concepts and attitudes. In E.E. Maccoby (Ed.), *The development of sex differences* (pp. 82-172). Stanford, CA: Stanford University Press.

Liben, L.S., & Signorella, M.L. (1980). Gender related schematic and constructive memory in children. *Child Development, 51,* 11-18.

Martin, C.L., & Halverson, C.F. (1981). A schematic processing model of sex-typing and stereotyping in children. *Child Development, 49,* 1119-1134.

Mischel, W. (1966). A social learning view of sex differences. In E.E. Maccoby (Ed.), *The development of sex differences* (pp. 56-81). Stanford, CA: Stanford University Press.

Perry, D.G., White, A.J., & Perry, L.C. (1984). Does early sex typing result from children's attempts to match their behavior to sex role stereotypes? *Child Development, 55,* 2114-2121.

Slaby, R., & Frey, K. (1975). Development of gender constancy and selective attention to same-sex models. *Child Development, 46,* 849-856.

Williams, J.E., Bennett, S.M., & Best, D.L. (1975). Awareness and expression of sex stereotypes in young children. *Developmental Psychology, 11,* 635-642.

Learning and Teaching: Behavioural Approaches

Despite the current ascendancy of the cognitive perspective in psychology, few would deny the importance of behavioural principles in the learning-teaching process. Much of the behavioural literature involves the use of various kinds of reinforcement to increase desirable student behaviour. Reinforcement schedules are only as effective as the people dispensing them, however, so the question Andrews and Kozma asked in their study was how to train a teacher to use positive reinforcement appropriately and systematically. In the first phase of their study, the teacher praised any child doing what he or she was supposed to be doing, every time the teacher heard a tone in her earphone. During the second phase of the experiment, the teacher focused two-thirds of her praise on the group of children identified as lowest in on-task behaviour. During this phase, the teacher herself was praised for her efforts at the end of each teaching session. The results of the study are fascinating. First, when the teacher was free to choose which children she would praise for on-task activity, she distributed her praise equally among all the children in the class. Although this approach seems fair, it meant that the consistently high on-task children were getting more praise than they needed, and the consistently low on-task children were not getting enough. In phase two, when the teacher praised the low on-task children more often than the other children, their level of on-task activity increased markedly. Second, when the experimenters stopped praising the teacher, she stopped praising the students. It would seem that teachers need positive reinforcement too!

The authors of the second article in this section propose a more radical approach to increasing positive behaviours even in relatively young children. Why not structure the child's physical environment to dispense rewards independent of the teacher's presence? This is exactly what Partridge, Gehlbach, and Marx did with their sand-play machine. In the baseline condition, each of the two 5-year-old boys, one on either side of the machine, could fill the sand chute on his side which led to his own conveyor belt and then he could turn a crank and "deliver" the sand out of the bottom. In the hard contingency or "pure" prosocial condition, each boy could only fill the sand chute on his side which led to his partner's conveyor belt. Each boy's sand supply was totally dependent on the prosocial behaviour of the other boy. In the soft contingency condition, each boy could fill both his own and his partner's sand chute from his side, but it was easier to fill the partner's chute. The results suggested, first, that the boys' behaviour *was* influenced by the sand-play machine and second, that the soft contingency condition was as effective in encouraging prosocial behaviour as the hard contingency condition. Of course, parents might not be completely comfortable with the idea that their children were being taught by their toys instead of their teachers.

Increasing Teacher Praise and Altering its Distribution to Children of Differing On-Task Levels

Lynn Andrews and Albert Kozma
Memorial University of Newfoundland

The present investigation had a two-fold purpose: It assessed the distribution in teacher praise for on-task activity among high, medium, and low on-task children following an audio-cuing training procedure; and it evaluated the feasibility of changing the preferred distribution in favour of a subgroup of low on-task children. Following baseline observations, 37 Grade 5 children were divided into high, medium, and low on-task groups. Treatment phases included general audio-cuing for teacher praise, cuing combined with instructions, feedback and praise to focus 67% of the teacher praise on the low on-task subgroup, cuing with focussing instructions removed, and cuing with daily feedback. The increase in teacher praise resulting from audio-cuing was relatively evenly distributed among the three subgroups, but increased to 67.3% of the total in favour of the low on-task group with the focussing package. Removal of the focussing procedure decreased the praise rate to this group to 19.4%. Changes in on-task student behaviour varied as a function of base rate and treatment condition.

*　　*　　*

NUMEROUS STUDIES HAVE BEEN REPORTED SHOWING AN INCREASE IN THE frequency of on-task activity when such activity is followed immediately by praise (Cossairt, Hall, & Hopkins, 1973; Fontenelle & Holliman, 1983; Hall, Lund, & Jackson, 1968; Schutte & Hopkins, 1970; Thomas, Becker, & Armstrong, 1968). This finding has led to numerous procedures for increasing teacher praise rates. Those found to be effective include videotape feedback (Thomas, 1971), verbal feedback (Parsonson, Baer, & Baer, 1974), self-control techniques (Szykula & Hector, 1978; Workman, Watson, & Helton, 1982), and audio cuing (Kozma, Noseworthy, & Ingraham, 1977; Van Houten & Sullivan, 1975).

One deficiency in studies concerned with teacher praise has been a failure to monitor how increases in praise rates are distributed among children who differ on levels of on-task activity. If the frequency of on-task activity determines probability of praise, then most of the praise should be directed at high on-task children rather than the low on-task group whose behaviour is in greatest need of modification. Accordingly, the utility of these techniques for use with regular classes, in which on-task activity is known to vary significantly among pupils, would seem to be limited, unless it can be demonstrated that low on-task children receive their fair share of the increased praise. Hence, it would seem desirable to determine the distribution of praise among groups of children who differ in levels of on-task behaviour, especially if the increase in teacher praise is to be used as the primary strategy for increasing children's on-task activity. While any of the listed strategies for increasing teacher praise rates could be employed in such an investigation, the audio-cuing procedure employed by Kozma et al. (1977) is the one preferred by us. The procedure makes few demands on teacher time, is easy to implement, produces rapid changes in teacher praise rates, and leads to minimal interference with the teaching process (Van Houten & Sullivan, 1975).

A second issue that needs to be addressed in the teacher praise literature is the feasibility of altering the distribution of teacher praise from whatever preferred mode he/she possesses. Data on this issue are important, since posttreatment teacher praise rates, even if they were evenly distributed among all students, may not be sufficiently high to bring about a change in the appropriate behaviour in low on-task children. In such a case, the praise rate directed at low on-task children would have to be selectively increased to bring about the appropriate programme effects. The success of such a focussed praise strategy can be evaluated by instructing the teacher to direct two-thirds praise on a designated group of low on-task children and by providing daily feedback on the success with which this criterion is achieved. The additional instructions and feedback are necessary to maximize rate of training (Mace, Cancelli, & Manos, 1983).

The present investigation, therefore, had a dual purpose. First, we wanted to determine the distribution of teacher praise directed at groups of high, medium, and low on-task children in an auto-cuing programme. It has been pointed out that such information is necessary in evaluating the usefulness of programmes designed to increase teacher praise rate as the basis for enhancing on-task pupil activity. Second, we wanted to test a procedure involving feedback and additional instructions for differentially increasing the distribution of teacher praise to low on-task children. By demonstrating that a modified auto-cuing strategy can be used not only to increase overall teacher praise rate, but also to raise rates of praise to targeted subgroups, we will have enhanced the flexibility of this procedure far beyond its current application.

Method

Subjects and Setting

A female teacher with 17 years of teaching experience and her fifth grade class of 19 girls and 18 boys participated in this study. The teacher was the first one from the selected school district to respond to our request for a volunteer. The St. John's, Newfoundland, Canada class was judged to be average in amount of on-task behaviour emitted.

Design

It was felt that an A, B1, B+C, B2 design, in which A represented the baseline condition, B the auto-cuing manipulation, and C the focussed praise instructions and feedback, would be adequate for obtaining answers to our two questions. However, a methodological problem made it necessary to add a B+D phase to the study. During this phase, cuing (B1) was supplemented by feedback on the effectiveness of praise (D) to retain some of the increases in teacher praise rates obtained during B1.

Observational Methods

The teacher and children were observed at the beginning of every morning during the study for approximately 30 to 60 minutes. Activities occurring during this time were roll call, religious instruction, and mathematics instruction.

Teacher praise. Teacher praise was defined as a commendatory statement made by the teacher to an individual child or group of children upon the occurrence of an on-task behaviour. Phrases such as "that's right, " "that's correct, " and "okay" were not scored as praise. Each praise statement emitted by the teacher was counted and was coded according to the specific child praised. When a praise statement was directed to a number of children, then it was considered to be directed to the class as opposed to an individual student.

Child behaviour. Each child was observed, in turn, for 10 seconds. The order of observation began with the child at the front of the row and continued to the child at the end of the row. This procedure was repeated for each line of seats. When all rows had been observed, the process was repeated until the end of the session. The row to be observed first was changed in a sequential order each morning.

Child behaviour was scored as being either on-task or off-task. On-task activity involved all of the following characteristics: (a) The child's hands were manipulating only items necessary in the on-going teacher specified activity; (b) the child was sitting at his/her desk with his/her feet planted firmly on the floor or tucked under him/her; and (c) the child's head was oriented in a direction dictated by the teacher-specified activity.

The child's behaviour was scored as off-task if he/she engaged in any of the following behaviours at any point during the 10-second interval: (a) The child was talking to a neighbour; (b) the child's head was oriented towards and/or the child's hands were manipulating objects other than those required by the task at hand; (c) the child was using task-required materials in an inappropriate manner; and (d) the child was disturbing a neighbour by making physical contact with the child.

Each on-task and off-task observation was coded according to the seat in which the behaviour was emitted. At the end of each session, a class seating diagram was used to determine which child emitted each on-task behaviour. The percentage of on-task behaviours for each child per interval was calculated from these data by dividing the total number of on-task behaviours by the total number of observation intervals and multiplying the result by 100.

Changes in observational methods. When the baseline observations began, child behaviour and teacher praise were observed simultaneously. After Day 20, teacher behaviour and child behaviour were observed sequentially, since observers were not able to accurately record child and teacher behaviour simultaneously once the teacher's praise rate was increased. Whether child behaviour or teacher praise was observed first was alternated daily. Within each session, the observers would alternate between observing child behaviour and teacher praise, with 5 minutes at a time devoted to each category.

Reliability. Reliability values for appropriate praise were obtained by having a second person observe behaviours at randomly selected sessions throughout the study. Reliability checks were obtained at least once per phase.

When audio cuing 1 (B1) was first introduced, the teacher had problems with giving praise. She spoke in a lowered voice, omitted the children's names, and described behaviours without praising. Because of these difficulties, reliability for the first 7 B1 days was unacceptably low (50%), and these data must be interpreted with caution.

The reliability for recipient of praise was calculated by dividing the number of agreements on a recipient of praise by the total number of observations and multiplying the quotient by 100. A disagreement for recipient of praise was recorded if observers agreed that praise occurred but disagreed on the recipient, or if one observer recorded a praise statement but the second observer did not. Reliability for recipient of praise ranged from 83.3% to 100%.

Reliability for child behaviour was calculated by dividing the number of agreements for the occurrence of on-task behaviour by the total number of observations and multiplying by 100. Reliability for child behaviour ranged from 86.6% to 98.2%.

The effects of cuing are reflected in the frequency of praise rates during cued intervals. Minimum rates of 30 per hour would indicate that the teacher followed cuing instructions. Accordingly, no other estimates of reliability were calculated for the cuing/praise relationship.

Procedure

Baseline. The main observer was present in the classroom for several weeks before the experiment began, allowing the teacher and children time to adapt to an observer's presence. The teacher was told that the experimenter was there to help her to increase the children's on-task behaviour. She was unaware that her praise was being observed. The children were told that the observer was helping the teacher. During baseline, classroom proceedings were conducted as usual.

After the last baseline session, the experimenter divided the children into high, medium, and low on-task groups, based on a rank ordering of the percentage of time that each child spent in on-task activity during the baseline condition. Children in the high on-task group ($n=12$) emitted on-task behaviour 92.1-98.9% of the time, in the medium on-task group ($n=12$) 82.9-90.7% of the time, and those in the low on-task group ($n=13$) 64.4-82.2% of the time. Neither the teacher nor the children were aware of this division.

Audio cuing 1 (B1). At the beginning of this phase the audio cuing system was introduced to the teacher. It was explained to her that the audio cues would help her to remember to praise and would assist her in spreading praise throughout the entire instructional period. On hearing a cue, she should look up and praise a child who was on-task, using both the child's name and a description of the child's behaviour. It was stressed that there would always be one child worthy of praise. The teacher was handed a sheet containing a definition of praise and a description of on-task behaviour. Studies on the effects of teacher praise on child behaviour were discussed. The teacher was given additional coaching during the first 7 days of this phase because she had difficulty giving praise and did not always use all of the required components of praise.

At the request of the experimenter, the teacher explained to the students that she would be carrying a tape recorder which would be giving her instructions to carry out. The audio cues, which consisted of the sound of a counter service bell struck once, were relayed to the teacher through a Sony M101 microcassette recorder. The cues were presented randomly at a rate of 30 per hour and were continued throughout the study at 30 per hour. The teacher wore the tape recorder in a leather purse hung over her shoulder. The teacher used an earphone so that the cues were audible only to her.

At the end of B1, the children were ranked once more on the percentage of on-task behaviour emitted over the entire phase. Only eight of the previously labelled low on-task children remained within the specified range of low on-task behaviour. These eight children will be referred to as the *consistently low on-task children* to distinguish them from the total low on-task group.

Audio cuing plus focussed praise (B+C). The teacher was instructed to focus 67% of her praise on eight children designated by the experimenter. She was told that these children had not improved as much as the others, but she was unaware that these were the only eight children still considered to be low on-task. One child of the eight consistently low on-task children was absent for 7 out of 10 treatment days, and his data had to be dropped from the analyses.

Feedback and praise were delivered by a written note given to the teacher at the end of each mathematics session. The note contained the percentage of praise directed to the targeted children. The note also praised the teacher when the criterion praise distribution was met or surpassed.

Audio cuing 2 (B2). The teacher was informed that she would no longer be provided with instructions, feedback, and praise regarding which children were to receive the higher praise rate. She was told that she could decide for herself which children to praise.

Cues continued to be provided at the rate of 30 cues per hour. However, the teacher's praise rate dropped significantly from the expected one per 2 minutes. It appeared that the teacher had become dependent on both cues and feedback for her praise. A feedback component, without focussed instructions, was added to the study to rapidly increase her general level of praise.

Audio cuing plus increased praise (B+D). The teacher was instructed to praise each time she heard the cue. At the end of each session, she was given a written note containing the observed praise rate. The note also contained instructions to increase the praise rate if the observed rate was below 30 praises per hour, or to maintain the current rate. The observer provided written praise for the teacher if she had improved from the previous day's rate. This package was different from the previous instructions, feedback, and praise package, in that it was directed towards increasing the teacher's praise rate rather than altering her distribution of praise.

Results

Mean teacher praise rates for A, B1, B+C, B2, and B+D were 2.1, 34.1, 28.7, 9.2, and 19.3, respectively. Rates in all treatment conditions were significantly above those of the precuing baseline condition. However, only B1 and B+C rates approximate the expected value of 30.

Distribution of Praise Among On-Task Subgroups

A one-way analysis of variance of praise data for B1 indicated that there was no significant difference in the percentage of praise directed to the high, medium, and low on-task children.

Effect of the Focussed Praise Package

A graph of the daily percentage of praise directed to the consistently low on-task children is presented in Figure 1. The effect of the focussed praise package can be determined by comparing the percentage of praise directed to the consistently low on-task children during B1, B+C, and B+D conditions. These conditions constitute a reversal design for the C component, despite the additional D component in the last phase. Although B2 is more similar to B1 than B+D, the praise rate during this phase was too low to provide an adequate test of the effects of C.

During B1, the consistently low on-task children received 25.7% of the praise. The percentage of praise directed to this group increased to 67.3% with the introduction of C and decreased to 19.4% during B+D when the focussing instructions were no longer in effect. These data suggest that the focussing strategy was effective in directing most of the praise to the designated group of children.

Changes in On-Task Behaviour for the High, Medium, and Low On-Task Groups

A graph comparing the percentage of on-task behaviour emitted by the high, medium, and low on-task groups is presented in Figure 2. The mean percentages of on-task behaviour for the three groups for each consecutive condition were: high on-task group, 94.6%, 95.3%, 96.1%, 95.6%, 96.2%; medium on-task group, 86.3%, 87.9%, 88.5%, 90.8%, 94.2%; and low on-task group, 76.9%, 84.9%, 89.7%, 90.4%, 92.7%. Increases in on-task behaviour over conditions appear to be most pronounced for medium and low on-task groups.

An analysis of variance for on-task behaviour resulted in significant main effects for groups, $F(2,33)=17.4$, $p<.01$, and treatment, $F(4,132)=12.3$, $p<.01$, and in a significant groups by treatment interaction, $F(8,132)=3.76$, $p<.01$. The groups by treatment effect may be attributed to group differences during baseline that disappeared by the end of

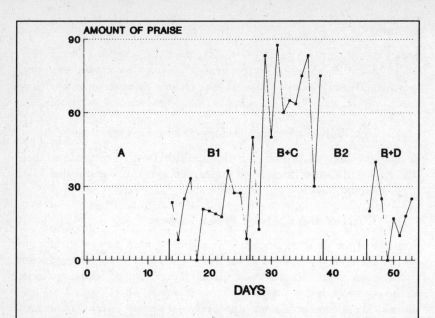

Figure 1. Daily percentage of praise directed to the consistently low on-task children.

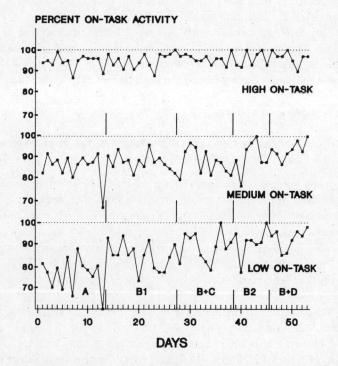

Figure 2. Percentage of on-task behaviour for the high, medium, and low on-task groups.

treatment (Fig. 2). A test of simple effects at Level A by means of the Tukey Honestly Significant Difference Test supported this conclusion. Mean differences substantially exceeded the critical value of 5.4 required for statistical significance ($r=3$, $df=33$, $p<.05$). None of the group differencs at B+D even approached this value.

The more appropriate series of difference tests for evaluating the sequential treatments compares treatment means within each on-task group. None of the mean differences across treatments in the high on-task group reached statistical significance. This group seemed to retain its task oriented behaviour independent of teacher praise. For the medium on-task group, B2 and B+D conditions resulted in significantly higher levels of on-task behaviour than the baseline condition, $D(5,132)>3.4$, $p<.01$, and the B+D condition was also superior over B1 and B+C conditions, $D(5, 132)>3.4$, $p<.01$. While some overall gains in on-task activity were obtained for this group, the critical factor appears to have been treatment length under praise conditions, rather than amount of praise per se during a particular praise condition.

For the low on-task group, all treatments resulted in improvement over baseline levels of on-task behaviour, $D(5,132)>3.4$, $p<.01$. Treatment effects were greater for this group with the introduction of focussed praise, in that B+C, B2, and B+D conditions produced significantly greater levels of on-task behaviour than B1, $D(5,132)>3.4$, $p<.01$.

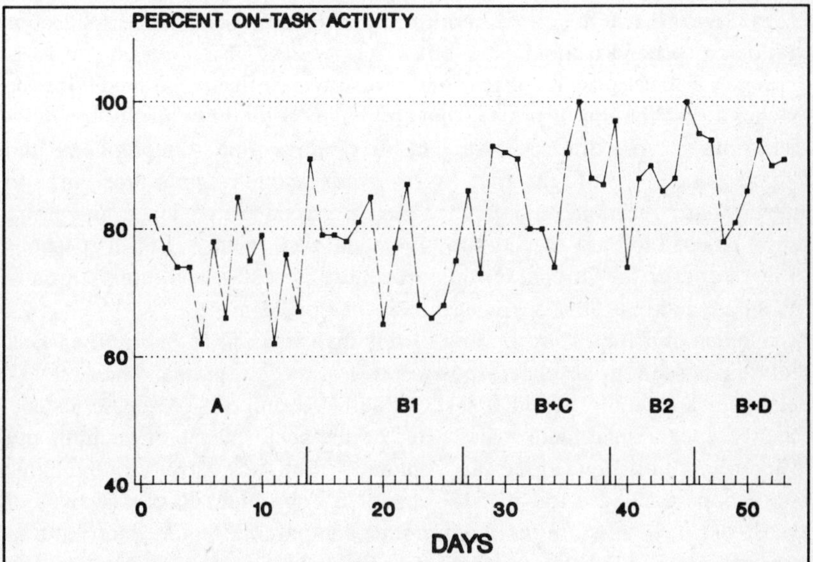

Figure 3. Percentage of on-task behaviour for the consistently low on-task group.

The Consistently Low On-Task Group

A graph of the percentage of on-task behaviour for the consistently low on-task group is presented in Figure 3. The mean percentage of on-task behaviour was 74.7% during baseline and 79.3% during B1. This level increased to 88.2% during the B+C condition and was maintained at this level during B2 (88.2%) and B+D conditions (88.2%).

A one-way analysis of variance on the on-task scores of the consistently low on-task children for treatment conditions yielded the expected significant treatment effect, $F(4,24)=5.7$, $p<.01$. The Tukey Honestly Significant Difference Test revealed significant improvement over the baseline level for B+C, B2, and B+D conditions, $D(5,24)>10.5$, $p<.05$. None of the significant conditions differed from each other. These results suggest that the consistently low on-task group improved with the introduction of focussed praise and that it remained at the same level throughout the rest of the study.

Discussion

The teacher in this study distributed praise equally among the high, medium, and low on-task children when audio cuing was first introduced. Since this study involved only one teacher, it is risky to generalize about how teachers in general distribute praise among different on-task groups. What is notable, however, is that focussing praise to a targeted population is feasible. Accordingly, audio-cuing can be used effectively both to increase overall teacher praise and to direct this praise to those subgroups that seem to need it most.

Since instructions, feedback, and praise were effective in modifying the teacher's distribution of praise, this combination might be useful for modifying other types of teacher/student interactions. For example, Gore and Roumagoux (1983) found that fourth grade teachers gave more time to answer math questions to boys than girls. Instructions, feedback, and praise might be used to train teachers to give equal time to answer math questions to boys and girls. Of course, this procedure is costly, and intervention is recommended only in cases where there is a problem.

The second important finding of this investigation is that high on-task individuals seem to be impervious to rates of teacher praise. Their on-task behaviour appears to be either task- or self-determined. To a lesser extent, the two unexamined factors also affected the performance of medium and low on-task children, since the frequency of on-task activity in the latter two groups exceeded the 50-60% observed in problem classes (Kozma et al., 1977). It is possible that high grades and parental praise contribute to this performance, but the present study lacks the necessary data to establish a relationship between on-task activity in the classroom and these two variables. The findings on high on-task children do not necessarily imply that this group should receive no praise at all, since receiving praise may be related to other important variables, such as self-esteem. For instance, Wilson (1976) found that teacher approval given for appropriate classroom behaviour resulted in increased feelings of self-esteem. Low self-esteem has been associated with depression in children (Kaslow, Rehm, & Siegel, 1984).

Hence, while high on-task children may not need praise to increase their on-task behaviour they may need it for the development of a positive self-concept and the avoidance of depression and other conditions correlated with low self-esteem.

The third finding of note is the effectiveness of the focussed praise condition for increasing on-task activity in consistently low on-task children. It was only after 67% of teacher praise was directed at them that this group approached the on-task levels of medium and high on-task children. These data suggest that consistently low on-task children may require far higher levels of praise than they would normally receive in class. If future studies substantiate this finding, it may be necessary to identify consistently low on-task children early in their education to reduce the frequency of later problems of inattentiveness, class disruption, and perhaps drop-out. While it does not seem feasible to introduce focussed praise intervention procedures in all existing classrooms, it would be advisable to raise these issues in teacher training programmes.

The changes in medium on-task children over treatment conditions are more difficult to interpret, as is the relative performance of this group in relation to low on-task subjects. Treatment effects for medium on-task subjects did not reach statistical significance until B2, while some low on-task subjects responded by B1. Even more disturbing is the finding that B2, with its relatively low rates of teacher praise, did not lead to drops in on-task behaviour. Differential training effects in medium and low on-task children will be addressed first. These effects are most consistent with the laws of initial values. This law relates increments in performance to the relative position of subjects on a postulated learning curve during base rate performance. The greater the base rate performance, the less the increment in performance under similar training conditions. In the present investigation, the medium on-task subjects were at a higher level on the curve for on-task activity, and the relative change under similar reinforcement contingencies would be expected to be slow (i.e., it would take more time for the training effect to be noticed). Thus, B1 was too short to produce a training effect, and a five-fold reduction in praise during B+C did little to increase training rate. The slow rate led to statistical significance in relation to base rate by B2, but on-task level in this group did not approximate that of high on-task children until B+D. Since the performance of low on-task subjects did not begin to approach that of medium and high on-task groups until B2, there was ample room for performance change in this group in earlier conditions, especially with the increases in teacher praise to over half the subjects in this group during B + C.

Failure to show a drop in performance by medium and low on-task groups during B2 may be attributed to resistance to extinction of a learned task under a partial reinforcement condition. It should be remembered that during B2, teacher praise rates were still four times as large as during baseline. Moreover, this resistance to extinction under decreased praise conditions is consistent with one of our earlier results. Kozma et al. (1977) found that the rates of on-task behaviour of a group of problem children who had exceeded a criterion level of 80% under a similar audio-cuing programme failed to drop significantly during the praise withdrawal condition. It would seem that once a high level of on-task activity is achieved, it takes only small rates of teacher praise to maintain it.

A more parsimonious interpretation for the behaviour of medium, low, and consistently low on-task children is that external or uncontrolled factors were responsible for increases in their on-task activities. One such possibility is negative reinforcement. The cuing for praise may have led to a decrease in aversive comments by the teacher, and if such a reduction had been consistent for B1, B + C, B2, and B + D, then the successive improvement in on-task activity over treatment conditions would have been expected. Just why it should take longer for medium than low on-task subjects to show a change in behaviour or why consistently low on-task subjects should show such a large change with the introduction of focussed praise would remain a mystery within this hypothesis. Nevertheless, future studies should monitor any changes in aversive comments by teachers as well as increases in praise statements.

The current study would also have benefitted by a monitoring of academic achievement and the addition of a follow-up phase, although our primary concern was the demonstration of targeted cuing. Correlations between achievement scores and on-task activity were relatively low, and several investigators have suggested that if the primary objective of an intervention strategy is to improve skill in a content area, that particular skill needs to be targeted (McLaughlin, Swain, Brown, & Fielding, 1986; Stewart & Singh, 1986). Accordingly, achievement deficiencies may not be solved simply by increasing on-task activity. There are, nevertheless, two reasons for increasing on-task behaviour. First, on-task behaviour may be considered a precondition to learning in the same way that attentional factors are. It is a necessary, but not sufficient, condition for learning. Second, since on-task activity frequently replaces disruptive classroom behaviour, it should make it easier for non-disruptive individuals to learn. Evidence for follow-up is more encouraging. For instance, Kozma et al.

(1977) found that teacher praise rates were at the cued level 4 months after cuing was terminated. Moreover, on-task levels still exceeded 85% in students whose pretreatment levels were under 60%.

Teacher behaviour during B2 posed an unexpected problem in this study. She began to ignore the audio cues and praised significantly below the cued rates. Both Kozma et al. (1977) and Van Houten and Sullivan (1975) found that the teachers in their studies praised when cued and suggested that audio cuing might be effective in the absence of an observer. However, the current findings indicate that an audio cuing system for increasing teacher praise rates may have to be monitored to ensure maximum benefit. If the teacher does ignore the cues, then a package such as the one used in the final phase of this study may be helpful in maintaining a high praise rate.

References

Cossairt, A., Hall, R.V., & Hopkins, B.L., (1973). The effects of experimenter's instructions, feedback and praise on teacher praise and student attending behavior. *Journal of Applied Behavior Analysis, 6,* 89-100.

Fontenelle, S., & Holliman, W. (1983). Social management techniques for classroom teachers. *Psychological Reports, 52,* 815-818.

Gore, D.A., & Roumagoux, D.V. (1983). Wait-time as a variable in sex-related differences during fourth-grade mathematics instructions. *Journal of Educational Research, 76,* 273-275.

Hall, R.V., Lund, D., & Jackson, D. (1968). Effects of teacher attention on study behavior. *Journal of Applied Behavior Analysis, 1,* 1-12.

Kaslow, N.J., Rehm, L.P., & Siegel, A.S. (1984). Social-cognitive and cognitive correlates of depression in children. *Journal of Abnormal Child Psychology, 12,* 605-620.

Kozma, A., Noseworthy, G.M., & Ingraham, W. (1977, June). *Audio cuing effects on teacher praise rate and student behaviour.* Paper presented at the annual meeting of the Canadian Psychological Association, Vancouver, Canada.

Mace, F.C., Cancelli, A.A., & Manos, M.J. (1983). Increasing teacher delivery of contingent praise and contingent materials using consultant feedback and praise. *School Psychology Review, 12,* 340-346.

McLaughlin, T.F., Swain, J.C., Brown, M., & Fielding, L. (1986). The effects of academic consequences on inappropriate social behavior of special education middle school students. *Techniques, 2,* 310-316.

Parsonson, B.S., Baer, A.M., & Baer, D.M. (1974). The application of generalized correct social contingencies: An evaluation of a training program. *Journal of Applied Behavior Analysis, 7,* 427-437.

Schutte, R.C., & Hopkins, B.L. (1970). The effects of teacher attention on following instructions in a kindergarten class. *Journal of Applied Behavior Analysis, 3,* 117-122.

Stewart, C.A., & Singh, N.N. (1986). Overcorrection of spelling deficits in moderately mentally retarded children. *Behavior Modification, 10,* 355-365.

Szykula, S.A., & Hector, M.A. (1978). Teacher instructional behavior change through self-control. *Psychology in the Schools, 15,* 87-94.

Thomas, D.R. (1971). Preliminary findings on self-monitoring for modifying teaching behaviors. In E.A. Ramp & B.L. Hopkins (Eds.), *A new direction for education: Behavior analysis* (Vol. 1), Lawrence, KS: The University of Kansas Support and Development Center for Follow Through, Department of Human Development.

Thomas, D.R., Becker, W.C., & Armstrong, M. (1968). Production and elimination of disruptive classroom behavior by systematically varying teacher's behavior. *Journal of Applied Behavior Analysis, 1*, 35-45.

Van Houten, R., & Sullivan, K. (1975). Effects of an audio cuing system on the rate of teacher praise. *Journal of Applied Behavior Analysis, 8*, 197-201.

Wilson, H.D. (1976). The effects of contingent and noncontingent teacher approval on reported feelings of self-esteem. *Dissertation Abstracts International, 36*, 5167A-5168A. (University Microfilms No. 76-1995, 100).

Workman, E.A., Watson, P.J., & Helton, G. (1982). Teachers' self-monitoring of praise vs. praise instructions: Effects on teachers' and students' behavior. *Psychological Reports, 50*, 559-565.

Social Contingencies, Physical Environment and Prosocial Behavior in Children's Play

Mary Janice Partridge, Roger D. Gehlbach, and Ronald W. Marx
Simon Fraser University

The purpose of this study was to test the effects on social behavior of alternate contingency systems in the physical aspects of children's play environments. Six 5-year-old boys were observed playing with a specially designed sand machine for 24, 10-minute sessions over 6 weeks. The machine was designed to structure the contingencies of reinforcement in three ways: (a) prosocial and nonsocial behaviors were reinforced equally; (b) only prosocial behaviors were reinforced; or (c) both types of behavior were reinforced, but prosocial behavior was reinforced more powerfully. Conditions were randomly assigned over time and player dyads were used as the unit of analysis. Results indicate that the frequency of occurrence of a target behavior can be increased, even when both target and nontarget behaviors are reinforced, if the reinforcement of the target behavior is the more powerful.

*   *   *

THROUGHOUT THE LITERATURE AND PRACTICE OF APPLIED BEHAVIOR analysis, the management of reinforcement contingencies is conducted largely by persons (e.g., teachers, therapists) who structure their behavior with respect to learners in certain specific ways (e.g., Bijou, 1976; Ullman & Krasner, 1965). In play situations, children's behavior has been managed largely through various means of "guiding" or "structuring" play through planned interventions, "in which space, materials, sometimes other children, and explicit or implicit instructions and guidance are provided in order for children to achieve some objective" (Bijou, 1976, p. 33). Innovations such as electronic and computer assisted learning games are not paradigmatically different from human mediated play environments, as the teacher-like behavior is simply programmed into the machines, creating in effect a surrogate teacher. For the most part, therefore, the physical environment has served merely as a place for human contingency management to happen.

Physical environment, however, can play a larger role in behavior control than is normally acknowledged either in theory or in practice (Ellis & Scholtz, 1978; Gehlbach, 1980). The design and placement of walls, windows, and doorways in an environment affect the behavior of those using the area, both in the direct channelling of behavior and in the structuring of contingent interactions among those using the environment (e.g., Gehlbach & Partridge, 1984).

One of the basic conventions in applied behavior analysis is that the schedule of reinforcement is continuous during the early stages of a behavior modification strategy and then normally converted to an intermittent schedule to achieve maintenance of the target behavior (e.g., Bijou, 1976; Ferster & Skinner, 1957). One may refer to continuous reinforcement systems as "hard contingency networks" since reinforcement is delivered if and *only if* the target behavior is performed. Such contingency systems are hard in the sense that the behavior is deprived of any reinforcement if target behaviors are not emitted.

In natural settings, of which play settings are a subset, it is often the case that both target and nontarget behaviors are reinforced. Nonetheless, only one (target) behavior ultimately and predominantly occurs. There are many instances of everyday knowledge and skills that children acquire in home and preschool settings, such as doorknob turning, aspects of verbal language, and social interaction, where the learner is reinforced for a wide variety of behaviors long before the knowledge or skill is fully acquired. Considered as contingency systems, such systems are not properly considered as shaping, since the reinforcement of off-target behavior is not systematically manipulated. Rather, they are what may be called "soft" contingency networks in which learning occurs (a) when both target and non-target behaviors are reinforced, either continuously or intermittently, and (b) in which a single behavior emerges predictably as dominant. The distinguishing feature of such soft networks is that it appears to be the level or strength of the reinforcers which is differentiated by the environment, not merely their occurrence or non-occurrence (as in differential reinforcement or shaping, where reinforcement is all or none and merely selective with respect to specific behaviors).

Most applications of behavioral psychology to problems in education utilize persons, such as teachers and trained parents, to manage whatever contingencies are to modify learner behavior. The present study was motivated in part by evidence that the physical environment in which children play can also be utilized in this effort in a more than contextual way (Gehlbach & Partridge, 1984). The idea is that during free play, when children are independent of adult-delivered reinforcement interventions, behavior can, in fact, be directed in desirable ways through the design of reinforcement-related features *into playthings themselves*. This is related to but significantly different from the work of Montessori (e.g., Montessori, 1967), who designed materials with built-in "control of error, " but with the introduction and use of them carefully controlled by trained teachers. The Gehlbach and Partridge work goes beyond that, to the design of physical environment for play which can manage, from start to finish, specific aspects of children's "free" play behavior. To the extent that this can be achieved, it may be expected that two useful things may be accomplished. First, teachers and parents will have genuine "teaching partners" in the *things* that children play with, thereby enhancing the overall power of their educational program. Second, achievement of this increased value of children's time in play does not require the management or training of nonprofessional staff, such as volunteer and untrained aides.

The first purpose of the present study was to test the hypothesis that the frequency of specific prosocial behaviors could be increased simply by reinforcing them more powerfully than other, competing non or antisocial behaviors. The second purpose of this study was to explore whether the management of the reinforcement contingency networks that control such behavior could be achieved simply through the design of a plaything, with absolutely no teacher intervention whatsoever. For this study, then, a plaything was designed to structure the social contingencies between players into three alternative contingency systems:

1. a "natural" contingency network, in which no specific social behavior was favored by the machine's behavior;

2. a hard contingency network, in which players were reinforced if and only if specific prosocial behaviors occurred, and

3. a soft contingency network, in which prosocial and nonsocial behaviors were reinforced, with prosocial behaviors reinforced more powerfully.

Method

Participants

Six five-year-old boys participated in the study. The boys attended kindergarten in a large suburban community in British Columbia, and were judged by their teacher to be representative of normal five-year-old children. There were three reasons for the choice of 5-year-old boys as participants.

1. prosocial development is a common objective in kindergartens, yet little has been done to structure environments to accomplish this objective (Gump, 1975; Orlick, 1981);

2. the use of only boys controlled for a sex variable; and

3. although Bar-Tal, Raviv, and Goldberg (1982) found that age alone is not a factor in preschool helping behavior, there is some indication that 5-year-old boys, when playing with a same-age male peer, are less prosocial than children in other preschool

age-sex combinations (Lewis, 1972). Thus, the possibility of a ceiling effect in the rate of prosocial behavior was reduced.

Conditions

A sand-play machine was especially designed for the study (see Figure 1). It was comprised of two identical sides, separated by an upright divider. Each side contained a vertical chute (A) which directed sand to an enclosed horizontal conveyer belt.

Each side also contained a second aperture (B) which directed sand to the partner's chute and conveyer belt. Each player's conveyer belt was activated by a hand crank on his side. Sand dropped through holes in the bottom of the horizontal enclosure (C), providing the opportunity to create sand "mountains" or to fill a container or truck appropriately placed by a player. By altering the accessibility of the filling apertures, the machine could be modified to structure the contingencies of reinforcement for social behaviors in three different ways:

1. In the baseline condition the filling apertures to the sand chutes of both players were fully open, so that prosocial and nonsocial behaviors were rewarded equally. Thus, "mountains" could be created, or trucks filled with equal ease and success by either type of behavior;

2. In the second, or "hard-contingency, " condition, the filling aperture to one's own sand chute was fitted with a cover, and the only aperture open to each player was to the sand chute of the *partner*, so that interaction with the machine was only possible if prosocial behavior occurred. Therefore only prosocial behavior was rewarded;

3. In the third, or "soft contingency, " condition, the filling apertures were open for both, but the one to each player's *own* sand chute was fitted with a *partial* cover, so that both nonsocial and prosocial behaviors were rewarded, but the reward was delivered more powerfully for prosocial behavior.

    Filling to one's partner was less difficult than filling to oneself, and sand delivery was faster over all if each filled the partner's sand chute.

Dependent variables

Social behavior was recorded and analyzed for each of the three conditions. Prosocial behavior was operationally defined to include the following behaviors: (a) filling sand to the partner's side of the apparatus; (b) verbal requests for sand; and (c) contracts in regard to mutual giving and receiving sand (e.g., "if you...then I will..."). These definitions are consistent with the current use of the prosocial construct (Bar-Tal, 1982; Mussen, Conger, Kagan, & Huston, 1984). Nonsocial behaviors (i.e., those behaviors which did not involve interacting with the other member of the dyad) included: (a) filling sand into the player's own side; and (b) simply cranking the machine. A single "fill" was operationally defined as a movement of one hand, or both hands in concert, from a sand source to an aperture, together with delivery of any amount of sand *into* the aperture. A crank was a full 360 degree turn of the handle.

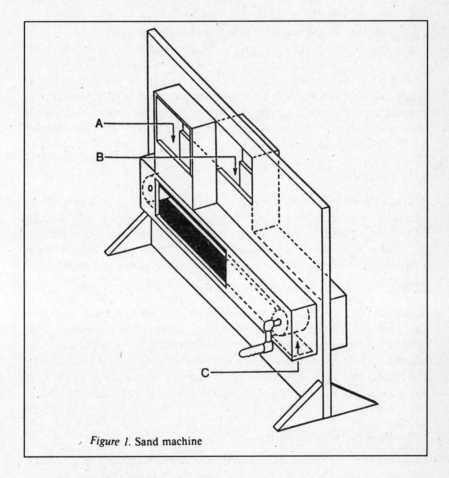

Figure 1. Sand machine

Procedures

A single-case analysis-of-variance design with two replications was employed, with conditions randomly assigned over time (Herson & Barlow, 1976). Players were randomly assigned to dyads which remained the same throughout the study. The dyad was the unit of analysis. The experiment was conducted in 24 sessions over 6 weeks. Conditions, which lasted for a full session, were randomly distributed in two blocks of 12 sessions each over 3-week units of time. All sessions were videotaped, and subsequently blind-coded by a naive coder. The following dependent variables were measured:

1. number of fills of sand into one's own part of the machine;
2. number of fills of sand into the partner's part of the machine;
3. number of cranks of the machine;
4. number of requests for fills from the partner; and
5. number of verbal contracts for mutual fills.

Behavior frequencies were recorded by dyad totals, rather than for individuals. Halfway through the experiment, a minor change was made to increase appeal without changing the structure of interaction. A plexiglass panel was inserted in the front surface of the horizontal enclosures, making the chain conveyors visible.

Scoring

Behaviors were individually coded for each subject. From the videotapes, a trained observer blind-coded occurrences of: (a) putting sand in one's own chute, or "filling to self"; (b) putting sand into the partner's chute, or "filling to partner"; (c) turning the crank; (d) requests for sand from a partner; and (e) verbal contracts related to the giving and receiving of sand.

Three randomly chosen sessions were independently coded by the experimenter, and scores were compared with those of the trained coder. The total score for one dependent variable, for one subject in one session, constituted one opportunity for agreement. The coefficient of agreement was computed by dividing actual agreements by the number of opportunities for agreement. The totals which the coders recorded were identical in 81 of the 90 possible opportunities, resulting in a coefficient of agreement of .91.

Results and Discussion

The modification of the machine halfway through the study produced no statistically reliable differences for fills to self, fills to partner, requests or contracts. There was a statistically significant difference ($p < .05$) for cranking. An examination of the new data revealed that 40% of the cranking behavior in the two parts was probably due to a novelty effect at the onset of the experiment, rather than to the modification of the machine itself.

Analyses of variance indicated significant treatment effects on the variables of fills to self $(F(2,71)=12.85, p<.01)$, fills to partner $(F(2,71)=6.71, p=.01)$ and verbal requests $(F(2,71)=4.60, p=.02)$. The effect of treatment on contracts was not statistically reliable. (Table 1 reports the details of these analyses.) The median intercorrelation among the five dependent variables, disregarding size, was .12 (ranging from -.22 to .32). These data indicate that the dependent variables shared only minimal variance.

Table 1
Means and Standard Deviations by Cell

		Treatment			
Variable	Dyad	NC	HC	SC	Total
Fills to Self	A	25.38 (18.15)	0.75 (2.12)	5.63 (9.52)	10.92 (16.06)
	B	17.87 (17.07)	3.13 (6.27)	3.15 (3.69)	8.08 (12.44)
	C	4.13 (4.39)	1.25 (2.43)	8.50 (11.74)	4.63 (7.67)
	Total	16.13 (16.80)	1.70 (4.03)	5.79 (8.86)	7.88 (12.63)
Fills to Partner	A	1.25 (1.67)	12.50 (11.51)	11.13 (8.54)	8.29 (9.57)
	B	4.38 (6.26)	10.38 (9.09)	6.75 (5.97)	7.17 (7.36)
	C	0.13 (0.35)	3.50 (3.81)	1.00 (2.07)	1.54 (2.81)
	Total	1.92 (4.02)	8.79 (9.23)	6.29 (7.23)	5.67 (7.62)

Note: Upper figure is mean. Lower figure is standard deviation.
NC = no contingency; HC = hard-contingency; SC = soft-contingency

Results of the study confirmed the hypothesis that a soft-contingency network could produce the target behavior at a level well above the baseline, or no-contingency, network. A post-hoc Newman-Keuls test indicated that although there was not a statistically reliable difference $(p<.05)$ between the hard and soft-contingencies, there was, overall, a reliable difference $(p<.05)$ between both contingencies treatments and the baseline condition.

These results also indicate that physical features of a plaything can manage the structure of social contingencies between players to produce measurable effects in social behavior. In this study, the physical structure of the plaything acted as an agent, which managed the reinforcement contingencies for free play behavior of the players. The only physical changes in the environment were alterations in the relative access to filling apertures.

One question arising from this study is whether instructional playthings should be designed to incorporate a hard- or soft-contingency network. The results of this study indicate that soft-contingency network reinforcement is at least as effective as a hard-contingency one. With a hard-contingency network in operation, the plaything is instructional only to the degree that the child interacts with it. If the child is relatively unskilled in the target behavior interaction with the plaything or the other player, instruction simply may not occur, since the child is effectively blocked from access to reinforcement. With non-target behaviors reinforced at least to some degree, the unskilled child may be expected to interact with the plaything more frequently than she or he would otherwise. In other words, the design of a soft-contingency system into the plaything allows the player who is unskilled in the target behavior (in this case, prosocial, sharing skills) *access* to the learning system without forcing that entry via an all-or-none contingency system.

In the 1970s, many suggestions for training prosocial behavior in children emphasized contingent reinforcement (Combs & Slaby, 1978) and modelling (Dodge, 1984; Zahn-Waxler, Radke-Yarrow, & King 1979). More recently, more emphasis has been seen on cognitive approaches, such as self-concept training (Grusec & Redler, 1980), inductive discipline (Brody & Shaffer, 1982), and coaching (Bierman & Furman, 1984). All of these methods are teacher-intensive and require both time and training for the adult. This study, in combination with other empirical work on the relationship between the nature of children's play and the design of the play environment (Ellis & Scholtz, 1978; Gehlbach, 1980; Gehlbach & Partridge, 1984), suggests that the *systematic design* of playthings and the settings in which they are used may become an important independent supplement to the utilization of well-trained personnel in the provision of educationally sound early childhood play experiences.

References

Bar-Tal, D., Raviv, A., & Goldberg, M. (1982). Helping behavior among preschool children: An observational study. *Child Development, 53*, 396-402.

Bierman, K.L., & Furman, W. (1984). The effects of social skills training and peer involvement on the social adjustment of preadolescents. *Child Development, 51*, 1231-1238.

Bijou, S.W., (1976). *Child Development: The basic stage of early childhood.* Englewood Cliffs, NJ: Prentice-Hall.

Brody, G.H., & Shaffer, D.R. (1982). Contribution of parents and peers to children's moral socialization. *Developmental Review, 2*, 31-75.

Combs, M.L., & Slaby, D.A. (1978). Social skills training with children. In B.B. Lahey & A.E. Kazdin (Eds.), *Advances in clinical child psychology.* New York: Plenum Press.

Dodge, M.K. (1984). Learning to care: Developing prosocial behavior among one- and two-year-olds in group settings. *Journal of Research and Development in Education, 17,* 26-34.

Ellis, M.J., & Scholtz, G.J., (1978). *Activity and play of children.* Englewood Cliffs, NJ: Prentice-Hall.

Ferster, C.B., & Skinner, B.F. (1957). *Schedules of reinforcement.* New York, NY: Appleton-Century Croft.

Gehlbach, R.D. (1980). Instructional play: Some theoretical prerequisites to systematic research and development. *Educational Psychologist, 15*(2), 112-124.

Gehlbach, R.D., & Partridge, M.J. (1984). Physical environmental regulation of children's verbal behavior during play. *Instructional Science, 13,* 225-242.

Grusec, J.E., & Redler, E. (1980). Attribution, reinforcement and altruism: A developmental analysis. *Developmental Psychology, 16,* 524-534.

Gump, P.V. (1975). Ecological psychology and children. In M. Hetherington (Ed.), *Review of child development research* (Vol. 5). Chicago, IL: University of Chicago Press.

Herson, M., & Barlow, D. (1976). *Single case experimental designs.* New York, NY: Pergamon Press.

Lewis, M. (1972). Sex differences in play behavior of the very young. *Journal of Health, Physical Education and Recreation: Leisure Today, 43*(b), 38-39.

Montessori, M. (1967). *The discovery of the child.* New York, NY: Random House.

Mussen, P.H., Conger, J.J., Kagan, J., & Huston, A.C. (1984). *Child development and personality* (6th Ed.). New York, NY: Harper & Row.

Orlick, T.D. (1981). Positive socialization via cooperative games. *Developmental Psychology, 17,* 426-429.

Ullman, L. & Krasner, L. (1965). *Case studies in behavior modification.* New York, NY: Holt, Rinehart & Winston.

Zahn-Waxler, C., Radke-Yarrow, M., & King, R.A. (1979). Child rearing and children's prosocial initiations toward victims of distress. *Child Development, 50,* 319-330.

Learning and Teaching: Cognitive Approaches

The first two articles in this section focus on the learning component of the learning-teaching process and illustrate the importance
of understanding all the cognitive steps which intervene between
the teacher's provision of information and the student's mastery
of the material. Try to calculate the product of 17 and 99 in your
heads. How many of you said to yourselves, "17 times 100 is
1700; subtract 17 and the answer is 1683?" And how many of
you are still muttering, "7 times 9 is 63, put down the 3 and carry
the 6, 7 times 9 is 63 plus 6 is 69, 1 times 9 is 9, put the 9 in
the second row under the 9 in the first row...?" In Hope and
Sherrill's study, the Grade 11 and 12 students enroled in a university entrance mathematics course knew their basic multiplication
facts very well. However, when Hope and Sherrill analyzed what
actually went on inside these students' heads when they tried to
solve a series of multiplication problems, the differences between
the unskilled and skilled mental calculators were striking, with the
former group seemingly unaware of or unable to use "shortcut"
strategies and relying instead on a cumbersome mental paper-and-
pencil approach. Can these shortcut mental calculations be
taught? It seems worth a try. At the least, student and teacher
awareness of these strategy differences might alleviate the mutual
frustration experienced when some students just don't seem to
"get it."

As a teacher, I am often frustrated when the results of a test
indicate that most of my students missed a question based on
material I am sure I covered in one of my brilliant lectures. The
problem may be that my lectures are more boring than brilliant.

The explanation I prefer is that some of my students do not know how to take good notes. Some record irrelevant information, while others try to write down every single word in the lecture rather than using more efficient summarizing strategies. Kobasigawa, Chouinard, and Dufresne examined the relevancy and efficiency of study notes taken by Grade 4 and Grade 8 children. The results of their first study indicated that Grade 8 students were much more efficient note takers than Grade 4 students. In terms of relevancy, although students in both grades copied down more relevant than irrelevant facts, they also copied down irrelevant facts, with about one-third of the students being totally nonselective. Kobasigawa and his colleagues reasoned that Grade 4 students might be nonselective because they could not keep the reason for taking notes in mind while they took them. Grade 8 students might be nonselective because their note-taking skills were good enough so that they had enough time to copy down both relevant and irrelevant facts. The results of the second study tended to confirm this reasoning. Grade 4 children who were told to be selective in their note taking took more relevant notes than those not so instructed, and, given the same amount of time, Grade 8 students given a longer story copied fewer irrelevant facts than those given a shorter story.

The second two articles in this section involve the assessment of specific teaching techniques based on what we know of cognitive functioning. Numerous studies have shown that it is easier to learn facts if we have some kind of cognitive "peg" on which to hang these facts. Pressley and Brewster suggested that such a peg could involve the elaboration of a particular image or picture. For example, if I learn to associate a picture of Banff with the name of the province in which it is located (Alberta), and I then imagine a lot of buffalo in the Banff picture, it should be easier for me to remember that a lot of buffalo live in Alberta than if I did not have the Banff picture-Alberta name "peg" on which to hang the buffalo fact. This was exactly what Pressley and Brewster found in their field experiment with Grade 5 and Grade 6 students. The imaginal elaboration technique worked well, but only when students were asked to imagine the new fact in the picture. Even if they had mastered the connection between the picture and the province name, merely showing students the picture and asking them to memorize a fact associated with the province was not sufficient. This finding suggests that the picture in school textbooks can aid in learning facts, but only if students can reliably recall what the pictures represent and then can construct internal images involving the placement of new facts in the picture.

In 1963, Ausubel proposed that teachers should start their lessons with advance organizers, in order to provide students with a conceptual framework for new information. Kloster and Winne compared student use of two "true" advance organizers, concept and analogy, with their use of two "false" advance organizers, an outline and a dummy. Students who used true advance organizers correctly performed significantly better than students using outline or dummy organizers on a number of achievement measures. However, less than half of the students in the concept and analogy advance organizer groups knew how to use these organizers correctly. It would seem that efforts to improve teaching effectiveness may often be sabotaged by invalid teacher assumptions regarding student familiarity with these and other potentially useful cognitive tools.

Characteristics of Skilled and Unskilled Mental Calculators

John A. Hope
University of Saskatchewan
James M. Sherrill
University of British Columbia

Fifteen skilled and 15 unskilled students were selected from 286 Grade 11 and 12 mathematics students as a result of their performances on a mental multiplication test. Introspective reports during mental multiplication tasks yielded 4 methods of solution and 12 calculative strategies. The unskilled students used strategies more suited to written than mental computation, and the skilled students used strategies based upon the number properties suggested by the factors in the task. The skilled students recalled more large products to aid in a mental calculation than the unskilled students did. Mental multiplication performance had a low positive correlation with forward and backward digit span and with multiplication fact recall.

*   *   *

BECAUSE MANY EVERYDAY USES OF MATHEMATICS INVOLVE A RAPID MENtal calculation, teaching children to calculate mentally meets an important practical need (Committee of Inquiry into the Teaching of Mathematics in Schools [Cockcroft Report], 1982; B.J. Reys, 1985; R.E. Reys, 1984). Apart from this practical significance, many researchers believe that mental calculation is one of the best means of developing and deepening a child's understanding of numbers and their properties (Menchinskaya & Moro, 1975; R.E. Reys, 1984). Notwithstanding the many avowed benefits of mental calculation, studies (Cockcroft Report, 1982; National Assessment of Educational Programs [NAEP], 1983) have demonstrated that many children and adults cannot perform even the most straightforward calculations mentally. For example, 45% of the 17-year-olds sampled by the Third National Mathematics Assessment were unable to multiply 90 and 70 "in the head" (NAEP, 1983, p. 32).

Why do some people have such difficulty calculating in the head? Researchers such as Hunter (1962, 1978), Hitch (1977, 1978), and Howe and Ceci (1979) believe that skilled mental calculators make different uses of their long-term and short-term memory systems than unskilled mental calculators do. Expert mental calculators such as Aitken, Klein, and Bidder accomplished their extraordinary calculative feats by using a wide variety of unconventional but efficient strategies, recalling large numerical equivalents to reduce the number of calculative steps, and using an extraordinary memory for numbers to retain each step of a calculation (Hunter, 1962, 1978; Smith, 1983).

Thus, individual differences in mental calculation performance can be argued to reflect differences in the choice of a calculative strategy, the knowledge of useful numerical equivalents, and the capacity to process numbers. Because this argument is based primarily on the study of atypically proficient calculators, any generalizations about the differing performances of lesser skilled calculators are very speculative.

This study characterized the performances of unskilled and skilled mental calculators by addressing the following research questions. Do skilled and unskilled mental calculators (a) use different methods and strategies to calculate mental products, (b) recall different types of numerical equivalents during the solution of a mental calculation, (c) differ in the ability to quickly and accurately recall the basic facts of multiplication, and (d) possess different short-term memory capacities?

Method

Instruments

The Screening Test CAL1. The Screening Test CAL1 was designed to identify skilled and unskilled mental calculators who participated in the study. Twenty mental multiplication tasks selected from an 80-item pool that had been used in an initial pilot study formed CAL1. To allow the students to apply a diversity of strategies, the majority of items were selected so that the factors satisfied various number properties (Hope, 1984, p. 76). Ten easy and ten difficult items were chosen to ensure that the test would discriminate between extreme and nonextreme performances. For example, the items 30×200 and 8×99 were designated as easy, and the items 32×64 and 24×24 were designated as difficult. Each item was recorded on audio tape using an item-presentation rate of 20 seconds.

The group administration of CAL1 posed special problems: Each student needed a pencil to record a solution, but a pencil could not be used as a calculative aid. All students were instructed to record only the solutions and to record neither the factors nor any intermediate calculations. All answers were scored as either correct or incorrect. The internal consistency reliability of CAL1 (Kuder-Richardson 20) was calculated to be .80.

The Probing Test CAL2. The Probing Test CAL2 was used to determine each participating student's methods of solution and consisted of 30 mental multiplication tasks. Some sample items are 25×48, 25×120, 32×32,

8×999, and 49×51. The item selection process for CAL2 as for CAL1 was guided by the expected strategies that an item might elicit.

CAL2 was administered individually. As soon as both factors were stated, the student was to determine the solution by using any mental method that seemed "natural." Whether or not a correct solution was stated, the student was asked to explain the calculative method applied. If the method could not be clearly identified, the student was asked to provide more detail. All explanations were recorded on audio tape for later analysis. Because the function of CAL2 was to identify the procedures used, performance scores were not necessary, and a reliability coefficient was not determined.

The Basic Fact Recall Test BFR. Because the basic number facts are the fundamental building blocks of most calculations, an assessment of basic fact recall was vital in characterizing skilled and unskilled mental calculation performance. The Basic Fact Recall Test BFR consisted of a sheet listing in scrambled order the 100 multiplication facts formed from single-digit factors. All students were tested individually and told to state each product as quickly as possible. Each answer was scored as either correct or incorrect.

Several weeks after the initial testing, BFR was readministered to all students in the sample. The test-retest reliability of BFR was calculated to be .77.

Tests of Short-Term Memory Capacity. The forward and backward digit span subtests of the Wechsler Adult Intelligence Scale (Wechsler, 1955) were used to estimate each student's short-term memory capacity. Each subtest was administered individually. Each subtest contains two lists (Trial I and II) of seven series of digits. In the forward digit span subtest the series vary in length from 3 to 9 digits, and in the backward digit span subtest the series vary from 2 to 8 digits. A student's digit span (forward or backward) was the number of digits in the longest series repeated without error in Trial I or II on the appropriate subtest. Wechsler (1955) reports a reliability for the combined subtests of .71.

Sample

The participants in the study were senior high school students enrolled in a Grade 11 or 12 university entrance mathematics course. The 286 students who participated in the screening phase were given the CAL1 mental multiplication test and were eligible to participate in the subsequent interview phase only if they exhibited extreme performance on the screening test. The 15 most skilled and the 15 most unskilled mental calculators were selected. (See Hope, 1984, for details of the selection procedure.)

Procedure

The 900 transcribed introspective reports resulting from the administration of the test CAL2 were examined to identify the primary or dominant strategy used by each student to solve each mental multiplication task. Another mathematics educator was provided with a written description of the resulting classification scheme and asked to classify a 10% randomly selected sample of the reports. There was mutual agreement on 95% of the classifications.

Results

Mental Calculation Methods and Strategies

The analysis of the introspective reports revealed that 4 methods of solution and 12 calculative strategies were used to solve the CAL2 mental multiplication tasks.

PENCIL-AND-PAPER MENTAL ANALOGUE (P&P)

A mental counterpart of the conventional pencil-and-paper algorithm was used to solve many of the tasks. Four main variations of this method were identified: (a) no partial product retrieved (P&P0), (b) one partial product retrieved (P&P1), (c) two partial products retrieved (P&P2), and (d) stacking.

P&P0. Students who used the P&P0 strategy made no attempt to adapt pencil-and-paper methods to a mental medium. Each partial product was calculated digit by digit, and no numerical equivalent larger than a basic fact was retrieved during the calculation. One unskilled subject's unsuccessful attempt to solve 25×480 provides a good illustration: "Let's see. 480 is on the top and 25 on the bottom. 5 times 0, 5 times 8 is 40, carry 4, and 4 is 24. I have to realize that the second number is one over. 2 times 0, 2 times 8 is 16, carry 1; 2 times 4 is 8 and 1 is 9, so 960, 9600. So 9600 and 2400 is 0, 0,..., 19 thousand and...860."

P&P1. Rather than completing the calculation of each partial product by proceeding digit by digit, students who used P&P1 retrieved a numerical equivalent for one partial product. The following report involved an application of P&P1 to calculate 25×48: "5 times 48 is...5 times 8=40, carry 4, 24, 240. And 2 times 48 is 96. I know that. I think of 96 brought over one. So it's 1200." Notice that the first partial product 240 was calculated digit by digit, but the second partial product 96 was retrieved as a numerical equivalent.

P&P2. To apply P&P2, students arranged the calculation so that two partial products were retrieved as numerical equivalents rather than calculated digit by digit. One student's explanation of 12×250 illustrates an application of this strategy. She explained, "2 times 250 is 500, and 1 times 250 is 250. Move over one, 3000."

Stacking. The stacking strategy was applied only to questions involving one-digit by multiple-digit factors. Each partial product was completed digit by digit and visualized as a stacked arrangement. One reported solution of 8×999 is a good example: "I thought 8 times 9 is 72, 72, and 72, right across." The student who provided this report said that she never "carried" during the calculation.

DISTRIBUTION

The distribution method of calculation was initiated by transforming one or more factors into a series of either sums or differences. The calculation proceeded by applying one of four strategies: additive, subtractive, fractional, or quadratic distribution.

Additive distribution. The additive distribution strategy is based on the principle of the distributive law of multiplication over addition. As the calculation progressed, each partial product was added successfully to produce a running sum. The following solution of 8×4211 involved an application of additive distribution: "8 times 4000 is 32 000; 8 times 200 is 1600; so it's 33 600. 8 times 11 is 88; so the answer is 33 688."

Fractional distribution. The fractional distribution strategy was usually applied to those tasks in which at least one factor contained 5 as a unit digit. For example, 15×48 was calculated by one student as, "10 times 48, 480, and half of 480 is 240; so it's 720." Although factoring is needed to complete a portion of the calculation, the strategy was classified as a type of distribution rather than as a type of factoring because the calculation proceeded by partitioning each factor initially into a sum rather than a product.

Subtractive distribution. To use the distributive principle of multiplication over subtraction, students expressed a factor as a difference between two numbers that they thought made the calculation more tractable. For example, $8 \times 999 = 8 \times (1000-1) = 8000-8 = 7992$.

Quadratic distribution. Certain properties of quadratics were used by some students as a calculative aid. The algebraic identity for the difference of squares $(x-y)(x+y) = x^2 - y^2$ is one form of quadratic distribution that was used by some students. For example, 49×51 was recast as $50^2 - 1$.

FACTORING

The factoring method differed from distribution in that one or more factors in the task were transformed into a series of products or quotients rather than into a series of sums or differences. Four types of factoring strategies were identified: general, half-and-double, aliquot parts, and exponential factoring.

General factoring. To apply the general factoring strategy, students factored one or more of the factors before applying the associative law for multiplication. To calculate 25×48, one student factored 25 into 5×5 and reasoned, "5 times 48 is 240, and 5 times 240 is 1200." This student applied additive distribution to determine the intermediate calculations 5×48 and 5×240: $5\times48=(5\times40)+(5\times8)$ and $5\times240=(5\times200)+(5\times40)$. Despite the additional use of additive distribution, the student's reasoning was classified as general factoring rather than distribution because the computation was transformed initially into a series of products rather than sums. Additive distribution can be thought of as playing an ancillary rather than a primary calculative role during an application of factoring. The remaining variations of factoring could all be considered, in a mathematical sense, as special cases of general factoring, but were classified as separate strategies.

Half-and-double. When one factor in a multiplication task was a multiple of 2, a special form of factoring was often employed. The calculation proceeded by halving the multiple of 2 and doubling the remaining factor. This process continued until the student completed the calculation, usually by applying another strategy.

One student reported that to calculate 12×16, "I did doubling and halving again. I did half of 12 is 6. Doubling 16 gives 32. And 6 times 30 is 180, so 192." Another student explained, "I just decided to multiply by 2, or 12 times 2, four times."

Aliquot parts. Instead of transforming a factor into two or more factors, students who used aliquot parts transformed one factor into a quotient. This strategy was applied frequently to those computations where one factor [*f*] was a factor of a power of 10 [*p*] and the remaining factor was a multiple of the quotient p/f. Products such as 25×48 and 12×250, for example, were sometimes calculated through an application of aliquot parts: $25\times48=100/4\times48=100\times48/4=100\times12=1200$ and $12\times250=12\times100/4=12/4\times1000=3\times1000=3000$.

Exponential factoring. The exponential factoring strategy was used to calculate the products of powers through the application of an exponential rule. To find 32×32, one student reasoned, "I solved it by thinking powers of 2. 32 is 2 to the fifth, and squaring this is 2 to the tenth, which I just

know is 1024." If some knowledge of exponential arithmetic was incorporated into the calculation, the strategy was classified as exponential factoring.

RETRIEVAL OF A NUMERICAL EQUIVALENT

Some products were retrieved from memory rather than calculated. For
example, many skilled students stated "625" immediately when presented
with the task 25×25. To ensure that the solution was retrieved and not
calculated, each student was asked if any intermediate calculations had
been attempted. Typically, a student would respond to this query with
phrases such as, "I just know it," "I memorized it," "It's a fact," or as
one student said, "It's common knowledge; everyone knows that." But
the response, "I did 5 times 25, then I kind of remembered that 25 times
25 is 625," was classified as general factoring rather than retrieval because
the student had indicated that some calculation was necessary. Very short
solution times (1 to 3 seconds) also suggested a retrieval rather than a
calculative process.

Choices of Methods of Solution

Skilled and unskilled mental calculators could be characterized by the
methods they chose to solve calculation tasks. The frequency and proportion of methods used by the unskilled and skilled groups to solve the 30
CAL2 mental multiplication items are summarized in Table 1, and the
frequency and proportion of strategies are summarized in Table 2.

Table 1
*Frequency and Percent of Methods Used by Skilled and Unskilled Students to Solve CAL2
Mental Multiplication Tasks*

Method	Unskilled (n = 15)		Skilled (n = 15)	
	Frequency	%	Frequency	%
Mental pencil-and-paper	387	86.0	101	22.4
Distribution	53	11.8	244	54.2
Factoring	7	1.6	61	13.6
Retrieval, no calculation	2	0.4	44	9.8
Guess	1	0.2	0	0.0

To determine if the choices of methods of solution were different for
skilled and unskilled mental calculators, a chi-square test for independent
samples was used. The invalid incomplete distribution and guess responses
were not included in this analysis. The magnitude of the calculated X^2 (3,
$N=886)=393, p<.001$.

Table 2
Frequency and Percent of Strategies Used by Skilled and Unskilled Students to Solve CAL2 Mental Multiplication Tasks

Strategy	Unskilled ($n = 15$)		Skilled ($n = 15$)	
	Frequency	%	Frequency	%
P&P0	320	71.1	28	6.2
P&P1	52	11.6	51	11.3
P&P2	15	3.3	18	4.0
Stacking	0	0.0	4	0.9
Additive distribution	36	8.0	187	41.6
Fractional distribution	0	0.0	15	3.3
Subtractive distribution	4	0.9	32	7.1
Quadratic distribution	0	0.0	8	1.8
Incomplete distribution	13	2.9	2	0.4
General factoring	2	0.4	15	3.3
Half-and-double	3	0.7	15	3.3
Aliquot parts	2	0.4	30	6.7
Exponential factoring	0	0.0	1	0.2
Retrieval, no calculation	2	0.4	44	9.8
Guess	1	0.2	0	0.0

CHARACTERIZING THE METHODS OF THE UNSKILLED STUDENTS

The unskilled students favored the pencil-and-paper mental analogue and therefore made little attempt to examine the calculative task for even the most transparent number properties that might aid in the calculation. For example, 11 of the 30 items in CAL2 included factors having 1 as a digit in the units or tens place value position (e.g., 12×81, 17×99, and 12×15). Surprisingly, 61% of the unskilled group's attempts to solve these 11 items did not incorporate the identity principle for multiplication to expedite the calculation.

The most graphic example of unnecessary and excessive calculation was an unskilled student's attempted solution of the straightforward mental calculation 20×30. She explained, "30 is on the top, and 20 is on the bottom. 0 times 0 is 0; 0 times 3 is 0. Put down the 0. And 2 times 0 is 0, and 2 times 3 is 6. And then you add them together, and you'd get...6....600?" Her calculation took 34 seconds to complete.

Most unskilled students used a digit-by-digit, right-to-left calculative process during the additive phase of a mental calculation. As one student explained, "I do it [addition] from right to left and then read the answer out backwards." This tendency of unskilled students to fragment a calculation could have been one of the reasons that even the most obvious sums were calculated rather than retrieved. In calculating 12×250, one student was heard to say, "So five hundred and two thousand five hundred" before beginning the process of addition. But instead of retrieving a sum of 3000, she immediately began to say, "5, 0, 0, and 2, 5, 0, 0, ...would be...0, 5,

7, 2...2, 7, 5, 0?" She was asked later in the interview to add 2500 and 500, and again used a digit-by-digit, right-to-left additive process.

The use of P&P0 and P&P1 was often accompanied by motions indicating that the student was attempting to "write" each stage of the calculation. Fingers were used to form calculations either in the air or on a table. One student used a pencil poised just above the table to record her calculative stages. Eleven of the 15 unskilled subjects used an imaginary writing instrument to solve the majority of the mental calculation tasks.

CHARACTERIZING THE METHODS OF THE SKILLED STUDENTS

The pencil-and-paper mental analogue was used infrequently by the skilled students. Those few skilled students who did use the method retrieved larger numerical equivalents than basic multiplication facts to minimize the number of calculation steps.

Distribution was the method used most frequently by the skilled students. Over half of their attempted solutions involved a distribution strategy. The additive distribution strategy was initiated by determining the product of the most significant digits of each factor and annexing the appropriate number of zeros. The direction of the calculation progressed from the more significant to the less significant digits in each factor.

A running sum of the partial products was completed rather than delaying the addition until all partials had been calculated. Many skilled subjects believed that such progressive addition helped minimize forgetting. One skilled student said, "I try to add the numbers as I go along and forget the others. I usually start at the left, add, and drop those numbers." When asked to explain why he added in this manner, he said, "There is too much to remember otherwise."

Subtractive distribution was used by the majority of skilled students to find products such as 8×99, 17×99, and 8×999 where each item included a factor whose magnitude was close to a multiple of a power of 10. For the three items, 8×99, 17×99, and 8×999, 28 of 45 solutions incorporated subtractive distribution. In comparison, only 3 of the unskilled students' solutions to the three items involved this strategy. Subtraction strategies that differed from pencil-and-paper methods generally accompanied an application of subtractive distribution.

Seven of the eight instances of quadratic distribution were reported in the calculation of 49×51. One skilled student used differences of squares to calculate 23×27 by reasoning $25^2 - 2^2 = 625 - 4$.

In contrast to the infrequent use of factoring by the unskilled students, the majority of skilled students used factoring to solve some calculative tasks.

The most common factoring strategy applied by the skilled group was aliquot parts. Half the number of attempted applications of this strategy involved three items: namely, 25×48, 25×120, and 25×32. One student solved 25×65 in a novel manner by incorporating decimal arithmetic into his calculation: "65 divided by 4 is 16.25. Move the decimal over two places. So the answer is 1625."

Several students applied aliquot parts by reformulating the task into a monetary situation. For example, one skilled student commented, "When I multiply by 25, I think of money, like quarters. So I divided by 4 to calculate dollars." She thought this strategy was learned through practical life experiences. She explained, "When I was in Brownies, we always used to sell cookies, and they were $1.25. So I got used to adding, subtracting, and multiplying by quarters."

Retrieval of Numerical Equivalents

There were a number of ways that the skilled and unskilled groups differed in the ability to retrieve numerical equivalents useful for mental multiplication.

RECALLING BASIC MULTIPLICATION FACTS

Each group exhibited close to perfect multiplication fact recall. More than 70% of all the participating students made less than three errors on the basic multiplication fact test BFR. The median score for the combined groups was 99.06. The mean scores on the BFR for the skilled and unskilled groups were 99.9 ($SD = 0.35$) and 96.7 ($SD = 3.10$). The covariance information strategy (Alf & Abrahams, 1975) was used to determine the strength of the relationship existing between accuracy of multiplication fact recall and CAL1 mental multiplication performance. The correlation r for the intact sample (see Alf & Abrahams, 1975) was estimated to be .33, $p < .001$.

RECALLING LARGER NUMERICAL EQUIVALENTS

The skilled students solved 44 problems by recalling rather than calculating a product, whereas the unskilled students solved only 2 problems by recall. These differences were so large that a test for statistical significance seemed unnecessary. Forty-four of the 46 tasks solved by retrieval were squares: namely, 13^2, 15^2, 16^2, 24^2, and 25^2. The only square in CAL2 not solved by retrieving a numerical equivalent was 32×32, the largest square on the test.

Short-Term Memory Capacity

The results of each group's performances on forward and backward digit span are presented in Table 3. The skilled students had greater mean scores than the unskilled students on each memory measure. The correlation between CAL1 performance and each measure of memory capacity was determined using the covariance information statistic. The values and statistical significance of each *r* are presented in Table 3.

Table 3
Means and Standard Deviations for Digit Span Measures and Their Correlation with CAL1 Mental Multiplication Performance

Measure	Skilled (n = 15)		Unskilled (n = 15)		
	M	SD	M	SD	r
Forward digit span	7.8	1.2	6.3	1.2	.33*
Backward digit span	6.2	1.3	4.8	1.3	.30*

*p < .01.

Discussion

Processing Efficiency of Calculative Strategies

Because of the design of the study, efficient students and efficient strategies cannot be disassociated from one another. However, the findings suggest that efficient strategies may be those that (a) eliminate the need for a carry operation, (b) proceed in a left-to-right manner, and (c) progressively incorporate each interim calculation into a single result.

Research has demonstrated the difficulty of the carry operation in calculating mentally (Hitch, 1977, 1978; Merkel & Hall, 1982). If a calculation involves only a few carries, the additional burden imposed by the carry operation can likely be handled by short-term memory. But with some particularly complex calculations such as 25×48, the burden of a carry can become so excessive that performance suffers.

An analysis of the strategies used by the proficient mental calculators indicates that carrying was conspicuous by its absence. The carry operation was eliminated in several ways. For example, the skilled students rarely used the digit-by-digit, paper-and-pencil mental analogue, a strategy that can involve many carries both in the multiplicative and additive stages of the calculation. Instead, they tended to use additive distribution and eliminated carrying by arranging the calculation so that each factor had only one significant digit. To calculate the product of 9 and 742, for example, the factors became 9, 700, 40, and 2. No carries were required to calculate the partial products 6300, 360, and 18. An analysis of the other strategies used by the proficient students revealed a similar absence of the carry operation.

The carry operation was also eliminated by retrieving rather than calculating a partial product. For example, one skilled student used no carry operations to complete the calculation of 15×16: "80 and 16, move one over, 160. And, 160 and 80 is 200, and 40 more, which equals 240."

Another common characteristic of the proficient students was their tendency to complete a calculation in left-to-right fashion. Because studies have demonstrated that "interim information produced in the course of computation will undergo rapid forgetting if it is not immediately utilized" (Hitch, 1978, p. 306), it can be hypothesized that left-to-right mental calculation methods are less demanding on short-term memory than right-to-left methods. It can also be hypothesized that the accuracy of an estimate can be improved by using left-to-right methods because fewer errors would be made in calculating with the most significant digits. Further research is needed to evaluate these hypotheses.

Another feature of proficient mental calculation was the tendency to incorporate progressively the interim calculations into a single result. In the case of distribution, for example, the retention of a single result was accomplished by continually retrieving a sum, updating by adding a newly calculated partial product, and storing the new sum. In the case of factoring, a running product rather than a sum was continually modified.

What seems to be the purpose behind this technique? The proficient students said that retaining a running total was less demanding on their memory than the mathematically equivalent procedure of computing a total in the last stages of the calculation. Likewise, expert calculators such as Bidder believe that their memory demand is significantly reduced by focussing on only one result (Smith, 1983). Because a proficient calculator can jettison unneeded calculations like so much excess memory-baggage, the load on short-term memory is presumably lightened. Whether or not the running total technique reduces one's memory load, as its proponents have claimed, will have to be decided by future studies.

Memory of Numerical Equivalents

The difference between the skilled and unskilled groups in recalling the basic multiplication facts was statistically significant but not substantial. Both skill groups had attained a considerably high level of mastery. This finding indicates that the basic fact mastery of young adults is likely not an important factor contributing to differences in their mental calculation performance.

Although the two skill groups differed in their ability to retrieve large numerical equivalents used to aid a mental calculation task, the extended mental multiplication tables of the skilled calculators went only slightly beyond 10×10. This specialized numerical information seems to have been memorized through the pursuit of some interesting mathematical activity rather than through a deliberate intention to commit such numerical facts to memory. For example, several students commented that they had memorized powers of 2 such as 16^2 and 32^2 by "working with computers and the binary system." One student, when asked why he knew immediately that 1024 was a large power of 2, replied:

> When I was a little kid, we'd go on these long trips, and I used to sit in the back of the car and think 1 + 1 is 2, 2 + 2 is 4, and go all the way, just for something to occupy my mind. I would recognize that 1024 is a power of 2, but I wouldn't know that it was 2 to the 10th.

Another student was asked why he remembered that 36^2 equalled 1296. He explained, "Probably working with probability. In rolling dice you have a chance of one sixth of rolling a 1. So if you do that 4 times in a row, it would be one sixth to the 4th or 1 in 1296."

Short-Term Memory Processes

The finding that forgetting the interim calculations was a great source of error in calculating mentally seems to be consistent with the notion of a short-term memory system with a limited capacity to store and process temporary information. But the finding that only a weak relationship existed between mental calculation performance and short-term memory capacity seems to weaken the argument for the important contribution that the short-term memory system supposedly makes to this type of reasoning process. These discrepant findings can be explained in several ways.

On the technical side, the low correlations reported in this study could have been attenuated by the somewhat restricted range of the memory capacity scores. Perhaps the relationship between capacity and mental calculation performance would be more evident if a greater range of memory span estimates were considered: those students with exceptionally low estimates being more likely to be poor mental calculators than those with particularly high estimates.

However, the lack of a strong relationship could be more than a statistical one produced solely by studying students who differed very little in memory capacity. Perhaps a strong relationship between capacity and mental calculation exists only when all students are required to use the same strategy. In this study, the students' choice of strategies were left unconstrained, and as Hitch (1977, 1978) and Hunter (1978) have argued, the resourceful person can always find a way to ease the memory burden by selecting a strategy that requires little information processing. Through the judicious selection of a calculative strategy, a skilled calculator can get by with fewer short-term memory resources than the selection of more inefficient strategies would necessitate. Further research into the relationship between short-term memory capacity and the processing efficiency of different mental calculation strategies is needed.

References

Alf, E.F. Jr., & Abrahams, N.M. (1975). The use of extreme groups in assessing relationships. *Psychometrika, 40,* 563-572.

Committee of Inquiry into the Teaching of Mathematics in Schools. (1982). *Mathematics counts.* London, UK: Her Majesty's Stationery Office.

Hitch, G. (1977). Mental arithmetic: Short-term storage and information processing in a cognitive skill. In A.M. Lesgold, J.W. Pellegrino, S. Fokkema, & R. Glasser (Eds.), *Cognitive psychology and instruction* (pp. 331-338). New York, NY: Plenum Press.

Hitch, G.J. (1978). The role of short-term working memory in mental arithmetic. *Cognitive Psychology, 10,* 302-323.

Hope, J.A. (1984). *Characteristics of unskilled, skilled, and highly skilled mental calculators.* Unpublished doctoral dissertation, University of British Columbia, Vancouver, BC.

Howe, M.J.A., & Ceci, S.J. (1979). Educational implications of memory research. In M.M. Gruneberg & P.E. Morris (Eds.), *Applied problems in memory* (pp. 59-94). London, UK: Academic Press.

Hunter, I.M.L. (1962). An exceptional talent for calculative thinking. *British Journal of Psychology, 53,* 243-258.

Hunter, I.M.L. (1978). The role of memory in expert mental calculations. In M.M. Gruneberg, P.E. Morris, & R.N. Sykes (Eds.), *Practical aspects of memory* (pp. 339-345). London, UK: Academic Press.

Menchinskaya, N.A., & Moro, M.I. (1975). Instruction in mental and written calculation. In J. Kilpatrick, I. Wirszup, E. Begle, & J. Wilson (Eds.), *Soviet studies in the psychology of learning and teaching mathematics* (Vol. 14, pp. 73-88). Stanford, CA: School Mathematics Study Group.

Merkel, S.P., & Hall, V.C. (1982). The relationship between memory for order and other cognitive tasks. *Intelligence, 6,* 427-441.

National Assessment of Educational Progress. (1983). *The Third National Mathematics Assessment: Results, trends, and issues.* Denver, CO: Author.

Reys, B.J. (1985). Mental computation. *Arithmetic Teacher, 32*(6), 43-46.

Reys, R.E. (1984). Mental computation: Past, present and future. *Elementary School Journal, 84,* 547-557.

Smith, S.B. (1983). *The great mental calculators: The psychology, methods, and lives of calculating prodigies, past and present.* New York, NY: Columbia University Press.

Wechsler, D. (1955). *Manual for the Wechsler Adult Intelligence Scale.* New York, NY: Psychological Corporation.

Characteristics of Study Notes Prepared by Elementary School Children: Relevancy and Efficiency

Akira Kobasigawa, Maureen A. Chouinard, and Annette Dufresne
University of Windsor

The characteristics of study notes prepared by children were examined. Grades 4 and 8 students read prose passages and prepared study notes for a subsequent test in which they would be asked to recall four different attributes of different kinds of bears. In general, students' notes at both grade levels contained more task relevant than task irrelevant information. However, only 35% of the students even at grade 8 recorded task relevant information to the exclusion of irrelevant information (selective note taking); 40% of the grade 8 students copied both relevant and irrelevant information to the same degree. Grade 4 students tended to record information verbatim, whereas grade 8 students tended to be more efficient at note taking, writing many facts using fewer words. It was also demonstrated that many grade 4 students could be easily induced to use the highly selective and more efficient note taking strategy.

*   *   *

ACCORDING TO BROWN, BRANSFORD, FERRARA, AND CAMPIONE (1983), PRE-vious research concerning children's learning in school settings has focused on how well students do on tests, rather than on what activities children engage in while studying. One common activity to use in school when studying is that of taking notes. In this context, then, the present research was conducted to characterize study notes prepared by children while reading prose passages for a later test.

Two functions of note taking have been identified in the research. One frequently suggested by college students as well as researchers is that the process of taking notes will facilitate the learner's subsequent recall (Hartley & Davis, 1978; Howe, 1974). Another function of note taking is

We wish to acknowledge the excellent cooperation from the administrative staff, teachers, and students of the Essex County Separate School System, the Windsor Separate School System, and the Kent County Separate School System in conducting this research. We would like to thank D. Carroll for collecting the data and P. Tumolo for initiating the present research. The research was supported by a grant from the Social Sciences and Humanities Research Council of Canada to the first author.

to keep a record of information gained through listening to a lecture or reading a text for a subsequent review (Hartley & Davies, 1978; Howe, 1974; Rohwer, 1984). This second function of note taking is the focus of the present research.

What are some characteristics of children's notes that may be useful for investigation? One important feature of good study notes is that they contain information relevant to performance objectives to the exclusion of task irrelevant information (note relevancy). If the notes include only the task relevant information, students will not have to decide which parts to study in a later review situation. In addition to screening information, a note taker does not have to copy the task relevant information verbatim. Since study notes are simply for one's own use, the use of point form, thereby eliminating redundant words and phrases, permits the notes to be written more quickly (note efficiency). Copying task relevant information by deleting redundant words represents the simplest form of note taking strategies (Brown, Day, & Jones, 1983). These two characteristics (relevancy and efficiency) conform to two important decisions that students must make when they take notes, namely: (a) what information should be included in notes, and (b) in what form (Hartley & Davies, 1978). In light of these considerations, children's notes were characterized in the present research in terms of their relevancy and efficiency.

The two studies reported here were patterned after an experiment conducted by Tumolo and Kobasigawa (1976). In that study, grades 3, 5, and 7 children were asked to read and take notes on prose passages containing factual information (attributes of different bears) in preparation for a test. These investigators reported that the percentage of relevant facts contained in children's notes increased with age. For example, 63% of children's notes contained relevant facts at grade 3, while the corresponding figure was 73% at grade 7. This finding even for the grade 7 level, however, is not particularly impressive when we consider that nearly 70% of the facts included in the original reading passage were task relevant. Apparently, many of the students in the Tumolo and Kobasigawa study used a nonselective strategy, copying both relevant and irrelevant facts in their notes. With regard to note efficiency, it was found that the number of students copying the information in the passage verbatim clearly decreased between grades 5 and 7, whereas the difference between grades 3 and 5 was not significant.

To investigate further the characteristics of children's notes, two studies were carried out using grades 4 and 8 students. While general procedures and reading materials were similar to those used in the previous study (Tumolo & Kobasigawa, 1976), there were several differences between the present and previous investigations. First, the same number of task relevant and task irrelevant facts were included in the present reading material so that the relevancy of notes could be compared with the irrelevancy of notes more directly. Second, in the previous study the same amount of study time for taking notes was used regardless of grade. A pilot study was conducted to determine the time needed for note taking for respective grades, and the time allotted for each grade level in the present research was adjusted accordingly. Third, students were given one trial to prepare notes in the previous experiment, whereas participants were given two trials to make notes in the present research. An additional trial was included to ensure that younger students were familiar with the procedure.

Study 1 was concerned with the manner in which children would spontaneously prepare notes when they had received instructions as to kinds of questions they would have in a later test (performance objectives). To demonstrate the replicability of our data, findings from a replication study are also provided in Study 1. Study 2 was conducted to explore why some students do not take notes selectively or efficiently.

Study 1

Method

Participants. The participants were 25 grade 4 (*M* CA=9.9 years) [CA=chronological age] and 25 grade 8 (*M* CA=13.9 years) students drawn from a predominantly middle-class parochial school in Windsor, Ontario. The participants for our replication study consisted of 20 grade 4 and 20 grade 8 students of comparable chronological ages drawn from a parochial school located in the outskirts of Windsor, Ontario. Within each grade, approximately half of the students were male and half were female. According to their teachers' judgments, none of the participants should have had difficulty in reading the materials used in the present research.

Materials. The materials prepared for each student were two story booklets, a note taking booklet, and a test sheet. The first story booklet consisted of two pages: a cover sheet and a page containing the instructions and the reading passage. The instructions indicated the task objectives and stated: "This is the first of two stories about different types of bears. You have to remember where each kind lives, what each kind eats, how fast each kind can run, and how much each kind weighs." These instructions, then, "defined" what kinds of factual data in the reading material would constitute task relevant information. The reading passage consisted of two paragraphs (111 words long) describing various characteristics of grizzly and polar bears, with the readability at a grade 3 level (Spache, 1953). The passage contained 11 task relevant facts (bears' food, weight, speed, and location) as well as 11 task irrelevant facts (e.g. bears' temperament, life expectancy, color). These pieces of task relevant and irrelevant information were randomly arranged in the reading material. The second story booklet was constructed in the same manner as the first except that its reading passage contained information about major characteristics of black and brown bears.

The note taking booklet consisted of three pages: a cover sheet with a space for a participant's name, grade, and birth date and two pages on which students prepared their notes. The test sheet contained 32 completion items (e.g. Brown bears can run _____ miles per hour) designed to assess children's recall of 21 task relevant and 11 task irrelevant facts.

Procedure. The students were tested in their respective classes. Each student received a package of the two story booklets (sets 1 and 2) and the note booklet. The experimenter initially told the students that they would read two stories about different types of bears and have an opportunity to make notes for a subsequent review.

The experimenter then told the students to turn to the first page of the first story booklet and read the instructions and passage with students. The instructions, as stated previously, described four types of questions (i.e., bears' food, speed, weight, and location) that would appear in a subsequent test. Grade 4 students were then given 10 minutes to read and take notes while grade 8 students were given five minutes. (In a pilot study, grade 4 students needed approximately twice as long as grade 8 students to read and copy a comparable passage.) This procedure was repeated for the second booklet.

Just to be consistent with the initial instructions that the notes would be prepared for a subsequent review, the students were given five minutes to examine their notes. This was followed by a 10-minute recall test. The entire test session was supervised by the experimenter and one adult assistant.

Scoring. Each child's notes for each trial were scored for note relevancy, irrelevancy, and efficiency. A note relevancy score was obtained by counting the number of task relevant facts recorded in the child's notes (i.e., 11 attributes contained in each set of booklets describing the bears' food, speed, weight, and location). When more than one fact defined the relationship between a particular type of bear and "items" (e.g., Polar bears eat *seals* and *walruses*), each fact was counted separately. A note irrelevancy score was defined as the total number of irrelevant facts recorded in notes (i.e., 11 attributes contained in each set of booklets describing the bears' temperature, color, life expectancy). Thus on each note taking trial, the maximum relevant or irrelevant score was 11. These two types of scores were used to examine the selective aspects of students' note taking behavior.

A note efficiency score was obtained by dividing the total number of words contained in the notes by the total number of relevant and irrelevant facts recorded in the notes (see also Howe, 1970). Consequently, a child's note taking was judged to be more efficient when the obtained ratio was lower.

Results and Discussion

Relevancy. The mean relevancy and irrelevancy scores for grades 4 and 8 students on each trial are presented in Table 1. Because the number of students sampled was different between the two schools, these data were analyzed by the general linear models procedure described in the Statistical Analysis System (Type III SS, 1979). Variables involved in the analysis were school (2), grade (2), relevancy-irrelevancy (2), and trial (2), the last two being within-subject variables. Follow-up mean comparisons were made using the Tukey (A) test (Cichetti, 1972).

The most pertinent finding to the present study was that, irrespective of school, grade, or trial, students' notes contained more task relevant facts ($M=9.61$) than task irrelevant facts ($M=5.12$), and consequently, the main effect of note relevancy was significant, $F(1,86)=127.27, p<.001$. Interactions involving the relevancy variable were not significant.

Next, for each child, the number of relevant facts recorded was divided by the total number of relevant and irrelevant facts included in the notes (trial 2). Children whose proportion scores thus obtained were .85 (e.g., notes containing 11 relevant facts and 2 irrelevant facts) or higher were judged to have allocated their note taking effort exclusively or nearly exclusively to the recording of the relevant facts (highly selective strategy). In contrast, those children whose proportion scores were between .45 and .55 were judged to have used a nonselective strategy copying everything in an indiscriminate manner. After combining the data from the two schools, 27% of the grade 4 and 38% of the grade 8 students used the highly selective note taking strategy (i.e., proportion scores .85 or higher), whereas 33% of the grade 4 and 38% of the grade 8 students used the nonselective strategy. The age-related differences reported here were not statistically reliable. However, these data indicate that about one-third of children recorded information in an indiscriminate manner, although the group scores suggested, as previously described, that students' notes contained more task relevant than task irrelevant items.

Efficiency. The mean efficiency scores for grades 4 and 8 students on each trial are summarized in Table 2. These scores were analyzed by the general linear models procedure involving variables of school (2), grade (2), and trial (2), the last factor being a within-subject variable. Students in School B ($M=4.05$) were significantly more efficient than those in School

		Trial 1		Trial 2	
		Relevancy	Irrelevancy	Relevancy	Irrelevancy
School A	Grade 4 ($N=25$)	6.80	3.44	8.96	5.04
	Grade 8 ($N=25$)	10.84	6.60	10.64	6.84
School B	Grade 4 ($N=20$)	8.85	3.90	9.40	4.55
	Grade 8 ($N=20$)	10.70	5.50	11.00	4.70

TABLE 1

Mean Relevancy and Irrelevancy Scores
for Grades 4 and 8 Students (Study 1)

Note: highest possible relevancy and irrelevancy = 11

TABLE 2

Mean Efficiency Scores for Grade 4 and 8 Students (Study 1)

		Trial 1	Trial 2
School A	Grade 4 ($N=25$)	5.37	5.38
	Grade 8 ($N=25$)	3.52	3.40
School B	Grade 4 ($N=20$)	4.53	5.04
	Grade 8 ($N=20$)	3.34	3.29

Note: A note efficiency score = total number of words in notes/total number of facts in notes. The lower score indicates more efficient note taking by students.

A ($M=4.42$), $F(1,86)=5.47$, $p<.02$. A main effect of grade and an interaction of grade by trial were significant, $F(1,86)=114.10$, $p<.001$ and $F(1,86)=5.26$, $p<.02$, respectively. This significant interaction emerged because grade 4 students' note taking became slightly less efficient with trial (trial 1 $M=4.99$ and trial 2 $M=5.23$) while grade 8 students' note taking became slightly more efficient with trial (trial 1 $M=3.44$ and trial 2 $M=3.35$). On each trial, grade 8 students were significantly more efficient than grade 4 students, $p<.01$. Because there were 22 facts in each story booklet with 111 words, the efficiency score would be 5.32 if students copied the text verbatim. Grade 4 students' efficiency scores suggest, then, that many of these students copied the text word-for-word, as illustrated by Example 1 in Table 3. In contrast, nearly 80% of the grade 8 students utilized point form as illustrated by Example 2.

Although both grades 4 and 8 students copied significantly more relevant than irrelevant facts, only a small proportion of them selected relevant material exclusively. Why did they not copy relevant material exclusively? One reason may be that these students were not able to discriminate relevant from irrelevant material. This, however, is unlikely. When grade 4

TABLE 3

Examples of Study Notes*

Example 1

Many polar bears weigh about 1200 pounds. They eat seals and walruses. Polar bears can run as fast as 25 miles per hour. They live in areas around the Arctic Ocean.

Example 2**

Polar (Bears)
  (live)—Arctic Ocean
  (eat)—seals, walruses
  (run)—25 mph
  (weigh)—1200 pounds

---

*Both of these notes are equally selective, recording only task relevant facts. However, Example 2 is more "efficient" than Example 1, containing fewer words.
**A few grade 8 students deleted the words in parentheses.

---

students in a preliminary study were explicitly asked to select those units of the passage relevant to each of the four questions one at a time, they underlined 85% of the relevant factual data, but no irrelevant material.

Another reason may be that the nonselective strategy is much easier to use than the selective strategy. To use the selective strategy, a child must keep in mind the performance objective during an entire period of note taking and decide whether a particular fact is relevant or irrelevant. Perhaps this may be a difficult task for grade 4 students to carry out. Some of the older students, in contrast, may not show the selective note taking because they now have skills to use point form or to pick up "key words" that enable them to write down everything in the allotted study time. In addition, the tendency to use the nonselective strategy may reflect students' assumption that information not stressed at the outset may nevertheless appear on a later test.

In view of these considerations, Study 2 was conducted. To examine whether grade 4 students have the ability to use the highly selective strategy, half of them were explicitly instructed to write down only task relevant information in their study notes while the remaining children were tested using the same procedure as used in Study 1. Study 1 also showed that grade 4 students were likely to copy information verbatim, although grade 8 students were likely to delete redundant words. This age-related difference in note efficiency may simply reflect age-related differences in usual note taking practices in classrooms rather than in their basic abilities. To determine this possibility, as a last task, all of the grade 4 students were explicitly asked to use point form.

It was argued previously that grade 8 students, because they were efficient at note taking, might have had sufficient time to copy everything, and consequently some of them were not selective in note taking. In other words, older students may show more selective note taking behavior if given a longer passage with more relevant facts to record than the passage used in Study 1. Based on this reasoning, half of the grade 8 students in Study 2 received longer booklets containing more relevant facts while the remaining students received the same booklets used in Study 1.

Finally, a second session was included in which both grades 4 and 8 students were interviewed to assess their ideas about note taking strategies.

Study 2

Method

Participants. The participants were 25 grade 4 (*M* CA=9.9 years) and 26 grade 8 (*M* CA=13.9 years) students drawn from a predominantly middle-class parochial school in Chatham, Ontario. Within each grade, approximately half of the participants were male and half were female. Twelve grade 4 students were randomly assigned to a control condition in which they were tested using the same procedure as used in Study 1, whereas the remaining 13 students were assigned to a condition in which they were explicitly instructed to be selective in their note taking (explicit condition). Fourteen grade 8 students were randomly placed in a control condition in which they received the same reading material used in Study 1 while the remaining 12 grade 8 students were placed in a condition in which they received longer story booklets (longer story condition).

Materials. The story booklets, note taking booklets, and test sheets were identical to those used in Study 1. For the grade 8 students in the longer story condition, however, two sets of longer story booklets were prepared. The reading passage of each of the longer story booklets contained three paragraphs describing major characteristics of three types of bears. Two of these bears were identical to those included in the shorter version of story booklets. While the shorter version contained 11 relevant and 11 irrelevant facts, the longer version contained 18 relevant and 18 irrelevant facts. The test sheet for the longer story condition also consisted of completion items: 36 items assessed children's recall of relevant material and 16 items assessed children's recall of irrelevant material.

Procedure. There were two sessions in Study 2. The characteristics of students' notes were obtained in the first session. Children's ideas about note taking and grade 4 students' ability to use point form were assessed in the second session.

During the first session, participants were tested in groups of 12 to 14 by two experimenters. Each group consisted only of students in the same note taking conditions and grade level. The procedures were identical to those used for Study 1 with the addition to be described. Similar to the first study, students received two story booklets and a note booklet appropriate to their assigned conditions. The experimenter then told students to read stories and make notes, and explained why they would need their notes later. The grade 4 students in the explicit condition were additionally told to pay special attention to the reading material related to the four questions that would appear in a subsequent test. They were instructed to write down only the answers to the four questions. Similar to Study 1, grade 4 students had two 10-minute note taking trials while grade 8 students had two 5-minute note taking trials.

On the following day (i.e., second session), children were interviewed individually to assess their ideas about note taking strategies. They were asked (a) whether they had copied information not asked for by the performance objectives and why, and (b) which method would be better to use, a nonselective strategy copying both relevant and irrelevant facts or a selective strategy copying only relevant information. Grade 4 students were then shown a sample of study notes written in point form (see Example 2, Table 3) and given a new story booklet that contained both relevant and irrelevant facts. They were asked to prepare study notes (where sun bears live, what sun bears eat, how fast sun bears run, and how much sun bears weigh) "in the same way the study notes (Example 2) are done for polar bears."

Scoring. Each child's notes were scored for note relevancy, irrelevancy, and efficiency for each trial separately using identical procedures to those used in Study 1. Because numbers of facts contained in the shorter and longer versions of booklets were different, proportion scores were obtained for the analyses of grade 8 students' data by dividing the note relevancy scores (note irrelevancy scores) by the appropriate number of relevant (irrelevant) facts contained in the story booklets.

Results

Relevancy. The data for Study 2 were analyzed in terms of the general linear models procedure (SAS, 1979). Each of the analyses involved one between-subject variable (grade or group) and two within-subject variables (relevancy-irrelevancy and trial). Because the main interest of the analyses was to determine the presence or absence of a significant main effect of relevancy and a significant interaction of relevancy by grade (or group), only these results will be summarized.

First, grade 4 and grade 8 control groups were compared to examine whether older children were more selective than younger children in their note taking activities. The analysis of the data revealed that the main effect of relevancy was significant, $F(1,24)=21.94$, $p<.001$, as was the interaction of relevancy by grade, $F(1,24)=4.65$, $p<.05$. This significant interaction indicated that grade 8 control children attained significantly higher relevancy scores $(M=10.53)$ than irrelevancy scores $(M=5.50)$, $p<.01$, whereas grade 4 control children showed comparable relevancy $(M=9.67)$ and irrelevancy $(M=7.80)$ scores. Approximately 30% of the grade 8 and 0% of the grade 4 control subjects used the highly selective strategy while 43% of the grade 8 and 67% of the grade 4 students used the nonselective strategy recording both relevant and irrelevant facts equally frequently.

Second, one question raised in Study 2 was "Do grade 4 children have the ability to select task relevant information to the exclusion of irrelevant information?" To examine this question, grade 4 control and explicit groups were compared. Both the main effect of relevance and an interaction of relevancy by group were statistically reliable, $F(1,23)=42.98$ and $F(1,23)=14.42$, respectively, $ps<.001$. The significant interaction reflects the fact that grade 4 students copied significantly more of the relevant $(M=10.85)$ than irrelevant $(M=3.85)$ facts when they were explicitly instructed to be selective (explicit group), but they did not show such selectivity under a spontaneous condition (control group). Under the explicit condition, approximately 70% of the grade 4 students used the highly selective strategy on at least one trial. About 15% of the grade 4 children still used the nonselective strategy even under the explicit condition.

Third, another question raised in Study 2 was "Do grade 8 students show better selectivity by not recording task irrelevant information if the quantity of factual data is increased?" This question was examined by comparing the grade 8 control group with the grade 8 "longer story" group. Because the number of facts contained in the reading materials was different between these two groups, the relevancy and irrelevancy scores were transformed into proportion scores (e.g., number of relevant facts copied in notes divided by the number of relevant facts contained in the text). The analysis revealed that the main effect of relevancy was significant, $F(1,24)=67.33$, $p<.001$; grade 8 students wrote down relevant facts $(M=.96)$ more frequently than irrelevant facts $(M=.41)$. As expected, students in the longer story group copied relatively fewer irrelevant facts $(M=.33)$ than those in the control group $(M=.50)$, although this difference was not statistically reliable. As compared with the grade 8 control subjects (selective strategy users = 30% and nonselective strategy users = 43%), more of the grade 8 students in the longer story group (50%) used the selective strategy and fewer of them (8%) used the nonselective strategy.

Efficiency. Efficiency scores were initially examined by comparing the two control groups (grade 4 vs. grade 8) to determine whether age-related differences in note efficiency observed in Study 1 would be found in Study 2. The analysis involved one between-subject variable (grade) and one within-subject variable (trial). As was found in Study 1, grade 8 students obtained significantly better efficiency scores ($M=3.66$) than grade 4 students ($M=4.51$), $F(1,24)=4.83, p<.05$. In addition, students at both grade levels were significantly more efficient at note taking on trial 2 ($M=3.91$) than on trial 1 ($M=4.19$), $F(1,24)=5.64, p<.03$.

One question raised in Study 2 concerning note efficiency was whether grade 4 children could be induced to attain better efficiency scores by merely showing them an example of highly efficient study notes. To this end, grade 4 students were exposed to such notes at the end of the second session and prepared their own notes regarding a new story (hereafter trial 3). After combining the two groups of grade 4 (control and explicit), mean efficiency scores were 4.52, 4.02, and 3.08 for trials 1, 2, and 3, respectively. The analysis of these scores revealed that grade 4 children obtained significantly better efficiency scores on trial 3 than on trial 1, $p<.05$, indicating that brief exposure to efficient notes was sufficient to improve younger children's note taking behavior. It is also interesting that no grade 4 children recorded any task irrelevant information in their study notes prepared on trial 3, demonstrating that these children had the ability to use the highly selective note taking strategy.

Interview data. One purpose of the interview questions was to find out why children include task irrelevant information in their notes. Thus those children (20 grade 4 and 18 grade 8 students) who recorded irrelevant information were asked why they copied material unrelated to the performance objective (four specific questions). The most frequent answer was that "irrelevant facts" might be asked in the test (81% of grade 4 and 72% of grade 8). Other major reasons were "I had extra time" and "they were important to me."

Another purpose of the interview was to obtain information concerning how children assess the relative usefulness of two strategies, a nonselective strategy copying both relevant and irrelevant information and a selective strategy copying only relevant information. One interesting observation was that grade 4 children in the control group and those in the explicit group tended to give different assessments: 67% of the control children indicated that the nonselective strategy was better while 77% of the explicit children said that the selective strategy was better. This difference was statistically significant, $p<.05$ (Fisher's exact probability test). Like the grade 4 children in the explicit group, a large majority of the grade 8 students (88%) thought that the selective strategy would be more useful.

Many children (67%) who selected the nonselective strategy justified their choice by referring to its benefit for the test situations ("You may need them for the test," "So you don't miss anything for the test"). Some of the students indicated that the non-selective strategy would be better because "you don't have to think about what to write down." Most of the younger students (70%) who selected the selective strategy said that this strategy would be useful because of the time factor during note taking while most of the older students (70%) said that such note taking strategy would facilitate subsequent study.

General Discussion

The present research was conducted to characterize children's notes prepared for a subsequent review for a test. The following two characteristics are of particular interest: (a) the extent to which children selectively record task relevant material in their notes, and (b) the efficiency with which children record factual data.

With regard to selectivity, students' notes prepared under spontaneous situations revealed three major types of note taking strategy users: (a) those who recorded task relevant information to the exclusion of irrelevant information (selective strategy); (b) those who recorded mainly relevant information but also added some irrelevant information (partially selective strategy); and (c) those who copied both relevant and irrelevant information to the same degree (nonselective strategy). As one may expect from previous studies on children's selective attention, (e.g., Hagen & Hale, 1973), more of the grade 4 (67%) than grade 8 (43%) students tended to use the non-selective strategy in Study 2. On the other hand, grade 4 students in Study 2 rarely used the highly selective strategy while about 30% of the grade 8 students did so. However, the present research also has shown that younger children's lack of selectivity is somewhat dependent on schools.

Unlike the findings of Study 2 (67%), the percentage of grade 4 students who used the nonselective strategy was smaller (40%) in Study 1. Furthermore, about 30% of the grade 4 children in that study copied the relevant information exclusively. As a result, grade 4 students in Study 1, just as grade 8 students did, recorded significantly more relevant than irrelevant facts in their notes. However, the present research (3 schools involved) as well as the Tumolo and Kobasigawa (1976) study (2 schools involved) indicated that only a small proportion (40% or less) of grade 7 and 8 students utilized the highly selective strategy, and approximately the same proportion (40%) of these older students used the nonselective strategy, copying both task relevant and irrelevant information to the same degree.

The highly selective strategy examined in the present research calls for children's skills to divide a reading passage into task relevant and irrelevant units in terms of an instructional objective given in the reading booklet. Our findings suggest that many children have the ability to carry out these skills by the time they reach grade 4. About 70% of the grade 4 students selected relevant facts exclusively when they received explicit instructions to do so (Study 2). In addition, no grade 4 children included even a single task irrelevant fact in their notes when they were requested to make notes using point form (Study 2). Given that many children had the ability to use a highly selective strategy, why did they not use that strategy spontaneously? Below we examine four factors leading to children's failure to use the selective strategy.

First, the use of the selective strategy assumes that children attend to the instruction that defines what information is task relevant. The use of the nonselective strategy may be, at least in part, due to the children's failure to attend to the task demand. Second, children may use the nonselective strategy even when they attend to the performance criterion, as some of the grade 4 students indicated in Study 2, simply because they believe that this strategy is easier to use than the highly selective strategy. Third, even if children believe that their note taking should be selective, some of them still use the nonselective strategy and others may use the partially selective strategy, as many of these children think that task irrelevant information might be asked in the test. Fourth, whether children choose the nonselective or partially selective strategy may be affected by another factor, the children's assessment of task difficulty. Thus more of the grade 8 students in Study 2 used the nonselective strategy when the reading material contained 22 pieces of factual information (relatively easy to copy all) than when it contained 36 pieces of factual information (relatively hard to copy all in the allotted time).

With regard to the second characteristic of study notes, this study as well as the Tumolo and Kobisagawa study clearly indicated that grade 8 students obtain consistently better efficiency scores than grade 4 students. In the case of the selective note taking strategy, the major task was to delete task irrelevant material. In the case of note efficiency, the most common strategy was to delete redundant words, especially the names of bears once they had been used as headings or at the beginning of each paragraph. A few grade 8 students obtained still better efficiency scores by deleting the word "bear" completely as the heading "polar" or "brown" is sufficient for indicating the content of the paragraph that follows, or by deleting such verbs as "live" and "weigh" because such phrases as "the Arctic Ocean" and "1200 pounds" are sufficient to imply that these pieces of information are related to "where bears live" and "how much bears weigh" respectively.

It is reasonable to assume that opportunities for note taking and the amount of learning material presented to students should increase with age.

As a result, older students are likely to realize that copying information verbatim from the text would be an inefficient strategy to complete the task within the allotted time. In contrast, teachers of younger children are likely to present information in the form of full sentences and encourage students to copy the presented information verbatim. The observed age-associated differences in the present research in note efficiency probably reflect such age-related differences in note taking practices in school. It was demonstrated in Study 2 that grade 4 students could be induced to improve efficiency scores rather easily.

In summary, the present research shows that many grade 4 children are capable of (a) recording information in their notes selectively according to a performance objective, and (b) deleting redundant words or phrases to increase their note efficiency, although many of these children may not use these skills spontaneously. Initially, children presumably take study notes using a nonselective strategy, copying every piece of information verbatim (absence of both [a] and [b]). Eventually, children's spontaneous note taking shows a shift from this strategy of "copy all verbatim" to a selective but inefficient strategy (absence of [b]) or to a nonselective but efficient strategy (absence of [a]). Because skills to make notes selectively and skills to make notes efficiently are available in grade 4 children if age-appropriate material is used, there is no logical sequence in which these two types of shifts should emerge. The available data, however, indicate that the former type is more likely to appear than the latter type. Although many grade 8 students appear to think that selective note taking is desirable, they also think that task irrelevant information may be asked in the test. As a result, only a small proportion of grade 8 students actually use the highly selective strategy. In contrast, efficient note taking is highly useful whether one uses the nonselective or selective strategy. Perhaps, for this reason, students rarely copy information verbatim by the time they reach grade 8.

The strategy of recording relevant material in notes by deleting unnecessary words and phrases is applicable to a wide variety of learning situations and, therefore, should be taught to young students. However, what is required for a student to do in using this "copy-delete" strategy (Brown, Day, & Jones, 1983) is merely to list important items in point form in the same sequence in which they appear in original materials or in lectures. In certain situations, though, the original material may be condensed more efficiently by combining several pieces of information from different paragraphs. In addition, notes sometimes can be made in a diagramatic format showing various relationships among different key concepts. How readily do young students learn to use these more advanced note taking strategies? Research is needed that includes learning materials that make more "cognitive transformational demands" (Rohwer, 1984) on students than those used in the present studies.

References

Brown, A.L., Bransford, J.D., Ferrara, R.A., & Campione, J.C. (1983). Learning, remembering, and understanding. In P.H. Mussen (Ed.), *Handbook of child psychology: Cognitive development*, Vol. III. New York, NY: Wiley.

Brown, A.L., Day, J.D., & Jones, R.S. (1983). The development of plans for summarizing texts. *Child Development, 54*, 968-979.

Cicchetti, D. (1972). Extension of multiple-range tests to interaction tables in the analysis of variance. *Psychological Bulletin, 77*, 405-408.

Hagen, J.W., & Hale, G.A. (1973). The development of attention in children. In A.D. Pick (Ed.), *Minnesota symposia on child psychology* (Vol. 7). Minneapolis, MN: University of Minnesota Press.

Hartley, J., & Davies, I. (1978). Notetaking: A critical review. *Programmed Learning and Educational Technology, 15*, 207-224.

Howe, M.F.A. (1970). Using students' notes to examine the role of the individual learner in acquiring meaningful subject matter. *Journal of Educational Research, 64*, 61-63.

Howe, M.F.A. (1974). The utility of taking notes as an aid to learning. *Educational Research, 16*, 222-227.

Rohwer, W.D. (1984). An invitation to an educational psychology of studying. *Educational Psychologist, 19*, 1-14.

SAS user's guide. (1979). Cary, NC: SAS Institute.

Spache, G.D. (1953). A new readability formula for primary grade reading materials. *The Elementary School Journal, 53*, 410-413.

Tumolo, P.J., & Kobasigawa, A. (1976). *Note-taking behavior of primary school children*. Unpublished manuscript, University of Windsor.

Imaginal Elaborations of Illustrations to Facilitate Fact Learning: Creating Memories of Prince Edward Island

Michael Pressley and Mary Ellen Brewster
University of Western Ontario

Canadian students in grades 5 and 6 studied facts about the 10 Canadian provinces (e.g. Many very good plays are put on in Prince Edward Island). At study, each fact was accompanied by a picture of a stereotypical setting in the province (e.g. a picture of the lush farmland in Prince Edward Island). Half the subjects were instructed to learn by imagining the fact as stated occurring in the depiction (e.g. very good plays being produced in the lush farmland setting); half were told only to try hard to remember that the fact occurred in the particular province. The imagery instruction was effective, but only when children had previously mastered associations between the provinces and the pictures of the provinces. Naturalistically occurring pictures can be used by grade-school children to create elaborative images that facilitate acquisition of confusing facts, but only if children first know what the illustrations represent.

*   *   *

CHILDREN ARE OFTEN CALLED UPON TO LEARN FACTUAL INFORMATION, including scientific facts (e.g. characteristics of chemical elements), biographical content, and information about particular places. These tasks can be difficult even for proficient adult learners (e.g. Bransford, Stein, Vye, Franks, Auble, Mezynski & Perfetto, 1982; Pressley, Symons, McDaniel, Snyder, & Turnure, 1988), let alone children, who were studied in the investigation reported here. Although we do not agree with extreme arguments that even more fact learning should be presented in school (e.g. Hirsch, 1987; Ravitch & Finn, 1987), the frequency of fact learning, and the challenges it poses, combine to fuel the search for mechanisms that promote learning of facts. Our position is that if children are going to be required to learn facts, they should be armed with procedures that permit acquisition of factual content. To date, most procedures that have been studied are various forms of elaboration (Pressley, 1982; Pressley, Johnson & Symons, 1987).

This research was funded by a grant to the first author from the Natural Sciences and Engineering Research Council of Canada.

For instance, Bransford and his associates demonstrated that children experience difficulty when attempting to learn sentences containing mutually interfering pieces of information, such as the following:

The hungry man got into the car.
The strong man helped the woman.
The brave man ran into the house.

When children are taught to elaborate these sentences so that it makes clear why each particular man performed the action that he performed (e.g. The hungry man got into the car *to go to the restaurant*; The brave man ran into the house *that was on fire to save the baby*), learning is facilitated. The problem with this approach, however, is that it requires that the learner possess a knowledge base that is extensive enough to permit generation of precise elaborations. This is a serious limitation given that children are often required to learn information about domains in which they have little prior experience or knowledge.

An alternative method of elaboration, one that can be used when prior knowledge is low, is based on keyword mnemonics. For instance, Levin, Shriberg, and Berry (1983) presented grade-8 students with passages describing the attributes of fictitious towns (i.e. towns about which children could not possess prior knowledge). One of their towns was Fostoria which was noted for abundant natural resources, advances in technology, considerable wealth, and a growing population. Students were then provided a word that was acoustically similar to the town name (this was the keyword), a word that represented a well-known concept. Thus, for Fostoria, the keyword was frost. The students then generated an interactive scene in which frost covered natural resources, technological advances, wealth, and the growing population. Doing so promoted later recall of the four attributes given the town name as a cue. In general, the available data support the conclusion that the keyword strategy can be taught during late childhood and early adolescence, assuming that good keywords are provided (e.g. Peters & Levin, 1986).

The rub is that some people (e.g. Sternberg, 1987) are turned off by the 'unnaturalness' of this method. Images based on keywords are considered unnatural in the sense that keywords often refer to concepts that are not meaningfully related to the to-be-remembered material. For example, frost has nothing to do with any of the attributes of the town Fostoria. In fact, frost might never occur in Fostoria if it were a town in southern Florida or some other semitropical climate. Modern critics such as Sternberg are in good company in shying away from mnemonic methods, even as they acknowledge the effectiveness of keyword-like approaches—Erasmus, Descartes, Galileo, and Kepler voiced similar arguments (e.g. Bolles, 1988, Chapter 1). Those who support the teaching of 'artificial' mnemonic methods also have respectable intellectual bedfellows, however, including

Cicero (Herrmann & Chaffin, 1988), Fenaigle (1813), and Miller, Galanter and Pribram (1960)—see Desrochers and Begg (1987) for more extensive commentary. Moreover, keyword methods are natural in another sense of the word—efficient associate learners invariably use them on their own to mediate fact learning (e.g. Beuhring & Kee, 1987; Pressley, 1982; Pressley, Levin & McDaniel, 1987; Schneider & Pressley, 1989, Chapter 6). In short, the argument that keyword-like mnemonic methods are unnatural is controversial at best, as eloquently summarized by an anonymous reviewer for this journal [*Applied Cognitive Psychology*]: "How do we decide what is natural or unnatural for the mind or cognitive system to do? Are mental operations that require a great deal of cognitive control necessarily unnatural? Are mental operations that seem more complex than the information to be learned necessarily unnatural? I am not sure."

Even so, the concerns raised by both modern and ancient critics of keyword-like interventions motivate the investigation of elaboration procedures that (a) can be applied when learners have a low knowledge base but (b) do not depend on use of keywords. One such procedure was evaluated here in the context of a particular fact-learning task, acquisition of information about Canadian provinces by Canadian grade-school children.

Consistent with other work on elaboration, we assumed that it would be good first to represent the unfamiliar concepts (i.e. the provinces) correctly, and thus, provided potential pegs (e.g. Paivio, 1971) that could be used to elaborate the to-be-learned information. This was accomplished by presenting a stereotypical picture for each province (e.g. a scene from Banff Park in Alberta) Half the subjects mastered associations between these pictures and the provincial names so that they could recall each province given its picture. The remaining subjects were provided the pictures when they were presented facts to learn, although they had not mastered the picture-province associations. Within the picture-province association mastery and non-mastery conditions, half the subjects were instructed to use an imagery strategy to learn the facts, and half were instructed only to try hard to learn the associations. The imagery instruction was to construct an internal image with the to-be-learned fact integrated into the image depicted in the picture associated with the province. Thus, to learn that "Very good plays are put on in Prince Edward Island," subjects were to imagine plays being produced in the lush farming scene depicted in the illustration that represented Prince Edward Island. Presumably, when asked later about where good plays are produced, the scene with the lush fields would be recalled. If it were, and the field scene were clearly associated with Prince Edward Island (as it would be for students who had mastered the picture-province associations), then the learner should recall the name of the province.

Method

Subjects

The subjects were 66 students (32 females, 34 males) enrolled in grades 5 (mean age 10 years 7 months; range = 9 years 8 months to 11 years 5 months) and 6 (mean age 11 years 6 months; range = 10 years 11 months to 12 years 8 months) in public schools serving a medium-sized Canadian city. Approximately half of the subjects were randomly assigned to the imagery-strategy training condition; the remaining subjects were assigned to the control condition. Within the imagery and control conditions, half the subjects were randomly assigned to master associations between provincial names and pictures depicting stereotypical scenes associated with the provinces (mastery condition); the remaining subjects (non-mastery condition) completed an exercise designed to activate the names of the provinces without exposure to accompanying pictures.

Although these students had studied the names of the provinces in previous classwork, they had not received instruction about the geography or history of the provinces. Discussion with school officials and informal pilot testing confirmed that the children had very little prior knowledge about the distinctive physical characteristics or cultural features of the Canadian provinces.[1]

Materials

Thirty facts about the ten provinces (three per province) were obtained from *The Canadian Encyclopedia* (Marsh, 1985). These were the to-be-learned materials in the study. Two facts about each of the two territories (Yukon, Northwest Territories) served as examples. All of these items are presented in the Appendix.[2]

Each fact was typed on a separate piece of paper and placed in a three-ringed binder. Each fact was accompanied by a picture of a stereotypical scene for the province (placed facing the fact in the ring binder, so that when the binder was open, both the fact and the picture were visible). The same picture was used for each of the three facts for a province. The pictures were selected from calendars, government of Canada publications, and other picture books. The two experimenters agreed that the scenes were distinct from one another.

An extra unbound set of the twelve pictures (ten for provinces, two for territories) was used in the picture-province mastery condition.

A second binder held a set of fill-in-the-blank exercises for the non-mastery condition. These required non-mastery subjects to produce the full names of provinces, given only some of the letters in their proper positions and the remaining letters represented as blanks.

A tape recorder played a tape containing the facts about the provinces (one fact every 15 seconds). There were two different versions, one presenting the facts proceeding from the front to the back of the binder, and the other from the back to the front of the binder. Half the subjects in each condition heard each of the two orders.

Procedure

On entering the testing room, each subject was given a list of names of the ten provinces and two territories. Subjects were asked to read this list aloud as a warm-up task. Subjects then completed one of two different tasks. Subjects in the picture-province mastery condition were shown the set of twelve pictures representing each of the provinces. They were instructed as follows:

> I have some pictures here. There is one picture from each of the Canadian provinces. I am going to show you each picture and tell you where it was taken. I want you to try to remember which picture goes with which province. After I have shown you all the pictures once, I will hold them up again and I want you to tell me the province that the picture represents.

The experimenter kept track of whether each picture was identified correctly or incorrectly, and gave the subject immediate feedback after each response. If incorrect, subjects were told the correct province. After each test trial the experimenter went over all the pictures that had been missed. Then the testing with feedback process was repeated using all twelve pictures until the subject could correctly identify all the pictures on a single test trial. Time to learn the picture-province associations was recorded with a maximum time limit of 12 minutes.

Subjects in the non-mastery condition were required to complete province-name exercises during the time corresponding to picture-province learning in the mastery condition. They were instructed as follows:

> Now we will do some exercises where you must recall the name of each province. I'll show you the name of the province, given only some of the letters, and you have to tell me the whole name of the province.

There were five pages of exercises. Each page included twelve items, one for each of the province and territory names. Subjects responded aloud to each item. The experimenter recorded the correctness of responses and provided immediate feedback about the adequacy of these responses. When subjects were incorrect they were told the province name. Time on this task was determined by the amount of time taken by a yoked subject in the corresponding picture-province-association-mastery condition. That is, the time taken by an imagery/mastery subject to learn the picture-province associations determined how long an imagery/non-mastery subject spent working on the name completion task.

Following either picture-province mastery or the province-name completion task, subjects participated in one of two instructional conditions, either imagery-training or a no-strategy-control condition. The subjects in both conditions were first informed that they should try to learn the facts about the provinces, so that, when presented a fact later, they could recall the appropriate province name.

Imagery subjects were informed that they would be taught a special method to help them remember the facts. The subsequent imagery instructions varied slightly as a function of whether the subject was in the mastery or non-mastery condition. Imagery subjects who had mastered the picture-province associations were instructed as follows:

> I am going to teach you a special method to help you remember the facts. It will involve using the pictures that you already learned about.

Imagery subjects in the non-mastery condition were told:

> I am going to teach you a special method to help you remember the facts. It will involve using pictures of each province.

Four instructional examples (two facts for each of the two territories) were presented in the same fashion to all imagery subjects. While viewing the fact, "Moose is a favourite food in the Yukon," and the picture of a Yukon scene, imagery subjects were instructed to do the following:

> The way to remember that moose is a favourite food in the Yukon is to make up a picture in your head showing people eating moose in this scene from the Yukon. Can you do that? Can you imagine people eating moose in this setting? Perhaps you see them hunting for moose and then having a moose barbeque. What is your image like?

After presentation of the four examples the imagery subjects were given a practice test over the four practice items. Just before taking this practice test they were reminded to think back to their images in order to remember the territory corresponding to the fact. Following this practice test, subjects were told that thirty items would be presented, three for each of the ten provinces. They were instructed to use the pictures accompanying each fact to construct an image representing the fact.

Control subjects were provided no instruction about the use of strategies. They were told instead that they were to try hard to remember the facts about each of the provinces. For instance, when they were presented the sample item, "Moose is a favourite food in the Yukon," and the accompanying picture, they were instructed as follows:

> Try hard to remember that moose is a favourite food in the Yukon. Can you do that? Here is the/a picture of the Yukon. Try hard to remember this fact about the Yukon.

Following presentation of the four examples, control subjects were given the practice test. Before this test they were instructed to try hard to answer each of the questions. Following the practice test, control subjects were informed that the thirty facts would be presented, and they were reminded that they should try hard to remember each one.

The thirty facts were presented over a tape-recorder in either the forward or backward order (i.e. the experimenter paged from front to back or back to front) at a rate of 15 seconds per item. There were three 15-second breaks in the presentation to permit the experimenter to remind the subjects of their learning instructions (i.e. to make an image for each fact or to try hard to learn each fact). After all of the facts had been presented, a test was given in which subjects were required to respond with the provincial names when given the facts. Imagery subjects were instructed at this point to "Think back to the images you made," and control subjects were told to "Try hard to remember the answer."

Following the test, the experimenter selected five facts from the list. Imagery subjects were asked to describe their images for each of these facts. Control subjects were asked what they did to try to learn each fact. All answers were recorded on audiotape for later transcription.

Results and Discussion

The first learning task in the picture-province association mastery conditions was to learn the twelve associations so that each picture reliably evoked recall of the appropriate province. Because different children took different amounts of time on various phases of this task (e.g. time to respond to a probe, number of incorrect items that was repeated during a test trial), the best metric for amount of study to mastery was time spent learning picture-province associations (12 minutes maximum) rather than other measures (e.g. number of learning trials). Imagery/mastery subjects required 6 minutes 16 seconds on average (SD=2 minutes 39 seconds) compared to 7 minutes 8 seconds (SD=3 minutes 47 seconds) in the control condition, a non-significant difference $t(31)=0.78, p>.40$ (e.g. Kirk, 1982). That learning the stereotypical picture-province associations was not particularly rapid (averaging more than 30 seconds for each association) reinforced our belief that the children's prior knowledge about the provinces was low.

The mean number of provinces recalled in each condition are recorded in Table 1. These means were analysed with a set of four planned comparisons, one for each of the four unconfounded pairwise comparisons that are possible given the design used here. Each comparison was conducted at a Type 1 error rate less than .0375 (cutoff $t=2.13$). Thus, the overall error rate ($p<.15$) was comparable to the overall rate had an alternative 2×2

Table 1. Mean recall (and standard deviations for recall) of provinces given facts

Instructional condition	Picture–province associations	
	Mastered	Not mastered
Imagery	21.24 (5.53) $n = 17$	14.00 (7.36) $n = 17$
Control	16.50 (6.35) $n = 16$	13.56 (4.82) $n = 16$

$MS_E = 37.247$.

analysis of variance been conducted with Type 1 rate of .05 per effect (Kirk, 1982).

When no picture-province associations were mastered, the difference between the two instructional conditions were not significant, $t(62)=0.21$. When picture-province associations were mastered, recall in the imagery condition exceeded recall in the control condition, $t(62)=2.23$. Within the control condition the difference in performance between mastery and non-mastery subjects was not significant, $t(62)=1.36$. The corresponding difference in the imagery instructional condition was significant, $t(62)=3.46$. In short, the imagery instruction was effective only if picture-province associations were mastered previously. Mastery of the picture-province associations alone, however, was not sufficient to increase learning of facts.

The post-test interview suggested that the imagery subjects could execute the strategy. They reported doing so for 90 per cent of the probed items. Imagery subjects reported making an elaboration that did not involve imagery for 1.8 per cent of the probes, and reported no mediators for the remaining 8.2 per cent of the probes. Control subjects reported memorizing by rote 55 per cent of the time (47.5 per cent in the control/mastery condition; 62.5 per cent in the control/non-mastery cell). There were some reports of not very meaningful associations between physical features depicted in the illustrations and physical attributes of objects mentioned in the to-be-learned facts (e.g. The boats in the picture are white and so is cauliflower). These occurred 37.5 per cent of the time in the control/mastery condition and 17.5 per cent of the time in the control/non-mastery condition. More meaningful elaborations of the facts (e.g. I have friends that went to see a play in Prince Edward Island) were reported 15 per cent of the time in the control/mastery condition and 20 per cent of the time in the control/non-mastery condition. In short, imagery subjects reported following the directions as given; control subjects reported meaningful elaborations less than one-fifth of the time, a result consistent with the general failure of grade-school children to use elaboration strategies that might facilitate their learning (e.g. Beuhring and Kee, 1987).

Although there are many demonstrations that instructions to construct interactive mental images are effective with 10–12-year-olds (Pressley,

1982), such directions were not sufficient to promote learning in this study (i.e. there was no performance gain in the imagery/non-mastery condition relative to control performance). Interactive imagery instructions cannot be effective if the cue provided at testing cannot re-integrate an image that leads to recall of the correct answer (e.g. Anderson, Goetz, Pichert & Halff, 1977; Desrochers & Begg, 1987). This condition probably held only in the imagery/mastery condition of this experiment.

Imagery/mastery subjects presumably constructed an image for each fact using the picture of the province that was in front of them. At testing, mention of the fact should have elicited a concrete image associated with the fact, one that had also been activated during encoding of the fact (e.g. when asked about where plays were produced, the image of a play should have followed, presumably the same image of a play that was activated at study). Because the play had been imagined in interaction with the provincial setting in the picture, the stereotypical scene of the province should also have been elicited by the question about the play (e.g. Bower, 1970). That is, the image of the play would be contained in a larger image based on the context of the stereotypical scene of Prince Edward Island. Since the picture-province associations were mastered in this condition, ready retrieval of the province name would be possible once this interactive image was recovered.

The most likely explanation for the lower performance in the imagery/non-mastery condition (compared to the imagery/mastery condition) was that children in that condition were not able to retrieve the correct provincial name, even if they recalled the interactive image (i.e. the stereotypical image-province association was not well established in these learners). The most likely explanation for the lower performance in the control/mastery condition is that even if the question about a play elicited an image of a play, this image would not be embedded in a larger scene including the stereotypical depiction of the province (since no such interactive image would have been constructed at encoding). Thus, there would be no imagery-based route to the province name.

We believe that there are clear messages here for those who wish to teach students to use imaginal coding to learn factual material. To-be-learned facts are often accompanied by illustrations (e.g. pictures in content-area textbooks). Such pictures rarely depict all of the to-be-acquired factual content, however. The usual conclusion is that such pictures do not improve learning of facts that are not depicted (e.g. Levie, 1987). The data presented here suggest that such pictures have the potential to do so, however, if two conditions hold. (1) Students should know the picture content well enough that the pictures reliably evoke verbal recall of what they represent (e.g. in this experiment, ready recall of provinces given the pictures). Although these associations were taught explicitly here, we suspect that useful associations to pictures are often created as part of ongoing instruction. For instance, a key element in elementary geography instruction seems to be presentation of pictures depicting the landscapes of regions that are studied. We suspect that it does not matter how picture-label associations are established, just so long as the learner has mastered them. (2) When they are mastered, the pictures can be used in the construction of internal interactive images that encode non-depicted information (e.g. facts about provinces) that relate to material referred to by the illustrations (e.g. the provinces). This two-step elaborative method could be adapted to many other domains, and studies of imaginal elaboration of other types of pictures (e.g. depictions of historical events and of scientific content) should be conducted.

Because imaginal elaboration of illustrations does not require use of mnemonic elements that may not be semantically consistent with the content being learned (e.g. keywords), it might be appealing to those who are critical of other elaborative approaches to learning. Nonetheless, we suspect that imaginal elaboration of illustrations would be most effective as one of a number of elaborative strategies possessed by a learner. Students can be taught elaborative strategies that exploit natural associations and meaningful connections between to-be-learned content and prior knowledge (e.g. Pressley *et al.*, 1988) as well as keyword-type mnemonic approaches that can be applied when meaningful associations are not obvious. See Scruggs and Mastropieri (in press) for a initial study of how to coordinate use of several types of elaborative activities simultaneously. That new elaborative procedures are still being devised (albeit based in part on well-known mechanisms—concrete pegs in the present case; e.g. Paivio, 1971) and that work on how to coordinate various elaborative strategies is only beginning (Mastropieri & Scruggs, 1988; Scruggs & Mastropieri, in press) makes it obvious that a lot of research will be required before the power and flexibility of elaborative techniques is understood well.

Appendix

Sample items (front-to-back order)
Moose is a favourite food in the Yukon.
There are a lot of grizzly bears in the Yukon.
Copper was first used in Canada in the Northwest Territories.
There is only one large bakery in the Northwest Territories.

To-be-learned items (front-to-back order)
The biggest geese in Canada are in Manitoba.
Canada's first apple trees were in Nova Scotia.
There is more coal in Alberta than in any other province.

A lot of grapes are grown in British Columbia.
Canada's first museum was in Ontario.

(15-second pause to remind subject of directions)

Lots of blueberries are grown in New Brunswick.
Almost everyone in Saskatchewan has a job.
Newfoundland was the first province to be mapped.
Prince Edward Island is famous for its potatoes.
Canada's first astronaut was born in Quebec.
Many famous authors of books live in Manitoba.
Canada's first dentist was in Nova Scotia.
A lot of buffalo live in Alberta.
Canada's first judo experts were in British Columbia.
Canada's first soccer game was in Ontario.

(15-second pause to remind subject of directions)

Many foxes are raised in New Brunswick.
The hottest day in history was in Saskatchewan.
The taxes in Newfoundland are very high.
Many very good plays are put on in Prince Edward Island.
Canada's first cartoonist lived in Quebec.
The worst flood in Canadian history was in Manitoba.
Canada's first magazine was published in Nova Scotia.
A lot of buildings burn down in Alberta.
The worst Canadian earthquake was in British Columbia.
A lot of cauliflower is grown in Ontario.

(15-second pause to remind subject of directions)

The worst pest in New Brunswick is a type of moth.
A lot of dinosaur bones have been found in Saskatchewan.
Newfoundland has a very famous airport.
Many people from England settled in Prince Edward Island.
The first school for deaf children was in Quebec.

Notes

1   As part of the investigation, we had considered a prior-knowledge-activation condition. In anticipation of this condition a separate sample of grade-5 and -6 children at the school were provided each fact and its corresponding provincial picture. They were asked to explain why it would make sense that the fact occurred in the province where it occurred. Children could construct adequate answers only 19 per cent of the time, which discouraged further development of the treatment. In this context this pilot finding is additional evidence that the grade-5 and -6 students were low in prior knowledge about the provinces.

2   Most of the facts used here had been employed in a study of adult learning (Pressley et al., 1988). As part of that study, Canadian university students were asked to match each fact with its province, before they were provided exposure to the province-fact

associations. Performance on this task was at near-chance levels, making clear that even Canadian adults do not have the facts used in this study encoded into long-term memory.

References

Anderson, R.C., Goetz, E.T., Pichert, H.M., and Halff, H.M. (1977). Two faces of the conceptual peg hypothesis. *Journal of Experimental Psychology: Human Learning and Memory, 3,* 142-149.

Beuhring, T., and Kee, D.W. (1987). Elaborative propensities during adolescence: The relationships among memory knowledge, strategy behavior, and memory performance. In M.A. McDaniel and M. Pressley (eds.), *Imagery and related mnemonic processes: theories, individual differences, and applications,* pp. 257-273. New York, NY and Berlin, Germany: Springer-Verlag.

Bolles, E.B. (1988). *Remembering and forgetting: inquiries into the nature of memory.* New York, NY: Walker & Co.

Bower, G.H. (1970). Imagery as a relational organizer in associative learning. *Journal of Verbal Learning and Verbal Behavior, 9,* 529-533.

Bransford, J.D., Stein, B.S., Vye, N.J., Franks, J.J., Auble, P.M., Mezynski, K.J., and Perfetto, G.A. (1982). Differences in approaches to learning: an overview. *Journal of Experimental Psychology: General, 111,* 390-398.

Desrochers, A., and Begg, I. (1987). A theoretical account of encoding and retrieval processes in the use of imagery-based mnemonic techniques: The special case of the keyword method. In M.A. McDaniel and M. Pressley (eds.), *Imagery and related mnemonic processes: theories, individual differences, and applications,* pp. 56-77. New York, NY and Berlin, Germany: Springer-Verlag.

Fenaigle, G. von. (1813). *The new art of memory.* London, UK: Sherwood, Neely & Jones.

Herrmann, D.J., and Chaffin, R. (eds.). (1988). *Memory in historical perspective: the literature before Ebbinghaus.* New York, NY and Berlin, Germany: Springer-Verlag.

Hirsch, E.D. Jr. (1987). *Cultural literacy: what every American needs to know.* New York, NY: Houghton Mifflin.

Kirk, R.E. (1982). *Experimental design,* 2nd edn. Belmont, CA: Brooks/Cole.

Levie, W.H. (1987). In D.M. Willows and H.A. Houghton (eds.), *The psychology of illustration,* Vol. 1: *Basic research,* pp. 1-50, New York, NY, and Berlin, Germany: Springer-Verlag.

Levin, J.R., Shriberg, L.K., and Berry, J.K. (1983). A concrete strategy for remembering abstract prose. *American Educational Research Journal, 20,* 277-290.

Marsh, J. (ed.). (1985). *The Canadian encyclopedia.* Edmonton, AB: Hurtig.

Mastropieri, M.A., and Scruggs, T.E. (1988). *Increasing the content area of learning disabled students: research implementation.* Technical report. West Lafayette, IN: Purdue University, Department of Special Education.

Miller, G.A., Galanter, E., and Pribram, K.H. (1960). *Plans and the structure of behavior.* New York, NY: Holt, Rinehart & Winston.

Paivio, A. (1971). *Imagery and verbal processes.* New York, NY: Holt, Rinehart & Winston.

Peters, E.E., and Levin, J.R. (1986). Effects of mnemonic strategy on good and poor readers' prose recall. *Reading Research Quarterly, 21,* 179-192.

Pressley, M. (1982). Elaboration and memory development. *Child Development, 53,* 296-309.

Pressley, M., Johnson, C.J., and Symons, S. (1987). Elaborating to learn and learning to elaborate. *Journal of Learning Disabilities, 20*, 76-91.

Pressley, M., Levin, J.R., and McDaniel, M.A. (1987). Remembering versus inferring what a word means: Mnemonic versus contextual approaches. In M. McKeown and M.E. Curtis (eds.), *The nature of vocabulary acquisition*, pp. 107-127. Hillsdale, NJ: Lawrence Erlbaum.

Pressley, M., Symons, S., McDaniel, M.A., Snyder, B.L., and Turnure, J.E. (1988). Elaborative interrogation facilitates acquisition of confusing facts. *Journal of Educational Psychology, 80*, 268-278.

Ravitch, D., and Finn, C.E., Jr. (1987). *What do our 17-year-olds know?: A report of the first national assessment of history and literature*. New York, NY: Harper & Row.

Schneider, W., and Pressley, M. (1989). *Memory development between 2 and 20*. New York, NY, and Berlin, Germany: Springer-Verlag.

Scruggs, T.E., and Mastropieri, M.A. (1988). Reconstructive elaborations: a model for content area learning. *American Educational Research Journal*. (In press.)

Sternberg, R.J. (1987). Most vocabulary is learned from context. In M.G. McKeown and M.E. Curtis (eds.), *The nature of vocabulary acquisition*, pp. 107-127. Hillsdale, NJ: Lawrence Erlbaum.

The Effects of Different Types of Organizers on Students' Learning From Text

Aldona M. Kloster
Burnaby School District, Burnaby, British Columbia
Philip H. Winne
Instructional Psychology Research Group, Simon Fraser University

Prior to reading a text about computer crime and prevention, eighth graders read one of four types of operationally defined organizers: concept, analogy, outline, or dummy. While reading the text, students matched paragraphs of the text to numbered sections in the organizer, leaving a trace that was scored to reflect their actual use of the organizer while reading the text. Multiple regression analyses of multiple-choice and short answer achievement measures showed no main effects of type of organizer. However, students in true advance organizer groups (concept and analogy) who were able to use the organizers effectively, as indicated by the higher trace scores, outperformed students in the outline and dummy groups. Analysis of trace scores revealed that students had difficulty connecting information in the concept and analogy organizers to the text. These findings indicate that simply presenting a genuine advance organizer does not guarantee that students will use it effectively. However, when students did use an advance organizer effectively, achievement increased slightly.

* * *

TWENTY YEARS OF RESEARCH ON ADVANCE ORGANIZERS HAVE PRODUCED inconsistent findings. Some studies indicate that advance organizers facilitate learning; others do not (see Barnes & Clawson, 1975; Hartley & Davis, 1976; Mayer, 1979b). In general, advance organizers do not show effects when measures of general or overall learning are used. However, advance organizers influence qualitative features of learning. Specifically, organizers (a) promote retention of conceptual but not factual details (Mayer & Bromage, 1980), (b) enhance problem solving that involves transfer (Mayer, 1980), but (c) may retard the recall of specific details (Mayer, 1980). Several studies also have examined aptitude-organizer interactions, but results are inconsistent. Advance organizers have positive

---

This article is based on the first author's master's thesis, supervised by the second author and Tom O'Shea.

effects for inexperienced or low-ability learners relative to higher ability learners (Mayer, 1979b, 1980) and vice versa (Derry, 1984).

Two recurring problems plague previous research on advance organizers. First, operational definitions for organizers, if provided, are imprecise (see Hartley & Davis, 1976). Second, only a subset of studies (Derry, 1984; Mayer, 1976) specifically instruct learners to use the advance organizer. *No* study has verified operationally that students actually link information in the advance organizer to new material during study. Our experiment addresses both shortcomings. We operationally define different types of advance organizers and relate their effects to observed traces (Winne, 1982, 1983b) of students' assimilation processes (Mayer, 1979a) while they study new information.

Operational Information in Advance Organizers

Advance organizers are theorized to promote learning either because they cue students to assemble links between new information and more abstract, general and inclusive information that the students already know (Ausubel, 1963); or because an advance organizer supplies a learner with a new cognitive structure so that new information can be connected to it (Mayer & Greeno, 1972). Because both explanations emphasize aspects of cognitive structure, we operationalized different types of organizers in structural terms, specifically, hierarchical structure.

Figure 1 represents a hierarchical structure for some hypothetical content. In the figure, X represents an abstract, general concept. The numbers 1, 2, and 3 are features or chunks of information specifically about X. Concepts A, B, and C are specific items relating to X. Concepts a_m, a_n, a_o, a_p are yet more specific elaborations of concept A, and so on.

In this example, we define the information about concept A to be *congruent* with information about concept B because both the amount and the organization of information about concept A are identical to those for concept B. In contrast, information about concept C is not congruent to A or to B. In the following discussion, let A and its subordinate parts (a_m, a_n, a_o, a_p) represent new information that a student is to learn. Furthermore, assume the learner already knows X and has some prior knowledge about B.

Different types of organizers can be classified by their location in this map. Information about concept X could serve as an expository advance organizer (Ausubel, 1963). We label this expository organizer *concept*—it presents information more abstract and higher in the hierarchy than information to be learned (i.e., concept A in Figure 1). Mayer's (1979b) assimilation theory suggests that a learner provided with a concept organizer would make vertical external connections to link information about X with new information about A. An "analogy" organizer is defined here as information that is congruent to material to be learned, which is about a different topic, and therefore, which the learner can map onto the new information part for part (e.g., see Holyoak, 1984, Table 5.2). In Figure 1, because the learner is already familiar with concept B, B and its parts could serve as an analogy organizer. To use an analogy organizer, a learner would make predominantly specific lateral external connections between the new material about A (e.g., a_m) and its analog information in B (i.e., b_g). The analogy organizer operationalizes some features of Ausubel's comparative organizer (Ausubel, 1963) and Mayer's concrete model (Mayer, 1975), but is not identical to either.

An "outline" organizer consists of labels for several levels in the hierarchical map of new material to be learned. An outline does not fit Ausubel's definition of a "true" advance organizer because it does not draw on prior knowledge. Instead, when students use an outline, they assemble (Winne, 1985) new labels in the outline with new elaborations in the text to produce what Mayer and Greeno (1972) labeled internal connections. In terms of Figure 1, the learner would make vertical internal connections between labels in the outline (e.g., labels for a_m, a_n, a_o, and a_p) and the new material (all of A and its constituent parts). A "dummy" introduction can not meaningfully be assembled with the new material to create either internal or external connections. Therefore, information in a dummy introduction theoretically cannot help the learner organize or learn the new material. For ease of presentation, we use the general label "organizers" to refer to all four introductory aids, recognizing that the outline and the dummy are false organizers according to Ausubel and others.

In this study, students read a text about computer-related crimes that had been developed and mapped as a hierarchy (like Figure 1) based on Armbruster and Anderson's (1984) procedure. Four types of advance organizers—concept, analogy, outline, and dummy—were developed to conform to the operational definitions just provided.

Operationalizing Students' Use of Advance Organizers

Advance organizers are theorized to promote learning because they cue students to assemble connections between new information and information they already know. Cues may help students learn only when four conditions apply: students (a) attend to a cue, (b) correctly perceive which cognitive operation(s) have been cued, (c) are able to carry out the cognitive operation(s), and (d) are motivated to perform the cognitive tasks that result in learning (Winne, 1982). To test hypotheses about whether cues such as advance organizers affect learning, data are needed to verify that all four conditions hold. Such data are called traces (Winne, 1982, 1983b) because they "trace" in observable form the unobservable cognitive operations that students carry out while learning.

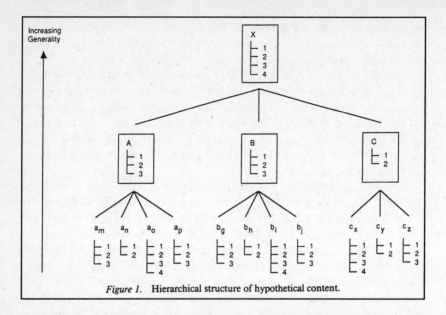

Figure 1. Hierarchical structure of hypothetical content.

In this study, we traced students' use of information in organizers by having them write codes for sections of the organizer next to paragraphs in the text they read. Students' traces could be scored to verify how well they connected information in the text to information in the organizer.

Method

Participants

The population available to us was 227 students from all eighth-grade mathematics classes in one high school in Burnaby, British Columbia. Because mathematics is a required subject for all students in this grade, choice of these classes provided a sample that represented the school's population. Students participated with permission from the school board and parents. The final sample was 199 students for whom data were complete. The 28 students whose data were not included were either absent for one of the days when the study was done or spoiled at least one of the evaluation instruments.

Materials

For each task in the experiment, students were given written instructions first describing what they had to do and then illustrating those operations. Classroom teachers clarified instructions for students who required extra help.

Text. The material to be learned was a 2,000-word article titled "Computer Crime and Prevention." The article was written to be at a seventh-eighth-grade reading level. It described methods and examples of computer crimes, problems in controlling such crimes, and methods for preventing them. Information in the article was organized hierarchically starting with broad general concepts such as "theft of software by thieves can be prevented" (parallel to A in Figure 1) and moving to very specific technical details such as "programs can be locked by writing extra information between tracks" (corresponding to features that would appear under a_p in Figure 1). The structure of the text at the global level was a collection of descriptions, with comparative and causal structures at lower levels (see Meyer & Freedle, 1984). The 30 paragraphs in the text were presented to students in a booklet of eight double-spaced pages. A box (to be used to code the paragraph) was placed in the right margin at the end of each paragraph.

Organizers. Four different organizers were developed: a concept, an analogy, an outline, and a dummy introduction. The concept, analogy and dummy organizers were presented on one page and consisted of 4 paragraphs numbered in sequence 1–4. The outline was presented on one page and each main section was numbered 1–4.

The concept organizer described the idea that new inventions give rise to new abuses, which in turn give rise to new methods for controlling those abuses. No specific computer-related technology, invention, or crime was named in the concept organizer. It referred only to "inventions" and "methods" for dealing with problems that arise as new inventions are introduced into society. This organizer is equivalent to X in Figure 1.

The analogy described misuses of office photocopiers and efforts to control these abuses. It was an analogy to computer crime and prevention because it could be mapped part for part (Holyoak, 1984) to high-level nodes in the map of content for the 2,000-word article (A as in Figure 1). Thus, the analogy is equivalent to B in Figure 1 and congruent to parts of A. No mention was made in the analogy of links that could be used to assemble information in it with information in the longer passage. We assumed students were generally familiar with office photocopiers and their uses.

The outline was a point-form list of topics covered in the article. It contained four main headings, each with three subheadings. It was a summary of labels for high-level entries in the spatial map of the article on computers and computer crimes.

The dummy was a general passage about computers. It mentioned nothing about computer crime or methods for preventing computer crime.

Tracing

While reading the article with the organizer at hand, students coded each paragraph in the article by writing the number (0–4) of the matching organizer section in the box beside each paragraph of text. All students had been instructed to code a zero if they thought that there was no relation between a paragraph in the text and a section of their organizer. This allowed all students the option of recording the absence of relations. In the dummy introduction treatment, zeroes should be coded for every paragraph. To code paragraphs according to numbered sections of the organizer, it was assumed that students had to activate information from each source and assemble a link between the text and particular information in the organizer. Thus, by coding a paragraph, students leave a trace of their cognition while reading the text. Because each paragraph in the text had only one correct code, a correct trace satisfies all four conditions for testing whether students linked information in an organizer with information in the text (Winne, 1982). The trace score for each student in the study was the number of correct traces.

Achievement Instruments

Free-recall test. This test measured recall through five short-answer questions about representatively selected sections of the text. Questions targeted at the top, middle, or lowest level of the hierarchical content map of the article allowed us to explore whether treatments affected recall at different levels of the hierarchy. Students were instructed to write as many "points" as they could remember to answer each question.

For each question, a model answer was written in terms of idea units, that is, noun or verb phrases from the text that corresponded to the "points" students were to write. For example, one of the free-recall questions was "According to the article, why do people commit computer crimes?" The model answer was "for gain, for power, for money, out of spite, for information." The score for each free-recall question was the number of idea units from the model answer that appeared verbatim or paraphrased in the student's answer. A total score on free recall was the sum of scores over the five free-recall items.

Multiple-choice tests. This test was divided into two parts. Multiple-choice Part 1 tested comprehension of details (Anderson, 1972). It was a conventional achievement test containing 15 items sampled evenly across the paragraphs in the article. Each item contained four alternatives, only one of which was correct. The score for this part of the test was the number of correct responses.

Multiple-choice Part 2 presented 15 multiple-choice items covering content sampled evenly across the full text. It was used to explore whether treatment groups preferentially chose as correct answers information expressed in terms of their organizer. The four options for each item contained three correct alternatives and one wrong alternative. Each correct alternative was phrased to match the way that information was presented in either the concept organizer, the analogy organizer, or the outline. Students ranked the four alternatives from best to worst by judging the correctness of each alternative. Their first choice corresponded to the best answer and their fourth choice to the worst. Items that students ranked in the first and last positions were scored. Four scores were generated. The worst-answer score was the number of incorrect alternatives that were ranked last. The concept score was the number of times that the alternative expressed in concept terms was ranked first.

Aptitude measures. Average school letter grade was used as a measure of students' general aptitude to test for aptitude-treatment interactions. The school uses a seven-point scale to which we assigned scores as follows: A=7, B=6, C+=5, C=4, C-=3, D=2, and E=1. An average letter grade was computed for each student by averaging point values over four core subjects: English, social studies, mathematics, and science. Letter grades were taken from students' Spring report cards which had been distributed a few weeks before the study.

Design and Procedure

Students in intact classrooms were randomly assigned to one of four groups by randomly distributing packages of material. Each group received a different organizer but the same article. All students were administered the same instruments.

The study's procedures were implemented by students' regular classroom teachers. The procedures had been explained to teachers in a 1-hr meeting. Teachers were given a script of detailed instructions to follow and directions to read verbatim to students while administering the conditions. The study was carried out on two consecutive days.

Day 1. Students were instructed how to code paragraphs in a text as descriptions or extensions of information presented in a section of introductory material. An example was provided. After the classroom teacher asked for questions about the procedure and answered any that students raised, the teacher handed out the reading materials for the study. Students read the organizer first. Second, they read the article with the organizer at hand and completed the tracing activity described earlier. Students were given 25-30 minutes for this activity. Next, the text materials were collected and a 16-item questionnaire was administered. It asked how interesting the article was and how familiar students were with topics relating to computers. Answering the questionnaire functioned solely as an interpolated activity between reading the text and the free-recall test. Data from this questionnaire are not analyzed. Finally, students were given 20-25 minutes to complete the free-recall test.

Day 2. Students first participated in a categorizing task used for exploratory purposes. After materials from this task were collected, teachers gave out Part 1 of the multiple-choice test. As students completed the first part of the test, the teacher collected it and issued Part 2 of the test. All students finished the various activities in one class period.

Results and Discussion

Table 1 presents descriptive statistics for aptitude and achievement measures. Correlations among predictor and achievement variables are presented in Table 2.

One-way analyses of variance revealed that there were no differences among treatment groups on average letter grade, $F(3,195)=.24, p>.10$, $MS_e=2.78$. There were statistically reliable differences among groups on trace scores, $F(3,195)=16.48, p<.01, MS_e=48.89$. Mean correct trace

Table 1

Means, Standard Deviations, and Ranges of Scores for Predictor and Achievement Variables

Variable	Range	Group 1: Analogy (n = 50)		Group 2: Concept (n = 49)		Group 3: Outline (n = 49)		Group 4: Dummy (n = 51)		All groups (n = 199)	
		M	SD	M	SD	M	SD	M	SD	M	SD
Letter grade	1–7	4.60	1.73	4.35	1.51	4.43	1.71	4.57	1.71	4.49	1.66
Trace	0–30	11.42	5.69	8.86	3.96	18.37	5.94	11.82	10.49	12.60	7.77
Free recall	0–71 (22)	6.84	3.64	6.02	3.24	7.02	3.21	7.04	3.72	6.73	3.46
Multiple-choice											
Part 1	0–15	8.54	2.56	9.06	2.80	9.22	2.73	8.90	2.86	8.93	2.73
Worst answer	0–15 (14)	6.74	2.84	6.90	3.05	7.08	2.55	6.73	2.81	6.86	2.80
Concept	0–15 (8)	2.68	1.90	2.91	1.63	2.80	1.77	2.86	1.52	2.81	1.70
Analogy	0–15 (9)	1.78	1.47	2.04	1.66	2.00	1.89	2.39	2.11	2.06	1.80
Outline	0 (1)–15	8.68	3.51	8.00	2.92	8.71	3.32	8.12	2.90	8.38	3.16

Note. Where values for a range appear in parentheses, this indicates where actual scores differed from a scale's possible minimum and maximum. For example, the maximum possible score for free recall was 71, but the maximum observed score was 22.

scores expressed as percentages were: concept 30%, analogy 38%, outline 61% and dummy 38%.

Higher trace scores were expected for the outline group. Because the outline included phrases and terms appearing verbatim in the passage students were reading, they simply had to recognize common information. The low scores of the students in the concept and analogy organizer groups indicate that linking a new material with information in a true organizer was a difficult task.

Effects on Achievement

Achievement measures served as criterion variables in three separate multiple regression analyses in which all predictors were forced into the re-

Table 2
Correlations Among Predictor and Achievement Variables

Variable	1	2	3	4	5	6	7	8	9	10	11	12	13	14	15	16	17
1. Free-recall total	—	.48*	.42*	−.19*	−.22*	.41*	.40*	.24*	.08	.00	−.09	.10	.03	−.02	.08	−.02	−.05
2. Multiple-choice 1		—	.52*	−.28*	−.35*	.58*	.32*	.24*	−.07	.04	−.05	−.03	.08	−.03	−.07	.00	−.04
3. Multiple-choice 2: Worst-answer			—	−.22*	−.21*	.56*	.38*	.14	−.02	.05	−.01	−.02	.12	.05	.00	.04	−.01
4. Multiple-choice 2: Concept				—	−.04	−.57*	−.17*	−.15	−.05	−.01	−.01	−.09	−.01	.01	−.08	−.03	.02
5. Multiple-choice 2: Analogy					—	−.62*	−.24*	−.06	−.05	−.08	−.08	−.10	−.09	−.11	−.07	−.08	−.14
6. Multiple-choice 2: Outline						—	.31*	.21*	.08	.07	−.01	.13	.12	.03	.12	.08	.02
7. Letter grade							—	.20*	.05	−.03	−.01	.08	.02	−.01	.08	−.03	−.03
8. Trace								—	.11	.29*	−.31*	.15	.10	−.53*	.12	.31*	−.30*
9. Analogy–concept contrast (C1)									—	.00	.01	.90*	.00	.07	.94*	.00	.03
10. Outline–dummy contrast (C2)										—	.01	.00	.86*	−.15	.00	.94*	.02
11. True organizer– false organizer contrast (C3)											—	.09	−.12	.86*	.03	.02	.94*
12. Trace × C1												—	−.01	.17*	.89*	.00	.11
13. Trace × C2													—	−.14	.00	.84*	−.12
14. Trace × C3														—	.09	−.15	.85*
15. Letter grade × C1															—	.00	.05
16. Letter grade × C2																—	.03
17. Letter grade × C3																	—

*$p < .01$.

gression equation followed by backward deletion of statistically unreliable predictors. Predictor variables were letter grade and trace score as aptitudes; three a priori contrasts representing group differences; and six aptitude-treatment interactions formed by multiplying each aptitude vector by each of the group contrasts. The contrasts between groups were: analogy versus concept (C1), outline versus dummy (C2) and combined true organizer groups (concept and analogy) versus false organizer groups (outline and dummy) (C3). For statistically reliable effects, simplified regression equations were calculated to show the effect of a single predictor variable using a method described in Winne and Marx (1983; see also Pedhazur, 1982).

Caveat. In the following discussion, it is important to recognize that statistically reliable effects refer to relations between residualized variables. Because residualized variables are not perfectly correlated with their unresidualized parents, the construct of a residualized variable is not identical to the original construct. The changes to construct validity are proportional to the correlations among predictor variables (see Winne, 1983a).

Main effects. Three achievement scores measured quantity of learning: free recall, multiple-choice Part 1 and multiple-choice Part 2 worst-answer scores. Regression analyses showed statistically reliable effects due to letter grade and trace score on all three measures (see Table 3). As expected, achievement improved with a student's aptitude and with the ability to trace. The low correlation between letter grade and trace ($r = .20$, $p < .01$; see Table 2) indicates that correct tracing reflects a construct different from general success in school.

Table 3
Backward Rejection Regression Analyses on Achievement Variables: Specific Effects of Individual Predictors

Variable	Free recall			Multiple-choice Part 1			Multiple-choice Part 2											
							Worst answer			Concept			Analogy			Outline		
	b	t	R^2_s	b	t	R^2_s	b	t	R^2_s	b	t	R^2_s	b	t	R^2_s	b	t	R^2_s
LG	.70	5.20	.11	.38	3.37	.05	.58	5.19	.11	−.15	−1.98	.02	−.27	−3.71	.06	.43	3.27	.05
Trace	.14	3.94	.06	.14	4.54	.09	.09	2.98	.04	−.03	−1.69	.01				.14	3.81	.06
C1																		
C2																−1.67	−2.50	.03
C3	−1.52	−3.32	.04				−1.09	−2.82	.03				.88	2.52	.03			
LG × C1				−.12	−2.31	.02												
Analogy*				.25														
Concept				.50														
LG × C2				−.37	−3.41	.05												
Outline				.00														
Dummy				.75														
LG × C3													−.23	−3.13	.05			
True organizer													−.50					
False													−.04					
Trace × C1							−.05	−2.08	.02									
Analogy							.04											
Concept							.15											
Trace × C2				.10	3.46	.05										.11	3.03	.04
Outline				.24												.25		
Dummy				.05												.03		
Trace × C3	.13	3.56	.05	.04	2.49	.03	.11	3.50	.05							.05	2.72	.03
True	.27			.19			.20									.19		
False	.02			.11			−.01									.09		
R^2 adjusted	.22			.18			.19			.03			.10			.16		

Note. LG = letter grade; C1 = analogy–concept contrast; C2 = outline–dummy contrast; C3 = true organizer–false organizer contrast. Regression coefficients are for the equation at the last step and are adjusted for the degrees of freedom adsorbed by predictors. R^2_s is the squared semipartial correlation coefficient. Blank spaces in the table indicate results which were not statistically reliable.
* Regression coefficients for individual groups describe the slopes of an achievement score regressed onto the aptitude (letter grade or trace score). The difference between these regression coefficients describes the aptitude–treatment interaction.

Group contrasts. Statistically reliable group contrasts on free recall and multiple-choice Part 2 worst-answer showed that the combined false organizer groups performed better than the true organizer groups.

Because separate analyses of each question on the free-recall test revealed the same patterns as analysis of the total score, only the latter is reported. The free-recall and multiple-choice Part 2 worst-answer scores measured memory for and comprehension of details in the text and, as such, constitute near transfer tasks. Our results are consistent with assimilation theory and other studies (Mayer, 1979a, 1979b, 1980): students' use of conceptual organizers may impede recall of low-level details.

Interaction effects. An interesting picture emerges in findings about interactions. Free-recall, multiple-choice Part 1, and multiple-choice Part 2 worst-answer scores showed statistically reliable Trace×Contrast interactions. Successful tracing had very little relation to scores in the false organizer groups, but it was reliably and positively related to higher scores in the true organizer groups. This indicates that when students do assemble information in a true advance organizer with new material, as reflected by traces, learning increases. Recall that trace scores for students in the true organizer groups were very low (<40%). We suggest that the apparent lack of effects associated with exposing students to advance organizers in other previous research may be due to subjects' inability to use the organizer effectively. Analysis of scores of the multiple-choice test Part 1 yielded two interesting interactions. Letter Grade×Contrast interactions indicated that students using the concept organizer showed a greater improvement in scores with increasing letter grade than did students using the analogy organizer. This is consistent with Derry's (1984) findings that concept advance organizers have most value for high-ability students. Perhaps using concept advance organizers requires higher level or more thorough cognitive processing than using analogies.

Trace×Contrast interactions showed that better tracing had little impact on performance in the dummy introduction group. Because the dummy introduction had nothing to do with the text, a student who recognizes that fact, as signaled by accurate tracing, gains no advantage in learning the text material. On the other hand, for the outline group, achievement improved proportionally to trace scores. Links that a student made to the outline helped to organize the information needed for a task involving near transfer.

It was predicted that students would show a preference for multiple-choice alternatives expressed in terms corresponding to the type of organizer they used. The interesting finding here is that better students with higher aptitude and more accurate tracing, regardless of group, generally chose the outline alternative as the best answer and avoided the other two correct alternatives. An explanation for this finding can not be grounded directly in this study. We are tempted to speculate, however, that better students' idea of the "most correct answer" is the answer that is most like the text that they read. The outline alternatives were verbatim and near-verbatim samples of the text.

Conclusions

Achievement measures showed a statistically reliable main effect due to level of tracing: achievement increased with increasing trace scores. This is an important result because it indicates that the effectiveness of an organizer depends on the student's ability to relate new information in a text to the organizer.

The apparent advantage of the false organizer treatments shown in statistically reliable group contrasts was reversed when interactions were examined. When students were able to accurately link information in true organizers with the text, achievement improved. Success in using the false organizers did not enhance achievement. This finding is particularly important because the traces show that students use true organizers with different degrees of accuracy, and there is a proportional relation between using the organizer accurately and achievement.

The overall conclusion we draw is that true advance organizers promote learning conditionally, the condition being whether the organizers are used appropriately and accurately. A student's ability to link information in the advance organizer correctly with new information is critical. When students are unable to link correctly, their achievement may suffer relative to groups that have not been given an advance organizer.

The general difficulty we observed students to have in connecting information in true organizers to the text they read has major implications for interpreting previous research. The lack of effects often reported for types of organizers may be due to students' ineffective use of the organizers rather than to characteristics of the organizers themselves. Studies that compare a group receiving an organizer to another group that does not, and that do not trace whether the organizer is actually used, may be comparing a group that was not able to make proper use of an organizer with a control. Failing to notice this possibility will misdirect interpretations. We note that the cognitive operations reflected by a trace need to be specified more precisely in the future. Further research is needed to analyze the cognitive procedures that students perform as they relate information in the two sources.

This study provides weak indications that the concept and the analogy organizers had different effects. In recent research, the general umbrella of "advance organizer" has not distinguished these two types of organizers. This potential difference should be pursued in further research. Previous studies have explored the interactions between student ability and learning with advance organizers. Results of our study do not shed much more light on this topic. Several statistically reliable Aptitude×Treatment interactions indicated that the effects of true organizers were proportional to student ability. However, the effects were small in magnitude and were not observed for all the measures of achievement. This topic needs further investigation with emphasis on more precise understanding of what "ability" is and how ability is applied in the process of learning.

A major focus of previous research has been interactions between types of organizers and learning outcomes. These studies generally show that true organizers promote far transfer but not low-level recall or near transfer. Unlike the findings of previous studies, and counter to the predictions of assimilation theory, this study found that true advance organizers appeared to promote near transfer quite successfully when students used them appropriately. Greater precision in interpreting this finding awaits clearer operational definitions for both near and far transfer.

Theoretical predictions about the effects of advance organizers are totally bound up with cognitive processes that learners are hypothesized to perform while they use an advance organizer as a backdrop to learning from a text. This study has shown that merely exposing students to an advance organizer does not guarantee students will use the organizer as a theory describes. If there is a single recommendation for further research to be drawn from this study, it is that future research must identify these cognitive processes and gather traces reflecting students' use of them.

References

Anderson, R.C. (1972). How to construct achievement tests that assess comprehension. *Review of Educational Research, 42*, 145-170.

Armbruster, B.B., & Anderson, T.H. (1984). Mapping: Representing informative text diagrammatically. In C.D. Holley & D.F. Dansereau (Eds.), *Spatial learning strategies: Techniques, applications, and related issues* (pp. 189-209). Orlando, FL: Academic Press.

Ausubel, D.P. (1963). *The psychology of meaningful verbal learning.* New York, NY: Grune & Stratton.

Barnes, B.R., & Clawson, E.U. (1975). Do advance organizers facilitate learning? Recommendations for further research based on an analysis of 32 studies. *Review of Educational Research, 45*, 637-659.

Derry, S.J. (1984). Effects of an organizer on memory for prose. *Journal of Educational Psychology, 76*, 98-107.

Hartley, J., & Davies, I.K. (1976). Preinstructional strategies: The role of pretests, behavioral objectives, overviews and advance organizers. *Review of Educational Research, 46*, 239-265.

Holyoak, K.J. (1984). Analogical thinking and human intelligence. In R.J. Sternberg (Ed.), *Advances in the psychology of human intelligence* (Vol. 2, pp. 199-230). Hillsdale, NJ: Erlbaum.

Mayer, R.E. (1975). Different problem-solving competencies established in learning computer programming with and without meaningful models. *Journal of Educational Psychology, 67*, 725-734.

Mayer, R.E. (1976). Some conditions of meaningful learning for computer programming: Advance organizers and subject control of frame order. *Journal of Educational Psychology, 68*, 143-150.

Mayer, R.E. (1979a). Can advance organizers influence meaningful learning? *Review of Educational Research, 49*, 371-383.

Mayer, R.E. (1979b). Twenty years of research on advance organizers: Assimilation theory is still the best predictor of results. *Instructional Science, 8*, 133-167.

Mayer, R.E. (1980). Elaboration techniques that increase the meaningfulness of technical text: An experimental test of the learning strategy hypothesis. *Journal of Educational Psychology, 72*, 770-784.

Mayer, R.E., & Bromage, B.K. (1980). Different recall protocols for technical texts due to advance organizers. *Journal of Educational Psychology, 72*, 209-225.

Mayer, R.E., & Greeno, J.G. (1972). Structural differences between learning outcomes produced by different instructional methods. *Journal of Educational Psychology, 63*, 165-173.

Meyer, B.J.F., & Freedle, R.O. (1984). Effects of discourse type on recall. *American Educational Research Journal, 21*, 121-143.

Pedhazur, E. (1982). *Multiple regression in behavioral research: Explanation and prediction* (2nd ed.). New York, NY: Holt, Rinehart & Winston.

Winne, P.H. (1982). Minimizing the black box problem to enhance the validity of theories about instructional effects. *Instructional Science, 11*, 13-28.

Winne, P.H. (1983a). Distortions of construct validity in multiple regression analysis. *Canadian Journal of Behavioural Science, 15*, 187-202.

Winne, P.H. (1983b). Training students to process text with adjunct aids. *Instructional Science, 12*, 243-266.

Winne, P.H. (1985). Steps toward promoting cognitive achievements. *Elementary School Journal, 85*, 673-693.

Winne, P.H., & Marx, R.W. (1983). *Students' cognitive processes while learning from teaching* (Final Report, National Institute of Education Grant NIE-G-79-0098). Burnaby, British Columbia, Canada: Instructional Psychology Research Group, Simon Fraser University.

Motivation

The most sophisticated educational resources in the world will work only if students are motivated to learn, and motivation can be enhanced or diminished by many factors. Rosenthal and his colleagues showed that teachers' expectations about their students' abilities could actually change their students' behaviour. Could students' behaviour also be influenced by their expectations about their teachers' abilities? Jamieson, Lydon, Stewart, and Zanna believed that students might be more motivated to learn if they believed that their teacher was above average in competence. The authors conducted a field experiment with four classes of Grade 11 students. After only three weeks, students in the two experimental classes, who had been led to believe that their teacher was especially capable and motivated, demonstrated significantly more appropriate nonverbal behaviour and attained significantly higher grades than did students in the control classes, whose expectations had not been manipulated.

Traditional classrooms are very competitive places, in which only a few students are consistently rewarded for their efforts. As a result, lower ability students often stop trying to do well. When children of varying ability levels work together on academic tasks in structured cooperative groups, lower ability students realize that their contributions are necessary for the group's success, and so their achievement and motivation improve. But what happens if the cooperative groups or teams compete with each other? Chambers and Abrami believed that being a member of a losing team could be just as negative an experience as losing individually. They also believed that members of losing teams would think they lost because they weren't as smart or lucky as the winners and would be especially discouraged because ability and luck cannot be controlled. The results of their five-week field study of a cooperative learning strategy called Teams-Games-Tournaments (TGT) generally supported these hypotheses. Students who had been low achievers before participating in TGT, and who had experienced consistent individual and team failure during TGT, performed worse on the final achievement test than any other group. Although students on both winning and losing teams believed effort was the most important determinant of team outcome, students on losing teams rated their ability and luck as lower than did students on winning teams. Chambers and Abrami suggest that cooperative learning strategies requiring inter-team cooperation would be more beneficial for all students.

The relationship between attributions and academic achievement is also the focus of the study conducted by Perry and Palmer. Some students believe that they have no real control over their academic outcomes. Sometimes this feeling is transient, and sometimes it reflects a more stable personality trait called locus of control (LOC). As defined by Perry and Penner, internal LOC students attribute failure to lack of effort (a controllable cause) while external LOC students attribute failure to lack of ability (an uncontrollable cause). The university students in Perry and Penner's experiment were all given a transient sense of control when they completed a multiple-choice test on which they received immediate feedback as they answered each question. Perry and Penner reasoned that this treatment would make no real difference for internal LOC students but would make external LOC students more receptive to subsequent interventions. Half the students were then given attributional retraining—a videotaped talk by a psychology professor encouraging them to attribute poor performance to lack of effort and good performance to ability and proper effort. All students then watched another videotaped lecture by a different professor, who was very expressive for half the students and unexpressive for the other half. A week later, all students completed tests on the lecture and related homework. As expected, external LOC students who had received the attributional retraining did much better than external LOC students who had not received the retraining on both tests. Similarly, external LOC students with a highly expressive teacher did much better on both tests than external LOC students with an unexpressive teacher. Since internal LOC students were already making internal attributions, the attributional retraining made no difference to their performance. For related reasons, their performance was not positively influenced by the highly expressive instructor.

In her article, Haggerty analyzed the results of recent studies on gender differences in science achievement and participation in Canadian high school science classes. In terms of achievement, girls do as well as or better than boys on course marks; however, they do not perform as well on standardized tests. The evidence suggests that girls' better study habits and greater skill at rote learning give them the advantage on class tests, but that boys understand the science they are learning better than girls, due in part to more informal science learning experiences, and can therefore apply it in new contexts like standardized tests. Attitudes toward science seem to become less positive as children approach adolescence, especially for girls, and influence participation rates in elective science courses. Overall, for Anglophones, the three largest and most industrialized provinces were least successful in attracting girls to these courses. Finally, male and female participation rates and interaction styles in science classrooms seem to differ significantly, with males more likely to ask questions and participate actively, even with teachers who consciously encourage their female students to get involved.

Pygmalion Revisited: New Evidence for Student Expectancy Effects in the Classroom

David W. Jamieson, John E. Lydon, Glenn Stewart, and Mark P. Zanna
University of Waterloo

We conducted a field experiment to test the idea that students' expectations regarding their teacher's competence would influence their classroom behavior and academic achievement. At the end of a 3-week teaching unit, students in two high school classes who had been given an initial positive expectancy about their teacher's ability and motivation engaged in more appropriate and less inappropriate nonverbal behavior and received significantly higher final grades on the unit than did their peers in two no-expectation control classes. We speculate about both the direct (student-mediated) and indirect (teacher-mediated) processes by which students' expectations came to affect their academic outcomes. We also discuss the importance of group-level expectancies and some ethical issues in student expectancy research.

*   *   *

THE EXPECTATION THAT A TEACHER HAS ABOUT A PARTICULAR STUDENT'S ability sometimes acts as a self-fulfilling prophecy, bringing about the very level of academic attainment for that student that was originally expected. Initial research on teacher-student interactions (Rosenthal & Jacobson, 1968) has been followed by theory and research articulating the process by which differential teacher expectancies for student achievement produce actual differences in student performance (Braun, 1976; Brophy & Good, 1974; Cooper, 1979; Cooper & Good, 1983). Partially as a result of such efforts, investigators have recently recognized the active role played by students in the teaching situation (Weinstein, 1983).

Student perceptions of teacher behavior have been shown to mediate the relation between teacher expectations and student outcomes (Brattesani, Weinstein, & Marshall, 1984). Yet, in addition to their role as mediators of the teacher expectation communication process, students are also agents

This article is based largely on thesis research conducted by the third author (Stewart, 1975). We wish to thank John Holmes, Shelley Hymel, and Elise Ditner for their comments on earlier aspects of the research and on previous versions of this article.

of influence in their own right, acting on the perceptions and expectations they hold about the learning experience. Thus, experimental studies of students' expectations for their own achievement have amply demonstrated the impact of this belief on subsequent academic attainment (Rappaport & Rappaport, 1975; Zanna, Sheras, Cooper, & Shaw, 1975). In addition, research on student expectation about such teacher variables as expressiveness (Ware & Williams, 1975) and the warm-cold dimension of personality (Manni, 1975) can influence student ratings of teacher ability and student achievement under certain circumstances.

Perhaps one of the most interesting and influential teacher variables examined in this context is the student-perceived competence of the teacher. A perfect complement to the kind of expectancy first investigated in this research literature (viz., teacher expectancies for student ability), student expectancies for teacher competence are likely to influence student motivation and performance. It seems highly plausible that the belief that one is to be taught by a particularly skilled, intelligent, and motivated teacher may enhance one's own motivation to learn and may ultimately heighten one's academic outcomes. It also seems plausible that students form expectations about their teachers' abilities in the first place: Just as individuals and classes develop academic and behavioral reputations that are communicated among teachers, teachers develop similar reputations that are communicated among students, both within and across grades (cf. Kulik & Kulik, 1974).

In search of evidence for such student expectancy effects, Feldman and Prohaska (1979) created a laboratory interaction situation that cast pairs of undergraduates in the roles of teacher and student for short, one-time dyadic teaching sessions. Positive versus negative expectations about their teacher's competence produced a consequent difference in students' achievement on one of the two performance measures employed. A second experiment with a similar manipulation yielded a marginally significant effect on the multiple-choice test used (Feldman, Saletsky, Sullivan, & Theiss, 1983). In fact, the results of only one study conducted by these workers failed to show support for the effects of this type of student expectancy on actual student performance (Feldman & Theiss, 1982).

Other investigators have explored student expectations through noninteractional studies in which college students are exposed to carefully crafted lecture materials. For example, Perry and his colleagues (Perry, Abrami, Leventhal, & Check, 1979; Perry, Niemi, & Jones, 1974) manipulated the teaching reputation of a college instructor and then had subjects watch a videotape of him lecturing. In one of the two experiments in which achievement was assessed, a marginal main effect of expected teacher competence on student performance was found. Thus, two independent laboratory paradigms have provided convergent (if somewhat weak) evidence regarding the causal importance of student expectations about teacher competence for students' own academic attainment.

It was also clear from the results of each of these experimental approaches that manipulations of expected teacher competence reliably and powerfully affected students' perceptions of their instructors. That such effects were not as strong on the measures of achievement used may seem disappointing, given the high degree of control normally afforded by laboratory methods. However, in defense of these ingenious studies, it must be noted that manipulated expectations are generally weaker than naturalistic ones in educational research (Braun, 1976) and that the causal connections between expectancies and one-time laboratory performance are likely to be weak and indirect. Thus, although the laboratory evidence obtained by the researchers was mixed, it is possible to conclude that the experimenters mainly accomplished what they set out to do, namely, to demonstrate that student expectations of teacher competence can, in principle, affect student performance outcomes.

Nevertheless, there remains the need to demonstrate whether such expectancies might have a meaningful impact in real teaching contexts. Feldman and Prohaska (1979) signaled the need for more fieldwork in this area, noting that the artificiality of laboratory paradigms may severely limit the generalizability of their findings: "Future research must examine the phenomenon of student expectation effects in more naturalistic and applied settings" (p. 492). Our purpose in the present study, therefore, was to address the ecological question of whether this phenomenon can occur in real classrooms. We expected that in a real classroom, where teacher-student contacts may be characterized as frequent, lengthy, nondyadic, and of unequal status, students' expectancies about their instructor's competence might meaningfully influence their ongoing classroom behavior and, ultimately, their academic performance.

Method

Participants

Four classes of Grade 11 students served as subjects in the study ($N=64$, 40 girls and 24 boys). A female teacher, who had recently been transferred to the school, taught these students a 3-week unit on oral and written English skills in the weeks immediately preceding their annual spring break.

Experimental Situation

The fortuitous transfer of a new teacher to the school provided optimal conditions for a test of expectancy effects at a time during the academic year when we otherwise might not have anticipated significant results. Because the students had no prior contacts with, knowledge of, or expectations about the instructor, an experimental situation was created in which conditions were equivalent to those at the beginning of a school year, when the impact of (teacher) expectancies has been shown to be strongest (Cooper & Good, 1983; Raudenbush, 1984). In addition, the course content of English-language instruction, owing to its more subjective nature, has been found to be a teaching area particularly amenable to expectancy effects (Smith, 1980).

We recognized that by using so few classes and only one teacher we would limit the generality of our findings. However, because this was our first attempt to study the phenomenon in the field, we believed that the execution of an "experimental case study" might nevertheless provide useful information. With these caveats in mind, we worked within the constraints of this unique research opportunity.

Procedure

Initial expectations. On the first day of the unit, all participants completed a questionnaire designed to measure their initial perceptions of the new teacher's competence, defined here as her ability to teach and motivate. This instrument was based on the work of French-Lazovik (1974), who examined variables important for the perception of teacher effectiveness. Subjects rated the teacher on 14 characteristics with a 5-point scale labeled *below average* (1), *average* (2), *above average* (3), *superior* (4), and *excellent* (5). These ratings were averaged into three 5-point subscales representing the dimensions of teacher behavior found by French-Lazovik to predict student satisfaction with teachers: clarity of exposition, ability to arouse student interest, and ability to motivate intellectual activities. A 15th question was also added in order to assess the perceived fairness of the teacher's grading practices. In all, four general categories of teacher competence were assessed.

An analysis of these perceived competency ratings revealed no initial differences between classes. In particular, the expectations held by students later assigned to the positive-expectancy condition in this study did not differ from those held by students assigned to the control condition in any of the four domains of teacher competence assessed; clarity of exposition: positive-expectancy $M=2.48$ versus no-expectancy $M=2.55$, $t(58)<1$; ability to arouse student interest: $M=2.38$ versus $M=2.13$, $t(52)=1.56$, *ns*; ability to motivate intellectual activities: $M=2.42$ versus $M=2.35$, $t(59)<1$; and fairness of grading practices: $M=2.32$ versus $M=2.26$, $t(54)<1$.[1]

Manipulation of expectations. On the 6th teaching day of the unit, two classes were randomly assigned to a positive-expectancy condition, whereas the remaining two classes served as a no-expectation control. Raudenbush (1984) argued that more than 2 weeks of teacher-student contacts prior to an induction of teacher expectations is sufficient to render expectancy effect sizes nonsignificant. Assuming that there was a similar premanipulation time frame for student expectancies, we ensured that our induction of positive expectations occurred well within this limit. Note that by contrasting a positive-expectancy condition with a neutral one, we conducted a more conservative test of the hypothesis than would have been possible if positive and negative expectancies had been imparted.

We manipulated positive expectancy by conducting individual interviews with each of the students from the two experimental classes (except for two pupils who were absent that day). We presented these interviews as a means of soliciting student feedback on general aspects of school courses, and we emphasized that students' responses to their questionnaires would in no way influence their grades.

Positive-expectancy subjects were led to believe that their peers, the experimenter and the teacher herself all saw her as highly capable and motivated to teach the English unit. We did this primarily by showing these students the (bogus) high mean ratings of the teacher previously made by their classmates. We carefully explained to each person that across the 15 characteristics of performance on which the teacher had been rated by the class on the first day of the unit, she had received a total of 5 *excellent*, 8 *superior*, and 2 *above average* ratings. We emphasized that these were considered very high scores. In addition to communicating to students the enthusiasm of their peers, we informed them that we had rated the teacher and their class quite highly and that the teacher had expressed excitement about the unit and her new students.

At the end of the interview, these students once again anonymously completed the teacher perception questionnaire as a check on the impact of the manipulation. As a result of this intervention, students in the positive-expectation condition significantly changed their expectations about the teacher's competence relative to their initial baseline expectancies in each of the four competence domains assessed; clarity of exposition: postmanipulation versus premanipulation $M = 0.79$; dependent $t(21) = 4.88$, $p < .001$; ability to arouse student interest: $M = 0.86$, $t(20) = 4.95$, $p < .001$; ability to motivate intellectual awareness: $M = 0.61$, $t(21) = 3.46$, $p < .01$; and fairness of grading practices: $M = 0.71$, $t(20) = 3.63$, $p < .01$. In summary, with this manipulation we successfully persuaded the experimental subjects to expect that the teacher was more competent than they had originally anticipated.

Because of time limitations, students in the control classes could not be interviewed. As a result, no new expectations whatsoever were imparted to them on the 6th day of the unit, and their perceptions of the teacher were not reassessed at this time.[2] Although this may have engendered some suspicion on the part of the subjects, we attempted to control for the possible perception of preferential treatment between classes by having all four classes sign up initially for the interviews, with the proviso that we would call on only a limited number of students.

The teacher was not informed about which classes had been manipulated because we scheduled the interviews on a day she had planned to be (and was) absent from school. Moreover, she was informed of neither the content of the manipulation nor the experimental hypotheses under investigation. Told only that the experimental team was interested in the difference between traditional versus open classrooms, the teacher admitted no awareness of the experimental inductions or hypotheses when she was later debriefed.

Dependent Measures

Student classroom behavior. Six prime and two alternate target students from each class were randomly selected for systematic time-sampling observation. In the 7 teaching days following the expectancy induction, the prime students in each class or, in the event of absenteeism, their alternates were observed daily during the middle part of their English class period for between 20 and 30 minutes. (This varied with the teaching curriculum and format for that day.) Recording intervals of 30 seconds were used: Targets were observed for the first 20 seconds and behaviors coded in the remaining 10 seconds.

Student behaviors were coded by two trained observers into three mutually exclusive categories: appropriate nonverbal behavior, inappropriate nonverbal behavior, and verbal behavior. Appropriate behaviors included paying attention during a lecture or exercise and reading and writing during reading and writing sessions. Inappropriate behaviors included inattention, gross motor responses, and talking out of turn or when silence was required. Verbal behavior was annotated in three subcategories: teacher-afforded response opportunities, teacher-afforded communications, and student-initiated actions (Brophy & Good, 1970). The quality of student responses and teacher feedback was also recorded in an attempt to gauge the extent to which student expectation differences might manifest themselves in differential teacher behavior.

Because one observer, the third author, was not unaware of the experimental conditions, the second observer was brought in on several occasions for joint observation sessions in order to examine the possibility of systematic observer bias. Twelve separate reliability checks interspersed over the 7-day observation period produced an average interrater agreement of 90% on the behavioral categorizations; this argues against an interpretation of the results as stemming from observer bias.

Student performance. Students' academic performance was assessed in two ways. First, each student's final mark for the unit was noted. This final grade was an overall evaluation of student performance made by the teacher after consideration of each student's test performances, class contributions, effort, diligence in completing homework assignments, absenteeism, and so forth. In addition, students' marks for all the graded tests and assignments completed during the unit were recorded. Some of these grades reflected subjective assessments made by the teacher of students' oral and written work; others were objective measures of students' performances on tests of English proficiency.

Results

Results for each measure are summarized below. Data from the two experimental and two control classes are combined within condition in this presentation.

Student classroom behavior. In the 7 days following the experimental induction, the positive-expectancy target students displayed significantly more appropriate nonverbal behavior and significantly less inappropriate nonverbal behavior than did their no-expectancy control counterparts. Whereas 75.9% of the positive-expectancy students' total classroom activity was categorized on average as appropriate nonverbal behavior, only 60.5% of the control students' behaviors were deemed to be appropriately nonverbal, $SE_M = 5.76$, $t(27) = 2.68$, $p < .02$. At the same time, positive-expectancy students were engaging in only 19.3% inappropriate nonverbal behavior, as compared with 31.7% inappropriate nonverbal behavior for the controls, $SE_M = 5.90$, $t(27) = 2.10$, $p < .05$.

Because of an insufficient number of observations, an analysis of verbal behavior was, unfortunately, disallowed. The verbal interaction subcategories, even when combined, accounted for less than 5% of the sampled behavior among students in the positive-expectation condition and only about 8% of students' behavior in the no-expectancy control. As a result of such low frequencies, no reliable inferences regarding the teacher's behavior or her use of praise and criticism were made possible by our behavioral time-sampling procedure.

Student performance. It is important to note that there were no initial differences in the English grade point averages (GPAs) achieved by members of the two expectation groups on the five teaching units completed prior to the unit under study. The students' first teacher had awarded a mean grade of 81.57% to students in the positive-expectancy condition and an average of 80.32% to students in the control classes, $SE_M=2.12$, $t(60)<1$. However, overall final grades for the subjects indicated that students in the experimental condition received significantly higher grades (83.95%) than did the control students (73.98%) on the 3-week teaching unit, $SE_M=3.76$, $t(60)=2.66$, $p<.01$.[3] Interestingly, this disparity in final grades seems to have been more attributable to a difference between the two groups in their performance on the unit's objective tests and assignments, positive-expectancy $M=89.78$ versus control $M=84.79$, $SE_M=2.48$, $t(56)=2.01$, $p<.05$, than to a difference in their performance on the more subjective tests, $M=87.91$ versus $M=87.67$, $SE_M=2.18$, $t(56)<1$. Note that both the objective and subjective test grades were higher than the overall grades assigned by the teacher, indicating that her comprehensive criteria for performance on the unit were more stringent than were her standards for performance on these tests.[4]

Discussion

In contrast to the mixed or weak results formerly obtained in laboratory simulations of the teacher-student interaction, the results of this field study show that a positive expectation about their teacher's competence caused changes in students' ongoing nonverbal behavior and academic performance relative to control students given no expectancy. This was true despite the initial equivalence of the two groups on relevant variables, such as perceptions of the teacher and prior academic attainment. Thus, although Feldman and Prohaska (1979) suggested that the opportunity for students to communicate their expectations to a teacher might be limited by the unequal-status arrangements of real classroom situations, the present data suggest that in a real classroom, students' expectations can have a meaningful impact on their own behavior and performance. Whether such expectations typically do have such an impact is nevertheless still open to question because the experimental conditions described here may have maximized our chances of obtaining expectancy effects. Conceptual replications of this study will therefore be necessary in order to explore the prevalence of the phenomenon among students of differing ages, genders, and abilities; among different teachers; at different times of the year; with different and less artificial means of inducing expectancies; and with different instructional subject matters.

Several processes, acting either individually or additively, may be suggested as possible mediators of our findings. For example, students' beliefs about their teacher's competency may have affected their achievement as mediated (indirectly) by the teacher. The relatively more favorable classroom behavior of students in the positive-expectancy classes may have caused the teacher to form differential expectancies for these two classes and perhaps even to change her instructional behavior to reflect these standards (even though, if they existed, such differences were apparently not perceived by students in the two groups; see footnote 2). Alternately, the expectancy-achievement relation may have resulted from the more direct causal effect of students' beliefs in their own work motivation and conduct (Cooper & Good, 1983). As a result of believing that they were to be taught by a highly competent teacher, students may have perceived a greater potential for learning, been more tolerant of teacher ambiguity, set higher standards for their own achievement, expected a stronger general contingency of outcomes with effort, or formed stronger self-efficacy expectations. Future work is needed in order to disentangle the direct and indirect mediators of student expectancy effects.

Although the generality of the present design was limited by our random assignment of whole classes rather than individuals to conditions, we believe that group-level factors deserve future research attention as variables in their own right. Among the possible social moderators of teacher-student interaction are focused group influence and shared group consensus. For example, to the extent that teacher behavior may have been the primary mediator of the expectancy-achievement relation obtained here, the strength of our findings may be attributable to the fact that the expectancies of entire classes were brought to bear on the teacher in this research. In general, student expectancy effects may prove to have much more impact when a group of students holds a single shared expectancy regarding a teacher than when individual students hold differential expectancies. Teachers may more readily perceive and react to such focused group-level expectations (Brophy, 1983).

By the same token, to the extent that students' behavior and performance may have been directly influenced by their own beliefs, our manipulation of a group-level expectancy for teacher competence may have had its strong effect because of the expectancies of many students acting on each other. Knowledge of their peers' competency expectations and perceptions of the class's cooperative behavior were probably powerful forms of social influence on the subjects in our positive-expectancy condition, especially because this consensus was shared by nearly all the students in those classes.

Although it may be argued that our manipulation of a univalent, shared expectancy about the teacher was artificial, we believe that its psychological effect was at least conceptually representative of the effect in classrooms in which teachers have well-developed reputations that precede them. Moreover, a relatively direct analogue to our procedure exists in the popular practice of publishing student evaluations of college course instructors. It would be useful to determine whether such information has constraining effects on subsequent teacher effectiveness. In sum, the influence of many students whose beliefs are conjointly brought to bear on both the teacher and each other may result in powerful group-fulfilling or group-sustaining effects (cf. Cooper & Tom, 1984), and these warrant future inquiry.

Finally, a note about the apparent decline in final academic performance among our control subjects relative to their baseline English GPAs is in order. This decline may represent an interesting phenomenon in its own right. For example, because the unit was shortened to accommodate spring break, student motivation may have been undercut by the prospect of the impending school recess. Studies of performance changes immediately preceding school holidays would be needed to explore this hypothesis. Alternately, the importation of the new instructor to the classrooms may have caused a lowering of intrinsic motivation when students had to discern the classroom's new reward structure. Studies of new, substitute, and short-term replacement teachers might evidence similar student achievement deficits. Whatever its root cause, to the extent that a declining academic baseline may have been a real phenomenon in this study, the factors that produced it were common to both the experimental and control groups. This could imply that the positive-expectancy manipulation successfully inoculated students against performance drops that they would have experienced in the absence of our intervention.

Of course, a second possible reason for the declining control baseline is the unfortunate prospect that despite our efforts to conduct a conservative test of the hypothesis, the single-teacher experimental intervention may have itself caused a decrement. Although there was little evidence that the teacher viewed her classes differently (as assessed by ratings collected in her debriefing) and despite the fact that the students in both conditions perceived her teaching effectiveness similarly by the end of the unit, the possibility of a contrast effect on the part of the teacher in the way she perceived or treated the different experimental groups raises obvious concerns about the ethics of conducting research by using the experimental case study approach. Because the roots of such contrast effects may potentially reside in either "Pygmalion-prone" instructors (Babad, Inbar, & Rosenthal, 1982) or particularly compelling expectancy manipulations, future field investigators may be better advised to use multiple-teacher paradigms and to rely more heavily on correlational methods that capitalize on naturally occurring student expectations.

In sum, this experiment demonstrated the important influence that students' expectancies can have on their own academic attainment. Subsequent studies of student expectancy effects need to chart a course parallel to that described in the teacher expectancy literature so that researchers can discover how expectancies are formed and communicated by students and how they are perceived and acted on by teachers. Only then will investigators articulate the most complete theoretical model of a student-teacher interaction that accounts for the translation of student expectancy to student fact.

Notes

1 The degrees of freedom for various tests presented throughout this article vary because of missing data due to uncompleted questionnaire items and to absenteeism.

2 The questionnaire assessing student perceptions of the teacher was also administered to all four classes on the last day of the unit as a final measure of students' impressions of the teacher's competence. Positive-expectancy subjects' final perceptions of the teacher remained significantly higher than their initial perceptions in all four domains of teacher effectiveness, at about the same levels as the postmanipulation data. Control subjects' perceptions were favorably altered in all four domains by the end of the unit relative to the beginning (and significantly so in three of these). Although there was one between-groups difference (for clarity of exposition) at this time, the general pattern of final perceptions was that the teacher was considered to be of above-average ability by all the classes. This was true despite the behavioral and performance differences that we report and may indicate that the teacher, who was in fact competent, eventually came to be perceived in that way by all her classes. Such an interpretation may argue against an explanation of the behavioral and performance data in terms of differential teacher behavior.

3 An analysis of change scores (unit grade minus pre-unit GPA) within our two groups suggested both that the positive-expectation students' performance improved and that the control students' performance declined, relative to their prior levels of achievement: positive-expectancy $M=2.39$, dependent $t(21)=2.11$, $p<.05$, and control $M=-6.35$, $t(39)=3.05, p<.01$. The appropriateness of the GPAs as a baseline is somewhat questionable, however, because they were determined by another teacher, whose grading practices may have differed from those used by our instructor.

4 We examined all the data reported to determine if the effects were localized to particular classes. There were no significant differences between the pairs of classes within each condition in perceived teacher competence, appropriate behavior, inappropriate behavior, final grades, objective grades, subjective grades, or, for the two positive-expectancy groups, postmanipulation teacher perceptions (e.g., the final grades for the positive-expectancy classes were 83.13% and 85.71%, whereas those for the control classes were 72.79% and 75.75%).

References

Babad, E.Y., Inbar, J., & Rosenthal, R. (1982). Pygmalion, Galatea and the Golem: Investigations of biased and unbiased teachers. *Journal of Educational Psychology, 74,* 459-474.

Brattesani, K.A., Weinstein, R.S., & Marshall, H.H. (1984). Student perceptions of differential teacher treatment as moderators of teacher expectation effects. *Journal of Educational Psychology, 76,* 236-237.

Braun, C. (1976). Teacher expectation: Sociopsychological dynamics. *Review of Educational Research, 46,* 185-213.

Brophy, J.E. (1983). Research on the self-fulfilling prophecy and teacher expectations. *Journal of Educational Psychology, 75,* 631-661.

Brophy, J.E., & Good, T.L. (1970). Teachers' communication of differential expectations for children's classroom performance: Some behavioral data. *Journal of Educational Psychology, 61,* 365-374.

Brophy, J.E., & Good, T.L. (1974). *Teacher-student relationships.* New York, NY: Holt, Rinehart, & Winston.

Cooper, H.M. (1979). Pygmalion grows up: A model for teacher expectation communication and performance influence. *Review of Educational Research, 49,* 389-410.

Cooper, H.M., & Good, T.L. (1983). *Pygmalion grows up: Studies in the expectation communication process.* New York, NY: Longman.

Cooper, H.M., & Tom, D.Y.H. (1984). Teacher expectation research: A review with implications for classroom instruction. *Elementary School Journal, 85,* 77-89.

Feldman, R.S., & Prohaska, T. (1979). The student as Pygmalion: Effect of student expectation on the teacher. *Journal of Educational Psychology, 71,* 485-493.

Feldman, R.S., Saletsky, R.D., Sullivan, J., & Theiss, A.J. (1983). Student locus of control and response to expectations about self and teacher. *Journal of Educational Psychology, 75,* 27-32.

Feldman, R.S., & Theiss, A.J. (1983). The teacher and student as Pygmalions: Joint effect of teacher and student expectations. *Journal of Educational Psychology, 74,* 217-223.

French-Lazovik, G. (1974). Predictability of students' evaluations of college teachers from component ratings. *Journal of Educational Psychology, 66,* 373-385.

Kulik, J., & Kulik, C. (1974). Student ratings of instruction. *Teaching of Psychology, 1,* 51-57.

Manni, J.L. (1975). The effect of the warm-cold variable on students' expectations for teacher performance and students' learning (Doctoral dissertation, Temple University, 1975), *Dissertation Abstracts International, 36,* 3518A-3519A.

Perry, R.P., Abrami, P.C., Leventhal, L., & Check, J. (1979). Instructor reputation: An expectancy relationship involving student ratings and achievement. *Journal of Educational Psychology, 71,* 776-787.

Perry, R.P., Niemi, R.P., & Jones, K. (1974). Effect of prior teaching evaluations and lecture presentation on ratings of teacher performance. *Journal of Educational Psychology, 66,* 851-856.

Rappaport, M.M., & Rappaport, H. (1975). The other half of the expectancy equation: Pygmalion. *Journal of Educational Psychology, 67,* 531-536.

Raudenbush, S. (1984). Magnitude of teacher expectancy effects on pupil IQ as a function of the credibility of expectancy induction: A synthesis of findings from 18 experiments. *Journal of Educational Psychology, 76,* 85-97.

Rosenthal, R., & Jacobson, L. (1968). *Pygmalion in the classroom: Teacher expectation and pupils' intellectual development.* New York, NY: Holt, Rinehart, & Winston.

Smith, M. (1980). Meta-analysis of research on teacher expectations. *Evaluations in Education, 4,* 53-55.

Stewart, G. (1975). *Analysis of the student expectancy effect in teacher-pupil interactions.* Unpublished bachelor's thesis, Princeton University, Princeton, NJ.

Ware, J.E., & Williams, R.G. (1975). The Dr. Fox effect: A study of lecture effectiveness and ratings of instruction. *Journal of Medical Education, 50,* 149-156.

Weinstein, R.S. (1983). Student perceptions of schooling. *Elementary School Journal, 83,* 151-188.

Zanna, M.P., Sheras, P.L., Cooper, J., & Shaw, C. (1975). Pygmalion and Galatea: The interactive effects of teacher and student expectancies. *Journal of Experimental Social Psychology, 11*, 279-287.

The Relationship Between Student Team Learning Outcomes and Achievement, Causal Attributions, and Affect

Bette Chambers and Philip C. Abrami
Department of Education, Concordia University

The field investigation examined the relationship between prior achievement (high vs. average vs. low), individual outcome (success vs. failure), team outcome (success vs. failure) and students' achievement and academic perceptions. One hundred and ninety students in 7 elementary school classes learned mathematics for 5 weeks with the Teams-Games-Tournaments cooperative learning strategy. Team outcome was significantly related to achievement and academic perceptions and was independent of prior achievement and individual outcome. Members of successful teams attributed their team's performance more to ability and luck than did members of unsuccessful teams, believed themselves to be more successful, more deserving of reward, and happier about their team outcome. Alternatives such as criterion-referenced team goals and between-team cooperation are recommended.

*　　　*　　　*

REVIEWS OF RESEARCH ON THE EFFECTS OF COOPERATIVE LEARNING HAVE established positive and substantial effects on achievement (Johnson, Maruyama, Johnson, Nelson, & Skon, 1981; Slavin, 1990) and other outcomes (Johnson, Johnson, & Maruyama, 1983). Less is known about the mechanisms behind these cooperative learning strategies and the processes that take place in cooperatively structured classrooms. Consequently, research is moving beyond the question of whether cooperative learning enhances achievement and affect to address questions about the conditions under which cooperative learning works. Such research may lead to a better understanding of the factors that promote effective group learning.

One aspect of cooperative learning that may have a powerful impact on students is team outcome, in which some teams succeed and others fail. The general purpose of this research was to determine the relationship be-

This research was supported by grants to Bette Chambers and Philip C. Abrami from the Ministry of Education, Province of Quebec, and the Social Sciences and Humanities Research Council, Government of Canada. We acknowledge the assistance of Linda Stroh and Jenny Schaeff, who assisted in data collection and analysis, respectively.

tween team outcome (along with prior achievement and individual outcome) and student achievement and beliefs.

In many cooperative learning strategies for classroom use, each team is composed of students of varying ability levels such that overall the teams are equal in average ability. With group rewards, heterogeneous teams, and varying team outcomes, which are characteristic of cooperative learning strategies, the distribution of winners and losers changes from the distribution in traditional instruction. Students usually perceive traditional instruction as competitive (Johnson et al., 1981), with the most able students usually achieving the highest and the least able students usually achieving the lowest. Thus, in contrast to competition, success in cooperative learning should be perceived by students as dependent more on the effort of each team member than on student ability. For a team of students to do well, each team member is generally required to try hard, especially when there is individual accountability.

Ames (1984a) hypothesized that the motivational systems that underlie classroom reward structures vary. However, the effects of failure on student beliefs about learning may be negative regardless of the reward condition. For example, Ames (1981) suggested that the final impact of failing in a cooperative condition was similarly debilitating compared with losing in a competitive condition: "Cooperative settings that end in group failure have substantial negative consequences for children's self-adaptive and interpersonal behavior" (p. 286). In the cooperative condition, one would expect team outcome to have a major effect on attributions to effort. However, Ames (1981) found that team outcomes caused ability (and luck) attributions to vary considerably, whereas effort (and task) attributions varied slightly, if at all.

Why might this be? If the task is the same for all teams, then perception of task difficulty should not vary. If effort is perceived as important and if all students work hard to achieve for their team, then perceptions of the importance of effort should be uniformly high and invariant. This explanation is consistent with the findings of Ames (1981).

If task difficulty is not a factor and if students try hard to learn, team outcome may be a function of the remaining causes, primarily luck (if the task is a novel one) but also ability (if students perceive teams to be unequal in ability). Ames (1981) found significant effects of team outcome on both ability and luck, which are uncontrollable causes for success (Weiner, 1980). However, does the relationship between team outcome and uncontrollable causal beliefs generalize from the laboratory to the classroom?

Ames (1981) tested children in like-sex pairs; the children either competed or cooperated in the solution of line drawing puzzles. However, Ames did not assess the influence of team success and failure on a critical factor for classroom instruction: individual achievement and retention of the subject matter. For example, would subjects in the groups that succeeded perform better on future, similar tasks?

Ames' (1981, 1984b) research was largely short-term, carefully controlled experimentation. It differed from the classroom setting in a host of ways that may qualify its applicability. The research was of short duration (a small part of one day). In addition, the research involved a novel task (line puzzles) of questionable importance to the participants, which by its nature may have enhanced attributions to effort and luck. Ames controlled for performance, manipulating team outcome so that some puzzles could not be solved, and used smaller group sizes (two-member groups) than those that have been used in most small-group learning (Kagan, 1985). Finally, the subject pairs neither knew each other nor were permitted to interact with each other, limiting the development of helping strategies (Slavin, 1983a).

In their meta-analysis of research on children's causal attributions, Whitley and Frieze (1985) called for attributional research in more naturalistic settings because of the potential mediational effect that factors such as task importance and ego-involvement may have. In the case of cooperative learning research, Slavin (1983b) convincingly argued that the best evidence will be found in studies that take place in actual classrooms, in which students learn actual course content over several weeks.

Consequently, the purpose of this field research was to contribute to the understanding of how the structure of team learning mediates learning. Is team outcome a salient factor in the achievement, causal attributions, and affect of students participating in a cooperative learning strategy? We also discussed the influences of prior achievement and individual outcome variables. This study compensated for the problems of laboratory studies by having students in real classrooms work together, in teams of 4, on actual academic material for a 5-week period.

The main hypothesis of this study was that team outcome would relate positively to subsequent individual achievement. Consistent with Ames' (1981) findings, we hypothesized that members of successful teams, compared with members of unsuccessful teams, would perceive the uncontrollable causes (ability and luck) of their outcome as greater, would see themselves and their teams as more successful and more deserving of reward, and would be happier with their outcome.

Method

Subjects

One hundred and ninety students (89 boys and 101 girls) and their teachers in suburban Montreal, Canada, participated in the research. There were two third-grade classes, one fourth-grade class, two fifth-grade classes, one sixth-grade class, and one seventh-grade class distributed among four English elementary schools. The teachers volunteered to participate in the study after participating in an in-service workshop on Teams-Games-Tournaments (TGT; DeVries, Slavin, Fennessy, Edwards, & Lombardo, 1980; Slavin, 1980).

Procedure

The teachers conducted a 5-week mathematics unit with their classes, using the TGT strategy and curricular materials adapted from those developed by Slavin (1980). Teachers ranked the students in their classes on the basis of students' mathematics grades from the first report period and then used these rankings to assign students to heterogeneous 4-member teams according to the method outlined in the TGT teachers' manual (Slavin, 1980, p. 16). The assignment of students to teams was closely supervised, and the mean ability rank of each team was calculated to verify that the teams were as equal in prior achievement as possible. The assignment of teams is important in cooperative learning, especially in strategies that involve interteam competition (DeVries & Slavin, 1978), as the teams must be equal in ability for the interteam competition to be fair.

Each team was given two copies of a worksheet that contained approximately 30 mathematics questions. The group members worked together to answer these questions. After studying the material within the teams, each student played a game, which involved answering questions similar to those on the worksheets, with two students of similar ability from other teams. Students earned points for their teams based on the relative number of questions answered correctly compared with their competitors. Thus, all students, regardless of ability level, had an equal chance of contributing points to their team.

The TGT strategy calls for the winner at each tournament table to be "bumped" up to a higher ability table for the next tournament and the loser at each table to be "bumped" down to the next lower ability table. This procedure serves several purposes: to insure that any improper tournament assignments will eventually be adjusted, guaranteeing that each team has a similar chance of obtaining points; to vary the tournament competition from week to week, maintaining a gamelike atmosphere; and finally to change the difficulty level of bumped students, thereby enhancing student motivation.

The individual and team scores were calculated, and weekly newsletters were written by the researchers to announce the weekly standings and to congratulate the teams and individuals with the highest scores. The purpose of the newsletters was to reinforce the teams that performed well and to motivate all students to try hard.

At the end of the program, the teachers administered objective math tests on material covered in the 5-week TGT program. On the day after the students received their test marks, the researcher administered attribution and satisfaction measures.

Measures

The academic tests typically included a selection of 30 objective items taken from the mathematics curriculum studied in each class during the 5-week TGT program. The academic perceptions measured were causal attributions, affect, and perceptions of deserved reward and degree of success for each of three situations: individual TGT performance, team TGT performance, and test performance. We predicted that prior achievement would most strongly relate to beliefs about test performance, that individual outcome would most strongly relate to individual TGT performance, and that team outcome would most strongly relate to team TGT performance. We also were interested in the relationship of team outcome to individual TGT and test performances.

Causal attributions were assessed with 9-point Likert scales ranging from *not at all* to *very much*, on which students rated the degree to which ability, effort, luck, and task difficulty applied to each situation (e.g., "How bright were you on the math tournaments?"). Students responded by marking an "X" on one of nine graduated circles, which represented the scale responses.

Perceived success was the degree of success, rated on Likert scales, that was experienced on the test, on individual TGT, and on team TGT. Deserved reward was operationally defined as the degree of reward that individual students felt they deserved in each situation. It was measured by asking the children to circle the number of stars between 0 and 9 that they felt they earned. To assess affect, students circled one of five faces that demonstrated varying degrees of happiness (see Ames, 1981).

Design and Analysis

The design of the study was a $3 \times 2 \times 2$ factorial: Prior Achievement (high vs. average vs. low) × Individual TGT Outcome (success vs. failure) × Team TGT Outcome (success vs. failure). Grade level and gender were also included in the initial analyses, but they explained less than 1% of the variance in the dependent measures either as main effects or in interactions with other factors. Subsequently, we collapsed the analyses across these factors. This study is a comparison of team success and team failure and not a comparison of cooperative and traditional instruction; therefore we did not include a traditional instruction control group.

Prior achievement was operationally defined as the mathematics achievement of the students as determined by their mathematics grades for the first term. Students were ranked within classes and then divided into categories of high, average, and low prior achievement.

Individual outcome was operationalized as a student's average TGT score over the 5-week treatment. Individual outcome was divided by median split into successful and unsuccessful students within each class. Team outcome was also determined by a median split within each class into successful and unsuccessful teams; the criterion was the total TGT score for each team for the entire TGT program.

The students in different grades and different classes completed different tests. Therefore, we transformed the raw test scores within classes to make the achievement measures equivalent. To transform raw scores, we computed z scores for each class on the basis of the class mean achievement and the square root of mean square error from a Prior Achievement×Individual Outcome×Team Outcome analysis of variance (ANOVA) for each class. (See Table 1 for the class means and mean square error terms for the raw test scores.) This method of analysis allowed the main and interaction effects to vary from class to class even though mean class achievement was now zero and did not vary across classes (cf. Abrami, Perry, & Leventhal, 1982). Estimates of omega squared (Hays, 1981) were calculated for all significant ($p < .05$) univariate effects in order to determine the percent of variance accounted for by each factor.

Table 1

Class Means and Mean Square Error Terms for Achievement Raw Scores

Class	M	MS_e
1	56.01	431.30
2	23.85	20.82
3	18.90	18.04
4	20.39	15.79
5	16.04	21.63
6	17.70	14.66
7	22.95	21.42

As teacher reports of student ability can be subjective and more unreliable than standardized tests, we analyzed the bumping process. We determined that the initial rankings and tournament table assignments were quite accurate.

Results

The hypotheses relating to the relationship between team outcome and achievement, causal attributions, and affect were largely supported. First the achievement data are presented, followed by presentation of the students' perceptions of their individual TGT performance, team TGT performance, and test performance. Table 2 presents the sample sizes, cell means, and standard deviations for the transformed test scores.

Achievement

A 3 (prior achievement)×2 (individual outcome)×2 (team outcome) factorial ANOVA on the transformed test scores confirmed the hypothesis that members of successful teams would perform better on the test than members of unsuccessful teams, $F(1,178)=4.407, p<.05, w^2=.012$. In addition, both prior achievement and individual outcome main effects were significant, $F(1,178)=36.041, p<.05, w^2=.253$, and $F(1,178)=9.796, p<.05, w^2=.032$, respectively. There were no significant interaction effects. Inspection of the means in Table 2 shows the combined effects of prior achievement, individual outcome, and team outcome. The highest test scores were obtained by prior high-achieving students who individually succeeded aand whose teams succeeded ($M=0.94$), whereas the lowest test scores were obtained by prior low-achieving students who individually failed and whose teams failed ($M=-1.44$), a difference of almost 2.5 standard deviations.

TABLE 2

Cell Means, Sample Sizes, and Standard Deviations for Achievement (z Scores)

Prior achievement	Team outcome	Individual outcome	n	M	SD
High	High	High	23	0.94	0.67
		Low	7	0.21	0.93
	Low	High	12	0.76	0.99
		Low	19	0.74	0.67
Average	High	High	23	0.52	0.63
		Low	11	-0.15	0.96
	Low	High	13	0.14	0.97
		Low	19	-0.47	1.27
Low	High	High	18	-0.19	1.11
		Low	12	-0.70	1.32
	Low	High	19	-0.82	1.19
		Low	14	-1.44	1.17

Academic Perceptions

Initially, we computed Prior Achievement×Individual Outcome×Team Outcome multivariate analyses of variance (MANOVAs) on the set of academic perceptions for each of the three different situations: individual TGT outcome, team TGT outcome, and test performance. Multivariate and univariate tests for the attribution and affect measures are summarized in Table 3, along with estimates of omega squared.

Table 3
Summary of Main Effects of Prior Achievement, Individual Outcome, and Team Outcome on Attributions and Affect: Multivariate and Univariate F Ratios and Estimates of Omega-Squared[a]

Outcome measure[b]	Prior achievement		Individual outcome		Team outcome		MS_e[c]
	F	ω^2	F	ω^2	F	ω^2	
Perceptions of individual TGT performance							
MANOVA	2.56*		3.05*		3.25*		
Ability	6.70*	.06	3.88*	.01	0.84		1.15
Effort	0.01		0.62		0.54		2.14
Luck	0.11		1.40		1.07		4.17
Task	3.11*	.02	1.77		0.47		4.79
Success	1.31		10.08*	.04	4.39*	.02	2.47
Affect	2.49		23.35*	.10	8.53*	.03	0.65
Rewards	0.18		7.28*	.03	1.20		3.56
Perceptions of team TGT performance							
MANOVA	1.48		0.54		9.61*		
Ability	1.41		0.16		21.23*	.10	2.05
Effort	0.85		0.03		3.51		2.05
Luck	0.01		0.01		20.69*	.09	4.17
Task	0.08		0.26		0.04		4.46
Success	0.47		0.31		58.10*	.23	2.87
Affect	0.17		1.33		30.88*	.13	0.91
Rewards	2.86		0.15		29.33*	.13	2.84
Perceptions of test performance							
MANOVA	2.91*		1.01		1.77		
Ability	8.86*	.07	2.57		3.70		3.07
Effort	3.48*	.03	0.94		0.54		2.14
Luck	4.69*	.04	3.29		5.73*	.02	4.91
Task	2.78		1.95		0.30		4.70
Success	16.75*	.14	3.34		6.76*	.03	3.85
Affect	9.46*	.08	4.02*	.01	2.75		1.40
Rewards	8.09*	.07	1.56		1.25		6.32

Note. TGT = Teams–Games–Tournament; MANOVA = multivariate analyses of variance.
[a] The interactions are not tabulated because there were no significant ($p < .05$) multivariate effects and very few significant univariate effects. Estimates of omega-squared (ω^2) are reported only for significant ($p < .05$) univariate effects.   [b] For groups of measures, the multivariate test results precede the univariate results.   [c] Multivariate error df for individual outcome and team outcome = 162; df for ability = 324; univariate error $df = 178$.
* $p < .05$.

There were significant ($p < .05$) main effects of prior achievement on the perceptions of individual TGT results and test scores. There was a significant main effect of individual outcome, only on perceptions of individual TGT results. More importantly, there were significant main effects of team outcome on perceptions of team and individual TGT results but not on test performance.

Consistent with the results for the achievement data, there were no significant multivariate interaction effects in any of the three sets of perceptions. There were also very few univariate interaction effects (about the number expected by chance), and they were small in size. Consequently, we chose to ignore the interaction effects and concentrate only on the main effects. We report in detail the results related to team outcome, as this is the focus of the study, and only briefly describe the results related to prior achievement and individual outcome. As might be expected and as Table 3 indicates, prior achievement related most strongly to perceptions of test performance, individual outcome related most strongly to perceptions of individual TGT outcome, and team outcome related most strongly to perceptions of team performance. The significant relationships between team outcome and perceptions of individual TGT performance and test performance are interesting to note. (See Table 4 for means and standard deviations for the attribution and affective measures.)

Prior achievement. Students' prior achievement substantially predicted their perceptions of the test and somewhat predicted their perceptions of individual TGT performance. However, prior achievement had no significant relationship with perceptions of team TGT performance. High achievers rated their ability, effort, and luck on the test higher than did low achievers. As might be expected, high achievers felt happier, more successful, and more deserving of reward regarding their test score than did low achievers. With regard to their individual TGT performances, high achievers found their ability more important and found the task easier than did low achievers.

Individual outcome. Overall, individual outcome had only a modest relationship with student perceptions, and this relationship was generally concerned with TGT performance. Individual outcome was significantly related to ability attributions, perceived success, deserved reward, and affect, with regard to individual TGT performance.

For reactions to test performance, only affective perceptions were related to individual outcome. Perceptions of team TGT performance were not influenced by individual outcome.

Team outcome. As predicted, team outcome played a role in students' perceptions: Not only was it strongly related to most aspects of team TGT performance but it also was related to some of the individual TGT performance and test score measures. Team outcome was significantly and substantially (estimates of omega squared were almost .10) related to ability and luck attributions. There were no significant relationships between team outcome and effort or between team outcome and task attributions. However, regardless of team success or failure, students rated the importance

Table 4
Means and Standard Deviations for the Attribution and Affective Measures

Outcome measure	Prior achievement			Individual outcome		Team outcome	
	High	Average	Low	Success	Failure	Success	Failure
Perceptions of individual TGT performance							
Ability							
M	7.41	6.97	6.71	7.18	6.83	7.14	6.92
SD	0.69	1.08	1.34	1.02	1.18	0.77	1.35
Effort							
M	7.90	7.88	7.92	7.99	7.78	8.00	7.80
SD	1.59	1.56	1.32	1.49	1.49	1.38	1.59
Luck							
M	6.43	6.04	6.32	6.52	6.09	6.53	6.14
SD	1.93	1.80	2.01	2.05	1.98	1.81	2.21
Task							
M	3.79	4.48	4.73	4.18	4.56	4.40	4.28
SD	2.00	2.10	2.36	2.08	2.30	2.16	2.21
Success							
M	7.13	6.83	6.68	7.25	6.39	7.21	6.55
SD	1.35	1.63	1.88	1.50	1.70	1.29	1.87
Affect							
M	3.77	4.08	3.98	4.23	3.57	4.19	3.71
SD	0.90	0.86	0.99	0.71	0.98	0.74	0.97
Reward							
M	6.46	6.53	6.35	6.81	5.98	6.69	6.21
SD	1.73	1.96	2.06	1.80	1.97	1.52	2.21
Perceptions of team TGT performance							
Ability							
M	7.07	7.44	7.44	7.38	7.24	7.81	6.84
SD	1.60	1.48	1.41	1.39	1.64	1.18	1.62
Effort							
M	8.08	7.83	7.76	7.94	7.82	8.10	7.69
SD	1.12	1.45	1.77	1.39	1.51	1.19	1.62
Luck							
M	6.39	6.38	6.37	6.49	6.21	7.06	5.69
SD	2.83	2.10	2.14	1.98	2.35	1.58	2.39
Task							
M	4.70	4.58	4.71	4.73	4.57	4.65	4.68
SD	2.11	2.13	2.18	2.06	2.23	2.14	2.13
Success							
M	6.95	7.12	6.76	7.19	6.62	7.95	5.97
SD	1.68	1.90	2.31	1.82	2.14	1.02	2.19
Affect							
M	3.93	4.03	3.92	4.11	3.77	4.38	3.55
SD	1.01	0.94	1.18	0.99	1.09	0.76	1.12
Reward							
M	6.98	7.45	7.68	7.56	7.15	8.07	6.70
SD	1.99	1.94	1.52	1.74	1.96	1.07	2.35
Perceptions of test performance							
Ability							
M	7.20	6.61	5.87	6.78	6.26	6.86	6.25
SD	1.25	1.83	2.15	1.78	1.93	1.51	2.11
Effort							
M	8.23	8.15	7.59	7.91	8.10	8.05	7.93
SD	1.46	1.42	1.78	1.56	1.40	1.41	1.58
Luck							
M	6.33	5.92	5.13	6.12	5.35	6.27	5.32
SD	2.01	2.32	2.42	2.30	2.25	2.08	2.42
Task							
M	4.67	5.33	5.56	4.98	5.48	5.05	5.33
SD	2.25	1.92	2.33	2.30	2.01	2.34	2.03
Success							
M	7.20	6.59	5.21	6.62	5.94	6.79	5.88
SD	1.33	2.02	2.48	2.04	2.26	1.75	2.42
Affect							
M	4.03	3.50	3.11	3.72	3.30	3.73	3.35
SD	0.89	1.29	1.35	1.17	1.31	1.03	1.41
Reward							
M	6.70	5.83	4.89	6.04	5.49	6.07	5.53
SD	2.03	2.59	2.80	2.56	2.62	2.22	2.90

Note. TGT = Teams–Games–Tournament.

of effort highest. In contrast, attributions to task difficulty were overall the lowest. Ability and luck causes were second and third most important, respectively.

Perceived success, affect, and deserved team reward were significantly related to team outcome for team TGT performance. The measure of perceived success served as a check that the students accurately perceived the TGT team results; the effect was very large (estimates of omega squared were almost .250).

Of additional interest was the effect of team outcome on perceptions of individual TGT performance and test performance. Team outcome was significantly related to perceived success and affect for individual TGT performance. Members of successful teams rated their individual TGT performance as more successful and felt happier about it than did members of failing teams.

Team outcome was significantly but modestly related to two of the seven measures of individual test performance, namely, luck attributions and perceived success. Members of successful teams felt luckier and more successful with regard to their test scores than did members of failing teams.

Although team outcome was significantly related to only a single attributional category (luck) on individual test performance, the overall pattern of attributional responses in this situation was similar to the pattern of responses on team TGT performance. That is, the highest-rated attribution was effort, followed by ability, luck, and task difficulty, respectively.

Discussion

The major findings of this study are those related to the effects of team outcome. Team outcome was significantly related to both achievement and student perceptions. Members of successful teams performed better on the individually completed test and rated their ability and luck higher than did members of unsuccessful teams.

The implications for student learning are that students low in prior achievement who work in successful teams can benefit academically. However, students low in prior achievement who work in unsuccessful teams are at a disadvantage academically. What feature of the teams resulted in members of successful teams actually learning the material better than those of unsuccessful teams? Because the teams were equal in average ability, the differences in learning cannot be attributed to differences in team ability. Webb's (1982, 1984, 1985) work indicates that the gender and personality mix of small groups influenced group functioning, as well as giving and receiving explanations (Peterson & Swing, 1985).

Interestingly, members of successful teams felt happier and more successful not only with their team performance but also with their individual

TGT performance. This is an important finding as it shows that team outcome can moderate the effects of individual success or failure as well as the effects of team performance. The attributional and affective findings of this field study corroborate the experimental findings of Ames (1981) and extend them to students who learn curricular material in cooperative groups over several weeks as part of an actual classroom routine. In particular, there were significant relationships between team outcome and causal beliefs about the importance of ability and luck in the team learning situation. Both ability and luck are uncontrollable causal factors.

Like Ames (1984b), we found that attributions to effort were the highest-rated cause, regardless of whether teams succeeded or failed. Furthermore, the relative importance of the four attributional categories—effort, ability, luck, and task difficulty—was invariant across situations. Students perceived effort rather than ability, which was of secondary importance, as the single most important cause of their individual achievement results. This finding raises questions about the long-term impacts of cooperative learning.

The dilemma is the following: Will effort be perceived as the single most important element in team learning and be unaffected by outcome after students have multiple success and failure experiences learning in teams, or will students come to see their success as increasingly uncontrollable?

Proponents of cooperative learning argue that it can be used for mainstreaming and in schools in which there are a wide range of ethnic and student ability differences (Aronson & Osherow, 1980; Slavin, Madden, & Leavey, 1984). Indeed, team learning is increasingly used when classes of students are very heterogeneous. However, it is important to consider the evidence on learned helplessness among schoolchildren (Diener & Dweck, 1980; Dweck & Reppucci, 1973).

If students with very low ability in heterogeneous classes perceive themselves as ineffective or helpless learners, then they take little personal responsibility for individual learning and view learning outcomes as dependent on their lack of ability rather than on their lack of effort. The effect of team success for these students may be positive, although Diener and Dweck (1980) suggested that helpless students tend to discount success experiences. For these students the effect of team outcome and individual ability may no longer be additive; it may be multiplicative. That is, outcome and ability may interact such that helpless students whose teams fail may learn much less and be more negative about learning than other students. Future research should explore this question.

The results of this study have implications for the type of instructional strategies used in schools. If being a member of a successful team has the positive results indicated by this study, increasing the possibility of team success makes sense. One method would be to set a reasonable criterion that teams would be able to reach and thus be rewarded, rather than norm-referencing team success, which guarantees winning and losing teams. In fact, Slavin previously advocated between-team competition but now suggests using criterion-referenced rewards when using TGT (Slavin, 1986). This may decrease the number of students who experience failure and the negative effects associated with it. However, the problem of determining appropriate criteria that will challenge students without frustrating them accompanies this type of strategy. If an educator's goals are to promote student affect, then successful group experiences should be created.

The teachers in this study volunteered to participate and were especially interested in improving their teaching. The effects of teacher motivation and experience in cooperative learning are not yet clear (Talmage, Pascarella, & Ford, 1984). In addition, the variables of prior achievement, individual outcome, and team outcome were not manipulated; therefore, causal interpretations of the findings are not definitive. In particular, we do not know what caused teams to succeed or fail, an area for futher study (Solomon, 1988). This study took place in suburban middle class schools; therefore, generalizations can only be made to similar populations and settings.

Future research should address the question of what teaching strategies best enhance the motivation and achievement of all students. Do cooperative instructional strategies that de-emphasize the success or failure of learning teams result in the same degree of influence on individual achievement and perceptions of team performance as found in this study? Kagan, Zahn, Widaman, Schwarzwald, and Tyrrell (1985) found that for some minority students TGT was detrimental to achievement and affect, whereas student teams-achievement divisions, a strategy that does not involve face-to-face competition, was not. Very few of the widely used cooperative strategies involve between-team cooperation such that when all of the groups reach a criterion, the whole class is rewarded. Between-teams cooperation may provide an incentive without the failure that may be debilitating for subsequent achievement and motivation.

References

Abrami, P.C., Perry, R.P., & Leventhal, L. (1982). The relationship between student personality characteristics, teacher ratings, and student achievement. *Journal of Educational Psychology, 74*, 111-125.

Ames, C. (1981). Competitive versus cooperative reward structures: The influence of individual and group performance factors on achievement attributions and affect. *American Educational Research Journal, 18*, 273-287.

Ames, C. (1984a). Competitive, cooperative, and individualistic goal structures: A cognitive-motivational analysis. In R.E. Ames & C. Ames (Eds.), *Research in motivation in education: Vol. 1, Student motivation* (pp. 177-208), San Diego, CA: Academic Press.

Ames, C. (1984b). Achievement attributions and self-instructions under competitive and individualistic goal structures. *Journal of Educational Psychology, 76,* 478-487.

Aronson, E., & Osherow, N. (1980). Cooperation, prosocial behavior, and academic performance: Experiments in the desegregated classroom. *Applied Social Psychology Annual, 1,* 163-196.

DeVries, D.L., & Slavin, R.E. (1978). Teams-Games-Tournaments (TGT): Review of ten classroom experiments. *Journal of Research and Development in Education, 12,* 28-38.

DeVries, D.L., Slavin, R.E., Fennessy, G.M., Edwards, K.J., & Lombardo, M.M. (1980). *Teams-Games-Tournaments: The team learning approach.* Englewood Cliffs, NJ: Educational Technology Publications.

Diener, C.I., & Dweck, C.S. (1980). An analysis of learned helplessness: II. The processing of success. *Journal of Personality and Social Psychology, 39,* 940-952.

Dweck, C.S., & Reppucci, N.D. (1973). Learned helplessness and reinforcement responsibility in children. *Journal of Personality and Social Psychology, 25,* 109-116.

Hays, W.L. (1981). *Statistics* (3rd ed.). New York, NY: Holt, Rinehart & Winston.

Johnson, D.W., Johnson, R., & Maruyama, G. (1983). Interdependence and interpersonal attraction among heterogeneous and homogeneous individuals: A theoretical formulation and a meta-analysis of research. *Review of Educational Research, 53,* 5-54.

Johnson, D.W., Maruyama, G., Johnson, R., Nelson, D., & Skon, L. (1981). Effects of cooperative, competitive, and individualistic goal structures on achievement: A meta-analysis. *Psychological Bulletin, 89,* 47-62.

Kagan, S. (1985). *Co-operative learning: Resources for teachers.* Riverside, CA: University of California, Riverside Press.

Kagan, S., Zahn, G., Widaman, K.F., Schwarzwald, J., & Tyrrell G. (1985). Classroom structural bias: Impact of cooperative and competitive classroom structures on cooperative and competitive individuals and groups. In R. Slavin, S. Sharan, S. Kagan, R.H. Lazarowitz, C. Webb, & R. Schmuck (Eds.), *Learning to cooperate, cooperating to learn* (pp. 227-312). New York, NY: Plenum Press.

Peterson, P.L., & Swing, S.R. (1985). Students' cognitions as mediators of the effectiveness of small-group learning. *Journal of Educational Psychology, 77,* 299-312.

Slavin, R.E. (1980). *Using student team learning.* (Rev. ed.). Baltimore, MD: Johns Hopkins University.

Slavin, R.E. (1983a). *Cooperative learning.* New York, NY: Longman.

Slavin, R.E. (1983b). When does cooperative learning increase student achievement? *Psychological Bulletin, 94,* 429-445.

Slavin, R.E. (1986). *Using student team learning.* (3rd ed.). Baltimore, MD: Johns Hopkins University.

Slavin, R.E. (1990). *Cooperative learning: Theory, research, and practice.* Englewood Cliffs, NJ: Prentice-Hall.

Slavin, R.E., Madden, N.A., & Leavey, M. (1984). Effects of cooperative learning and individualized instruction on mainstreamed students. *Exceptional Children, 50,* 434-443.

Solomon, G. (1988, April). *When teams don't function the way they ought to.* Paper presented at the annual meeting of the American Educational Research Association, New Orleans, LA.

Talmadge, H., Pascarella, E.T., & Ford, S. (1984). The influence of cooperative learning strategies on teacher practices, student perceptions of the learning environment, and academic achievement. *American Educational Research Journal, 21,* 163-179.

Webb, N.M. (1982). Peer interaction and learning in cooperative small groups. *Journal of Educational Psychology, 74,* 642-655.

Webb, N.M. (1984). Sex differences in interaction and achievement in cooperative small groups. *Journal of Educational Psychology, 76,* 33-44.

Webb, N.M. (1985). Student interaction and learning in small groups: A research summary. In R. Slavin, S. Sharan, S. Kagan, R.H. Lazarowitz, C. Webb, & R. Schmuck (Eds.), *Learning to cooperate, cooperating to learn* (pp. 147-172). New York, NY: Plenum Press.

Weiner, B. (1980). *Human motivation.* New York, NY: Holt, Rinehart & Winston.

Whitley, B.E., & Frieze, I.H. (1985). Children's causal attributions for success and failure in achievement settings: A meta-analysis. *Journal of Educational Psychology, 76,* 608-616.

Enhancing Academic Achievement in College Students Through Attributional Retraining and Instruction

Raymond P. Perry and Kurt S. Penner
University of Manitoba

Attributional retraining is a therapeutic method for reinstating psychological control that may be useful for improving students' achievement in the college classroom. After attributional retraining or no training, internal- and external-locus students observed a videotaped lecture presented by either a low- or a high-expressive instructor in a simulated college classroom. One week later they wrote a test on the lecture and on a homework assignment. Attributional retraining improved external, but not internal, students' performance on both the lecture and homework tests. Expressive instruction also enhanced lecture- and homework-related achievement in external students but not in internal students. These results suggest that cognitive factors influencing students' perceived control (e.g., internal/external locus) must be taken into consideration when remedial interventions for academic achievement are developed. The results are interpreted within a social cognition framework.

*   *   *

PERCEIVED CONTROL REFERS TO A PERSON'S ABILITY TO PREDICT AND TO influence the surrounding environment. Control theory (e.g., Carver & Scheier, 1982; Rothbaum, Weisz, & Snyder, 1982) suggests that perceived control is likely to play an instrumental role in college students' academic development and, ultimately, in their overall adjustment. Periodically, college students are threatened with loss of control through academic failure, personal trauma, and financial insecurity. These events can place some of them at risk, in part because loss of control impedes their capacity to benefit from effective instruction (Perry, 1985). The potential consequences range from boredom and apathy to absenteeism and dropping out. Improving the quality of instruction for these students will do little to promote

This research was based on an honors thesis carried out by Kurt S. Penner under Raymond P. Perry's direction. Support for this research was provided to Raymond P. Perry by the University of Manitoba Research Board and the Center for Higher Education Research and Development. We are grateful to Connie Perry and Scott Stephen for their assistance in data collection and to Jamie-Lynn Magnusson for her assistance in data analysis.

better academic performance unless perceptions of uncontrollability can be modified. Attributional retraining is one therapeutic technique for reinstating psychological control that appears to have considerable potential.

Perceived Control and Quality of Instruction

Effective teaching has long been considered instrumental to students' learning and performance. As such, it potentially represents a viable remediation for poor academic achievement in college students. Recent research on college teaching in both laboratory and field settings has revealed a number of teaching behaviors that can have positive consequences for students' academic development (e.g., Abrami, Leventhal, & Perry, 1982; Marsh, 1984; Murray, 1983). Accordingly, a relatively simple solution would be to ensure that marginal, at-risk students are enrolled in programs having high-quality instruction. Unfortunately, the solution is not so simple because poor performance is frequently associated with low perceived control. As Perry and Dickens (1984) have shown, students lacking control over academic performance are incapable of benefiting from good instruction. Ironically, the students who are in most need of effective teaching are least likely to gain from it.

Subsequent research has provided further insight into this relation between perceived control and instruction. The research also offers useful guidance into the development of remedial interventions for improving achievement in college students. Perry and Dickens (1984) originally demonstrated the relation by presenting college students with either contingent or noncontingent feedback on a prelecture aptitude test that temporarily altered their perceptions of control in accordance with helplessness theory (Seligman, 1975). After the aptitude test, half of the students in each feedback condition viewed a 25-minute videotaped lecture presented by a low-expressive instructor, and the other half saw the same lecture given by a high-expressive instructor. Students who received contingent feedback reported more control over their postlecture achievement test when taught by the high-expressive instructor than when taught by the low-expressive instructor. More important, they actually performed better with the expressive instructor. In contrast, students who received non-contingent feedback suffered temporary loss of control and did not perform well with the expressive instructor (see Figure 1, left panel). These results were replicated in three follow-up studies with similar experimental procedures (Perry & Magnusson, 1987; Perry, Magnusson, Parsonson, & Dickens, 1986; Perry & Tunna, 1988). Invariably, expressive instruction was an effective teaching behavior only when students perceived some control over their academic performance.[1]

Throughout these studies, loss of control was deemed to be the result of transient *situational* factors that periodically occur in college classrooms.

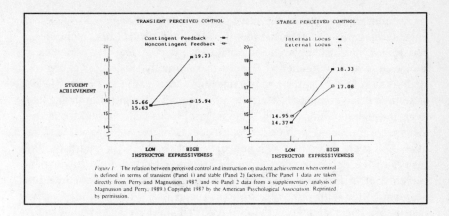

Figure 1 The relation between perceived control and instruction on student achievement when control is defined in terms of transient (Panel 1) and stable (Panel 2) factors. (The Panel 1 data are taken directly from Perry and Magnusson, 1987, and the Panel 2 data from a supplementary analysis of Magnusson and Perry, 1989.) Copyright 1987 by the American Psychological Association. Reprinted by permission.

Contingent and noncontingent feedback on an aptitude test was used to represent such environmental events. In addition to noncontingent feedback (e.g., Brophy, 1981), unannounced tests, excessive content, and poor organization are common classroom events that can lead to loss of control. The manipulation of feedback on aptitude tests provides a precise method for experimentally manipulating perceived control. Two additional experimental conditions were included in the core experimental design as levels of the contingency feedback variable: (a) no feedback, which requires students to respond to the aptitude test by using a standard IBM sheet (students are thus provided with no information about the accuracy of the answers) and (b) no training, which omits the aptitude test before the lecture.

But control theory specifies also that *stable* cognitive schemata, in addition to transient, environmental events, can determine students' perceptions of control. Internal locus of control (Rotter, 1966) and Type A personality (Glass, 1977), for example, are two constructs that describe people who have relatively enduring perceptions of control. Magnusson and Perry (1989), using a version of Rotter's (1966) scale modified for college classrooms (B. Weiner, personal communication, February 1981), examined how stable cognitive schemata might affect students' perceptions of control. If internals and externals differ in their stable perceptions of control (Lefcourt, 1980; Rothbaum et al., 1982), a pattern that is similar to that reported by Perry and Dickens (1984) for transient perceptions of control should emerge. As Figure 1 (right panel) indicates, internal-locus students in the study by Magnusson and Perry (1989) performed better for the expressive instructor than for the unexpressive instructor: however, external-locus students showed no comparable improvement in performance. Thus whether loss of control is considered in terms of temporary (state) or enduring (trait) qualities, it can consistently impede the benefits of effective instruction.

Of course, *both* stable cognitive schemata and transient environmental events *simultaneously* affect students' perceived control in actual college classrooms. For example, an internal-locus student may be periodically subjected to an environmental episode that normally causes loss of control, such as failure on a test or social rejection. Magnusson and Perry (1989) examined these combined determinants of perceived control in their other experimental conditions. Half of the internal-locus and external-locus students were presented with contingent feedback on the aptitude test, and the other half were presented with noncontingent feedback. In contrast to the results of the earlier studies, *noncontingent* feedback did not lower perceived control for internal-locus students. As a result, they continued to perform better with the expressive instructor than with the unexpressive instructor. Perry and Tunna (1988) reported similar results with Type A students. These students did better with the expressive instructor, even though before the lectures, they suffered loss of control as a result of receiving noncontingent feedback. On the other hand, *contingent* feedback presented before the lecture resulted in external-locus students' performing better with the expressive instructor than with the unexpressive instructor. Contingent feedback appears to serve a remedial function by increasing perceived control and thereby allowing the external-locus students to benefit from expressive instruction.

Together, these studies provide some guidance for developing remediation strategies to improve academic achievement. First, they show that loss of control, whether caused by transient environmental events or by preexisting cognitive schemata, impairs the achievement-enhancing capacity of effective instruction. Moreover, student achievement deteriorates in direct relation to the amount of uncontrollability induced before instruction (Perry & Dickens, 1988). Second, they indicate that some students are more resistant to loss of control because of cognitive schemata associated with internal locus of control and Type A personality. Despite the occurrence of events that normally lower perceived control, these students manage to retain or regain control so that they benefit from good instruction. Finally, contingent feedback appears to serve as a rudimentary intervention for one group of at-risk students (namely, those having an external locus) and to thereby enable effective instruction to increase achievement.

Attributional Retraining: Improving Academic Performance

If perceived control can be increased in at-risk students, then their achievement should improve as a result of both their own efforts and the quality of instruction. Attributional retraining is one remediation technique that appears to be gaining considerable prominence as a technique for restoring perceived control and self-efficacy (Försterling, 1985). Weiner (1974) and others (e.g., Abramson et al., 1980; Dweck, 1975) have argued that attributional retraining can be used to modify causal attributions, which in turn can lead to an increase in perceived control. Attribution theory has been used to design one-shot interventions in which ability and effort are linked to success and lack of effort to failure (Weiner, 1979). For example, Zoeller, Mahoney, and Weiner (1983) examined this technique with mentally retarded adults who observed a peer perform a psychomotor task on film. A commentator verbalized the desirable attribution following each success and failure. A second intervention procedure involved in vivo feedback given directly to subjects following each success and failure. Both interventions caused subjects' performance on a related task to improve more than the performance of an experimental group that received no intervention.

Attributional retraining has been used with different subjects in a variety of settings, but other than Wilson and Linville's (1982, 1985) research, few studies have focused on college students and academic achievement (Försterling, 1985). Wilson and Linville gave college students concerned about their academic performance a brief, one-shot attributional retraining session. The students saw videotaped interviews in which senior students described how their grade point averages (GPAs) improved substantially from their first to later academic years. The information was intended to change attributions for performance from stable to unstable causes and to show that although many students had problems initially, their performance improved dramatically in later years. Attributional retraining increased performance for men on a Graduate Record Examination (GRE) type test immediately after the session and enhanced GPA for both men and women in the next academic term. These results underscore the potential utility of attributional retraining for improving academic achievement in college students, although further development and closer scrutiny are required (e.g., Block & Lanning, 1984).

Attributional retraining was used here to induce a mastery orientation in college students who had either an internal or external locus of control (Rotter, 1966). It was combined with selected instructional variables to determine whether it can assist potentially at-risk students who are unable to benefit from effective teaching. External locus of control identifies a specific group of students who may have perceptions of low control (e.g., Rothbaum et al., 1982). Their beliefs that factors outside themselves determine important outcomes could result in lower control and, in some cases, helplessness (e.g., Dweck, 1975; Lefcourt, 1980). Magnusson and Perry's (1989) study is relevant to this issue because they examined external-locus students in relation to three types of prelecture feedback: contingent, noncontingent, and no feedback. External students were unable to improve their performance with the expressive instructor in the no-feedback condition (Figure 1, right panel). Yet, when presented with contingent feedback, they did better with the expressive instructor than with the unexpressive instructor.

The attributional retraining procedure used in our study was a short videotape intervention that was given before simulated classroom manipulations. Internal- and external-locus students received either attributional retraining or no training, after which they took an aptitude test that provided immediate contingent feedback. This phase was followed by a videotaped lecture that was presented by a low-expressive instructor to half of the retraining and no-training students and by a high-expressive instructor to the other half. Before departing, students received study material unrelated to the lecture and were told to return in 1 week to be tested on the lecture material and on the homework. These procedures depart from previous research by Perry and associates in that (a) an improved locus of control measure was used, (b) achievement was measured 1 week later rather than immediately after the lecture, and (c) a homework assignment provided a different type of achievement task.

Attributional retraining was expected to increase performance on both achievement measures 1 week following the lecture. If effective, it should have had immediate motivational consequences for students during the lecture, thereby improving their learning and ensuring better performance at a later date. It should also have motivated students to tackle the homework assignment in view of the impending test. A main effect would occur on the two achievement tests if both internal- and external-locus students benefited equally from the attributional retraining. If, however, either type of student benefited more than the other from the intervention, then a Locus of Control×Attributional Retraining interaction would occur. This is possible if differences in causal attributions and perceived control exist between internal- and external-locus students. For example, external-locus students could benefit from attributional retraining because it changes their causal attributions to a more internal locus. Internal-locus students may show little or no improvement if their attributions are congruent with the mastery orientation depicted in the attributional retraining.

Attributional retraining should also enable external-locus students to benefit from effective instruction. As demonstrated by Magnusson and Perry (1989), external-locus students performed better with an expressive instructor than with an unexpressive instructor when they received contingent feedback on a test before the lecture. In contrast, external-locus students who received no feedback before the lecture did not improve their performance with the expressive instructor. These results would be expected if contingent feedback led to an increase in perceived control in the external-locus students. The attributional retraining procedures employed in this study are more congruent with standard practices (e.g., Fösterling, 1985) and therefore are likely to augment the effects of Magnusson and Perry's rudimentary contingent feedback manipulation.

Method

Subjects

Subjects were 198 male and female students enrolled in a multi-section introductory psychology course of approximately 3,000 students at the University of Manitoba. Subjects volunteered for two sessions, and experimental conditions were assigned to sessions, as described in the *Procedure* section. Students received credit toward a course requirement for research participation.

Materials

Locus of control. The Multidimensional Multiattributional Causality Scale (MMCS) was used to assess internal-external locus of control (Lefcourt, Von Baeyer, Ware, & Cox, 1979). It is an attributional questionnaire for college students that focuses on two specific areas: academic achievement and affiliation. The psychometrics of the scale were described in detail by Lefcourt et al. Subjects responded to 48 Likert scale items that can be analyzed separately according to achievement versus affiliation, attributions for success/failure, and four kinds of attributions (ability, effort, context, and luck). Ability and effort attributions to failure were used to classify subjects into internal- and external-locus groups. The ratings for ability minus effort yield possible scores ranging from -15 to +15; higher scores indicate greater externality. This computational procedure separates students who attribute failure to lack of effort (internal locus of control) from those who attribute failure to lack of ability (external locus of control).

Our use of the terms *internal* and *external* depart from the original formulation as proposed by Rotter (1966). He would view an attribution of limited ability as an internal cause, although it implies an absence of self-contingency and a lack of control. A problem exists because this attribution does not conform with the general definition of internal locus, which suggests the presence of self-contingency and control. Because of this confusion, some researchers have deemed a limited ability attribution following failure as implying an external locus (e.g., Diener & Dweck, 1978; Lefcourt, 1976). An external locus is logically inferred because the person does not possess the resources (i.e., ability) necessary to produce success. This issue has been discussed at length elsewhere (e.g., Janoff-Bulman, 1979; Rothbaum et al., 1982). For our purposes, external locus was considered as involving an attribution to limited ability following failure. Without prejudging the resolution of this issue, our use of the term *external locus* implies differences in causal attributions and perceived control. Of course, an attribution to limited ability on the MMCS does not guarantee the absence of self-contingency because, owing to its construction, the scale does not assess other internal attributions that may be salient.

Only failure items were used to differentiate internal locus from external locus, on the basis of reviews of the learned helplessness literature that show that negative outcomes are the primary determinants of uncontrollability (e.g., Miller & Norman, 1979; Rothbaum, et al., 1982). Perry and Dickens (1988) found similar patterns in their simulated college classroom, in which noncontingent failure caused loss of control but noncontingent success caused no comparable effect. A median-split procedure was used to classify students as internal (MMCS score $\leq$ -4) or external (MMCS score $\geq$ -3); scores ranged from -12 to +5 ($M = -4.22$). The mean ratings were -6.68 for internals and -0.67 for externals; higher ratings denoted greater externality.

Contingency task. An aptitude test that provided *contingent* feedback to all students was given before the videotaped lecture. It was a shortened version (30 items) of Perry and Dickens's (1984) contingency task, which has been shown to enable students to retain control over their academic performance (Perry & Dickens, 1984, 1988). The task consisted of verbal analogies and quantitative items similar to those found on the Miller's Analogies Test and on the GRE. Multiple-choice answer sheets provided immediate feedback to the subjects when a special pen was used to mark the chosen alternative. Irridescent properties of the ink interacted with the invisible type on the answer sheet so that the contingent feedback was immediately visible. The answer sheet had four alternatives for each question, and a *C* or an *X* indicated whether the choice was correct or incorrect. Subjects were given 20 minutes to complete the questions.

Attributional retraining. Attributional retraining involved an 8-minute color videotape in which a male psychology professor described his freshman year at university. He recounted a critical incident in which, in the face of repeated failure, he persisted only at a friend's urging and went on to succeed in university, and graduate school. He encouraged students to attribute poor performance to lack of effort and good performance to ability and proper effort. He also explained that persistence is a major part of successful effort and that long-term effort enhances ability (ability is unstable and increasing). He emphasized that the amount of effort that a person expends is not a stable personality trait but is actually controllable.

The videotape intervention ensured better experimental control than did an in vivo technique, while maintaining comparable effectiveness (Schunk,

Hanson, & Cox, 1986; Zoeller et al., 1983). The attributional retraining stressed that poor performance is often due to lack of effort and that greater effort and ability can enhance performance significantly. Both effort and ability were depicted as unstable factors to ensure common consensus in their interpretation and to increase the number of factors affecting subsequent performance. Weiner (1979, 1986) has repeatedly stated that attributions can have several interpretations, and so their placement may vary in his three-dimensional taxonomy. In contrast to the usual interpretation, effort may sometimes be considered as a stable trait, as in "a hard worker," and ability may be viewed as unstable, as in "a skill" that can be acquired. The procedure used here fosters a consistent interpretation by the students in which both are viewed as unstable.

Instructor expressiveness. Instructor expressiveness (low and high) was manipulated with two 25-minute color videotapes. A male psychology professor, different from the one in the training tape, presented a lecture on the topic of repression that was based on actual lecture notes. His presentation varied in expressiveness, defined in terms of physical movements, eye contact, voice inflection, and humor. Decreased or increased frequencies of these behaviors represented the low- and high-expressiveness conditions as determined by Perry, Abrami, and Levanthal (1979). Lecture content was based on the number of teaching points covered in the presentation and was restricted to Perry, Abrami, Leventhal, and Check's (1979, Study 2) high-content tapes. An Advent 1000A Videobeam Color Projection Unit was used to project a life-size image on a 2.2-metre diagonal screen.

Dependent measures. The dependent variables were administered as part of a questionnaire package 1 week after the videotaped lecture. Two achievement tests were used to assess students' academic performance: one related to the lecture and the other to the study materials. The lecture test contained 30 multiple-choice items, each with four response alternatives, designed to measure retention and understanding (Perry & Dickens, 1984). The homework test was similar and consisted of 10 multiple-choice items. The study materials were two pages of text summarizing a chapter entitled "The Nature of Anxiety-Based Problems" and written by the same professor who presented the videotaped lecture (Martin, 1983). Russell's (1982) Causal Dimension Scale (CDS) was used to assess students' causal perceptions of their performance on the two achievement tests. It consisted of nine Likert scales measuring the relative locus, stability, and controllability of a given cause. Each of these three attribution dimensions consisted of three Likert scales with a combined range of 1-27. Higher scores on these dimensions defined the cause as being more internal, stable, and controllable.

Procedure

The experimental procedures involved a two-stage sequence in which subjects volunteered to participate in a 2-hr session followed by a 1-hr session 1 week later. The first session involved the independent variable manipulations (attribution retraining and expressiveness); the second session was used to administer the achievement tests and the CDS. Before the first session began, the subjects were informed that the experiment concerned teaching processes and that they would first complete a questionnaire and an aptitude test and then view a videotaped lecture. They were also told that in the second session, they would take a test on the lecture and homework material and complete a questionnaire related to their performance. To prevent detailed discussions of the manipulations, the no-training conditions were run before the attribution retraining conditions. This reduced the possibility that the attribution retraining information would be disseminated to no-training condition subjects. Expressiveness conditions were randomly assigned to an equal number of morning and afternoon sessions. Lefcourt et al.'s (1979) MMCS was administered at the beginning of the first session.

In Session 1, subjects participated in groups of 15-25 in a simulated college classroom with rows of desks and blackboards and a video-projector unit. The subjects received the MMCS and then were given the aptitude test providing immediate contingent feedback. In the attributional retraining condition, the subjects were told that they would view a short videotaped interview on the student role in the learning process. The attributional retraining videotape was shown, followed by the aptitude test and then the lecture with the low- or high-expressive instructor. Subjects in the no-training conditions did not view the retraining videotape but simply proceeded to the aptitude test and to the lecture. After the lecture, subjects were told that they were to return to a specified room 1 week later to take a test and complete a questionnaire. They received the study materials before departing.

For Session 2, subjects returned to a different room than the one used for Session 1 and were introduced to a second experimenter. They participated in groups of 20-40 in which two Session 1 groups were tested on the same day when possible. Subjects wrote the lecture test and the homework test and then completed the CDS on the basis of their perceived performance on the two achievement tests. Debriefing involved a detailed explanation of the rationale for the experiment and the expected results.

Results

Preliminary Analyses

The experiment consisted of a lecture session that included the three independent variables and a testing session in which the dependent variables were administered 1 week later. A Locus of Control (internal and external)×Attributional Retraining (training and no-training)×Instructor Expressiveness (low and high) 2×2×2 factorial design was used to test student achievement and causal perceptions. The initial sample contained 267 subjects; however, 18 subjects were removed from the analyses because they failed to return for Session 2. A Locus×Retraining×Expressiveness chi-square analysis was computed for Session 2 attendance. An expressiveness main effect, $X^2(1, N=249)=4.40, p<.05$, (critical $X^2(1, N=249)=3.05$), revealed that attendance in Session 2 was higher with expressive instruction than with unexpressive instruction (96.6% vs. 90.4% of Session 1).

The complete Session 1/Session 2 sample was screened to remove subjects not suitable for the attributional retraining procedure developed for this study. Attributional retraining is intended to modify motivational deficits that cause students to perform below their capacity (e.g., Dweck, 1975; Wilson & Linville, 1982). The brief, one-shot videotape procedure used here would not be appropriate for students suffering extreme motivational deficits. Rather, they would require a lengthier, more personalized intervention than the short, group-administered videotape procedure. Consequently, students were not included if they were likely to be suffering extreme motivational deficits according to the following criteria: GPA < 2.10 (i.e., D average) and lecture achievement $<27\%$ (i.e., 8/30). These criteria would also likely remove some students with marginal ability who would not be receptive to attributional retraining because it cannot correct intellectual deficits.[2] These criteria excluded approximately the same number of internal- and external-locus students (23 vs 28) but excluded more students who had attributional retraining than those who had no training (34 vs 17).

Lecture and Homework Achievement

Attributional retraining was predicted to improve learning during a lecture and to increase the use of study materials. It should be noted that the attributional training and no-training conditions both included contingent feedback on the aptitude test before the lecture. It was expected that external-locus students would benefit more from retraining than would internal-locus students because of external students' lower level of perceived control. Students' lecture and homework achievement was analyzed in separate Locus of Control×Attributional Retraining×Instructor Expressiveness 2×2×2 factorial analyses of variance (ANOVAs). See Table 1 for means and standard deviations.

Attributional retraining had a significant effect on lecture achievement, $F(1, 190)=6.56$, $MS_e=11.38$, $p<.01$, and on homework achievement, $F(1, 190)=4.07$, $MS_e=3.82$, $p<.05$. Students who received retraining performed better than those who received no training on the lecture test ($Ms=16.21$ and 14.94) and on the homework test ($Ms=4.88$ and 4.30). Attributional retraining also interacted with locus to affect lecture performance, $F(1,190)=3.03$, $p=.08$, and homework performance, $F(1,190)=9.48$, $p<.01$ (see Figure 2). Planned comparisons of the interactions indicated that attributional retraining improved achievement on the lecture test for external-locus students more than for their no-training coun-

Table 1
Means and Standard Deviations for the Postlecture Measures

	Attributional retraining				No training			
	Internal		External		Internal		External	
Measure	Low[a]	High[a]	Low	High	Low	High	Low	High
Lecture achievement[b]								
M	15.36	15.97	15.33	18.17	14.67	15.84	13.19	16.05
SD	3.03	3.36	3.40	3.63	2.55	4.48	2.50	3.44
Homework achievement[c]								
M	4.87	4.00	4.80	5.83	5.17	4.31	3.35	4.36
SD	1.86	1.62	2.18	2.18	2.08	2.15	1.65	2.06
n	31	30	15	18	24	32	26	22
Causal Dimension Scale (CDS)								
Internality[d]								
M	17.94	18.17	16.53	16.24	14.92	14.41	15.34	16.55
SD	5.54	4.50	4.94	4.67	5.31	4.38	5.38	5.43
n	31	30	15	17	24	32	26	22
Control[e]								
M	20.35	18.63	18.87	16.56	19.44	15.44	18.80	17.25
SD	4.22	5.12	4.31	4.05	3.91	4.81	4.44	3.95
n	29	30	15	18	23	32	25	20
Stability[f]								
M	9.36	8.93	9.00	11.83	8.29	8.41	9.50	10.32
SD	4.88	4.75	4.99	4.59	4.26	4.54	3.54	5.46
n	31	30	15	18	24	32	26	22

[a] Refers to low- and high-expressive instructor. [b] Lecture achievement range is 0–30. [c] Homework achievement range is 0–10. [d] Internality dimension on the CDS: range = 1–27. [e] Control dimension on the CDS: range = 1–27. [f] Stability dimension on the CDS: range = 1–27.

terparts, $t(190)=2.74$, $p<.01$. For internal students, attributional retraining did not increase achievement more than did no training, $t(190)<1$. Homework achievement revealed a similar pattern in which attributional retraining improved the performance of external-locus students, $t(190)=3.24$, $p<.01$, but not of internal-locus students, $t(190)<1$. Thus attributional retraining enabled external-locus students to perform better on both the lecture and homework tests, but it provided no comparable advantage for internal-locus students.

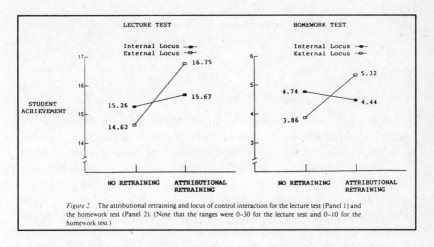

Figure 2. The attributional retraining and locus of control interaction for the lecture test (Panel 1) and the homework test (Panel 2). (Note that the ranges were 0–30 for the lecture test and 0–10 for the homework test.)

It was expected that the Locus of Control×Expressiveness relation reported by Magnusson and Perry (1989; see Figure 1, right panel) would change because attributional retraining elevated students' perceptions of control. Instructor expressiveness had a main effect on lecture performance, $F(1,190)=14.23$, $p<.001$, and interacted with locus on both performance measures. For lecture achievement, the Locus of Control×Expressiveness interaction, $F(1,190)=3.87$, $MS_e=11.38$, $p<.05$, indicated that external-locus students achieved more with an expressive instructor than with an unexpressive instructor, $t(190)=3.59$, $p<.01$. However, internal-locus students did not perform better with the expressive instructor, $t(190)=1.44$, $p>.05$ (see Figure 3, left panel).

For homework achievement, a similar pattern emerged. The Locus×Expressiveness interaction, $F(1,190)=10.88$, $MS_e=3.82$, $p<.01$, revealed that external-locus students performed better if they had had an expressive instructor than if they had had an unexpressive instructor, $t(190)=2.31$, $p<.01$. Of interest is that the internal-locus students performed *worse* after having had the expressive instructor, $t(190)=2.38$, $p<.01$ (see Figure 3, right panel).

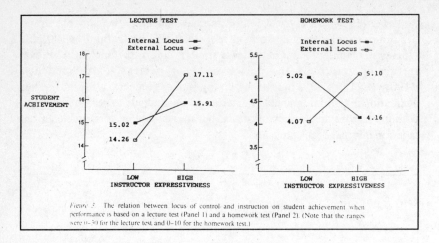

Figure 3 The relation between locus of control and instruction on student achievement when performance is based on a lecture test (Panel 1) and a homework test (Panel 2). (Note that the ranges were 0–30 for the lecture test and 0–10 for the homework test.)

Causal Perceptions of Performance

A Locus of Control×Attributional Retraining×Instructor Expressiveness 2×2×2 factorial ANOVA was computed for Russell's (1982) CDS. Students' causal perceptions of their performance were analyzed separately for each of the three dimensions (see Table 1 for means and standard deviations). Attributional retraining had a significant main effect on the locus of perceived causes, $F(1,189)=6.33$, $MS_e=25.30$, $p<.01$, and it interacted with locus of control, $F(1,189)=4.22$, $p<.05$. Internal-locus students perceived the causes of their performance as more internal after attributional retraining than after no training, $t(116)=3.64$, $p<.01$, whereas external-locus students showed no similar increase in internality ($t<1$). The attributional retraining main effect confirms predictions and is congruent with the achievement results. Although external-locus students did not increase their internality after attributional retraining, their mean ratings were within the range for internal-locus students. Thus their ratings were reasonably comparable but likely influenced by factors other than attributional retraining, such as the contingency feedback presented before the lecture.

Expressiveness influenced the controllability of causes, $F(1,184)=13.13$, $MS_e=19.67$, $p<.01$; the unexpressive instructor produced higher ratings than did the expressive instructor ($Ms=19.36$ and 16.97). This pattern suggests a hedonic bias in which students are willing to give control for poor performance to the unexpressive instructor but are unwilling to attribute control for good performance to the expressive instructor. Locus affected students' perceived stability of causes, $F(1,190)=4.35$, $MS_e=21.42$, $p<.05$; external-locus students viewed the causes as more stable than did internal-locus students ($Ms=10.16$ and 8.75).

Discussion

Attributional Retraining

Loss of control represents a serious threat to college students' academic development because it causes helplessness-related cognitive, motivational, and affective deficits. Attributional retraining can provide remedial assistance for these at-risk students by restoring perceived control. In our study, attributional retraining enabled external-locus students to learn more during a lecture and to make better use of study materials than they had before. Of significance is that it improved their performance on both lecture and homework material 1 week after the lecture and assignment were given. In contrast, attributional retraining offered no advantage to internal-locus students.

One explanation for this difference is that the retraining procedure introduced new causal attributions to external-locus students, whereas it simply reiterated existing options for internal-locus students. The potential for change, therefore, would be greater in external-locus students because they had a greater attributional deficit. An alternative explanation may lie in the students' capacity to incorporate the causal attributions presented in the retraining procedure. Not surprisingly, external-locus students would have more difficulty incorporating the ability and effort attributions into their achievement schemata than would internal-locus students, who would already have considerable familiarity with them. But of the two attributions, effort requires less cognitive restructuring than does ability, which could require major changes to one's self-concept, among other things. Consequently, effort would likely be the more salient explanation for performance in external-locus students and would be readily used. This would create optimal motivational conditions for subsequent achievement striving (Weiner, 1986) and more uniform performance across different achievement tasks.

Internal-locus students would not show similar performance gains because both effort and ability can be salient and each can have different consequences for motivation. An ability attribution could actually inhibit achievement striving if the student believes that his or her ability is sufficient to ensure success without trying hard. A perception that "I'm smart and I don't need to work at this" would lower motivation and impair performance, especially on learning tasks requiring greater self-initiative. Learning during a lecture requires passive participation in which lack of motivation can be compensated for by extra effort from the instructor. But a homework assignment requires self-initiated activity, which is vulnerable to an ability attribution that lowers motivation in this way.

Thus attributional retraining appears to benefit external-locus students in disparate achievement tasks that require either cooperative or autonomous learning activities. The lecture format is a ubiquitous instructional method in college classrooms in which the teacher assumes a primary responsibility for the learning process. The student is expected to participate in a generally passive but cooperative role in activities ranging from information acquisition to teacher-initiated questioning. It is noteworthy that attributional retraining ensured the retention of information for at least 1 week after the presentation of the lecture material. Homework assignments, however, require considerable self-initiative by the student, who must take the major responsibility for mastering the task. Here again, attributional retraining facilitated performance 1 week after the assignment was given.

The retraining procedure used here would be suitable for remediation in large universities with its videotape format, short duration, and group-administration capabilities. It could be particularly useful as an instructional aid to reach those students who otherwise would not seek assistance from the instructor, their peers, or counseling services. For these students, loss of control exacerbates academic failure by preventing them from seeking help. The retraining procedure would, however, exclude students suffering extreme motivational or intellectual deficits. These students would be better served with a more individualized intensive intervention typically offered through student counseling or learning centers.

These results are important in view of Försterling's (1985) review of the attributional retraining literature, which identified only two studies in which academic achievement by college students was directly examined (Wilson & Linville, 1982, 1985). Our study incorporated several improvements to those studies. First, it included achievement measures that are based on two types of learning activities. The lecture test reflects learning that takes place in the confines of a classroom under the direction of an instructor. The homework test depicts self-initiated learning in which greater responsibility is placed on the student. Wilson and Linville used two measures, the Graduate Record Exam (GRE) and grade-point average (GPA), which are overdetermined and do not differentiate between dependent and autonomous learning activities. The achievement measures used here were derived from specific lecture content and study materials and are more representative of curriculum-related achievement tests than are the global GRE and GPA measures.

Second, this study combined locus of control with attributional retraining. Locus of control is a theoretically relevant student variable that has important consequences for academic achievement (e.g., Stipek & Weisz, 1981). External locus identifies one potentially at-risk group of college students who exhibit a stable attributional pattern sometimes associated with low perceived control. This relation has not been considered in college students previously, but it has been examined to some extent in elementary school students (e.g., Dweck, 1975). Finally, an instructional variable was included on the basis of the premise that teachers make an important contribution to students' academic development. Instructor expressiveness was identified as an important college teaching behavior from an extensive literature of field and laboratory studies. Its inclusion in the simulated college classroom provides a more systematic analysis of how instructional factors contribute to locus of control and attributional retraining.

Effective Instruction and Perceived Control

The Locus of Control×Instructor Expressiveness interaction replicates and extends Magnusson and Perry's (1989) study. They found that external-locus students performed better with an expressive instructor than with an unexpressive instructor if contingent feedback preceded the lecture. With similar procedures, our study revealed that a comparable pattern occurred 1 week after the lecture. These results are noteworthy because existing research has documented expressiveness effects on student achievement only immediately after a lecture. It is clear, however, that expressive instruction can increase both short-term recall *and* long-term retention of information at least for external-locus students. Of particular note is that expressiveness increased homework-related achievement, which required self-initiated learning activities rather than passive lecture participation. These results demonstrate that expressive instruction has a motivational influence extending beyond the immediate constraints of the classroom.

Expressive instruction was of little benefit, however, to internal-locus students. It did not improve performance on the lecture test and actually reduced achievement on the homework test. This pattern could occur if ability was the primary attribution used by internal-locus students to explain their performance as discussed in relation to the attributional retraining results. When presented with poor instruction, internal-locus students would strive harder to avoid failure and ensuing threats to their self-concept. When faced with good instruction, they would work less because of a lower probability of failure and a reduced threat to their self-concept. This rationale presumes that students are preoccupied with their level of ability and that they are motivated to protect it when threatened with failure (e.g., Perry & Magnusson, 1989; Rothbaum et al., 1982).

An attributional analysis may also account for the achievement results in the external-locus students. Perry and associates (Perry & Dickens, 1984; Perry & Magnusson, 1987; Perry et al., 1986) have noted that although expressive instruction did not increase achievement in students experiencing temporary loss of control, it did enhance their tendency to view internal attributions as responsible for their performance. This would serve to heighten the salience of both the ability and effort attributions. As described previously with attributional retraining, however, an effort attribution would be much easier for external-locus students to incorporate with other schemata than would an ability attribution.

These results augment previous research showing that for some students, expressive instruction (a) increases their achievement immediately after a lecture and their perceived success of and control over the performance, (b) instills greater confidence in their achievement, and (c) causes them to believe that they tried hard and to have more responsibility for their successes and failures. The results provide a more complete profile of instructor expressiveness as an effective teaching behavior in college classrooms. Expressive instruction enhances achievement in some students for as long as 1 week after the actual lecture is given and on tasks that require self-initiated learning outside the classroom. Thus expressive instruction is effective because of its cognitive and motivational impact on students. It appears to activate information-processing activities that ensure both immediate performance benefits and long-term retention of material. It also serves an important motivational function by initiating learning activities that are not directly related to the original teaching setting.

Finally, expressive instruction ensured better attendance at the second experimental session than did unexpressive instruction. These data raise some interesting implications for course enrollments and class attendance. They are consistent with evidence that instructor reputation is one of the most important factors influencing enrollment patterns in multi-section undergraduate courses (Leventhal, Abrami, Perry, & Breen, 1975). If effective teaching is an integral part of a "good reputation," then expressiveness may be the element responsible for influencing enrollments. Thus expressiveness may serve to both increase enrollments and ensure class attendance. Of course, actual classrooms differ from our laboratory analogue in many ways, and further research is needed to examine these broader implications.

Notes

1   The impairment of the achievement-enhancing capacity of effective instruction can be understood in terms of information-processing theory. According to Perry and Magnusson (1987), teaching behaviors are effective because they prime cognitive mechanisms involved in academic achievement. Expressiveness, for example, is effective because it activates selective attention. The basic dimensions that constitute expressiveness—namely, physical movement, voice inflection, eye contact, and humor (Perry, Abrami, & Leventhal, 1979)—have stimulus-cuing properties that serve to elicit selective attention. Other teaching behaviors, such as instructor organization, engage different components of the information processing system. Thus instructor organization is effective because conceptual structures inherent in organized lectures provide "chunking" strategies that can enhance long-term memory capacity. Cognitive, motivation, and emotional deficits associated with loss of control (Abramson, Garber, & Seligman, 1980) would interfere with mechanisms responsible for the storage and retrieval of achievement-related material.

Under these conditions, effective teaching behaviors such as expressiveness would have greater difficulty activating information processing mechanisms.

2   Although it may seem improbable that students with marginal ability would be at university, recent changes in entrance requirements make this likelihood more feasible. In the last two decades, universities have moved to increase accessibility through various procedures, including lower entrance standards, open admissions for special students, and so forth. Some universities also have a mandate to serve the general public in the broadest capacity, necessitating less stringent admissions policies.

References

Abrami, P.C., Leventhal, L., & Perry, R.P. (1982). Educational seduction. *Review of Educational Research, 52,* 446-464.

Abramson, L.Y., Garber, J., & Seligman, M.E.P. (1980). Learned helplessness in humans: An attributional analysis. In J. Garber & M. Seligman (Eds.), *Human helplessness: Theory and applications* (pp. 3-34). Toronto, ON: Academic Press.

Block, J., & Lanning, K. (1984). Attribution theory requestioned: A secondary analysis of the Wilson-Linville study. *Journal of Personality and Social Psychology, 46,* 705-708.

Brophy, J. (1981). Teacher praise: A functional analysis. *Review of Educational Research, 51,* 5-32.

Carver, C.S., & Scheier, M.F. (1982). Control theory: A useful conceptual framework for personality-social, clinical, and health psychology. *Psychological Bulletin, 92,* 111-135.

Diener, C.I., & Dweck, C.S. (1978). An analysis of learned helplessness: Continuous changes in performance, strategy, and achievement cognitions following failure. *Journal of Personality and Social Psychology, 36,* 451-462.

Dweck, C.S. (1975). The role of expectations and attributions in the alleviation of learned helplessness. *Journal of Personality and Social Psychology, 36,* 451-462.

Fösterling, F. (1985). Attributional retraining: A review. *Psychological Bulletin, 98,* 495-512.

Glass, D.C. (1977). *Behavior patterns, stress, and coronary disease.* Hillsdale, NJ: Erlbaum.

Janoff-Bulman, R. (1979). Characterological versus behavioral self-blame: Inquiries into depression and rape. *Journal of Personality and Social Psychology, 37,* 1798-1809.

Lefcourt, H.M. (1976). *Locus of control: Current trends in theory and research.* Hillsdale, NJ: Erlbaum.

Lefcourt, H.M. (1980). Personality and locus of control. In J. Garber & M. Seligman (Eds.), *Human helplessness: Theory and applications* (pp. 245-259), Toronto, ON: Academic Press.

Lefcourt, H.M., Von Baeyer, C.L., Ware, E.E., & Cox, D.J. (1979). The Multidimensional-Multiattributional Causality Scale: The development of a goal specific locus of control scale. *Canadian Journal of Behavioural Science, 11,* 286-304.

Leventhal, L., Abrami, P.C., Perry, R.P., & Breen, L. (1975). Section-selection in multisection courses: Implications for the validation and use of teacher rating forms. *Educational and Psychological Measurement, 67,* 885-895.

Magnusson, J.-L., & Perry, R.P. (1989). Stable and transient determinants of perceived control: Implications for instruction in the college classroom. *Journal of Educational Psychology, 81,* 362-370.

Marsh, H. (1984). Students' evaluations of university teaching: Dimensionality, reliability, validity, potential biases, and utility. *Journal of Educational Psychology, 76,* 707-754.

Martin, D.G. (1983). *Counseling and therapy skills*. Monterey, CA: Brooks/Cole.

Miller, I.W., & Norman, W.H. (1979). Learned helplessness in humans: A review and attribution theory model. *Psychological Bulletin, 86*, 93-118.

Murray, H.G. (1983). Low-inference classroom teaching behaviors and student ratings of college teaching effectiveness. *Journal of Educational Psychology, 75*, 138-149.

Perry, R.P. (1985). Instructor expressiveness: Implications for improving teaching. In J.G. Donald & A.M. Sullivan (Eds.), *Using research to improve teaching* (pp. 35-49). San Francisco, CA: Jossey-Bass.

Perry, R.P., Abrami, P.C., & Leventhal, L. (1979). Educational seduction: The effect of instructor expressiveness and lecture content on student ratings and achievement. *Journal of Educational Psychology, 71*, 107-116.

Perry, R.P., Abrami, P.C., Leventhal, L.,. & Check, J. (1979). Instructor reputation: An expectancy relationship involving student ratings and achievement. *Journal of Educational Psychology, 71*, 776-787.

Perry, R.P., & Dickens, W.J. (1984). Perceived control in the college classroom: The effect of response outcome contingency training and instructor expressiveness on students' attributions and achievement. *Journal of Educational Psychology, 76*, 981-996.

Perry, R.P., & Dickens, W.J. (1988). Perceived control and instruction in the college classroom: Some implications for student achievement. *Research in Higher Education, 27*, 291-310.

Perry, R.P., & Magnusson, J.-L. (1987). Effective instruction and students' perceptions of control in the college classroom: Multiple-lectures effects. *Journal of Educational Psychology, 79*, 453-460.

Perry, R.P., & Magnusson, J.-L. (1989). Causal attributions and perceived performance: Consequences for college students' achievement and control when instruction fails. *Journal of Educational Psychology, 81*, 164-172.

Perry, R.P., Magnusson, J.-L., Parsonson, K.L., & Dickens, W.J. (1986). Perceived control in the college classroom: Limitations in instructor effectiveness due to noncontingent feedback and lecture content. *Journal of Educational Psychology, 78*, 96-107.

Perry, R.P., & Tunna, K. (1988). Perceived control, Type A/B behavior, and instructional quality. *Journal of Educational Psychology, 80*, 102-110.

Rothbaum, F., Weisz, J.R., & Snyder, S.S. (1982). Changing the world and changing the self: A two-process model of perceived control. *Journal of Personality and Social Psychology, 42*, 5-37.

Rotter, J.B. (1966). Generalized expectancies for internal versus external control of reinforcement. *Psychological Monographs, 80*, 1-28.

Russell, D. (1982). The Causal Dimension Scale: A measure of how individuals perceive causes. *Journal of Educational Psychology, 42*, 1137-1145.

Schunk, D.H., Hanson, A.R., & Cox, P.D. (1986, August) *Peer models: Effects on children's achievement behaviors*. Paper presented at the meeting of the American Psychological Association, Washington, DC.

Seligman, M.E.P. (1975). *Helplessness: On depression, development and death*. San Francisco, CA: Freeman.

Stipek, D.J., & Weisz, J.R. (1981). Perceived control and academic achievement. *Review of Educational Research, 51*, 101-138.

Weiner, B. (1974). *Achievement motivation and attribution theory*. Morristown, NJ: General Learning Press.

Weiner, B. (1979). A theory of motivation for some classroom experiences. *Journal of Educational Psychology, 71*, 3-25.

Weiner, B. (1986). *An attribution theory of motivation and emotion*. New York, NY: Springer-Verlag.

Wilson, T.D., & Linville, P.W. (1982). Improving the academic performance of college freshmen: Attribution therapy revisited. *Journal of Personality and Social Psychology, 42*, 367-376.

Wilson, T.D., & Linville, P.W. (1985). Improving the performance of college freshmen with attributional techniques. *Journal of Personality and Social Psychology, 49*, 287-293.

Zoeller, C., Mahoney, G., & Weiner, B. (1983). Effects of attribution training on the assembly task performance of mentally retarded adults. *American Journal of Mental Deficiency, 88*, 109-112.

Gender and School Science:
Achievement and Participation in Canada

Sharon M. Haggerty
University of Western Ontario

A review of recent studies of gender differences in science achievement and participation suggests that achievement differences cannot be understood or addressed without considering the effects of both attitude and participation. Canadian findings on achievement and participation support the suggestion that females and males approach school science differently and that those approaches are an important factor in the achievement differences that are observed. Enrolment data from ministries and departments of education reveal marked differences in participation in elective sciences, with the smaller provinces appearing to be more successful at encouraging students to persist in their science studies at the senior high school level.

*   *   *

THE ISSUE OF GENDER DIFFERENCES IN SCIENCE AND MATHEMATICS achievement has probably received more attention than in any other subject. Concern for girls and science has existed internationally since the publication of the results of the first international science assessment (Comber & Keeves, 1973; Kelly, 1978). Arising from this concern, an international organization, Gender and Science and Technology (GASAT), was established in 1981 and continues to meet biennially[1] to work toward achieving educational equity in science, mathematics, and technology. Canadians have participated in GASAT since its inception.

The Science Council of Canada (1984) conducted a major study of science education in Canada. Among its many recommendations were two specifically developed to increase the participation of girls in science. At the provincial level:

> Ministries should outline, in all policy documents relating to science and technology education, concrete steps to be taken by educators to increase the participation of girls in science and technology. (p. 48)

and at the national level:

The author would like to thank Paul Nagy, the anonymous reviewers, and particularly Todd Rogers for their many helpful suggestions.

The Minister of State for Science and Technology and the Minister responsible for the Status of Women should together sponsor a large-scale public information program directed especially towards parents and designed to raise public awareness of the need for girls and young women to participate in science and technology education. (p. 63)

Attention has also been drawn to gender differences in favor of males in science achievement[2] as measured in various provincial (e.g., Bateson, Anderson, Dale, McConnell, & Rutherford, 1986) and international assessments (e.g., Connelly, 1987; Connelly, Crocker, & Kass, 1985; Lapointe, Mead, & Phillips, 1989).

While gender differences continue to be reported, debate persists as to their extent and their validity and significance. Not all studies have detected achievement differences; and in studies where differences are found there are a number of views as to the reasons why they occur. Some suggest that gender differences can be accounted for by differential course taking, while others believe the causes are more deeply embedded in factors related to differential socialization of females and males.

As well as achievement and participation in science, attitudes toward science are considered in this article. A recent longitudinal study of influences on attitude toward and achievement in high school science conducted in the United States revealed a strong relationship between achievement and attitude (Simpson & Oliver, 1990). It was found that school variables strongly influenced attitudes, and that attitudes of grade 10 students successfully predicted which students would not pursue future elective science courses in 90% of the cases studied. Hence the view taken in this article is that achievement and attitudes should not be examined in isolation from each other. It is also suggested that merely examining gender differences is little more than an academic exercise. We must also be prepared to develop and implement strategies aimed at ensuring that both females and males in Canada are equally successful in school science. Suggestions as to how that might be addressed are presented.

Achievement in Science

As indicated above, recent science assessments in Canada and elsewhere have found gender differences in favor of males in science achievement, and that these differences first become noticeable at early adolescence, increasing during the high school years. Individual science teachers, however, may dispute their existence, stating there are no differences between the achievement of females and males in their classes (Sadker & Sadker, 1986; Tobin & Garnett, 1987). Moreover, average grade 12 final marks obtained from the British Columbia Ministry of Education reveal little difference between the final marks of male and female grade 12 students in science in that province (Kozlow, personal communication, 1986). Thus there is conflicting evidence as to whether gender differences in science achievement really do exist.

In order to account for this apparent discrepancy, Haggerty (1987) suggested that there may be two distinctly different kinds of achievement measures in science. In the first instance, a test score is being considered. Generally, the test is externally prepared and presented in a multiple choice format. It covers a wide range of content that the students are expected to have encountered in their previous science studies. The students generally do not know what specific content is covered on the test. Further, the context of the items may be quite different from the context in which the particular scientific principles were studied in school, and at times the students do not have the opportunity to study a particular body of content to be tested. Perhaps most importantly the students are aware that the results of such tests will not influence their marks in any way. The second type of achievement measure is a mark or grade obtained by students for a particular science course in school. Such a mark is a composite of test scores and marks/grades received on various assignments. The tests in this instance are very different in nature. Generally, the content tested has been recently studied in a particular science course. The students study content identified by the teacher. A portion of the mark may be given for work effort in class and for completion of assigned homework. Haggerty suggested these two kinds of achievement measures (i.e., scores on standardized tests and course marks) are actually measuring distinctly different sorts of achievement. To investigate this possibility, she examined data from three British Columbia sources.

In the first analysis, scores on the British Columbia science assessment achievement scales showed superior performance by males for almost all science topics (Bateson et al., 1986; Hobbs, Boldt, Erickson, Quelch, & Sieben, 1979; Taylor, Hunt, Sheppy, & Stronck, 1982). The gender differences were greatest for physical and earth science topics and on questions requiring higher level thinking skills. Moreover, the differences increased with age. In the second analysis, final marks obtained by grade 12 students in British Columbia were examined. In contrast to the assessment results, these final marks are comprised of two equally weighted components: one the mark assigned by the classroom teacher and the other the score on a provincial school leaving examination.[3] It was found that in the sciences the average marks obtained by females ranged from 0.8% less than those obtained by males in chemistry to 2.9% more than males in physics. Thus looking at gender differences on these two kinds of measures (i.e., provincial science assessment achievement scales and blended final marks in biology, chemistry and physics) yielded different findings.

In the third analysis, Haggerty (1986, 1987) drew on data from a study of a grade 9 science class during a unit on heat and temperature. In the study, scores were obtained on a posttest measure that tested how well students could apply scientific knowledge related to a variety of phenomena[4] they had studied in school. The contexts of the items in this posttest, and in a similar pretest administered prior to instruction, were different from those used by the teacher to teach the unit. And, as in the case of the provincial assessment, the students could not study for this test by learning a particular set of facts and the students knew the results of the test would not be included in their course marks. The pretest revealed no significant gender differences in understanding the heat and temperature concepts tested. Similarly, there were no significant gender differences in the scores obtained by the students on the unit test (set by the teacher and limited to questions that could be answered correctly by a student who had memorized key definitions and other facts), and on combined notebook, homework, and unit test marks assigned by the teacher for the unit as a whole. In contrast, the posttest did reveal significant gender differences. After completing the heat and temperature unit, the boys seemed better able than the girls to apply what they had learned to the novel situations presented in the posttest measure. This finding suggests that males understood the science they learned more effectively than the females, in spite of the marks obtained in their science course. Similar findings have been reported by Bejar and Blew (1981), De Boer (1984), Levin and Fowler (1984), Maccoby and Jacklin (1974), Sadker, Sadker, and Klein (1986), Simpson and Oliver (1990), and Zarega, Haertel, Tsai, and Walberg (1986). Researchers have attempted to identify plausible explanations for why girls receive course marks comparable to those of boys, yet apparently are not able to apply what they learned as well as boys. One suggestion is that better work habits of females provide them with an advantage on school achievement measures (De Boer, 1986; Maccoby & Jacklin, 1974; Walberg, 1969; Zarega et al., 1986). Ridley and Novak (1983) have suggested that females are socialized toward rote learning strategies. Concern for right answers among females is often noted by teachers and was clearly evident in the classroom study conducted by Haggerty (1986). Such findings reinforce the contention that the important question is not whether gender differences exist, but rather, under what circumstances do gender differences exist and, most importantly, what can be done to provide both females and males with opportunities to understand the science they learn and to have that understanding reflected in their achievement?

As noted earlier, there appear to be three plausible explanations as to why males outperform females on standardized tests (such as the British Columbia Science Assessment and the American National Assessment of Educational Progress or NAEP). Eylon and Linn (1989) are among those who support the differential course taking hypothesis, suggesting that because males take more science, they perform better. Erickson and Erickson

(1984), however, using data from the British Columbia science assessment, dispute that. Similarly, Mullis and Jenkins (1988), using American NAEP data, found that course enrolment had no effect on the magnitude of the gender difference. In the second international science assessment (International Association for the Evaluation of Educational Achievement, 1988), when students enroled in their final year of secondary science were tested by subject, there were still significant gender differences in Canada and most other countries (differences for chemistry and physics were greater than for biology).

In their recent review of gender and mathematics and science, Linn and Hyde (1989) concluded that informal as well as formal learning experiences were important. They noted:

> Gender differences in science knowledge and scientific reasoning reflect both formal and informal learning experiences. Overall gender differences in science (a) are larger for science knowledge than for science processes, (b) are declining among high school students, and (c) accompany gender differences in formal and informal learning experiences. (p. 22)

Other British Columbia work by Erickson and Farkas (1987) suggests that males and females tend to draw on different sources of personal knowledge when confronted with questions on a standardized test, and that a lack of relevant prior informal experiences contributes to females' inferior performance. Students were questioned as to what they had been thinking about as they chose their answers to science assessment questions on which significant achievement differences between females and males had occurred. Females more than males indicated that they recalled an incident that had occurred in school science classes, whereas males more than females recalled an incident outside of formal school science. Similarly, Linn and Hyde noted that "males compared with females report substantially more informal experience with physical science" (1989, p. 22). Haggerty (1987) has suggested that females may do better on test questions that can be answered by rote learning, whereas the reverse may be true for males. This suggestion is consistent with the findings of both Erickson and Farkas (1987) and Linn and Hyde (1989) and could also account for males' superior performance on higher level assessment questions and for females' superior performance on lower level questions. Similarly, school science course marks are more likely to reflect good work habits and to be based on tests that ask predominantly lower level questions, thereby contributing to the relatively higher achievement of females on these measures.

One additional explanation has been proposed to account for the differences on British Columbia assessment scales. Bateson and Parsons-Chatman (1989) suggest that the differences may be due to gender bias in the content of the items. Erickson and Farkas's (1987) findings do not support that explanation. At best, the content of the items appears to be insufficient to account for the explanations given by students in Erickson and Farkas's study.

The view that any one factor such as differential course taking, prior informal experiences, or content of items is responsible for gender differences in achievement is not supported by the studies reviewed above.

There is now considerable evidence that achievement is influenced by a complex of factors.

Attitudes Toward Science

In a meta-analytic study of gender and science, Steinkamp and Maehr (1984) concluded that although in general females were more motivated to achieve than males, the reverse was true at the junior high level in the United States. There, adolescent males' motivation to succeed exceeded that of females and the gap between the two had been increasing during the preceding decade. Since then, Simpson and Oliver (1990) have conducted a longitudinal study with adolescents in the United States. Using extensively revised existing instruments, as well as developing additional instruments for their work, they finally produced and utilized a 60-item, 14-subscale attitude survey. In their study, females scored consistently higher on motivation to achieve in science (among other subscales), whereas males had significantly more positive attitudes toward science. Simpson and Oliver noted, as have others (e.g. Duncan & Haggerty, 1985; Yager & Yager, 1985), a general decline in attitudes toward science during the adolescent years. In a Saskatchewan study of 43 grade 7 to 9 science classes, Wideen (1974) found that interest in science was greater for males than females, and that for students who indicated that a subject other than science was their favorite subject, there was a decline in science interest from grade 7 to grade 9. The decline did not occur among students who chose science as their favorite subject in school. Similarly, Kelly (1986) included gender as a factor in a longitudinal study of science attributes. She found that from ages 11 to 13 children's attitudes toward science declined significantly and noted that "their personal liking for science showed a particularly marked drop, especially among girls" (p. 402). These declines in adolescents' attitudes toward science should be of concern to those involved in science education during the middle school/junior high school years.

Linn and Hyde (1989) discussed three aspects of attitude (or what they call *psychosocial*) differences: aggression (e.g., males' greater participation in class activities and discussions), confidence (e.g., males overestimate their abilities, females are realistic), and interest. They noted that gender differences were heterogeneous and interacted both with the particular situation and with cultural factors. Linn and Hyde concluded that the only interest factor that seemed to influence persistence in science and mathematics was perceived usefulness, and suggested that this may be related to the frequently reported concern that the science taught in the schools is not seen as addressing relevant topics or problems. As most provinces have expressly developed curricula with relevance to students (particularly at the middle school/junior high school level), this is a concern. It appears that although curriculum developers believe the curriculum addresses topics that are socially relevant to adolescents, that relevance is not apparent to the students. If Linn and Hyde are correct that science participation is related to perceived relevance, then perhaps we might hope to increase participation if we can make that relevance apparent to the students. Similarly, we might look to perceived relevance as we ponder explanations for low participation in elective science courses.

Simpson and Oliver (1990) have come to somewhat different conclusions. Data were initially collected on 4,500 grade 10 students. To determine the extent to which further participation in science could be predicted, additional data were collected five years later from these students. Student attitudes toward science and success in science in grade 10 were a strong predictor of subsequent science achievement in high school, and science self concept at grade 10 was a significant predictor of future course participation. In particular, students with low science attitudes did not take elective science courses. The authors concluded, "A major finding of this study, therefore, is that attitudes toward science play a key role in influencing the amount of exposure to science a student experiences" (p. 13). The longitudinal nature of this study appears to have allowed more precise identification of the relationship between attitude and both achievement and participation in elective sciences. Simpson and Oliver also found, contrary to their expectations, that school variables were more strongly related to attitude toward science than were family variables. This is encouraging for educators who are sometimes discouraged from attempting to address student attitudes due to the perception that the home is the major influence on student attitudes. Simpson and Oliver's finding suggests that it is important to consider the school environment when addressing both achievement and attitude issues.

Participation in Science

Two aspects of participation are considered—choosing to enrol in elective science courses and student participation in discussions and activities in the science classroom.

Enrolments in Elective Science

Studies reviewed in the previous section suggest that attitude is an important factor in a student's choice to enrol in science courses. Ridley and Novak (1983) have suggested that the socialization of females toward rote learning strategies may be related to low female participation in advanced science and mathematics courses. In order to examine the pattern of student enrolments in science, representatives of each of the 10 provincial departments/ministries of education were asked to provide student enrolment data for grade 10 to 12 science courses. In the first analyses of these data, male and female enrolments in grade 11 sciences were compared with the corresponding populations in each province. Generally, grade 11 marks the point at which enrolment in a science course becomes optional rather than compulsory, that is, science becomes an elective rather than a required course. To obtain an estimate of the total number of females and males who might potentially enrol in a grade 11 science, the population of 15- to 19-year-olds (Statistics Canada, 1988) was divided by five. There is greater participation by both males and females in some provinces than in others. For example, in Saskatchewan the percentages of females enroled in biology, chemistry, and physics were respectively, 76%, 61%, and 47%. The corresponding data for Ontario were 43%, 32%, and 20%. This result illustrates a second point: higher enrolments in grade 11 science tend to be inversely related to total grade 11 population size across the six provinces for which there were sufficient data (see Table 1). Thirdly, examination of the corresponding course percentages for females and males reveals that across all provinces a greater percentage

Table 1
Estimated Participation of Females and Males in Grade 11 Biology,
Chemistry, and Physics by Province
1987/1988

Province	Female Pop'n X1000 (15-19)	Biol.	Females Chem.	Phys.	Male Pop'n X1000 (15-19)	Biol.	Males Chem.	Phys.
B.C.	101.8	45%	34%	19%	106.9	40%	34%	34%
Alberta	89.3	67	58	24	92.9	54	55	38
Saskatchewan	38.3	76	60	47	40.3	64	55	50
Ontario	336.4	43	31	20	352.7	29	34	28
N.B.	29.4	34	40	28	31.0	30	36	33
P.E.I.	5.2	73	60	30	5.6	49	46	39

Note: Data not included for some provinces because of insufficiency (Manitoba and Newfoundland/Labrador) or because not all sciences are offered at the grade 11 level (Nova Scotia and Quebec).

of females than males enrol in biology; in contrast, the percentage of females in physics is lower. The pattern of differences for chemistry is less clear.

To further examine the relative participation of females and males enroled in each science course offered in grades 10, 11, and 12 in each province, the proportion of males and females enroled in each subject is shown in Table 2. A number of observations can be made. First, in agreement with the data provided in Table 1, more females than males studied biology, and, except among francophones in Ontario and Quebec, more males than females studied physics. For chemistry, the proportions of males and females were more nearly equal. There were more males in chemistry in British Columbia and Newfoundland and among central Cana-

Table 2
Percentage of Females in Canadian Secondary Science Classes, 1987/88

Province	Science	Biology			Chemistry			Physics		
Grade:	10[a]	11	12	13	11	12	13	11	12	13
B.C.	50	57	61		49	43		35	21	
Alberta	53/50/49[b]	55	59		50	51		38	33	
Saskatchewan	50	53	55[c]		51	52		47	44	
Manitoba[d]		(57)			(49)			(36)		
Ontario Fr.[e]	56	63	50	63	53	58	47	53	52	41
Eng.	51	59	61	59	48	48	44	43	39	32
Quebec Fr.	53/50[f]				53					
Eng.	49/38				45		47			
N.S.	50/46[g]		58		52	52		45	36	
P.E.I.	54	60	61		55	56		42	43	
N.B: Fr.		68[h]	63		53	57		48	47	
Eng.		53	58		51	51		45	44	
Nfld/Lab.[i]		60			43			27		

[a]In most provinces general science is compulsory in grade 10.

[b]In Alberta in 1987/88 each of biology, chemistry, and physics was offered in grade 10. Each student was required to take at least *one* of the three courses. In 1990/1991 general science will replace the three separate courses.

[c]Francophone biology 12 classes were 57% female.

[d]Data for Manitoba were estimated from a bar graph; grade was not indicated.

[e]Ontario, Quebec, and New Brunswick maintain separate records for francophone and anglophone classes. Ontario is the only province that provides a 13th year of schooling.

[f]In Quebec there is no grade 12. Chemistry and physics are offered at years 10 and 11, respectively. Biology is not offered after year 9.

[g]In Nova Scotia biology and physical science are offered in grade 10.

[h]The first year of biology in New Brunswick is a grade 10 course.

[i]Newfoundland/Labrador did not respond to the request for data. Figures given are taken from Scott (1982) and are for the final year of secondary school which at that time was grade 11. Since then grade 12 has been introduced as well.

dian anglophones, but more females among the francophones and in the Maritime provinces. The greater participation by females in francophone classes is interesting and probably warrants further examination.

Although it is impossible to explain these course enrolment variations with certainty, some patterns have been identified and some speculations can be made. The smaller, more rural regions of Canada (i.e., the prairies and Atlantic provinces) tend to have higher science participation. This is particularly so for Saskatchewan and for females in Prince Edward Island. New Brunswick, however, is an exception. New Brunswick differs from the others in that it offers a greater variety of academic and nonacademic courses. In New Brunswick, students who will be continuing to postsecondary education take different courses than those who will not. New Brunswick also has a relatively higher proportion of females in physics than any other province except Saskatchewan (not including francophone classes) and has made an effort to attain gender equity in education (Department of Education, 1987). Physics participation by females is particularly dismal in the final year of schooling in British Columbia, Ontario, and Alberta. These three provinces are more industrialized and economically advantaged than the others.

The differences between Saskatchewan and Alberta are of interest. In both of these provinces approximately half of those enroled in chemistry are female. In Alberta, however, the typical gender bias (more females take biology, more males take physics) is more pronounced in biology and physics. Historically, these provinces have much in common. There are differences in the dominant economic base and the dominant political philosophy of these neighboring provinces. In Alberta the oil industry is particularly significant in the provincial economy, whereas farming dominates in Saskatchewan.

Overall, among anglophones the gender bias is most pronounced in the three provinces that not only have the larger populations, but also are more industrialized than the others (i.e., Alberta, British Columbia, and Ontario)—the question is, is this merely a coincidence, or is there any possible significance to such trends?

Differences in course participation across Canada illustrate the complexities involved in the issue. Sociocultural influences are undoubtedly involved. However, it behooves those of us in the educational community to focus on school and curriculum variables in the hope that we can have some impact on how students experience school science. The following section examines how the school science experience differs for females and males.

Participation in Science Classes

Differences in the way females and males interact and respond in the classroom have been well documented in a variety of subject areas and at all age levels (Becker, 1981; Bossert, 1981; Haggerty, 1987; Linn & Hyde, 1989; Sadker & Sadker, 1986; Tobin & Gallagher, 1987; Wienekamp, Jansen, Fickenfrerichs, & Peper, 1987; Whyte, 1984). For example, females appear less likely to engage in high risk situations (Lolley, Davies, & Scott-Hodgetts, 1986). And, although females are more likely to respond "I don't know," they are less likely to give wrong answers than males (Linn, De Benedictis, Delucchi, Harris, & Stage, 1987).

Table 3
Student-Teacher Dialogue During Class Discussion

	Male		Female		Total
	N	%	N	%	N
Number of Students	9	39.1	14	60.9	23
Students Called on by Teacher	43	58.1	31	41.9	74
Student Responses to Questions					
Correct Answer	100	63.7	86	75.4	186
Incorrect Answer	14	8.9	13	11.4	27
Partially Correct	13	8.3	10	8.8	23
Alternative Belief	21	13.4	6	5.3	27
No Response	6	3.8	2	1.8	8
Total	157	100.0	114	100.0	271
Student Initiated Dialogue					
Question	37	55.2	12	36.4	49
Information	30	44.8	30	60.6	50
Total	67	100.0	32	100.0	99
Teacher Responses to Students					
Encourage, Explore	100	33.9	71	38.2	171
Acknowledge Answer	65	22.0	44	23.7	109
Wrong Answer	11	3.7	2	1.1	13
Provide Information	38	12.9	19	10.2	57
Explanation	28	9.5	27	14.5	55
Demonstration	2	0.7	0		2
Redirect Question	7	2.4	1	0.5	8
Repeat	24	8.1	19	10.2	43
Ignore or Dismiss	16	5.4	2	1.1	18
Managerial	4	1.4	1	0.5	5
Total	295	100.0	186	100.0	481

In Haggerty's (1986) classroom study of a grade 9 science class studying heat and temperature, the frequency of different forms of teacher-student verbal interactions was recorded during two weeks of class discussion (Table 3). Although only 39% of the students in the class were male (9 of 23), males were called upon to answer 58% of the questions and males initiated 67% of the student-initiated dialogue (see Table 3). When students did initiate dialogue, females were more likely to provide information, whereas males were more likely to ask a question. Although females comprised 61% of the class, they responded to only 42% of the teacher's questions. However, 75% of their responses were accepted as correct by the teacher. The males, who responded to 58% of the questions asked by the teacher, provided correct responses 64% of the time. When the teacher responded to students' responses, she was more likely to encourage further responses or to provide explanations when responding to a female student, and less likely to redirect a question or ignore a response from a female student. Taken together, these two forms of response (student, teacher) suggest that in spite of the teacher's positive and encouraging responses to female students, females were still much less responsive than the males. These findings are consistent with those reported in other studies in the United States and Australia (Sadker & Sadker, 1986; Tobin & Gallagher, 1987).

Kahle, Matyas, and Cho (1985), Tobin and Garnett (1987), and Zimmerer and Bennett (1987) all found that males reported different perceptions of their activities in school science than did females in the same classes. Males reported greater time spent in activities than did females in the same classes. Haggerty (1987) suggested these differing perceptions may be related to the ways in which males and females go about doing science. Males appear to be more involved in manipulative laboratory activities and females to be more concerned with finding the right answers.

The issue of male dominance in classrooms is a difficult one. In classes taught by teachers who claimed to actively encourage participation of female students, males still dominated the activities and discussions, a situation that was not recognized by the teachers concerned (Duncan & Haggerty, 1985; Sadker & Sadker, 1986; Tobin & Garnett, 1987). Observers noted that even when a teacher deliberately called on students proportionally, males were more likely to attempt a response when they were unsure about a question. This provided an advantage for the males, as even an incorrect answer provides the teacher with a basis for continuing to probe and draw out a more acceptable response. Alternatively, a response of "I don't know" gives the teacher nothing to build on and she or he typically passes on to another student. If we wish to overcome this problem, teachers will need to develop strategies to draw out and encourage all students, both female and male, to make an attempt to answer questions.

Teachers must convince students (and be convinced themselves) that giving the correct answer should not be the major goal in science classrooms. Rather, the process of developing and evaluating alternative answers is the essence of doing science. As Tobin and Garnett (1987) have noted, the first step is for teachers to recognize the tendency for students to want to identify a single correct answer to any question as problematic.

Conclusions

This article reviews recent studies of gender differences in science achievement, attitude, and participation. Achievement differences are often considered to be related to attitudes toward science and to different participation rates in science. The studies reviewed suggest that these three factors are interrelated and that each contributes to the other.

At the present time, although participation varies across Canada, generally fewer than half of our students choose to study elective science courses. Differences in participation of francophone and anglophone females were unexpected. Some sociocultural factors that might possibly influence participation have been speculated on, but these would require considerably more investigation before any claims could be made.

Studies completed in Canada and elsewhere are reviewed in this article and suggest that for females more than for males success in school science is attained by learning right answers. It is suggested that the result of this approach to learning is that girls more than boys frequently do not understand the science they learn. This approach to learning may contribute to females' lower level of achievement on standardized tests. In turn, failure to understand the science that is being learned leads females to feel that science, particularly physics, is not for them. Consequently, they are less likely to participate in elective physical science courses. If females' disadvantage with respect to both participation and achievement is to be overcome, it will be necessary for middle school/junior high school science to be taught in a more meaningful and relevant way, involving girls as well as boys as active participants in science classes. Oliver and Simpson (1988) stress the importance of "structuring the science classroom learning environment to improve the student's belief that he or she can succeed in science" (p. 154). Parker and Rennie (1986) found that teacher in-service aimed at reducing gender stereotyping of science had positive effects on 10-year-olds in Australia. Kelly (1986) reported that interventions aimed at improving attitudes of 11- to 13-year-olds in several British schools also had positive effects. Duncan and Haggerty (1985) found that in one of two Canadian high schools they studied, the science department head/chemistry teacher successfully recruited large numbers of female students into grade 11 chemistry. Informal anecdotal information from teachers also suggests that individual, enthusiastic teachers can make a difference. Studies currently underway in British Columbia are aimed at identifying characteristics of schools that do have above average participation of females in science. Hopefully, this work will assist teachers and schools to identify ways of increasing participation in science.

Overall, the findings from these studies are encouraging, and teachers should feel empowered by such research. Teachers can have an impact on the achievement and participation of their students in school science.

Notes

1   The 1993 GASAT conference will be held in Canada at the University of Waterloo. Only once before has GASAT met in North America (at the University of Michigan in 1987).

2   Although this article specifically deals with science, many of the situations and views described apply equally to mathematics.

3   At the time of this study, grade 12 final marks in academic courses were determined by a combination of a teacher-assigned mark and the score obtained on the provincial examination. The two scores were equally weighted.

4   For example, students were told that if there were a large ice cube and a small ice cube in a beaker of water, the large ice cube would take longer to melt than the smaller one. They were then asked if that meant it took more heat to melt the larger cube. On both the pretest and the posttest many students replied no, because ice always melts at 0 degrees. Such students clearly did not distinguish heat and temperature appropriately, although that was a major goal of the unit, and all students were able to define the two terms correctly on the unit test.

References

Bateson, D., Anderson, J., Dale, T., McConnell, V., & Rutherford, C. (1986). *British Columbia science assessment: General report.* Victoria, BC: Ministry of Education.

Bateson, D.J., & Parsons-Chatman, S. (1989). Sex-related differences in science achievement. *International Journal of Science Education, 11,* 371-385.

Becker, J.R. (1981). Differential treatment of females and males in mathematics classes. *Journal for Research in Mathematics Education, 12,* 40-53.

Bejar, I.I., & Blew, E.O. (1981). Grade inflation and the validity of the Scholastic Aptitude Test. *American Educational Research Journal, 18,* 143-156.

Bossert, S.T. (1981). Understanding sex differences in children's classroom experiences. *Elementary School Journal, 81,* 255-266.

Comber, L.C., & Keeves, J.P. (1973). *Science education in nineteen countries.* Stockholm, Sweden: Almquist and Wiksell.

Connelly, F.M. (1987). *Ontario science education report card: Canadian national comparisons.* Toronto, ON: Queen's Printer.

Connelly, F.M., Crocker, R.K., & Kass, H. (1985). *Science education in Canada: Policies, practices and perceptions.* Toronto, ON: Ontario Institute for Studies in Education.

De Boer, G.E. (1984). A study of gender effects in the science and math course-taking behavior of a group of students who graduated from college in the late 1970's. *Journal of Research in Science Teaching, 21,* 95-103.

De Boer, G.E. (1986, April). *Perceived science ability and effort among males and females: Relationships to persistence in undergraduate science studies.* Paper presented to the Annual Meeting of the American Educational Research Association, San Francisco, CA.

Department of Education. (1987). *Educational opportunities for girls and boys: A commitment to sex-equity.* Fredericton, NB: Author.

Duncan, M.J., & Haggerty, S.M. (1985). *Action plan for girls in science in British Columbia.* Report prepared for the Department of the Secretary of State, Canada, Women's Programs.

Erickson, G.L., & Erickson, L.J. (1984). Females and science achievement: Evidence, explanations, and implications. *Science Education, 68,* 63-89.

Erickson, G., & Farkas, S. (1987). Prior experience: A factor which may contribute to male dominance in science. In J.S. Daniels & J.B. Kahle (Eds.), *Contributions to the Fourth GASAT Conference* (vol. 1, pp. 49-56), Ann Arbor, MI: University of Michigan.

Eylon, B., & Linn, M.L. (1989). Learning and instruction: An examination of four research perspectives in science education. *Review of Educational Research, 58,* 251-301.

Haggerty, S.M. (1986). *Learning about heat and temperature: A study of a grade 9 science class.* Unpublished doctoral dissertation, University of British Columbia.

Haggerty, S.M. (1987). Gender and science achievement: A case study. *International Journal of Science Education, 9,* 271-279.

Hobbs, E.D., Boldt, W., Erickson, G., Quelch, T., & Sieben, G. (1979). *British Columbia science assessment: General report.* Victoria, BC: Ministry of Education.

International Association for the Evaluation of Educational Achievement. (1988). *Science achievement in seventeen countries.* Oxford, UK: Pergamon.

Kahle, J.B., Matyas, M.L., & Cho, H. (1985). An assessment of the impact of science experiences on the career choices of male and female biology students. *Journal of Research in Science Teaching, 22,* 385-394.

Kelly, A. (1978). *Girls and science.* Stockholm, Sweden: Almquist and Wiksell.

Kelly, A. (1986). The development of girls' and boys' attitudes to science: A longitudinal study. *European Journal of Science Education, 8,* 399-412.

Lapointe, A.E., Mead, N.A., & Phillips, G.W. (1989). *A world of difference: An international assessment of mathematics and science.* Princeton, NJ: Educational Testing Service.

Levin, J., & Fowler, H.S. (1984). Sex, grade, and course differences in attitudes that are related to cognitive performance in secondary science. *Journal of Research in Science Teaching, 21,* 151-166.

Linn, M.C., De Benedictis, T., Delucchi, K., Harris, A., & Stage, E. (1987). Gender differences in National Assessment of Education Progress items: What does "I don't know" really mean? *Journal of Research in Science Teaching, 24,* 267-278.

Linn, M.C., & Hyde, J.S. (1989). Gender, mathematics, and science. *Educational Researcher, 18*(8), 17-19, 22-27.

Lolley, M., Davies, S., & Scott-Hodgetts, R. (1986). Teachers as researchers. *Mathematics Teaching, 118,* 46-47.

Maccoby, E.E., & Jacklin, C.N. (1974). *The psychology of sex differences.* Stanford, CA: Stanford University Press.

Mullis, I.V.S., & Jenkins, L.B. (1988). *The science report card, elements of risk and recovery: Trends and achievement based on the 1986 national assessment* (Report No. 17-S-01). Princeton, NJ: Educational Testing Service.

Oliver, J.S. & Simpson, R.D. (1988). Influences of attitude toward science, achievement motivation, and science self-concept on achievement in science: A longitudinal study. *Science Education, 72,* 143-155.

Parker, L.H., & Rennie, L.J. (1986). Sex stereotyped attitudes about science: Can they be changed? *European Journal of Science Education, 8,* 173-183.

Ridley, D.R., & Novak, J.D. (1983). Sex-related differences in high school science and mathematics enrolments: Do they give males a critical headstart toward science- and math-related careers? *Alberta Journal of Educational Research, 29,* 308-318.

Sadker, D., & Sadker, M. (1986). Sexism in the classroom from grade school to graduate school. *Phi Delta Kappan, 56,* 512-515.

Sadker, D., Sadker, M., & Klein, S.S. (1986). Abolishing misconceptions about sex equity in education. *Theory into Practice, 25,* 219-226.

Science Council of Canada. (1984). *Science for every student: Educating Canadians for tomorrow's world.* Ottawa, ON: Author.

Scott, J. (1982). Is there a problem? In J. Ferguson (Ed.), *Who turns the wheel?* (pp. 21-44). Ottawa, ON: Science Council of Canada.

Simpson, R.D., & Oliver, J.S. (1990). A summary of major influences on attitude toward and achievement in science among adolescent students. *Science Education, 74,* 1-18.

Statistics Canada. (1988). *Canada Yearbook: 1988.* Ottawa, ON: Supply and Services Canada.

Steinkamp, M.W., & Maehr, M.L. (1984). Gender differences in educational motivations toward achievement in school science: A quantitative synthesis. *American Educational Research Journal, 21,* 39-59.

Taylor, H., Hunt, R., Sheppy, J., & Stronck, D. (1982). *British Columbia science assessment: General report.* Victoria, BC: Ministry of Education.

Tobin, K., & Gallagher, J.J. (1987). The role of target students in the science classroom. *Journal of Research in Science Teaching, 24,* 61-75.

Tobin, K., & Garnett, P. (1987). Gender related differences in science activities. *Science Education, 71,* 91-103.

Walberg, H.J. (1969). Physics, femininity, and creativity. *Developmental Psychology, 1,* 47-54.

Whyte, J. (1984). Observing sex stereotypes and interactions in the school lab and workshop. *Educational Review, 36,* 75-86.

Wideen, M.F. (1974). Division III science: An in depth evaluative study. *Saskatchewan Journal of Educational Research and Development, 5*(1), 15-20.

Wienekamp, H., Jansen, W., Fickenfrerichs, H., & Peper, P. (1987). Does unconscious behaviour of teachers cause chemistry lessons to be unpopular with girls? *International Journal of Science Education, 9,* 281-286.

Yager, R.E., & Yager, S.O. (1985). Changes in perceptions of science for third, seventh, and eleventh grade students. *Journal of Research in Science Teaching, 22,* 347-358.

Zarega, M.R., Haertel, G.D., Tsai, S., & Walberg, H.J. (1986). Late adolescent sex differences in science learning. *Science Education, 70,* 447-460.

Zimmerer, L.K., & Bennett, S.M. (1987, April). *Gender differences on the California statewide assessment of attitudes and achievement in science.* Paper presented to the Annual Meeting of the American Educational Research Association, Washington, DC.

Classroom Management and Communication

Twenty years ago, teachers did most of the talking in elementary school classrooms. Since then, much research has suggested that learning is facilitated when students have the chance to talk to each other, especially in teacher-led, student-centred activities like discussion groups. Given this history, Staab wanted to find out whether the pattern of teacher domination of classroom talk had changed and in which activities students were encouraged to talk. Her findings suggest that children today probably do not get to talk much more in class than their parents did. Furthermore, the inclusion of child-centred activities like brainstorming, group problem solving or role playing seems to be the exception rather than the rule. In her study of 24 Grade 3 and Grade 6 classrooms, Staab reported that students spent almost one-third of their time working quietly and independently and another half of their time listening to the teacher. They were allowed to talk to each other informally during work times (about 15% of the total activity time), but all other kinds of student talk accounted for only 7% of activity time, and activities like problem solving were limited to one or two of the 24 classes. Despite these figures, 98.5% of the teachers whose classrooms were studied believed that oral language should be part of learning in all content areas! Obviously the discrepancy between the teachers' own ideal and the reality is an important topic for future research.

Netten and Spain were intrigued by research indicating discrepancies between cognitive ability and academic achievement for children enroled in Newfoundland French immersion classes. They hypothesized that these discrepancies might be related to different levels of competence in French which in turn might be related to differences in teaching styles. In their article, Netten and Spain focus on three Grade 2 French immersion classrooms, and the results they report tend to confirm their hypotheses. Comparison of scholastic ability and French language achievement indicated that the class with the lowest relative ability had higher French language achievement than would have been expected, while the class with moderately high ability had lower French language achievement than expected. Examination of teaching strategies indicated that the teacher in the latter classroom relied primarily on lectures and formal drill-type activities, while the teacher in the former classroom almost never lectured and instead spent a lot of time working with individual students and small groups. Students also interacted more with each other in this classroom than in the others. Further analysis of communication patterns between each teacher and high- and low-achieving students indicated that the teacher with the best relative achievement in her class communicated more with her low-achieving students than the other two teachers. Both low- and high-achieving students in her class initiated more communication with her than did low and high achievers in the other two classes.

Although the concept of classroom control is central to discussions of effective teaching, it has had different meanings for different researchers. In an effort to identify the dimensions of classroom control, Crocker and Brooker observed 36 Grade 2 and 39 Grade 5 classes over the course of a year, noting the occurrence of 30 different classroom processes. Factor analysis of these process variables indicated that classroom control consisted of three factors. Boundary control referred to the limits the teacher placed on classroom activities like movement, talk or task choice. The second factor, which the authors called disruptive behaviour, referred to the action taken by the teacher when a classroom rule was broken. The third factor, discussion-recitation, referred to the way in which the teacher organized student talk in the classroom. Overall, the classrooms studied could be characterized as very task-oriented and teacher-directed. High teacher direction was associated with higher cognitive performance while student-chosen activities were associated with lower cognitive performance.

Teachers' Practices With Regard to Oral Language

Claire F. Staab
University of British Columbia

The study investigated how elementary teachers structure their classroom and the school day to permit students to talk. Detailed observations over a week were made in 12 randomly selected grade 3 classrooms and 12 randomly selected grade 6 classrooms to determine the amount of time spent under the conditions of Teacher Talking, Students Speaking Formally, Students Speaking Informally, and Quiet over all curriculum areas. Results indicated that most of the school day (78% of the activity time) was spent in either quiet work time or the teacher talking. Activities such as brainstorming, oral problem solving, student-led discussions and role playing received minimal time (in combination, less than 1% of the instructional activity time). Students Speaking Informally occurred most often during art, physical education, and writing periods. Female teachers allowed significantly more Students Speaking Formally than did male teachers (F=4.97, p=.036) but neither grade level taught nor numbers of years of teaching experience was significant with regard to any talk structure.

*   *   *

DURING THE LATE 1960s AND EARLY 1970s, SEVERAL STUDIES INDICATED that talk in elementary school classrooms was dominated by the teacher. Teachers talked and students listened. Partly as a reaction to this teacher domination, and partly as a result of increasing attention being focused on the relationship of talk to learning (Britton, 1970; Langer, 1960, Vygotsky, 1962), the professional literature of the 1970s and the 1980s abounded with articles suggesting that students be given increased time during the school day for talking and that this talking be done during many different types of activities. The purpose of this study was to investigate whether there has been a shift in this teacher domination of classroom talk during the past 20 years and to investigate during which activities, if any, teachers encourage students to talk.

Furst and Amidon (1967) found that teachers talked during 45-50% of all class time, students talked during 27-30% of all class time, and 15-20%

This study was funded by the Social Sciences and Humanities Research Council of Canada.

of the time the classroom was silent. Bellack, Kliebard, Hyman, and Smith (1966) found that 15 teachers talked 50% more than 345 pupils and that three fifths of all teacher talk was for the purpose of soliciting a student response. Flanders (1970), in analyzing teachers' classroom behavior, found approximately the same ratio of teacher to student talk as did Furst and Amidon. Several researchers (Edwards & Furlong, 1978; Hennings, 1975) replicated the general findings of Flanders during the 1970s. None of these studies indicated during which specific activities students were encouraged to talk, but clearly past research has revealed that teacher talk dominated the school day.

In the minds of many theorists and educators, this teacher domination of classroom talk was unfortunate as it seemed inconsistent with the growing knowledge of how children learn (Vygotsky, 1962). The idea that talk is central to the process of learning has gained prominence during the past 15 years (Chorny, 1981; Jones, 1988). The literature of the 1970s, 1980s, and early 1990s evidenced an abundance of articles suggesting that if teachers want children to take an active part in learning, it is important for the child to talk (Barnes, 1976, 1990; Barnes & Todd, 1977; Beebe, Steven, & Masterson, 1982; Edwards & Mercer, 1987). Students need time to talk and for this to happen, teachers must talk less.

Before proceeding, it seems important to note that not all research done in the 1970s and 1980s advocated the importance of student talk in the classroom. Researchers on teacher effectiveness have found that engaged time on task, academic emphasis in teaching content, and direct instruction carried out by the teacher were included among the correlates of effective teaching as measured by student achievement on standardized tests (Brophy & Evertson, 1974, 1976; Brophy & Good, 1986; Evertson, Anderson, & Brophy, 1978; Evertson, Emmer, & Brophy, 1980; Fisher et al., 1978; McDonald & Elias, 1976; Rosenshine, 1976; Soar & Soar, 1972; Tikunoff, Berliner, & Rist, 1975). Subsets of these studies conducted during reading and math lessons have suggested that students who were academically engaged under direct teacher supervision scored higher on standardized measures (Anderson, Evertson, & Brophy, 1979; Good & Grouws, 1977, 1979; Stallings, Cory, Fairweather, & Needels, 1977, 1978). Several studies (Brophy & Evertson, 1976; Soar, 1977; Solomon & Kendall, 1979; Stallings et al., 1977, 1978; Stallings & Kaskowitz, 1974) have shown that successful teachers were strong, businesslike leaders who had high academic expectations for students. Less successful teachers were more child centered in that they allowed students to select their own activities and working arrangements (Good & Beckerman, 1978; Soar, 1977; Solomon & Kendall, 1979; Stallings & Kaskowitz, 1974; Stallings, Needels, & Stayrook, 1979). These child centered teachers often allowed students to talk with peers.

Clearly inconsistencies exist between a variety of teacher effectiveness studies and studies in language learning. Resolving these inconsistencies is impossible without further research. From the data presented in the above teacher effectiveness studies, it is difficult to ascertain the intent or amount of teacher organization present in the classrooms of less successful teachers. Did the teachers structure tasks that were to be completed by groups or pairs of individuals, or was the "talk time" simply time off task? In the Stallings and Kaskowitz (1974) and the Soar (1977) studies, nonacademic activities were defined as dramatic play, games, talk about home and family—not structured discussion groups or students helping one another on academic tasks. What parameters, if any, were placed on student self-selection? Were the students trained in any way to be self selecting or were they left entirely to their own devices? These questions need to be answered. Certainly studies in which a child centered teacher was highly successful have been reported (Edelsky, Draper, & Smith, 1983; Gunderson & Shapiro, 1986; Hansen, 1987; and Platt, 1984), and the social and academic contexts of these types of classrooms need to be compared with the social and academic contexts in the types of classrooms included in the teacher effectiveness studies.

Another important issue is the length of the data collection period. In general, observation during most of the teacher effectiveness studies took place over a period of a few days or weeks. Data from cooperative learning studies have suggested that to be successful groups must be well organized by the teacher, students must learn to work effectively in these groups, and that this learning takes time (Logan, 1986; Sharan & Shachar, 1988; Slavin, 1983). Groups of this nature need to operate for several months before a realistic evaluation is possible (Damon & Phelps, 1989; Wasserman, 1989).

Another possible reason for the discrepancies lies in the evaluation instrument. Standardized tests may not be the best means of evaluation when testing the benefits of talk in the classroom. Research has indicated that peer instruction and cooperative learning groups have led students to higher level cognitive responses than they were able to produce individually (Gilbert & Pope, 1986; Graybeal & Stodolsky, 1985; Sharan & Shachar, 1988; Trudge & Caruso, 1988). Damon and Phelps (1989), in working with 4th and 5th graders on problems in mathematics, found that students achieved deeper insights into concepts when allowed to collaborate with peers, but that peer collaboration was less successful for those tasks that relied on formulas and procedures. It is difficult to measure higher level cognitive responses on standardized tests. Phillips (1988) has suggested that the best measure of assessment is not a standardized test but the language of students in terms of their ability to put a point across, produce supporting facts, and sustain an argument.

Regardless of the inconsistencies that need to be resolved by further research, studies do exist that link student talk to learning. King (1989), in working with grade 4 students of high and average ability on computer assisted problem solving tasks, found that students working in small groups did use language to clarify meaning and to try a number of strategies for solving the problem. Webb and Kenderski (1984) reported that students' providing explanations for other students was associated with achievement, and current research is indicating that intermediate students can improve their reading comprehension through literature response groups (Eeds & Wells, 1989; Strickland, Dillon, Funkhouser, Glick, & Rogers, 1989).

Assuming, then, that talk can be a factor in the process of learning, several researchers, theorists, and educators have attempted to further explain the relationship between talking and learning. Edwards and Westgate (1987) have stated that talk allows the speaker to investigate how relationships and meanings are organized. Barnes (1990), Lindfors (1987), and Staab (1990) have noted that talk plays an important part in learning in that it helps one focus information, clarify ideas, and formulate opinions.

It is not only talk in general that is important but specifically talk with peers or talk in which the teacher acts as a facilitator (e.g., brainstorming sessions) rather than as a leader in absolute control. Chang and Wells (1988) have noted that in collaborative talk the learner must have ownership of the task. When a teacher is in control of a group, the freedom of pupils to introduce their own ideas is highly curtailed (Edwards & Mercer, 1987). The teacher retains control over what is said and done, what decisions are reached, and what interpretations are put on experiences. Often in this situation students may not have an opportunity to clarify their ideas or to formulate their own opinions.

Recent research has indicated that students are able to formulate opinions and to clarify ideas in situations where the teacher is not in control. Eeds and Wells (1989) reported that grade 6 students were able to engage in active inquiry in literature response groups in which the teacher was only a participant. Webb, Ender, and Lewis (1986) found that in debugging computer problems, groups that carried out abstract planning strategies without the teacher were more likely to learn the material.

The benefits of peer interaction are numerous. Talk with peers often clarifies both ideas and instructions (Cohen, 1989). Exploratory talk of students in small groups (i.e., peer talk) is one means by which assimilation and accommodation of new knowledge to the old is carried out. Cazden (1986) has stated that students are given more opportunity during talk with peers to ask questions of an informational nature and that questions asked of teachers are often procedural rather than informational. The asking of informational questions is critical to the learning process.

Talk is important not only for learning but as a way to improve oral communication skills. Children should be offered many opportunities to talk, and it should not be assumed that they enter the classroom being able to communicate effectively (Berliner & Casanova, 1988; Pigford, 1988; Stewig, 1988). To improve oral communication skills, students should be offered opportunities to talk to each other as well as to the teacher (Pigford, 1988; Stewig, 1988). Peer interaction provides important social experiences that foster skill development not achieved during interaction with adults (Cryan, 1984).

Given that the past 10 to 15 years have produced an explosion of information on why student talk is important in the classroom and that this information has, in many cases, reached the form of teacher manuals (Inner London Education Authority, 1984; Province of British Columbia Ministry of Education, 1989), one might wonder to what extent this information has changed the pattern of teacher domination of talk in the classroom. No recent studies have been reported, but several educators have expressed opinions. Gambell (1980) has stated that students today are probably being given more opportunities than ever to talk, to interact orally with their peers and to learn through oral communication. Edwards and Westgate (1987) have noted that innumerable teachers are now becoming interested in oral language in the classroom and are enrolling in inservice courses that are increasing their awareness of the place of oral language in the school day. Awareness of the value of oral language does not necessarily translate into increased student talk, however.

Not all educators agree that change is taking place at the level of classroom interaction. Jones (1988) has stated that in spite of the quantity of theoretical work in the area, there has been very little real change in the extent of productive talk that students actually engage in during the teaching day. This opinion was based on informal classroom observation rather than research. Chilcoat (1987) has agreed that little has changed since the studies conducted in the late '60s, but again this opinion is not based on recent research.

Research is needed to determine if the information on the value of oral language has reached the classroom at the level of day-to-day interaction. If change has occurred, is it more evident among any particular group of teachers? Allen, Brown, and Yatvin (1986) have suggested that if a change in the ratio of teacher to student talk has been made, it is more evident in primary classrooms than in intermediate classrooms. Edwards and Westgate (1987) have suggested that change may be more evident in the classrooms of teachers who have had advanced training (e.g., inservice) in the area of oral language. The following study is one validation of the opinions that have been expressed in the literature over the past several years.

Specifically the researcher asked the following questions:

1. How do teachers structure the school day with respect to quiet time, student talk, and teacher talk across various curriculum areas?

2. Does the way a teacher structures the school day with respect to quiet time, student talk, and teacher talk differ on the basis of grade level taught, sex of the teacher, number of years of teaching experience, or the number of reading and/or language arts courses taken?

Method

Subjects

The subjects in the study were 12 randomly selected grade 3 and 12 randomly selected grade 6 teachers from a pool of over 150 teachers at each grade level. The subjects taught in a large suburban area of Vancouver, British Columbia, Canada. In selecting the subjects for the study, the researcher obtained a list of all grade 3 and all grade 6 teachers from the school district office. Grades 3 and 6 were chosen because the researcher wanted to obtain a representation from both a primary and an intermediate grade level.

Procedure

The randomly selected subjects were telephoned at their schools and asked to participate in a classroom interaction study. At no time was oral language mentioned. Subjects were told that they would be given the details of the study when it was finished, but to preserve the integrity of the study no specific details could be provided before the data were collected. Subjects were told that a research assistant would observe in their classrooms for a period of one week and code the classroom interaction.

Classroom observations took place during the months of October and November, excluding the week before Halloween. All classroom observations in each classroom were for a period of one week and included all classroom activities from the beginning of school Monday morning until the close of school Friday afternoon. Periods before school, recess, and lunch time were not observed. Each research assistant observed in one classroom for a period of one week; thus it took four research assistants a period of six weeks to observe in the 24 classrooms. On average each classroom was observed for about 1,300 minutes during the week.

On the Friday following each classroom observation, teachers were asked by the research assistant to provide some demographic information. Teachers were asked how many years they had taught and how many reading and/or language arts courses had been taken at the university level. The research assistant also noted the sex of the teacher and the grade level taught.

Prior to data collection, the four research assistants received one week's training on the use of the classroom observation form which appears as Table 1. Training took the form of initial explanation of the form, the coding of videotapes of classrooms, and the coding of actual sample classrooms. No sample classrooms used for training were part of the randomly selected sample used in the study.

The classroom observation form appearing as Table 1 was designed to record four basic classroom conditions: Teacher Talking, Students Talking Formally, Students Talking Informally, and Quiet Classroom. The category of Teacher Talking included four subcategories: the teacher reading aloud, the teacher lecturing, the teacher leading a question-and-answer session, and the teacher talking to individual students as he or she was helping them with their work. If the teacher spoke continuously for more than 30 seconds, the talk was coded as teacher lecturing. If the teacher asked a question of students within that 30 seconds, the talk was coded as question-and-answer even though the teacher was doing the majority of the questioning.

The category of Students Speaking Formally included those times when the teacher specifically called on one or more students to give a presentation to the class or a small group. The teacher expressly had given the floor to one student or a group of students. The subcategories for Students Talking Formally were an individual giving an oral report, group choral reading or speaking, a dramatic production, an individual student reading aloud to a group, or a student debate.

The category of Students Speaking Informally included those times when students had the teacher's permission to speak but the talk was of a less formal, spontaneous nature. The teacher was allowing talk, but had not given the floor expressly to one student or group of students. The sub-categories for Students Talking Informally were a student-led discussion either in small or large groups (the teacher may have been a participant but was not the designated leader, or the teacher was not a direct member of the group), role playing or spontaneous drama, brainstorming, group problem solving, students informally helping each other such as in a partner situation, and student initiated questions.

The category of Quiet Times was recorded when there was no oral language in the room and when the students were talking without the teacher's permission. If students were talking informally during a work time and the teacher either gave them permission to do so or made no effort to stop the talking, the time was recorded as SIHX (students informally helping one another). If students were talking during work time and the teacher asked them to be quiet, or indicated that quiet was required, then

Table 1
Instruction Page of the Classroom Observation Form

General Instructions for Structured Observation Form

General Rules

1. Only oral language will be observed.
2. Focus of the observation is on the teacher or on the activity that the teacher assigned, not on what the students are doing if these differ.
3. The unit of observation is an entire activity (e.g., the morning exercises or the brainstorming session).
4. Each activity will be timed to the nearest minute. If an activity lasts less than 30 seconds, it will not be recorded.

Abbreviations or codes

Talk Structure

Note who is talking and in parentheses the nature of that talk. TT = Teacher talking, STF = formal student talk, STI = informal student talk, QC = quiet classroom.

TTRA	=	teacher reading aloud
TTLX	=	lecture
TTQA	=	question/answer/comment
TTSX	=	teacher helping individual student
SFRT	=	individual student giving oral report
SFCS	=	group choral reading or speaking
SFDR	=	dramatic production
SFRX	=	individual student reading aloud to group
SFDT	=	student debate
SIDX	=	student led discussion
SIRP	=	role playing or spontaneous drama
SIBX	=	brainstorming
SIPS	=	group problem solving
SIHX	=	students informally helping each other, reading to each other or talking with permission
SIQX	=	student initiated questions
QCQX	=	no oral language — quiet work time
QCUS	=	quiet work time, students talking without permission

Curriculum Activity

ME	=	morning exercises	AX	=	art
TX	=	transition	FT	=	free time
RX	=	reading	HX	=	housekeeping activities
LO	=	language arts oral	OL	=	oral language instruction
LW	=	language arts written	ST	=	show and tell or news
MX	=	math	PE	=	P.E.
SS	=	social studies	MU	=	music
SX	=	science	FR	=	French

Note: < indicates that two or more activities are happening simultaneously.

the time was scored as QCUS (quiet work time, students talking without permission).

These four talk conditions (i.e., Teacher Talking, Students Talking Formally, Students Talking Informally, and Quiet) were measured across all curriculum areas. The codes for these curriculum areas appear at the bottom of Table 1. Four general rules for the observations are also shown in Table 1.

The second page of the classroom observation form, which is shown in Table 2, gives an example of how the coding was actually recorded. The coder indicated the talk structure (e.g., TTQA-teacher question/answer/comment) in the first column, the curriculum area (e.g., MX-mathematics) in the second column, the time the activity began in the third column, and the time the activity stopped in the fourth column.

If two talk structures were happening simultaneously in the classroom (e.g., one group was working quietly while the teacher was lecturing to a second group), both activities were coded and these simultaneous talk structures were indicated by a < mark.

The researcher spent one day per week with each of the research assistants to independently code the oral language in the classroom. This procedure was done for the purpose of providing a measure of interrater reliability. Two measures of time were taken. The total amount of time spent under one talk structure in one curriculum area was calculated and labeled T time (i.e., total time). The number of times a talk structure occurred under each curriculum area was calculated and labeled N time (number of incidents). N time was the total number of times a talk structure occurred without regard for its duration, and T time was the duration measured to the nearest minute. Pearson Product Moment Correlations were calculated for both T time and N time as the coding of the research assistant was correlated with the independent coding of the researcher. The correlation between the two codings for T time was equal to .8252 and the correlation between the two codings for N time was equal to .9030.

Results

Table 3 indicates the total number of minutes spent in each talk structure across all curriculum areas. SFDR (student dramatic production) and SFDT (student debate) have not been included in the table or subsequent tables as no evidence of these talk structures was observed. The number in each row indicates the total number of minutes that each individual teacher spent under the condition of each talk structure. The categories are not mutually exclusive, because if two or more talk structures were occurring simultaneously all talk structures were recorded. The total shown in the right-hand column, Total Activity Time, is the sum of the values in the row. It is an indication of the gross amount of activity in the class.

Table 2
Mock Sample of a Coded Observation Form

Teacher's Name_____ Grade____ School_____ Date____

Time Observation Began_____ Time Ended_____ Recess_____ Lunch_____

Talk Structure	Curric. Area	Time Started	Time Ended
TTQA	MX	10:42	10:43
TTLX	MX	10:43	10:44
QCQX	MX	10:44	10:45
⟨ QCQX / TTSX	MX	10:45	10:46
⟨ QCQX / TTQA	MX	10:46	10:47
⟨ QCQX / TTSX	MX	10:47	11:08
TTQA	OL	11:08	11:10
QCQX	MX	11:10	11:31
QCUS	TX	11:31	11:32
TTLX	SS	11:32	11:33
TTQA	SS	11:33	11:34
TTLX	SS	11:34	11:35
⟨ TTSX / QCQX	SS	11:35	11:59
TTLX	TX	11:59	12:00

Table 4 indicates the proportion of total activity time each teacher spent in each of the major talk structures. The values were determined by cumulating the categories from Table 3 and dividing by the total activity time.

Table 5 indicates the total number of minutes spent in each of the four major categories of talk structures (i.e., Teacher Talking, Students Speak-

Table 3
Duration in Minutes per Teacher of Talk Structures Over One Week

Teacher	QCQX	QCUS	SFRT	SFCS	SFRX	SIDX	SIRP	SIBX	SIPS	SIXH	SIQX	TTRA	TTLX	TTQA	TTSX	Total*
1	796	221	5	36	9	0	0	0	0	244	24	19	293	250	472	2369
2	284	467	11	99	9	0	0	9	1	376	0	58	259	248	490	2311
3	94	68	93	43	34	31	0	2	1	760	0	24	93	146	880	2238
4	287	186	91	10	22	0	0	7	0	469	72	12	160	202	676	2215
5	620	78	45	29	48	0	0	1	0	211	4	55	49	389	614	2120
6	489	100	37	0	59	0	0	3	0	276	7	29	96	437	533	2092
7	712	87	40	8	16	0	0	0	0	159	19	96	289	210	498	2075
8	750	37	0	0	16	0	0	0	0	173	0	31	302	170	501	2047
9	339	143	94	15	15	0	0	34	9	366	0	54	198	114	654	2026
10	166	16	0	125	31	70	0	0	0	633	100	16	190	83	555	1894
11	435	75	46	30	80	0	4	5	111	106	4	35	531	126	415	1884
12	685	46	44	5	18	100	10	24	0	97	0	0	71	175	515	1857
13	362	39	32	63	2	7	0	7	0	311	0	78	339	223	342	1848
14	546	44	56	0	26	0	0	0	2	251	13	135	244	176	346	1807
15	340	80	82	15	0	0	0	0	0	267	21	63	202	265	498	1751
16	194	85	63	62	3	12	0	0	3	515	18	0	209	252	321	1734
17	786	31	0	0	14	0	0	0	0	241	44	6	206	116	286	1693
18	600	8	104	22	64	14	0	0	0	206	7	26	164	242	274	1679
19	312	26	0	15	31	0	0	0	0	254	2	81	472	181	194	1653
20	344	60	46	109	0	10	0	0	0	317	5	30	175	266	302	1641
21	591	39	0	0	37	0	19	0	0	94	11	28	224	186	360	1635
22	528	8	13	41	109	0	0	4	1	125	15	84	111	194	368	1590
23	441	76	23	14	10	10	0	0	0	42	0	51	193	288	386	1546
24	437	12	62	5	17	0	0	0	0	317	0	50	190	113	324	1542
Totals	11,138	2,032	987	746	670	254	33	96	128	6,710	368	1,061	5,260	5,062	10,714

QCQX — quiet, no oral language
SFCS — group choral reading/speaking
SIRP — role playing
SIXH — students helping one another
TTLX — teacher lecturing

QCUS — students talking without permission
SFRX — student reading to group
SIBX — brainstorming
SIQX — student initiated questions
TTQA — teacher question/answer

SFRT — student giving oral report
SIDX — student led discussion
SIPS — group problem solving
TTRA — teacher reading aloud
TTSX — teacher helping individual student

* Note: Total = total number of activity minutes. Categories of talk structures are not mutually exclusive.

Table 4
Proportion of Total Activity Time for Each Major Talk Structure

I.D. From Table 3	QC	SF	SI	TT	Grade Level Taught
2	32	4	16	46	3
3	7	8	34	51	3
5	33	4	10	52	3
6	28	6	13	52	3
9	24	7	18	51	3
10	10	9	37	44	3
11	27	8	6	59	3
13	22	6	19	53	3
15	24	7	16	53	3
19	21	5	19	56	3
23	34	3	5	59	3
24	29	5	22	43	3
1	43	2	11	44	6
4	21	5	25	47	6
7	38	1	8	53	6
8	39	3	9	49	6
12	39	2	16	41	6
14	32	3	14	50	6
16	16	8	32	46	6
17	48	0	15	36	6
18	36	8	13	45	6
20	25	9	19	47	6
21	38	5	8	49	6
22	34	11	8	47	6

ing Formally, Students Speaking Informally, and Quiet) categorized by each curriculum area. The final column in this table indicates the proportion of time spent in each curriculum area over the total number of minutes all subjects were observed.

Tables 3, 4, and 5 present a picture of how teachers structured their school day but do not answer the second research question. The second research question explored the notion of demographics. Does the way a teacher structures the school day with regard to Teacher Talk, Students Talking Formally, Students Talking Informally, and Quiet differ on the basis of grade taught, number of years of teaching experience, number of reading or language arts courses taken at the university level, or sex of the teacher? For the purpose of analysis, the sex of the teacher and whether the teacher taught grade 3 or grade 6 was obvious. Years of teaching experience was divided into two groups, those teachers who had taught 10 years or less and those teachers who had taught more than 10 years. Number of reading and/or language arts courses taken was divided into two groups— five or less and more than five. The data were subjected to a one-way

Table 5
Amount of Activity by All Teachers on Each Talk Structure for Each
Curriculum Area

Curriculum Area	OC	SF	SI	TT	Total	Proportion of Total Activity
Art	320	0	1,026	1,371	2,717	6
Computer Instruction	5	0	69	60	134	0
French	41	29	5	147	222	0
Free Time	225	3	858	602	1,688	4
Housekeeping	808	74	711	2,484	4,077	9
Library	176	0	157	188	521	1
Language Arts, Oral	74	220	96	370	760	2
Language Arts, Written	2,952	182	1,041	4,744	8,919	20
Morning Exercises	102	56	186	481	825	2
Music	237	432	50	340	1,059	2
Math	2,402	74	845	4002	7,323	16
Oral Language Instruction	197	0	23	337	557	1
Physical Education	218	16	905	846	1,985	4
Reading	3,085	501	291	2,727	6,604	15
Socials	947	224	539	1,305	3,015	7
Show-tell	16	530	30	115	691	2
Science	470	62	259	1,117	1,908	4
Transition	895	0	498	841	2,234	5
Totals:	13,170	2,403	7,589	22,077	45,239	100

Codes:

    QC—quiet classroom
    SF—students talking formally
    SI—students talking informally
    TT—teacher talking

analysis of variance for both T time and N time across each of the above demographic variables across each of the four major talk structures (i.e., Teacher Talking, Students Talking Formally, Students Talking Informally, and Quiet). For the purpose of these analyses, all curriculum areas were combined. The only significant difference at the .05 level appeared in T time for sex of teacher during Students Talking Formally. Female teachers had significantly more Students Talking Formally than did male teachers ($F=4.97$, $p=.036$). A significant difference was not found in any other analysis of variance.

Discussion

The total activity time varied from teacher to teacher because several activities could occur simultaneously. On average, although there is a variation of 7% to 48%, teachers spent 29% of the activity time during the school day asking students to work quietly and independently. Another 49% of the activity time was consumed by teachers talking. These percentages were similar to those found by Furst and Amidon (1967). When students were allowed to talk, this talk was evidenced mostly by students helping one another informally during work times. During these work times, typically, students were allowed to chat with one another, to ask each other questions regarding their work, or to share what they were doing. Earlier studies did not describe student talk, so a comparison of the activities that elicited student talk is impossible. This informal talk consumed 15% of the activity time. If these figures for Teacher Talk, Quiet Time, and Informal Student Talk during work time are totalled, they account for 93% of the activity time during the school day.

These figures leave 7% of the activity time to be accounted for by other forms of talk. Students spent very little time reading aloud to one another or in small groups. Reading aloud accounted for 1% of the activity time and 12 of the 24 teachers spent less than 20 minutes in a week at this talk structure. Students talking in front of a large or small group such as Show-and-Tell, or reporting the news or a current event, occurred slightly more often—2.2% of the total activity time. Eight of the 24 teachers spent less than 20 minutes per week at this talk structure. The talk structures of student-led discussions (e.g., small group discussions in which the teacher was not conducting a question-and-answer session), role playing, brainstorming time and problem solving, in combination, comprised about 1% of the activity time. Where these types of talk structures did occur, they were localized largely in one to two classrooms and absent in other classrooms (e.g., one teacher spent a total of 111 minutes in one week in a problem solving activity whereas the other 23 teachers spent a combined total of 17 minutes).

If one simply looks at the figures, one must conclude that the overall amount of students' oral language in the classroom has not changed significantly in the past 20 years. Even though numerous articles have been published and recommendations have been made that children be encouraged to engage in many types of oral language activities as a means for learning, it is apparent that these recommendations have not become a reality in today's classrooms. Corson (1984) speculated that talking takes time, and upper elementary grade teachers are too busy covering curriculum to allow time for discussion and generating ideas by means of talk. According to the present study this also is true in the primary grades.

The study did provide information as to the type of activity students engaged in when talk was encouraged. This information was not available in previous studies. Even if this information is now available, it is difficult, if not impossible, to state how much time during the school week teachers should spend on various types of talking activities. In effect, it is difficult to answer the question of how much is enough. It would be unwarranted to state that teachers should spend 10% of the school day on brainstorming, another 10% on problem solving, and so forth. Neither should teachers feel that these talk structures should be practiced for themselves as isolated activities. If students are to use oral language as a means for learning, then teachers should consider many types of talk structures as integral to curriculum areas (Staab, 1990). In mathematics children may need to brainstorm as a means of thinking through possible methods for solving a problem. In science children may need to problem solve as a way to discover alternative means for completing an experiment. In reading children may need to role play as a means for understanding a character's motivation. In social studies children may need to form small discussion groups as a means to review what they have learned. If any tie-in can be made with the teacher effectiveness studies, time spent talking must be time on task. To increase student talk in the classroom teachers need to vary the pattern of lecturing or leading a question-and-answer session and then assigning seat work. If students are to use oral language as a means for learning, then they need many opportunities to talk about what they are doing (Beebe, Steven, & Masterson, 1982; Edwards & Mercer, 1987; Lindfors, 1987).

It is also important to note that in the study there was considerable variation among individual teachers. Previous studies simply quoted averages. It may be misleading to state what "all" teachers do. All teachers asked for quiet work time, allowed students to talk within work times, lectured, asked questions, and helped individual students, yet the range of time spent during each of these talk structures was large. Individual variation was not connected to grade level taught, number of years of teaching experience, the number of reading and/or language arts courses taken at the university level, or sex of the teacher. Female teachers did provide significantly more opportunities for students to speak formally than did male teachers, yet beyond this one difference individual teachers seemed to vary in the use of talk structures in accordance with their own teaching style and not in accordance with the above demographics. Even though it is true that few teachers engaged in such talk structures as brainstorming and role playing, there was much individual variation in the use of the more common talk structures (e.g., teacher talking, quiet time). In discussing their individual profiles with the teachers involved in the study, many seemed surprised at the lack of various talk structures that had been observed.

In interviews only 21% of the subjects felt that a quiet classroom is a more productive classroom, and 98.5% felt that oral language should be a way to learn in all content areas. Even teachers who favored a quiet classroom felt that productive talk (i.e., talk for the purpose of learning) was valuable. Perhaps teaching is such a complex act that teachers often are unaware of the amount of time they spend talking and the amount of time they allow students to talk. The reasons for this discrepancy between belief and action need to be explored in further research.

In examining the number of minutes spent in each of the four main categories of talk structures (i.e., Teacher Talking, Students Speaking Formally, Students Speaking Informally, and Quiet) over each curriculum area, it seems that teachers allow students to talk mainly during art, free time, and physical education. This may be one indication that teachers still feel that talk is not something one uses for serious learning but rather a time merely to chat. The one exception to this notion was the amount of Students Speaking Informally that occurred during language arts, written. The writing process as elaborated by Graves (1983) is a method for teaching writing that encourages students to work together and to serve as audiences for each other's writing. As many classrooms included in the study were engaged in this form of writing instruction, much of the language categorized as Students Speaking Informally happened during the language arts, written period.

In examining the amount of total time over all talk structures spent in each curriculum area, it became apparent that language arts/reading consumed 38% of the week's activity time. Mathematics consumed 16% of the week's activity time. If transition times and housekeeping activities were combined, they consumed 14% of the week's activity time, while science consumed 4% of the time and social studies consumed 7%. It seems desirable that transition and housekeeping procedures become streamlined so that the extra time might be distributed over such curriculum areas as social studies and science. None of the teachers in the study had less than five years teaching experience, so it seems that this need to streamline peripheral activities is not symptomatic of only the beginning teacher.

If talk is so important for learning, why is not more of it going on in today's classroom? Is the old adage, "A quiet classroom is a good classroom" still being given credence? Are teachers unaware of the talk structures that are happening within their classrooms? Do teachers view talk as only a way to socialize rather than a way to learn? Are teachers unaware of specific techniques for conducting brainstorming sessions and for structuring small group discussions? Whatever the cause, it seems important for researchers, teacher educators, and curriculum specialists within school districts to discover the answers to these questions so that practice is more aligned with recent theory and research.

References

Allen, R., Brown, K., & Yatvin, N. (1986). *Language learning through communication.* Belmont, CA: Wadsworth.

Anderson, L., Evertson, C., & Brophy, J. (1979). An experimental study of effective teaching in first grade reading groups. *Elementary School Journal, 79,* 193-223.

Barnes, D. (1976). *From communication to curriculum.* Harmondsworth, UK: Penguin.

Barnes, D. (1990). Oral language and learning. In S. Hynds & D.L. Rubin (Eds.), *Perspectives on talk and learning* (pp. 41-57). Urbana, IL: National Council of Teachers of English.

Barnes, D., & Todd, F. (1977). *Communicating and learning in small groups.* London, UK: Routledge and Kegan Paul.

Beebe, W., Steven, T., & Masterson, J. (1982). *Communicating in small groups.* Glenview, IL: Scott Forsman.

Bellack, A., Kliebard, H., Hyman, R., & Smith, F. (1966). *Language of the classroom.* Columbia, MO: Teachers College Press.

Berliner, D., & Casanova, U. (1988). Are schools hampering language competency? *Instructor, 97*(7), 14-15.

Britton, J. (1970). *Language and learning.* London, UK: Penguin Press.

Brophy, J., & Evertson, C. (1974). *Process-product correlations in the Texas teacher effectiveness study: Final report* (Research report no. 74-4). Austin, TX: Research and Development Center for Teacher Education, University of Texas at Austin. (ERIC Document Reproduction Service No. ED 099345)

Brophy, J., & Evertson, C. (1976). *Learning from teaching: A developmental perspective.* Boston, MA: Allyn and Bacon.

Brophy, J., & Good, T.L. (1986). Teacher behavior and student achievement. In M.C. Wittrock (Ed.), *Handbook of research on teaching* (3rd ed., pp. 328-375). New York, NY: Macmillan.

Cazden, C. (1986). Classroom discourse. In M.C. Wittrock (Ed.), *Yearbook of research on teaching* (pp. 432-463). New York, NY: Macmillan.

Chang, G.L., & Wells, G. (1988). The literate potential of collaborative talk. In M. Maclure, T. Phillips, & A. Wilkinson (Eds.), *Oracy matters* (pp. 95-110). Philadelphia, PA: Open University Press.

Chilcoat, G.W. (1987). Teacher talk: Keep it clear. *Academic Therapy, 22,* 263-271.

Chorny, M. (1981). A Canadian perspective: Focus on talk. *English Education, 13*(1), 32-35.

Cohen, E.G. (1989). Can classrooms learn? *Sociology of Education, 62*(2), 75-94.

Corson, D. (1984). The case for oral language in schooling. *Elementary School Journal, 83,* 265-285.

Cryan, J.R. (1984). Forms and functions of child-to-child interaction in classroom settings: A review, *Childhood Education, 60*(5), 354-360.

Damon, W., & Phelps, E. (1989). Critical distinctions among three approaches to peer education. *International Journal of Educational Research, 13*(1), 9-19.

Edelsky, C., Draper, K., & Smith, K. (1983). Hookin' em in at the start of the school year in a "whole language" classroom. *Anthropology and Education Quarterly, 14*(4), 257-281.

Edwards, A., & Furlong, V. (1978). *Language and teaching: Meaning in classroom interactions.* London, UK: Heinemann.

Edwards, A.D., & Mercer, N. (1987). *Common knowledge: The development of understanding in the classroom.* New York, NY: Methuen.

Edwards, A.D., & Westgate, D.P.G. (1987). *Investigating classroom talk*. London, UK: Falmer.

Eeds, M., & Wells, D. (1989). Grand conversations: An exploration of meaning construction in literature study groups. *Research in Teaching English, 23*(1), 4-29.

Evertson, C., Anderson, L., & Brophy, J. (1978). *Texas junior high school study: Final report of process-outcome relationships* (Report No. 4061). Austin, TX: Research and Development Center for Teacher Education, University of Texas.

Evertson, C., Emmer, E., & Brophy, J. (1980). Predictors of effective teaching in junior high mathematics classrooms. *Journal for Research in Mathematics Education, 11*, 167-177.

Fisher, C., Marliave, R., Cahen, L., Dishaw, M., Moor, J., & Berliner, D. (1978). *Teaching behaviors, academic learning time and student achievement: Final report of Phase III-B, beginning teacher evaluation study*. San Francisco, CA: Far West Laboratory for Education Research.

Flanders, N. (1970). *Analyzing teacher behavior*. Reading, MA: Addison-Wesley.

Furst, N., & Amidon, E. (1967). *Interaction analysis: Theory, research and application*. Reading, MA: Addison-Wesley.

Gambell, T.J. (1980). *Talk contexts and speech styles: Planning for oral language*. Paper presented at annual meeting of Canadian Council Teachers of English, Halifax, NS. (ERIC Document Reproduction Service No. ED 193637)

Gilbert, J., & Pope, M. (1986). Small group discussions about conceptions in science: A case study. *Research in Science and Technological Education, 4*(1), 61-76.

Good, T., & Beckerman, T. (1978). A naturalistic study in sixth grade classrooms. *Elementary School Journal, 78*, 192-201.

Good, T., & Grouws, D. (1977). Teaching effects: A process-product study in a fourth grade mathematics classroom. *Journal of Teacher Education, 28*(3), 49-54.

Good, T., & Grouws, D. (1979). The Missouri mathematics effectiveness project: An experimental study in fourth grade classrooms. *Journal of Educational Psychology, 71*(3), 355-362.

Graves, D. (1983). *Writing: Teachers and children at work*. Exeter, NH: Heinemann.

Graybeal, S., & Stodolsky, S. (1985). Peer work groups in elementary schools. *American Journal of Education, 93*(3), 409-428.

Gunderson, L., & Shapiro, J. (1986). Some findings on whole language instruction. *Reading-Canada-Lecture, 5*, 22-26.

Hansen, J. (1987). Organizing student learning. Teachers teach what and how. In J. Squire (Ed.), *The dynamics of language learning* (pp. 321-335). Urbana, IL: NCTE.

Hennings, D.T. (1975). *Mastering classroom communication: What interaction analysis tells the teacher*. Pacific Palisades, CA: Goodyear.

Inner London Education Authority. (1984). *Improving secondary schools*. Report of the Committee on the Curriculum and Organization of Secondary Schools. London, UK: ILEA.

Jones, M. (1988). *Lipservice: The story of talk in schools*. Philadelphia, PA: Open University Press.

King, A. (1989). Verbal interaction and problem solving within computer-assisted cooperative learning groups. *Journal of Educating Computing Research, 5*(1), 1-15.

Langer, S. (1960). *Philosophy in a new key* (3rd ed.). Cambridge, MA: Harvard University Press.

Lindfors, J. (1987). *Children's language and learning* (2nd ed.). Englewood Cliffs, NJ: Prentice-Hall.

Logan, T. (1986). Cooperative learning: A view from the inside. *The Social Studies, 77*(3), 123-126.

McDonald, F., & Elias, P. (1976). *The effects of pupil performance on pupil learning. Final report. Beginning teacher evaluation study, Phase II, 1974-1976.* Princeton, NJ: Educational Testing Service.

Phillips, T. (1988). Why successful small-group talk depends upon not keeping to the point. In M. Maclure, T. Phillips, & A. Wilkinson (Eds.), *Oracy matters* (pp. 69-81). Philadelphia, PA: Open University Press.

Pigford, A.B. (1988). Teachers let students talk. *Academic Therapy, 24*(2), 193-197.

Platt, N. (1984). How one classroom gives access to meaning. *Theory Into Practice, 23,* 239-245.

Province of British Columbia Ministry of Education, Student Assessment Branch. (1988). *Oral communication in the primary grades: Teachers' resource package.* Victoria, BC: Author.

Province of British Columbia Ministry of Education, Program Development. (1989). *Primary program.* Victoria, BC: Author.

Rosenshine, B. (1976). Recent research on teaching behaviors and student achievement. *Journal of Teacher Education, 27*(1), 61-64.

Sharan, S., & Shachar, H. (1988). *Language and learning in the cooperative classroom: Recent research in psychology.* New York, NY: Springer-Verlag.

Slavin, R. (1983). *Cooperative learning.* New York, NY: Longman.

Soar, R. (1977). An integration of findings from four studies of teacher effectiveness. In G. Borich (Ed.), *The appraisal of teaching: Concepts and processes.* Reading, MA: Addison-Wesley.

Soar, R., & Soar, R. (1972). An empirical analysis of selected follow-through programs: An example of a process approach to evaluation. *National Society for the Study of Education Yearbook, 71*(2), 229-259.

Solomon, D., & Kendall, A. (1979). *Children in classrooms: An investigation of person-environment interaction.* New York, NY: Praeger.

Staab, C. (1990). Talk in whole language classrooms. In V. Froese (Ed.), *Whole-language: Practice and theory* (pp. 15-47). Scarborough, ON: Prentice-Hall.

Stallings, J., Cory, R., Fairweather, J., & Needels, M. (1977). *Early childhood education classroom evaluation.* Menlo Park, CA: SRI International.

Stallings, J., Cory, R., Fairweather, J., & Needels, M. (1978). *A study of basic skills taught in secondary schools.* Menlo Park, CA: SRI International.

Stallings, J., & Kaskowitz, D. (1974). *Follow-through classroom observation evaluation 1972-1973* (SRI project URU-7370). Stanford, CA: Stanford Research Institute.

Stallings, J., Needels, M., & Stayrook, N. (1979). *The teaching of basic reading in secondary schools, Phase II and Phase III.* Menlo Park, CA: SRI International.

Stewig, J.W. (1988). Oral language: A place in the curriculum. *Clearing House, 62*(4), 171-174.

Strickland, D., Dillon, R., Funkhouser, L., Glick, M., & Rogers, C. (1989). Research currents: Classroom dialogue during literature response groups. *Language Arts, 66*(2), 192-201.

Tikunoff, W., Berliner, D., & Rist, R. (1975). *An ethnographic study of the forty classrooms of the beginning teacher evaluation study known sample* (Technical Report No. 75-10-05). San Francisco, CA: Far West Laboratory for Educational Research and Development.

Trudge, J., & Caruso, D. (1988). Cooperative problem solving in the classroom: Enhancing young children's cognitive development. *Young Children, 44,* 46-52.

Vygotsky, L.S. (1962). *Thought and Language.* Cambridge, MA: MIT.

Wasserman, S. (1989). Children working in groups? It doesn't work! *Childhood Education, 65*(4), 201-205.

Webb, N., Ender, P., & Lewis, S. (1986). Problem-solving strategies and group processes in small groups learning computer programming. *American Educational Research Journal, 23*(2), 243-261.

Webb, N. & Kenderski, C. (1984). Student interaction and learning in small-group and whole-class settings. In P. Peterson, L. Wilkinson, & M. Hallinan (Eds.), *The social context of instruction: Group organization and group processes* (pp. 153-170). New York, NY: Academic Press.

Student-Teacher Interaction Patterns in the French Immersion Classroom: Implications for Levels of Achievement in French Language Proficiency

Joan E. Netten and William H. Spain
Memorial University of Newfoundland

The purpose of this article is to report the initial analysis of a study of student-teacher interaction patterns in the French immersion classroom, by describing specific differences found in the classrooms of three grade two teachers. The statistical findings are discussed from the point of view of trend and consistency. The procedure is exploratory, and the purpose is to generate hypotheses for further study and closer analysis. Indications are given of the degree to which the nature of communication in these three classrooms differs. Possible links between teaching style and communication in the classroom are explored. The probable significance of teacher priorities in creating the communication patterns in the classroom is also presented.

*   *   *

BILINGUAL EDUCATION IN THE FORM OF FRENCH IMMERSION INSTRUCTION is being chosen by increasing numbers of Canadian parents as an alternative form of schooling for their children. Currently, it is reported that there are over two hundred thousand pupils enrolled in immersion classes in Canada.[1] The basic assumption in these programs is that subject matter can be learned in French while, at the same time, competence is acquired in the second language. It is widely held that this process takes place with no long-term loss to either mother tongue development or content comprehension. It has also been generally assumed by program evaluators that the French language would be acquired equally well by all children participating in the programs, given usually anticipated individual differences in cognitive abilities. In making this assumption it does not seem to have been foreseen that instructional differences in the classroom could have an effect

The research from which these data were taken is part of a larger study which has been funded by the Social Sciences and Humanities Research Council of Canada and the Office of the Secretary of State through the Department of Education and the Province of Newfoundland and Labrador.

on the level of competence attained in the second language by individual pupils.

The success of immersion pupils in achieving considerably higher levels of competence in French than those normally reached by children participating in regular French instruction in the schools has generally been attributed in large measure to the use of French as a vehicle of communication.[2] The second language is primarily acquired by use through learning subject matter in the classroom, not through being taught as an academic subject. Consequently, the nature of communication in the classroom is of prime importance in the successful implementation of bilingual programs of this type.

A number of evaluation studies have been conducted of French immersion programs in several provinces since the inception of the program.[3] These studies tend to indicate that average levels of performance in French immersion classrooms are similar to average levels of performance in regular English comparison classrooms. However, evaluation studies undertaken in the province of Newfoundland and Labrador have tended to indicate that, while average levels of performance may be similar, actual levels of achievement for individual pupils vary greatly.[4]

One of the most persistent findings in the Newfoundland data was the unaccounted variance both within and between classrooms. There was a general tendency for the variance in achievement levels in the French immersion classrooms to be greater than that of the regular English comparison classes, even though immersion classrooms tended to have more homogeneous cognitive ability scores at the beginning of the school year. It was also noted that there were extremely wide variations in results between classrooms on the standardized measures of French achievement used in the evaluations.

The differences in achievement levels in French are of considerable significance in the immersion classroom. Achievement in subject matter appears to be positively correlated with achievement in the second language. Consequently, the level of achievement which pupils attain in French will ultimately affect their overall scholastic achievement. Since no evidence as yet links these findings to the capabilities of the teacher in the second language it seems reasonable to consider the hypothesis that differences in classroom processes may explain these findings.

Classroom Processes Study

To investigate further this phenomenon a study of classroom processes was initiated. It was felt that, by focusing on the high and low achieving pupils in each classroom, some light could be shed on the question of the instructional processes which affect language learning. The nature of the differences between high and low achievers should vary across classrooms, reflecting differences in teaching, and also providing hints as to the kind of teaching that is most effective in promoting the learning of a second language. The study undertaken proposed to describe differences in classrooms, linking these differences, where possible, to achievement in the second language.

The study was based on a number of theoretical assumptions, of which the following were of prime importance.

- In an immersion classroom the learning of the second language takes place within the context of communication in the classroom. This is the major assumption on which school immersion programs are based.

- The nature, and quality, of this communication will govern the acquisition of the second language. It is the communication acts in which an individual participates, either overtly or covertly, within the classroom which will determine the level of development of the second language for the pupil.

- Communication in the classroom carries two sets of messages with each utterance. There is the cognitive message which has to do with the classroom situation and the content being learned. There is also the affective message that is carried simultaneously and affects the pupil's motivation to learn.

- The influence of the cognitive content of a message to a pupil depends on the influence of the affective content of the communication. The child's ability, or willingness, to assimilate the content of a communication can be enhanced, or depressed, by the affective content which accompanies the cognitive message.

- The role of the teacher is of prime importance in determining the nature of communication within the classroom. The cognitive and affective content of communication in the classroom depends upon the priority which the teacher places on these two aspects. It also depends on how the teacher construes cognitive outcomes in relation to affective outcomes.

The study procedures included observations of a total of twenty-three Grade one, two, and three classrooms, and interviews with the twenty-three teachers. The classrooms involved in the larger study included the majority of those on the island of Newfoundland where immersion programs were offered. The total numbers of pupils involved in the study was 524, distributed as indicated in Table 1.

Within each classroom, six pupils were chosen as target students. Three of the pupils were identified as high achievers, while the other three were pupils who tended to achieve less well. Target pupils were selected on the basis of achievement data and teacher report at the end of the year.

Table 1
Characteristics and Number of Classrooms Studied

Grade Level	I	II	III	Total
Number of Classes	11	6	6	23
Number of Pupils				
Smallest Class	10	7	11	
Largest Class	29	34	28	
Median Class Size	24	24	20.5	
Total Number of Pupils	259	143	122	524

The study examined the teaching style of the teachers involved. Teaching style, as used here, is a generalization of the way that teachers conduct their classrooms, and deals with the use of verbal and non-verbal messages, the reliance on each to convey cognitive and affective content, as well as the type of lessons used, and general classroom organization. Additional data not discussed here were also collected.

Achievement Outcomes

It may be helpful to examine some of the evidence found in the outcome measures which have led to the hypothesis of between classroom differences with respect to process.

Scholastic Ability

Table 2 gives an indication of the English language scholastic ability of the pupils as measured by the Canadian Cognitive Abilities Test (CCAT). These results are reported both as national norms and as Newfoundland norms based on the number of French immersion classrooms in the province. It may be seen that the pupils in all three classrooms possess generally high ability and would normally be expected to achieve well in school.

With respect to the relative ability of the three classrooms, it is apparent that Classroom A has the lowest relative ability. Classroom B has the highest, and that of Classroom C is moderately high. From the information provided by the Newfoundland norms it may be seen that Classroom A would normally be expected to achieve less well than the majority of immersion classrooms in the province. Classroom B would be expected to perform better than the majority of French immersion classrooms, and Classroom C would be expected to attain a level of achievement somewhat better than that which is typical in the province. It would usually be antic-

Table 2
Scolastic Ability: Three Grade II Classrooms

Measure	Classroom A		Classroom B		Classroom C	
	Mean	*SD*	*Mean*	*SD*	*Mean*	*SD*
CCAT National %ile	54.1	24.46	83.7	18.82	72.7	22.84
CCAT Nfld %ile Rank	58	5	95	7	70	46

Note 1: The mean national percentile rank is the mean of the individual percentiles taken from the published Canadian national norms for the CCAT. The standard deviation of the national percentiles has a similar basis.

Note 2: The Newfoundland percentile refers to the position of the raw score mean or standard distribution of 45 means from grade II early French immersion classrooms in Newfoundland and Labrador. A Newfoundland percentile rank of 58 for a mean would indicate that 58% of Newfoundland grade II classrooms had raw score means lower than the mean listed. The Newfoundland percentile rank for standard deviations would be interpreted the same way.

ipated that the relative level of average performance would be reflected in the French language achievement outcomes for the three classrooms.

The dispersion of scholastic ability in the classrooms is also of interest. Classroom B is a very homogeneous class relative to the other two classrooms. Both Classrooms A and C have a spread of ability which is about average for the province. Again, it would usually be anticipated that this same relative dispersion would occur in the French language achievement outcomes.

French Language Achievement

The results of the achievement testing are reported in Table 3. The Tourond *Test diagnostique de lecture* (TDL) was used as an indicator of French language achievement. The assumption was made that reading ability depends on communicative competence to a considerable degree. In this way the Tourond test can be considered as an indirect measure of achievement in oral French and perhaps, in particular, of oral comprehension. Considering that a similar curriculum was used in all classrooms, it may be hypothesized that departures from expectations with respect to achievement levels and variance in the three classrooms indicate differences in classroom processes. Reference to this problem is made in Table 3 which discusses comprehension of the second language.

Considering Classroom B first, it may be seen that the relative expectations for achievement for this classroom are met. It achieved among the highest of Newfoundland classrooms, with a corresponding homogeneity of outcomes, as well. Classrooms A and C, however, present a different pic-

	Comparison of Achievement Outcomes in French of Three Grade II Classrooms					
	Classroom A		Classroom B		Classroom C	
Measure	Mean	SD	Mean	SD	Mean	SD
TDL I						
Raw Score	31.9	2.43	34.6	1.50	32.3	7.30
Nfld %ile rank	35	62	97	13	40	98
TDL II						
Raw Score	22.8	3.27	23.8	2.49	20.1	6.39
Nfld %ile rank	89	20	97	4	42	98
TDL III						
Raw Score	21.0	4.39	23.3	3.11	19.0	6.92
Nfld %ile rank	80	27	98	9	53	89
TDL IV						
Raw Score	18.3	4.12	19.1	4.15	17.0	6.68
Nfld %ile rank	87	22	93	24	55	98

Note 1: The Newfoundland percentile refers to the position of the raw score mean or standard deviation in a distribution of 45 means or standard deviations from grade II early French immersion classrooms in Newfoundland and Labrador. A Newfoundland %ile rank of 53 for a mean would indicate that 53 percent of Newfoundland grade II classrooms had raw score means lower than the mean listed.

Table 3

ture. In Classroom A, the data suggest that, with the exception of subtest I of the Tourond test, achievement was among the best for Newfoundland classes, even though the scholastic ability of this group was relatively the lowest. Furthermore, the class seemed to be relatively more homogeneous than predicted, suggesting relatively greater achievement of the poorer students than typical for Newfoundland. Finally, Classroom C shows generally lower achievement than expected, with a very heterogeneous distribution, indicating in particular that poorer students achieved relatively less well than was expected. This seems clearly to point to differences in process within these classrooms that lead to differences in language achievement.

	Correlation of Teacher Rankings of Oral Attainment with Achievement on the Tourond *Test diagnostique de lecture*		
Measure	Classroom A	Classroom B	Classroom C
TDL I	.51	.03	.40
TDL II	.60	.44	.71
TDL III	.30	.34	.70
TDL IV	.31	.32	.77

Note 1: TDL Subtests - Gr. 2
    i) La synthèse de mots de la discrimination de graphèmes.
    ii) La lecture de mots.
    iii) Les phrases à compléter.
    iv) La compréhension de textes.

Table 4

Table 4 provides a look at the assumption that oral achievement and reading achievement are related. The differences between teachers provide additional evidence of process differences. Teacher ranking of oral achievement and Tourond scores correlate differently indicating:

- that there is less relation in some classes than in others between oral and reading achievement,

or

- that teachers differ in the ways that they assess oral achievement.

In particular, the contrast between Classrooms B and C is evident. In Classroom B, the oral rankings of the teacher show a consistently lower correlation with all the Tourond subscales. In Classroom C, the same correlations are consistently quite high. The differences in Classroom A are mixed, the two lower Tourond subscales correlating somewhat more positively with the oral rankings than do the higher subscales. Finally, Table 5 examines the relationship of scholastic ability to French achievement scores. The correlations generally tend to be low, with one exception which may possibly be explained by the nature of the Tourond subtest. The tendency appears to be toward lower correlations in Classroom A than in either of the other two classrooms, though these differences are not large. All three teachers seem to be exceptional in the Newfoundland context in that the correlations that have been observed in their cases are much lower

Table 5
Correlation of Canadian Cognitive Abilities:
Percentile Ranks with Achievement on the
Tourond *test diagnostique de lecture*

Measure	Classroom A	Classroom B	Classroom C
TDL I			
Correlation	0.28	0.10	-0.10
Nfld %ile Rank	49	24	7
TDL II			
Correlation	0.09	0.24	0.23
Nfld %ile Rank	8	27	27
TDL III			
Correlation	0.10	0.29	0.25
Nfld %ile Rank	10	25	24
TDL IV			
Correlation	-0.02	0.42	0.24
Nfld %ile Rank	2	34	28

Note 1: The Newfoundland percentile refers to the position of the correlation in a distribution of 45 correlations from grade II early French immersion classrooms in Newfoundland and Labrador. A Newfoundland percentile rank of ten would indicate that 10% of Newfoundland grade II classrooms had correlations lower than the correlation listed.

than typical for grade two classrooms in Newfoundland. In general, the outcomes in French in these classrooms are much less predictable than is usually the case, suggesting very important process differences from the normative classroom. Teacher mother tongue is not an evident cause in this case.

Process Hypothesis

A process hypothesis may be advanced to suggest an explanation for these lower correlations. It may be hypothesized that in all classrooms the teacher responds to pupil factors which are not associated with scholastic ability directly, but which are, none the less, related to the achievement process. Responding differently to pupils thought to be high or low achievers, for example, would have the appearance in this analysis of an apparently random influence, operating to make mean scores higher and pupil outcomes more homogeneous, as is the case in Classroom A, or mean scores lower and pupil outcomes more heterogeneous, as is the case in Classroom C.

It is important to remember that the factors triggering these process differences are most likely different for each teacher so that classrooms must be examined on a case by case basis. It is suggested in this analysis that these differences may possibly be related to teacher priorities in the classroom. It is also important to remember that the results may have either positive or negative consequences for the pupils. The low correlations in Classroom C, for example, suggest a less effective learning environment for all pupils, but particularly low achievers. The low correlations in Classroom A, on the other hand, suggest much more positive results for all pupils, particularly low achievers, when the actual levels of achievement are taken into consideration.

Process Differences in the Classrooms

In the following paragraphs some of the process differences which have been uncovered at the present time are discussed.

Process Structure

Although the three teachers followed the same prescribed curriculum, there were significant differences between the classrooms with respect to teaching strategies used, and to the percentage of time spent on different types of activities in the classrooms. These differences may have implications of considerable import for second language learning in the immersion classroom. Table 6 presents a comparison of the three classrooms with respect to the amount of time spent on each of the types of activity observed.

Percentage of Messages per Classroom Respecting Process Structure			
Process Structure		% Messages	
	A	B	C
Lecture	1.3	8.9	20.2
Questions	12.6	11.0	9.8
Drill	2.9	10.9	15.1
Expressive Language Exercise	3.4	3.5	.6
Discussion	5.0	1.9	.9
Seatwork (Monitoring)	8.0	1.5	3.4
Seatwork (Piloting)	26.8	34.8	17.6
Boardwork	2.4	3.8	7.1
Group Activity	2.3	1.6	3.4
Group Piloting	10.1	6.2	3.7
Organization/Administration	13.9	12.3	15.5
Control	.8	.2	.7
Social with Teacher	.8	.7	.5
Social with Peers	9.4	2.3	1.3
Non-Interacting	.1	.2	.2
Number of Messages	1967	2594	2032

Table 6

In Classroom C about one-fifth of class time was spent on lessons in which the teacher instructed the pupils in a relatively formal fashion. Another third of class time was taken up with administration or organizational activities and drill-type activities, although the drills often took the form of a game. Altogether, one-half of class time was consumed in activities where the pupils were listening to the teacher or producing relatively stereotyped language responses.

In Classroom B there was considerably less lecture and drill-type activity than in Classroom C, and almost twice as much activity where the teacher interacted on an individual basis with the pupils. In fact, over one-third of class time was spent in this type of activity. Classroom B, then, appears to be a classroom in which pupils made less use of the second language in structured situations and more use of the second language in individual interchanges with the teacher.

The third classroom, Classroom A, presents another different learning environment. In this classroom there was virtually no lecture type activity. The teacher used a question/answer technique with the pupils. In addition, about 25% of class time was spent in seat work with the teacher assisting individual pupils. Approximately 10% of class time was spent in group work activity, with the teacher giving assistance to each group. In this classroom there was also considerably more interaction between peers than in the other two classrooms (almost 10% of class time). This pattern is reflected in a lower number of messages from the teacher. It appears, then, that this classroom was one in which individual pupils used the second language regularly to express themselves about both academic and social matters to the teacher and to each other.

The differences between the classrooms are also further reinforced by looking at the percentage of class time spent in several of the other categories observed. The amount of boardwork was much higher in Classroom C than in the other two classrooms, and was particularly low in Classroom A. The percentage of class time spent in discussion, on the other hand, was much higher in Classroom A than either of the other two classrooms. Expressive language use exercises were employed more often in both Classrooms A and B than in Classroom C. These types of differences tend to reinforce the hypothesis that Classroom C provided a rather formal learning atmosphere where pupils had limited opportunities to use the second language to engage in real communication acts. On the other hand, Classroom A presented a learning environment where the pupils were constantly using, and experimenting with, the second language as they engaged in communications of an academic and social nature with their peers and the teacher.

Messages in the Classroom

These process differences between classrooms are further reinforced by the data collected with respect to messages in the classroom. Tables 7, 8 and 9 give some information about the number of messages coded in each classroom. Nearly two-thirds of the messages in Classroom C were initiated by the teacher. In Classroom A, less than one-half the messages were initiated by the teacher. With respect to messages from the teachers to the target pupils, there were more messages to low achievers than to high achievers in all classrooms, but, in Classroom A, there were twice as many messages to low achievers as to high achievers. In all, the number of messages to target students in Classroom A was nearly four times the number of messages to target students in Classroom C. Of the total number of messages from teacher to pupil, nearly 20% were directed at the target students in Classroom A, while only about 7% were directed at the target students in Classroom C.

The difference between the number of messages from the target pupils to the teacher is even more dramatic. The number of messages from high achievers to the teacher in Classroom A was almost double that in Classroom B, and four times as many as in Classroom C. In Classroom A, the number of messages from low achievers was half as many more again as those from high achievers, nearly six times that in Classroom B and ten times that in Classroom C.

These data appear to indicate that there was more active communication in classroom A than in the other two classrooms. They would also appear

Percentage of Messages per Classroom by Initiator of the Message			
		% in the classroom	
Message Initiator	A	B	C
Teacher	44.2	58.7	62.1
Students	54.7	35.7	29.8
Targets	28.9	22.0	13.7
Total #	1967	2594	2032

Table 7

Number of Messages from Teacher to Targets			
	A	B	C
High Achievers	117	104	57
Low Achievers	220	139	77
Subtotal	337	243	134
% Total Number of Messages per Classroom	17.1	9.4	6.6

Table 8

Number of Messages from Targets to Teacher			
	A	B	C
High Achievers	105	59	27
Low Achievers	154	28	16
Subtotal	259	87	43
% Total Number of Messages per Classroom	13.2	3.4	2.1

Table 9

to indicate that the low achieving pupils in Classroom A were participating in communication acts much more often than their peers in Classroom C.

Task Orientation of Messages

It is also interesting to note the relative amounts of on-task behaviours in the three classrooms. The information is summarized in Table 10. On-task messages from the teacher were generally higher in Classroom A, though this category was also high in Classroom C. Off-task disruptive messages from targets were higher in Classroom B. Off-task disruptive messages from pupils were highest in Classroom A. These data seem to suggest that communication in Classroom A was usually on-task, but that individual pupils also felt free to initiate conversation with the teacher on other matters. In Classroom B, there were many more messages of an ambiguous nature present in the classroom, particularly from low achieving pupils, which suggests that communication in the classroom tended to be somewhat

Task Orientation of Messages Given as Percentage of Total Messages per Classroom				
Teacher to Target		A	B	C
On Task	H*	92.3	88.5	87.7
	L**	87.7	90.6	85.7
Off Task Disrupt	H	4.3	10.6	12.3
	L	9.4	7.2	10.4
Non-disrupt	H	4.3	0	0
	L	2.7	0	2.7
Target to Teacher				
On Task	H	83.8	71.2	88.8
	L	77.9	42.9	81.2
Off Task Disrupt	H	2.9	22.0	3.7
	L	7.4	53.6	6.2
Off Task Non-disrupt	H	12.4	3.3	7.4
	L	11.7	0	3.1
*H = High Achievers **L = Low Achievers				

Table 10

unfocused for a considerable percentage of class time. In Classroom C, there were fewer off-task messages than in Classroom B, but not quite as much on-task behaviour as in Classroom A. If the absolute number of messages is taken into account, as previously indicated in Table 9, the amount of purposeful interaction in Classroom A is considerably greater than that in either Classroom B or C.

Messages to Low and High Achieving Pupils

Another interesting difference is shown in Table 11, which suggests different priorities on the part of the teachers relative to high and low achieving pupils, with respect to the learning of subject matter content. There were about one-fifth more messages from the teacher to low achieving pupils than to high achievers in both Classrooms B and C. However, the data for Classroom A suggest that about two-thirds of the messages in that classroom were directed to low achievers. This finding suggests that the teacher in Classroom A spends considerable time interacting with low achievers with respect to the learning of content.

The differences between the classrooms were more extreme when the number of messages from target to teacher were examined. The percentage of messages from low achieving pupils in Classroom A is very similar to the percentage of messages from high achievers in Classrooms B and C. Furthermore, the percentage of messages about content learning from low achieving pupils to the teacher in Classroom A is nearly double the percentage of such messages in both Classrooms B and C. Again, when the absolute number of messages is taken into consideration, there would ap-

Percentage of Total Number of Messages per Classroom Respecting the Learning of Content			
	A	B	C
Messages from Teacher to Target H*	34	42	42
L**	66	58	58
Messages from Target to Teacher H	41.3	67.8	62.8
L	58.7	32.2	37.2

*H = High Achievers   **L = Low Achievers

NOTE: Percentages are given on a per classroom basis.

Table 11

pear to be much more opportunity for low achievers in Classroom A to engage in communication with the teacher about the learning of subject matter than in either of the other two classrooms.

These findings suggest that the nature of communication was very different for the pupils in each of the three classrooms described. They also point to differences within the same classroom for individual pupils. Some pupils have considerably more opportunity than others to participate in meaningful acts of communication. To the extent that this type of participation is essential to the learning/acquisition of a second language, some pupils have more opportunity to learn the target language than others. These opportunities are governed, not so much by factors associated with the pupil, but more by the teaching style, or priorities, of the instructor. The teacher, then, plays a highly significant role in determining the nature, and the quality, of the communication acts in which each pupil is able to participate. The teacher behaviours which control the quality of the second language environment for each pupil, though, are often not obvious, even to the teacher.

Teacher Priorities

The question may be raised at this point as to why processes in the three classrooms were so different. An interesting area to explore may well be that of teacher priorities. Teachers, though they follow a common curriculum, do place different emphases on the various goals of instruction. Without specific guidelines as to the relative importance of each of the instructional goals in French immersion programs, teachers will rank the variety of objectives presented to them according to their own philosophy of education, their personality, or their intuitive feelings about immersion teaching. In this way, despite the use of the same curriculum materials in all classrooms, very different learning environments are created for pupils, depending upon the particular teacher to whom they are exposed.

With respect to the classrooms under study, teacher self-report data relating to priorities were collected in the interviews. An interview format was used, including both formal and informal collection techniques. In the structured part of the interview, teachers were asked to priorize objectives from several suggested to them. In the unstructured part of the interview teachers were able to indicate other areas which had not been suggested to them which they felt to be important.

For the structured part of the interview priorities were chosen in accordance with what the researchers identified as the major goals of instruction in immersion classrooms. The goals selected for this purpose were the following:

- cognitive learning, or the learning of the subject matter for each of the prescribed content areas,

- second language learning, in this case the learning of French,

- social and emotional development of the child, which had added importance in the context of learning in the second language classroom, where a new means of expression is being taught,

- control, or discipline in the classroom. This latter priority is not associated only with second language learning, but is one which is of major importance to all teachers. However, it, too, appears to have special significance in the second language classroom, at least for some teachers, who feel that pupils must be attending more closely to the teacher in an immersion classroom than in the regular classroom.

The teacher self-report data collected with respect to these priorities showed very considerable differences amongst the three teachers. While all teachers placed considerable importance on all of these goals, there was a tendency for each teacher to place somewhat more importance on one of the goals. This emphasis in personal approach to teaching in the immersion classroom is not without interest, particularly since there appear to be some interesting hypotheses which might be advanced with respect to the priority of the teacher and the actual classroom process data.

As shown in Table 12, indications from the teacher interviews are that the teacher in Classroom C, for example, placed a very high priority on classroom control. This is also the classroom where a considerable amount of class time was spent in lecture and drill type activities. It was also the classroom with the highest percentage of teacher-talk. The teacher in Classroom B placed a very high priority on the affective development of the pupils. In this classroom, there was evidence of a higher tolerance of off-task disruptive behaviours. In Classroom A the teacher gave cognitive learning of the subject matter the highest priority. It was this classroom

Classroom Control Priority			
Messages	A	B	C
Organization	13.9	12.3	15.5
Control	.8	.2	.7
On-Task	82.9	79.9	92.1
Off-Task	15.9	19.4	7.9
Classroom Activities			
Lecture	1.3	8.9	20.2
Questions	12.6	11.0	9.8
Drill	2.9	10.9	15.1

NOTE: Messages Coded
      Message Initiator Contrast

Table 12

where most evidence was observed of language-oriented behaviours; more use of verbal cues was observed, as well as more attention given to understanding the target language used. It was also this classroom in which more attention was paid to the low achiever with respect to the learning of content.

These types of findings suggest that there is a distinct possibility the underlying priorities of the teacher affect the processes in the classroom. It therefore seems that the area of teacher priorities may well be a fruitful one to explore further with respect to differences between classrooms, particularly with respect to classroom processes. It would also seem that a possible way of intervening in the processes of the classroom in order to bring about change to more effective processes may be by means of talking to teachers about priorities. As teacher priorities change it may be that strategies used in classrooms may be altered in order to enhance the use of those which are most effective for the learners in the classrooms. It will also be important to continue to try to identify the types of learning strategies for French immersion teaching which are most effective for different types of learners.

Conclusions

What do these findings tell us about classroom processes and achievement in French immersion classrooms? First of all, they indicate that different processes are in evidence in different classrooms, and these different processes bring about very different results for pupils. Despite a common curriculum, teachers organize and instruct their classes differently, and these differences are significant with respect to the learning outcomes for pupils.

Second Language Learning

With respect to second language learning in immersion classrooms, the differences brought about by the different processes observed in the classrooms appear to have a significant effect on language learning. All pupils in an immersion program do not have equal opportunity to learn the second language as they are learning the subject matter. Language learning is much more clearly a goal of instruction in some classrooms than in others. In addition, more language-oriented behaviours are used, and encouraged, in some classrooms than in others. It is likely that pupils in a classroom where there is a richer language environment, from the point of view of more opportunity to interact in communicative exchanges that have direction and meaning for the child, will learn the second language better than would be the case if they were in a more restricted classroom environment from the point of view of language interaction. Furthermore, some pupils within a classroom will have more occasion to develop language than will others.

Opportunities to learn the second language are not equal for pupils who are high or low achievers, particularly in some classrooms. It would appear that there may be fewer occasions for low achievers to use language in the classroom, and this lack of opportunity to communicate may have a negative effect on the learning of the second language for the low achiever. The findings suggest that there is a considerable chance low achievers may receive less attention than high achievers. Data in addition to those discussed here support the tendency noted for low achievers in some classrooms to have fewer opportunities to interact verbally with the teacher, or with peers. Low achievers may also receive more non-verbal messages than high achievers, and more negative feedback. These differences will cause low achievers to react to teachers in ways that are different from high achievers. It seems reasonable to hypothesize that these instructional differences will affect the level of performance that pupils are able to attain in French immersion programs.

This study has attempted to determine to what extent high and low achieving pupils find themselves in different learning environments despite the fact that they are in the same classrooms. Some indications of the differences with respect to the use of language between these pupils and the teacher have been recorded. In addition, the study has tried to examine whether the learning environment in the French immersion classroom could be made more effective for all learners. The data seem to suggest that it could indeed be improved. The findings also suggest that some of our conventional wisdom about good immersion teachers may need re-appraisal. Fluency in the target language, beyond a certain point, may be less essential than the ability to encourage pupils to communicate. In preparing immersion teachers, considerably more emphasis should be placed on developing an awareness of the differences which process makes in creating an effective communicatively oriented learning environment. Certainly, the findings of this study point to the conclusion that processes which encourage active and purposeful communication on the part of as many pupils as possible in the classroom are of the utmost importance in any bilingual education program.

Notes

1 Annual Report of the Commissioner of Official Languages (1988) pp. 306-309.

2 Stern (1983) p. 426. Supports this point of view.

3 The first studies were carried out by Lambert and Tucker at McGill University and results published in several joint articles and summarized in a book (1972). Very complete evaluations were conducted by the Ottawa-Carleton Project and the Bilingual Education Project at the OISE Modern Language Centre. Swain (1978), Stern (1978, 1978a, 1983), Swain and Lapkin (1981), and Bibeau (1982) among others have reviewed the programs, and various studies undertaken. The studies undertaken in Ontario and the rest of Canada have been regularly reported in the *Canadian Modern Language Review*; for example Harley, (1976).

4 Netten and Spain (1983).

References

Alatis, J.E., Stern, H.H., & Stevens, P. (Eds.), (1983). *Georgetown University Round Table on Languages and Linguistics 1983. Applied linguistics and the preparation of second language teachers: Toward a rationale.*

Bibeau, G. (1982). *L'éducation bilingue en Amérique du Nord.* Montréal, PQ: Guérin.

Commissioner of Official Languages. (1989). *Annual Report 1988: From Act to Action.* Ottawa, ON: Minister of Supply and Services Canada.

Harley, B. (guest editor). (1976). Alternative programs for teaching French as a second language in the schools of Carleton and Ottawa School Boards. *Canadian Modern Language Review, 33*(2).

Lambert, W.E., & Tucker, G.R. (1972). *Bilingual education of children: the St. Lambert experience.* Rowley, MA: Newbury House.

Netten, J.E., & Spain, W.H. (1983). Immersion education research in Newfoundland: Implications for the classroom teacher. *Journal of the Canadian Association of Immersion Teachers.*

Netten, J.E., & Spain, W.H. (1982). Bilingual education in Newfoundland. *The Morning Watch, 10,* 33-41.

Stern, H.H. (1978). Bilingual schooling and foreign language education: some implications of Canadian experiments in French immersion. *Alatis* 1978: 165-188.

Stern, H.H. (1978a). French immersion in Canada: Achievements and directions. *Canadian Modern Language Review, 34,* 836-854.

Stern, H.H. (1983). *Fundamental concepts of language teaching.* Oxford, UK: Oxford University Press.

Swain, M. (1978). Bilingual education for the English-speaking Canadian. *Alatis* 1978: 141-154.

Swain, M., & Lapkin, S. (1981). *Bilingual education: A decade of research*. Toronto, ON: Ontario Ministry of Education.

Classroom Control and Student Outcomes in Grades 2 and 5

Robert K. Crocker and Gwen M. Brooker
Memorial University of Newfoundland

This study sought to identify dimensions of classroom control derived from factor analysis of selected classroom process variables, to interpret these dimensions in relation to two contemporary models of classroom control, and to explore the relationships between dimensions of control and certain cognitive and affective outcomes. Data used in the study were drawn from a larger data base developed from some 30 hours of observation per classroom, pre- and posttesting, teacher interviews, and other data sources in a sample of 36 second grade and 39 fifth grade classes. Results of the study indicate that dimensions of boundary control and disruptive behavior are readily identifiable but, contrary to what has been suggested by other authors, warmth or emotional climate cannot be clearly separated from disruptive behavior or discussion-recitation. Correlations with outcomes are generally consistent with those found in other process-product studies.

*   *   *

As WELL AS BEING A MATTER OF SUBSTANTIAL PUBLIC CONCERN, THE QUESTION of classroom control has been a pervasive one in studies of teaching. In fact, it might be argued that control is one of a small number of broad concepts that underlie and serve to unify the diverse body of theoretical and empirical research on teaching. This study sought to examine the dimensions of classroom control and to explore the relationships between the dimensions of control and a range of cognitive and affective outcomes.

Research on control suggests that the concept is by no means a unitary one. For example, specific lines of investigation have been concerned with such aspects of control as discipline and group management (Kounin, 1970), pupil control ideology (Willower, Eidell, & Hoy, 1973), and teacher directedness versus indirectedness (Flanders, 1970). Control has also been treated broadly, as in studies of openness in classrooms (e.g., Bennett, 1976; Sharp & Green, 1975). Major classroom process studies (e.g., Evertson, Anderson, & Brophy, 1978; Stallings & Kaskowitz, 1974) have typically included many process variables that may be identified with various aspects of control. In fact, the "direct instruction" model (Rosenshine, 1979), which seems to capture the results of many such studies, may be viewed as a model of control.

Relatively little research has addressed specifically the question of the possible dimensions of control. A major exception is the work of Soar and Soar (1979, 1983). Drawing on their own empirical studies, as well as other major classroom process studies of the 1970s, Soar and Soar have distinguished between emotional control and control as management. Emotional control refers to positive and negative affect, where the positive teacher is viewed as warm and supportive and the negative teacher as strident and critical. Within the management dimension, a further distinction is made between management of behavior, of learning tasks, and of thinking processes. Each of these is posited to occur on a continuum based on the degree to which an established structure exists for the conduct of certain management tasks.

A somewhat different approach has been taken by Morrison (1974). On the basis of a review of research up to that time, Morrison proposed that control be treated as having three dimensions, which he labeled warmth, boundary control, and control of deviant behavior. Warmth refers to emotional climate, specifically to whether a classroom is relaxed and comfortable or tense and uncomfortable. This dimension appears to be similar to Soar and Soar's emotional climate. Boundary control refers to constraints on movement, talk, task choice, and similar features of the classroom setting. This corresponds approximately to Soar and Soar's management dimension. Control of deviant behavior refers to action taken when some implicit or explicit rule of the classroom is broken. This appears to cut across both major dimensions of the Soar and Soar model.

Research on the relationship of control to achievement is difficult to interpret because the dimensions of control have not been clearly distinguished. For example, a general conclusion from work based on the Flanders model would suggest that indirect teaching is associated with higher achievement (Flanders, 1970). However, the Flanders model does not separate emotional climate from response to deviant behavior or from more substantive matters of teacher-student interaction. Thus, praise, use of student ideas, and acceptance of student feelings are all included in the numerator of the Flanders indirect/direct (I/D) ratio, while lecturing and giving directions are combined with criticism in the denominator.

Reviews by Rosenshine (1979) and Gage (1978) seem to suggest the opposite results from those of Flanders. Using the results of a series of comprehensive classroom process studies conducted during the 1970s, these reviewers conclude that increased cognitive achievement is associated with high teacher control of time allocations and a high degree of attention to task. In Morrison's terms, these processes seem to be associated with the dimension of boundary control. On the other hand, one variable that is closely associated with emotional climate, that of praise, has yielded quite inconsistent results, leading Brophy (1981) to argue that even an apparently simple concept such as praise is not unitary in its usage or its effects. Control of deviant behavior seems not to have been addressed in these reviews, although it is possible to identify appropriate variables in the classroom observation schedules used in most of the major empirical studies.

Again, it is Soar and Soar (1979) who provide the clearest statements about the relationship of control to achievement. These authors report that their own studies provide no support for the belief that a warm emotional climate is superior for learning. An affectively neutral classroom can also be seen as effective. What is important, however, is the avoidance of a negative emotional climate. On the question of management of behavior, Soar and Soar support the direct instruction model by concluding that freedom of behavior is negatively related to achievement. Similarly, the results for management of learning tasks indicate that high on-task behavior is important for learning. Other behaviors associated with task management tend to show nonlinear relationships, with an intermediate level of control being optimal for learning.

Relatively few studies have addressed the question of the relationship of control to affective outcomes. Most such studies have been concerned with the broad issue of open education rather than with specific classroom processes. Reviews of such studies (e.g., Horowitz, 1979; Peterson, 1979) suggest that, contrary to the findings for cognitive outcomes, affective outcomes tend to be positively associated with more open forms of classroom functioning.

The study reported here was part of a larger investigation of teacher perceptions, classroom processes, and outcomes. In order to examine the dimensions of classroom control, a selection of 30 classroom process variables was made from a larger set of some 150 variables available. The selection was based on the investigators' judgment of variables that could represent one or another of the aspects of control in either the Soar and Soar or Morrison models. This set of variables was factor analyzed, and the factors were examined in terms of the models available. Factor scores were then developed for each class, and these were used as independent variables in the investigation of relationships of the dimensions of control to outcomes.

Method

Population and Sample

The immediate population consisted of all second and fifth grade classrooms in schools located in Eastern Newfoundland, Canada. The population included some 200 schools, with approximately 350 classrooms at each of the designated grades. Schools were located in a variety of rural, suburban, and urban settings. School sizes ranged from fewer than 100 to more than 600 students. A wide range of socioeconomic classes was represented in the schools, but all schools were relatively homogeneous in racial and ethnic makeup.

The sampling procedure was designed to yield a random sample of approximately 40 classes at each grade level. Since participation in such a study had to be voluntary, it was decided to follow an opting-out procedure in which teachers were selected randomly and asked to participate, with the clear understanding that participation was voluntary. Since there were relatively few refusals, the procedures can be said to have been successful in achieving the aim of a random sample. The final sample size was 36 classes in grade 2 and 39 classes in grade 5.

Data Sources

Observational data were gathered over a period of one school year, with each class being observed on 20 occasions averaging 90 minutes each. Observation occasions were chosen on an essentially random basis, with some restrictions to allow for specialist subjects and noninstructional events. The observation system was a three-part, time-sampling category system (Crocker, Brokenshire, Boak, Fagan, & Janes, 1978) with alternating focus on the teacher, six target students, and global classroom events. Observers coded on optically scorable forms all categories occurring during a 30-second time unit. The observation data were aggregated to the lesson level and reported in terms of proportions of time occupied by each category. As already indicated, 30 of the 150 available observation variables were used as independent variables in the study of control.

The following measures were used as dependent variables:

(1) reading—the Gates-MacGinitie Reading Test;

(2) mathematics—curriculum-specific tests developed by the research team;

(3) self-concept—McDaniel-Piers Young Children's Self-Concept Scale; and

(4) sociometric status—the Ohio Social Acceptance Scale

All instruments were administered as pre- and posttests near the beginning and end of the school year. The measures used in the analysis were residualized gain scores. Acceptable local reliability coefficients of at least .80 were found for all outcome measures. Selection of acceptable observation categories was based on a generalizability study incorporating the facets of classes, observers, and subjects. The results of this study were used to adjust for observer differences as required, and to determine which categories were stable enough to include in certain aspects of the analysis.

Data Analysis

Factor analysis of the initial set of 30 process variables was conducted by the principal components method. Three factors were extracted, as suggested by the three dimensions of Morrison's model. (A subsequent four-factor solution, designed to determine whether an emotional response factor could be separated from others, was discarded because it did not add appreciably to the interpretability of the pattern.) The initial extraction was followed by orthogonal and oblique rotations. Since the latter revealed that the factors were essentially uncorrelated, only the orthogonal (varimax) rotation is reported. No grade or subject breakdowns were carried out for the factor analysis since the models of control under investigation were presumed to be general rather than context-specific in nature.

Results

Descriptive Statistics

Definitions of the process variables and their means and standard deviations appear in Table 1. The descriptive picture is one of classrooms that are highly task oriented and highly teacher directed, with relatively little disruptive behavior. Students tended to spend most of their time at their desks either attending to the teacher or engaged in other teacher-directed tasks. A good deal of the activity could be classed as recitation, with the teacher leading the discussion, selecting students for response, and reacting, usually positively, to the responses. Certain kinds of activities, such as academic focus or teacher-chosen tasks, were quite stable across classes, while others, such as teacher presentation or questioning, showed considerable interclass variation.

Although this is not shown on the table, there were relatively few grade level differences in classroom behavior. However, subject differences were more in evidence. In particular, language lessons showed substantially more variation in behavior than mathematics. Also, discussion-recitation was more characteristic of subjects such as science, religion, and social studies than of language or mathematics.

It should be noted that certain variables, especially those in the disruptive behavior cluster, occurred with very low frequency. Observers' field notes suggest that these behaviors tended to be quite fleeting and were easily overlooked in the 30-second observation interval, despite the instruction to code a category if it occurred at any time during the interval. The restriction of variance in such categories tends to reduce and render unstable the correlations involving these variables. The importance of these variables is thus likely underestimated in the analysis.

TABLE I

Means, Standard Deviations, and Factor Pattern: Classroom Process Variables

Variable definition	$\bar{X}$[a]	SD	Factor pattern[b]		
			1	2	3
			Boundary control	Disruptive behavior	Discussion-recitation
Teacher focus					
TEC01 academic	.95	.02		−.50	
TEC03 behavioral	.01	.01		.79	
TEC25 imperative mood	.25	.08	.43		
TEC26 interrogative mood	.34	.07			.65
TEC28 student selected by name	.09	.04			.38
TEC31 accepts call-out	.10	.05			.35
TEC34 positive reaction	.25	.06		.51	.79
TEC36 negative reaction	.03	.03		.51	
TEC37 private disruptive behavior	.02	.02			
TEC38 public disruptive behavior	.02	.02		.50	
TEC39 group disruptive behavior	.01	.02		.46	
TEC40 mild reprimand	.04	.04		.56	
TEC41 severe reprimand	.01	.01		.71	
TEC42 threat	.01	.01		.59	
TEC43 punishment	.01	.01		.51	
Student focus					
CL02 desk	.87	.07	−.58		
CL03 on-task	.87	.05	−.73		
CL05 teacher chosen task	.84	.05	−.79		
CL06 student chosen task	.09	.05	.81		
CL14 attending	.46	.10	−.66		.57
CL15 talking	.07	.03			.44
CL20 waiting	.04	.03	.59		
CL21 idling	.05	.03	.72		
Lesson focus					
LES13 teacher presentation	.57	.13		.43	
LES14 discussion	.37	.13			.76
LES27 independent	.04	.06	.64		
LES28 teacher directed	.11	.07	.41		
LES30 waiting	.05	.07	.59		
LES34 warmth	3.90	.45		−.50	.47
LES35 enthusiasm	3.76	.38			.56
Eigenvalue			6.49	3.84	3.14
Percent variance			21.7	12.8	10.5

[a] Means and standard deviations are reported as proportions of all recorded events except for warmth and enthusiasm, which were coded as a 5-point rating scale.

[b] Factor loadings < .35 are omitted.

Dimensions of Control

Table 1 shows that Factor 1 is strongly bipolar, with one pole incorporating variables that are characteristic of a low degree of teacher orchestration of task orientation and choice, and the opposite pole having high loadings for variables that suggest high teacher control of tasks. This factor thus

Discussion

The factor analysis revealed a pattern that corresponds well to two of the three dimensions of Morrison's model. Similarly, the variables making up the boundary control and disruptive behavior factors can be identified with Soar and Soar's definitions of learning task and behavior management, respectively. The major difference between these results and the existing models is that emotional climate or warmth could not be distinguished as a separate factor but, instead, was embedded within two other factors. Clearly, positive emotional climate is linked to low incidence of disruptive behavior and to greater student participation in classroom communications.

Observers' field notes provide a possible explanation for the failure to separate emotional climate. Warmth was operationalized in terms of presence or absence of tension, and enthusiasm in terms of voice inflections, apparent liking for the subject, and the like. However, it is clear from the field notes that observers were using many low inference indicators to capture these high inference concepts. In particular, direct behavioral events such as positive or negative teacher reactions, student communication with the teacher, or the manner in which the teacher selected students for response were used as indicators. Emotional climate may thus be simply a high inference way of expressing a particular combination of low inference events.

The appearance of discussion-recitation as a separate factor allows a broader interpretation of control than is inherent in either of the models considered here. The added dimension is associated with the classroom as a setting for oral discussion. It seems plausible to consider the orchestration of discussion as an aspect of control that is distinct from boundary control, task management, or control of disruptive behavior. In fact, sociological studies using concepts such as power (e.g., Sharp & Green, 1975) or negotiation (Martin, 1976) suggest that the degree of student participation in classroom events and the differential power of teacher and students in determining participation levels are important aspects of control. While it is beyond the scope of this paper to examine sociological models of control, it is suggested that such models might help resolve the anomalies in the more narrowly based approaches of classroom process researchers.

In general, the direction of the correlations of process variables and factor scores with cognitive outcomes is consistent with the pattern that has become established in recent research on teacher effectiveness (Brophy & Good, in press). Although these correlations are fairly small, as is generally the case in such studies, they do point in a consistent direction that supports the concept of direct instruction (Rosenshine, 1979). Correlations with the boundary control and disruptive behavior variables suggest that higher achievement is attained in classrooms that function in a businesslike manner, under high teacher direction, with a minimum of lost time or task disruption. It is interesting to note that many of the strongest correlations are negative. This supports the suggestion by Soar and Soar (1979) that what is most important is to avoid certain negative behaviors. This point is reinforced by the general lack of correlation with achievement of variables under the discussion-recitation cluster. Overall, it appears to be easier to identify behaviors that should be avoided than behaviors that might be augmented to improve learning.

The results for affective outcomes show less consistent patterns than those for achievement. Significant correlations occurred only for grade 2. The negative association of self-concept with discussion-recitation and with the variables of attending and discussion in second grade is especially difficult to understand. One hypothesis is that the public nature of discussion may draw attention to student academic weakness, reticence, or similar characteristics, and thus detract from enhancement of self-concept.

The relationships that appear for sociometric status support the intuitively plausible hypothesis that sociometric status is enhanced by a type of classroom structure that is less teacher directed. On the other hand, of course, the direction of causation may be opposite, in that classrooms with students of high sociometric status may naturally operate under less direct teacher control. In any case, it appears that the conditions associated with higher sociometric status are opposite of those associated with higher achievement. Again, this is consistent with the indications in the literature (Horowitz, 1979; Peterson, 1979) that affective outcomes are positively associated with more open classroom environments. However, the findings in this area are by no means as consistent as those for cognitive outcomes. More important, it is much more difficult to determine a causal direction in the case of affective outcomes. Further research is clearly required on this issue.

References

Bennett, N. (1976). *Teaching styles and pupil progress*. London, UK: Open Books.

Brophy, J. (1981). Teacher praise: A functional analysis. *Review of Educational Research, 51*, 5-32.

Brophy, J.E., & Good, T.L. (in press). Teacher behavior and student achievement. In M.C. Wittrock (Ed.), *Third handbook of research on teaching*.

Crocker, R., Brokenshire, G., Boak, T., Fagan, M., & Janes, E. (1978). *Teacher Strategies Project: Manual for classroom observers*. St. John's, NF: Institute for Educational Research & Development, Memorial University of Newfoundland.

Evertson, C., Anderson, L., & Brophy, J. (1978). *Texas Junior High School Study: Final report of process-outcome relationships* (Report No. 4061). Austin, TX: Research & Development Center for Teacher Education, University of Texas.

Flanders, N. (1970). *Analyzing teacher behavior*. Reading, MA: Addison Wesley.

Gage, N. (1978). *The scientific basis of the art of teaching.* New York, NY: Teachers College Press, Columbia University.

Horowitz, R. (1979). Effects of the "open classroom." In H. Walberg (Ed.), *Educational environments and effects: Evaluation, policy and productivity.* Berkeley, CA: McCutchan.

Kounin, J. (1970). *Discipline and group management in classrooms.* New York, NY: Holt, Rinehart and Winston.

Martin, W. (1976). *The negotiated order of the school.* Toronto, ON: Macmillan.

Morrison, T. (1974). Control as an aspect of group leadership in classrooms. *Journal of Education, 156,* 38-64.

Peterson, P. (1979). Direct instruction reconsidered. In P. Peterson & H. Walberg (Eds.), Research on teaching: Concepts, findings and implications. Berkeley, CA: McCutchan.

Rosenshine, B. (1979). Content, time and direct instruction. In P. Peterson & H. Walberg (Eds.), *Research on teaching: Concepts, findings and implications.* Berkeley, CA: McCutchan.

Sharp, R., & Green, A. (1975). *Education and social control.* London, UK: Routledge and Kegan Paul.

Soar, R.S., & Soar, R.M. (1979). Emotional climate and management. In P. Peterson & H. Walberg (Eds.), *Research on teaching: Concepts, findings and implications.* Berkeley, CA: McCutchan.

Soar, R.S., & Soar, R.M. (1983). *Context effects in the teaching-learning process.* Paper presented at meeting of the American Association of Teacher Education, Detroit, MI.

Stallings, J., & Kaskowitz, D. (1974). *Follow-through classroom observation evaluation, 1972-1973.* Stanford, CA: Stanford Research Institute.

Willower, D., Eidell, T., & Hoy, W. (1973). *The school and pupil control ideology* (2nd ed.). University Park, PA: Pennsylvania State University Press.

Student Diversity

The fact that all students are not alike seems fairly obvious. However, the implications of this fact for learning and teaching are profound. Barnes and McCabe provide evidence that even "typical" students in "typical" high school classrooms vary widely in terms of ability levels. None of the high school students in their study had been identified as having special learning problems. Yet, according to their data, more than one-third of the students in compulsory courses and more than half the students in optional courses had arithmetic and language skills one or more grades below the required skill level. At the same time, some students had skills more than two grade levels above those required for the course. In fact, Barnes and McCabe reported that teachers commonly had a student ability range of seven or eight grade levels in their classes. With this kind of diversity, it is not surprising that some students are bored, some students are frustrated, and some teachers are burned out.

Until recently, children with learning disabilities were often placed in classes for the mentally retarded or regarded as unmotivated underachievers who just did not want to learn. We now know that some children of average or above-average intelligence score consistently below grade level because they have great difficulty learning specific skills in specific areas. The article by Snart, Spencer, and Das reports the results of the use of a remediation model involving the cognitive processes of coding, attention and planning (CAP) to teach spelling to learning disabled elementary school students. Experimental group students completed 20 hours of remedial work, consisting of five CAP tasks and five related spelling tasks focusing on successive cognitive processing skills. At post-test, the experimental students did significantly better than control students on a sequential cognitive coding task, and their spelling of both predictable and unpredictable words improved relative to the performance of the control group, which had also received remedial training.

The current position regarding children with mental and/or physical exceptionalities is that they should be integrated into regular classes to the greatest extent possible. What sort of reception can exceptional children expect from their classmates when they are mainstreamed? King, Rosenbaum, Armstrong, and Milner explored this question by asking almost 2,000 elementary school children in two school boards to respond to a scenario about a boy or girl with cerebral palsy or mental retardation. Among other findings, girls had more favourable attitudes towards children with mental or physical disabilities than boys, and those with a handicapped friend or relative had more favourable attitudes than those who had not had the opportunity for such contact.

At the same time that educators are advocating the mainstreaming of most children with physical and mental exceptionalities, many school boards have established separate classes or schools for gifted students. This move is controversial for many reasons; some parents believe that such segregation may be good for intellectual development but bad for social development, and some teachers argue that pulling the brightest children out of regular classrooms makes their job more difficult. The results of the study by Schneider, Clegg, Byrne, Ledingham, and Crombie do not provide definitive answers to this debate. However, they did find that the social and physical self-concepts of gifted children in regular classes did not differ from those of children in segregated gifted classes. Interestingly, the gifted children in regular classes had higher academic self-concepts than those in segregated classes, suggesting that direct social comparison with classmates is a more potent influence on self-esteem than more abstract knowledge than one's entire class is perceived to be academically superior.

The Academic Slipstream: Diversity Within Secondary School Classrooms

Michael J. Barnes and Ann E. McCabe
University of Windsor

According to the evidence offered in this article, Ontario's three educational streams for differing academic abilities are not accommodating the majority of high-school students. Basing their research on more than eleven hundred students in courses at the advanced and general levels, the investigators found that, overall, less than half of these students were performing at the level of grade placement in the five courses examined.

*　　　*　　　*

REGULAR CLASSROOM TEACHERS FREQUENTLY COMMENT ON THE PRESENCE of a wide range of student aptitudes and skills within the classes assigned to them for instruction. Almost as frequently, they describe this range as being too wide to expect that appropriate and effective instruction can be provided for each student. Often, these same teachers associate classroom management difficulties, presented by some students' academic or social behaviours, with the presence of this wide range. Many teachers report experiences of high and continuing stress as a consequence of their attempts to meet both the professional and legal obligations to teach each student assigned to their classes.

Educators in the field of special education claim also that a wide range of student characteristics is present in many regular classrooms. Kirk (1972) restated his 1941 observation

Every classroom teacher must organize his instructional methods and assignments to meet the needs of children who vary one to three grade levels above and below the grade in which they have been placed.

Heron and Harris (1982) describe an almost identical condition that regular classroom teachers should expect to encounter.

Recently, as a preliminary to the present investigation, 121 elementary and secondary regular classroom teachers completed questionnaires concerning estimated ability levels of students within their own classes. These teachers estimated that only 50 to 60% of their students demonstrated skills in language or arithmetic that approximated the requirements of the instructional level at which they had been placed. The remainder were estimated to possess skill levels considerably above or below placement level.

If these educators are correct in their estimates, then students whose skill levels are substantially above or below that expected in a given classroom may be caught in a kind of academic slipstream. In aerodynamics, some of the air that is forced aside by a forward moving mass follows it in an eddying wake. The amount of turbulence associated with the wake is relative to the size and speed of the moving mass. This phenomenon is termed a slipstream. In education, an analogous phenomenon may occur. Students significantly above or below expected levels of skill may well be forced aside by the mass of students in the middle ranges of ability. Such students would have little choice but to follow along in the wake of the moving mass. Turbulence in the form of inappropriate academic and social behaviours is a likely result. The amount of turbulence would be expected to be closely related to the number of students in the extremes of ability in a class, and the extent to which their skills vary above or below those required by the level at which they have been placed for instruction.

Are wide ranges of student skills a common phenomenon? If they do exist, do they have any common characteristics or do the profiles vary by subject, grade level or program orientation? Is there substance to the expressions of concern by classroom teachers and in the authoritative opinions? Despite the consistency in statements of belief, there is a lack of supporting empirical evidence. The purpose of the present investigation was to determine the extent to which the language and arithmetic skills of secondary students do vary above and below the levels at which they have been placed for instruction.

Method

Subjects

In three Ontario counties, 1,162 secondary school students in 41 class groups were tested. The tests were administered in each of the school years 1979-80 through 1983-84. The total secondary school population for these counties ranged from approximately 14,700 students in 1979-80 to 13,200 students in 1983-84. The distribution of the subjects by grade level of placement, course, course level of difficulty and type of course is illustrated in Table 1. In the Ontario secondary school system there are five grade levels, 9 through 13. In each of the grades 9 through 12, students may select or be assigned to courses at three levels of difficulty: advanced, general, or basic. Only two levels of difficulty, general and advanced, were included in the present investigation. Basic, the level of least difficulty, was excluded as it is generally considered a remedial level. Of the total number of subjects, 579 were enrolled in English or mathematics, two of the courses designated as compulsory by regulation or program orientation. The remaining 583 subjects were enrolled in five

Table 1
Study Population

Grade Level	Course & Level of Difficulty		Compulsory Courses		Optional Courses	
			No. of Classes	No. of Students	No. of Classes	No. of Students
9	English	-General	-	-	2	60
		-Advanced	1	29	-	-
	Math.	-General	1	31	2	60
		-Advanced	1	29	-	-
10	English	-General	1	32	2	71
		-Advanced	1	26	-	-
	Math.	-General	1	32	4	136
		-Advanced	1	28	-	-
11	English	-General	2	60	3	72
		-Advanced	1	27	-	-
	Math.	-General	2	54	3	84
		-Advanced	1	31	2	46
12	English	-General	1	29	2	54
		-Advanced	2	51	-	-
	Math.	-General	1	27	-	-
		-Advanced	1	25	-	-
13	English	-Advanced	2	45	-	-
	Math.	-Advanced	1	23	-	-
	(Only Advanced Courses offered at this level)					

courses designated as optional: An Introduction to Business; Marketing; Business Mathematics; Accounting; and Law. Students in compulsory mathematics and English courses were assessed on mathematical, vocabulary and comprehension scores, respectively. Students in optional courses were assessed on either mathematics- or English-related skills. In each of the mathematics-tested optional courses, mathematics skills are required. Vocabulary and comprehension testing in optional courses was not specifically related to course content, but is justified on the basis that for even textbook reading these abilities are required.

There were 510 male and 652 female subjects. Some subjects were tested in one class group for mathematics skills and as members of another class group for vocabulary and comprehension skills. In all, 1,718 test scores were obtained. None of the subjects had been identified as having a learning exceptionality.

Test Instruments

Arithmetic skills were assessed by the Wide Range Achievement Test (JASTAK Assessment Systems, 1978), Arithmetic, Level II, Written Part. This test includes tasks that range from the addition and subtraction of single digits and operations with fractions and decimals, to algebraic factoring and geometric and logarithmic calculations. Test scores are convertible to grade-level equivalent scores that range from preschool levels to grade 17.5.

Arithmetic skills also were assessed by The Key Math Diagnostic Arithmetic Test, Canadian Edition (Connolly, Nachtman and Pritchett, 1977). This test includes tasks in addition, subtraction, multiplication, and division that range from single-digit to fractional and decimal calculations. The test scores are convertible to grade-level equivalent scores that range from preschool levels through to grade 8, or nonspecifically higher than grade 8.

Language skills were assessed by the Gates-MacGinitie Reading Test, Levels E and F, Form 1 (MacGinitie, 1980), Vocabulary and Comprehension subtests. Both subtests use a multiple-choice format. The vocabulary tasks require the selection of synonyms for target words. The comprehension tasks require the selection, from among words provided, of those that best complete sentences summarizing descriptive paragraphs. Norms are provided for conversion of test scores to grade level equivalent scores ranging from grade 3.4 to 12.8. For scores above or below these grade-level equivalents, grade level was interpolated.

Procedure

Of the 1,162 subjects, 638 were from among those assigned to the first author for instruction over the period of the investigation. They represent 24 of the 41 class groups in the investigation and were tested for relevant skills as part of normal pre-instruction planning. The remaining 524 subjects, in 17 class groups, were from among those assigned to colleagues who agreed to have testing take place. The testing of 670 subjects took place at the beginning of September-December terms and 492 subjects were tested at the beginning of January-June terms.

Results

For analysis, test scores were grouped into the following five intervals: more than 2.0 grade levels above actual grade placement, 1.0 to 2.0 grade levels above actual grade placement, within .9 grade levels of actual grade placement, 1.0 to 2.0 grade levels below actual grade placement and more than 2.0 grade levels below actual grade placement. Scores for optional and compulsory courses and for each relevant skill tested were categorized separately. The distribution of scores within each of the categories is presented in Table 2. An overall summary is presented in Table 3. Overall, only 30% of scores of these students fall at the level of grade placement. This is roughly equivalent to the percentage of student scores which are more than two grade levels away from actual placement (26.8%). Students in optional courses have fewer scores at grade level (25.1%) than do students in compulsory courses (36.2%). Similarly, students in compulsory courses have a smaller percentage of scores widely discrepant (i.e., more than 2 grade levels) from grade placement (21.5%) than do students in optional courses (32.3%).

Table 2
Summary of Slipstream Distribution by Type of Course & Skill

Students' Scores Relative to Actual Placement	Compulsory Courses			Optional Courses		
	Mathematics	Vocabulary	Comprehension	Mathematics	Vocabulary	Comprehension
More than Two Grade Levels Above Placement	12.14%	15.05%	5.02%	5.20%	2.33%	0.00%
From One to Two Grade Levels Above Placement	19.29%	13.71%	17.06%	15.03%	20.23%	6.61%
Within One Grade Level of Placement (±.9)	32.86%	37.12%	38.46%	23.93%	31.13%	20.61%
From One to Two Grade Levels Below Placement	24.28%	23.08%	29.43%	28.53%	26.07%	30.74%
More than Two Grade Levels Below Placement	11.43%	11.04%	10.03%	27.30%	20.23%	42.02%
No. of Test Scores:	280	299	299	326	257	257

Most of this latter difference is attributable to the much higher percentage of scores (29.6%) in the lowest category for optional courses than for compulsory courses (10.8%). As can be seen in Table 2, the major contributor to the high proportion of very low scores in optional courses is the comprehension test scores of which a substantial percentage (42.02%) is more than two grade levels below actual grade placement. No distribution differences between advanced and general level courses were detected.

The pattern of scores shows considerable consistency across grade and difficulty levels, at least for compulsory courses. Group percentages across

Table 3
Summary of Slipstream Distribution by Type of Course

Student's Scores Relative to Actual Placement	All Compulsory Courses	All Optional Courses	All Courses
More than Two Grade Levels Above Placement	10.7%	2.7%	6.8%
From One to Two Grade Levels Above Placement	10.6%	14.0%	15.3%
Within One Grade Level of Placement (±.9)	36.2%	25.1%	30.8%
From One to Two Grade Levels Below Placement	25.6%	28.4%	27.0%
More than Two Grade Levels Below Placement	10.8%	29.6%	20.0%
No. of Test Scores	878	840	1718
No. of Subjects	579	583	1162

skills within optional and compulsory courses were used to generate expected frequencies for Goodness of Fit Chi Square tests. For these analyses individual classes within courses were combined whenever possible to provide acceptable expected frequencies. This combination resulted in 28 course groups for Goodness of Fit testing. Observed frequencies and Chi Square values are presented in Table 4.

For compulsory mathematics courses none of the distributions of mathematics test scores differed substantially from expectation, even at $p=.50$. For compulsory English courses, only 25% of Chi Squares of vocabulary scores differed from expectation at $p=.30$. For comprehension test scores in those same classes, three or 37.5% differed significantly from expectation at $p=.30$. Scores in optional courses were more variable. Mathematics scores in optional courses differed significantly from expectation in five of the six courses at $p<.10$. In the five English-tested optional courses, vocabulary scores yielded significant Chi Square values in three courses ($p<.10$), while for comprehension scores the distribution in one of the classes differed significantly at $p<.10$. Of the remaining four, three had probabilities less than .30. The lack of fit among optional courses appears to be due primarily to the tendency for scores in the earlier grades to be distributed fairly symmetrically around grade level, while scores in the later grades tend to be more concentrated in the below grade level categories. Nevertheless, even in grades nine and ten, 23% of scores are more than two grade levels away from actual placement, and in grades eleven

Table 4
Observed frequencies and Chi Square values for Goodness of Fit Tests

Compulsory Mathematics Courses — Math Scores

Grade Level	9 G	9 A	10 G	10 A	11 G	11 A	12 G	12 A	13 A
+2	3	4	4	4	8	1	4	3	3
+1	7	6	6	6	11	6	3	4	5
0	10	9	10	8	17	12	9	8	9
−1	9	7	6	6	13	10	7	6	4
−2	2	3	6	4	5	2	4	4	2
X^2	1.50	1.16	2.86	1.67	1.81	3.01	1.38	.81	1.24

Compulsory English Courses — Vocabulary Scores

Grade Level	9 A	10 G	10 A	11 G	11 A	12 G	12 A	13 A
+2	4	3	4	5	6	3	9	11
+1	6	4	5	7	5	2	7	5
0	12	10	9	19	13	9	21	18
−1	5	9	6	20	2	11	9	7
−2	2	6	2	9	1	4	5	4
X^2	2.02	2.54	.96	3.91	9.23	4.00	4.22	10.86

Compulsory English Courses — Comprehension Scores

Grade Level	9 A	10 G	10 A	11 G	11 A	12 G	12 A	13 A
+2	1	0	2	3	2	0	3	4
+1	5	6	5	9	4	6	7	9
0	14	13	14	19	15	9	13	18
−1	7	9	4	20	5	11	22	10
−2	2	4	1	9	1	3	6	4
X^2	3.03	5.84	4.78	4.62	4.10	5.27	9.10	.98

and twelve 20% of scores are at grade placement level. Regarding the shift from symmetrical distributions in the earlier grades to a primarily below-grade-level distribution in the later grades, one might suspect ceiling effects on the tests if it were not for the fairly symmetrical distributions of scores on the same tests across the five grade levels in compulsory courses.

Using group percentages within skills across compulsory and optional courses to generate expected frequencies yields a similar pattern, although a somewhat less good fit. Again compulsory courses best fit the overall percentages with compulsory mathematics courses providing the best fit.

Across all class groups there was considerable consistency in the proportion of scores at grade level. Of the 41 class groups 30 (73.2%) had

Optional Courses — Math Scores

| Grade | 9 | 10 | 10 | 11 | 11 | 11 |
Course	Business	Marketing	Business Math I	Accounting	Business Math II	Business Math III
+2	6	1	6	1	2	1
+1	12	9	6	8	7	7
0	21	21	20	9	5	2
-1	15	26	25	4	12	11
-2	9	14	8	3	33	25
X^2	23.64	5.15	19.14	11.05	21.92	17.82

Optional Courses — Vocabulary Scores

| Grade | 9 | 10 | 11 | 11 | 12 |
Course	Business	Marketing	Accounting	Business Math	Law
+2	6	0	0	0	0
+1	12	13	12	7	8
0	19	25	4	17	15
-1	17	20	6	11	13
-2	6	13	4	11	18
X^2	21.92	8.80	22.84	4.71	2.26

Optional Courses — Comprehension Scores

| Grade | 9 | 10 | 11 | 11 | 12 |
Course	Business	Marketing	Accounting	Business Math	Law
+2	0	0	0	0	0
+1	7	5	0	3	2
0	17	17	7	11	1
-1	24	23	7	15	10
-2	12	26	12	17	41
X^2	6.82	6.04	7.25	4.25	58.11

1 G=General; A=Advanced
2 $X^2(4)=3.356$, p=.50; $X^2(4)=4.878$, p=.30; $X^2(4)=7.779$, p=.10

between 25% and 40% of students scoring at grade level. In three classes (7.3%) the percentage of students scoring at grade level ranged from 45% to 52%, while for eight classes (19.5%) fewer than 25% of students scored at grade level. The latter were all optional courses and mainly at the upper grade levels. (For these comparisons vocabulary and comprehension percentages were averaged.)

Throughout, a test score difference of 7 to 8 grade levels between the lowest and highest scores in a class group was common. This range of difference was consistent for all class groups although the difference was most commonly seven grade levels in the early years of secondary school and eight grade levels in the later years. For three class groups, the difference was nine grade levels. These three classes represented optional courses at the grade 12 level of difficulty, one in Business Mathematics and two in Law.

Although no specific hypotheses were formulated regarding differences between male and female test scores, it was convenient to draw comparisons from the data. A higher percentage of females' scores fell at and above the level of placement than males' scores. This was consistent across the three skills tested and across optional and compulsory courses with a single exception. For mathematics-tested optional courses males had a higher proportion of scores at level and above level than did females. This was in contrast to the scores in compulsory mathematics courses where females' scores were higher than males' scores. Overall, the differences were small and no significant advantage was found for either sex. However, there was an indication that where an entry skill advantage exists in class groups, females tend to have it.

Discussion

The present data confirm the belief of educators that the skill levels within secondary school classes vary considerably. This variability was found to exist in both compulsory and optional courses at advanced as well as general levels of difficulty. Although the precise profiles were found to vary, each could be considered to present formidable challenges to the classroom teacher. The problem is magnified when it is remembered that the secondary school teacher faces as many as five or six classes of students in each academic year.

Thus, the potential exists for an educational slipstream. It may affect as many as 15 to 25% of students in compulsory courses and, because of more flexible prerequisites, an even larger proportion of students in optional courses.

The slipstreamed student frequently will be labelled as being weak, lazy, uninterested, not motivated, careless or disruptive. The underlying cause of these behaviours may be either a deficit in or surplus of one or more of the basic entry skills in language or mathematics implied by placement.

The present data indicate that approximately 30 to 40% of students in a given class bring significant deficits in skills relevant to their placements. Many of these students are unable to achieve the teacher's goals and objectives adequately because they lack the skills to do so. However, their academic or social behaviours are likely to be such that they will be described as unwilling rather than unable.

The data also indicate that approximately 20 to 25% of the students in the same class bring significant surpluses in relevant skills to their placements. Some of these students will achieve the teacher's goals and objectives easily and impressively but others may perceive a lack of personal challenge or relevance. These students may exhibit behaviours quite similar to those of students with skill deficits. There is a risk of the symptom being mistaken for cause; thus both types of students may acquire the same labels and, more importantly, the same low expectations may be set for them.

Within the present data there is evidence that is consistent with the notion of the slipstream. In optional courses, as grade level increases, there is an increasing percentage of students scoring in the lowest categories. This phenomenon is present in all three skills tested. Such findings suggest that these low scoring students have not been adequately served in earlier grades and have been pushed aside by the moving mass of average students.

The time, effort and personal stress associated with attempts to manage and teach a class including a slipstream, in ignorance of the specific characteristics of its skills profile, is likely to be counterproductive for both teacher and students.

Experience suggests that the inappropriate academic or social behaviours most difficult to manage will be exhibited by males. Given a relationship between students' entry skills and their classroom behaviours, it follows that slipstreamed male students will be more numerous and more apparent to classroom teachers than will slipstreamed female students. There is continuing debate on issues related to the superiority of one sex in a particular ability. For example, Benbow and Stanley (1980) conclude in favour of male superiority in mathematical ability. Grey, Fennema and Sherman, as reported by Kolata (1980), disagree. It may be that a distinction should be made as to the context from which such data are obtained. When large numbers of subjects are tested under conditions that are not usual or familiar, as with Benbow and Stanley, the results may differ from those obtained in a more familiar context. The present data suggest that when male and female students, already grouped together for instruction, are tested in familiar settings by familiar testers for study related purposes, females show a general advantage in entry skills. The observation is of significance to classroom teachers because it is in classroom settings that students' skills, male and female together, are elicited and applied to specific educational activities.

Several cautions must be kept in mind in evaluating the present data. First, although the data are based on a fairly large number of students of different ability levels and from different school systems, we cannot provide assurances that they are representative of students in any other given school system. While it seems likely that similar distributions of abilities within class groupings exist elsewhere, only further research can answer the question of how general a phenomenon is the academic slipstream. Secondly, considering optional courses, we have assumed in our argument that grade level skills in mathematics, vocabulary, and comprehension are required for success in these courses. There may be instances where this assumption is invalid, where skills required in these areas are less than grade level. Thus, students who possess a lower level of skill may not encounter difficulties.

Conclusion

There appears to be considerable substance to the expectation of diverse ability levels within secondary school classes. The academic slipstream is a reality. The range of abilities found can reasonably be regarded as too wide to expect that effective instruction is being provided for each student in the range.

Ysseldyke (1983) reported that the overwhelming majority of teachers sampled attributed deviant classroom behaviours to the home, the family, or deficits, disorders and dysfunctions inherent in the students. Fewer than 2% attributed such behaviours to instructional or school system inadequacies. While one might debate the sources of the academic deficits, it is their existence that must be dealt with within the classroom and it is unlikely that they can be dealt with effectively when class groups are so varied. It is reasonable to expect that the slipstream contributes substantially to the burnout experienced by many teachers.

References

Benbow, C. & Stanley, J. (1980). Sex differences in mathematical ability: Fact or Artifact? *Science, 210*(12) (December), 1262-1264.

Connolly, A.J., Nachtman, W., & Pritchett, E.M. (1977). *Key Math Diagnostic Arithmetic Test/Canadian Edition*. Willowdale, ON: Psycan Ltd.

Heron, T.E., & Harris, K.C. (1982). *The educational consultant*. Toronto, ON: Allyn & Bacon.

Jastak Assessment Systems (1978). *Wide Range Achievement Test (1978). Norm Revisions*. Wilmington, DE: Guidance Associates of Delaware Inc.

Kirk, S.A. (1972). *Educating exceptional children* (2nd ed.). New York, NY: Houghton Mifflin.

Kolata, G.B. (1980). Math and sex: Are girls born with less ability? *Science, 210*(12) (December), 1234-1235.

MacGinitie, W.H. (1980). *Gates-MacGinitie Reading Tests, Canadian Edition*. Toronto, ON: Nelson Canada.

Ysseldyke, J.E. (1983). Current practices in making psychoeducational decisions about learning disabled students. *Annual Review of Learning Disabilities, 1*, 31-37.

A Process-Based Approach to the Remediation of Spelling in Students with Reading Disabilities

Ferne Spencer
Edmonton Public School District
Fern Snart and J.P. Das
University of Alberta

Aspects of Das and Conway's (1986) remedial program CAP *(Coding, Attention, and Planning training) were combined systematically with a spelling program designed to reflect the same global cognitive processing strategies. Daily intervention, consisting of training in both the global tasks and the specific spelling tasks, was provided for 10 learning disabled students with particular deficits in spelling, to a total of 20 hours of remediation. Ten matched, learning disabled students received 20 hours of the normal classroom remedial spelling program. Following remediation the experimental group performed significantly better than did the control group on the* K-ABC *sequential subtests, selected* CAS *planning subtests, and the Test of Written Spelling (Larson & Hammill, 1986). Results are discussed as supportive of an appropriate and viable remedial option for spelling with learning disabled students.*

*   *   *

Some children are just born poor spellers. (Flaro, 1985, p. 4)

The ability to spell well is a gift from God. (Lerner, 1981, p. 337)

THE ABOVE SUGGESTIONS TYPIFY THE ATTITUDES OF MANY EDUCATORS regarding the ability to spell. The implication is that spelling ability is innate, and as such the onus on educators to influence the success of their students in this area is certainly lessened. It has been noted by several researchers that teachers spend relatively little time teaching spelling, particularly when compared with an area such as reading, and that often techniques for teaching spelling are disregarded even when they have been empirically validated (Gerber & Hall, 1987; Wallace & Larsen, 1978). Yet spelling ability, or lack of such ability, can influence a child's total experience, affecting as it does one's ability to communicate in written form (Hammill & Noone, 1975; Wallace & Larsen, 1978).

The close relationship between reading and spelling is reflected by the fact that most children who experience reading difficulties invariably have difficulty learning to spell (Gerber, 1984; Rieth, Polsgrove, & Eckert,

1984; Wong, 1986). Such children with specific learning disabilities are particularly vulnerable to the emotional burden of their academic deficiencies, and the related lowering of self-esteem, in that "incorrect spelling often creates an unfavorable impression beyond its true significance" (Otto & McMenemy, 1966, p. 203). It thus seems vital that attention be given to remediation of a skill which may otherwise persist as a serious problem with children who are already struggling with learning problems in areas such as reading.

Initially, traditional spelling programs were the only viable option available for the reading disabled student. The majority of these programs reflected a linguistic theory wherein emphasis was placed on the teaching of phonology, morphology, and syntactic rules (Hammill, Larsen, & McNutt, 1977). For most reading disabled students, these programs proved to be ineffective. More recently there have been several attempts to gain a "process-based" understanding of spelling and its remediation in learning disabled students (Englert, Hiebert, & Stewart, 1985; Gettinger, 1985; Kaufman, Hallahan, Haas, & Boren, 1978; Wong, 1986), but the results to date remain equivocal.

The objective of the present study was to design and test instructional procedures that would facilitate spelling ability in students with reading disabilities. The procedures are based on the cognitive processing model of Das and colleagues at the University of Alberta (Das, Kirby, & Jarman, 1975, 1979).

This "information-integration model" involves an integration of neuropsychology and information processing psychology, and within the model the conceptualizations of Soviet psychologist Luria (1970, 1980) have been used to describe three global but interactive cognitive processes: coding, attention, and planning. Coding involves the manner in which information is organized by the brain, successively and/or simultaneously, and is largely accomplished within the temporo-frontal and occipito-parietal cortex. Empirical evidence for successive and simultaneous processing has been generated in a large set of studies in which the performance of normal and disabled children on a diverse set of cognitive measures has been factor analyzed (Das et al., 1979). Similar processes have also been described by cognitive psychologists, for example, Neisser (1976). The attention component of the model includes arousal, a subcortical function, as well as modulation of arousal regulated via the frontal cortex in concert with subcortical processes. Planning, the third component, is broadly defined as the generation, selection, and execution of programs, either conceptual or behavioral. Kirby (1984) has identified at least four factors within the planning domain including search and metacognition.

Based on the information integration model, Das and his associates have developed a cognitive approach to remediation founded on three premises:

(a) children learn most effectively by dynamically interacting with adults and peers; (b) remediation is most effective when done from a theoretical perspective in which the cognitive processing of children is related to the processing requirements involved in learning academic skills; and (c) transfer of learning will be maximized if general, nonthreatening tasks are combined with academic bridging tasks. Support for the first premise of dynamic interaction is provided in the writing of Vygotsky (1962) and Feuerstein (1979) and in the research of Tizard and her colleagues (Tizard & Hughes, 1984). Empirical support for the second premise of the remediation model, that global cognitive processes (successive and simultaneous coding, attention, and planning) related to academic skill processes can be used to effectively remediate skill deficiencies, is provided by a series of studies done over the years by Das and associates (Kaufman & Kaufman, 1979; most recently through development and use of the Coding, Attention and Planning [CAP] remediation program by Das & Conway in 1986) and by independent investigators (Garolfo, 1986; McRae, 1986). Finally, support for the third premise of the remedial model, that academic bridging tasks may enhance the transfer of global processing to academic skills, is found in the writings of Douglas (1980), Kirby (1984), and Leong (in press).

Based on the above premises, the model for spelling remediation within the present study was developed through an extension of aspects of the global CAP program (Das & Conway, 1986). In particular, specific bridging tasks involving spelling were created to accentuate transfer of successive coding skills to spelling ability. Because, as described previously, both successive and simultaneous coding, and attention and planning dimensions are implicated in all cognitive tasks, it was of interest to examine marker task results in each area as pretest/posttest measures. Unfortunately, at the time of the present study the "attentional" marker tasks were under extensive revision, and the focus was limited to an examination of scores for coding and planning. Actual remedial training focused on successive coding, following indications that initial spelling relies heavily on successive strategies (Brailsford, Snart, & Das, 1984), but it was felt that related improvements in other areas of cognition were possible, and worth noting. The remedial training aspects of attention and planning were addressed through specific and directed verbalizations with students. Strategy training for the reading/spelling disabled students involved five CAP tasks which focused on successive processing, and five spelling tasks which were developed to reflect the principles and skills underlying each CAP task. Following remediation it was hypothesized that the experimental students would exhibit substantial improvements in spelling ability and improvements on successive coding tasks. Pretest and posttest results for planning and simultaneous coding were examined on an exploratory basis.

Method

Subjects

Twenty learning disabled students in two special classes in the Edmonton Public School system served as participants in this study. The criteria for inclusion in a learning disabilities class within the Edmonton Public system consist of an IQ within the average range or above (WISC-R), and academic achievement in at least one area of more than two years below the expected level on standardized measures.

The students' ages ranged from 8 to 12 years, and WISC-R IQ means for each of the two classes ($N= 10$ per class) were within the average range. English was their native language, and they did not have either visual or auditory impairments. Means for age, IQ, and Schonell Spelling Inventory for each class are presented in Table 1 (t-tests comparing these means in each case revealed no differences between the two groups). Schonell test results were readily available through school files and provided initial data for group selection, though the more detailed analyses of spelling skills provided by the Test of Written Spelling (Larson & Hammill, 1986) were utilized in pretest/posttest comparisons. The students were also two or more years behind their age peers in reading achievement. One class of 10 students served as a control group who received the typical classroom remediation in spelling, while the other class received an equivalent number of hours of the experimental remedial program and no other intervention in spelling during this time period. When students from either group were absent they were given "make-up" hours of the appropriate spelling remediation. In both cases the "instructional word list," comprising those words used for remedial purposes, consisted of 39 words from grades 1 through 5 which had been carefully selected by the teachers from the lists constructed by Thomas (1974), and which were felt to be representative of words most frequently mispelled by Alberta schoolchildren.

Table 1
Means and Standard Deviations for Age, IQ, and Schonell Spelling Inventory
for Experimental and Control Groups

	Control Group	Experimental Group
Age in months	127.70 (7.24)	128.10 (15.73)
IQ	92.50 (9.06)	93.20 (8.32)
Schonell Spelling Inventory (Grade score)	2.50 (0.67)	2.30 (0.81)

Pretest and Posttest Battery

The pretest battery was administered during January and the posttest battery during April of the same year. In each case the testing was conducted in a quiet setting in the child's school. Tasks chosen as pretest and posttest indicators included spelling tasks which were felt to be valid and reliable indicators of spelling skills in elementary-aged students in Alberta, and marker tests for coding and planning. The latter marker tasks in the planning area are those which Das and Conway (1986) also used in pretest and posttest studies of the CAP remediation program of global cognitive functions. Though the planning marker tasks and marker tasks for coding and attention are currently under development by Das and colleagues as the Cognitive Assessment System (CAS, Naglieri & Das, 1987, 1988, in press), a decision was made to utilize tests for successive and simultaneous processing which had previously been published within the same theoretical framework and were better known at this time (Kaufman & Kaufman, 1983). Pretest and posttest tasks included the following:

Spelling Tests

1&2 *The Test of Written Spelling (TWS-2, Larson & Hammill, 1986)* was administered to the students in a group setting. This test is divided into two subtests to accommodate the theory that a child learns to spell in two ways. First, the child learns to apply rules and generalizations, and second, the child must rely on memorization skills. The former is instrumental when learning words that conform to the rules (i.e., "predictable words") while the latter is necessary to spell words that do not (i.e., "unpredictable words"). The students in this study were given both of the TWS-2 subtests. The TWS-2 was standardized on an American sample of 3,805 children across 15 states. The 50 words that comprise each of the subtests were carefully selected to ensure that they were actually taught in schools. The words up to grade 8 appear in five commonly used American basal spelling series and the words above grade 8 appear on word frequency lists. Within the present study, raw scores for each student were converted to standard scores for predictable words and unpredictable words. It is also noteworthy that the instructional word list used for both remedial groups did not contain any of the spelling words from the TWS-2.

The administration of the TWS-2 involved the examiner first saying the word in isolation, then using the word in a sentence, and finally saying the word again in isolation. The subjects were required to write the dictated words.

Cognitive Assessment System (CAS) Tests (Naglieri & Das, in press).

3   *Visual Search* is one of the Planning subtests of the CAS. It comprises 20 search tasks grouped under either the Automatic Search or Controlled Search component. The child's task is to find a picture, number, or letter identical to one located in a box in the center (called the Target) somewhere within the group of stimulus items (called the Field). The score is the time in seconds to locate the Target embedded in a field of similar items (picture among pictures, number in numbers, letter in letters) or dissimilar items. Automatic Search time is the sum of times for searching where the Target differs in kind from the Field items (e.g., a picture among letters) whereas Controlled Search time refers to those where Target and Field items are the same. Automatic Search is essentially a measure of attention as the target "pops up" from the field, whereas in controlled or planned search the child has to make a deliberate effort to locate the target. Alpha reliability of the test is .64 based on 135 children in grades 3 through 5.

4   *Crack the Code* is a Planning subtest from the CAS. In this subtest the student's task is to determine the correct sequence of a number of colored chips when given a limited amount of information. The subject is given two or three trials with feedback to determine the one correct order of chips for each of the 7 items. The subtest is organized into 7 items with 2 or 3 trials per item and a 3-minute limit per item. The score is determined considering the number of trials necessary to produce the correct sequence. Alpha reliability is .68 based on 140 children in grades 5 and 6.

5   *Planned Connections* is a CAS Planning subtest. The child's task in this subtest is to connect, using a regular pencil, a series of numbered boxes in correct numerical sequence as quickly as possible. There are two kinds of items in this subtest: those that include numbers only, and those that include numbers and letters. The latter items involve connecting the boxes using numbers and letters alternately (1-A-2-B-3-C etc.). The overall score for all items is the time in seconds required to complete them. Alpha reliability is .64 based on 70 children in grades 5 and 6.

Subtests from the Kaufman Assessment Battery for Children (K-ABC) (Kaufman & Kaufman, 1983)

6   The *Hand Movements* subtest of the K-ABC is a Sequential processing task in which the child is required to reproduce a series of hand movements in the same sequence as the examiner. As with all the K-ABC processing tasks, the raw score is converted to a scaled score. The reliability of this test and the others which follow are given in the K-ABC manual.

7   *Number Recall* is a K-ABC Sequential task, in which the child attempts to repeat a series of numbers in the same sequence as the examiner.

8   *Word Order* is a K-ABC Sequential task which involves the child touching a series of silhouettes of common objects in the same sequence as the examiner has verbalized the names of the objects. (More difficult items include an interference task between the stimulus and response.)

9   *Gestalt Closure* is a Simultaneous processing task from the K-ABC. The child is required to name an object or scene presented as a partially complete "inkblot" drawing.

10   *Triangles* is a K-ABC Simultaneous task in which the child assembles several plastic triangles into patterns to try to match a series of models.

11   *Matrix Analogies* is a K-ABC Simultaneous task, requiring that children select a meaningful picture or abstract design which best completes a visual analogy.

12   *Spatial Memory* is a K-ABC Simultaneous task which involves recall of the placement of a set of pictures on a page which was exposed briefly.

13   *Photo Series* requires students to place photographs of an event in chronological order, and is one of the K-ABC Simultaneous tasks. The K-ABC was standardized on more than 4,100 administrations. Split-half reliability was established with the use of the Rasch-Wright model. The mean value for coefficients of internal consistency for 12 of the 16 subtests was .80 or above. Support for the construct validity of the K-ABC mental processing subtests was established through a correlation study between K-ABC and Factor scores on the Das-Kirby-Jarman Successive-Simultaneous battery (see K-ABC Interpretive Manual).

Intervention Program

Five global CAP tasks which had loaded most clearly on successive processing in factor analytic studies were selected and five spelling tasks were created, modeled after each of the CAP tasks. Representative examples of two of the global tasks are presented in the Appendix, along with the related spelling task in each case. One important component of the remedial training was having students talk about their approaches to the tasks, how they might change an approach to have it "work better," and so on. Within such discussions with the teacher the growth of planning ability was predicted.

The remedial sessions for the intervention group took place on a daily basis for each child, according to a prepared schedule, and were located at stations in the student's classroom. A total of 20 hours of global and content-specific training was given to each child in the experimental class, while children in the control class received an equivalent number of hours of the "I-Can-Spell" program (Rodgers, Covell, & Slade, 1978). In this approach students were presented with words from the instructional word list at their respective ability levels, in a pretest-study-posttest fashion. Each word list was accompanied by workbook activities prior to posttest.

The daily remediation session in the intervention program involved training at two stations. Each station trained a different CAP task. A student would receive 5 minutes of training on a CAP task and then 10 minutes on the associated spelling task at each station (as in the control group the spelling words were those from the instructional word list). Following the training at both stations a cumulative spelling test was administered bringing the total time of the session to 35 minutes. The stations were operated by the classroom teacher and the classroom aide.

The remedial training was scheduled for the mornings. The students were on individual programs and worked independently on assignments until they were called on for their remedial session. After the remedial session, students returned to their individual assignments. Each day the students were provided with schedules for their morning assignments. The instructional component of the students' school day was scheduled for the afternoons.

The students' daily performance on the CAP and spelling training was recorded. Specific record forms were used for each activity. The information obtained from the CAP record forms provided the basis for establishing a starting point for training the student the next time the task was used. The spelling record forms provided the teacher with diagnostic information in terms of how particular students were misspelling words, as well as an ongoing indication of words which were spelled correctly.

Results and Discussion

Of vital importance in this study was an examination of the actual improvement in spelling achievement. This emphasis was reflected in the fact that two thirds of remedial training time was spent on spelling tasks, with one third spent on training with the global tasks. An expectation for concurrent improvement on the global tasks existed whereby specific training would enrich global processing in addition to task-related processing. As a limitation of the present study, it must be noted that results may be directly generalized only to populations within segregated classes for students with learning disabilities, and that further research will be necessary to determine broader implications of the method.

Student scores on the Test of Written Spelling were analyzed using a 2 (Group)×2 (Pretest/Posttest)×2 (Predictable/Unpredictable words) ANOVA, and group means are presented in Table 2. Main effects for Pretest/Posttest, $F(1,18)=68.2$, $p<.001$, and Word Type, $F(1,18)=70.7$, $p<.001$, reflected the superior performance overall at posttest, and for predictable words. A significant Group×Pretest/Posttest interaction occurred $(F(1,18)=14.2$, $p<.001)$ with spelling scores at posttest significantly higher for the experimental students thus providing support for the effect of the remedial program. It is also of interest to note that, although the small N per cell contributed to the lack of a significant Group×Pretest/Posttest or Group×Pretest/Posttest×Word interaction in the ANOVA, the means in Table 2 certainly suggest that the experimental students were better able than the control students to handle unpredictable words at posttest. Because predictable words conform to rules and generalizations, while unpredictable words demand that the student focus on and analyze the letters sequentially, it might be further suggested that the latter skill may be enhanced through successive strategy training.

Results of the present remedial program hold promise for assisting disabled learners in their ability to spell. Anecdotal evidence from the 10

Table 2
Mean Scores on the Test of Written Spelling (TWS-2)
for Experimental and Control Students

		Pre	Post
Experimental (N = 10)	Predictable Words	9.60 (SD = 5.38)	13.60 (SD = 6.10)
	Unpredictable Words	6.80 (SD = 3.77)	10.30 (SD = 4.27)
Control (N = 10)	Predictable Words	10.40 (SD = 2.72)	12.50 (SD = 3.34)
	Unpredictable Words	7.00 (SD = 2.31)	7.70 (SD = 3.02)

students in the experimental group, when compared with their 10 peers in the control group, suggests some positive and more broad-based effects of the remedial program. In all cases, the experimental students gained confidence in their ability to write as their spelling skills increased, and their written expression as analyzed through actual work sample comparisons was markedly improved. The fact that the negative "set" toward writing was lessened allowed these students to practice their writing skills, and of course one success built on another! The experimental students also became aware of their own learning and became "active learners" during the remedial sessions, which is evident not only in the planning posttest results described later, but also in their more optimistic and flexible approaches to problem solving in the classroom in general.

Table 3
Mean Cognitive Coding Scores for Experimental and Control Students

	Sequential Score		Simultaneous Score	
	Pre	Post	Pre	Post
Experimental	21.50	27.20	46.50	52.00
(N = 10)	(SD = 3.66)	(SD = 5.20)	(SD = 10.65)	(SD = 12.28)
Control	26.20	28.40	46.10	50.30
(N = 10)	(SD = 5.81)	(SD = 4.17)	(SD = 10.52)	(SD = 10.60)

To examine the results for global processing and provide direction for future studies having larger sample sizes, a series of t-tests was performed on Pretest-Posttest means for each group (means are presented in Table 3). Significant improvements were revealed for the experimental group in sequential coding ($t(1,9) = 3.64$, $p < .005$), and for both the experimental ($t(1,9) = 3.44$, $p < .010$) and control group ($t(1,9) = 3.84$, $p < .005$) in simultaneous coding. Certainly a case can be made for an increase in cognitive coding ability over time for all students, based on maturity and living experience, academic experience, and so on. However, there seems to be a more complex issue at hand when one examines sequential or successive processing. Past research has suggested that successive coding is particularly implicated in early reading skills such as basic decoding (Brailsford, Snart, & Das, 1984; Cummins & Das, 1977), and that even intellectually advanced students with learning difficulties may require specific successive training prior to achieving these basic skills (Snart, Das, & Mensink, 1988). The active intervention with the experimental group, using successive coding tasks, was apparently a factor in the differential improvement of sequential ability for these students, and the impact of this improvement is emphasized when we examine actual spelling achievement.

Planning ability within the information integration model has generally been understood as a superordinate ability relating to a student's foresight and flexibility in problem solving. Taking into consideration again the small N per cell, t-tests of Pretest-Posttest means on planning marker tasks were examined for each group. Significantly better performance at posttest was found for the experimental students on the Visual Search (Automatic) task ($t(1,9)=3.42$, $p<.01$) and Planned Connections task ($t(1,9)=2.73$, $p<.05$), with none of the planning tasks showing pretest/posttest differences for the control students (means are presented in Table 4). Automatic search requires little planning; it is a test of attention. Of course, one can only speculate based on these results, but it seems that remedial training, encompassing as it did the verbalization of students in problem solving, may have contributed to an improved attention and planning ability overall. An initial indication such as this opens the door to continued research in this area.

Table 4
Mean Scores for Planning Marker Tasks at Pre/Post Test

Task	Experimental Group		Control Group	
	Pre	Post	Pre	Post
Visual Search	34.47	28.73	35.08	29.10
(Automatic)	(SD = 8.15)	(SD = 8.09)	(SD = 11.16)	(SD = 12.70)
Visual Search	121.78	102.94	118.75	121.15
(Controlled)	(49.34)	(19.48)	(25.95)	(29.88)
Planned	136.00	100.67	130.06	114.08
Connections	(52.71)	(43.54)	(36.62)	(35.13)
Crack the	1.80	3.80	3.10	3.80
Code	(2.20)	(1.75)	(1.79)	(1.81)

In summary, the notion of spelling ability (or disability) as an immutable factor in students is certainly challenged by the present data which support a remedial option for disabled students. It appears initially that global plus bridging tasks focusing on successive coding and spelling could be successfully incorporated into the whole class instruction for students with learning problems, and that they could impact positively on spelling achievement. Perhaps even more importantly, this study provides direction and optimism for future research into the use of such a model, utilizing nonacademic global tasks plus bridging tasks to an academic area, in subject areas beyond spelling (e.g., a simultaneous coding emphasis plus bridging tasks in reading comprehension). Further, such a remedial model may have direct application within a resource room situation, or even within a regular classroom with a preventive focus. The fact that strategies rather than merely academic content are actively taught, and that attention and planning abilities receive consideration within the context of the "delivery" of the remedial teaching, makes this intervention more motivating for the students and more likely to generalize to other academic pursuits of the student.

References

Brailsford, A., Snart, F., & Das, J.P. (1984). Strategy training and reading comprehension. *Journal of Learning Disabilities, 17,* 287-290.

Cummins, J. & Das, J.P. (1977). Cognitive processes and reading difficulties: A framework for research. *Alberta Journal of Educational Research, 23,* 245-256.

Das, J.P., & Conway, R. (1986). *CAP training manual.* Edmonton: University of Alberta, Developmental Disabilities Centre.

Das, J.P., Kirby, J., & Jarman, R.F. (1975). Simultaneous and successive synthesis: An alternative model for cognitive abilities. *Psychological Bulletin, 82,* 87-103.

Das, J.P., Kirby, J.R., & Jarman, R.F. (1979). *Simultaneous and successive cognitive processes.* New York, NY: Academic Press.

Douglas, V.I. (1980). Treatment and training approaches to hyperactivity: Establishing internal or external control. In *Hyperactive children—The social ecology of identification and treatment* (pp. 283-317). New York, NY: Academic Press.

Englert, C., Hiebert, E., & Stewart, S. (1985). Spelling unfamiliar words by an analogy strategy. *Journal of Special Education, 19,* 291-306.

Feuerstein, R. (1979). *The dynamic assessment of retarded performers.* Baltimore, MD: University Park Press.

Flaro, L. (1985, October). Learning disabilities and neuro-linguistic programming: An introduction. *Focus,* pp. 4-5.

Garofalo, J. (1986). Simultaneous synthesis, regulation, and arithmetical performance. *Journal of Psychoeducational Assessment, 4,* 229-238.

Gerber, M. (1984). Techniques to teach generalizable spelling skills. *Academic Therapy, 20,* 49-57.

Gerber, M., & Hall, R. (1987). Information processing approaches to studying spelling deficiencies. *Journal of Learning Disabilities, 20,* 34-42.

Gettinger, M. (1985). Effects of teacher-directed versus student-directed instruction and cues versus no cues for improving spelling performance. *Journal of Applied Behavior Analysis, 18,* 167-171.

Hammill, D., Larsen, S., & McNutt, G. (1977). The effects of spelling instruction: A preliminary study. *Elementary School Journal, 78,* 67-72.

Hammill, D., & Noone, J. (1975). Improving spelling skills. In D.D. Hamill & N.R. Bartel (Eds.), *Teaching children with learning and behavior problems* (pp. 89-106). Boston, MA: Allyn & Bacon.

Kaufman, A.S., & Kaufman, N.L. (1983). *Kaufman assessment battery for children: Interpretive manual.* Circle Pines, MN: American Guidance Service.

Kaufman, D., & Kaufman, P. (1979). Strategy training and remedial techniques. *Journal of Learning Disabilities, 12,* 416-419.

Kaufman, J., Hallahan, D., Haas, K., & Boren, R. (1978). Imitating children's errors to improve their spelling performance. *Journal of Learning Disabilities, 11*, 217-222.

Kirby, J. (Ed.) (1984). Educational roles of cognitive plans and strategies. In *Cognitive strategies and educational performance* (pp. 51-88). New York, NY: Academic Press.

Larson, S., & Hammill, D. (1986). *Test of written spelling.* Austin, TX: Pro-ed.

Leong, C.K. (in press). Neuropsychological models of learning disabilities: Contribution to remediation. In C.R. Reynolds (Ed.), *Handbook of clinical neuropsychology.* New York, NY: Plenum.

Lerner, J.W. (1981). *Learning disabilities: Theories, diagnosis, and teaching strategies* (3rd ed.). Boston, MA: Houghton Mifflin.

Luria, A.R. (1970). The functional organization of the brain. *Scientific American, 222*(3), 66-78.

Luria, A.R. (1980). *Higher cortical functions in man* (2nd ed.). New York, NY: Basic Books.

McRae, S.G. (1986). Sequential-simultaneous processing and reading skills in primary grade children. *Journal of Learning Disabilities, 19*(8), 509-511.

Naglieri, J.A., & Das, J.P. (1987). Construct and criterion related validity of planning, simultaneous, and successive cognitive processing tasks. *Journal of Psychoeducational Assessment, 4*, 353-363.

Naglieri, J.A., & Das, J.P. (1988). Planning—arousal—successive—simultaneous (PASS): A model for assessment. *Journal of School Psychology, 26*, 35-48.

Naglieri, J.A., & Das, J.P. (in press). *Cognitive assessment system (CAS).* Psychological Corporation.

Neisser, U. (1976). *Cognition and reality: Principles and implications of cognitive psychology.* San Francisco, CA: Freeman.

Otto, W., & McMenemy, R.A. (1966). *Corrective and remedial teaching.* Boston, MA: Houghton Mifflin.

Rieth, H.J., Polsgrove, L., & Eckert, R. (1984). A computer-based spelling program. *Academic Therapy, 20*, 59-65.

Rodgers, D., Covell, H., & Slade, K. (1978). *The I-Can-Spell program.* Toronto, ON: Heath Canada.

Snart, F., Das, J.P., & Mensink, D. (1988). Cognitive processing in high I.Q. reading disabled students: A comparative examination. *Journal of Special Education, 22*(3), 344-357.

Thomas, V. (1974). *Teaching spelling: Canadian word lists and instructional techniques.* Toronto, ON: Gage.

Tizard, B., & Hughes, M. (1984). *Young children learning.* Cambridge, MA: Harvard University Press.

Vygotsky, L.S. (1962). *Thought and language.* Cambridge, MA: MIT Press.

Wallace, G., & Larsen, S. (1978). *Educational assessment of learning problems: Testing for teaching.* Boston, MA: Allyn & Bacon.

Wong, B. (1986). Cognitive approach to teaching spelling. *Exceptional Children, 53*(2), 169-173.

Appendix

Descriptions of Two CAP Global Tasks and Related Spelling Remedial Tasks

CAP TASK 10 BEAD THREADING

Strategy: Successive

Objective: To thread a bead pattern by recall following either teacher demonstration or card study.

Instructions:

1. A "bead pole" is used: This has a cardboard cover around it and a window cut out in the cardboard cover. The teacher drops beads in a predetermined order, ensuring that the beads can be seen briefly as they pass through the window.

2. Learner copies the pattern using his or her own frame.

3. Correctness of sequence is checked by lifting the cover off the frame.

4. Student should repeat the task if incorrect (provide more cues).

5. Teacher records response (1 for correct, 0 for incorrect).

or

1. Teacher holds up a card with a picture of beads on a bead pole for the student to study.

2. Card is removed.

3. The student then attempts to duplicate the pattern observed.

4. Student then checks the card for accuracy. Teacher records the response (1 for correct, 0 for incorrect).

5. Student should repeat the task if incorrect. (Discussion of clues and strategies should precede the next attempt.)

SPELLING TASK TO FOLLOW CAP TASK 10

Instructions:

1. Teacher presents a card with letters arranged on it, says, "This word is _____," and turns the card over immediately saying, "Use the letters in front of you to make this word" (student places letter cards in a card holder). Teacher records the response and asks the student to mix up the letters.

2. Teacher presents a window chart to the student. Each window has a strip of paper with a letter on it. The teacher says, "Watch carefully." The teacher then pulls the strips through the windows

one at a time, saying the letter name. The letter is exposed for no longer than 5 seconds. Student is then asked to arrange the letters in front of him in the card holder as he remembers seeing them. Teacher records the response. Student checks his response by exposing the letters in the windows. Each letter is left exposed to allow student to check. Student corrects errors as they are discovered.

3. Teacher takes the chart from the child and holds it up for the child to see that the letters are still exposed. Teacher then says the name of each letter and pulls the letter out of sight. Teacher says the whole word after the last letter has been named and pulled out of sight. The student is then asked to place the letter cards in the holder in the correct order. Teacher records the response. The student is then given the window chart to check his or her response. Student checks his or her response by exposing the letters in the windows. Each letter is left exposed to allow student to check. Student corrects errors as they are discovered.

4. Repeat step 3.

5. Repeat step 1.

CAP TASK 16 TELEPHONE

Strategy: Successive.
Objective: To dial from memory telephone numbers of increasing length.

Instructions:

1. The teacher reads a digit number sequence (allow 1 second delay between each digit).

2. Learner then dials this sequence on a telephone. Teacher records response (1 for correct, 0 for incorrect).

3. Repeat sequence if incorrect—discuss ways of remembering.

4. Discuss student's correct response.

SPELLING TASK TO FOLLOW CAP TASK 16

Instructions:

1. Student finds the correct envelope for the spelling word (envelopes are numbered). Inside the envelope are the materials required:
    -   language master card (side 1 and side 2);
    -   letter cards inside a small white envelope (15 letters in each envelope);

- 3 yellow sheets numbered 1, 2, 3 respectively. Student's spelling word is recorded on the language master card. On side (1) the word is said and then used in a sentence. On side (2) the word is spelled, that is,

  > Side (1) turkeys—turkeys are birds
  > (2) t-u-r-k-e-y-s.

  Student takes everything out of the envelope.

2. Student is instructed to listen to side one of the language master card. The student is to print the spelling word he or she heard on yellow sheet numbered (1) and place it in the box beside him or her. Student is reminded to check that his or her name is on the sheet. (The sheets have been predated.)

3. Student is to empty the letters from the white envelope and arrange them in a line.

4. Then the student listens to side 2 of the language master card.

5. The student has extra letters. He or she must choose the correct ones to make the word after he or she has heard the spelling. The letters are spread out on the table. He or she must choose from the selection—10% of the spelling words will have misinformation, that is, not all of the required letters will have been included—the student will be encouraged to solve the problem.

6. Student then listens to side 2 again to check his or her arrangement. If there are errors student fixes them and then again checks by listening once more.

7. Student mixes up the letters and repeats steps 4 through 6 two more times.

8. Now the student writes his or her arrangement for the spelling word on the yellow sheet numbered (2). The student then places this sheet in the box beside him or her.

9. The student puts everything back in its place and then writes the spelling word on the yellow sheet numbered (3) and then places it in the box.

An Epidemiological Study of Children's Attitudes toward Disability

Susanne M. King, Peter Rosenbaum, Robert W. Armstrong,
and Ruth Milner
McMaster University

In this epidemiological study the authors recorded the attitudes of children in Hamilton, Ontario, to physically disabled and mentally handicapped children. Univariate analyses confirmed the importance of female gender, friendship and contact with handicapped persons as determinants of more accepting attitudes. Type of disability and the presence or absence of disabled children in respondents' schools were not found to influence attitudes in a systematic manner. Correlations between attitudes and children's self-esteem or sociometric ratings were not significant, nor were parent-child attitude correlations. Maternal language of origin was found to influence children's attitudes, in favour of children of English-speaking mothers. These results are discussed with reference to their practical applications by community and educational systems seeking to foster integration of disabled children.

*   *   *

SUCCESSFUL INTEGRATION OF DISABLED CHILDREN IS THOUGHT TO BE greatly influenced by the attitudes of able-bodied children (Bender, 1980). There is considerable evidence that disabled children are perceived in negative and prejudiced ways by their non-handicapped peers (Johnson, 1950; Goodman et al., 1972; Gottlieb & Budoff, 1973; Gottlieb, 1974; Gottlieb et al., 1974), and that integration may even increase prejudice and the stereotyping and rejection of handicapped children. The negative attitudes of able-bodied children thus are obstacles to integration. We need to understand more fully the nature of these attitudes in order to change them.

The authors gratefully acknowledge the co-operation and support of the Hamilton Board of Education and the Hamilton-Wentworth Roman Catholic Separate School Board in providing access to the children and families who participated in this study. Cathy Graham and Tim Young were responsible for the data collection, coding and entry, and Joanne Miles typed innumerable revisions of this paper with her usual skill, speed, and cheerfulness. This study was made possible by an operating grant from The Easter Seal Research Institute of Ontario (formerly the Conn Smythe Research Foundation for Crippled Children).

A number of determinants of children's attitudes to disability have been described. These include gender (females generally more positive than males), volunteering for contact with disabled peers, experience of contact with disabled people, parental attitudes, age, and the geographical layout of the school (see Rosenbaum et al., 1988 for a review of these issues). The contribution of the school 'climate' to children's expressed attitudes has been assessed by Gottlieb et al. (1974), who found that attitudes were more favourable in schools in which there was no contact with children requiring special education. On the other hand, there are reports of a significant association between children's expressed attitudes and schools in which integration with severely handicapped schoolmates occurred regularly (Voeltz, 1982), and in which a 'high contact' integration program was offered to promote opportunities for contact (Towfighy-Hooskyar & Zingle, 1984).

In contrast to the external determinants of attitudes are the influences of respondents' characteristics as perceived by self and peers. In studies of adults' attitudes toward the physically disabled, persons with low self-esteem were more likely to show prejudice toward this group (Eisenman, 1970), while more positive attitudes are associated with higher self-esteem and personal adjustment (Epstein & Shontz, 1961; Eisler, 1964). No published evidence has been found concerning this relationship in children. Similarly, the role of a child's social status, as judged by his peers, has received little attention. Children who are socially valued by others may have a stronger sense of security and consequently feel more confident in their relationships with others, which might predispose them to more favourable attitudes to the disabled.

The nature of the disability is often thought to affect children's expressed attitudes. Richardson's work (Richardson et al., 1961; Richardson, 1970), described the hierarchy of physical disabilities to which children respond, but did not address the effects of varying types of handicapping conditions on response patterns. Gottlieb and Gottlieb (1977) reported that a physically disabled child was evaluated significantly more favourably than a mentally retarded child on an adjective checklist, although there were no significant differences on a social distance scale. Similar findings were reported with an adult population by Furnham and Pendred (1983), using a modified version of Yuker's ATDP (Yuker et al., 1966).

In order to evaluate the role and relative importance of these several factors as determinants of children's attitudes, an epidemiological survey was conducted in which these potential influences were assessed simultaneously.

This study was carried out in Hamilton, Ontario, a community of 310,000 people, with the full collaboration of two area School Boards, each of which reviewed and consented to the project. At the time of the study there were 61,000 children in schools administered by the non-denominational Hamilton Board of Education (HBE) (41,000 students) and the Hamilton-Wentworth Roman Catholic Separate School Board (RCB) (20,000 students). The RCB has had a long-standing policy of integrating disabled children into regular classrooms, while the HBE has traditionally segregated disabled students.

The sampling frame for this investigation included 536 classrooms of students in grades 5 to 8 in the two School Boards. Classes were only excluded if they contained primarily or exclusively children in a special education program. A stratified random selection of classes was performed to achieve a balanced number of children from each grade, in proportions which reflected the overall student populations of the two School Boards. Sixty-six classes with 1831 children were randomly selected, including 46 classes (1277 students) from 19 different schools in the HBE, and 20 classes (554 students) from 20 different schools in the RCB. The students were approximately equally divided between boys (N=909) and girls (N=922), and among the four grades (438, 458, 425 and 510 in grades 5 to 8, respectively).

This survey was conducted during the months of April to June 1985. The children's package of questionnaires included an attitude measure (CATCH), a self-esteem measure and a classroom sociometric rating form. Before completing the attitude measure, the children were asked to read a 'stimulus scenario' (see Appendix) which was attached to the questionnaire. They were instructed to respond to the CATCH statements with the stimulus child in mind.

Children in each classroom were randomly assigned to receive one of two gender-specific scenarios. Each scenario described a child either functioning in a manner characteristic of a physical disability (the 'cerebral palsy' scenario) (N=915) or displaying features and performance of mental handicap (the 'mental retardation' scenario) (N=916). Furthermore, half of each of the scenarios randomly contained a concluding sentence 'labelling' the disability (e.g., 'Melissa is mentally retarded'), while the other half presented the identical information without any label.

The children's questionnaires were administered during a single one-hour classroom visit by one of three trained research assistants. Instructions to the students on how to complete the forms were fully detailed so that the presentation was uniform to each class. Each child was also given a package to take home which contained a letter of explanation about the survey, two parent attitude questionnaires (PATCH), a family demographic information sheet, and a consent form for the parents to sign. Although the School Boards granted permission to administer the children's questionnaire on a group basis, consent was obtained for parent participation. To ensure confidentiality, all child and parent forms were coded with an individual number and no names were required on any forms.

All parent questionnaires were returned to the school in numbered, sealed envelopes. These were then collected by the research assistants, who left a McDonald's coupon for the child, regardless of the parents' decision to participate. Since we did not have identifying information such as phone numbers, a reminder note was left for any child who had not yet returned the package. The School Exposure Questionnaire was completed by the school Principal, either at the time of the initial visit or within a week of the visit.

Measures

Chedoke-McMaster Attitudes Toward Children with Handicaps (CATCH)

CATCH is a 36-item self-administered scale to which children respond on a five-point Likert scale to statements concerning their cognitive understanding of disabled children ('Handicapped children feel sorry for themselves'); their affective response to disabled children ('I would be happy to have a handicapped child for a special friend'); and their behavioural intentions toward disabled children ('I would talk to a handicapped child I didn't know'). Standardized scores range from 0 to 40, with a higher score indicating more positive attitudes.

CATCH is reliable (coefficient alpha = 0.90) and is able to detect differences in children's attitudes according to gender, volunteering to be involved with disabled children and having a friend who is disabled (Rosenbaum et al., 1986a). Further validation of the measure includes a significant improvement in attitude scores following a 'buddy' intervention program (Armstrong et al., 1987) and a differential change in scores when comparing a 'buddy' program (positive change) with an educational program (no change or negative change) (Rosenbaum et al., 1986b).

Perceived Competence Scale

This is a self-report instrument suitable for classroom use (Harter, 1982). Four dimensions of competence are assessed: cognitive ('Some kids often forget what they learn, but other kids can remember things easily'); social ('Some kids have a lot of friends, but other kids don't have very many friends'); physical ('Some kids are among the last to be chosen for games, but other kids are picked first'); and general ('Some kids are very happy being the way they are, but other kids wish they were different'). The scale is reliable (test-retest 0.73 to 0.84, internal consistency 0.73 to 0.83) and has demonstrated construct and discriminant validity.

Classroom sociometrics

Classroom sociometrics are designed to assess the social status of an individual child by having each student in the class evaluate every other class-mate. Students are provided with an alphabetical classlist and for each name they are asked to respond to the question 'How much would you like to be friends with this person outside of school time?'. Response options vary from 0 ('not at all') to 4 ('very much'), and a child's score reflects the mean of same-sex class-mate answers. Sociometrics are reliable, stable for periods as long as three years, and are powerful predictors of later psychiatric problems (Milich & Landau, 1980). Classroom sociometrics have been used extensively in peer interaction research.

Parental Attitudes Toward Children with Handicaps (PATCH)

This 30-item measure is modelled on the CATCH questionnaire. It is designed to assess parents' perception of disabled children and the degree to which they would allow their child to associate with disabled children. Scoring is done on a five-point Likert scale, with transformed scores ranging from 0 to 30, a higher score indicating a more positive attitude. Coefficient alpha is 0.88. PATCH is able to detect differences in parents' attitudes according to gender; stimulus scenario (mentally retarded or cerebral-palsied child); presence of a disabled child in the family; and familiarity with a disabled person (Rosenbaum et al., 1987). In a randomized controlled trial of a 'buddy' program, parents of 'buddy' children had a significant positive change in PATCH scores compared with parents of control children (Armstrong et al., 1987).

Sociodemographic data

The demographic information sheet completed by the parents included marital status, the number of children in the family and, for each parent, the birthplace (country), language first spoken, education level and occupation. The socio-economic index used for this study was based on the scale developed by Blishen and McRoberts (1976). Using data on the Canadian work-force, the index ranks occupations in terms of education and income. The classification system gives continuous ordered data which can be aggregated by deciles into six classes, with level I indicating the lowest socio-economic status and level VI the highest.

Familiarity with disabled people

Children were asked if they knew any handicapped person(s), and if so to indicate whether they were family members, relatives or friends. In addition, they were asked if they had played with a handicapped child in the previous week. Children were also asked whether they themselves were handicapped, and if so in what way. This information was all obtained before the completion of the attitude measure.

School exposure questionnaire

A questionnaire modelled on an unvalidated measure by Stainback and Stainback (1982) was completed by the Principal of each school and provided information about the exposure of able-bodied children to disabled children within that school. A total school exposure score was calculated, based on responses to 14 questions about the number and kinds of disabilities of disabled students and their involvement in school routines. Scoring was on a five-point scale from 0 ('not at all') to 4 ('full-time [100%]'). Total scores ranged from 0 (reflecting absence or total segregation of disabled students in the school) to 56 (full integration of disabled children with regular students).

Analysis

Data were analyzed using both ANOVA and multiple regression. Because of the large number of analyses undertaken, results were considered statistically significant only when the p value was ≤ 0.001 (except where noted otherwise).

One-way ANOVAs were done with CATCH as the dependent variable and each of the following as the independent variable: gender, having a handicapped friend, recent contact with a handicapped child, having a handicapped relative, and scenario. Pearson product moment correlations of CATCH scores with each of the perceived competence component scores and sociometric ratings were also performed.

The importance of several parent-related variables was also analyzed. Pearson product moment correlations of CATCH and PATCH scores were performed separately by gender. Analyses of variance were done to evaluate the impact of parental education (four levels), parents' occupation (six levels) and parents' first language (English or non-English).

In order to assess a number of child variables thought to contribute to the explanation of variance in CATCH scores, a stepwise multiple regression analysis was performed. These variables were gender, grade, the four component-perceived competence scores, the sociometric rating, scenario, being handicapped, having a handicapped friend or relative, and contact with a disabled child. The native language (English or other) of the child's mother was also added as an independent variable. PATCH scores were not included because data were available for only 61% of mothers and 45% of fathers.

S.M. King, P. Rosenbaum, R.W. Armstrong, & R. Milner

Results

Complete data for the three child measures were obtained for 1819 students (99.3%); in 12 cases perceived competence scores were not available. The overall rate of return for the parent packages was 75%, including both consenting and non-consenting parents. Of this group, 81.6% consented to participate in the survey and completed some or all of the appropriate forms. Of the total sample of 1831 subjects, family background data were provided for 1138 (62%).

Sociodemographic information was supplied by parents completing the Family Background Form, a large proportion (83%) of whom lived in two-parent families. The majority of both fathers (71%) and mothers (74%) indicated that English was their first language and over half the parents had completed high-school or further education. In comparison with the demographic profile of the community, based on the 1981 Canadian census, the socio-economic status of the parents was shifted slightly toward the higher occupational levels (38.3% of respondents in levels V and VI, compared with approximately 30% in the population).

Children's responses

The mean CATCH score was 26.8 (SD 4.7, median 26.7, mode 25.8). Scores varied from 8.3 to 39.2, with 7.6% of children scoring 20 or less, 66% scoring between 21 and 30, and 26.3% scoring above 30. Girls scored significantly higher on CATCH than boys (27.8 *vs.* 25.8) ($F(1,1829)=86.51, p<.001$, SD 0.43). Table 1 shows that on each of the variables 'having a handicapped friend.' 'recent contact with a handicapped child' and 'having a handicapped relative' there were significant differences, with children who answered 'yes' having more positive attitudes than those answering 'no.'

TABLE I
Mean CATCH scores for three dimensions of familiarity with handicapped (HC) persons

	Yes	No	SD (%)
Have HC friend	(N=780) 28·3	(N=1045) 25·7	0·55
	$F(1,1821)=121·58, p<0·001$		
Recent contact with HC child	(N=604) 28·1	(N=1218) 26·2	0·40
	$F(1,1818)=61·93, p<0·001$		
Have HC relative	(N=495) 27·6	(N=1332) 26·3	0·28
	$F(1,1823)=17·34, p<0·001$		

No significant difference was detected in expressed attitudes in response to the vignette describing the mentally retarded child compared with the scenario describing the physically disabled child. Within each type of scenario, comparison between labelled and unlabelled descriptions indicated no differences.

Correlations between CATCH scores and each of the four components of the Perceived Competence Scale revealed no significant associations, with values ranging from -0.08 to 0.10. Similarly, there was no significant correlation ($r=0.01$) between CATCH scores and sociometric ratings.

School

Mean CATCH scores across the 39 schools (66 classes) varied from 22.6 to 29.7. Children in HBE schools scored higher (27.1) than children in the RCB schools (26.2), ($F(1,1827)=13.15, p<0.001$). There was also a significant main effect for grade ($F(3,1823)=9.87, p<0.001$). Scheffé analysis revealed that the grade 8 students (ages 14 to 16 years) had a significantly lower mean CATCH score ($p=0.05$) compared with each of the other three grades (25.9 for grade 8 vs. 26.9, 27.1, 27.5 for grades 5 to 7 [ages 10 to 13], respectively). No differences were found between the means of the other three grades.

The School Exposure Questionnaire was returned by all but one school Principal. All but five of the schools had at least one visibly disabled student, with a range from less than 1% to 9% (median 2%). The pattern of school exposure scores bore no relationship to the mean CATCH scores of students in that school, nor was there any relationship between the percentage of visibly disabled students in the school and mean CATCH scores.

Parents

There were no significant differences in attitudes scores between children whose parents consented and those who refused to be involved in the study. There were also no significant differences in the children's CATCH scores across educational or occupational levels of either parent. However, children whose mother's first language was English scored significantly higher than those whose mother's language was not (27.4 vs. 26.1; $F(1,1103)=10.32, p=0.001$; 0.28 SD difference). There was no significant difference for fathers' language of origin.

Correlations between attitude scores of parents and children were small (0.08 to 0.21) and non-significant. Mothers had higher correlations with their children than did fathers, and the correlation of either parent was higher with daughters than with sons.

Multiple regression analysis

Table 2 presents the results of the multiple regression analysis, in which 13.7% of the variance in CATCH score was accounted for by nine variables. Of these, only three (having a handicapped friend, gender and mother's native language) contributed more than 1% each to the explanation of the outcome.

TABLE II
Results of multiple regression analysis

Step	Variables	Multiple R	R^2	F^*
1	Handicapped friend	0·258	0·067	77·68
2	Gender	0·302	0·091	54·48
3	Language of mother	0·323	0·104	42·02
4	Cognitive perceived competence	0·336	0·113	34·56
5	Handicapped relative	0·346	0·120	29·51
6	Grade	0·353	0·125	25·68
7	Contact	0·360	0·129	22·95
8	Scenario	0·365	0·133	20·77
9	Physical perceived competence	0·370	0·137	19·04

*Significance: $p < 0.001$.

Discussion

The results of this survey can be summarized in terms of 'positive' and 'negative' findings. In addition to providing further evidence of the relationship between expressed attitudes and gender, contact and familiarity, the role of the mother's native language emerges. There are also important contributions made by the 'negative' results. Attitudes were not found to be associated with the child's perceived self-esteem, social status as judged by peers, educational and SES levels of the parents, parents' expressed attitudes, or type of disability scenario used to evaluate attitudes.

Children whose mothers' native language was English had more positive attitudes than children whose maternal language of origin was not English, while paternal language of origin did not show this effect. Language of origin (English or non-English) has been shown to be an important determinant of parental attitudes to disability (Rosenbaum et al., 1987). Other data have demonstrated stronger correlations between mothers' and children's attitudes than between fathers' and chidren's attitudes (Rosenbaum et al., 1988). Both these findings support the inference that the mechanism of the observations reported in this study operates via parental influences, particularly mothers' impact on their children.

The absence of an effect of attitude referent (stimulus scenario) on expressed attitudes is in contrast to findings in other studies which have found either a hierarchy of preference for various disabilities (Richardson, 1970; Miller et al., 1981; Miller, 1984; Weiss, 1986); a labelling effect (Budoff & Siperstein, 1977; Bak & Siperstein, 1986); or preference for the physically disabled over the mentally retarded (Willey & McCandless, 1973; Gottlieb & Gottlieb, 1977). It is possible that written descriptions of function may not have been powerful enough to elicit any differentiating effects on children's attitudes. However, since adults in this survey were able to discriminate between the disabilities on the basis of written information (Rosenbaum et al., 1987), and we have no evidence that children had difficulty doing the same, we conclude that the lack of differences is a 'real' finding. These results support the use of the generic or non-categorical term (i.e., disabled or handicapped) to describe children with functional differences (Jones, 1974).

What other factors not explored here contribute to children's attitudes? Disabled children themselves clearly play a part in affecting the able-bodied child's attitudes. Competence of the disabled child leads to more positive attitudes and willingness to interact with mentally handicapped schoolmates (Siperstein & Bak, 1985; Bak & Siperstein, 1986). Further study is required of characteristics of physically disabled children and their impact on able-bodied peers.

These findings modestly support the notion that contact between able-bodied and disabled children is associated with more positive attitudes and has the potential to promote relationships. There is evidence that the kind of contact matters and that social opportunities should be of a structured, co-operative nature (Donaldson, 1980; Armstrong et al., 1987). While it may be useful to work with those having poorer attitudes, there is no evidence that interventions to improve a child's self-esteem or social position among peers would be the appropriate means of changing attitudes toward disabled schoolmates. The perceptions of boys and girls vary, and what they respond to may also be different. All of these factors need to be considered in planning integration and in promoting positive attitudes.

Appendix

'Cerebral palsy' scenario

PLEASE READ THE FOLLOWING PARAGRAPH ABOUT A BOY WHO IS HANDICAPPED. WHEN YOU ANSWER THE QUESTIONS ON THE NEXT FOUR PAGES, THINK ABOUT THIS BOY WHEN YOU SEE THE WORD 'HANDICAPPED'.

John is a boy your age who has just moved to this area of the city and may be starting at your school next week. He walks with braces on his legs, uses crutches for balance, and sometimes needs a wheelchair for long trips with his family. About one day a month John misses school to go to a doctor's appointment or to have treatment to help him walk better. John can learn in a regular class. He uses a typewriter at school because he writes slowly. Sometimes he speaks unclearly and sounds like he has an accent. John has cerebral palsy.

(The identical paragraph for girls had the name Jennifer substituted for the name John, with appropriate adjustment of all gender-specific words. Half of these scenarios omitted the concluding sentence.)

'Mental retardation' scenario

PLEASE READ THE FOLLOWING PARAGRAPH ABOUT A GIRL WHO IS HANDICAPPED. WHEN YOU ANSWER THE QUESTIONS ON THE NEXT FOUR PAGES, THINK ABOUT THIS GIRL WHEN YOU SEE THE WORD 'HANDICAPPED'.

Melissa is a girl your age who has just moved to this area of the city and may be starting at your school next week. She is just beginning to learn to read and write, and has trouble learning math. She can run and play like other kids, but sometimes forgets the rules of the game. She will need extra time to learn about school, and to remember who people are and where everything is. Melissa has a deep voice, but can speak clearly using simple words. She asks a lot of questions about people and things. She goes to a special class for part of the day for extra help with school. Melissa is mentally retarded.

(The identical paragraph for boys had the name Mark substituted for the name Melissa, with appropriate adjustment of all gender-specific words. Half of these scenarios omitted the concluding sentence.)

References

Armstrong, R.W., Rosenbaum, P.L., & King, S.M. (1987). A randomized controlled trial of a 'buddy' program to improve children's attitudes toward the disabled. *Developmental Medicine and Child Neurology, 29*, 327-336.

Bak, J.J., & Siperstein, G.N. (1986). Protective effects of the label "mentally retarded" on children's attitudes towards mentally retarded peers. *American Journal of Mental Deficiency, 91*, 95-97.

Bender, L.F. (1980). Attitudes towards disabled people. *Developmental Medicine and Child Neurology, 22*, 427-428 *(Editorial).*

Blishen, B.R., & McRoberts, H.A. (1976). A revised socioeconomic index for occupations in Canada. *Canadian Review of Sociology and Anthropology, 13*, 71-79.

Budoff, M., & Siperstein, G.N. (1977). Low-income children's attitudes toward mentally retarded children: effects of labelling and academic behavior. *American Journal of Mental Deficiency, 82*, 474-480.

Donaldson, J. (1980). Changing attitudes toward handicapped persons: a review and analysis of research. *Exceptional children, 46*, 504-514.

Eisenman, R. (1970). Birth order, sex, self-esteem, and prejudice against the physically disabled. *Journal of Psychology, 75*, 147-155.

Eisler, R. (1964). The relationship between stability of self-concept and acceptance of the disabled and aged. Unpublished master's thesis, Hofstra University, Hempstead, NY.

Epstein, S., & Shontz, F. (1961). Attitudes toward persons with physical disabilities as a function of attitudes toward one's own body. Paper presented at the meeting of the American Psychological Association, New York, NY.

Furnham, A., & Pendred, J. (1983). Attitudes toward the mentally and physically disabled. *British Journal of Medical Psychology, 56,* 179-187.

Goodman, H., Gottlieb, J., & Harrison, R.H. (1972). Social acceptance of EMRs integrated into a nongraded elementary school. *American Journal of Mental Deficiency, 76,* 412-417.

Gottlieb, J. (1974). Attitudes toward retarded children: effects of labelling and academic performance. *American Journal of Mental Deficiency, 79,* 268-273.

Gottlieb, J., & Budoff, M. (1973). Social acceptability of retarded children in nongraded schools differing in architecture. *American Journal of Mental Deficiency, 78,* 15-19.

Gottlieb, J., & Gottlieb, B.W. (1977). Stereotypic attitudes and behavioral intentions toward handicapped children. *American Journal of Mental Deficiency, 82,* 65-71.

Gottlieb, J., Cohen, L., & Goldstein, L. (1974). Social contact and personal adjustment as variables relating to attitudes toward educable mentally retarded children. *Training School Bulletin, 71,* 9-16.

Harter, S. (1982). The perceived competence scale for children. *Child Development, 53,* 87-97.

Johnson, G.O. (1950). A study of the social position of mentally handicapped children in regular grades. *American Journal of Mental Deficiency, 55,* 60-89.

Jones, R.L. (1974). The hierarchical structure of attitudes toward the exceptional. *Exceptional Children, 40,* 430-435.

Milich, R., & Landau, S. (1980). Socialization and peer relations in hyperactive children. *In* Gadow, K.D., & Biales, L. (Eds.) *Advances in learning and behavior disabilities.* Greenwich, CN: JAI Press.

Miller, M. (1984). Social acceptability characteristics of learning disabled children. *Journal of Learning Disabilities, 17,* 619-621.

Miller, M., Armstrong, S., & Hagan, M. (1981). Effects of teaching on elementary students' attitudes toward handicaps. *Education and Training of the Mentally Retarded, 16,* 110-113.

Richardson, S.A. (1970). Age and sex differences in values toward physical handicaps. *Journal of Health and Social Behavior, 11,* 207-214.

Richardson, S.A., Goodman, N., Hastorf, A.H., & Dornbusch, S.M. (1961). Cultural uniformity in reaction to physical disabilities. *American Sociological Review, 26,* 241-247.

Rosenbaum, P.L., Armstrong, R.W., & King, S.M. (1986a). Children's attitudes toward disabled peers: a self-report measure. *Journal of Pediatric Psychology, 11,* 517-530.

Rosenbaum, P.L., Armstrong, R.W., & King, S.M. (1986b). Improving attitudes toward the disabled: a randomized controlled trial of direct contact versus Kids-on-the-Block. *Journal of Developmental and Behavioral Pediatrics, 7,* 302-307.

Rosenbaum, P.L., Armstrong, R.W., & King, S.M. (1987). Parental attitudes toward children with handicaps: new perspectives with a new measure. *Journal of Developmental and Behavioral Pediatrics, 8,* 327-334.

Rosenbaum, P.L., Armstrong, R.W., & King, S.M. (1988). Determinants of children's attitudes toward disability: a review of evidence. *Children's Health Care, 17,* 32-39.

Sipstein, G.N., & Bak, J.J. (1985). Effects of social behavior on children's attitudes toward their mildly and moderately mentally retarded peers. *American Journal of Mental Deficiency, 90,* 319-327.

Stainback, S. & Stainback, W. (1983). A severely handicapped integration checklist. *Teaching Exceptional Children, 15*, 168-171.

Towfighy-Hooskyar, N., & Zingle, H.W. (1984). Regular-class students' attitudes toward integrated multiply handicapped peers. *American Journal of Mental Deficiency, 88*, 630-637.

Voeltz, L.M. (1982). Effects of structured interactions with severely handicapped peers on children's attitudes. *American Journal of Mental Deficiency, 87*, 380-390.

Weiss, M.F. (1986). Children's attitudes toward the mentally ill: a developmental analysis. *Psychological Reports, 58*, 11-20.

Willey, N.R. & McCandless, B.R. (1973). Social stereotypes for normal, educable mentally retarded, and orthopedically handicapped children. *Journal of Special Education, 7*, 283-287.

Yuker, H., Block, J.R., & Young, J.H. (1966). The measurement of attitudes toward disabled persons. *Human Resources Study No. 7*. Albertson, NY: Human Resources Centre.

Social Relations of Gifted Children as a Function of Age and School Program

Barry H. Schneider, Marjorie R. Clegg, Barbara M. Byrne,
Jane E. Ledingham, and Gail Crombie
University of Ottawa

This study examined social and personal concomitants of exceptional academic capability in the context of various educational settings. Students in Grades 5, 8, and 10 participated in the study. At each grade level, there were students in classes for the gifted (self-contained gifted), gifted students in regular classes (integrated gifted), and classmates of the integrated gifted (matched and random controls). Subjects completed self-report scales of social competence and feelings about school. Peer nominations for social competence were also obtained from children in the integrated classes. The integrated gifted children at all three grade levels had higher scores for academic self-concept than the other groups; there were no differences in social or physical self-concept. In Grade 5 only, the integrated gifted were rated by their classmates as higher in social competence than were controls. Although there were no significant differences among groups in terms of attitude towards school, feelings toward school became less positive as age increased.

*   *   *

THE EDUCATIONAL TREATMENT OF THE GIFTED CHILD HAS RECEIVED INcreased scrutiny in recent years. Jellen and Verduin (1986) have emphasized the need for the development of differential education for the gifted. However, separate special programming for the gifted has been criticized for depriving regular children of appropriate models and opportunities for association with the gifted, and some have contended that a "good" program for gifted is the same as a "good" program for all children (Marland, 1972). Although "mainstreaming" has been advocated for gifted children (Henson, 1976), a recent Richardson Foundation study was highly critical of the fragmented educational experience of many gifted children in regular classes (Cox, Daniel, & Boston, 1986).

The classroom experience of gifted children in regular classrooms is profoundly different from that of their counterparts in separate special pro-

This research was financially supported by the Social Sciences and Humanities Research Council of Canada and the Ontario Ministry of Education. This report reflects the views of the authors and not necessarily those of the funding agencies.

grams. In a regular class, gifted children compare themselves and their achievements with others of lesser academic ability. These social comparisons may lead to high self-perceptions of ability for the gifted. However, lower achieving students' comparisons with such high-ability classmates may generate hostility (Levine & Wang, 1983). Social comparisons, nevertheless, can also serve positive functions by acting as cues to identify which classmates can be sought out for help (Marshall, Weinstein, Sharp, & Brattesani, 1982).

Marshall and Weinstein (1984) argued that dimensions such as social comparison must be considered within the context of multiple classroom factors that interact in determining student outcome. Other elements of their model are useful in conceptualizing the influence of school program options for the gifted. For example, in regular classes, the gifted child's repeated task success may lead to differential teacher treatment and the communication of higher teacher expectations (Brophy, 1983). These teacher variables should influence self-perceptions of academic ability and, perhaps, self-perception in general.

Schneider (1987) reviewed theoretical arguments that suggest that children of higher intellectual ability should be expected to display advanced social development. Most models of intelligence include component abilities that relate to social competence, either as applications of general ability or as more or less distinct subcomponents (see, e.g., Abroms, 1985; Sternberg & Davidson, 1986; Walters & Gardner, 1986). These social-cognitive skills include social perspective and social problem solving. One would expect gifted children to excel in peer relations because of these intellectual abilities. However, extremely high levels of these abilities have not been seen as entirely positive. Savage (1985) noted that high levels of perspective-taking ability may lead to emotional turmoil, which may exact a toll on children's social relationships. Furthermore, gifted behaviors such as artistic creativity or academic excellence may at times require a child to withdraw from social interaction (Getzels & Jackson, 1962).

Self-Concept of the Gifted

Although some researchers have found gifted children to exhibit significantly higher levels of self-concept than their nongifted peers (Lehman & Erdwins, 1981; O'Such, Twyla, & Havertape, 1979), others have reported no significant differences (Bracken, 1980; Ketcham & Snyder, 1977). There are many factors that may underlie these seemingly conflicting results. First, investigators have used a variety of criteria to identify gifted children. Second, potentially important moderating variables such as grade, sex, sociometric status, and classroom setting have been frequently overlooked. Third, most researchers have not considered the multidimensionality of self-concept, although construct validity research has repeatedly demonstrated that any comparison of mean differences is meaningful only when it bears on a specific facet of self-concept (Byrne & Shavelson, 1986; Marsh & Shavelson, 1985). Finally, many studies have not compared gifted youngsters with adequate local nongifted comparative groups, but have contrasted data from gifted samples with the normative data reported in test manuals (Janos, Fung, & Robinson, 1985; Maddux, Scheiber, & Bass, 1982; Tidwell, 1980).

Social comparison theory (Festinger, 1954) predicts that, with the transition from regular class to special program, the self-concepts of gifted children should decrease, because comparisons will then be made to a group with generally higher ability levels. Kulik and Kulik (1982) conducted a meta-analysis of fifteen studies which investigated the self-concept of gifted students in self-contained special programs and integrated settings. Seven of these studies showed a slight advantage for gifted students in special programs. Six found slightly lower self-concepts in similarly-placed gifted children, and two reported no significant differences. Because the direction of program effect was variable and the absolute effect sizes small, these authors concluded that the effect of special programming on self-concept was minor. Nevertheless, there is still a definite need for more research on the self-concept of gifted children because of the methodological limitations in previous research, the paucity of research into age and sex differences in gifted children's self-concept, and the limited attention given to domain-specific self-concepts.

This study sought to determine whether the self-concepts (academic, social, physical, and global) of bright students differ markedly from those of their academically less capable peers. It also explored differences in the self-concepts of gifted children as a function of educational setting, gender, and IQ.

Peer Acceptance of the Gifted

Challenging the folk notion of gifted children as social isolates, many researchers have endeavored to establish the social status of the gifted in comparison with their nongifted peers. Several reviews of this literature (Austin & Draper, 1981; Gamble, 1975; Schneider, 1987) have concluded that gifted elementary children are indeed well accepted by their nongifted peers. However, these results may vary as a function of gender and IQ. Solano (1976) found that gifted boys were better liked than gifted girls by their regular-class peers. Several researchers have also suggested the possibility of a maximum IQ level (150 or higher) above which popularity declines (Austin & Draper, 1981; Gallagher, 1958; Hollingworth, 1926, 1942). Hollingworth (1942) found that the greater the IQ difference was between gifted and nongifted children in a group, the lower the acceptance was of gifted children.

In contrast with the social status of younger gifted children, the peer relationships of gifted children in high school have received little attention. In an early study by Keisler (1955), high-ability girls in high school were found to be less popular with opposite-sex peers than were average-ability girls. This relation did not hold for high-ability boys.

There is some reason to believe that placement of gifted children in self-contained classrooms may also affect peer acceptance. Maddux, Scheiber, and Bass (1982) found that initial placement in a totally self-contained program for the gifted resulted in less favorable ratings by special class peers during the first year (Grade 5). However, by Grade 6, peer ratings had improved, suggesting that, with time and increasing familiarity, the peer relations of gifted children in special classes tend to normalize. Gallagher, Greenman, Karnes, and King (1960) also noted a decrease in popularity for gifted elementary children after their placement in a special program. Further research is necessary to clarify the effects of age and sex as they mediate the impact of special programming on the social adjustment of the gifted. A major goal of the present study was to determine how well peers accept gifted children in integrated settings, and to examine sex and age differences in this regard, as well as the impact of higher levels of IQ within the gifted range.

Attitudes Toward School

One other adjustment variable of educational relevance is the attitude of gifted children toward school. Two studies (Bracken, 1980; Tidwell, 1980) have found that gifted students enrolled full time in special classes had fairly positive attitudes toward school. Unfortunately, neither of these studies included an adequate comparison group of nongifted students. In a study that did use this control, Maugh (1977) found that gifted students placed in special classes displayed less favorable attitudes toward school than did their nongifted counterparts. However, another study by Miller (1983) reported no significant differences in attitudes between these two populations. Given these conflicting results, it was felt that further investigation of this relation was warranted. The present study was therefore designed to evaluate whether integrated gifted children, gifted children in self-contained classes, and control children differed in their attitudes toward school.

Method

Subjects

The *self-contained gifted* sample consisted of 71 Grade 5, 59 Grade 8, and 20 Grade 10 pupils enrolled in special classes for the gifted, and included all but one of the 9 schools in the city with such classes. These children had achieved an IQ score of 129 or higher on the Henmon-Nelson Test of Mental Ability (Henmon & Nelson, 1973) or a score above the 97th percentile on the verbal section of the Canadian Cognitive Abilities Test (CCAT; Thorndike & Hagen, 1982). The self-contained classes for Grade 5 gifted children provided special programming for almost the entire school day. In Grades 8 and 10, special programming was generally provided in core academic subjects, encompassing most of the school day. All of the special classes were located in regular school buildings.

The *integrated gifted* sample consisted of 72 Grade 5, 59 Grade 8, and 73 Grade 10 students who met the same IQ criteria but were not enrolled in special classes for gifted students. These subjects were drawn from a total of 24 elementary schools and 9 high schools that had agreed to participate out of a possible 46 schools in a school system with no self-contained classes for gifted students. There was no self-selection factor in this school system as to whether a gifted child was placed in a self-contained or integrated program because the children in the integrated gifted sample did not have the option of electing self-contained class placement. Had this option been available, a confounding variable would have been introduced, as it could have been argued that considerations of social relations, the focus of the study, had entered into decisions about class placement.

Both school boards were public school systems in the Ottawa-Carleton Regional Municipality; schools in rural areas were excluded from the school system with integrated gifted programs only to make it more comparable to the urban environment of the system with self-contained classes. All pupils from the schools involved who met the inclusion criteria for gifted subjects and whose parents consented participated in the study.

The two comparison groups were drawn from the classmates of the integrated gifted pupils. These control group children did not meet the identification criteria for giftedness, but had agreed to participate in the study. The same routinely administered IQ tests were used to determine both gifted and control groups. For each integrated gifted subject, one classmate was chosen at random to serve as a control, and another non-gifted classmate was matched on the basis of sex, age, and number of years in the school. It would have been extremely difficult to locate a suitable control group for the self-contained gifted sample, because these children had been transferred from their feeder schools. However, it was assumed that the control groups would provide appropriate comparisons not only for the integrated group but also for the self-contained sample.

Group IQ tests were administered as a routine procedure in these schools. Thus, the measures we used to screen subjects had been administered to all gifted and control subjects by school-board personnel as part of a regular testing program prior to the beginning of the study. In most

B.H. Schneider, M.R. Clegg, B.M. Byrne, J.E. Ledingham,
& G. Crombie

schools, only one of two screening measures was administered (either the Henmon-Nelson or the verbal section of the CCAT). To minimize discrepancies among schools in screening criteria, the verbal section of the CCAT was used, because of its high correlation with the Henmon-Nelson ($r = .63$ for 267 enrichment candidates within the same jurisdiction; Bonyun, 1984).

Table 1 shows the sex, age, and IQ distributions of the different groups. In general, all groups were similar in sex and age comparison. One major difference between gifted groups in sample size was due to a decision not to participate by one of the two high schools with self-contained classes for the gifted. As a result, there were only 20 Grade 10 students from self-contained classes as compared with 73 from integrated classes.

Instruments

PERCEIVED COMPETENCE SCALE FOR CHILDREN (PCSC; HARTER, 1982)

The PCSC is a 28-item self-report instrument designed to measure the elementary-school-aged child's perceived competence across the cognitive (academic), social, and physical domains, and yields as well a measure

Table 1
Descriptive Statistics

Subjects	Sex %				Mean age				Mean IQ			
	IG	SG	MC	RC	IG	SG	MC	RC	IG	SG	MC	RC
Grade 5												
Boys	47.2	47.9	51.4	47.9	9.94	9.88	9.95	10.12	132.65	137.31	112.43	108.80
Girls	52.8	52.1	48.6	52.1	9.84	9.87	9.94	10.00	131.55	136.25	109.83	112.00
n	72	71	72	71								
Grade 8												
Boys	44.1	50.8	37.3	43.1	13.04	12.80	13.18	13.20	133.31	135.89	106.71	113.75
Girls	55.9	49.2	62.7	56.9	13.06	12.76	13.08	13.06	133.21	134.75	110.03	111.32
n	59	59	59	58								
Grade 10												
Boys	42.5	65.0	42.4	46.9	14.87	14.50	14.93	14.83	131.29	134.00	113.32	114.63
Girls	57.5	35.0	57.6	53.1	14.93	14.71	15.00	15.00	130.41	133.00	114.74	112.13
n	73	20	66	64								

Note. IG = integrated gifted; SG = gifted in self-contained classrooms; MC = matched control; RC = random control.

of general self-esteem. The subscales have internal consistencies ranging from .73 to .86 and test-retest stability coefficients from .69 to .87 have been reported (Harter, 1982). This instrument was used for children in Grades 5 and 8.

SELF DESCRIPTION QUESTIONNAIRE III (SDQ; MARSH & O'NEILL, 1984)

The SDQ is a self-report instrument designed to measure the multidimensional self-concepts of adolescents and was used in this study with Grade 10 students. Subscales measuring academic self-concept (ASC), social self-concept (SSC, including same-sex and opposite-sex social relations), physical self-concept (PSC, including physical ability and physical appearance), and general self-concept (GSC) were used. Internal consistency reliability coefficients ranging from .81 to .96 and convergent validity coefficients (based on inferred self-concept ratings by significant others) ranging from .45 to .78 have been reported (Marsh & O'Neill, 1984).

REVISED CLASS PLAY (RCP; MASTEN, MORISON, & PELLEGRINI, 1985)

The RCP is a peer nomination instrument on which elementary school-aged children select classmates for positive and negative roles in an imaginary class play. It includes 15 positive roles that load on a factor of Sociability/Leadership, and 15 negative roles which load on two additional factors (Aggressive/Disruptive and Sensitive/Isolated). As a reminder to the children of who is eligible for votes, an alphabetical roster listing all students in the class (including absentees, but excluding those for whom parental consent was not obtained) was included with the answer sheet. Internal consistency coefficients for the three factors range from .81 to .95. Test-retest stability of the RCP over a 6-month period has been shown to range from .77 to .87 for each of its three factors, and validity of the instrument has been demonstrated by moderately high correlations between peer nomination scores and teacher ratings of social competence (Masten et al., 1985). This instrument was used for children in Grades 5 and 8.

ADJUSTMENT SCALES FOR SOCIOMETRIC EVALUATION OF SECONDARY-SCHOOL STUDENTS (ASSESS; PRINZ, SWAN, LIEBERT, WEINTRAUB, & NEALE, 1978)

This peer nomination instrument was used to evaluate the Grade 10 samples. Five scales have been developed and cross-validated; Aggression/Disruptiveness, Withdrawal, Anxiety, Social Competence, and Academic Difficulty. The Aggression/Disruptiveness, Withdrawal, and Social Competence scales are quite similar to the three factors of the RCP. Coefficient alpha values for these dimensions are .96, .88, and .95, respectively, and after 3 weeks, test-retest stability values ranged from .72 to .91 (Prinz et al., 1978).

FEELINGS ABOUT SCHOOL (FAS; BILLS, 1975)

The instrument used in the present study was a 50-item short version of the scale. The FAS is one of a group of affective measures that together make up *A System for Assessing Affectivity* (Bills, 1975). The instrument is designed to measure a student's attitude toward school with respect to academic subjects, peers, teachers, overall milieu, scholastic standards, and provision of extracurricular activities. Split-half and internal consistency reliability coefficients of .88 and .91, respectively, have been reported for the short form; this short form was administered in all three grades.

B.H. Schneider, M.R. Clegg, B.M. Byrne, J.E. Ledingham,
& G. Crombie

Procedures

After parental consent was received, peer nomination forms were administered in each class that had at least one integrated gifted child. Peer nominations were not collected in self-contained classes because the primary question of interest involved the adequacy of gifted children's social adjustment relative to that of children not identified as gifted. However, all gifted and control children in integrated classes nominated themselves for appropriate items on the RCP.

Results

Comparison of Control Groups

Sex×Group Status multivariate analysis of variance (MANOVA) comparisons of the two control groups were carried out on the dependent measures. A separate MANOVA was performed for each grade level, and separately for the peer nomination and self-concept scores, respectively. For Grades 8 and 10, the control groups were not significantly different from each other. In Grade 5, however, there were some differences between them. The multivariate F for the RCP peer nominations was significant in Grade 5 for group status, $F(3,129)=2.72$, $p<.05$. Univariate analyses indicated that mean RCP withdrawal ratings were higher for the random control (RC) group than for the matched control group, $F(1,131)=6.59$, $p<.05$.

The multivariate F for the group status effect on self-concept scores was also significant, $F(4,122)=4.65$, $p<.001$, with univariate analyses indicating that mean perceived social competence scores were higher for the matched control group than for the random control group, $F(1,125)=5.63$, $p<.05$. Although there were no theoretical reasons to explain these differences, we decided that they were important enough to preclude combining the two groups in further analyses. To maintain consistency, the two control groups were not combined at any grade level.

MANOVA Results: Self-Concept and Peer Nominations

Separate MANOVAs were performed on the self-concept scales and on the peer nomination dimensions. Data from each grade level were analyzed separately. A 4 (group status) by 2 (sex) model was used for the MANOVAs. To reduce error rates, MANOVAs were followed by univariate MANOVAs only if the overall multivariate F was significant (Hummel & Sligo, 1971). The results are presented separately by grade in the following sections. Because no multivariate interaction effects reached significance, only the main effects are reported.

Grade 5

RESULTS FOR GROUP EFFECT

Self-concept. The MANOVA main effect for group status was significant, $F(12,662)=5.59, p<.01$. Subsequent univariate analyses indicated that the groups differed in terms of ASC, $F(3,253)=9.89, p<.001, MS_e=14.80$, $\eta^2=.10$. Tukey post hoc post analyses revealed that the ASC scores of the integrated gifted group were significantly higher than those for all of the other groups (including the self-contained gifted). There were no significant findings for general, social, or physical self-concept. Means and standard deviations on self-concept and peer nomination measures for subjects in Grades 5, 8 and 10 are presented in Table 2.

Peer nominations. The MANOVA main effect for group status was significant, $F(6,398)=4.47, p<.01$. Univariate analyses of variance indicated that there were significant differences on all three of the dimensions as a function of group status: aggression, $F(2,201)=4.53, p<.05, \eta^2=.03$, and

Table 2
Self Concept and Peer Nominations: Grade 5

| | Boys | | | | Girls | | | |
| | Gifted | | Control | | Gifted | | Control | |
Dependent variable	IG	SG	MC	RC	IG	SG	MC	RC
Self-concept								
General								
M	21.3	21.0	22.1	18.8	20.9	19.1	20.2	20.3
SD	4.6	3.3	4.4	4.3	4.9	3.5	4.3	4.4
Academic								
M	23.2	21.2	20.8	20.6	23.5	20.0	19.6	20.5
SD	3.4	3.2	3.8	4.4	3.3	3.0	4.6	4.8
Social								
M	20.0	21.0	20.5	17.6	19.3	19.2	20.8	19.3
SD	4.3	3.3	4.9	5.1	5.6	4.3	4.3	5.1
Physical								
M	18.5	19.8	20.4	19.8	17.7	17.3	18.8	19.8
SD	4.5	5.4	5.0	4.1	4.9	4.0	4.4	3.9
Peer nominations								
Social competence								
M	20.4	—	14.4	13.8	23.4	—	15.3	12.9
SD	14.8	—	13.1	15.2	18.0	—	10.5	12.9
Aggression								
M	10.4	—	13.2	21.1	6.1	—	7.5	9.8
SD	11.5	—	12.5	19.7	9.0	—	9.6	10.8
Withdrawal								
M	4.9	—	6.1	11.0	11.1	—	7.9	12.0
SD	5.3	—	7.2	11.7	16.5	—	9.7	12.4

Note. IG = integrated gifted; SG = gifted in self-contained classrooms;
MC = matched controls; RC = random control.

social competence $F(2,201)=7.35$, $p<.001$, $MS_e=203.85$, $\eta^2=.07$. Post hoc analyses showed that the integrated gifted group had significantly lower scores on aggression than did the random control group, and higher scores on social competence than either of the control groups.

RESULTS FOR SEX EFFECT

Only for the peer ratings was the MANOVA main effect for sex significant, $F(3,199)=9.65$, $p<.001$. Univariate analyses indicated that this effect was significant for the variables of aggression, $F(1,201)=16.13$, $p<.001$, $MS_e=149.46$, $\eta^2=.08$, and withdrawal, $F(1,201)=3.98$, $p<.05$, $MS_e=125.16$, $\eta^2=.02$, but not for social competence. Boys had higher scores for aggression, girls for withdrawal.

Grade 8

RESULTS FOR GROUP EFFECT

Group means on the self-concept ratings and peer nominations are presented as a function of sex in Table 3. There were no significant differences for the peer nomination dimensions.

The MANOVA group status effect for self-concept was significant, $F(12,580)=4.82$, $p<.001$. Univariate analyses of variance indicated that there were significant differences among the group means on the ASC scores, $F(3,222)=14.63$, $p<.001$, $MS_e=13.71$, $\eta^2=.16$. Post hoc analyses showed that the integrated gifted group had higher scores than did all three of the other groups, including the self-contained gifted. This latter group however, had higher mean scores than did the matched control group.

RESULTS FOR SEX EFFECT

Only for self-concept was the MANOVA main effect for sex significant $F(4,219)=9.17$, $p<.001$. Univariate analyses of variance indicated that the mean scores were higher for boys than for girls on the GSC, $F(1,222)=8.28$, $p<.01$, $MS_e=18.94$, $\eta^2=.04$, and PSC, $F(1,222)=9.98$, $p<.01$, $MS_e=24.80$, $\eta^2=.02$.

Grade 10

RESULTS FOR GROUP EFFECT

Group means for self-concept and peer nomination measures are presented as a function of sex in Table 4. The MANOVA group status effect on peer nomination measures was not significant.

The MANOVA main effect of group status for the self-concept ratings was significant, $F(18,529)=2.16$, $p<.01$, with univariate analyses of variance indicating that the significant group differences were on the ASC scores, $F(3,192)=6.02$, $p<.001$, $MS_e=143.58$, $\eta^2=.09$. Post hoc analyses

Table 3
Self-Concept and Peer Nominations: Grade 8

	Boys				Girls			
	Gifted		Control		Gifted		Control	
Dependent variable	IG	SG	MC	RC	IG	SG	MC	RC
	Self-concept							
General								
M	20.8	20.1	21.7	20.0	18.9	19.1	19.1	18.8
SD	3.5	4.8	3.1	4.3	5.2	3.9	4.7	4.3
Academic								
M	24.4	21.4	21.4	21.0	23.6	21.8	18.6	20.4
SD	2.1	3.4	3.3	3.8	3.8	3.9	4.1	4.3
Social								
M	18.3	18.3	20.6	19.1	19.6	19.6	20.2	20.7
SD	5.3	4.9	4.7	4.8	4.7	4.0	4.0	4.3
Physical								
M	19.8	20.1	19.4	21.1	16.4	18.3	18.7	18.8
SD	4.8	5.5	4.3	4.8	4.7	4.7	5.4	4.6
	Peer nominations							
Social competence								
M	16.4	—	17.0	22.8	17.9	—	15.8	18.9
SD	12.8	—	18.8	21.6	12.0	—	15.0	21.6
Aggression								
M	12.0	—	9.8	13.2	9.3	—	12.0	13.1
SD	13.3	—	12.0	12.4	10.3	—	13.6	13.8
Withdrawal								
M	14.6	—	15.1	14.0	9.2	—	14.2	8.5
SD	15.5	—	16.0	17.7	11.1	—	14.7	9.5

Note. IG = integrated gifted; SG = gifted in self-contained classrooms; MC = matched control; RC = random control.

showed higher mean scores on ASC for the integrated gifted group as compared with the two control groups.

RESULTS FOR SEX EFFECT

Self-concept. The MANOVA main effect for sex was significant, $F(6,187)=3.91$, $p<.001$. Univariate analyses of variance indicated that mean scores were higher for boys than for girls on PSC scores for physical ability, $F(1,192)=8.22$, $p<.001$, $MS_e=202.84$, $\eta^2=.04$; Appearance, $F(1,192)=8.19$, $p<.001$, $MS_e=115.15$, $\eta^2=.04$; and GSC, $F(1,192)=5.00$, $p<.05$, $MS_e=136.30$, $\eta^2=.03$.

Peer nominations. The MANOVA main effect for sex was significant, $F(5,192)=5.94$, $p<.001$. Girls had higher social competence scores, $F(1,96)=8.23$, $p<.001$, $MS_e=190.79$, $\eta^2=.04$, whereas boys had higher withdrawal scores, $F(1,96)=12.93$, $p<.001$, $MS_e=142.13$, $\eta^2=.06$, and

Table 4
Self-Concept and Peer Nominations: Grade 10

| | Boys | | | | Girls | | | |
| | Gifted | | Control | | Gifted | | Control | |
Dependent variable	IG	SG	MC	RC	IG	SG	MC	RC
	Self-concept							
General								
M	68.2	73.8	71.2	75.1	71.8	71.7	66.2	63.4
SD	15.9	9.7	8.8	8.2	10.4	8.8	11.1	14.3
Academic								
M	60.7	54.1	56.8	54.0	62.4	57.5	55.5	51.5
SD	11.7	12.9	11.7	14.1	10.5	2.2	12.3	12.6
Social (opposite sex)								
M	50.5	49.4	51.9	56.7	56.7	53.3	56.9	54.1
SD	15.4	12.2	11.8	10.4	13.3	10.8	11.6	13.1
Social (same-sex)								
M	61.6	60.9	56.2	56.5	60.2	58.0	58.1	57.6
SD	9.5	9.0	8.9	8.3	9.9	6.5	9.0	9.1
Physical appearance								
M	49.7	57.5	53.6	55.9	50.8	47.3	49.9	45.9
SD	10.8	6.9	13.6	9.9	9.7	6.6	9.6	12.5
Physical ability								
M	62.4	65.4	61.9	64.1	57.1	55.5	56.1	58.6
SD	12.0	10.6	13.4	13.6	16.5	17.0	15.2	14.0
	Peer nominations							
Social competence								
M	15.0	—	12.5	14.0	19.8	—	20.3	18.4
SD	11.7	—	13.4	15.6	11.8	—	16.2	13.7
Aggression								
M	6.7	—	4.6	8.5	4.9	—	5.0	4.9
SD	9.1	—	7.8	10.3	6.2	—	7.2	6.3
Withdrawal								
M	14.4	—	13.9	12.1	7.9	—	6.6	7.7
SD	14.2	—	14.8	12.1	11.2	—	9.8	9.5
Anxiety								
M	5.8	—	7.3	5.2	5.2	—	5.2	7.1
SD	5.8	—	5.9	4.7	5.8	—	4.9	9.7
Academic								
M	7.3	—	6.0	6.8	3.1	—	4.3	4.8
SD	10.6	—	7.0	7.7	6.0	—	6.4	5.0

Note. IG = integrated gifted; SG = gifted in self-contained classrooms; MC = matched control; RC = random control.

higher academic difficulty scores, $F(1,96)=6.85$, $p<.01$, $MS_e=51.99$, $\eta^2=.03$.

Correlations Between IQ and Social Competence

Of particular interest were any differences in the relation between IQ and self-perceptions of social competence within three of the groups: integrated gifted, self-contained gifted, and random controls. The random controls were assumed to be more representative of the general population for these analyses than were the matched controls. Pearson correlation coefficients were computed separately within each group between IQ scores and self-nominations on the sociability/leadership dimension of the RCP in Grades 5 and 8, and between IQ scores and self-nominations on the social competence dimensions of ASSESS in Grade 10. There was a significant negative correlation between IQ and self-nominations for sociability/leadership in the integrated group in Grade 5, $r=-.22$, $p<.05$, and in Grade 8, $r=-.23$, $p<.05$. The correlation was not significant in Grade 10. Correlations between IQ and self-perceptions of social competence were not significant at any grade level for the self-contained gifted group. However, in contrast to the negative correlation between these variables for the integrated gifted, IQ and self-nominations of social competence within the random control group were found to be positively correlated in Grade 5, $r=.52$, $p<.001$, and there was a trend in the same direction in Grade 8, $r=.20$, $p<.10$. The correlation between IQ and self-nominations of social competence for the random control group in Grade 10 was not significant.

A second set of correlations was calculated to determine whether acceptance by peers was related to the difference in IQ between gifted and control classmates. Within each integrated class, mean IQ scores were calculated separately for the gifted subjects and for the combined matched and random control subjects. Difference scores between these two means were then correlated for all classes at a given grade level with the mean peer nomination scores on the social competence dimension for the gifted subjects in the class. The correlation between IQ difference scores for each class and for the mean peer nomination score on sociability/leadership for integrated gifted subjects in each class was significant and negative in Grade 5, $r=-.33$, $p<.05$, but not at any other grade level.

Feelings About School

The FAS was the only measure whose wording was suitable for use in all three grades. A Grade×Sex×Group Status analysis of variance (ANOVA) was performed on the data. Although group status was not a significant source of variation, grade level was, $F(2,656)=26.27$, $p<.001$. Mean FAS scores were significantly lower in the higher grades than in the lower grades, indicating that older children's feelings about the school experience were less positive. There was also a significant Grade×Sex interaction, $F(2,656)=4.54$, $p<.05$, with girls having higher scores than boys in Grade 5, and lower scores than boys in Grade 10. These data are presented in Figure 1.

B.H. Schneider, M.R. Clegg, B.M. Byrne, J.E. Ledingham, & G. Crombie

Summary of Major Findings

SELF-CONCEPT

On only one aspect of self-concept, perceived cognitive competence, did the groups differ significantly. The integrated gifted group's ASC was higher than that of the two control groups in all three grades. The self-

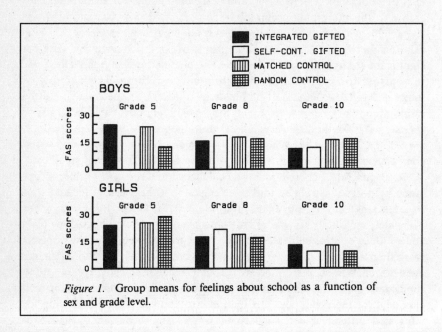

Figure 1. Group means for feelings about school as a function of sex and grade level.

contained gifted had higher perceived cognitive competence scores than did the matched controls in Grade 8 only.

With regard to school placement effects for the gifted (self-contained vs. integrated), the only significant difference was found on perceived cognitive competence: in Grades 5 and 8, the integrated gifted had higher ASC scores than did the self-contained gifted. Differences were nonsignificant but in the same direction for the students in Grade 10. Thus, although equally gifted, the self-contained gifted tended to view themselves as less academically competent than did their counterparts in integrated classes.

PEER ACCEPTANCE

The integrated gifted were seen by peers as more socially competent and as having more leadership skills than were the control groups, but only in Grade 5.

SEX AND IQ DIFFERENCES

Contrary to predictions, there were no significant interactions of gifted status with sex, indicating that there were similar patterns in the social development of gifted and normal children as a function of sex.

Although higher IQ within the normal range was generally associated with enhanced social competence, the correlations tended to be in the negative direction for the gifted groups. The brighter children among the integrated gifted group tended to nominate themselves less often for social competence items. Also, the greater the difference in IQ between gifted and control children in the same class, the lower was the peer acceptance of the gifted child, at least in Grade 5.

ATTITUDES TOWARD SCHOOL

There were no significant differences in attitudes toward school between gifted and nongifted children, or between gifted children in regular and self-contained classes. However, there were differences by grade and sex: Both boys and girls in the higher grades had less positive feelings about school. This was more pronounced for girls than for boys: Girls felt better than boys about school in Grade 5, but worse in Grade 10.

Discussion

These results in general portray the gifted child as a relatively well-adjusted individual. There is little support here for the folk notion of the bright child as a social isolate, or for the myth that the intellectually gifted are destined to excel in all areas of their development. Conclusions from research on the social development of gifted children must take into account developmental differences. Gifted children in Grade 5 were held higher in the esteem of their peers than were controls. This effect was not evident in later years, where gifted children were not differentiated on social behavior from their average classmates.

The findings related to self-concept are not inconsistent with social comparison theory, and with inferences about the effects of the repeated task success of gifted children in regular classrooms. Differences in self-perceptions between gifted children in regular and special programs were limited to the academic domain. This is logical, as academic self-perceptions of the integrated gifted should more directly reflect favorable comparisons with classmates who are less successful in school, as well as differential teacher responses to their work. Although academic success does not appear to elevate social and personal self-perceptions, it is also important to remember that the integrated gifted group did not display any deficits in the personal, emotional and social aspects of self-evaluation.

This underscores the importance of domain-specific conceptualizations for the analysis of self-perceptions.

We did not explore possible differences in classroom organization that may mediate the relation between school program and student social development: Classrooms vary greatly in terms of the importance of ability grouping, the visibility of the basis for such grouping, and the amount of comparison of students' work (Marshall & Weinstein, 1984). In some classrooms, there are different groupings according to distinct task-specific skills rather than a single grouping procedure that applies to all subjects (Rosenholtz & Wilson, 1980; Simpson, 1981). The effects of academic talent may be attenuated in environments where explicit evaluations of academic ability are less central to the structure and organization of the classroom.

Although we obtained data in three grades, there are important limitations to the comparability of the data at the three grade levels. Separate ANOVAs and correlations were computed at each grade level for all instruments except the FAS. Grade was not introduced as an additional variable in the analyses because different instruments were used in elementary and high schools to accommodate their different social realities and reading levels. Further limitations on comparisons among our three grade levels are dictated by the tendency for congregated special programs for the gifted to encompass less of the pupils' school day in the higher grades.

Some caution is indicated in the interpretation of these findings because of several limitations of the study. As in many other studies of gifted children, it was necessary for us to rely on preexisting group test data for the identification of the gifted sample. The alternative—administering individual tests of intelligence to all children in the target grades in each of the schools that participated—was simply impossible. These group tests tend to have a rather low ceiling, which limits their value when one is discriminating between the very highly gifted children and the moderately gifted. However, despite the probable existence of an IQ ceiling effect, the brighter children in our gifted sample nominated themselves as less socially competent than their moderately gifted peers, at least in Grade 5.

Owing to our sampling procedure and screening measures, the data do not accurately represent the full range of IQ values. Nevertheless, they do suggest that if we were able to generate a complete scatterplot describing the relation between IQ and social competence, that relation would not be fully linear. After a certain maximal IQ level, social competence seems to decline.

The group tests tapped only certain gifted behaviors. For this reason, some gifted children, such as the artistically creative and those whose cognitive strengths were specific to certain areas of intellect, were not included. IQ was used as the most valid, reliable means of identifying a population of gifted youngsters for a large-sample study. This does not imply disagreement with the widespread call for identification criteria that go beyond IQ to other factors that help determine the actualization of intellectual potential (cf. Sternberg & Davidson, 1986). Our sample was restricted to urbanized areas where parental education levels exceeded those of the Canadian national average. The average IQs for control subjects, although significantly lower than those of the gifted groups, were considerably above average. Nevertheless, the peer acceptance of gifted children was lower in classrooms in which there was a greater discrepancy between the IQs of the gifted and control youngsters. The social status of gifted children in less privileged areas may be quite different from the optimistic situation reported here.

There are certain limitations to the comparability of our gifted samples from self-contained and integrated programs. The subjects were not randomly assigned to self-contained or integrated programs. Although this would have provided a more definite guarantee of comparability of the samples, this would have been impossible under existing special education legislation in Ontario, as in most other jurisdictions.

The size of our sample and the number of schools from which it was drawn are a clear strength of this study. The exception is the Grade 10 self-contained group, for which only 20 participants were available. Those results should be considered very tentative until they are replicated.

Some of the studies reviewed earlier (e.g., Maddux et al., 1982) have suggested that gifted children in self-contained programs display lower self-concepts and less satisfying peer relations than their counterparts in integrated settings. The results of the present study, however, indicate that the enhanced academic input provided by the special classes can be accomplished without detriment (or benefit) to the children's self-perceptions of their social adjustment. It must be emphasized that this study is not intended as an evaluation of any existing program. To adequately evaluate the impact of special class programming on gifted youngsters, it would be necessary to establish the degree to which their cognitive as well as social development was facilitated. That information was not available here.

We found no significant differences between gifted and nongifted children in terms of attitudes toward school. We might expect the academically talented child to perceive school more positively than others just as the athlete should perceive the gym, and the actor theater. On the other hand, the gifted child may have higher standards and tend to be more critical. Nevertheless, those who plan educational programs for the gifted should renew their efforts to capture the interest of these children.

It may be profitable to conceptualize the gifted population as a heterogeneous one, rather than searching for attributes that pertain to the entire group. Many parents are deeply concerned about the social adjustment of their gifted youngsters, and about the effects of academic talent on their children's peer relations. Rather than dismiss these as isolated or exaggerated concerns, they should be taken seriously. The minority of gifted children who do suffer peer relations difficulties may require specific assistance in overcoming them.

References

Abroms, K.I. (1985). Social giftedness and its relationship with intellectual giftedness. In J. Freeman (Ed.), *The psychology of gifted children* (pp. 201-218). Chichester, UK: Wiley.

Austin, A.B., & Draper, D.C. (1981). Peer relationships of the academically gifted: A review. *Gifted Child Quarterly, 25*, 129-133.

Bills, R.E. (1975). *A system for assessing affectivity.* University: University of Alabama Press.

Bonyun, R. (1984). *Enrichment candidates: Basic statistics.* Unpublished manuscript, Research Department, Ottawa Board of Education, Ottawa, ON.

Bracken, B.A. (1980). Comparison of self-attitudes of gifted children and children in a non-gifted comparative group. *Psychological Reports, 47*, 715-718.

Brophy, J.E. (1983). Research on the self-prophesy and teacher expectations. *Journal of Educational Psychology, 71*, 733-750.

Byrne, B.M., & Shavelson, R.J. (1986). On the structure of adolescent self-concept. *Journal of Educational Psychology, 78*, 474-481.

Cox, J., Daniel, N., & Boston, B.O. (1986). *Educating able learners: Programs and promising practices.* Austin, TX: University of Texas Press.

Festinger, L.A. (1954). A theory of social comparison processes. *Human Relations, 7*, 117-140.

Gallagher, J.J. (1958). Peer acceptance of highly gifted children in elementary school. *Elementary School Journal, 58*, 465-470.

Gallagher, J.J., Greenman, M., Karnes, M., & King, A. (1960). Individual classroom adjustments for gifted children in elementary schools. *Exceptional Children, 26*, 409-432.

Gamble, A.D. (1975). The gifted and their non-gifted peers. *North Carolina Association for the Gifted and Talented Quarterly Journal, 2*, 22-31.

Getzels, J.W., & Jackson, P.W. (1982). *Creativity and intelligence: Explorations with gifted children.* New York, NY: Wiley.

Harter, S. (1982). The Perceived Competence Scale for Children. *Child Development, 53*, 87-97.

Henmon, C., & Nelson, M.J. (1973). *Henmon-Nelson Tests of Mental Ability.* Boston, MA: Houghton Mifflin.

Henson, F.O. (1976). *Mainstreaming the gifted.* Austin, TX: Learning Concepts Press.

Hollingworth, L.S. (1926). *Gifted children: Their nature and nurture.* New York, NY: MacMillan.

Hollingworth, L.S. (1942). *Children above 180 IQ. Stanford-Binet: Origin and development.* Yonkers, NY: World Book.

Hummel, T.J., & Sligo, J.R. (1971). Empirical comparison of univariate and multivariate analysis of variance procedures. *Psychological Bulletin, 76*, 49-57.

Janos, P., Fung, H., & Robinson, N. (1985). Perceptions of deviation and self-concept within an intellectually gifted sample. *Gifted Child Quarterly, 29*, 78-82.

Jellen, H.G., & Verduin, J.R. (1986). *Handbook for the differential education of the gifted.* Carbondale, IL: Southern Illinois University Press.

Keisler, E.R. (1955). Peer group ratings of high school pupils with high and low school marks. *Journal of Experimental Education, 23,* 375-378.

Ketcham, B., & Snyder, R. (1977). Self attitudes of gifted students as measured by the Piers-Harris children's self-concept scale. *Psychological Reports, 40,* 111-116.

Kulik, C.C., & Kulik, J.A. (1982). Effects of ability grouping on secondary school students: A meta-analysis of evaluation findings. *American Educational Research Journal, 19,* 415-428.

Lehman, E., & Erdwins, C. (1981). Social and emotional adjustment of young intellectually gifted children. *Gifted Children Quarterly, 25,* 134-138.

Levine, J.M., & Wang, M.C. (Eds.) (1983). *Teacher and student perceptions: Implications for learning.* Hillsdale, NJ: Erlbaum.

Maddux, C.D., Scheiber, L.M., & Bass, J.E. (1982). Self-concept and social distance in gifted children. *Gifted Children Quarterly, 26,* 77-81.

Marland, S.P., Jr. (1972). *Education of the gifted and talented.* Washington, DC: U.S. Government Printing Office.

Marsh, H.W., & O'Neill, R. (1984). Self Description Questionnaire III: The construct validity of multi-dimensional self concept ratings by late adolescents. *Journal of Educational Measurement, 21,* 153-174.

Marsh, H.W., & Shavelson, R.J. (1985). Self-concept: Its multifaced, hierarchical structure. *Educational Psychologist, 20,* 107-123.

Marshall, H.M., & Weinstein, R.S. (1984). Classroom factors affecting students' self-evaluations: An interactional model. *Review of Educational Research, 54,* 301-325.

Marshall, H.M., Weinstein, R.S., Sharp, L., & Brattesani, K.A. (1982, March). *Student descriptions of the educational environment for high and low achievers.* Paper presented at the annual meeting of the American Educational Research Association, New York, NY.

Masten, A.S., Morison, P., & Pellegrini, D.S. (1985). A revised class play method of peer assessment. *Developmental Psychology, 21,* 523-533.

Maugh, V.M. (1977). An analysis of attitudes of selected academically talented elementary school students toward self-concept and school and selected elementary teachers toward the academically talented student (Doctoral dissertation, University of Southern Mississippi, 1976). *Dissertation Abstracts International, 38,* 2458-A.

Miller, W. (1983). A comparative analysis of segregated versus non-segregated educational programming for school gifted students on self-concept and selected other variables (Doctoral dissertation, Pennsylvania State University, 1982). *Dissertation Abstracts International, 43,* 2288-A.

O'Such, K., Twyla, G., & Havertape, J. (1979). Group differences in self-concept among handicapped, normal, and gifted learners. *The Humanist Educator, 18,* 15-22.

Prinz, R.L., Swan, G., Liebert, D., Weintraub, S., & Neale, J. (1978). ASSESS: Adjustment Scales for sociometric evaluation of secondary-school students. *Journal of Abnormal Child Psychology, 6,* 493-501.

Rosenholtz, S.J., & Wilson, B. (1980). The effects of classroom structure on shared perceptions of ability. *American Educational Research Journal, 17,* 75-82.

Savage, L.B. (1985, August). *Empathy in gifted children: Gift or curse?* Paper presented at the Sixth World Congress on the Gifted and Talented, Hamburg, (West) Germany.

Schneider, B.H. (1987). *The gifted child in peer group perspective.* New York, NY: Springer-Verlag.

Simpson, C. (1981). Classroom structure and the organization of ability. *Sociology of Education, 54,* 120-132.

Solano, C.H. (1976, September). *Teacher and pupil stereotypes of gifted boys and girls*. Paper presented at the Annual Conference of the American Psychological Association, Washington, DC.

Sternberg, R.J., & Davidson, J.E. (Eds.) (1986). *Conceptions of giftedness*. Cambridge, UK: Cambridge University Press.

Thorndike, R.L., & Hagen, E. (1982). *Canadian Cognitive Abilities Test*. Scarborough, ON: Nelson Canada.

Tidwell, R. (1980). A psycho-educational profile of 1,593 gifted high school students. *Gifted Child Quarterly, 24*, 63-68.

Walters, J., & Gardner, H. (1986). The crystallizing experience: Discovering an intellectual gift. In R.J. Sternberg and J.E. Davidson (Eds.), *Conceptions of giftedness*. Cambridge, UK: Cambridge University Press.

Bilingualism and Multiculturalism

One area in which Canada differs from the United States is in its endorsement of bilingual education. In every province, increasing numbers of children are attending immersion schools in order to learn Canada's other official language. Consistent with Canada's commitment to multiculturalism, increasing numbers of minority language children are attending heritage language classes in order to learn or maintain the language of their country of origin. In terms of research in these areas, Canadian educational psychologists continue to make substantial contributions. In terms of broader social implications, it remains to be seen whether this new concern with appreciating and empowering *all* the members of Canada's cultural mosaic will be sufficient to keep us from fragmenting into two or more distinct societies.

The four articles in this section deal with Anglophone, minority language, and Francophone students. Despite their generally favourable reaction to the immersion option, one concern of Anglophone parents and educators is whether children should enrol in early immersion programmes, beginning in kindergarten or first grade, or wait until later. Some parents favour the latter option so their children can get a good grounding in English, while educators have pragmatic concerns such as finding an adequate number of French-speaking teachers to staff immersion schools. The evidence presented by Day and Shapson suggests that, on balance, early immersion is better, not only for the development of language skills but also for the cultivation of positive attitudes about the French language and French speakers. Although early immersion and late immersion students in the three school districts included in their sample did not differ in French language arts skills, early immersion students in all three districts had better French comprehension than their late immersion counterparts. Early immersion students were also more positive than late immersion students about bilingualism and French-Canadian culture and, in one district, were less anxious about using French.

But what happens to one's English language skills if French is the predominant language of instruction throughout elementary school? The Grade 8 Anglophone students in Laing's study provide a credible answer to this question. Since kindergarten, they had attended a French-speaking school, in which English instruction did not start until Grade 4 and then was limited to 40 to 50 minutes a day. Laing's study is also informative because students were assessed in terms of their ability to write compositions rather than on standardized tests of discrete language skills. His results should be reassuring to potential parents considering the pros and cons of French language immersion. Laing's Grade 8 immersion students did not differ from Grade 8 students attending an English-speaking school on any of the measures of writing ability used. These results are also interesting theoretically, since they suggest that children are capable of transferring or generalizing information learned in one language about literacy-related skills to another language, with little formal instruction in how to do so.

What about children whose first language is neither French nor English? Should they be encouraged to learn both official languages or is this imposing too much of a cognitive burden on them? In their first study, Swain and Lapkin compared the French proficiency of three groups of Grade 8 French immersion students; those whose first language was English, those whose first language was Italian (a Romance language closely related to French), and those whose first language was one of a number of non-Romance languages. The three groups did not differ significantly in their French vocabulary use, and the two minority language student groups demonstrated significantly better grammatical knowledge than the English first language group. Although the Italian speakers tended to do better than the non-Romance language speakers, the differences between the two groups were not significant. Swain and Lapkin reasoned that the non-Romance students did almost as well as the Italian students because, in addition to speaking their heritage languages, they were more proficient than the Italians at writing them. The second study reported in this article supported this conjecture. Literate minority language students, who could read and write as well as speak their first language, were significantly more proficient in French than either the English first language students or the minority language students who could only speak their first language. Literacy skills are an important component of heritage language programs. These results suggest, therefore, that the inclusion of heritage language classes in the regular school curriculum would enhance the first and third language performance of minority language children.

The fourth article in this section is important because it provides a Francophone perspective on bilingualism. The Grade 12 Francophone students surveyed by Landry, Allard, and Théberge attended French-speaking high schools in Manitoba, Saskatchewan, and Alberta, provinces in which Francophone Canadians are a minority. All the students in the study spoke both French and English, and the authors wanted to determine whether the students' bilingualism could best be characterized as additive or subtractive. Additive bilingualism occurs when acquisition of the second language does not diminish use of one's first language or positive identification with one's first language community. Subtractive bilingualism refers to the loss of first language ability and the development of negative feelings about one's first language and first language community. Previous studies have indicated that Francophones outside Quebec demonstrate subtractive bilingualism, and the results of this study were no different. In theory, strongly Francophone school and family influences could counterbalance the dominance of English language and culture in the students' environment. In practice, however, the vitality of their Francophone identity only came close to that found among Quebec Francophone students for those students attending high French ambience schools or those attending moderate French ambience schools who also had high French ambience families.

A Comparison Study of Early and Late French Immersion Programs in British Columbia

Elaine M. Day and Stan Shapson,
Simon Fraser University

This study compared the French language skills and attitudes of grade 7 early and late immersion students in three school districts in British Columbia. Statistical comparisons in each district revealed that only in one (District C) did early immersion students perform significantly higher than late immersion students in both French language arts and French comprehension. In the two other districts, early immersion students performed significantly higher than late immersion students in French comprehension but not in French language arts. Early and late immersion students in one district (District A) did not differ significantly on attitudinal measures, whereas in the other two districts early immersion students displayed significantly more positive attitudes to their schooling than their late immersion counterparts. The British Columbia results show some of the same variations that have been found in comparisons of early and late program options conducted elsewhere in Canada.

*   *   *

IN THE LAST DECADE BRITISH COLUMBIA HAS DRAMATICALLY EXPANDED second-language programs that teach all or a major part of the curriculum in French. Until 1976, early French immersion was the only option other than the basic French as a second language, and it was offered in only three of the province's seventy-five school districts. However, since then the number of school districts offering early immersion has risen to nearly forty, and late immersion programs have been introduced and are offered in approximately twenty school districts.[1] Enrolment in immersion programs at the elementary level has risen from under 1,000 in 1976 to nearly 20,000 students.

Because of this rapid growth, British Columbia's Ministry of Education contracted an evaluation study of immersion programs on a provincial level.[2] One objective of the provincial study was to compare the attitudes and French language skills of students enrolled in the early and late immersion programs at grade 7, the final year of elementary school in British Columbia. The *early immersion* program begins in kindergarten and offers 100% instruction in French from kindergarten through grade 2, 80% instruction in French in grade 3, and from 50 to 70% in grades 4 to 7. The *late immersion* program is a two-year program beginning in grade 6 offering from 60 to 100% instruction in French in grades 6 and 7. In secondary school (grades 8-12), both early and late immersion students are offered a follow-up program (secondary immersion), in which French is the language of instruction for 40 to 50% of the time.

Literature Review

Considerable research has been conducted on early and late immersion programs in many regions of Canada (e.g., in British Columbia, Shapson & Day, 1982a, 1982b; in Quebec, Genesee, 1978a, 1978-1979; in New Brunswick, Gray, 1981, 1985; and in Ontario, Swain & Lapkin, 1982). This research has consistently demonstrated that students in both programs (a) suffer no harm to their cognitive or native-language (English) development through being schooled in a second language; (b) master content subjects such as mathematics and science as well as their unilingually educated peers; and (c) develop high levels of French language skills.

Because each program has proven effective at enabling students to develop high levels of proficiency in French and at the same time to maintain normal academic progress, studies have also been undertaken to compare the levels of French language proficiency attained by students in the two programs. The relative effectiveness of the programs raises theoretical issues in second-language learning having to do with the supposed advantages of an early starting age and greater amounts of instructional time for achievement in a second language. The benefits of an early starting age have been debated extensively for several years (for reviews, see Genesee, 1978b; Krashen, Long, & Scarcella, 1979; Stern, 1976). However, empirical studies have uncovered little evidence of the superiority of younger second language learners. They suggest on the contrary that older learners are quicker and more efficient because of their more advanced cognitive skills. Nevertheless, because research has also demonstrated a strong relationship between achievement and amount of time spent learning a second language (Carroll, 1975; Swain, 1978), many researchers have hypothesized that those who start earlier may ultimately be able to reach a higher level of language proficiency (Genesee, 1978b; Stern, 1976). Since early and late immersion programs differ in the starting age (age 5-6 years rather than 12-14 years) and in the number of years spent in immersion (12-13 years rather than 6-7 years), comparisons of outcomes of the two programs can shed light on this hypothesis.

Comparisons of the French language skills attained by students in early and late immersion programs have been conducted in the Protestant School Board of Greater Montreal (Genesee, 1978-1979; Genesee & Morcos, 1978), in the Ottawa and Carleton School Boards (Morrison, Walsh, Pawley, & Bonyun, 1979; Pawley & Walsh, 1980) and more recently in the provinces of Manitoba (CERCO [Centre for Research and Consultation], 1983) and New Brunswick (Lapkin & Swain, 1984).[3] These comparisons involved students in grades 8 and 9 who had been enrolled in an early immersion program from kindergarten or grade 1, or in a late immersion program from grade 6 or 7. The results in Ottawa and Carleton revealed that grade 8 early immersion students were superior to their late immersion counterparts on all French language skills tested.[4] In contrast, results in Montreal indicated that grade 8 and 9 early and late immersion students were equivalent on all French language skills except listening comprehension for one cohort of grade 9 students, where the differences favoured the early immersion students. Results in Manitoba and New Brunswick showed a disparity similar to that between Ottawa and Carleton and Montreal. Whereas grade 9 early immersion students in Manitoba were superior to their late immersion counterparts on most French language measures, grade 9 early immersion students in New Brunswick were superior only in listening comprehension.

To account for the disparity between the findings in Ottawa and Carleton and those in Montreal, Genesee (1984) has suggested that early immersion students in Montreal may not have had the advantage of an optimal program design. The activity-based instructional approach of Ottawa and Carleton and the higher percentage of French instructional time after grade 3 (i.e. 60-80% in grades 4 and 5, and 50% thereafter in Ottawa and Carleton, as opposed to 40% in Montreal) may be factors that have contributed to Ottawa and Carleton early immersion students' superiority over their late immersion counterparts. However, it is interesting to note that the New Brunswick early immersion students also had received a high percentage of their instructional time in French after grade 3 (i.e., 85-90% in grades 4 to 6, and 50-60% in grades 7 and 8), and yet they were not superior to their late immersion counterparts on most French language measures— which suggests that instructional time alone may not be the critical variable.

In Ottawa and Carleton and Montreal, the relative benefits of early and late immersion programs were also investigated in the late secondary grades (grades 10 and 11). In Montreal, the two groups of students were comparable in their French language skills in grade 10 and 11 (Adiv, 1980). In Ottawa and Carleton (Morrison, Pawley & Bonyun, 1982), while one cohort of late immersion students still lagged behind their early immersion counterparts in grade 10, a subsequent cohort attained comparability on French language arts and writing in this grade. In addition, a recent study of grade 12 students in Ottawa and Carleton (Morrison & Pawley, 1985) revealed fewer differences between early and late immersion students as they approached the end of secondary school. In this study, early immersion students did better than their late immersion counterparts on a locally developed French Speaking Test, but were equivalent on listening, reading, dictation, and cloze tests developed by the University of Ottawa. The authors suggest that the instruments may not have been sensitive enough to capture the differences between the two groups of students. Thus, cohort variation and instrumentation bear on comparisons of early and late immersion, and the relative effectiveness of the two programs remains uncertain.

To date, most comparisons between early and late immersion programs have emphasized students' linguistic achievements. The affective and attitudinal outcomes of the two programs can also be compared. However, the little research that has been conducted in this area suggests no clear pattern of results. For example, although early immersion students in Manitoba (CERCO, 1983) did better than their late immersion counterparts on most French language tests, the two groups of students did not differ significantly in areas such as motivation for learning French, anxiety in using French, and attitudes towards French-speaking Canadians. On the other hand, although in New Brunswick (Lapkin & Swain, 1984) early immersion students were equivalent to late immersion students in most of their French language skills, they were clearly superior in such areas as self-perceptions of their ability in French and feelings of comfort and ease in using the language. Similar findings were reported in the early/late comparisons conducted in Peel County, Ontario (Lapkin, Swain, Kamin, & Hanna, 1983).

Because the findings of previous comparison studies to date were disparate, the study reported here was undertaken to determine the relative effectiveness of early and late immersion programs in the British Columbia context. In British Columbia, students have much less French second-language instruction prior to entering late immersion than their counterparts in other regions of Canada (1-2 years as opposed to 5-6 years in Ottawa, Carleton, and Montreal). Financial considerations precluded collecting background data on the students (e.g., socioeconomic and cognitive abilities levels) and testing them for a wider range of language skills, in particular for oral communications skills.[5]

Description of the British Columbia Study

The study was conducted in three school districts in British Columbia. These districts were the first in the province in which early and late immersion programs reached grade 7. The early immersion programs in the three districts were similar to one another in the percentage of instructional time in French they had offered in the primary grades (i.e., kindergarten through grade 2, 100%; grade 3, 80%), but they differed in the intermediate grades (grades 4-7), with one district (District A) offering 50% instructional time in French, another (District B), 60% and the third

(District C), 70%. The three districts' late immersion programs offered the same amounts of instructional time in French in both grade 6 (100%) and grade 7 (80%).

Sample

The sampling included all schools (10) housing grade 7 early and late immersion programs in the three districts. The class sample for early immersion consisted of all classes (7) and for late immersion, of all classes in two districts and two out of three classes in one district (i.e., five out of six classes for the three districts).

Measurement Instruments

TEST DE RENDEMENT EN FRANÇAIS (SEC. LEVEL 1, 1982-83)

This French language arts test was developed for grade 7 French-speaking children in Montreal by the Bureau de l'Évaluation, La Commission des Écoles Catholiques de Montréal. It is a 40-item paper and pencil test measuring a variety of French language arts skills including spelling, vocabulary, grammar, reading comprehension, and logical sequencing. Norms are available to make comparisons with Francophone children in Montreal, who are tested in November of the school year.

TEST DE COMPREHENSION AUDITIVE, NIVEAU A (REVISED 1978)

This test was designed by the Bilingual Education Project, Ontario Institute for Studies in Education, to measure comprehension of French in "communicative" situations. It is a tape-administered test consisting of six passages recorded from radio broadcasts, interviews, and similar situations; the student listens to each passage and answers multiple-choice questions on it.

STUDENT OPINIONS SCALES (KAUFMAN, D., SHAPSON, S., & DAY, E., 1982)

This instrument was originally developed for high school and university students studying French as a second language in summer immersion programs. The present study utilized the first section in a format altered slightly to suit younger students; it is composed of a series of five-point Likert-type items (28 in all) which form six sub-scales: attitudes toward French-speaking Canadians (8 items); attitudes toward English-speaking Canadians (5 items); attitudes toward bilingualism (6 items); motivation for learning French (4 items); anxiety about using French (4 items); and perceived understanding of French-Canadian culture (1 item). Most items were taken or adapted from existing scales and are used with permission of the authors (Clement, Smythe, & Gardner, 1976). Reliability coefficients (Cronbach's Alpha) were determined for the present study; the reliability coefficients for the total scale were 0.83 and 0.78 for the early and late immersion students, respectively.

This questionnaire, which was designed for the present study, is composed of a combination of closed- and open-ended questions asking students about their use of French, their perceptions of their knowledge in French, reasons for learning French, and their satisfaction with the program and desire to continue.

Analysis

The analyses were conducted separately within each district in an attempt to validate the findings with three different groups of early and late immersion students. Mean raw scores and standard deviations were computed, and the performance of the early immersion students was compared statistically with that of the late immersion students in their districts on all measures. In addition, a two-way analysis of variance was conducted on the French language measures to examine the main effects of district and program.

Results

French language skills

The performance of the early and late immersion students in each district on the French language measures is illustrated in Figure 1. Statistical comparisons of the mean scores indicated that early immersion students in only one of the districts (District C) performed significantly higher than late immersion students in their district in both French language arts ($t[1,41]=3.47$, $p<.001$) and French comprehension ($t[1,42]=4.05$, $p<.001$). Early immersion students in the two other districts (Districts A and B) also performed significantly higher than their late immersion counterparts in French comprehension (District A: $t[1,97]=2.75$, $p<.01$; District B: $t[1,85]=3.47$, $p<.001$). However, unlike those in District C, the early and late immersion students in these districts performed at a similar level in French language arts (District A: $t[1,96]=0.47$; District B: $t[1,88]=1.28$).[6]

The results of the two-way analysis of variance (see Table 1) revealed that overall there was a significant program effect, with early immersion programs superior to late immersion programs in both French language arts ($F=4.0$, $p<.05$) and French comprehension ($F=32.1$, $p<.001$). However, there was also a significant district effect on the French comprehension test ($F=21.3$, $p<.001$) and a significant program by district interaction on the French language arts test ($F=4.4$, $p<.01$).

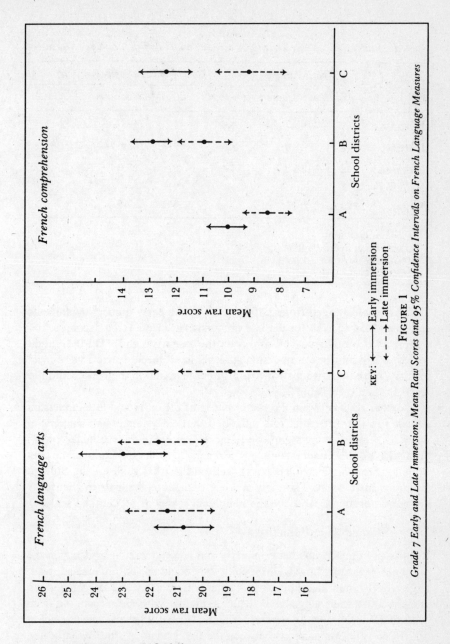

FIGURE 1

Grade 7 Early and Late Immersion: Mean Raw Scores and 95% Confidence Intervals on French Language Measures

Attitudes and Opinions

The performance of the early and late immersion students in each of the districts was compared on the Student Opinions Scales (see Table 2). Student attitude scores were positive in all three districts: mean scores on

TABLE 1
Results of the Two-way Analysis of Variance on the French Language Measures

Effects	French Language Arts			French Comprehension		
	df	Mean Square	F-value	df	Mean Square	F-value
Program	1	105.7	4.0*	1	246.8	32.1***
District	2	43.0	1.6n.s.	2	163.6	21.3***
Program x District	2	115.2	4.4**	2	10.6	1.4n.s.
Within	225	26.5		224	7.7	

n.s.= not significant
* Significant at the .05 level.
** Significant at the .01 level.
*** Significant at the .001 level.

the total scale ranged from 2.19 to 2.36 for the early immersion students and from 2.34 to 2.54 for the late immersion students (on a 5-point scale, with 1 as the positive end and 5 as the negative end). On individual scales, early and late immersion students in all three districts were most positive in their attitudes toward bilingualism and in their motivation to learn French (see Table 2).

Comparisons between the performance of the early and late immersion students in the three districts indicated that early immersion students in Districts B and C were significantly more positive in their attitudes toward bilingualism, their understanding of French-Canadian culture, their anxiety in using French (District B only), and on the total scale of the Student Opinions instrument. The early and late immersion students in District A did not differ significantly on the individual scales or on the total scale.

Student Questionnaire

Results of comparisons between early and late immersion students on the questions regarding how well they felt they could speak, understand, read, and write French also appear in Table 2. Both early and late immersion students rated their language skills quite highly, with means ranging from 1.36 to 2.11 (on a scale where 1 equals "fluently" and 4 means "not at all" fluently). Comparisons between the two groups of students indicated significant differences in favour of early immersion students in Districts A and B in ratings of ability to speak French, and in Districts B and C in the ratings of ability to understand French. However, there were no

TABLE 2

Comparisons Between the Performance of Early and Late Immersion Students in Three School Districts: Student Opinions Scales and Students' Self-Rating of their Knowledge of French

	District A			District B			District C		
	Early Mean Rating	Late Mean Rating	t-value	Early Mean Rating	Late Mean Rating	t-value	Early Mean Rating	Late Mean Rating	t-value
Student Opinions Scales[a]									
Attitudes toward French-speaking Canadians (8 items)	2.52	2.46	0.50 n.s.	2.65	2.66	0.14 n.s.	2.45	2.52	0.50 n.s.
Attitudes toward English-speaking Canadians (5 items)	2.82	2.75	0.56 n.s.	2.79	2.89	0.90 n.s.	2.82	3.00	1.13 n.s.
Attitudes toward bilingualism (6 items)	1.98	1.86	1.09 n.s.	1.91	2.17	2.47*	1.58	1.89	2.44**
Motivation to learn French (4 items)	2.06	1.84	1.34 n.s.	2.00	2.02	0.11 n.s.	1.85	1.71	0.87 n.s.
Anxiety about using French (4 items)	2.38	2.59	1.22 n.s.	2.02	2.71	3.97***	2.15	2.59	1.84 n.s.
Perceived understanding of French-Canadian culture (1 item)	2.52	2.78	1.65 n.s.	2.53	3.13	3.17**	2.36	3.18	3.30**
TOTAL SCALE (28 items)	2.36	2.34	0.27 n.s.	2.34	2.54	2.77**	2.19	2.40	2.15*

(continued next page)

TABLE 2 continued

Comparisons Between the Performance of Early and Late Immersion Students in Three School Districts: Student Opinions Scales and Students' Self-Rating of their Knowledge of French

	District A			District B			District C		
	Early Mean Rating	Late Mean Rating	t-value	Early Mean Rating	Late Mean Rating	t-value	Early Mean Rating	Late Mean Rating	t-value
Student Self-Ratings[b] *of Knowledge of French*									
How well do you feel you:									
Speak French?	1.68	1.93	2.87**	1.58	1.91	3.15**	1.86	2.00	1.40 n.s.
Understand French?	1.66	1.82	1.65 n.s.	1.36	1.85	4.69***	1.67	2.05	2.88 n.s.
Read French?	1.94	2.11	1.49 n.s.	1.82	1.91	0.74 n.s.	1.81	2.00	1.32 n.s.
Write French?	1.89	1.96	0.72 n.s.	1.82	2.03	1.67 n.s.	1.90	2.09	1.26 n.s.

n.s. = not significant

* Significant at the .05 level.

** Significant at the .01 level.

*** Significant at the .001 level.

[a] The Student Opinions Scales are based on a five-point scale with 1 as the positive end and 5 as the negative end. *A lower mean rating indicates more positive findings.*

[b] Based on a four-point scale, where 1 = Fluently, 2 = Fairly well, 3 = A little, and 4 = Not at all.

significant differences in any of the districts in student ratings of their ability to read and write French.

The results of remaining questions on the Student Questionnaire, which assessed the students' use of French, their opinions of the program, and their desire to continue in French immersion, indicated a similar pattern of results for all three districts. In all districts, English was the language first learned and the language most often spoken in the home for the great majority of early and late immersion students. There were no significant differences between ratings given by early and late immersion students to the question asking why they thought it was important for them to learn French. All students rated the following as the most important reasons for learning French: "It will be useful when visiting places where French is spoken" and "It will be useful in getting a good job some day." In addition, all students appeared to be enthusiastic about their immersion experience. When asked whether they would recommend a French immersion program to a friend, the majority of early and late immersion students said they would. The majority also indicated they would like to continue in a French immersion program in the following year.

However, late immersion students in two districts (A and C) were more willing to speak French in their home and outside of school than their early immersion counterparts. Over half of the late immersion students, compared to less than half of the early immersion students, reported that they "occasionally," "frequently," or "always" spoke French at home (District A, 78% vs. 47%; District C, 64% vs. 48%) or with French-speaking people outside of school (District A, 56% vs. 45%; District C, 55% vs. 38%). In addition, a greater percentage of late than of early immersion students in Districts A and B (District A, 58% vs. 39%; District B, 43% vs. 15%) reported that they would like to be able to speak French more often with French-speaking people outside of school.

Summary and Discussion

Comparisons between early and late immersion programs in three British Columbia school districts showed variations that also have been found in other Canadian comparisons of the two program options (e.g., in Manitoba, CERCO, 1983; in Montreal, Genesee & Morcos, 1978; in New Brunswick, Lapkin & Swain, 1984; and in Ottawa and Carleton, Morrison et al., 1979). The findings in one district (District C) paralleled the Manitoba and Ottawa and Carleton findings in showing the superiority of early over late immersion students in their French language skills. The findings in the two other districts (Districts A and B) paralleled the New Brunswick and Montreal findings, where early immersion students were equivalent to their late immersion counterparts on most French language skills, but maintained superiority in listening comprehension (in Montreal, for one cohort of grade 9 students only).

As was the case with the linguistic measures, comparisons of the performance of the early and late immersion students on the attitudinal and opinions measures were also not consistent for the three districts. Early immersion students in one district (District A) did not differ significantly from late immersion students on the individual scales or on the total scale of the Student Opinions instrument. However, the early immersion students in the two other districts (B and C) were significantly more positive than the late immersion students in the same districts in their attitudes toward bilingualism and understanding of French-Canadian culture, and showed less anxiety in using French (District B only).

Early immersion students in two districts rated their ability to speak French (Districts A and B) and their ability to understand French (Districts B and C) more highly than their late immersion counterparts, but late immersion students in Districts A and C were more willing to use French in their homes and outside of school. Early immersion students also rated their linguistic skills more highly than their late immersion counterparts in New Brunswick (Lapkin & Swain, 1984) and in Peel County, Ontario (Lapkin, Swain, Kamin, & Hanna, 1983). Further research would show whether these perceptions result in better French language development and increased use of French in and outside of school. Previous research (Gardner & Lambert, 1972; Gardner, Smythe, Clement, & Gliksman, 1976) suggests that affective and attitudinal variables should be given more consideration in weighing the effectiveness of the two programs.

Research on early and late language learning has provided much evidence of late language learners' abilities to attain levels in their second language equivalent to those who start early. Although late immersion students in two districts in this study were able to catch up to their early immersion counterparts in French language arts, they were not able to do so in French listening comprehension. It is possible that this skill develops more slowly than other language skills. If so, late immersion students may attain equivalence with their early immersion counterparts in future grades. However, it is also possible that the development of this skill is so closely related to the amount of instructional time in the second language that the early immersion students may always maintain their advantage. It is interesting that listening comprehension was the only advantage retained by early as compared to late language learners in a study of French second-language programs in Great Britain (Burstall, Jamieson, Cohen, & Hargreaves, 1974). Comparisons of the linguistic levels attained by early and late immersion students at the end of secondary school would shed more light on this question.

While considerable research has been conducted on student perfor-mance, relatively little is known about how immersion programs operate in practice. Variations in the findings of comparisons between early and late immersion programs across Canada suggest that detailed investigations be conducted especially to examine intervening programs and instructional factors that contribute to the relative effectiveness of these two program options.

Notes

1 French immersion programs are intensive second-language programs designed for An-glophone students. A separate program for Francophone students, the *programme-cadre de français* (minority language program), is also offered in many school districts in the province. In this program, French is the only language of instruction except for the time given to English language arts, and the curriculum parallels the prescribed English core curriculum.

2 This project included surveys of parents, teachers, and administrators; instrument devel-opment; and collection of normative data on French language skills of grade 3 early and grade 7 early and late immersion students. The survey results are presented in Day & Shapson (1983), and the test results in Shapson & Day (1984).

3 The Protestant School Board of Greater Montreal offers a one-year and a two-year late immersion program beginning in grade 7. Only the findings of the two-year program are discussed in this review because this program's format is more consistent with that of others discussed.

4 Comparisons of early immersion students with late immersion students who had begun their immersion experience somewhat later than those reviewed (i.e., grade 8 vs. grade 6 or 7) were also conducted in Ontario's Peel County by Lapkin, Swain, Kamin, & Hanna (1983). These comparisons, too, revealed consistent differences in favor of the early immersion students.

5 Since this study was conducted, a French Speaking Test for grade 7 immersion students has been developed under contract to the British Columbia Ministry of Education (Day, Shapson, & Rivet, 1985) in preparation for a more comprehensive study of early and late immersion students.

6 Comparisons of the results on the French language arts test with the norms for native French-speaking students in Montreal indicated that all groups of British Columbia stu-dents performed in a similar percentile equivalent range (i.e., 24th to 39th percentile range) except for the late immersion students in District C, who performed in a lower range (i.e., 11th to 23rd percentile range). The results of item analyses conducted on this test revealed that early and late immersion students in all three districts tended to perform less well on the items measuring vocabulary and reading than on those measuring technical skills and grammar. Although it was not possible to compare directly the performance of the immersion students with that of the Francophone students in the norming group, the results suggest that there may be considerable room for growth in the vocabulary and reading skills of both the early and late immersion students if they are to attain comparability with native French speakers.

References

Adiv, E. (1980, November). *A comparative evaluation of three French immersion programs: Grades 10 and 11.* Paper presented at the Fourth Annual Convention of the Canadian Association of Immersion Teachers, Winnipeg, MB.

Burstall, C., Jamieson, M., Cohen, S., & Hargreaves, M. (1974). *Primary French in the balance.* Windsor, UK: NFER.

Carroll, J.B. (1975). *The teaching of French as a foreign language in eight countries.* New York, NY: John Wiley.

Centre for Research and Consultation [CERCO] (1983). *The French immersion research project, Manitoba, 1983.* Winnipeg, MB: Ministère de l'Éducation du Manitoba, Bureau de l'Éducation Française.

Clément, R., Smythe, P.C., & Gardner, R.C. (1976). Échelle d'attitudes et de motivations reliées à l'apprentissage de l'anglais, langue seconde. *Canadian Modern Language Review, 33,* 5-26.

Day, E.M., & Shapson, S.M. (1983). *Elementary French immersion programs in British Columbia: A survey of administrators, teachers, and parents. Part I: Summary of findings; Part II: Detailed findings.* Burnaby, BC: Simon Fraser University, Faculty of Education, B.C. French Study.

Day, E.M., Shapson, S.M., & Rivet, M. (1985). *Examiner's manual. British Columbia French speaking test: Grade 7.* Burnaby, BC: Simon Fraser University, Faculty of Education, B.C. French Study.

Gardner, R.C., & Lambert, W.E. (1972). *Attitudes and motivation in second-language learning.* Rowley, MA: Newbury House.

Genesee, F. (1978a). A longitudinal evaluation of an early immersion school program. *Canadian Journal of Education, 3*(4), 31-50.

Genesee, F. (1978b). Is there an optimal age for starting second language instruction? *McGill Journal of Education, 13,* 145-154.

Genesee, F. (1978-1979). Scholastic effects of French immersion. An overview after ten years. *Interchange, 9,* 20-29.

Genesee, F., & Morcos, C. (1978). *A comparison of three alternative French immersion programs: Grades 8 and 9.* Montreal, PQ: Protestant School Board of Greater Montreal, Instructional Services Department.

Gray, V. (1981). *Evaluation of the grade six French immersion programme in Fredericton, New Brunswick.* Fredericton, NB: University of New Brunswick, Psychology Department.

Kaufman, D., Shapson, S.M., & Day, E.M. (1982). An evaluation study of the summer language bursary program. *Canadian Journal of Education, 7*(3), 62-83.

Krashen, S., Long, M., & Scarcella, R. (1979). Age, rate and eventual attainment in second language acquisition. *TESOL Quarterly, 13,* 573-582.

Lapkin, S., & Swain, M. (1984). *Final report on the evaluation of French immersion programs at grades 3, 6 and 9 in New Brunswick.* Toronto, ON: OISE.

Lapkin, S., Swain, M., Kamin, J., & Hanna, G. (1983). Late immersion in perspective: The Peel study. *Canadian Modern Language Review, 39,* 182-206.

Morrison, F., & Pawley, C. (1985). French speaking proficiency of Ottawa area immersion students at the grade 12 level. *CAIT News, 8*(3), 20-21.

Morrison, F., Pawley, C., & Bonyun, R. (1982). *After immersion: Ottawa and Carleton students at the secondary and post-secondary level. Evaluation of the second language learning (French) programs in the schools of the Ottawa and Carleton Boards of Education. Ninth Annual Report.* Ottawa, ON: Ottawa Board of Education.

Morrison, F., Walsh, M., Pawley, C., & Bonyun, R. (1979). *French proficiency of grade 8 primary- and late-entry immersion students, Ottawa and Carleton Boards*. French Working Paper #131. Ottawa, ON: Ottawa Board of Education.

Pawley, C., & Walsh, M. (1980). *French proficiency and general achievement of grade 8 students in primary- and late-entry immersion, Carleton and Ottawa*. French Working Paper #135. Ottawa, ON: Ottawa Board of Education.

Shapson, S.M., & Day, E.M. (1982a). A longitudinal evaluation of an early immersion program in British Columbia. *Journal of Multilingual and Multicultural Development, 3,* 1-16.

Shapson, S.M., & Day, E.M. (1982b). A comparison study of three late immersion programs. *Alberta Journal of Educational Research, 28,* 135-148.

Shapson, S.M., & Day, E.M. (1984). *Evaluation study of the grade 3 early and grade 7 early and late French immersion programs in British Columbia*. Burnaby, BC: Simon Fraser University, Faculty of Education, B.C. French Study.

Stern, H.H. (1976). Optimal age: Myth or reality? *Canadian Modern Language Review, 32,* 283-294.

Swain, M. (1978). French immersion: Early, late or partial? *Canadian Modern Language Review, 34,* 577-585.

Swain, M., & Lapkin, S. (1982). *Evaluating bilingual education: A Canadian case study*. Avon, UK: Multilingual Matters.

A Comparative Study of the Writing Abilities of English-Speaking Grade 8 Students in French-Speaking Schools

Donald Laing
University of Windsor

This paper compares writing in two modes, narrative and argumentative, by English-speaking grade 8 students educated in French-speaking schools with that done by a group of similar children in a regular English program. The students' papers are compared for overall quality as measured by holistic scoring, for syntactic maturity as measured by T-unit analysis, and for surface feature control as measured by frequency of selected errors. In addition, the scores for syntactic maturity are compared to those presented in major studies of this aspect of writing development. Fifty writing variables do not differ significantly at the .05 level. The study strongly supports the view that education in a second language does not impair native-language abilities.

*   *   *

RESEARCH ON BILINGUAL EDUCATION IN CANADA HAS FOR FIFTEEN YEARS questioned whether French immersion programs are detrimental to children's English language abilities. Parents and administrators have worried that when thousands of hours of instruction normally given in English are switched to French, students' skills in English may suffer.

The question is urgent for English-speaking children who attend French-speaking schools in the Roman Catholic Separate School Board in the city of Windsor, Ontario. Although these students are not enrolled in an immersion program, they experience an intensive form of immersion education. As students in French-speaking schools, rather than in immersion classes within English-speaking schools or in special immersion schools, these children experience from kindergarten to grade 8 many more hours of instruction in French than do those in most immersion programs. French is commonly the dominant language of instruction up to grade 5 in even the most intensive immersion programs, but then the use of English increases, until in grades 7 and 8 half the curriculum is taught in English and half in French (Swain & Lapkin, 1981). For these Windsor children,

Research for this paper was supported by a grant from the Research Board of the University of Windsor.

French remains the dominant language of instruction throughout their elementary education. Apart from a required class in English language arts amounting to 40 minutes a day in grade 4, 60 minutes in grade 5 and 6, and 50 minutes in grades 7 and 8, the students receive no formal instruction in English at all.

In one important aspect these students' education stands apart from typical immersion and comes closer to what has been called submersion (Swain, 1978; Cummins, 1979): they share classrooms with children more advanced in the language of the school, that is with children whose mother tongue is French. However, since non-Francophone children constitute such a large presence in these schools—32 out of 65 students in the grade 8 cohort studied—primary grade teachers often find themselves introducing practices more common in immersion than in native language classrooms. For example, they respond in French to youngsters who must still express their ideas or needs in English. Programs in these schools exhibit none of the other important characteristics of submersion. The Windsor children, from the dominant linguistic group of their community, make a home-school language switch by parental choice rather than necessity; they are praised for their growing competence in French rather than simply expected to have it; and English is itself a subject within the curriculum. The most accurate view, then, is to see these students as receiving an atypical but comparatively intensive form of second-language immersion as defined by Swain (1978):

> Immersion refers to a situation in which children from the same linguistic and cultural background who have had no prior contact with the school language are put together in a classroom setting in which the second language is used as the medium of instruction. (p. 238)

Although Windsor pupils may be studied to see whether French immersion has a negative effect on English language skills, strictly empirical research will not finally decide the issue. Subjects cannot be randomly assigned to treatments since students are generally placed in immersion programs in advance of any research and for reasons beyond the researchers' control. Researchers have had to resort to what Carey (1984) has called "a model of necessity" rather than one of choice, and to compare the progress of immersion students with those in regular programs. The question has thus been altered: "How do the English language skills of French immersion students compare with those of similar students following the same curriculum in English?"

Even this question presents difficulties, most notably how to establish comparison groups that are similar. As Carey stresses (1984, p. 252), although it is almost impossible to control for the attitudes of parents, students and teachers, and for many other variables associated with the social milieu, there is evidence such factors strongly influence language acquisition and school achievement. Given these difficulties, it is important to interpret cautiously the results of research based on comparison groups.

Still, the research is impressively consistent. In their comprehensive survey, Swain and Lapkin (1981) conclude that, after a "temporary lag" in English language skills to the end of grade 3, "The overall trend in subsequent grades is for immersion students to perform as well as or, in the case of early total immersion students, better than their English-educated counterparts" (p. 127). Although this is an accurate enough report of the evidence, the conclusion is not entirely justified by it, or by certain other studies. Indeed, English language ability has been assessed largely through language subtests of such standardized tests as the Canadian Tests of Basic Skills and the Metropolitan Achievement Test. Results indicate that immersion children compare well with regular students in vocabulary, spelling, and punctuation. Grobe (n.d.) reports that grade 5 immersion students scored higher than their regular counterparts on all eleven objectives of the New Brunswick Language Arts Criterion-Referenced Test, performing significantly better on such writing-related items as using punctuation marks correctly and completing sentences to illustrate subject-verb agreement. However, such tests provide indirect and fragmentary pictures of students' writing.

Very few studies to date have examined samples of writing by children in immersion programs. Fewer still have employed the standard procedures used to assess writing ability in English. The earliest of the few studies is that of Lambert, Tucker, and d'Anglejan (1973). Thirty grade 4 and 20 grade 5 immersion students were given the language subtests of the Metropolitan Achievement Test and items from the Peabody Picture Vocabulary Test. Children's performance in such areas as spelling, word usage, and vocabulary was generally equivalent to that of comparison students in the regular English program, although the grade 4 immersion students scored lower in punctuation and capitalization. One teacher's evaluation of a composition showed grade 4 immersion students significantly below English controls, with a mean score of 6.06 compared to 7.84, and with "certain handicaps in expressing themselves through writing" (p. 145). The grade 5 immersion students performed "significantly better" than the regular students, with a mean of 7.90 compared to 6.80 (p. 151). Unfortunately, there is no information about the composition, how it was administered, or the procedures by which it was assessed. It may be inferred that one teacher evaluated the scripts holistically, on a 10-point scale. What the "certain handicaps" are or what "significantly better" means is never explained.

The most comprehensive and detailed study of immersion students' writing so far was done for the Protestant School Board of Greater Montreal, and reported in Genesee (1974) and Genesee and Stanley (1976). Fifty-four immersion students in grade 4, 26 in grade 6, 117 in grade 7, and 86 in grade 11 wrote narrative compositions in response to certain topic sentences. For the first three grades, each paper was scored "blind" by two markers on a five-point scale for six dimensions: spelling, sentence accuracy, sentence complexity, organization, originality, and overall quality. A sample of 20 grade 11 papers was scored by two markers, and the other 66 papers were divided evenly between them. All were judged appropriate or inappropriate for length and punctuation and superior, average, or below average for vocabulary.

At the grade 4 level, students in the regular program were found to spell significantly better, and students were rated significantly higher for originality. The differences were not significant on the other four dimensions. No significant differences on any dimension were found between the immersion and control groups at the grade 6 level. Grade 7 immersion students were rated significantly higher on overall quality and on sentence complexity; other differences were not significant. One group of grade 11 students who had been immersion students but were no longer taking French classes scored significantly higher on organization than did both a second group of immersion students still in the program, and the English controls. Other differences were not significant. Genesee and Stanley (1976) conclude that "the immersion students seemed to be at least as well equipped as the non-immersion students to express themselves in written English" (p. 15).

Although Genesee and Stanley must be commended for attending seriously to samples of writing and for the comprehensiveness of their study, some aspects remain problematic. The writing of grade 7 students in only their sixth month of an immersion program may not be fruitfully compared with that of students still in the regular program. Further, some of the criteria for the writing assessment are too vague to be informative or to be readily compared with other findings. A score of 5 in sentence complexity represents "superior use of complex and varied sentence types in a meaningful way," while 3 means that the "complexity and variety of sentence types is adequate for grade 7 level" (Genesee, 1974, p. 21). The immersion students' score of 3.00 for spelling is not significantly below the 3.46 scored by the control group since a score of 3 represents "4, 5 or 6 errors" without regard to the length of the composition (p. 21).

Swain (1975) compares two short stories written (in response to pictures) by each of 40 grade 3 immersion pupils with those done by 24 children from regular grade 3 classes. She finds that the immersion pupils' writing "compares favourably with that of their English-instructed peers" (p. 19). For example, they generally write longer stories (mean length 81.3 versus 61.6 words), use an equally varied vocabulary, make fewer morphological errors, and make proportionally fewer spelling errors. Examining syntax in greater detail than does Genesee, Swain finds that the immersion children are syntactically more mature and write "proportionately fewer simple and compound sentences and proportionately more complex and compound-complex sentences" (p. 20). It should be noted that the differences between the groups are very small and that the results were not analysed statistically.

Lapkin (1982) reports on holistic scoring of twenty-minute compositions written by grade 5 students in the immersion and regular programs of the Carleton and Ottawa Boards of Education. A random sample of 98 papers was assessed by three experienced teachers on a seven-point scale. The teachers did not know which students had written which papers. The mean scores were 4.09 (SD 1.14) for the immersion students and 4.13 (SD 1.36) for the regular students. In addition, as a measure of variety in vocabulary use, "type/token ratios" were calculated for nouns and verbs based on 50-word samples of good and poor writing drawn from the larger groups. The results are comparable. While Lapkin includes no statistical analysis of her findings, the data are so similar it is unlikely that any differences are statistically significant. She concludes: "The claim that the first language skills of immersion pupils do not suffer in comparison with those of pupils in a regular program is thus further substantiated by this analysis of their writing" (p. 28).

Although these studies support the view that the English writing skills of students in French immersion programs are not significantly different from those of similar students in the regular program, the studies are not extensive enough to be conclusive.

Aim of the Study

The present study provides a detailed and comprehensive comparison of the writing skills (in English) of grade 8 students at the end of an intensive immersion program with that of similar students completing the regular elementary school curriculum. Results are reported for three major aspects of written performance: overall quality; syntactic maturity; and surface feature control.

The syntactic maturity of the Windsor immersion students is compared not only to that of their counterparts in the regular program but also to the results for grade 8 students in three earlier major investigations of written syntax. Hunt (1970) reports the performance of a representative sample of students on his Aluminum passage, which measures how writers combine single-clause sentences into a more mature statement. Loban (1976) presents the findings of a longitudinal study into the increase in language skills of 211 Californian students from kindergarten to grade 12. Subsequent research has produced scores so consistent with those of these two studies that they (Hunt's and Loban's work) have been widely accepted as establishing norms for student performance (see Hillocks, 1986, pp. 63-76 for a review of research on syntactic maturity). The third investigation, that of Pringle and Freedman (1985) is the most comprehensive Canadian study to date. It gives the results for a random sample of students in two large Ontario school systems.

Method

Subjects

All the grade 8 students (N=65) in the four French-speaking schools of the Windsor Separate School Board and in four classes from three Anglophone schools located in comparable areas of the city (N=95) participated in the study. From this population, two subgroups were established: (a) immersion students (IMM), those within the Francophone schools who claimed English as their mother tongue and who had been educated predominantly in French; and (b) English students (ENG), those students within the regular program who claimed English as their mother tongue. On the basis of questionnaires concerning language use in their homes, completed by the students and corroborated by the principals, 33 students were initially classified as IMM. On further investigation, two students who claimed both English and French as their mother tongues but spoke predominantly French in their homes were disqualified, leaving a group of 31 subjects. These subjects represent an intensive form of immersion education; 28 received their entire elementary education, kindergarten to grade 8, in French-speaking schools, while the other three spent six years in such schools. To eliminate the possibility of second-language interference from the comparative data, 27 students who claimed a mother language other than English and who regularly used a second language at home were eliminated from the group. From the remainder a sample of 33 was drawn at random.

Some subjects were absent on the days the compositions were written, with the result that the data for the modes of writing are based on slightly different subject groups. In IMM, 28 narratives and 30 arguments were completed; in ENG, 32 narratives and 33 arguments. Table 1 provides descriptive statistics comparing by sex and age the students writing in each mode.

That there are more females (N=22) than males (N=9) in the immersion group leads to the question whether sex significantly affects comparisons. Chi square tests applied to the groups writing narratives ($X^2=1.35$, df=1) and those writing arguments ($X^2=2.39$, df=1) do not produce values for X^2 significant at the .05 level. Since the distribution of sex is not significantly different in the groups being compared, there is no reason to attribute significant effects to this variable. Differences in socioeconomic status (SES) are generally of concern in research into comparative perfor-

TABLE 1
Mean Age in Years and Months of Groups by Mode and Sex

Mode		IMM			ENG		
Sex		Females	Males	Total	Females	Males	Total
Narrative n		19	9	28	17	15	32
	M	13.8	13.10	13.9	13.11	13.11	13.11
Argument n		22	8	30	18	15	33
	M	13.9	13.10	13.9	13.11	13.11	13.11

mance and particularly in studies concerned with French immersion. The common view is that students in immersion programs tend to come from more privileged backgrounds. Employing a simplified version of the occupational categories and rankings of Pineo and Porter (1979), the subjects were rated according to parental occupation on a five-point scale using the following classifications:

1.   professionals, major proprietors, managers, and officials;

2.   semi-professionals, minor proprietors, managers, and officials;

3.   clerical and sales, skilled and semi-skilled workers;

4.   unskilled workers;

5.   unemployed, welfare, retraining allowances, etc.

Subjects with two parents employed at different levels were placed in the higher classification, on the assumption that socioeconomic status of the family is derived from the parent whose occupation is more highly ranked. Subjects in single-parent homes were rated according to the occupation of the parent they lived with. Table 2 shows the number of subjects in each

TABLE 2
SES for Subjects by Group and Mode

	IMM		ENG	
	Nar.	Arg.	Nar.	Arg.
1. Professionals	8	7	8	8
2. Semi-professionals	6	6	8	8
3. Clerical	12	15	13	14
4. Unskilled	1	1	1	1
5. Unemployed	1	1	2	2
Totals	28	30	32	33

classification for the two modes of writing and reveals that the two groups of students are remarkably similar in socioeconomic profile. A chi square test reveals that SES has the same distribution in both groups ($X^2 = 0.59$, df = 4); consequently, any differences between the groups cannot be attributed to SES.

Since the Windsor Separate School Board administers IQ tests only by referral in cases of evident need, no data are available on the intellectual ability of the students.

Procedures

The subjects were asked to write two compositions, one narrative, the other argumentative, two weeks apart in the final months of their grade 8 year. In six schools the compositions were written in May; in the seventh they were done in June. Both writing stimuli were selected from those proven successful in field trials for the Ontario Assessment Instrument Pool (1982). The narrative topic required the students to write from personal experience about someone, perhaps themselves, who always seems to cause trouble for others, and suggested as a possible title, "Trouble always starts when _____ is around." The arguments replied to the question, "Should young teenagers be spanked?" Students were invited to consider both sides of the question and to propose reasonable alternatives. Cooperating teachers provided a few minutes for the students to discuss the topics amongst themselves before settling in to write. Forty-five minutes were given one day for an initial draft, which was then collected, and 45 the next for revising and polishing the draft. Students could use dictionaries and other standard reference materials, but were not to seek assistance from others or to discuss their papers once writing had started. After the final writing sessions, the papers—identified only by number and photocopied—were returned to the teachers.

Analysis and Results

The immersion students wrote 28 narratives with a mean length of 328.04 words, while the regular pupils submitted 32 papers averaging 384.16 words. The 30 arguments by the immersion group had a mean of 239.90 words; those of the 33 regular students averaged 248.67 words. The differences between the groups are not significant at the .05 level.

Every script in the sample was scored in three ways corresponding to different aspects of writing performance: holistic scoring as a measure of overall quality; T-unit analysis as a measure of syntactic maturity; and error frequency as a measure of surface feature control. All results were tested by one-way analysis of variance for significant differences between the groups at the .05 level.

Holistic Scoring

To determine whether there were any differences in the overall quality of the compositions written by the two groups of students, the scripts were rated on a 10-point scale according to standard holistic scoring procedures by three experienced teachers with no connection to the participating schools. While the evaluators were aware of the nature of the research, the scripts were presented to them in a random sequence without identification as to group and with additional papers from the original population so that, as far as possible, the teachers were simply evaluating sets of narratives and arguments written by grade 8 students. The three scores were then averaged for each script. The results of the holistic scoring are given in Table 3. The differences between the immersion students and those in the regular English program are not significant in either set of comparisons.

TABLE 3
Statistics from Holistic Scoring

Mode	IMM	ENG	F	df
Narrative				
Mean	5.93	6.18	0.23	1,58
SD	2.22	1.79		
Minimum	1.33	2.67		
Maximum	10.00	10.00		
Argument				
Mean	5.47	5.62	0.09	1,61
SD	1.90	1.95		
Minimum	2.33	1.00		
Maximum	9.33	9.67		

Syntactic Analysis

Two scorers calculated independently four measures of syntactic maturity for each script following principles based on those of O'Hare (1973, pp. 48-49) for segmenting into T-units and for treating directly quoted discourse. Differences in scoring, of which there were remarkably few, were discussed until both scorers were in agreement. Three of the measures are those found by Hunt (1970) to be the most reliable indicators of syntactic maturity; words per T-unit (W/T), words per clause (W/C), and clauses per T-unit (p. 6). So that comparisons could more readily be made with Loban (1976) and Pringle and Freedman (1985), the clauses per T-unit were reported as dependent clauses per T-unit (DC/T), a change that reduces each score by one because the main clause in the T-unit is not counted. A fourth measure, the number of words in dependent clauses expressed as a percentage of the total number of words in the T-units (WDC/T%), was calculated for further comparison with Loban's reference study.

The scores for syntactic analysis of the narrative compositions are given in Table 4 and those for the arguments in Table 5. For comparison the scores from Hunt (1970) and for the students Loban (1976) selected at random from his larger sample are included in Table 4. These comparisons, however, should be made cautiously. Hunt's results are not based on students' compositions but on a test instrument. Loban's study does not differentiate between modes of writing. It has since been shown that mode significantly affects the complexity of written syntax. Argument makes the greatest demand on a writer's syntactic resources and narration the least (Crowhurst, 1980; Crowhurst & Piche, 1979). Loban's "typical samples of the subjects' written language were secured on an annual basis (one composition per year)" (p. 4). There is no way of knowing whether he reports scores for writing in modes other than narrative. Nevertheless, other studies have consistently reported scores similar to Hunt's and Loban's. This suggests that their scores may be taken to represent typical performance. Two measures—words per T-unit and dependent clauses per T-unit—can be compared more confidently with the results reported by Pringle and Freedman (1985), whose study does differentiate between modes. Table 4 includes their scores on these measures for personal narrative writing while Table 5 lists those for argument. Tables 4 and 5 show scores for syntactic maturity that are remarkably close on all four measures in each mode. Furthermore, the scores are in line with those reported by the studies cited for comparison. It should be noted too that neither group of students consistently displays higher mean scores. The immersion students score higher on two measures, in narrative writing, while the regular students are higher on three and the immersion students on one, in argumentative writing. The differences in the scores do not approach significance at the .05 level for any one of the eight measures reported.

Error Frequency

The scorers independently classified and counted the following surface errors in each script: spelling, sentence errors (e.g., comma splices, fragments), punctuation (e.g., periods omitted, unnecessary capitals), verb errors (e.g., subject-verb agreement errors, tense shifts, incorrect verb forms) and pronoun errors (e.g., shifts in person, incorrect forms). Differences in scoring were discussed until agreement was reached. To permit

TABLE 4

Means (Standard Deviations) for Syntactic Complexity in Narrative

	IMM	ENG	F	df	Hunt	Loban Random	Pringle/ Freedman
W/T	10.27 (1.66)	10.45 (1.82)	0.16	1,58	9.84 (3.06)	10.37 —	11.15 —
W/C	6.99 (1.12)	7.18 (1.10)	0.41	1,58	6.79 (1.12)	— —	— —
DC/T	0.48 (0.12)	0.46 (0.14)	0.41	1,58	0.43* —	0.50 —	0.43 —
WDC/T%	28.95 (5.64)	27.74 (7.41)	0.49	1,58	— —	26.30 —	— —

*Hunt's Subordinate Clause Index for grade 8 is 1.43. Subtracting 1 from each score will produce a mean score for DC/T that is 1 less than his reported figure. That score has been listed here for comparison.

TABLE 5

Means (Standard Deviations) for Syntactic Complexity in Argument

	IMM	ENG	F	df	Pringle/ Freedman
W/T	13.76 (2.51)	13.83 (3.01)	0.01	1,61	14.09
W/C	7.48 (0.93)	7.65 (1.61)	0.25	1,61	—
DC/T	0.82 (0.29)	0.85 (0.45)	0.14	1,61	0.84
WDC/T%	43.07 (11.98)	41.81 (14.90)	0.13	1,61	—

the analysis of scripts of varying length, the number of errors within a category was converted to a ratio expressing the frequency of the error per 100 words.

Since "error" in writing often varies with the eye of the beholder, the view of surface error taken in this study requires comment. To insure consistency the scorers adopted a rigid approach to the conventions of written language. In general, if a standard school composition text considered something an error, it was judged an error in this study. Consequently, errors were counted that in other contexts might well not have been considered errors at all. For example, sentence fragments were counted as errors even when they could reasonably be defended on rhetorical grounds. When an indefinite pronoun was followed by plural pronoun (e.g., "Anyone can see if they open their eyes"), it was counted an error in pronoun reference without regard to the defensible position (adopted by the National Council of Teachers of English in the United States, among others) that the plural "they" is preferable to the sexist "he."

TABLE 6
Means (Standard Deviations) for Misspellings per 100 Words

	IMM	ENG	F	df
Narrative				
All Misspelled Words	2.04 (2.23)	2.13 (1.63)	0.04	1,58
Different Misspelled Words	1.94 (2.00)	1.97 (1.47)	0.00	1,58
Argument				
All Misspelled Words	2.64 (3.20)	2.42 (2.50)	0.10	1,61
Different Misspelled Words	2.42 (2.57)	2.12 (1.98)	0.28	1,61

Tables 6 to 10 report for each mode of writing the frequency of the five major classifications of surface errors, together with the results of the statistical test for whether the educational stream of the students is a significant variable at the .05 level. The scores do not include every error the students made. In Table 7, for example, there is no entry for dangling participles. In Table 9 there is no entry for multiple negation. These and many other errors did occur in the students' writing, but with such low frequency that they have not been included in the tables.

As Table 6 makes clear, the educational stream of the subjects has no significant effect on their spelling in either mode of writing. The high standard deviations, particularly those greater than the mean, indicate that there is considerable variance within each group and that the mean has been influenced by very weak performance by a small proportion of the students in the group. Thus there are in both groups students who make very few spelling errors indeed.

TABLE 7

Means (Standard Deviations) for Sentence Errors per 100 Words

	IMM	ENG	F	df
Narrative				
Run-on Sentences	0.59 (0.96)	0.60 (1.01)	0.00	1,58
Comma Splices	0.25 (0.51)	0.51 (0.66)	2.69	1,58
Fragments	0.23 (0.37)	0.16 (0.35)	0.51	1,58
Argument				
Run-on Sentences	0.39 (0.61)	0.23 (0.53)	1.30	1,61
Comma Splices	0.29 (0.42)	0.41 (0.48)	0.98	1,61
Fragments	0.22 (0.33)	0.28 (0.43)	0.41	1,61

Analyses of variance also indicate that the subjects' educational stream does not significantly affect the frequency of the three major sentence errors in either mode of writing. For both groups the standard deviations on all measures are greater than the mean, an indication that only a small number of subjects make many of these errors while others make few, if any.

Statistical analysis shows no significant differences between the two groups in their control of those conventions of punctuation measured. This is surprising since quotation marks and capitalization are used differently in the two languages. Indeed, errors in use of quotation marks are the only ones made more frequently by the immersion students in both modes of writing. Immersion students also make more errors of capitalization in argument, as one might expect, but make fewer in narrative. As with spelling

TABLE 8
*Means (Standard Deviations) for Punctuation
Errors per 100 Words*

	IMM	ENG	F	df
Narrative				
Period Errors	0.15 (0.35)	0.39 (0.62)	3.37	1,58
Question Mark Errors	0.06 (0.18)	0.00 (0.23)	0.09	1,58
Comma Errors	0.91 (0.86)	1.23 (1.13)	1.50	1,58
Quotation Mark Errors	0.33 (0.87)	0.20 (0.75)	0.40	1,58
Capitalization Errors	0.35 (0.64)	0.57 (1.07)	0.86	1,58
Total Errors	1.83 (2.39)	2.54 (2.67)	1.16	1,58
Argument				
Period Errors	0.07 (0.25)	0.06 (0.17)	0.06	1,61
Question Mark Errors	0.10 (0.26)	0.08 (0.19)	0.06	1,61
Comma Errors	1.53 (1.61)	1.10 (0.91)	1.69	1,61
Quotation Mark Errors	0.12 (0.34)	0.03 (0.11)	2.14	1,61
Capitalization Errors	0.35 (1.11)	0.15 (0.30)	0.95	1,61
Total Errors	2.23 (2.08)	1.47 (1.16)	3.27	1,61

and sentence errors, consistently high standard deviations reveal that in both groups a small number of students make a good many of these errors, while other students make very few of them.

TABLE 9
Means (Standard Deviations) for Verb Errors

	IMM	ENG	F	df
Narrative				
Form Errors	0.03 (0.12)	0.07 (0.12)	0.98	1,58
Agreement Errors	0.01 (0.05)	0.04 (0.12)	1.18	1,58
Shift Errors	0.07 (0.16)	0.13 (0.26)	1.38	1,58
Total Errors	0.11 (0.19)	0.25 (0.32)	3.98	1,58
Argument				
Form Errors	0.03 (0.13)	0.14 (0.32)	2.88	1,61
Agreement Errors	0.09 (0.19)	0.04 (0.16)	1.10	1,61
Shift Errors	0.06 (0.15)	0.10 (0.25)	0.65	1,61
Total Errors	0.23 (0.28)	0.32 (0.52)	0.66	1,61

Analyses of variance reveal that no difference between the immersion students and the regular English students is significant at the .05 level, although the difference in the total number of verb errors in narrative writing comes very close to being so. Comparison favours the immersion students. Subjects from the regular English program make the greater number of errors as a group. The high standard deviations again indicate that some students in both groups make these errors with comparatively great frequency, while others make them seldom, if ever.

Once more the statistical procedure also reveals no significant differences between the groups, and, again, the high standard deviations show that a small number of students within the groups make many of these errors while the others make very few.

TABLE 10
*Means (Standard Deviations) for Pronoun
Errors per 100 Words*

	IMM	ENG	F	df
Narrative				
Form Errors	0.07 (0.14)	0.06 (0.14)	0.01	1,58
Shift Errors	0.03 (0.12)	0.03 (0.09)	0.00	1,58
Reference Errors	0.03 (0.11)	0.08 (0.18)	1.37	1,58
Total Errors	0.24 (0.37)	0.23 (0.31)	0.01	1,58
Argument				
Form Errors	0.14 (0.42)	0.02 (0.07)	2.76	1,61
Shift Errors	0.22 (0.32)	0.24 (0.30)	0.14	1,61
Reference Errors	0.27 (0.43)	0.54 (0.75)	2.90	1,61
Total Errors	0.68 (0.70)	0.84 (0.75)	0.79	1,61

Summary

In overall quality, syntactic resources, and control over surface conventions, no differences in the writing of students in French immersion and regular programs were found to be significant at the .05 level. In not one of the fifty measures of writing performance reported do differences between the two groups reach that level of significance. In only one measure, the total number of verb errors in narrative writing, does the difference even approach significance, and then comparison favours the immersion group.

Conclusion

The results of this study should be treated with caution. The two groups may not be similar where information about students' intellectual ability is lacking. Only one grade has been studied, an important restriction in the light of studies that suggest comparative differences vary with grade level (Lambert, Tucker, & d'Anglejan, 1973; Genesee, 1974; Genesee & Stanley, 1976). Although there is no reason to think so, it is possible that this cohort of students was exceptional and that others would perform differently on the same measures. One may find with further research that literary activity in students' homes, parental attitudes, reading habits, and other variables influence the development of writing ability.

Nevertheless, results comparing students' performance over a wide range of variables are impressively consistent. Furthermore, scores on those measures where comparison to other studies is possible are in line with established norms. On the evidence available, their performance is that of typical grade 8 students.

These results support the view that, in the long run, the amount of instructional time spent in a second-language immersion program has little effect on achievement in the native language. Despite thousands of hours of instuction in French, these grade 8 students display writing competence in English fully equal to that of children who received those thousands of hours of instruction in English. It seems improbable that their competence could be attributed to the relatively few hours of formal language arts instruction they received. What seems more likely is that cross-lingual transfer takes place, and that, as Cummins has argued, "literacy-related skills are manifestations of a common underlying proficiency" (1983, p. 123). Their education in French, along with unexamined contributions from their homes and lives outside the school, have made these French immersion students sufficiently literate to write well in their native language.

References

Carey, S. (1984). Reflections on a decade of French immersion. *Canadian Modern Language Review, 41*, 246-255.

Crowhurst, M. (1980). Syntactic complexity in narration and argument at three grade levels. *Canadian Journal of Education, 5*(1), 6-13.

Crowhurst, M., & Piche, G. (1979). Audience and mode of discourse effects on syntactic complexity in writing at two grade levels. *Research in the Teaching of English, 13*, 101-109.

Cummins, J. (1979). Linguistic interdependence and the educational development of bilingual children. *Review of Educational Research, 49*, 222-251.

Genesee, F. (1974). *Evaluations of English-writing skills of students in French-immersion programs*. Montreal, PQ: Protestant School Board of Greater Montreal.

Genesee, F., & Stanley, M.H. (1976). The development of English writing skills in French immersion school programs. *Canadian Journal of Education, 1*(3), 1-17.

Grobe, C. (n.d.). *Mastery level for grade five French immersion students on the 1977 New Brunswick Language Arts Criterion-Referenced Test.* Fredericton, NB: New Brunswick Department of Education.

Hillocks, G. (1986). *Research on written composition.* Urbana, IL: National Conference on Research in English.

Hunt, K.W. (1970). *Syntactic maturity in schoolchildren and adults.* Chicago, IL: University of Chicago Press for the Society for Research in Child Development.

Lambert, W.E., Tucker, G.R., & d'Anglejan, A. (1973). Cognitive and attitudinal consequences of bilingual schooling: The St. Lambert project through grade five. *Journal of Educational Psychology, 65,* 141-159.

Lapkin, S. (1982). The English writing skills of French immersion pupils at grade five. *Canadian Modern Language Review, 39,* 24-33.

Loban, W. (1976). *Language development: Kindergarten through grade twelve.* Urbana, IL: National Council of Teachers in English.

Ontario Ministry of Education. (1982). *Ontario assessment instrument pool: Report of the 1981 field trials in English, intermediate division.* Toronto, ON: Ontario Ministry of Education.

O'Hare, F. (1973). *Sentence combining: Improving student writing without formal grammar instruction.* Urbana, IL: National Council of Teachers in English.

Pineo, P.C., & Porter, J. (1979). Occupational prestige in Canada. In J.E. Curtis & W.G. Scott (Eds.), *Social stratification in Canada* (2nd ed., pp. 205-220). Scarborough, ON: Prentice-Hall.

Pringle, I., & Freedman, A. (1985). *A comparative study of writing abilities in two modes at the grade 5, 8 and 12 levels.* Toronto, ON: Ontario Ministry of Education.

Swain, M. (1975). Writing skills of grade three French immersion pupils. *Working papers on bilingualism, 7,* 1-38.

Swain, M. (1978). Home-school language switching. In J.C. Richards (Ed.), *Understanding second and foreign language learning* (pp. 238-250). Rowley, MA: Newbury House.

Swain, M., & Lapkin, S. (1981). *Bilingual education in Ontario: A decade of research.* Toronto, ON: Ontario Ministry of Education.

Heritage Language Children in an English-French Bilingual Program

Merrill Swain and Sharon Lapkin
Ontario Institue for Studies in Education

This article reports on two studies involving heritage language children enrolled in a bilingual (English-French) program beginning at grade 5. The maintenance and development of the heritage language with specific reference to literacy learning is shown to enhance the learning of French, which is a third language for these minority language students.

*   *   *

AMONG MINORITY LANGUAGE CHILDREN, THE DEVELOPMENT AND MAINTE-
nance of the home language, or heritage language, is often not seen as a
priority by either parents or educators. Immigrant parents may feel great
pressure for their children to function in the majority language (in this case,
English) quickly in order to integrate into the social mainstream and experience academic success. Educational institutions frequently provide little
or no heritage language instruction, in spite of research demonstrating that
second language learning and academic achievement may be enhanced by
valuing, using and teaching minority children's mother tongue (e.g.,
Cummins, 1981; Genesee, 1987; Hakuta, 1986; Krashen & Biber, 1988;
Rosier & Farella, 1976; Troike, 1978; Willig, 1985).

This paper reports on two studies conducted in Metropolitan Toronto
which underline the importance of heritage language maintenance and development, including literacy training, in second and third language learning.

Both studies (Bild & Swain, 1989; Swain, Lapkin, Rowen & Hart,
1991) involve heritage language children enrolled in a bilingual (English-
French) program beginning at grade 5 at a large Metropolitan Toronto
School board. In this program students study in English through to grade
4, taking French as a second language for twenty minutes a day as part of
their regular program. In grade 5, they begin a program in which half of
their instructional day is in French and half is in English. Throughout their
schooling, minority language children have the option of participating in a
Heritage Language Program. These are classes which instruct students in
and about their native language and culture and are offered outside of
school hours for a half hour each day, or two and a half hours on Saturday
mornings.

In the first study, Bild and Swain (1989) sought to determine how well minority language children in this bilingual program learned French relative to children whose first language was English. There were three groups of immersion students: a grade 8 English-background group and two grade 8 minority language background groups. One minority language group consisted of students whose first language was Italian. The second group was a heterogeneous group of non-Romance language speakers: 1 Armenian, 6 Croatians, 1 Czechoslovakian, 1 Greek, 1 Pole, 3 Slovenians, and 1 Ukrainian. There were two hypotheses. First, due to the historic linguistic connection among Romance languages, it was anticipated that the Italian speakers would, through positive linguistic transfer, perform better on measures of French proficiency than the non-Romance language speakers. Second, as Cummins' (1979, 1981) interdependence hypothesis would predict, learning a third language should be facilitated from other language learning, particularly with respect to literacy-related skills.

Students were selected on the basis of background information obtained from their teachers, school records, and a questionnaire which asked for information concerning language use patterns, own and parents' birthplaces, and parents' languages, level of education, and occupation. From the questionnaire it was determined that the home language use patterns of the minority language children involved the use of the minority language between the parents, between the student and at least one parent (often both), often between the student and grandparents, and only rarely between the student and siblings. According to self-ratings of written proficiency in the minority language, the non-Romance group rated themselves significantly higher than did the Italian group. Additionally, the Italian group had a significantly lower mean parental occupation score than did the English group.

Four different measures of French proficiency were used: 2 story retelling tasks and 2 cloze tasks. Scores for the story retelling task were calculated for such features as verb, prepositional, and syntactic accuracy; lexical diversity and lexical uniqueness; accent; fluency; and discourse and strategic performance.

The results indicate that the two groups of minority language students were significantly better than the English group on the French cloze tests and on most of the oral measures. This was the case in spite of the lower socioeconomic status (SES) as indicated by parental occupation of the Italian group. Interestingly, the minority groups were superior on all grammatical measures but not on measures of lexical uniqueness and lexical diversity. Thus, bilinguals show superior performance in the area of grammatical knowledge but not in lexical knowledge—in this case demonstrated in their learning of a third language. (See also Harley, Hart, & Lapkin 1986.)

The results also indicate that the Italian group consistently performed better than the non-Romance group. However no statistically significant differences were noted. As seen in the next study, literacy knowledge in the minority language appears to be a significant factor in French language performance. Thus, it may be that the higher minority language written proficiency (as indicated by self-ratings) of the non-Romance group relative to the Italian group has compensated for the greater "language distance" between their home and target languages. A significant positive correlation (found in the Bild and Swain study) between the number of years in heritage language classes and French proficiency supports this conjecture.

The second study (Swain et al., 1991) was carried out in the context of a large evaluation (Hart, Lapkin, & Swain, 1987) designed to compare the French performance of two immersion program groups: early immersion students and students enrolled in the bilingual program beginning in the "middle" years (grade 5) that was described above. The evaluation also documented the characteristics of the students who entered each type of program. We would like to have examined the French performance of minority students in the early immersion program relative to nonminority language students, but there were simply not enough minority language students in the early immersion sample to warrant such a study. However, in the Board of Education which housed the bilingual program, there were a large number of minority students enrolled in the program and therefore we were able to compare their performance in French relative to majority language students in the same program. In all, data were collected from 16 grade 8 bilingual classes.

There were three questions concerning minority language students' French performance relative to that of nonminority language (i.e., English background) students. First, we wanted to determine if the findings of the previous study were replicable—specifically whether minority language students' French proficiency would be superior to that of English background students and whether Romance and non-Romance students' performance would be similar. Second, we wished to explore the role of literacy in the minority language on third (i.e., French) language proficiency. Is there an additional impact that minority language literacy has above and beyond that provided by its oral use? And third, if there is a particular advantage in third language learning associated with first language literacy, could it be that SES is the critical variable rather than literacy per se? The relationship between SES and literacy in the minority language was therefore examined to be able to exclude SES as a confounding variable.

The set of French assessment instruments included a sentence repetition task, a listening comprehension test utilizing authentic passages from the radio, a cloze test, the writing of an opinion essay, and a discussion about a controversial but personal topic (parental strictness). The instruments, therefore, involved reading, writing, speaking, and listening.

Listening comprehension scores were based on both the comprehension test (multiple-choice) and the extent to which sentences were repeated in the sentence repetition task, thus indicating an understanding of what had been said, even if a precise repetition had not been given. For speaking, the discussion was scored for fluency, and the sentence repetition task was scored for various grammatical and discourse features. The opinion essay was scored for number of words written, nonhomophonous grammatical errors (i.e., errors which would sound incorrect if spoken), a global judgment of "good" writing involving two dimensions: complexity of sentence structure and phrasing and incidence of spelling, grammatical, and syntactic errors. Reading ability was assessed by the cloze score. Unfortunately, no measure of vocabulary knowledge was obtained.

Students were asked a number of questions (via a questionnaire) to determine minority language use patterns. To obtain categories which would indicate literacy knowledge in the minority language, information from several questions was combined. The questions asked students to list what languages, not counting English and French, they understand in written and spoken form and to indicate the main ways in which they use these languages (e.g., speaking to parents, writing to relatives, watching TV, reading letters or newspapers). Using this information, four categories were derived: 1) has no minority language; 2) has a minority language but is unable to understand the written form of it; 3) understands the minority language in the written form but does not indicate any use of it; 4) understands and uses the minority language in the written mode.

The results are striking. First, those students who do not have a minority language and those who do have a minority language but claim not to read or write in it are similar in their French test results; however those students who read and/or write in their minority language whether or not they claim to be currently making use of these skills are similar in their French test results. Second, with one exception, the literate minority language groups significantly outperform the English background group and the nonliterate minority language group on all measures of French language performance. The one exception is with respect to nonhomophonous grammatical errors where no significant differences were found. In other words, having a minority language in which one can or cannot engage in literacy activities appears to make no difference to the number of nonhomophonous grammatical errors the students make while writing in French. Why this finding should be unique to this measure is not at all clear.

In short, it appears that minority language literacy has a generalized positive effect on third language learning, that is, its positive impact is not limited to literacy-related activities in the third language. The results suggest that the effect is related to literacy knowledge rather than oral proficiency in the minority language.

One issue in interpreting these findings is whether the results could be due simply to a general high level of proficiency in the minority language, or whether they are specifically due to the impact of minority language literacy. In order to tease apart general minority language proficiency and minority language literacy, we examined test scores as a function of frequency of use of the minority language and literate versus nonliterate background. Doing so involved making the assumption that students who report frequent use of the minority language in the home are proficient in that language. Specifically, we looked to see if, among those who reported their minority language to be frequently used in the home, there was a tendency for those who are also literate in their minority language to do better on test measures relative to those who are not literate. The results significantly favour the literate group. Thus, it appears that minority language literacy has an enhancing effect on third language learning independent of overall general minority language proficiency.

Another issue in interpreting the above findings is a possible confounding of SES with literacy. If SES and literacy in the minority language are associated, then the higher French scores observed may be due to factors associated with social and economic class rather than literacy per se. The SES variables examined were father's educational level, mother's educational level, father's occupation and mother's occupation. The results show that students who are literate in their minority language are at least as likely to come from the lower categories of the SES variables as from the higher. That is, with respect to the educational attainment of fathers, those children who are literate in their minority language are at least as likely to come from families where the father has had only elementary school or some high school (approximately 32% of our sample) as they are to come from families where the father has completed a university, graduate, or professional degree (approximately 27%).

Similarly, with respect to the father's occupation, those children who are literate in their minority language are at least as likely to come from families where the father is a semiskilled or unskilled worker (approximately 33%) as they are to come from families where the father is a manager or a professional (approximately 19%). (The pattern is similar as concerns the mother's educational attainment and occupation.) Thus, among students who have a minority language, differences in third language proficiency associated with minority language literacy do not appear to be due to SES.

The final question that this study addressed was whether students speaking a Romance language would outperform their non-Romance peers in French. For this purpose, students were divided into two groups: a Romance group including students who reported using Italian, Spanish, or Portuguese, and a non-Romance group including students who reported using German, Polish, Hebrew, Filipino/Tagalog, Chinese, Greek, or Korean. As with the previous study, we found a trend for Romance background students to do better on the French measures than the non-Romance background students, but the differences were statistically significant on only two measures: fluency and global comprehension.

Taken together, these two studies show an enhanced proficiency in French among minority language students who read and/or write in their first language. This was suggested in the first study by a significant correlation between years in a Heritage Language Program (in which literacy skills are usually taught) and French performance. In the second study, the link between being literate in one's first language—as opposed to just having oral/aural skills in that language—and enhanced third language learning is quite clear. Moreover, the link does not appear to depend on generally high levels of oral/aural first language proficiency, SES, or the linguistic/historical relationship between the two languages.

Thus, for minority language children who have maintained their heritage language and supported it with literacy knowledge, we can expect superior third language performance relative to other minority language children who do not read or write in their heritage language. Moreover, we can expect superior performance from them also in relation to the French language skills of majority anglophones for whom French is a second, rather than a third language.

References

Bild, E.R., & Swain, M. (1989). Minority language students in a french immersion programme: Their French proficiency. *Journal of Multilingual and Multicultural Development, 10*(3), 255-274.

Cummins, J. (1979). Linguistic interdependence and the educational development of bilingual children. *Review of Educational Research, 49*, 222-251.

Cummins, J. (1981). The role of primary language development in promoting educational success for language minority students. In *Schooling and language minority students: A theoretical framework*, pp. 3-49. Los Angeles, CA: California State Department of Education, Evaluation, Dissemination and Assessment Center.

Genesee, F. (1987). *Learning through two languages: Studies of immersion and bilingual education*. Cambridge, MA: Newbury House.

Hakuta, K. (1986). *The mirror of language: The debate on bilingualism*. New York, NY: Basic Books.

Harley, B., Hart, D., & Lapkin, S. (1986). The effects of early bilingual schooling on first language skills. *Applied Psycholinguistics, 7*, 295-322.

Hart, D., Lapkin, S., & Swain, M. (1987). *Early and middle French immersion programs: Linguistic outcomes and social character*. Toronto, ON: Metropolitan Toronto School Board.

Krashen, S., & Biber, D. (1988). *On course: Bilingual education's success in California.* Sacramento, CA: California Association for Bilingual Education.

Rosier, P., & Farella, M. (1976). Bilingual education at Rock Point—Some early results. *TESOL Quarterly, 10,* 379-388.

Swain, M. (1975). Writing skills of grade three french immersion pupils. *Working Papers on Bilingualism, 7,* 1-38.

Swain, M., & Barik, H.C. (1976). A large scale program in french immersion: the ottawa study through grade three. *ITL: A Review of Applied Linguistics, 33,* 1-25.

Swain, M., Lapkin, S., Rowen, N., & Hart, D. (1991). The role of mother tongue literacy in third language learning. In *Foundations of literacy policy in Canada,* S.P. Norris & L.M. Phillips, Eds., pp. 185-206. Calgary, AB: Detselig Enterprises Ltd.

Troike, R.C. (1978). *Research evidence for the effectiveness of bilingual education.* Arlington, VA: National Clearinghouse for Bilingual Education.

Willig, A.C. (1985). A meta-analysis of selected studies on the effectiveness of bilingual education. *Review of Educational Research, 55,* 269-317.

School and Family French Ambiance and the Bilingual Development of Francophone Western Canadians

Rodrigue Landry, Réal Allard
Université de Moncton
Raymond Théberge
Collège Universitaire de Saint-Boniface

This paper examines the relative contributions of the school and of the family to the bilingual development of francophone minority group students in Western Canada. The subjects were grade 12 students in thirteen high schools that housed francophone students in the three prairie provinces. Data were analyzed from the perspective of a macroscopic model of the determinants of additive and subtractive bilingualism. The students were categorized into three groups: low, medium, and high French ambiance schools. These three groups were then further categorized according to the degree of French ambiance in the family (low vs high). The statistical analyses and the descriptive data clearly indicated a subtractive type of bilingualism for most of the students. Most students were dominant in their second language. French scores were higher in groups that came from high French ambiance schools and high French ambiance homes. Linguistic competence in English did not seem to be negatively affected by the higher French ambiance in the home and in the school. French ambiance scores were also positively related to the strength of personal beliefs of the students in the vitality of their language and also to the strength of their ethnolinguistic identity. The implications for the survival of the French language in Western Canada are discussed.

*   *   *

THE RECENT HISTORY OF FRANCOPHONES IN WESTERN CANADA CAN BE characterized as a struggle against the constant threat of linguistic and cultural assimilation. A survey of demographic data clearly demonstrates that

We wish to thank the Association canadienne-française de l'Alberta, the Association culturelle franco-canadiennne de la Saskatchewan, the Bureau de la minorité de langue officielle of the Department of Education of Saskatchewan and the Collège Universitaire Saint-Boniface for their financial and organizational contribution to the present study. We also express our gratitude to the school principals for their hospitality and their help in organizing the testing procedures in the schools and finally we are grateful to the students who participated by accepting to answer the numerous questionnaires involved.

linguistic assimilation has decimated the ranks of the francophone communities in these provinces (Denis & Li, 1988; Hébert & Bilodeau, 1987; Carey, 1987a; Allaire & Fedigan, 1989). This trend does not appear to be reversing itself. Numerous historical, constitutional, socio-political and educational factors have interacted to produce the current state of affairs (Aunger, 1989; Bastarache, 1989; Carey, 1989; Mahé, 1989; McMahon & Fedigan, 1989; Théberge, 1989). With respect to the area of education, the vast majority of francophones in western Canada have limited access to French instruction and to francophone schools that are intended specifically for minority language students (Aunger, 1989; Foucher, 1985; Théberge, 1987). The province of Saskatchewan plans to proceed with the implementation of a system of governance by francophones for a network of French schools in the province in the near future. The status of francophone education could be altered in the province of Alberta and Manitoba, depending upon the outcomes of current litigation. The outcomes of such conditions have been analyzed in Alberta, where francophone students tend to develop a subtractive type of bilingualism. Their performance on academic tasks in French has been found to approximate that of anglophone immersion students (Carey & Cummins, 1983; Carey, 1987a). In Manitoba, studies by Hébert et al. (1976) and Baril (1984) have shown that an increase in the amount of French schooling was related to gains in French linguistic competence with no negative effect on English linguistic competence when these students were compared to francophones schooled in English. Despite these results demonstrating the positive effects of French schooling, many francophone parents in western Canada are of the view that too much French schooling may be detrimental to their children's development of English language skills and therefore hamper their social mobility as western Canadians (Carey, 1987b; Ruest, 1988).

In this article, we examine the relative contribution of the school and of the family to the bilingual development of francophone minority group students in western Canada. This analysis is undertaken from both the perspective of a model of additive and subtractive bilingualism and that of empirical data collected in several high schools in Manitoba, Saskatchewan, and Alberta. The first part of the paper presents a global definition of additive and subtractive bilingualism and a social-psychological model of the factors related to these two types of bilingualism. In the second part, the predictions of the theoretical model relative to the schooling process and home language use are discussed. The third part of the paper presents data collected on most dimensions of the theoretical model on grade 12 students in thirteen high schools which housed francophone students in the three prairie provinces. In the final section, we conclude by discussing the role of the school and of the family as factors influencing the bilingual development of these minority group students.

Additive and Subtractive Bilingualism: A Theoretical Model

Lambert (1974, 1975), while in the process of trying to account for important contradictions in research results on the cognitive and affective consequences of bilingualism, was the first to coin the terms "additive" and "subtractive" bilingualism. He referred to additive bilingualism to denote the learning of a second language (L2) with no negative impact on the maintenance of the mother tongue (L1). Lambert also noted that, in some conditions, the learning of L2 led to less efficient L1 acquisition which could in turn be related to negative cognitive and affective consequences. He referred to this type of bilingualism as subtractive. Additive bilingualism is most common in majority group individuals, especially those who have been educated in intensive second language programs such as immersion programs for anglophones (Cummins & Swain, 1986; Genesee, 1983, 1987; Lambert & Tucker, 1972; Swain & Lapkin, 1982). Subtractive bilingualism seems to be most common in members of minority groups such as francophones outside Québec (Cummins, 1979; Hamers & Blanc, 1983, 1989; Landry, 1982; Lambert, 1974).

The use of the terms "additive" and "subtractive" bilingualism, however, has been largely restricted to the cognitive domain. Additive bilingualism has been associated with such positive cognitive consequences as mental flexibility, creativity and metalinguistic awareness, whereas subtractive bilingualism has been associated with poor cognitive abilities (Cummins, 1978, 1979; Hamers & Blanc, 1983, 1989). Although these cognitive consequences have been found to exist, they have tended to be of low magnitude when extraneous factors such as socioeconomic status and nonverbal intellectual aptitude were controlled, and no type of bilingualism has been found to be related to a significant increase or decrease in global intellectual functioning (Baker, 1988; Landry, 1984; McLaughlin, 1984). We contend that the exclusive focus on the cognitive domain deters from the strong social relevance of the concepts proposed by Lambert. We propose that the defining characteristic of additive and subtractive bilingualism should not be whether bilingualism is related to high or low levels of cognitive functioning (even though this does remain an interesting empirical issue), but whether conditions of bilingualism lead to the maintenance or loss of one's language, culture and ethnolinguistic identity. Bilingualism has important sociocultural aspects that cannot be neglected even when the intent is the study of the psychological aspects of bilingualism. Bilingualism is as much a societal as an individual phenomenon (Fishman, 1989). Additive and subtractive bilingualism need to be analyzed from several essential perspectives as an individual phenomenon, but must also be related to the social dimensions of linguistic communities. Without a minimum amount of ethnolinguistic vitality (Giles, Bourhis & Taylor, 1977), a linguistic community cannot survive as an active and distinct entity. When individuals lose the ability and the desire to use their mother tongue, the whole community loses in the dynamic process of cultural reproduction. Whenever individuals cease to participate in the process of the cultural reproduction of their linguistic community, there is a loss both for the individual and his or her linguistic community, and possibly for the society in general. Additive and subtractive bilingualism should encompass more than the absence or presence of cognitive and affective consequences. Even when a bilingual child is free of such problems as poor academic achievement and poor self-concept, and even if the bilingual experience did lead to increased cognitive functioning, bilingualism should not be said to be additive if this child has lost the opportunity to become an active member of his or her linguistic community. For bilingualism to be additive, both from the perspective of the individual and from that of the linguistic community, the dual language experience must allow the person to continue participating in the cultural reproduction of his or her linguistic community. The following modified definition of additive bilingualism is therefore proposed.

> Complete additive bilingualism should encompass: (a) a high degree of proficiency in both communicative and cognitive-academic aspects of L1 and L2; (b) maintenance of a strong ethnolinguistic identity and positive beliefs towards one's own language and culture while holding positive attitudes toward the second language; and (c) the opportunity to use one's first language without diglossia, that is without one's language being used exclusively for less valued social roles or domains of activity (Landry, 1987, p. 110).

The model shown in Figure 1 identifies factors which are instrumental in the development of additive or subtractive bilingualism. The model originated within a multidisciplinary approach to the study of bilingualism (Landry, 1982; Prujiner, Deshaies, Hamers, Blanc, Clement & Landry, 1984) and has been verified empirically (e.g., Landry & Allard, 1990, in press). The model links sociological and psychological variables, the two sets of variables being mediated by the individual's network of linguistic contacts. Language behavior is depicted as the end result of the interaction of these three sets of variables. The pattern of language use and the psychological disposition of the individual toward L1 and L2 can be analyzed to determine both degree and type of bilingualism.

As depicted in Figure 1 (Sociological level), a bilingual society can be conceived as being composed of two linguistic communities, each with a relative degree of ethnolinguistic vitality. Ethnolinguistic vitality is that which determines whether a community will remain an active and distinct entity (Giles et al., 1977). This dynamic process and "rapport de force" can be analyzed through various sociological procedures. Objective measures of the degree of vitality can be obtained by gathering indices of the structural variables involved. We have used the notion of "capital"

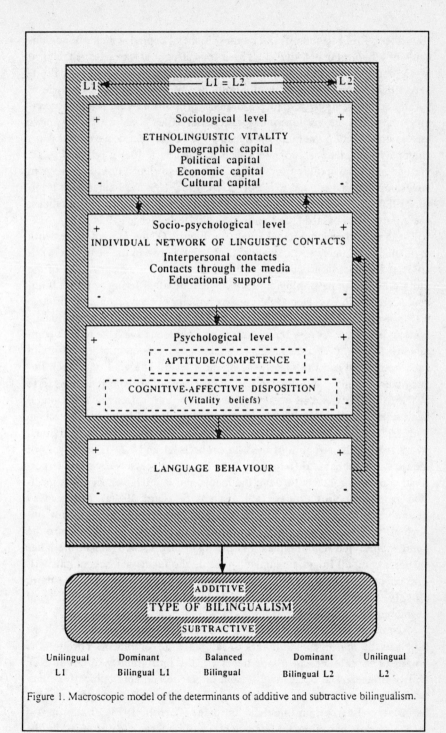

Figure 1. Macroscopic model of the determinants of additive and subtractive bilingualism.

(Bourdieu, 1980) to identify four types of social capital which are components of ethnolinguistic vitality. These four structural variables are defined as elements in a system of interacting forces (Prujiner et al., 1984; Prujiner, 1987). Empirical indices of vitality can be identified for each type of social capital; *demographic* (e.g., number, proportion, concentration, territory, exogamy, emigration, immigration; see Giles et al., 1977); *economic* (e.g., control and ownership of industry and commerce, occupation, salary, unemployment, language of work; see Vaillancourt, 1984); *political* (e.g., various indices of political power, legal language rights, use of language in government agencies; see Prujiner, 1984, 1987; Héraux, Lapierre, & Prujiner, 1984); and *cultural* (e.g., mass media, education, cultural institutions; see Allard, De la Garde, & Landry, 1984; De la Garde, 1984).

At the socio-psychological level (see Figure 1), the individual network of linguistic contacts (INLC) becomes the link between the structural variables at the sociological level and cognitive-affective dispositions of the individual at the psychological level. The individual living within a bilingual society will experience the relative vitality of each community through his or her network of linguistic contacts. To the extent that the individual's INLC is distributed across the spectrum of institutions available to both communities, the INLC becomes a micro-sociological reflection of the vitality of each community at the macro-sociological level. The vitality of each linguistic community, as reflected within each type of social capital (e.g., size of the community and its economic resources, political power and cultural institutions), will influence the quantity and quality of linguistic contacts in both L1 and L2. One can assess the bilingual experience of an individual by measuring the strength of the INLC in both L1 and L2. The analyses of the INLC can focus on different types of linguistic contacts such as interpersonal contacts, contacts through the media and language experiences mediated by the schooling process (e.g., Landry & Allard, 1987a). Another way of analyzing the INLC is to look at the relative contributions of three important "milieux de vie" in which the INLC is experienced. These are the *family milieu*, the *school milieu* and the *socio-institutional milieu* (the latter encompassing all linguistic contacts outside the family and school milieux). The concept of "milieux de vie" is discussed below as we analyze more closely the roles of the school and of the family as agents of bilingual development.

According to the model, the linguistic contacts experienced through the INLC are the major determinants of language development. Through the language experiences in his or her INLC, the individual will develop an ability to use L1 and L2 for different linguistic and communicative functions (the *aptitude/competence* factor). Though linguistic competence may be influenced by certain linguistic aptitudes (Carroll, 1973), it is proposed by the model that bilingual competence will be largely determined by the extent of opportunities to use L1 and L2 within the INLC. The model predicts that communicative competencies will be more closely related to the extent of interpersonal contacts than to media and schooling whereas cognitive academic linguistic proficiency, as defined by Cummins (1979, 1981), will be more closely related to literacy activities experienced in the language either in the school or in the home.

Linguistic contacts within the INLC will also largely determine the individual's cognitive-affective disposition toward the language, i.e., the willingness to learn and use the language. The ethnolinguistic identity of an individual is also part of the individual's psychological disposition toward the language. Allard and Landry (1986) have proposed that the cognitive-affective disposition of the individual toward the language can be conceptualized as the individual's "subjective ethnolinguistic vitality" (Bourhis, Giles, & Rosenthal, 1981) and effectively measured by an analysis of the individual's non-self and self beliefs reflecting the vitality of the language groups. Subjective ethnolinguistic vitality when conceptualized as a system of beliefs has been found to be a very strong predictor of language behavior (Allard & Landry, 1986, 1987a, 1988).

In a bilingual context, language behavior in L1 and L2 is hypothesized to be strongly related to the extent of the language contacts in both languages within the INLC and to the resulting psychological disposition toward each language. This hypothesis has been clearly supported by empirical data (Landry & Allard, 1988a, 1989, 1990, in press-a, in press-b). As shown in Figure 1, language behavior feeds back to the INLC because it is always experienced as part of the individual's network of language contacts and leads to further contacts in that language. The network provides the opportunities for language behavior and the actual behavior results from situational variables and the individual's psychological disposition.

Schooling, Family Milieu, and Additive Bilingualism

How can the school environment and the family milieu contribute to additive bilingualism? For minority group children, it is proposed that the school milieu and the family milieu act as counterbalancing forces to the socio-institutional milieu by providing linguistic contacts to help maintain L1. According to the counterbalance model of bilingual experience (Landry & Allard, 1987b, 1988b, in press-a), schooling in L1 or L2 and the use of L1 and L2 in the family milieu have different impacts depending on the vitality of the linguistic community of which the individual is a member. As shown in Figure 2, the school and family milieux play a role in the promotion of additive bilingualism. The particular role they play will depend on whether the student is a member of a low vitality or a high vitality group. In a low vitality group context, the prestige and the pervasive presence of L2 may be so strong as to dominate the student's INLC. Maintenance of L1 will be assured only if the family milieu and the school milieu can compensate for the dominance of L2 in the socio-institutional milieu. In such contexts, the ambiance of the school and of the family must be strongly dominated by L1. Increased efforts must also be made to assure the maximum amount of L1 contacts within the socio-institutional milieu. Without a certain degree of "institutional completeness," members of an ethnolinguistic group may not experience enough linguistic contacts for the long term maintenance of the language by the community (Breton, 1964).

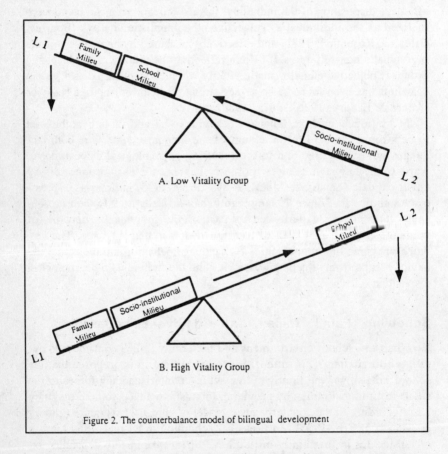

Figure 2. The counterbalance model of bilingual development

The situation is reversed for children in a high vitality group. For them, the language experiences provided by the socio-institutional and family milieux contribute to L1 unilingualism. Only the school can act as a counterbalancing force to increase the relative strength of the L2 network. Because of the clear dominance of L1 in the family and the socio-institutional milieux, intensive and long term second language programs are needed to foster a high degree of bilingualism for members of the high vitality group. Although French immersion has provided a relatively high level of additive bilingualism for anglophone students in Canada, some researchers are suggesting that if L2 contacts are limited to the school context, bilingualism for these students could be both restrained and short lived (Carey, 1984; Cummins & Swain, 1986; Genesee, 1987; Harley, 1984; Pellerin & Hammerly, 1986). The school milieu experience, therefore, may not be sufficient to foster stable bilingualism among children from a dominant high vitality group.

In low ethnolinguistic vitality situations such as those of western Canada's francophones, the counterbalance model of bilingual experience predicts that additive bilingualism would be better promoted under conditions of L1 schooling than under bilingual or L2 schooling. This prediction is consonant with the recent literature which shows that minority group children educated mainly via L1 not only better maintain their mother tongue but also learn L2 as well as minority students schooled via L2 (Cummins, 1984, 1986; Cummins & Mulcahy, 1978; Hamers & Blanc, 1983; Hébert et al., 1976; Landry & Allard, in press-a; Skutnabb-Kangas, 1977; Willig, 1985). This result is possible because L1 cognitive-academic linguistic competence transfers to L2 cognitive-academic linguistic competence (Cummins, 1981), this transfer being also facilitated by the oral competency in L2 acquired by language contacts in the socio-institutional milieu and also by the strong social pressure to learn L2 in a minority group context. In conditions of low ethnolinguistic vitality, it has even been suggested that the teaching of L2 be delayed and that the extra time be used to build a stronger L1 foundation, not only in competence but also in ethnolinguistic identity and beliefs (Landry & Allard, 1988).

In this article, we analyze the effects of the school and family milieux on various dimensions of bilingualism of grade 12 francophone students in Manitoba, Saskatchewan and Alberta. We were not able to test samples of the many francophone students who were educated exclusively via L2. Most students tested had received most of their schooling via the French language. Our sample is, therefore, reduced in variability on the variable of L1 schooling. We analyze in the remainder of this article the effects of the observed differences in the amount of L1 schooling and L1 use in the family on the development of both L1 and L2.

Method

Population

The francophone population of Manitoba is highly concentrated in the St. Boniface area and southeastern region of the province. The demographic base, though it is small, does occupy a specific territory. This is not the case for francophones in Saskatchewan and Alberta, where francophones are dispersed throughout the province due in great part to the trend of population movement from the rural to the urban area, where there are no traditional francophone enclaves. Participants in the study were grade 12 francophone high school students. Testing was done in six high schools in the province of Manitoba, most of them in the Winnipeg area or neighbouring communities (Précieux Sang, Windsor Park, Ile des Chênes, St-Jean Baptiste, St-Pierre and Louis Riel), four high schools in the province of Saskatchewan (one in each of the following rural communities: Bellevue, Bellegarde, Gravelbourg and Zenon Park) and three high schools in the province of Alberta (J.H. Picard in Edmonton, the community high school of Mallaig and the high school that housed the francophone students in the Bonnyville area). In the J.H. Picard school of Edmonton, anglophone French immersion students were also tested but are excluded from the analyses presented in this paper. A total of 301 francophone students constitute the sample tested in thirteen different high schools. The number of students tested varied considerably from school to school, from a low of 4 to a high of 71.

Materials

The questionnaire and tests used in this study have been extensively described in Landry and Allard (1987a) and are briefly presented here.

1. Non-verbal intellectual aptitude

    The abstract reasoning scale of the Differential Aptitude Tests (Bennett, Seashore, & Wesman, 1974) was administered. The maximum score is 50.

2. Socioeconomic status (SES)

    Occupation of the mother and father were categorized on a 1 to 7 scale based on Blishen and McRoberts (1976). Each parent's level of schooling was also categorized on a 1 to 7 point scale. Scores reported are the average for both parents' level of occupation and degree of schooling.

3. Individual network of linguistic contacts (INLC)

    Interpersonal contacts were measured by a questionnaire covering several structural dimension of L1, L2 and L1/L2 networks.

In this paper, only two scales are used: the proportion of francophones in the interpersonal network and the proportion of anglophones in the interpersonal network. Scores could range from 1 to 9 where 1 indicated that none of the persons constituting the network were francophones (anglophones) and 9 indicated that all were francophones (anglophones). *Contacts with the media* were measured by 12 questions pertaining to the access to several media sources in both French and English. The questions pertained to the availability of these media sources in their environment and not to their actual use. Total scores could range from 1 to 9, the latter referring to a high degree of contact. *Educational support* was measured by Likert-type scales indexing the language of schooling and the linguistic ambiance of the school from kindergarten to grade 12. For the degree of French schooling, average scores could range from 1 to 7, the latter indicating teaching exclusively in French. For the school French ambiance, scores could range from 1 to 5, the latter indicating a totally French ambiance.

4. Oral communicative competence

The students rated their ability to communicate in French and English in 15 different communicative situations ranging in levels of difficulty. The average score could range from 1 to 9, the latter indicating native-like ability.

5. Cognitive academic linguistic proficiency

French and English cloze-tests of approximately 325 words each were administered. The "exact word" scoring procedure was used and scores are reported as the number of words correctly identified. Scores could range from 0 to 65.

6. Beliefs in ethnolinguistic vitality

This questionnaire related eight different kinds of beliefs to twelve different indices of ethnolinguistic vitality (Allard & Landry, 1987b). Factor analyses of L1 and L2 beliefs have yielded two factor scores (non-self beliefs and self beliefs) in both French and English for minority francophone students (Allard & Landry, 1987a). Non-self beliefs refer to the perception of the "objective" vitality of the anglophones and francophones: the actual resources, the future resources, the legitimacy of the situation and the present language behavior of peers and models. Self beliefs consist of feelings of belonging, valorisation, personal efficacy at fulfilling one's needs in the language and personal goals. The scores reported here are the average score for the four non-self belief scales and the average score on the four self belief scales relative to both the francophone and anglophone linguistic communities.

7. Ethnolinguistic identity

The students rated their francophone and anglophone identity on a 1 to 9 scale from a variety of perspectives (culture, language, ancestors, ethnic origins, etc.), The mean scores for francophone and anglophone identity are reported. The higher the score the higher the ethnolinguistic identity.

8. Self-reported use of French and English

The students rated the frequency of use of French and English (1 = never, 9 = always) in 15 different linguistic contact situations. The mean score for degree of use of French and English with family members and the mean score for the degree of use of French and English in situations other than with family members are reported separately.

9. Language variety spoken

Each student indicated on a 1 to 7 scale the language variety most often spoken or the one he/she felt more at ease speaking. A score of 1 indicates that the most often used variety was English and a score of 7 indicates standard French as the most spoken variety. A score of 4 indicates a strong mixture of French and English. The lower the score, the stronger is the influence of English in the spoken variety.

Procedure

The testing in all 13 schools involved was done in October and November of 1988. Testing was done in groups of various sizes over two days and required a total of three 50-minute class periods (2 periods on day 1 and 1 period on day 2 or vice versa). Testing days were consecutive for most schools. The French and English cloze-tests (20 minutes each) and the non-verbal aptitude test (25 minutes) had time limits; the students responded to the remaining questionnaires at their own pace.

Design and Statistical Analyses

It is fair to say that francophone communities in the western provinces have very low ethnolinguistic vitality. In the 1986 Statistics Canada Census, the percentages of the total population that reported French as their mother tongue were respectively 4.3, 2.1 and 2.0 for the provinces of Manitoba, Saskatchewan and Alberta. The assimilation rates of francophones in these three provinces were 47, 67 and 63% respectively. Since ethnolinguistic vitality was uniformly low in all three provinces, the students were grouped in the following manner for the statistical analyses. First, the students were grouped according to the French ambiance of the school. Those who had scores below the 25th percentile constitute a "low French ambiance" group (LFA). Those who had scores between the 25th and 75th percentile constitute a "medium French ambiance" group (MFA). The third and final group is constituted of the students who had scores equal to or above the 75th percentile and is called the "high French ambiance" group (HFA). All students were further grouped according to the degree of French ambiance in the home. This variable was created by taking the mean score of the frequency of use of French when talking to the father, to the mother and to brothers and sisters. Those who had a mean score of 6.00 and more on a 9 point scale constitute the "high use of French" group (HUF) and those who had a mean score below 6.00 are part of the "low use of French" group (LUF). According to the counterbalance model of bilingual development described above, both the linguistic ambiance of the school and of the home should be related to the development of additive and subtractive bilingualism among these minority group students.

Statistical analyses were made using the SPSS-X programs (Statistical Package for Social Sciences, 1986). For each dependent variable, a 2×3 (LUF, HUF by LFA, MFA, HFA) analysis of covariance was made, the covariates being nonverbal aptitude, parents' degree of schooling, and parents' level of occupation. An a priori analysis of variance, using the same factors, was performed on the three variables used as covariates. A one-way analysis of variance was also performed on the data of the three school French ambiance groups to test for the significance of the linear trend component. A significant linear trend indicates that, as school ambiance increases, there is a concurrent increase in the analyzed dependent variable.

Results

The results are presented in three sections. The first results analyzed are those pertaining to the three variables that were used as covariates in the subsequent analyses of the study. In the second section, the results of the INLC scores (interpersonal network, contacts with the media and educational support) will be analyzed relative to the school and family ambiance groupings. These will be referred to as the *social psychological variables* because INLC scores refer to the socio-psychological level of the model. The latter represent opportunities to use L1 and L2 in different language contact situations. Finally, in the third section, the results on language competence, ethnolinguistic vitality beliefs, ethnolinguistic identity, degree of use of French and English and language variety used will be presented. The latter are called the *psychological variables* because they refer to the psychological and behavioral levels of the theoretical model. It is also these variables which represent the defining characteristics of additive and subtractive bilingualism (see theoretical model). The results of the third section will be presented both in table and graphic format whereas all other variables will be presented only in table format. The graphic format (explained below) will be used to compare the data with high vitality French and English norms.

Descriptive statistics for all the variables (including covariates) are shown in Table 1. Each of these scores can be interpreted according to the scale parameters described in the materials section (e.g., a mean score of 3.78 on a 9-point scale can be interpreted by using the scale's descriptors).

Covariates

The scores on the covariates for each school and family French ambiance group are presented in Table 1. On each covariate, a 2×3 analysis of variance was performed to verify for group differences. As shown in Table 1, group differences are very small on the degree of nonverbal intellectual aptitude. The analysis of variance failed to find significant group effects or interactions. There were also no significant differences in the parents' degree of schooling. Finally, there were also no significant differences in parents' level of occupation. Although statistically significant differences were not found for any of these variables taken individually, all three were included in the subsequent analyses of covariance to control for possible cumulative effects of two or more variables.

Social Psychological Variables

The French ambiance groups were compared on the six social psychological variables that constitute the INLC component of the model. These data illustrate the opportunities for contacts with the French and English languages via interpersonal contacts, contacts with the media and degree of educational support (degree of schooling in French and degree of French ambiance in the school). Analyses of covariance were performed on these variables to test for group differences. Descriptive statistics for these scores are shown in Table 1.

As expected, both the home language and the school language ambiance main effects were statistically significant in the analysis of covariance of the francophone interpersonal network scores, $F(1,265)=38.47, p<.001$, and $F(2,265)=12.59$, $p<.001$, respectively. The students whose family used more French had more francophones in their interpersonal network and the same was found for those who belonged to schools having a higher French ambiance. Post hoc comparisons indicate the LFA group to be significantly different from both the MFA and HFA groups. Both the linear component and the deviation from linearity were statistically significant, $F(1,293)=40.02, p<.001$, and $F(1,293)=6.84, p<.01$, respectively. Most

Table 1.
Descriptive statistics for the covariates, social psychological variables and the psychological variables relative to school and family French ambiance.

| | | | Family French ambiance | | | | |
| | | | Low | | | High | |
Variables	School French ambiance	N	Mean	S.D.	N	Mean	S.D.
Covariates							
1. Non-verbal aptitude	Low	48	40.00	6.21	23	38.35	6.91
	Medium	66	40.50	4.96	72	40.10	6.29
	High	18	38.83	7.47	53	39.43	5.36
2. Parents degree of schooling	Low	51	4.04	1.22	23	4.17	1.23
	Medium	68	4.28	1.24	80	4.09	1.45
	High	17	4.35	1.32	56	4.16	1.47
3. Parents level of occupation	Low	51	3.15	1.10	23	3.16	.98
	Medium	68	3.17	1.05	78	3.23	1.15
	High	18	3.22	1.20	56	3.20	1.13
Social psychological variables							
1. Francophone interpersonal network	Low	48	5.49	1.45	22	6.61	1.07
	Medium	66	6.36	1.22	70	7.21	.90
	High	17	6.44	.82	51	7.31	.75
2. Anglophone interpersonal network	Low	48	5.60	1.67	23	4.01	1.08
	Medium	66	4.82	1.68	70	3.64	1.38
	High	17	4.23	1.11	51	3.54	1.23
3. Contacts with French media	Low	48	3.14	1.17	23	3.69	1.43
	Medium	66	3.45	1.32	70	3.81	1.42
	High	17	3.55	.97	51	4.44	1.50
4. Contacts with English media	Low	48	7.64	1.18	23	7.48	1.24
	Medium	66	7.48	1.19	70	7.34	.86
	High	17	7.76	.85	51	6.80	1.26
5. Degree of French schooling	Low	48	4.56	1.09	23	4.55	1.19
	Medium	66	5.72	.55	70	5.53	.74
	High	17	6.15	.26	51	6.16	.22
6. Degree of school French ambiance	Low	48	2.96	.48	23	3.02	.35
	Medium	66	3.88	.25	70	3.92	.26
	High	17	4.50	.09	51	4.57	.15
Psychological variables							
1. French self-rated oral competence	Low	48	5.84	1.27	23	6.60	2.20
	Medium	65	6.38	1.40	67	6.85	1.20
	High	17	7.04	1.19	50	7.33	1.46
2. English self-rated oral competence	Low	41	7.89	1.66	21	7.51	2.45
	Medium	52	7.84	1.60	69	7.65	1.47
	High	15	8.49	.70	50	7.29	1.83

of the explained variance (85%) was linearly distributed, however. A larger proportion of francophones in the interpersonal network is associated with an increase in school French ambiance. The interaction component was not statistically significant. The covariates effect was significant, $F(3,265)=3.79$, $p<.05$, the latter being due to a single variable, parents'

3. Cognitive-academic French competency	Low	48	23.79	7.48	23	26.35	7.17
	Medium	66	25.27	6.30	70	25.09	6.66
	High	17	27.35	5.60	51	27.33	6.97
4. Cognitive-academic English competency	Low	48	27.50	5.96	23	27.91	7.98
	Medium	66	28.97	5.49	68	26.49	5.69
	High	17	28.35	5.76	51	26.29	6.33
5. Francophone ethno-linguistic vitality beliefs (non-self)	Low	48	5.25	.91	23	4.92	.86
	Medium	65	5.19	.71	70	5.38	.88
	High	17	5.19	.90	51	5.29	.67
6. Anglophone ethno-linguistic vitality beliefs (non-self)	Low	48	7.00	.83	23	6.93	.95
	Medium	65	7.07	.60	70	6.87	.73
	High	17	7.21	.68	51	7.10	.48
7. Francophone self beliefs	Low	48	5.84	1.17	23	6.49	1.10
	Medium	65	6.01	1.05	70	6.88	.96
	High	17	6.13	1.10	51	6.94	.80
8. Anglophone self beliefs	Low	48	7.31	.97	23	6.29	1.17
	Medium	65	7.01	.84	70	6.58	1.07
	High	17	6.94	.95	51	6.41	1.03
9. Francophone identity	Low	48	6.40	1.56	23	7.31	1.62
	Medium	65	7.45	1.14	70	8.20	.89
	High	17	8.09	.91	51	8.38	1.02
10. Anglophone identity	Low	47	6.36	1.79	23	4.04	1.82
	Medium	65	5.30	2.39	70	3.85	2.06
	High	17	4.92	2.43	51	3.68	1.98
11. Degree of use of French with family members	Low	48	3.56	1.37	23	7.36	1.01
	Medium	66	4.01	1.28	70	7.67	.94
	High	17	4.21	.94	51	7.89	.96
12. Degree of use of English with family members	Low	48	7.68	1.14	23	4.46	1.95
	Medium	66	7.21	1.39	67	3.69	1.92
	High	17	7.27	1.27	49	3.58	1.96
13. Degree of use of French in other situations	Low	48	3.19	1.04	23	4.31	1.05
	Medium	66	3.30	.89	70	4.72	1.19
	High	17	3.50	1.03	51	4.59	1.17
14. Degree of use of English in other situations	Low	48	7.88	.87	23	7.06	1.02
	Medium	66	7.59	.81	70	6.68	1.00
	High	17	7.74	.84	51	6.64	1.10
15. Variety of spoken language	Low	35	2.74	1.52	17	5.12	1.76
	Medium	57	3.05	1.76	60	4.95	1.59
	High	15	4.00	2.10	44	5.61	1.22

degree of schooling, which was negatively related to the strength of the francophone interpersonal network, $T = -2.78$, $p < .01$. Students who had a higher proportion of francophones as part of their interpersonal network tended to have parents with a lower level of schooling. This effect may be due to the fact that students who had a higher proportion of francophones in their interpersonal network came from rural areas.

The results of the anglophone interpersonal network were the converse of those of the francophone network. Both main effects were statistically significant: $F(1,266)=33.79$, $p<.001$, and $F(2,266)=5.96$, $p<.01$, for home language use and school ambiance, respectively. Students who lived in families where French was the dominant language and those who were schooled in a higher French ambiance tended to have fewer anglophones in their interpersonal network. All three school ambiance groups were found to be significantly different from each other by post hoc comparisons, and the linear trend component accounted for most (97%) of the explained variance, $F(1,294)=31.81$, $p<.001$. The effects of the covariates and the interaction component were not statistically significant.

For the degree of contact with the French media, only the home language use main effect was statistically significant, $F(1,266)=10.30$, $p<.001$. The students who used more French when talking with their family members also tended to be in more frequent contact with the French media. The school ambiance main effect was close to statistical significance ($p=.08$). In a one-way analysis of variance of the school ambiance effect, the linear trend component was found to be highly significant, $F(1,294)=19.56$, $p<.001$. An increase in contacts with the French media was associated with an increase in the French ambiance of the school. The opposite was found in the analysis of the scores for degree of contact with the English media. Only the home language use main effect was statistically significant, $F(1,266)=7.73$, $p<.01$. Students who used more French in the home also were in less frequent contact with the English media. The home language use by school ambiance interaction was close to statistical significance, $F(2,264)=2.72$, $p=.07$. As can be observed in Table 1, there is a tendency for students from schools with a high francophone ambiance to be less in contact with the English media but only if they also belong to a family that communicates most often in French. A one-way analysis of variance of the school ambiance factor showed the effect to be linearly distributed, $F(1,294)=9.76$, $p<.01$. There was a significant linear decrease of contacts with the English media as the French school ambiance increased.

Since the students were grouped according to degrees of French ambiance in the school, groups did differ significantly on this variable, $F(2,266)=399.97$, $p<.001$. Post hoc comparisons showed all 3 groups to be significantly different from each other. Although both the linear, $F(1,294)=1060.93$, $p<.001$, and the deviation from linearity, $F(1,294)=19.29$, $p<.001$, were highly significant, 98% of the between group effect was explained by the linear trend component. The home language use main effect was not statistically significant nor was the school ambiance by home language use interaction. The effect of the covariates was also not statistically significant.

It was also expected that the degree of French school ambiance would be positively related to the degree of French schooling. The analysis of covariance showed both the school ambiance main effect and the effect of the covariates to be statistically significant, $F(2,266)=74.37$, $p<.001$, and $F(3,266)=5.99$, $p<.01$, respectively. Post hoc comparisons found all 3 school ambiance groups to differ significantly from each other. The linear trend component explained 94% of the between-group effect, $F(1,264)=188.71$, $p<.001$, but the deviation from linearity was also statistically significant, $F(1,294)=12.45$, $p<.001$. School French ambiance increased as the degree of French schooling increased. Among the covariates, parents' education was positively related to degree of French schooling, $T=3.09$, $p<.01$. Students who had more schooling in French tended to have parents with a higher level of schooling. The main effect of home language use and the interaction component were not statistically significant.

Psychological Variables

The scores for the psychological variables which are also those that pertain to the defining characteristics of additive and subtractive bilingualism are presented in Table 1. As mentioned above, each variable is also presented in graphic format in order to better perceive the linearity of the school ambiance effect and the deviations from both the French and English high vitality norms.

In the graphic format, each dependent variable was transformed and standardized relative to a high vitality unilingual norm. The scores of a group of students from Rivière-du-Loup (Québec) who were tested in an earlier study using the same instruments (see Landry & Allard, 1987a) were used as a high vitality francophone norm. The scores of anglophone students from Moncton (New Brunswick) also tested in that earlier study were used as a high vitality anglophone norm. The norms were standardized as T-scores ($M=50.00$, $SD=10.00$) for each unilingual group. This allows the French scores to be compared to a Québec francophone norm (high vitality group) and the English scores to be analyzed relative to a high vitality anglophone norm. For example, a score of 40.00 in French can be interpreted as 1.0 standard deviation below the francophone norm and a score of 40 in English as being 1.0 standard deviation below the anglophone norm. These standardizations are intended for rough comparisons only. Deviations from normality on some scores and the low variability of the scores for the high vitality groups warrant caution in the interpretations. Standardized scores were presented in graphic format so that trends in the data relative to the two high vitality language groups could be more readily observed.

As shown in both Table 1 and Figure 3, French communicative competence was significantly related to both the degree of use of French in the home and the school ambiance, $F(1,261)=7.24$, $p<.01$, and $F(2,261)=6.41$, $p<.01$, respectively. Self-rated competence in oral French increased as both the use of French in the home and the French ambiance in the school increased. Post hoc comparisons found all three school ambiance groups to be significantly different from each other and the effect was clearly linear, $F(1,289)=28.40$, $p<.001$. An increase in school ambiance was positively associated with an increase in self-rated oral competency in French. Deviation from linearity was not statistically significant. The covariates effect and the interaction component were not statistically significant.

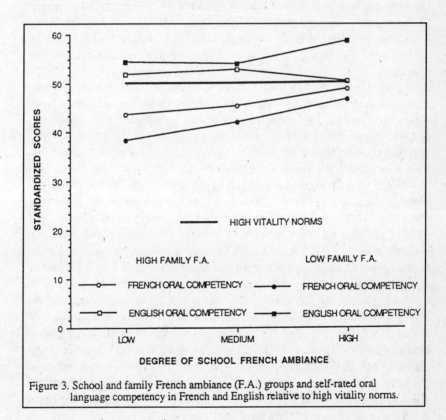

Figure 3. School and family French ambiance (F.A.) groups and self-rated oral language competency in French and English relative to high vitality norms.

On the English communicative competence scores, the school ambiance main effect was not statistically significant. The home language use main effect, however, was statistically significant, $F(1,239)=5.76$, $p<.05$. The students who used more French at home rated their communicative competence in English lower than did those who used French less often in the home. The interaction component was not statistically significant. The covariates had a significant effect on the results, $F(3,239)=2.94$, $p<.05$. This effect was mainly due to differences in nonverbal aptitude which were positively related to the self ratings on English communicative competence, $T=2.22$, $p<.05$. Students with higher aptitude scores rated their English communicative competence higher.

As shown in Figure 3, the students tended, on the average, to rate themselves below a high vitality norm in their competence to communicate in oral French. These scores are related to use of French with family members and also to degree of French ambiance in the school, as was confirmed by the analyses of covariance. Communicative competence in English, on the average, was rated to be equal to or above that of a high vitality anglophone norm. Although results were significantly affected by the use of French in the home, the self ratings of students from high French ambiance homes were still very high and at least equal to those of unilingual anglophones.

As can be observed in both Table 1 and Figure 4, the amount of French ambiance in the school was positively related to cognitive-academic proficiency in French. The effect is statistically significant, $F(2,266)=3.17$, $p<.05$. A one-way analysis of variance shows the effect to be linearly distributed, $F(1,282)=6.08$, $p<.05$. Scores increase as school French ambiance increases. Deviation from linearity was not statistically significant. The family French ambiance groups did not differ significantly. The largest effect, however, was due to differences between groups on the covariates, $F(3,266)=23.20$, $p<.001$. Both nonverbal intellectual aptitude and parents' education were positively related to these scores, $T=6.43$, $p<.001$ and $T=2.97$, $p<.01$. High aptitude scores for the students and a high degree of schooling for the parents were associated with high performance on the test of cognitive-academic proficiency in French.

As predicted by the model, the amount of French ambiance in the school had no negative impact on the scores of cognitive-academic proficiency in English. None of the main effects nor the interaction component was statistically significant. Only the covariates effect was statistically significant, $F(3,264)=29.87$, $p<.001$. Differences in non-verbal aptitude, $T=8.31$, $p<.001$, and differences in parents' degree of schooling, $T=2.11$, $p<.05$, accounted for this effect. Both variables were positively related to cognitive-academic proficiency in English.

As can be seen in Figure 4, the western Canadian francophone students scored below the high vitality francophone norms in French cognitive-academic proficiency. Deviations ranged from .3 to .8 standard deviations

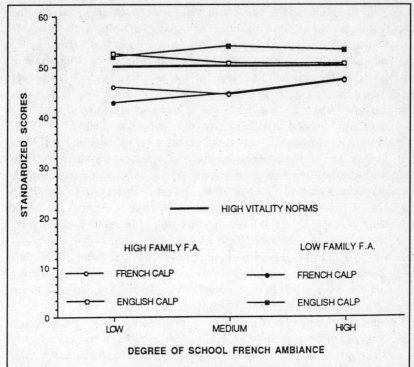

Figure 4. School and family French ambiance (F.A.) groups and cognitive-academic language proficiency (CALP) in French and English relative to high vitality norms.

below the Québec norm. Their performance was much better in English where average scores were either equal to or slightly above the New Brunswick (Moncton) anglophone norm. For the students from low French ambiance homes, there was a tendency for the English scores to increase when school French ambiance was high, whereas for the students from high French ambiance homes there was a tendency for English scores to decrease if the school French ambiance was also high, but this interaction did not reach statistical significance, $p = .10$. For all students taken together, there was no indication that an increase in school French ambiance was related to a decrease in scores of cognitive-academic proficiency in English.

Beliefs about the relative ethnolinguistic vitality of both francophones and anglophones were grouped into non-self beliefs and self beliefs (Allard & Landry, 1986, in press). Non-self beliefs refer to the perception of the "objective" vitality of the linguistic community whereas self beliefs reflect the personal aspirations of the individual (goals, feelings of belonging, self efficacy and valorisation of language). The model predicts that French ambiance in the home and in the school will be more strongly related to the self beliefs than to non-self beliefs. The results pertaining to these beliefs are shown in Table 1 and in graphic format in Figures 5 and 6.

The analyses of covariance on the non-self beliefs concerning francophone vitality found none of the main effects nor the interaction component to be statistically significant. Only the covariates had a significant effect and the latter was due to a single variable. Parents' degree of schooling was negatively related to perceptions of francophone vitality, $T=-2.10$, $p<.01$. Students whose parents had a higher level of schooling attributed less vitality to the francophone group. The results were similar on the scores of non-self beliefs concerning anglophone vitality. The only significant effect was that of the covariates, the latter due again to the single variable of parents' degree of schooling. This time, parents' degree of schooling was positively related to perceptions of anglophone vitality, $T=2.11$, $p<.05$. As shown in Figure 5, perceived anglophone vitality was much higher than perceived francophone vitality. The latter perceptions were on the average more than 3 standard deviations below the high vitality francophone norm whereas perceptions of vitality for the anglophone group approached the high vitality anglophone norm.

In the self beliefs concerning francophone vitality, the French ambiance of the school effect was not statistically significant but there was a highly significant effect of language use in the home, $F(1,265)=30.97$, $p<.001$. The students whose language use in the home was French dominant had much stronger self beliefs concerning francophone vitality. Although the school ambiance main effect was not statistically significant ($p=.12$), a one-way analysis of variance showed the effect to be linearly distributed; this effect was highly significant, $F(1,281)=17.25$, $p<.001$. None of the covariates had a significant effect nor was the interaction component significant.

Results followed the same patterns on the self beliefs concerning anglophone vitality. Only the home language use main effect was statistically significant, $F(1,265)=22.36$, $p<.001$. The students whose family environment was French dominant had lower self beliefs concerning anglophone vitality. The effects of use of French in the home on both francophone and anglophone personal beliefs can be clearly observed in Figure 6. All scores, however, were clearly below high vitality norms. Students from low French ambiance families tend to favor anglophone and francophone groups equally when they attend medium or high ambiance schools but to favor the anglophone group more than the francophone group when they attend a low French ambiance school. This interaction does not reach statistical significance, however ($p=.15$). For the group which used French to a high degree in the family, preference for the francophone group is dominant even for students in low French ambiance schools.

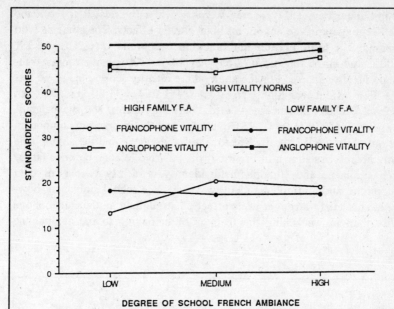

Figure 5. School and family French ambiance (F.A.) groups and non-self beliefs concerning francophone and anglophone ethnolinguistic vitality relative to high vitality norms.

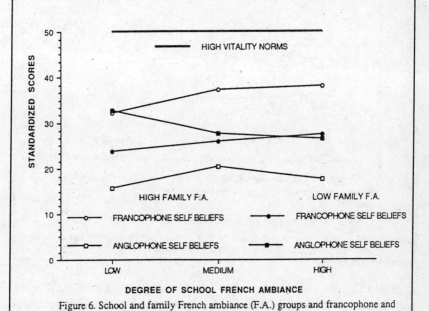

Figure 6. School and family French ambiance (F.A.) groups and francophone and anglophone self beliefs relative to high vitality norms.

Ethnolinguistic identity scores were significantly related to both the home language and the school ambiance main effects. The students who experienced a high French ambiance in the home, $F(1,265)=16.27$, $p<.001$, and in the school, $F(2,265)=21.24$, $p<.001$, had stronger francophone identity scores. For the anglophone identity scores, the home language main effect was highly significant, $F(1,264)=34.20$, $p<.001$, but the school French ambiance main effect only approached statistical significance, $F(2,264)=2.73$, $p=.07$. Covariates and the interaction component were not statistically significant for the francophone and the anglophone identity scores. As shown in Figure 7, the positive relation between family French ambiance and ethnolinguistic identity is clearly visible for both francophone and anglophone identity scores. The school ambiance, however, seems much stronger in its effect on strengthening the francophone identity than in weakening the feelings of belonging to the anglophone group.

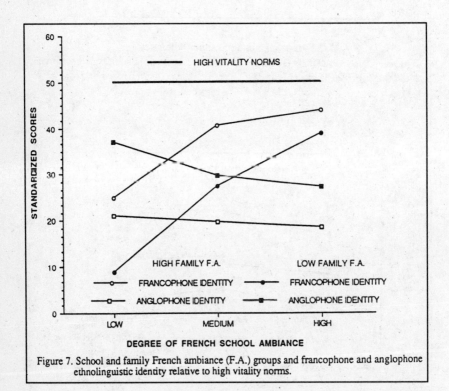

Figure 7. School and family French ambiance (F.A.) groups and francophone and anglophone ethnolinguistic identity relative to high vitality norms.

Since the students were grouped according to degree of use of French with family members, differences between groups on use of French and English in the home were expected to be statistically significant. As expected, the main effect of home language on use of French in the home was highly significant, $F(1,266)=569.88$, $p<.001$. However, the school ambiance main effect was also statistically significant, $F(2,266)=4.18$, $p<.05$ (see Figure 8). Post hoc comparisons found all three groups to be significantly different from each other and a one-way analysis found the effect to be linear, $F(1,289)=33.24$, $p<.001$, the deviation from linearity being nonsignificant. Students who were in schools with a higher French ambiance also used more French with their family members.

Both the family French ambiance and school French ambiance main effects were statistically significant for the ratings of use of English in the home, $F(1,261)=231.89$, $p<.001$ and $F(2,261)=3.24$, $p<.05$, respectively. The linearity of the school ambiance main effect approached the .05 level of statistical significance ($p=.07$).

As shown in Figure 8, the use of French in low French ambiance homes is negligible. These students are relatively close to a high vitality anglophone norm in their use of English but not even on the same distri-

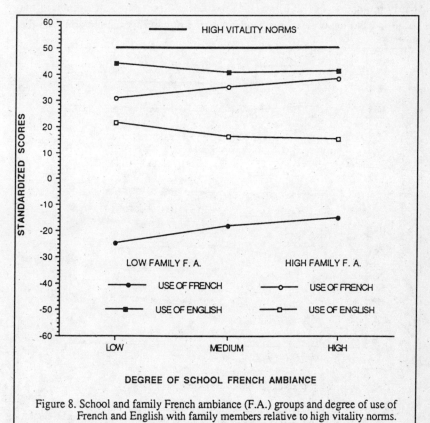

Figure 8. School and family French ambiance (F.A.) groups and degree of use of French and English with family members relative to high vitality norms.

bution as high vitality francophones on their use of French (approximately 7 standard deviations below the norm). Students from the high French ambiance homes were still between 1 and 2 standard deviations below the Québec francophone norm in their use of French. They scored approximately 3 standard deviations below the anglophone norm in their use of English. Therefore, in their home language use, LUF students were much more similar to anglophones than to francophones. Conversely, the HUF students were more similar to francophones than to anglophones but still used a considerable amount of English while talking to family members.

On the use of French in situations other than those involving family members, a significant effect was found for the home language use main effect, $F(1,266)=64.67$, $p<.001$. Students who used more French with family members also used more French in other communication situations (see Figure 9). The school effect and the interaction component were not statistically significant. The family French ambiance main effect was again highly significant for the use of English in contact situations other than with family members, $F(1,266)=51.55$, $p<.001$. Greater use of French in the home is also associated with less use of English in situations outside the

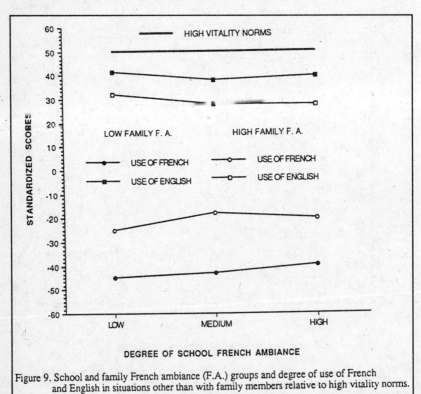

Figure 9. School and family French ambiance (F.A.) groups and degree of use of French and English in situations other than with family members relative to high vitality norms.

home. The school ambiance main effect approached statistical significance $F(2,266)=2.75$, $p=.07$. There is a tendency for a low French ambiance in the school to be related to a greater use of English in contact situations other than with family members. The covariates effect was also close to statistical significance, $F(3,266)=2.62$, $p=.05$. Students whose parents had a higher degree of schooling tended to use more English than students whose parents had a lower level of schooling. This finding could be a spurious relationship due to urban-rural differences in students' place of residence. Urban residency would be associated with both a greater use of English and a higher degree of parents' schooling.

Finally, analyses were also made of the self-rated language variety scores. High scores are associated with a greater use of standard French and lower scores indicate an influence of English in the spoken variety. On these scores, both the home language use and the school ambiance main effects were statistically significant, $F(1,210)=61.43$, $p<.001$, and $F(2,219)=4.08$, $p<.05$, respectively. In both cases, the greater the French ambiance in the students' environment, the closer the variety of spoken French was estimated to be to standard French (see Figure 10).

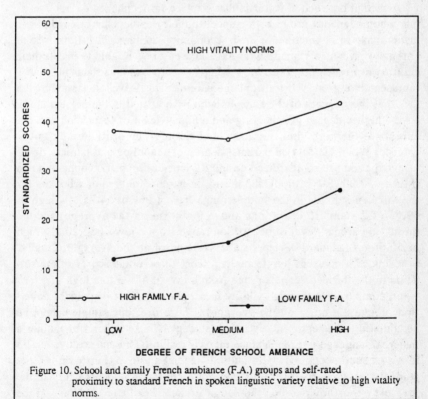

Figure 10. School and family French ambiance (F.A.) groups and self-rated proximity to standard French in spoken linguistic variety relative to high vitality norms.

Post hoc comparisons found the HFA group to be significantly different from the other two groups. A strong linear effect was also found, $F(1,240)=26.21$, $p<.001$. Deviation from linearity was not statistically significant. The use of standard French increased as degree of French ambiance increased in the school.

Discussion

Before discussing the results, these have to be placed in the particular context of the western francophone situation. This situation is characterized by high rates of linguistic assimilation: Manitoba (47%), Saskatchewan (67%), and Alberta (63%). An important consequence of this situation is that only a relatively small percentage of eligible children (as defined by section 23 of the Canadian Charter) are actually schooled in French: 30% out of a total of 18,000 in Manitoba, 11% out of total of 11,000 in Saskatchewan, and 8% out of a total of 21,000 in Alberta. A major factor responsible for these low rates of attendance is the relatively low vitality of the francophone minorities in western Canada, e.g., the relative lack of French school facilities and educational support in particular.

A second but related factor is that western francophones do not constitute a homogeneous group with respect to their demographic strength, their institutional infrastructure or their economic standing. The francophone parents of western Canada who have chosen or were able to enroll their children in French programs have a higher socioeconomic status than more representative groups of francophone parents. This is well illustrated by the fact that the parents of the students who participated in the present study have a higher degree of schooling and a higher level of occupation than the parents of the high vitality francophone norm group of Rivière-du-Loup, Québec. When the data on parents' degree of schooling and parents' level of occupation are standardized on the Rivière-du-Loup francophone norm (Mean=50.00, SD=10.00), the means on parents' degree of schooling for the thirteen schools in the sample range from a low of 54.75 to a high of 69.75 (1.2 standard deviations above the norm on the average) and the means on parents' level of occupation range from a low of 52.20 to a high of 60.66 (.7 standard deviations above the norm on the average). Finally, in terms of nonverbal intellectual aptitude, the average scores of the students in the thirteen schools range from a low of 48.95 to a high of 57.95 when compared to the high vitality francophone norm (.4 standard deviations above the norm on the average). Therefore, our sample cannot be considered to be representative of all students whose father's or mother's maternal language is French since there is a significant and positive bias in terms of socioeconomic status and intellectual aptitude. Furthermore, the students tested in the present study represent those students who had the greatest opportunity to be schooled in French. For these students, on the average, half or more of the courses were being taught in French; this is not typical for the overall francophone student population of the three prairie provinces. The situation depicted by the results cannot, therefore, be representative of the total francophone student population in western Canada, but it does seem to represent the situation of western Canada's more privileged francophone students in a context where francophones, in relative terms, are not generally privileged in terms of educational rights.

For the purposes of the statistical analyses in this study, groups from low, medium and high French ambiance schools were further categorized according to degree of French ambiance in the family (low vs. high). On the social psychological variables, these groups were significantly different from each other. Students from higher French ambiance schools had a greater proportion of francophones and a lesser proportion of anglophones in their interpersonal network. Students from higher French ambiance homes also had a greater proportion of francophones and a lesser proportion of anglophones in their interpersonal network. Overall, however, the interpersonal network of most of the students was constituted of only slightly more francophones than anglophones. Contacts with anglophone persons were very frequent for most students.

In their contacts with the media, students from higher French ambiance homes were more in contact with the French language than students from lower French ambiance homes. Although the school French ambiance main effect was not statistically significant, there was a significant linear increase in the contacts with the French media as school French ambience increased. The opposite trend was found for contacts with the English media. Nevertheless, the contacts with the anglophone media were clearly dominant for all groups. These results reflect the low availability of the French media in western Canada, a finding which is consistent with the generally low demographic capital of francophones.

Since the groups were constituted from the results of the self-reported French school ambiance experienced by the students from kindergarten to grade 12, they did differ significantly on this variable. In the higher French ambiance schools, the results approached those found in the higher vitality francophone communities (i.e., approximately 4.5 on a 5 point scale). But this level of French ambiance was reported by less than 25% of the students. For most students, the reported linguistic ambiance of the school tended to be strongly influenced by the English language. The schooling experience of these francophone students did not seem to offer the French ambiance needed to counterbalance the overall dominance of English in the socio-institutional milieu. It was also found that students who came from high French ambiance homes did not attend schools with a higher French ambiance than those attended by the students from lower French ambiance homes. As Desjarlais (1983) concluded, it may be that students who do not use French at home contribute to the decrease of French ambiance of the school. It must be noted, however, that when school ambiance groups were compared on the use of French with family members, there was a significant and linear increase of use of French in the home as school French ambiance increased.

The French ambiance of the school was strongly related to the degree of French schooling provided. The students from higher French ambiance homes, however, did not receive more French schooling than did the students from lower French ambiance homes. One variable that was significantly related to the degree of French schooling received was the parents' degree of schooling. The parents of students who had received more schooling in French had a higher degree of formal schooling. It must also be noted that most of the students tested had been schooled mostly in French. The effect of schooling in French and of the French ambiance of the school could have been better analyzed if a larger number of francophone students schooled mostly in the English language had been available for testing.

The data on the psychological variables allow us to determine whether the bilingual experience of these western Canada francophone students was subtractive or additive. The statistical analyses and the descriptive data clearly indicate a subtractive type of bilingualism for most of these students. In both oral and cognitive-academic linguistic competence, the scores indicated that the students were dominant in their second language. All groups scored higher in English than in French. But bilingualism was less subtractive for the students who came from high French ambiance schools and high French ambiance homes. Moreover, the French ambiance experienced by the students in the school and in the home did not seem to affect negatively their linguistic competence in English. As was found in other studies of low vitality francophone groups (Hébert et al., 1976; Baril, 1984; Landry & Allard, in press-a), the extent of French schooling for these students increased their competence in French with no negative impact on their English skills. The degree of French ambiance in the home was slightly but significantly related to a lower reported oral competency in English but was not related to cognitive-academic linguistic proficiency in English. As mentioned above, however, the linguistic competence scores may be affected by the relatively high socioeconomic status of the students who participated in the study. This would explain why francophones scored as high as or above the anglophone norm from New Brunswick in English.

In their perception of the relative ethnolinguistic vitality of both linguistic communities, as expected, all groups attributed more vitality to the anglophone group. The students attributed a moderate vitality to the francophone community. These perceptions, however, did not differ among groups. In the strength of their self beliefs concerning linguistic community, the expected effect of the French school ambiance was not statistically significant. The schooling experience did not seem to foster the self beliefs needed to maintain the desire to remain francophone (see Landry & Allard, 1988). In fact, many students seem to aspire more to be part of the anglophone community than to be part of the francophone community. The degree of French ambiance in the home, however, was strongly related to the strength of francophone self beliefs. Students from higher French ambiance homes aspired more to be part of the francophone community than of the anglophone community, although their francophone self beliefs were still much lower than those of the normative group from Québec. Students from lower French ambiance homes tended to aspire to belong to both groups with a stronger tendency toward the anglophone community if schooled within a low French ambiance school.

Ethnolinguistic identity was strongly related to both the home and the school French ambiance. Francophone identity approached the high vitality francophone norm only among students who had been schooled in high French ambiance schools or among subjects from the medium school French ambiance group coming from high French ambiance homes. Both the family and school milieux therefore seem to play a crucial role in the development and maintenance of a strong ethnolinguistic identity. These results do not support Edwards' (1985) hypothesis to the effect that the school would have very little or no positive impact upon the maintenance or development of the ethnolinguistic identity of members of low ethnolinguistic vitality groups.

The degree of subtractiveness of the bilingual experience of western Canadian francophones is most evident in the results relative to language behaviour. In their use of English, both with family members and in other contact situations, students from lower French ambiance homes were close to the anglophone norm in their language behaviour. They used French only sparingly and English was used in most language contact situations. The students from higher French ambiance homes used more French than English with family members but still used a considerable amount of English. In contact situations other than those with family members, however, the latter students used English more often than French. The home and the school clearly seem to be the only places where these minority francophone students tend to use their mother tongue and this is the case for only a portion of these students. Fishman (1967, 1972, 1989) would argue that this diglossic situation could help the students maintain their language despite the overall low vitality of their language. Fishman also contended, however, that in situations where there is diglossia with widespread bilingualism among community members, bilingualism tends to be unstable and there is a strong pull toward language shift. Therefore, unless more opportunities for the use of the mother tongue are provided in the socio-institutional milieu, it is not assured that the home and the school milieu will be able to counterbalance the dominance of the English language.

Positive relationships were found between the school and family milieux degree of French ambiance and the self-related language variety scores. The spoken variety of French was less infiltrated by the English language when the French ambiance was higher in both the home and the school. On the average, the variety of French spoken was approximately one standard deviation below the francophone norm for the students in the higher French ambiance homes but between 3 and 4 standard deviations below this norm for the students of lower French ambiance homes.

Conclusion

The counterbalance model of bilingual experience proposes that bilingualism for minority group students will be less subtractive if the family and school milieux act as counterbalancing forces to the dominance of the second language. The results in this study of western Canadian francophones give support to this model but also indicate that both the family and the school milieux need to be much more active in their role of strengthening the French language than they have been if these institutions wish to promote additive bilingualism for their children, or a bilingualism which is the least subtractive possible. If we consider the criteria of additive bilingualism given as part of the definition of this type of bilingualism earlier in the paper, bilingualism was subtractive on all three criteria. The degree of subtractiveness was not as pronounced on the criteria of linguistic competence as it was for those relative to the affective disposition toward their maternal language and their use of this language. The relatively better results on linguistic competence may be partly explained by the high socioeconomic status of the students sampled. The main effects of the school and/or the family milieux were statistically significant for linguistic competence, personal beliefs, ethnolinguistic identity and the reported language variety spoken. The relation of the school ambiance to the strength of personal beliefs and the use of French in daily contact situations was relatively weak. It must be understood that many francophones in western Canada did not have access to self contained francophone schools. With an increased control of their French schools, if they wish to develop additive bilingualism, francophone educators will need not only to focus on the teachinng of the language but also to develop specific and highly dynamic programs that will foster strong personal beliefs in the value of the French language and a strong ethnolinguistic identity. Pedagogical procedures to this effect have been suggested by Cummins (1986) and by Landry and Allard (1988b) but given the results analyzed in this article, it becomes clear that schools will have to spend much effort in the planning and implementation of these educational procedures.

References

Allaire, G., & Fedigan, L. (1989). *D'une génération à l'autre, le changement linguistique en Alberta*. Présentation au IXe Colloque annuel du Centre d'étude franco-canadienne de l'Ouest, Winnipeg, MB.

Allard, A., & Landry, R. (In press). *Ethnolinguistic vitality beliefs and language maintenance and loss*. Paper presented at the International Conference on Maintenance and Loss of Ethnic Minority Languages, Noordwijkerhout, The Netherlands.

Allard, R., & Landry, R. (1987a). *Contact des langues, vitalité ethnolinguistique subjective et comportement ethnolangagier*. Paper presented at the Conference "Contacts des langues: Quels modèles?" Nice, France.

Allard, R., & Landry, R. (1987b). Étude des relations entre les croyances envers la vitalité ethnolinguistique et comportement langagier des francophones en milieu minoritaire. In *Demain, la francophonie en milieu minoritaire*. R. Théberge & J. Lafontant (Eds.), pp. 15-41. Winnipeg, MB: Centre de recherche du Collège de Saint-Boniface.

Allard, R., & Landry, R. (1986). Subjective ethnolinguistic vitality viewed as a belief system. *Journal of Multilingual and Multicultural Development, 7*, 1-12.

Allard, R., De la Garde, R., & Landry, R. (1984). Le soutien éducatif. In *Variation du comportement langagier lorsque deux langues sont en contact*. A. Prujiner et al. (Eds.), pp. 69-72. Québec, PQ: Centre international de recherche sur le bilinguisme.

Aunger, E.A. (1989). Language and law in the province of Alberta. In *Language and law*. P. Pupier & J. Woehrling (Eds.), pp. 203-230. Montreal, PQ: Wilson & Lafleur.

Baker, C. (1988). *Key issues in Bilingualism and Bilingual Education*. Clevedon, UK: Multilingual Matters.

Baril, P. (1984). *L'étudiant franco-manitobain, conséquences des contacts interculturels*. Thèse de maîtrise. Université du Manitoba.

Bastarache, M. (1989). Le statut du français dans l'ouest canadien. In *Language and law*. P. Pupier & J. Woehrling (Eds.), pp. 203-230. Montreal, PQ: Wilson & Lafleur.

Bennett, G.K., Seashore, H.G., & Wesman, A.G. (1974). *Differential Aptitude Tests, Forms S and T (Fifth edition)*. New York, NY: Psychological Corporation.

Blishen, B.R., & McRoberts, H.A. (1976). A revised socioeconomic index for occupations in Canada. *Canadian Review of Sociology and Anthropology, 13*, 71-79.

Bourdieu, P. (1980). *La distinction*. Paris, France: Editions de Minuit.

Bourhis, R., Giles, H., & Rosenthal, D. (1981). Notes on the construction of a subjective vitality questionnaire for ethnolinguistic groups. *Journal of Multilingual and Multicultural Development, 2*, 145-155.

Breton, R. (1981). *Les ethnies*. Paris, France: Presses Universitaires de France.

Carey, S.T. (1989). La vitalité ethnolinguistique des Franco-Albertains en 1976. In *Écriture et politique*. G. Allaire, G. Cadrin, & P. Dubé (Eds.), pp. 233-245. Edmonton, AB: Institut de recherche de la Faculté Saint-Jean.

Carey, S.T. (1987a). Reading comprehension in First and Second Languages of Immersion and Francophone Students. *Canadian Journal for Exceptional Children, 3*(4), 103-108.

Carey, S.T. (1987b). Le débat sur l'école française et l'école d'immersion dans l'Ouest. In *Demain la francophonie en milieu minoritaire*. R. Théberge & J. Lafontant (Eds.), pp. 115-124. Winnipeg, MB: Centre de recherches du Collège de Saint-Boniface.

Carey, S.T., & Cummins, J. (1983). Achievement, Behavioral Correlates, and Teachers' Perceptions of Francophone and Anglophone Immersion Students. *The Alberta Journal of Educational Research, 29*(3), 159-167.

Carroll, J.B. (1973). Implications of Aptitude Test Research and Psycholinguistic Theory for Foreign Language Teaching. *International Journal of Psycholinguistics, 2*, 5-14.

Cummins, J. (1986). Empowering Minority Students: A Framework for Intervention. *Harvard Educational Review, 56*, 18-36.

Cummins, J. (1984). *Bilingualism and Special Education: Issues in Assessment and Pedagogy.* Clevedon, UK: Multilingual Matters.

Cummins, J. (1981). The Role of Primary Language Development in Promoting Educational Success for Language Minority Students. In *Schooling and Language Minority Students: A Theoretical Framework.* California State Department of Education, Los Angeles, CA: Evaluation, Assessment, and Dissemination Center.

Cummins, J. (1979). Linguistic Interdependence and the Educational Development of Bilingual Children. *Review of Educational Research, 49*, 222-251.

Cummins, J. (1978). Educational Implications of Mother Tongue Maintenance in Minority-language Groups. *The Canadian Modern Language Review/La Revue canadienne des langues vivantes, 34*, 395-416.

Cummins, J., & Mulcahy, R. (1978). Orientation to Language in Ukrainian-English Bilingual Children. *Child Development, 49*, 1239-1242.

Cummins, J., & Swain, M. (1986). *Bilingualism in Education.* London, UK: Longman.

De la Garde, R. (1984). L'accessibilité comparée aux médias de communication. In *Variation du comportement langagier lorsque deux langues sont en contact.* A. Prujiner et al. (Eds.), pp. 65-68. Québec, PQ: Centre international de recherche sur le bilinguisme.

Denis, W.B., & Li, P.S. (1988). The Politics of Language Loss: A Francophone Case from Western Canada. *Journal of Educational Policy, 3*, 351-370.

Desjarlais, L. (1983). *L'influence du milieu socio-linguistique sur les élèves franco-ontariens (une étude de cas).* Toronto, ON: Ministère de l'éducation et Ministère des collèges et universités.

Edwards, J. (1985). *Language, Society and Identity.* Oxford, UK: Basil Blackwell.

Fishman, J.A. (1989). *Language and Ethnicity in Minority Sociolinguistic Perspective.* Clevedon, UK: Multilingual Matters.

Fishman, J. (1972). *The Sociology of Language.* Rowley, MA: Newbury House.

Fishman, J. (1967). Bilingualism With and Without Diglossia, Diglossia With and Without Bilingualism. *Journal of Social Issues, 23*(2), 29-38.

Foucher, P. (1985). *Les droits scolaires constitutionnels des minorités de langue officielle au Canada.* Ottawa, ON: Conseil Canadien de documentation juridique.

Genesee, F. (1987). *Learning Through Two Languages.* Cambridge, MA: Newbury House.

Genesee, F. (1983). Bilingual Education of Majority Language Children: The Immersion Experiments in Review. *Applied Psycholinguistics, 4*, 1-46.

Giles, H., Bourhis, R.Y., & Taylor, D.M. (1977). Toward a Theory of Language in Ethnic Group Relations. In *Language Ethnicity and Intergroup Relations.* H. Giles (Ed.). pp. 307-348. New York, NY: Academic Press.

Hamers, J., & Blanc, M. (1989). *Bilinguality and Bilingualism.* Cambridge, UK: Cambridge University Press.

Hamers, J., & Blanc, M. (1983). *Bilingualité et bilinguisme.* Brussels, Belgium: Mardaga.

Harley, B. (1984). Mais apprennent-ils vraiment le français? *Langue et Société, 12*(hiver), 57-62.

Hébert, R., et al. (1976). *Rendement académique et langue d'enseignement chez les élèves franco-manitobains.* Winnipeg, MB: Centre de recherches du Collège de Saint-Boniface.

Hébert, R., & Bilodeau, M. (1987). Le français au Manitoba: Quelques tendances socio-démographiques. In *Demain, la francophonie en milieu minoritaire.* R. Théberge & J. Lafontant (Eds.), pp. 209-224. Winnipeg, MB: Centre de recherches du Collège de Saint-Boniface.

Héraux, P., Lapierre, J.W., & Prujiner, A. (1984). La dynamique des relations inter-communautaires dans le champ politique. In *Variation du comportement langagier lorsque deux langues sont en contact.* A. Prujiner et al. (Eds.), pp. 55-60. Québec, PQ: Centre international de recherche sur le bilinguisme.

Lambert, W.E. (1975). Culture and Language as Factors in Learning and Education. In *Education of Immigrant Students.* A. Wolfgang (Ed.), pp. 55-83. Toronto, ON: Ontario Institute cfor Studies in Education.

Lambert, W.E. (1974). The St. Lambert Project. In *Bilingualism, Biculturalism and Education.* S.T. Carey (Ed.). Edmonton, AB: University of Alberta Press.

Lambert, W.E., & Tucker, G.R. (1972). *Bilingual Education of Children: The St-Lambert Experiment.* Rowley, MA: Newbury House.

Landry, R. (1987). Additive Bilingualism, Schooling, and Special Education: A Minority Group Perspective. *Canadian Journal for Exceptional Children, 3*(4), 109-114.

Landry, R. (1984). In *Variation du comportement langagier lorsque deux langues sont en contact.* A. Prujiner et al. (Eds.), pp. 121-131. Québec, PQ: Centre international de recherche sur le bilinguisme.

Landry, R. (1982). Le bilinguisme additif chez les francophones minoritaires du Canada. *Revue des sciences de l'éducation, 8,* 223-244.

Landry, R., & Allard, R. (In press). Can Schools Promote Additive Bilingualism in Minority Group Children? In *Language, Culture and Cognition: A Collection of Studies in First and Second Language Acquisition.* L. Malave & G. Duquette (Eds.), Clevedon, UK: Multilingual Matters.

Landry, R., & Allard, R. (1990). Contact des langues et développement bilingue: Un modèle macroscopique. *The Canadian Modern Language Review/La revue canadienne des langues vivantes, 46*(3), 527-554.

Landry, R., & Allard, R. (1989). Vitalité ethnolinguistique et diglossie. *Revue Québécoise de linguistique théorique et appliquée, 8*(2), 73-101.

Landry, R., & Allard, R. (1988a). Ethnolinguistic Vitality and the Bilingual Development of Minority and Majority Group Students. Paper presented at the International Conference on Maintenance and Loss of Ethnic Minority Languages, Noordwijkerhout, The Netherlands.

Landry, R., & Allard, R. (1988b). L'assimilation linguistique des francophones hors-Québec, le défi de l'école française et le problème de l'unité nationale. *Revue de l'Association canadienne d'éducation de langue française, 16*(3), 38-53.

Landry, R., & Allard, R. (1987a). Étude du développement bilingue chez les Acadiens des provinces Maritimes. In *Demain, la francophonie en milieu minoritaire.* R. Théberge & J. Lafontant (Eds.), pp. 63-111. Winnipeg, MB: Centre de recherches du Collège de Saint-Boniface.

Landry, R., & Allard, R. (1987b). Développement bilingue en milieu minoritaire et en milieu majoritaire. In *L'école contribue-t-elle à maintenir la vitalité d'une langue minoritaire?* L. Péronnet (Ed.), pp. 11-30. Moncton, NB: Centre de recherche en linguistique appliquée.

MacMahon, F., & Fedigan, L. (1989). *École et culture: Le projet culturel des Franco-Albertains.* Edmonton, AB: Institut de recherche de la Faculté Saint-Jean.

Mahé, Y.T. (1989). L'évolution de l'enseignement du français en Alberta: Reflet d'orientations culturelles et idéologiques. In *Écriture et politique*. G. Allaire, G. Cadrin, & P. Dubé (Eds.), pp. 205-213. Edmonton, AB: Institut de recherche de la Faculté Saint-Jean.

McLaughlin, B. (1984). Early Bilingualism: Methodological and Theoretical Issues. In *Early bilingualism and child development*. M. Paradis & Y. Lebrun (Eds.), pp. 19-45. Lisse: Swets & Zeitlinger, B.V.

Pellerin & Hammerly (1986). L'expression oral après treize ans d'immersion française. *The Canadian Modern Language Review/La Revue canadienne des langues vivantes, 42*, 592-606.

Prujiner, A. (1987). Eléments de réflexion sur l'analyse des aspects sociétaux des contacts des langues. In *Problèmes théoriques et méthodologiques dans l'étude des langues/dialectes en contact aux niveau macrologique et micrologique*. J. Hamers & M. Blanc (Eds.), pp. 129-134. Québec, PQ: Centre international de recherche sur le bilinguisme.

Prujiner, A., Deshaies, D., Hamers, J.F., Blanc, M., Clément, R., & Landry, R. (1984). *Variation du comportement langagier lorsque deux langues sont en contact*. Québec, PQ: Centre international de recherche sur le bilinguisme.

Ruest, P. (1988). L'avenir éducatif des franco-manitobains: défi ou défaite? *Revue de l'Association canadienne d'éducation de langue française, 16*(3), 16-23.

Skutnabb-Kangas, T. (1984). Why Aren't All Children in the Nordic Countries Bilingual? *Journal of Multilingual and Multicultural Development, 5*, 301-315.

Skutnabb-Kangas, T. (1984). *Bilingualism or Not: The Education of Minorities*. Clevedon, UK: Multilingual Matters.

Skutnabb-Kangas, T., & Toukomaa, P. (1976). *Teaching Migrant Children's Mother Tongue and Learning the Language of the Host Country in the Context of the Socio-cultural Situation of the Migrant Family*. Helsinki, Finland: The Finnish National Commission for UNESCO.

Swain, M., & Lapkin, S. (1982). *Evaluating Bilingual Education: A Canadian Case Study*. Avon, UK: Multilingual Matters.

Théberge, R. (1989). *Les Fransaskois au XXIe siècle*. Winnipeg, MB: Centre de recherches du Collège de Saint-Boniface.

Théberge, R. (1987). Scandale national même là où le nombre justifie. *Revue de l'Association canadienne d'éducation de langue française, 15*(1), 12-19.

Toukomaa, P., & Skutnabb-Kangas, T. (1977). *The Intensive Teaching of the Mother Tongue to Migrant Children of the Pre-school Age and Children in the Lower Level of Comprehensive School*. Helsinki, Finland: The Finnish National Commission for UNESCO.

Vaillancourt, F. (1984). La détention des resources économiques et le statut socio-économique. In *Variation du comportement langagier lorsque deux langues sont en contact*. A. Prujiner et al. (Eds.), pp. 51-53. Québec, PQ: Centre international de recherche sur le bilinguisme.

Willig, A.C. (1985). A Meta-analysis of Selected Studies on the Effectiveness of Bilingual Education. *Review of Educational Research, 55*, 269-317.

Assessment and Evaluation

From the time they enter high school (and sometimes before), Canadian children are assessed and evaluated. Their promotion from grade to grade is dependent on their performance on tests assessing their grasp of course content, while their placement in particular classes or schools may be determined largely by their scores on standardized measures of intelligence and academic achievement.

Braun, Rennie, and Gordon explored the influence of different assessment contexts on children's reading performance. The reading ability levels of eight Grade 5 students identified by their teachers as the poorest readers in their classes were assessed in three different contexts for oral reading of words and three different contexts for oral reading of passages. The first context for both words and passages comprised the standard testing situation, as neutral as possible, with minimal interaction between child and tester. The second and third contexts for both the word and the passage reading assessments deliberately included different kinds of interaction between child and tester and were designed to identify each child's zone of proximal development (Vygotsky, 1978), the distance between actual performance on independent problem solving, and potential performance under adult guidance. The results were dramatic. When tested under the more interactive conditions, the range of performance for most of the children increased dramatically. In other words, although they were not capable of achieving a high reading level totally on their own, they had the potential for higher levels with just a little help from a friend. If the purpose of testing is to determine appropriate teaching interventions, the results of this study suggest that reliance on the conventional testing context is misplaced, leading teachers to underestimate their students' capabilities. In contrast, the information provided to teachers using a dynamic assessment context could be invaluable in structuring future learning/teaching situations.

Standardized intelligence tests are used extensively in Canadian schools in order to determine which students should be placed in special education classes at both the remedial and the gifted ends of the spectrum. Within the past decade, researchers in both the United States and Canada have debated the extent to which these tests are biased in favour of white, middle-class, English-speaking children. In their article, Common and Frost argue that the standardized intelligence tests most commonly used in Canada are not appropriate for assessing Native children. With regard to the Wechsler Intelligence Scale for Children (WISC), they discuss evidence indicating that the pattern of performance for Native children is consistently different from that of non-Native children, and so interpretation of test results for Native children according to the criteria applied to non-Native children leads to misidentification of some Native children as mentally deficient and a failure to recognize gifted Native children. Further, there is at least some evidence that a major justification for standardized intelligence tests—their value in predicting future school performance—does not hold for Native students. Rather than advocating the abandonment of intelligence tests, Common and Frost suggest that researchers investigate other ways of defining and measuring intelligence.

Many provincial Ministries of Education expend a lot of effort constructing standardized achievement tests to be administered to all the students in the province. The results of Anderson's analysis of more than 4,000 questionnaires from Grades 4, 7, and 10 teachers indicated that testing was a frequent classroom activity. However, although teachers assessed student achievement in a variety of ways, the most important components of student evaluation were teacher-made objective tests. Standardized tests were among the least emphasized measures, and the majority of teachers had no desire to base student assessment on provincial examinations. Anderson suggests, therefore, that educational measurement research should focus on the kinds of tests that teachers actually use.

An Examination of Contexts for Reading Assessment

Carl Braun, Barbara J. Rennie, and Christine J. Gordon
University of Calgary

In this descriptive study fifth-grade children were tested in three varying contexts to determine the effects of adult support and regulation on their ability to read words in isolation and to read connected discourse. This study provides support for dynamic assessment contexts which invite children to use language in more natural ways than has been possible in traditional assessment contexts. The findings are discussed in relation to Vygotsky's zone of proximal development.

*   *   *

CONVENTIONAL PRACTICE IN TESTING HOLDS TO THE BELIEF THAT LIMIT-ing, if not eliminating, contextual influence is a desirable prerequisite for the ideal testing situation. Such is the view articulated by Fuchs and Fuchs (1986): "Scientism appears to govern the way we administer tests as well as our understanding of what occurs during testing" (p. 243). They cite evidence for such a claim in the recently published *Standards for Educational and Psychological Testing* (American Educational Research Association, American Psychological Association, & National Council on Measurement in Education, 1985) in which testing is likened to formal experimentation. "This perspective encourages the examiner (i.e., unbiased investigator) to administer the test according to explicit non-varying instructions (i.e., experimental treatment) in a controlled setting (i.e., the laboratory)" (p. 243).

Such a statement endorses the perpetuation of the view that testing and teaching/learning situations are discrete entities. It leaves unchallenged the conventional examiner-examinee relationship as static, unidirectional, and predictable, reflected not only in the testing agenda, but also in the active control over the agenda. Further, this tradition places the examinee in a limiting language situation faced with a genre and circumstances which in any other life experience would be regarded as foreign, if not hostile.

It is only recently that challenges have been made to the powerful influence of positivism on teaching. Part of the challenge comes from the obvious disparity felt by teachers between their convictions about the best approaches to promote pupil learning and approaches which seem requisite for success on tests (Mayher & Brause, 1986). In addition, there is a growing body of research which challenges other basic assumptions underlying traditional testing. These studies suggest that test performance may be influenced by examiners' personality (Feldman & Sullivan, 1971); examiners' attitudes about the legitimacy of testing (Horne & Garty, 1981); and choice of test location (Labov, 1973; Stoneman & Gibson, 1978). There is evidence, further, that examiner-examinee familiarity influences test performance, and particularly so for low SES children (Fuchs & Fuchs, 1986; Fuchs, Fuchs, Power, & Dailey, 1985). In addition, research suggests that test performance can be influenced by examinees' interpretation of the purpose of tests and their comprehension of test instructions (Abramyan, 1977; Deyhle, 1983; Mehan, 1978). What is particularly relevant to this study are the findings which suggest that test performance appears to be influenced by the nature of the test and test situation (Cioffi & Carney, 1983; Feuerstein, 1979; Labov, 1973) and particularly, the evidence which points to the need for examiners and examinees to participate in dynamic, bidirectional, and idiosyncratic relationships, frequently resulting in unexpected behavior (Cioffi & Carney, 1983; Feuerstein, 1979; Fuchs, Zern, & Fuchs, 1983; Roth, 1974).

A significant challenge to the validity in testing comes from the realization that reading ability cannot be defined independent of the context in which reading is used. The transaction between reader and text during the reading process is dependent on such factors as the reader's interest in material being read, his or her purposes for reading it, and his or her background experiences relevant to the text. Of particular importance to reading during a testing situation is the chance element involved in accessing relevant background experience, especially under the pressure of the test context. Mayher and Brause (1986) suggest that such contextual variables are even more important for young and inexperienced readers than they are for skilled adults.

A consideration of the complexity of the reader/context interaction raises serious questions about traditional views of external validity. It suggests a need to look closely at internal validity (Johnston, 1986). This view is consonant with dynamic assessment methods which advocate inferences about children's learning based on improvement in learning observed during teacher/child (examiner/examinee) interaction (Budoff, 1974; Cioffi & Carney, 1983; Feuerstein, 1979). Such improvement can be conceptualized in terms of Vygotsky's zone of proximal development (Vygotsky, 1978). The zone has been described by Vygotsky as "the distance between the actual developmental level as determined by independent problem solving and the level of potential development as determined through problem solving under adult guidance or in collaboration with more capable peers" (p. 86).

A plausible interpretation of the zone of proximal development in reading assessment relates to the extent to which a given strategy is used independently, or with varying degrees of instructional assistance. Vygotsky (1978) believed that this difference between independent and assisted activity was important in that it defines mental operations which have not matured, but are in the process of maturing. Brown and Reeve (1985) corroborate this view when they suggest that any estimate of developmental status must depend critically on the environment in which it is revealed including social environments in which parents, teachers, peers, and experimenters provide degrees of contextual support for learning, sometimes without conscious attempts to do so. Such contexts, in their view, create development which in turn determines the level of learning for which a child is ripe.

The purpose of this study was to examine the impact of varying contexts in which processes of change could be observed as children navigated within their band-widths of competence with and without other regulation. In addition, the study aimed to determine children's perceptions of assessment in these varied contexts.

Method

Sample

The sample for the study consisted of eight fifth-grade children (six boys and two girls) selected from two classrooms. These children were judged by their teachers to be the lowest readers in the class. Comprehension scores on the Canadian Gates MacGinitie Reading Test (Level D) ranged between grades 3.1 and 3.9.

A brief description of the assessment contexts follows. Contexts one to three comprised the assessment scenarios for three separate sessions in which reading words in isolation was assessed. The materials used for the assessment were word lists from three different informal reading inventories judged to be equivalent in difficulty level. All words were printed on 3×7 inch cards. Context one consisted of reading words in an isolation assessment session. Every attempt was made to put the child at ease during the session, but no prompts of any kind were given. Context two consisted of reading the word lists followed by an opportunity for the child to listen to a taped version of his/her reading, and to check off the words in the list judged to have been read correctly. The children were encouraged to try the words missed on the initial trial. In addition, they were encouraged to ask any questions related to these words, except for the question "What is this word?" Because this procedure was assumed to be relatively foreign to the children, a number of questions were modeled. For example, "If I don't know the word *alligator*, I might ask you, 'Do the first three letters make the word *all?*' or 'Does the *g* in the word have the same sound as the *g* in *girl?*'"

Context three comprised the reading of another set of words, this time with prompts for any words not identified independently. These prompts involved cueing on sounds of specific words, for example, "That word starts the same as the word *gin.*" A very frequent prompt was that of progressively exposing a word, syllable by syllable, in order to highlight (visually only) the parts of polysyllabic words, as in false/hood, ob/ser/ving, gen/er/o/si/ty, among others. This was done by sliding a blank card across the word card from left to right.

Sessions for contexts one to three were conducted on three consecutive days, with contexts assigned randomly for each day's session.

Contexts four to six comprised the assessment scenarios for another three sessions, this time for the purpose of assessing oral reading of connected discourse. Three sets of oral reading passages were compiled from published informal reading inventories. Minor revisions were made to render the passages roughly equivalent. However, no attempt was made to justify equivalence on the basis of complex text analyses.

Context four consisted of the standard administration of the Informal Reading Inventory, IRI, oral reading passage. Wh-probes were used as the basis for comprehension assessment. Context five comprised another oral reading passage administration. Prior to the reading, children were encouraged to scan each passage for any help that they would like to receive before reading. Again, the only condition placed on their requests for help was that they could not ask, "What is that word?" A range of prompts was used to provide assistance for difficult words (e.g., placing a word in a strategic context; progressively exposing a polysyllabic word from left to right syllable by syllable; providing analogues to difficult parts of words; suggesting meanings for potentially difficult words; moving backward or forward in text for clues to meaning).

Context six comprised the reading of another set of passages. The scenario included a brief discussion about the topic, focusing on prior knowledge rather than on content from the passage, and culminating in establishing a purpose for reading. This was followed by an opportunity to scan for potential problems and to enlist assistance.

Sessions for contexts four to six were conducted on three consecutive days; again, contexts were assigned randomly for each day's session. All sessions were taped. Further, after each session, the classroom teacher conducted a brief, very informal, conference with the children to gain insights into their perceptions of the session.

Responses to the word list and passage reading were analyzed to determine maximum instructional levels for each child. Transcripts of tapes were analyzed. Descriptive analyses only were done.

Results

Contexts One to Three

The responses to the word list assessment within the three contexts are presented in Table 1.

Table 1 Highest Instructional Word Reading Level Achieved Within Assessment Contexts								
Context	1	2	3	4	5	6	7	8
One (*n*=8)	—	1	1	2	1	1	—	—
Two (*n*=8)	—	1	1	—	2	2	2	—
Three (*n*=7)	—	1	1	—	—	2	2	1

Intuition would suggest that increased time and increased input would result in commensurate improvements in student performance. This was so with six of the eight children in the study. It did not, however, apply to two of the children. These children remained within the level two to three instructional range irrespective of context. In context two, one of the children checked a total of three words (across three word lists) as correct when, in fact, the words had been read incorrectly. This child also failed to identify two words as having been read correctly. Another child failed to check two incorrect words as correct and failed to identify four words as having been read correctly. These were the two children with the lowest instructional level across the three contexts. One of the children was unable to think of a single question to ask; the other asked two questions which failed to result in successful responses. The prompts in context three produced one additional correct response for only one of the children ("about" was read correctly when the word was successively exposed).

For six of the children in the study, freedom to ask questions, and particularly, the occasion to receive prompts increased the range of performance markedly. One child moved from instructional level four to five to seven across the three contexts, respectively.

Contexts Four to Six

The results of the assessment of word passage reading are presented in Table 2.

Again, the range of instructional levels increased as the context allowed for increased prompting and interaction, that is for all but two children, who as in contexts one to three showed relatively stable performance across

Table 2
Highest Instructional Passage Reading Level Achieved Within
Assessment Contexts

Context	1	2	3	4	5	6	7	8
Four $(n=8)$	—	3	3	2	—	—	—	—
Five $(n=8)$	—	1	1	2	3	1	—	—
Six $(n=8)$	—	1	1	1	2	3	—	—

contexts. It became readily apparent that children varied widely in their abilities to scan for potential problems. Further, the range of questions varied widely across the sample. Three children in the sample gave no evidence of knowledge of context as a source for help.

A number of insights came from comments of the children. For example, one child who moved across levels three, five, and six (in contexts four to six) made the following comment relative to content six:

CHILD: Now that we have talked about the story, I know which words to look at.

INVESTIGATOR: How's that?

CHILD: Well, I know a lot about camping anyway and this makes it easy to see words that are hard (thinks for awhile)...but most of the words are not hard when you know something about the story...and you have done it (camping) before.

Another child who moved across levels four, five and six, made the following comment relative to context five:

CHILD: It's easy to find the words I can't do.

INVESTIGATOR: How do you do this?

CHILD: Well, I just go down the page and say, "Which words can't I read?" I just don't know what kinds of questions are right.

INVESTIGATOR: Try this one. Ask me a question about this (pointing to "through" which the child has identified as hard for him).

CHILD: You can't say the "gh." Right?

INVESTIGATOR: Right! Any other questions?

CHILD: I guess I should ask if reading further will be a good idea.

INVESTIGATOR: I think that is a good question.

CHILD: (Thinks) I guess good readers aren't only good readers. I guess they have to ask questions that fit.... Maybe then I don't always have to ask you...or like a teacher.

These types of comments from children provide evidence that children as they interact within the assessment context with another person not only act directly on prompts, but also interact with themselves as they make new discoveries about reading and especially their own reading. This corroborates a statement made by Brown and Reeve (1985) claiming that bandwidths of competence are created by contexts which vary in their degree of support. These contexts can be overtly social or covertly social as in the case of responding to an imagined internalized audience.

Another observation made during the sessions was that the slightest suspicion that real testing was occurring changed the behavior, more dramatically in some instances than in others. Karen's sudden shift in behavior illustrates the point.

Karen was reading with the investigator in a session she assumed to be instructional. She read, not exactly fluently, but with obvious meaning reflected in her voice, by the number and quality of self-corrections, and in the way in which she organized her oral production in relatively meaningful language clusters. When she noticed the investigator poising a pen to record comments on her performance, she interrupted her reading with "Oh, I didn't know this was a test." Immediately, her voice reflected strain, and her reading became labored and fragmented. Her word accuracy necessitated fewer corrections. However, the corrections she made were meaningless. There was an immediate change in Karen's sense of language marked by a decrease in the number of words clustered in her reading. Further, in two of the few instances in which she clustered more than one word, she did so across sentence boundaries.

Karen was asked to listen to her taped reading. The transcript which follows documents her perception about appropriate instructional context behavior and appropriate testing context behavior.

K: I changed my reading on line 8.

I: How did you change it?

K: I stopped being sloppy. I read real careful.

I: Were you not careful in the first part?

K: Not really. I read fast and I went back.

I: Why did you stop doing that in line 8?

K: Because I didn't know it was a test. And I just tried hard.

I: Do you try harder on tests than when you do other reading?

K: Yes!

I: Why?

K: Teachers (and...like you...) put things in our report and my mom wants me to try the best.

I: When we started reading, why did you think that this was not a test?

K: Well...like, we talked about it...to help me. And then I asked you questions.

I: And then it's not a test?

K: No. (Without hesitation) We just talked—and I just said what I thought in my reading. I wasn't really thinking hard. Also, you helped me.

Karen's test-taking register and her learning register are clearly differentiated. Further, like many children, she appears quite satisfied with this situation. Her test-taking register applies even to something as informal as an IRI. Under such circumstances, the question arises as to how one determines the instructional conditions under which Karen can best progress and the conditions under which her ability to learn can be altered. If the goal in assessment is to determine the minimal instructional adjustment necessary to succeed, then Karen's test-taking register represents a major obstacle to the realization of such a goal.

Teacher Interview Responses

The teacher interviews were very brief and meant to be as spontaneous and informal as possible. Despite the brevity, the interviews yielded interesting insights into the children's perception of appropriate test-taking register—both on their part and on the part of the examiner.

Contexts one and four were viewed as tests. The results of the tests were viewed as being passed on to the teacher, and from him or her to the parents, and then, as one child put it "then to other places." Consistently, the children were unable to think of what would happen to the results of their performance in contexts two, three, five, and six. When asked about their perceptions of the purpose of these sessions two children responded. One of them questioningly replied, "Maybe he wants to find out about kids." Another responded, "Perhaps he likes to teach children and takes us out to help us."

None of the eight children was able to verbalize why contexts one and four represented test situations. When the teacher asked how they knew, the typical response was a shrug of the shoulder and "I just know." Every child was able to provide reasons why contexts two, three, five, and six were not tests. The most common reason was that the investigator had helped them and that they could ask any questions they wished. One child responded, "He gave me answers" when this was not the case.

When asked how well they had done on context one, six of the eight thought they had done well, one thought she had done "ok," and one "wasn't sure." In response to the same question for contexts two and three, there wasn't one child who thought he/she had done well. The responses varied from "ok, maybe" to "terrible." Responses to their perceptions of their performance in contexts four to six were more variable. As compared with context one (no assistance), only three thought they had done well in context four (no assistance), two thought they had done quite well, and three thought they had performed poorly.

All children perceived themselves to have performed poorly in contexts five and six. None of them were able to provide reasons except for three children in context five, and two children in context six who all perceived themselves as having needed too much help.

Discussion

Generally, the aim in assessment is to determine the minimal instructional adjustments necessary to succeed with a particular type of text. A search for such minimal adjustments requires that the examiner look for peaks of performance, frequently considered to be aberrations and ignored during testing. Feuerstein (1979) feels that:

> these peaks of performance must be viewed as very important hints of the existence of a capacity that does not become generally manifest because of the individual's inefficiency in using it. The inefficiency may be transient or more permanent for reasons that have to be revealed by appropriate search. (p. 34)

Clearly, for most of the children in this study, termination of the testing cycle at conventional levels would have failed to reveal their peaks (some of them quite dramatic) of performance. Failure to recognize these peaks has serious implications for intervention plans. It would follow that interventions based on traditional assessment criteria would likely leave six of the eight children in the sample for this study with instructional programs considerably below their levels of potential performance.

The real significance of such searches for peaks goes far beyond a simple identification of levels at which children can perform. The essence lies in the identification of factors which either facilitate or inhibit learning. In other words, such a search specifies the conditions under which progress can be made and the conditions under which the ability to learn can be altered (Cioffi & Carney, 1983). What is noteworthy is the fact that a dynamic context has the potential to extend the range of insights under which learning can or will not occur. It provides insights into strategies which children possess under given conditions. It is significant that two of the children in this study experienced difficulty in identifying words that they had earlier read correctly. It is also significant that children varied in their abilities to anticipate difficulties as they scanned textual materials. Equally significant was the variability among children in the range of questions they were able to pose for the investigator—some no questions at all, others a wide range of questions highly pertinent to particular text reading problems. An assessment context which invites the examinee to expose process knowledge of this nature has implications for instruction which can

C. Braun, B.J. Rennie, & C.J. Gordon

lead to the development of "self improvement strategies rather than to the accumulation of learned items" (Clay, 1985, p. 57). In this sense, this study points to potential pitfalls of single assessments which rely on "static snapshot descriptions of developmental status frozen in time and welded to particular task environments" (Brown & Reeve, 1985, p. 71).

The children in this study, then, manifested varying zones or bandwidths of competence under conditions assumed to be supportive, and conditions which involved considerable interaction. These conditions did lead to the evaluation of cognitive processes and permitted investigators to see growth and change as opposed to fossilized or automated processes of static states of cognition. For Vygotsky (1978), it was necessary to "alter the automatic, mechanized, fossilized character of the higher forms of behavior and turn it back to its source through experiment to permit dynamic analyses" (p. 64). In other words, it was important to create environments in which cognitive processes underwent change right before one's eyes.

Vygotsky's (1978) view held that "learning should be matched in some manner with the child's developmental level" (p. 85). However, he maintained that it is impossible to understand a child's developmental level without considering two aspects of that level, that is, the actual developmental level and the potential developmental level. The actual developmental level is the result of already completed developmental cycles. Typically, standardized tests and measures such as informal reading inventories are designed to reflect a reasonable estimate of the child's actual developmental level.

An interactive environment involving demonstrations and leading questions provides the child with the necessary support to demonstrate his/her potential developmental level. It was Vygotsky's (1978) belief that the repertoire of behaviors manifested within the zone of proximal development (the zone marking the boundaries of competence between the two developmental levels) would in time become the learner's independent repertoire.

There are a number of ways in which Vygotsky's (1978) zone theory can be brought to an interpretation of the variant zone widths exhibited by children in this study. Indeed, considerable zones were evident in the case of six children. What about the apparently limited zones of two of the children, both in the word reading and passage reading tasks? One interpretation might be that these children, in fact, have limited zones at this point in time. That is, there is virtually no difference between their actual developmental level and their potential level. If this is found to be so, that is important information for the teacher to obtain.

Another interpretation begs the question, not of the existence of actual zones (or width of these zones), but rather whether or not the assessment environments in the study provided the kind of support, demonstrations, and prompts necessary for these children to reveal their bandwidths of competence. Stierer (1983) emphasizes that, in fact, assessment in a very real sense is a test of the tester:

> Coming to know the reader is, after all, a case of making meaning within a complex social context. Just as research and reading, a sociolinguistic emphasis makes explicit two vital aspects of reading assessment. First, it reinforces the sense-making nature of assessment, in contrast with the widely-held belief that it is an unambiguous mechanical operation. Second, it locates the assessment process within a situation which comprises a complex network of social structures and relationships. (p. 81)

Any dynamic assessment situation, then, stretches the competencies of the examiner to the limit. The most one can expect is for the examiner to provide the supportive environment which enables the development of a picture of many possible manifestations of reading, including manifestations which may well be contradictory in nature. Wertsch (1979) states "The issue is not simply one of whether or not the adult is providing strategic assistance—it is also an issue of what type of other regulation is being used" (p. 19). Johnston (1986) says "It would involve considering the teacher as the instrument to be developed rather than the task" (p. 86). Clearly, the teacher/examiner engages in a process of meaning-making as she/he, in turn, probes and observes the meaning-making manifestations of the learner, in sharp contrast with the widely held belief that assessment is an unambiguous mechanical operation.

This study highlights the range of perceptions of children of assessment constraints as well as a range of notions of perceived consequences of assessments. It is clear that children (at least those in this study) regard the testing situation as something totally different from any other context they are likely to encounter. It would appear from studies such as this that the assessment setting must be viewed as the stage for real language encounters. And there are significant differences between natural language encounters and invitations to use language in typical assessment situations.

In the first instance, the agenda in a typical testing situation is controlled by one of the persons, and a significant part of that agenda is secret. In fact, the rules of testing generally specify that the agenda must remain secret. In a natural language encounter each party is expected to contribute to the agenda; indeed, it is normally in the best interests of both parties to call for clarification if the agenda is unclear. Further, in natural discourse it is expected that the agenda may undergo at least some modification by mutual consent. Most testing situations make no provision for such modification.

Freedom of modification suggests freedom to explore and to risk temporary disagreement. The usual testing situation does not invite exploration and generally penalizes risk taking (or at least is assumed to operate in that way by the person being tested). Much of natural discourse invites pushing the limits of the imagination and intelligence. The language in most testing situations pushes persons to correct answers, especially answers assumed to be correct by other people. Finally, much of natural discourse happens without particular thought given to the consequences of what is being said. Or at the very least parties in conversation have a reasonable notion as to possible consequences. In the testing situation the person being tested seldom knows the consequences of the testing, and in many instances imagines the worst. This state of affairs is often exacerbated by the fact that much testing takes place between near or complete strangers, a circumstance which contributes significantly to the artificiality and limitations placed on the exercise of natural language functions.

In summary, this study provides additional support for dynamic assessment contexts which invite children (and adults) to use language in more natural ways than has been possible in traditional testing situations. It underlines the need for examiners/teachers to help children negotiate the zone of proximal development, gradually "luring them further and further into the task until, ultimately, the transition to self-regulation is complete" (Teale, 1981, p. 909).

References

Abramyan, L.A. (1977). On the role of verbal instructions in the direction of voluntary movement in children. *Quarterly Newsletter of the Institute for Comparative Human Development, 1*, 1-4.

American Educational Research Association, American Psychological Association, & National Council on Measurement in Education. (1985). *Standards for educational and psychological testing*. Washington, DC: American Psychological Association.

Brown, A.L., & Reeve, R.A. (1985). *Bandwidths of competence: The role of supportive contexts in learning and development* (Tech. Rep. No. 336). Urbana, IL: University of Illinois, Center for the Study of Reading.

Budoff, M. (1974). *Learning potential and educability among the educable mentally retarded*. Final Report Project No. 312312. Cambridge, MA: Research Institute for Educational Problems, Cambridge Mental Health Association.

Cioffi, G., & Carney, J.J. (1983). Dynamic assessment of reading disabilities. *The Reading Teacher, 36*, 764-769.

Clay, M.M. (1985). The reading recovery research reports: Part 1. *Reading-Canada-Lecture,4*, 93-106.

Deyhle, D. (1983). Learning failure: Test-taking and the Navajo student. (Summary). *Proceedings of the Fourth Annual University of Pennsylvania Ethnography in Education Research Forum, 5.*

Feldman, S.E., & Sullivan, D.S. (1971). Factors mediating the effects of enhanced rapport on children's performance. *Journal of Consulting and Clinical Psychology, 36*, 302.

Feuerstein, R. (1979). *The dynamic assessment of retarded performers: The learning potential assessment device, theory, instruments, and techniques*. Baltimore, MD: University Park Press.

Fuchs, D., & Fuchs, L.S. (1986). Test procedure bias: A meta-analysis of examiner familiarity effects. *Review of Educational Research, 56,* 243-262.

Fuchs, D., Fuchs, L.S., Power, M.H., & Dailey, A.M. (1985). Bias in the assessment of handicapped children. *American Educational Research Journal, 22,* 185-198.

Fuchs, D., Zern, D.S., & Fuchs, L.S. (1983). Participants' verbal and nonverbal behavior in familiar and unfamiliar test conditions. *Diagnostique, 8,* 159-169.

Horne, L.V., & Garty, M.K. (1981, April). *What the test score really reflects: Observations of teacher behavior during standardized achievement test administration.* Paper presented at the annual meeting of the American Educational Research Association, Los Angeles, CA.

Johnston, P.H. (1986). A Vygotskian perspective on assessment in reading. *Reading-Canada-Lecture, 4,* 82-92.

Labov, W. (1973). The logic of nonstandard English. In F. Williams (Ed.), *Language and poverty* (pp. 153-189). Chicago, IL: Markham.

Mayher, J.S., & Brause, R.S. (1986). Learning through teaching: Is testing crippling integrated language education? *Language Arts, 63,* 390-396.

Mehan, H. (1978). Structuring school structure. *Harvard Educational Review, 48,* 32-64.

Roth, D.R. (1974). Intelligence testing as a social activity. In A.V. Cicourel, S.H.M. Jennings, K.H. Jennings, K.C. Leiter, R. MacKay, H. Mehan, & D.R. Roth (Eds.), *Language use and school performance* (pp. 143-217). New York, NY: Academic Press.

Stierer, B. (1983). A research reading teachers reading children reading: Making sense of reading assessment in the classroom. In M. Meek (Ed.), *Opening moves: Work in progress in the study of children's language development.* London, UK: University of London.

Stoneman, Z., & Gibson, S. (1978). Situational influences on assessment performance. *Exceptional Children, 46,* 166-169.

Teale, W.H. (1981). Parents reading to their children: What we know and need to know. *Language Arts, 58,* 902-912.

Vygotsky, L. (1962). *Thought and language* (E. Hanfmann & G.G. Vakar, Trans.) Cambridge, MA: MIT Press.

Vygotsky, L. (1978). *Mind in society* (M. Cole, V. John-Steiner, S. Scribner, & E. Souberman, Trans.). Cambridge, MA: MIT Press.

Wertsch, J. (1979). From social interaction to higher psychological processes. *Human Development, 2,* 1-22.

The Implications of the Mismeasurement of Native Students' Intelligence Through the Use of Standardized Intelligence Tests

R.W. Common
Brock University
L.G. Frost
Ontario Institute for Studies in Education

*   *   *

We know that you esteem highly the kind of learning taught in those Colleges, and that the Maintenance of our young Men while with you, would be very expensive to you. We are convinced, that you mean to do us Good by your Proposal; and we thank you heartily. But you, who are wise, must know that different Nations have different Conceptions of things and you will therefore not take it amiss, if our Ideas of this kind of Education happen not to be the same as yours. We have had some Experience of it. Several of our Young People were formerly brought up at the Colleges of the Northern Provinces; they were instructed in all your Sciences; but, when they came back to us, they were bad Runners; ignorant of every means of living in the woods...neither fit for Hunters, Warriors, nor Counsellors, they were totally good for nothing.

We are, however, not the less obliged by your kind offer, though we decline accepting it; and, to show our grateful Sense of it, if the Gentlemen of Virginia will send us a Dozen of their Sons, we will take Care of their Education, instruct them in all we know, and make Men of them.

—the Chiefs of the Indians of the Six Nations at Lancaster, Pennsylvania in response to an offer from the commissioners of Maryland and Virginia to educate twelve young Indian men at William and Mary College, June 17, 1744 (McLuhan, 1971)

AT THE TIME THAT THIS STATEMENT WAS MADE, THE WHITE AND NATIVE peoples of North America had been in contact with each other for a relatively short time, and indeed some Native groups had had no exposure to Whites at all. Yet the Chiefs of the Indians of the Six Nations had recognized and articulated the problems that, to this day, plague cross-cultural education: the mismatch between the educational objectives of a school system based in one culture and the lifestyles, values, and goals of students attending it who come from a different cultural background. If this match is poor, then the culturally different student is faced with enormous problems of personal adjustment. When this student's intellectual potential is assessed with instruments developed for and normed on children from the majority population, then the student is faced with the prospect of being evaluated, not on the basis of his or her personal capabilities, but on the extent to which he or she has acculturated himself or herself. This certainly is the state of affairs for Native students in Canada today.

While the optimal course of action might be to discontinue the use of standardized intelligence tests with Native students, the reality of the situation is that the Department of Indian Affairs and Northern Development (DIA) insists that students referred for consideration for special education placement be assessed for their intellectual potential. This is particularly true of students being considered for identification as Gifted, Talented, and Creative (GTC), where in practice, at DIA—Local Education Authorities Join Assessment meetings, students must attain an Intelligence Quotient (IQ) of 130 in order to gain access to services appropriate to their needs.[1] This operational definition of Gifted, Talented, and Creative is in direct contradiction to the espoused DIA policy:

> It cannot be over-emphasized that the child's school performance must be fairly compared with the norms of the child's age group and *with the performance of the rest of the children in the community*. (*Special Education Handbook*, 1986, p.4, emphasis added).

Since all money provided to Natives for their education flows through DIA, and since DIA retains the prerogative to allocate funding, this authority is formidable and complete. Because of resource dependency, Natives have no alternative but to work within the limitations imposed by DIA. If these limitations include having Native children's intellectual abilities assessed through the use of such instruments as the Wechsler Intelligence Scale for Children—Revised (WISC-R), then the inappropriateness of these instruments becomes one more obstacle to be faced in the struggle for local control.

Assessing Native Intelligence: Historical Perspective

One of the earliest attempts to assess Native intelligence was conducted by Samuel Morton in the mid 1800s (Gould, 1981). Morton measured the volume in cubic inches of the skulls of 144 Amerindian people. The assumption that pervaded all of his work was that the volume of a skull was a direct measure of the intellectual capacity of the brain that had resided within it. Morton applied this technique to collections of skulls from different racial and ethnic groups and found different mean volumes for each group. Natives rated second from last in intelligence by Morton's accounts, with only the Negro group thought to be lower. His data, however, seem to have been deliberately compiled in order to prove his own preconceived ideas regarding racial origin and intelligence. Thus the assessment of Native intelligence was off to a less than illustrious start by being a vehicle for the perpetration of bias and prejudice.

Even in these times of supposedly more enlightened thinking, research has been conducted comparing Natives' cranial shapes to those of Caucasians (McShane, 1983; McShane, Risse, & Rubens, 1984; McShane, 1984). The finding of a more symmetrical head in Natives as compared to Caucasians, who have a pattern of larger left posterior and right anterior regions, has been interpreted to the detriment of Natives. The brains of Caucasians are supposedly better suited for language acquisition and the more oval heads of Natives explain the language delays and impairments that are more prevalent among them. Such a reductionistic and simplistic line of thinking is clearly not suitable to explain the differences in language functioning between Whites and Natives. To suggest that the shape of the head is related to the complex workings of the human brain is to ignore all that the fields of cognitive science and neuropsychology have contributed over the last century and a half to the understanding of thinking and brain function. To relate head shape to brain function is to discount all of the many factors known to influence human language and intellectual functioning, such as culture, personality, and life experience. The arguments based in McShane's research do not differ in substance from those suggested by Morton over 150 years ago and are equally erroneous.

Modern day studies of Native intelligence have relied heavily on the WISC-R and its forerunner, the WISC. The results of these studies have provided a consistent pattern of findings. Natives do not perform in the same manner as the White population on standardized tests of intelligence. Wilgosh, Mulcahy, and Watters (1986) report the assessment, using the WISC-R, of 366 Inuit children who were randomly selected from two districts in the Northwest Territories. The children covered the total age range testable with the WISC-R, 7 to 14.11 years. A Verbal Scale score of less than 70 was obtained for 77.4% of the children in the study. The percentage of children scoring below 70 on the Performance Scale was 5.74. The resulting Full Scale IQ scores indicated that 32.24% of the children in the sample scored below 70 and according to the test norms, would be classified as mentally retarded. None of the children in the study achieved a Full Scale IQ of 130 and therefore none would have been eligible for identification as GTC under the DIA criteria. Wechsler (1974) indicated that 2.3% of the norming population attained an IQ of 130 or higher. Application of this incidence figure to the 366 children in the Wilgosh, Mulcahy, and Watters study suggests that at least 8 children should have been identified as GTC. The report concluded that the WISC-R is not adequate for the assessment of Inuit children.

Similar results were obtained by St. John and Krichev (1976) who studied 160 Cree and Ojibwa children and young adults in Northwestern Ontario. The study was conducted because psychologists at Lakehead University and the Lakehead Board of Education had observed that the use of the WISC with Native students seemed to invariably result in the finding of subnormal functioning. Empirical data were sought.

The mean Verbal Scale IQs obtained ranged from 69.70 to 91.10 and all were significantly lower than the Performance IQs, which were average according to the test norm (about 100). The greatest differences were found among the younger children with the magnitude of the differences decreasing with age. The language of the home (English in unilingual or bilingual homes versus Native unilingual homes) was related to performance on the Verbal Scale only for the six- and seven-year-olds and the 14- and 15-year-olds. The children who spoke only a Native language at home scored lower.

This result is not surprising in the youngest children who were learning English as a second language. The researchers explain the relationship of language to Verbal IQ found in the 14- and 15-year-olds as due to the upheavals they were experiencing in their personal lives. This group was in a boarding home program in Thunder Bay and was encountering urban life for the first time. As only the six- and seven-year-olds had lower verbal scores than this group, the scores may not have been an artifact of the language of the home, but due rather to the changes in their lives.

The generally increasing scores as the children grew older may be the result of acculturation through the school system. Another finding that emerged from the St. John and Krichev study was that the WISC scores were nearly totally unrelated to school performance as measured by the grades achieved by the students. Since the purpose of administering measures of intelligence to students during the process of identifying them as exceptional is to make a prediction about the students' academic potential, then a finding of poor or nonexistent relationship between achievement and IQ scores renders the testing process a waste of time and resources. St. John and Krichev conclude that the use of the WISC with Native students could readily lead to the misclassification of large numbers of children as the average six- or seven-year-old in the study would have been diagnosed as mentally deficient.

Seyfort, Spreen, and Lahmer (1980) examined the WISC-R results of 177 Native children in southwestern British Columbia. The children all lived on reserves, but attended local community schools. While they did not report specific scores for the Verbal and Performance scales of the test, Seyfort, Spreen, and Lahmer state that they found the typical pattern of average Performance scores and poor Verbal scores. The three subtests of the Verbal scale which seemed to contribute to the differences between the children in the study and the test norming population were Information, Vocabulary, and Comprehension. Many items on these subtests were out of sequence in terms of difficulty when compared to the pattern obtained with the norming population.

An assumption underlying these subtests is a common body of experience from which more intelligent children will extract more in the way of knowledge and skills, and less intelligent children will extract less in the way of knowledge and skills. The logic of this line of thinking breaks down, however, when the tests thus constructed are applied to groups who operate from a different body of experience. Many aspects of the culture and the way of life of the children on these southwestern British Columbia reserves were highly different from those of the mainstream Canadian.

The inclusion of certain ethnic groups in the standardization of the WISC-R does not assure that the norms can be fairly applied to the members of those ethnic groups or others. The unique patterns exhibited by a certain cultural group will be lost in the total variance of the norming groups (Seyfort, Spreen, & Lahmer, 1980). Therefore, the minority groups effects will simply be averaged out over all the test scores and lost.

In general, Native children and young adults have exhibited a pattern of at least average Performance IQs and of significantly lower Verbal IQs. These results have been obtained by researchers working in different parts of Canada, and using Natives from different linguistic and indigenous peoples' groups. The groups have varied in the degree to which they have contact with White culture in that some children studied have lived in isolated settlements, others have attended integrated schools while living on their reserves, and still others were living in boarding home situations and attending school in large urban centers. Similar results to those of the three studies reported in detail above have been obtained by researchers spanning a half century of investigation of Native intelligence (Eells, Davis, Havighurst, Herrick, & Tyler, 1951; Havighurst, Gunther, & Pratt, 1946; Talford, 1932; Vernon, 1966).

A notable exception to this pattern was obtained by Rohrer (1942) who matched Natives and Whites for socioeconomic status, cultural opportunities, and comparable schooling, and found no differences in the IQs obtained. This finding suggests that the differences usually obtained may be artifacts of cultural differences as the Natives included in the study could be considered to have adopted the White culture (as opposed to being influenced by it or exposed to it). It may also be that the differences usually obtained are partially attributable to the socioeconomic disadvantages of Natives as compared to Whites.

There is obviously a need for an investigation along the lines of that conducted by Rohrer in 1942 to ensure that the results obtained can then be replicated in a modern day context. Such a study would serve to clarify the relationship of socioeconomic status and other potentially influential factors, to the IQ scores obtained by Natives. Without taking into account these kinds of factors, it is difficult to make statements about the underlying causes of the documented lower Verbal scores among Natives. However, since this result has been so consistently found, it must be considered as characteristic of the performance of Natives on standardized intelligence tests.

A Case in Point

For the past few years, the Ontario region of DIA has been funding an investigation into the use of standardized tests of intelligence with Native students. Funds for at least some of the testing costs have come from the Ontario Public School Teachers' Federation. One portion of the study was conducted in 1982 on two reserves, Caradoc and Oneida, by Scaldwell, Frame, and Cookson. Eighty-one children were included: 18 Oneida children and 63 Chippewa and Muncey children. Any conclusions one might wish to draw from this study about the functioning of Native children must be made with extreme caution due to the manner in which the sample was selected. While the Chippewa-Muncey group included all the children in the reserve school of testable age, the 18 Oneida children were the students who had been referred to their school's Special Education Committee because of learning difficulties. Therefore, 22% of the sample was comprised of children identified as having difficulties in school. This cannot be considered a random sample and the effects on the results can only be guessed. While Scaldwell, Frame, and Cookson state that the distribution of the group means was not different from each other, basic principles of experimental design have been violated in this study. The generalized statements about Native functioning made in the report have no validity due to the serious methodological error made in including a group of students who were known to function differently from the rest of their peers.

Scaldwell, Frame, and Cookson (1984) report a mean Verbal IQ of 92.18 (standard deviation = 13.87) and a Performance IQ of 105.07 (standard deviation = 12.16). This yields a Verbal-Performance difference of 12.89 points. Any discrepancy greater than 10 points between the scores for the two scales is considered significant (Wechsler, 1974). Therefore, the conclusion of the investigators that the WISC-R is appropriate because a Full Scale IQ of 97.98 (standard deviation = 12.34) was obtained, is not appropriate. Keeping in mind the flaws in sampling for this study, the Full Scale IQ masks a significant discrepancy between the Performance and Verbal Scales. Whether this pattern was obtained due to the inclusion of children with learning problems can not be determined.

Another portion of the ongoing DIA study into the assessment of Native children's intelligence was conducted by Scaldwell at Wikwemikong Un-ceded Indian Reserve in 1986. A sample of 47 children was randomly selected for the study. The WISC-R, Kaufman ABC (K-ABC), and Test of Nonverbal Intelligence-B (TONI-B) were all administered to the children. A mean WISC-R Verbal IQ of 86.69, mean Performance IQ of 109.55, and mean Full Scale IQ of 97.29 were obtained. The Performance-Verbal dis-crepancy is therefore 22.86 points, a highly significant difference. The per-formance of the Wikwemikong children on the Verbal subtests of Information, Similarities, Vocabulary, and Comprehension is significantly different from the norming population at the .001 level of confidence, with the Wikwemikong children obtaining lower scores on the subtests. On the Performance subtests of Block Design, Object Assembly, Coding, and Mazes, these children again showed a significant difference of .001 from the norms, but this time their scores were higher than the normative group. The Verbal and Performance Scale scores were both significantly different from the norms at the .001 level of confidence with the Verbal being lower and the Performance being higher.

Of the 18 subtests and scores reported for the K-ABC, there were signif-icant differences between the norming group and the Wikwemikong group on 13 and in all cases the Wikwemikong group scored lower. The levels of significance obtained for these differences ranged from .05 to .001, with five scores showing differences at a .001 level and two scores showing differences at the .005 level. This indicates that the children were unable to perform well on most aspects of this assessment and its use would be highly questionable for this group. The obtained mean IQ was 94.43.

The TONI-B yielded a mean IQ of 97.27 which is described by Scaldwell as being slightly below the mean of the normative group. The test results for the three scales used in the study are reported as being highly compa-rable in that the obtained scores are not significantly different from each other. Intercorrelations among the IQ scores obtained from the three tests were not reported. Unfortunately, a statistical comparison of the Perfor-mance Scale, WISC-R results, and the TONI-B results was not done. This would have been interesting because these scales supposedly measure the same general capabilities, yet the results were above average on the WISC-R Performance Scale and average on the TONI-B.

Scaldwell concludes that the WISC-R is the preferred instrument for use, with the Full Scale being a good estimate of general intelligence, and the Verbal Scale a good predictor of "academic prowess while in school." This position is considered unsupportable on two counts. The Full Scale score again masks the very wide range between the Verbal and Performance scales and as such blots out this group's unique style of functioning on the test. Second, Scaldwell has no basis for stating that the Verbal Scale is a good predictor of academic achievement because this study did not examine the relationship between the children's IQ scores and their achievement in school. St. John and Krichev (1976) found that neither the Verbal nor the Performance Scale of the WISC was a good predictor of academic achievement for Natives. Clearly, a thorough investigation must be made into the relationship between WISC-R scores and academic achievement before the WISC-R can be safely used as a predictor of "academic prowess."

Scaldwell's (1986) and Scaldwell, Frame, and Cookson's (1984) conclusions stand apart from those of other researchers who have investigated the assessment of Native intelligence. The discrepancies between Verbal and Performance Scales of the WISC-R found by Scaldwell follow the same pattern and are on the same order as those reported by others. These other researchers do not, however, conclude that the WISC-R is satisfactory for assessing Native children. Wilgosh, Mulcahy, and Watters (1986) stated that the Wechsler tests cannot assess the capabilities of children who are socially, culturally, and linguistically different from the children on whom the tests were originally normed. St. John and Krichev (1976) concluded that the Performance, Verbal, and Full Scale scores should be considered separately, because the use of the Full Scale score alone would likely lead to erroneous impressions of the child. Seyfort, Spreen, and Lahmer (1980) say that WISC-R results should be interpreted with caution. The WISC-R is not, therefore, generally regarded as a good instrument for measuring the intelligence of Native children, particularly if the WISC-R test norms are going to be applied to this culturally different group.

The review of the use of the WISC-R has shown that there is an obvious need to search for more appropriate and effective ways to assess the intelligence of Native students. The final section of the paper indicates areas of needed research in a move toward finding solutions to this complex problem.

A Contextualist Perspective on the Assessment of Native Intelligence

An important perspective on the performance of Native students on such tests of intelligence as the WISC-R is offered by Sternberg's (1984) contextualist view of intelligence whereby intelligence is considered in respect to the circumstances in which a given individual develops and operates. The contextualist view of intelligence then leads to a definition of intelligence. Tests developed and normed on the White population will reflect those skills and capabilities which are adaptive and relevant to the White culture and real-life situation. They will not necessarily be those which are adaptive and relevant to the Native way of life. Therefore, Native children being assessed with tests of intelligence developed for use with a culturally different group cannot necessarily be expected to have developed the skills being tested in the same manner or to the same degree.

That there are cultural differences between Natives and Whites has been documented over a period of some 380 years with current analyses of accounts from the 1600s taking on new perspectives (Hallowell, 1955). That these cultural differences have persisted has also been documented (Waltrous, 1949), although to a lesser extent in some families than in others (Red Horse, Lewis, Feit & Decker, 1978). Even when groups having a high degree of contact with Whites are compared to those having a low degree of contact, they are more similar to each other than different White groups tend to be to each other (Waltrous, 1949). Therefore, the assumptions of cultural similarity cannot be made between Whites and Natives.

In examining the typical Native Verbal-Performance discrepancy on the WISC-R, with respect to these cultural differences, the issue may be further clarified. Native parents tend to communicate with their children while performing tasks together and this communication usually does not go beyond the questions asked by the children. Further, the parents do not usually initiate the communication. Additionally, observations in Native homes have revealed that children are frequently found assisting with chores.

The implications for the development of a particular intellectual style are clear. Children in this type of situation will develop the ability to learn through observation and imitation. There is little use of language to communicate intent, expectations, and goals; rather, language is used minimally for clarification. A significant amount of time seems to be spent in this type of situation where there is little verbal communication, but undoubtedly a great deal of nonverbal communication occurring between parents and children. Performance-type skills, therefore, will likely be fostered to a greater degree than Verbal-type skills.

The influences of the experiential and performance contexts on the traditional Native culture from time immemorial have resulted in a unique pattern of intellectual competencies being developed. This pattern, which persists to this day, is at variance with the one which is evidenced in the White culture. Therefore, tests developed for the White culture cannot be considered appropriate for use with Natives.

Sternberg (1984) states that there is no evidence supporting differences in the anatomy or physiology of cognitive functioning between members of certain cultures or societies when compared to the members of others. Further, he states that there are probably no differences across cultures in cognitive processes, strategies, and other components of what he calls the software of cognitive functioning. It is the relative importance of various aspects of cognitive functioning which varies from culture to culture. Within any given culture, certain competencies are valued more than others, and individuals will develop these competencies in favor of others.

Therefore, the explanation of Natives' differential language functioning as a feature of a structural difference of their craniums, as has been recently offered by McShane, Risse, and Rubens (1984), is clearly inadequate in that it ignores this aspect of cultural influence on output.

Sternberg's theory of intelligence (1980) includes the metacomponents of what he believes are human universals. The particular forms that these metacomponents may take from culture to culture can be expected to vary widely in content. The metacomponents are:

1. recognizing the existence and nature of a problem;
2. deciding on the processes needed to solve the problem;
3. deciding on a strategy into which to combine these processes;
4. deciding on a mental representation on which the processes and strategy will act;
5. allocating processing resources in an efficacious way;
6. monitoring one's place in problem solving;
7. being sensitive to the nature and existence of feedback;
8. knowing what to do in response to this feedback;
9. actually acting on the feedback.

A given individual's ability to implement these metacomponents may be constrained by variables such as time, content, or size of the problem, or other forces in an individual's life which may prevent him or her from deploying his or her cognitive competencies in an optimal manner. These factors must be taken into consideration in the analysis of an individual's performance.

Neisser (1976) and Yussen and Kane (1984) have investigated the factors which individuals in the majority White culture of the United States consider to be indicative of intelligent behavior. Sternberg (1984) has classified the responses from these studies along with the results of his own as falling into three major categories: practical problem solving ability, verbal ability, and social competence. In the case of social competence, intelligent behavior is not reduced to the level of good manners or other equally superficial behaviors, but rather the intelligent individual is seen as one who can successfully interact with the people in his or her real-life situation and successfully achieve goals which necessitate communicating with and working with others.

Without similar studies having been conducted with Natives, it is difficult to speculate about the congruence that would be found between the two cultures on these factors. One might safely hypothesize that verbal skills are not as highly valued due to the profile that is typically found through psychometric evaluations of Native children and also due to the style of interaction, described above, between Native parents and children. Practical problem solving skills might receive more similar weightings across the cultures, again appealing to the same sources of information. However, an investigation of Native conceptions of intelligence would be required to clarify these issues.

Before the WISC-R or other tests of intelligence developed and normed within the White culture can be used with confidence with Native students, it must be demonstrated that the cognitive competencies being developed in children from the Native culture are the same and are equally weighted as those in the White culture. It is the contention of the writers that this cannot be demonstrated at this point in time. Therefore, the use of the WISC-R will result in incorrect and unfair assessments of Native children.

The renorming of tests as proposed by Wilgosh, Mulcahy, and Watters (1986) is one approach to the problem, but even they see this as not completely satisfactory. Instead of taking into consideration the uniqueness of children from the Native culture, this approach simply results in correcting superficially for the test bias, without making it congruent with the competencies of these children.

The extent to which Native children have been misclassified by the use of the WISC-R and other assessments in the school system over the years that such testing has been done can only be estimated, but it probably has been extensive. With the kinds of Verbal-Performance discrepancies found in the Native population, the application of the Full Scale norms indiscriminately, even when they "average out" to values close to that obtained by Whites, will not result in a fair appraisal of these children's abilities.

Ideally, basic research should be conducted into the components of Native intelligence and the forms this intelligence takes in terms of Sternberg's nine metacomponents. Once this kind of information is made available, a decision could be made as to which of the tests of intelligence, or portions of tests, available from any source are appropriate for assessing Native children. When one takes a contextualist view of intelligence, one would have to concede that it would be quite likely that no existing tests from the White culture could be demonstrated as sufficiently relevant to the Native culture for use. The logical course of action would be to construct a new test of intelligence for use with Natives that would be valid and reliable and would have good predictive ability for real-life performance of the individuals within the Native culture.

While the position of abandoning intellectual assessment for Natives altogether may be appealing, the reality of the school system as it stands today is that students are and will be assessed for their intellectual capabilities. Decisions which will have life long consequences will be made on the basis of the test results. If the ideal courses of action described above cannot be realized, then it behooves educators, psychologists, administrators, and any other persons involved in decisions about Native students based on tests of intelligence to make every effort to account for the test bias in these tests. Because these tests are often involved in placement decisions for students entering special education, consider the difference a low Verbal Score, which is 20 or 30 points below that usually obtained by a White child but which is average for a Native child, could make in the way a Native child is classified. It could make the difference between being classified as mentally deficient or normal, mentally deficient or learning disabled, gifted or average, and as such could lead to the placement of children in special education programs which are not appropriate for their needs. In the case of gifted Native students, it could mean no access to differential programming beyond that provided by the regular classroom teacher. In a school system and a society which values individual differences and, by implication, cultural differences, the misclassification of children due to those same cultural differences is an injustice.

Note

1   Corbiere, E. (1986). Personal communication. Principal, Pontiac School, Wikwemikong Unceded Indian Reserve.

Reference

Eells, K., Davis, A., Havighurst, R.J., Herrick, V., & Tyler, R.W. (1951). *Intelligence and cultural difference—A study of cultural learning and problem solving.* Chicago, IL: University of Chicago Press.

Gould, S.J. (1981). *The mismeasure of man.* New York, NY: Norton.

Hallowell, A.I. (1955). *Culture and experience.* New York, NY: Harcourt Brace.

Havighurst, R.J., Gunther, M.K., & Pratt, I.E. (1946). Environment and the Draw-A-Man Test; the performance of Indian children. *Journal of Abnormal and Social Psychology, 41,* 50-63.

McLuhan, T.C. (1971). *Touch the earth.* Toronto, ON: New Press.

McShane, D.A. (1983). Neurocranial form: Differentiating four ethnic populations using a simple CT scan measure. *International Journal of Neuroscience, 21,* 137-144.

McShane, D.A. (1984). Differences in cerebral asymmetries related to drinking history and ethnicity. *The Journal of Nervous and Mental Disease, 172,* 529-532.

McShane, D.A., Risse, G.L., & Rubens, A.B. (1984). Cerebral asymmetries on CT scan in three ethnic groups. *International Journal of Neuroscience, 23,* 69-74.

Neisser, U. (1976). *Cognition and reality: Principles and implications for cognitive psychology.* San Francisco, CA: Freeman.

Red Horse, J.G., Lewis, R., Feit, M., & Decker, J. (1978). *Family behavior of urban American Indians.* National Centre on Child Abuse and Neglect, Children's Bureau, OCD, OHD, DHEW, Grant No. 90-C624.

Rohrer, J. (1942). The test intelligence of Osage Indians. *Journal of Social Psychology, 16,* 99-105.

St. John, J., & Krichev, A. (1976). Northwestern Ontario Indian children and the WISC. *Psychology in the Schools, 13*, 4.

Scaldwell, W.A. (1986). *WISC-R, Kaufman ABC, and TONI results Wikwemikong, 1985-86.* Government of Canada: Department of Indian Affairs and Northern Development.

Scaldwell, W.A., Frame, J.E., & Cookson, D.G. (1984). *Individual intellectual assessment of Chippewa, Muncey and Oneida children using the WISC-R.* Government of Canada: Department of Indian Affairs and Northern Development.

Seyfort, B., Spreen, O., & Lahmer, V. (1980). A critical look at the WISC-R with Native Indian children. *The Alberta Journal of Educational Research, 26*, 14-24.

Special Education Handbook. (1986). Government of Canada: Department of Indian Affairs and Northern Development, Ontario Region.

Sternberg, R.J. (1980). Sketch of a componential subtheory of human intelligence. *Behavioral and Brain Sciences, 3*, 573-584.

Sternberg, R.J. (1984). A contextualist view of the nature of intelligence. *International Journal of Psychology, 19*, 307-334.

Talford, C.W. (1932). Test performance of full and mixed-blood North Dakota Indians. *Journal of Comparative Psychology, 14*, 139-148.

Vernon, P.E. (1966). Educational and intellectual development among Canadian Indians and Eskimos. Parts 1, 2. *Educational Review, 18*, 79-91, 186-196.

Waltrous, B. (1949). *A personality study of Ojibwa children.* Unpublished doctoral dissertation, Northwestern University, Evanston, IL.

Wechsler, D. (1974). *Manual: Wechsler Intelligence Scale for Children—Revised.* New York, NY: Psychological Corporation.

Wilgosh, L., Mulcahy, R., & Watters, B. (1986). Assessing intellectual performance of culturally different Inuit children with the WISC-R. *Canadian Journal of Behavioural Science, 18*, 270-277.

Yussen, S.R., & Kane, P. (1984). Children's concept of intelligence. In S.R. Yussen (Ed.), *The growth of insight in children.* New York, NY: Academic Press.

Evaluation of Student Achievement: Teacher Practices and Educational Measurement

John O. Anderson
University of Victoria

The evaluation of student achievement is a characteristic element of formal classroom education. Educational measurement addresses issues of and develops procedures for student evaluation. Recently there has been an increase in expressed interest in the relationship between educational measurement and the classroom practices used in evaluating student achievement (Stiggins, 1988). Questions have been raised as to the utility of procedures developed through educational measurement to teaching and learning. There appears to be a disparity between the science of measurement and the craft of evaluation as practiced in classrooms.

This study attempted to shed some light on classroom evaluation practices by considering whether testing is a common classroom practice, what kinds of student abilities or characteristics should be measured, what methods are used to collect this information, and what is the extent to which external sources of instrumentation or data are of interest to teachers. The 1986 British Columbia Provincial Science Assessment (Bateson, Anderson, Dale, McConnell, & Rutherford, 1986) provided data that could address these issues. This study reports the data derived from the teacher questionnaires in regard to the student evaluation practices and attitudes of science teachers in British Columbia and discusses some implications for the improvement of applied educational measurement.

*   *   *

THE EVALUATION OF STUDENT ACHIEVEMENT IS A CHARACTERISTIC ELEMENT of formal classroom education. Tests, assignments, and projects are developed, administered, and marked by teachers in order to generate information about the achievement of individual students. Educational measurement is a field of development and research which addresses issues of and develops procedures for the evaluation of student achievement. These issues include test reliability, validity, standard error of measurement, item bias, test equating, and models underlying response data. A large number of formalized procedures have been developed for test design and construction, item analysis, test scoring and analysis, and standard setting.

The relationship between educational measurement and classroom practice should be one of utility: Educational measurement should produce information and procedures which are useful in the evaluation of student achievement. Recently there has been an increase in expressed interest in the relationship between educational measurement and the classroom practices used in evaluating student achievement (Stiggins, 1988). Questions have been raised as to the utility of procedures developed through educational measurement to teaching and learning. There appears to be a disparity between the science of measurement and the craft of evaluation as practiced in classrooms.

Stiggins, Conklin, and Bridgeford (1986) noted in their extensive review of the literature on classroom assessment that the dominant paradigm in educational measurement is based on data generated from standardized paper-pencil tests used for the purposes of accountability. This focus of educational measurement is well illustrated in a recent description of the future of testing (Rudman, 1987). The article concentrates solely on published, standardized tests and does not mention the development and use of classroom tests by teachers. In contrast, Gullickson (1986) notes in his American study of teacher-perceived needs in measurement that teachers would favor more emphasis on the use of nontest methodologies including rating scales, observation, and anecdotal records. Teacher interest in measurement is directed toward a variety of instruments and procedures developed for instructional purposes and not toward the issues and procedures of mainstream educational measurement research and literature.

As a specific example of the disparity between measurement and instruction, consider a recent critique of the reporting of results of the National Assessment for Educational Progress (NAFP) project in the United States (McLean & Goldstein, 1988). It was noted that, after a great deal of complex analysis involving large data sets collected over several years, NAEP was able to report reading results on a single scale. McLean and Goldstein point out that this modeling of reading ability as a single trait does not coincide with conceptions of reading abilities that are current among those involved in the teaching of reading. The measurement project (NAEP) produced results that are meaningful within the measurement perspective of unidimensional human traits, but this perspective does not fit the multidimensional view of those involved in the study and teaching of reading.

Although the focus of educational measurement is on large-scale testing projects and standardized tests, it appears that most of the achievement testing done is in classrooms by teachers as part of ongoing evaluation of student achievement. An estimate of the number of tests a student completes during an academic career was provided by the results of a questionnaire administered by the author in the fall of 1987 to a group of 92 fourth- and fifth-year University of Victoria students in an educational measurement course. The students were asked, "How many formal tests or examinations (those counting for grades) would you estimate you have taken in your life?" The median response range was 500 to 600 such tests. The vast majority of these tests would not be standardized tests but rather tests developed by classroom teachers. In British Columbia, for example, a province that does have a provincial grade 12 examination program, a grade 12 scholarship exam program, and a provincial learning assessment program, most students continuing through to postsecondary levels would write fewer than 20 such tests in their public school (K to 12) career. It is likely, then, that most tests a student encounters are developed by classroom teachers to assess student achievement in specific instructional programs.

The purpose of this study was to explore a facet of the relationship between educational measurement and the evaluation of student achievement. Because it appears that most of the testing to which students are exposed over their educational careers consists of procedures and instruments developed by classroom teachers to assess student performance in instructional programs, a first step in exploring the utility of educational measurement is to investigate what goes on in the classroom. This could lead to the determination and perhaps the improvement of the fit between educational measurement and classroom practice.

This study attempted to shed some light on classroom evaluation practices by considering whether testing is a common classroom practice, what kinds of student abilities or characteristics should be measured, what methods are used to collect this information, and what is the extent to which external sources of instrumentation or data are of interest to teachers. The 1986 British Columbia Provincial Science Assessment (Bateson, Anderson, Dale, McConnell, & Rutherford, 1986) provided data that could address these issues. The 1986 British Columbia Science Assessment investigated the current state of science education in the province through the administration of achievement measures and attitude scales to all students in grades 4, 7, and 10, and the administration of questionnaires to all teachers of grades 4, 7, and 10 science. Data collection took place in the spring of 1986.

The teacher questionnaires focused on classroom practices and teacher attitudes toward various aspects of their teaching: teacher background and general information, coordination of science education, physical facilities, materials and equipment, science teaching, assessment and evaluation, and the science program. The grade 10 questionnaire contained 56 items. Grades 4 and 7 teachers were administered identical 34-item questionnaires.

This study reports the data derived from the teacher questionnaires in regard to the student evaluation practices and attitudes of science teachers in British Columbia. In total 1,895 grade 4 teachers, 1,519 grade 7 teachers, and 1,035 grade 10 teachers responded to the questionnaire. The grades 4 and 7 teachers were essentially classroom teachers, teaching science to their homeroom class in addition to teaching a broad range of other subjects to these students. Grade 10 students tended to be specifically assigned to teaching science (Bateson et al., 1986).

These data provide a start for a study of teachers' practices in and attitudes toward student evaluation. It is in this light that this article has been prepared. It is not to be inferred that these data fully answer the questions posed. However, the responses to the limited number of questionnaire items by science teachers in British Columbia suggest directions the answers would take if a broader sample of teachers were asked a broader sample of questions and if a more comprehensive set of methodologies were employed.

Results

In responding to the question: "Is testing a common classroom practice?" teachers of grades 4 and 7 science were asked to indicate how often 10 classroom activities were carried out in a typical week. The results (Table 1) indicate that, of those activities listed, testing was the most frequent

Table 1
Science Program — Activities in the Classroom
Grades 4 and 7

Item	Percentage of Teachers							
	Grade 4				Grade 7			
In a typical week of science classes, how often did you do the following?	A	O	S	N	A	O	S	N[1]
Carried out experiment for students	1	10	77	12	0	11	73	16
Handed out notes	1	12	52	35	0	13	56	31
Wrote out notes for students	2	22	60	16	2	23	62	13
Students conducted experiments individually	2	16	70	12	2	22	66	10
Students conducted experiments in small groups	2	19	64	15	2	31	55	12
Students used computer	0	2	15	83	0	3	19	77
Students used library books	5	25	67	3	2	14	76	9
Students chose topics to study	2	3	52	44	0	6	46	48
Students did homework	2	13	74	12	6	35	56	3
Students were tested	36	33	30	1	39	36	24	0

[1] A = Always, O = Often, S = Sometimes, N = Never

Table 2
Assessment and Testing — Curricular Goals Emphasis
Grade 10

Item	Percentage of Teachers
In the determination of the final grade, what emphasis should be placed on the following science goal areas?	
Attitudes	
0%	22
10%	56
20%	19
30%	2
40%	1
50%	0
60%	0
Skills and Processes	
0%	1
10%	10
20%	31
30%	44
40%	12
50%	3
60%	0
Knowledge	
0%	0
10%	1
20%	8
30%	23
40%	28
50%	22
60%	19
Critical Thinking	
0%	1
10%	22
20%	46
30%	23
40%	6
50%	1
60%	1

classroom activity, with approximately 70% of teachers reporting that students were tested "Always" or "Often" each week. Testing was a more frequent classroom activity than conducting science demonstrations or student experiments, using the computer, or doing homework. The pattern of responses was similar for both grades 4 and 7 teachers.

To answer the question of whether testing is a characteristic activity of the classroom, it is clear that testing is a common classroom activity.

In considering what kinds of student abilities or characteristics should be measured, grade 10 teachers were asked about the extent to which each of the four science goal areas—Attitude, Skills and Processes, Knowledge, and Critical Thinking (Ministry of Education, 1981)—should be tested in the determination of student achievement. In general, teachers indicated that all four areas should be tapped for student evaluation purposes.

Attitudes were considered to require less emphasis than the other areas, with over one-fifth of the teachers indicating that Attitudes should not be used at all in evaluating students. A majority of teachers (56%) indicated that Attitudes should count for 10% of the final grade. Essentially all teach-

Table 3
Assessment and Testing—Source of Assessment Data
Grades 4 and 7

Item	Percentage of Teachers							
	Grade 4				Grade 7			
What emphasis do you place on each of the below in deriving a final grade for a student in your science class?	N	L	S	M	N	L	S	M[1]
Anecdotal records	7	24	58	11	16	32	46	6
Teacher-made objective tests	1	3	48	48	0	2	43	54
Ministry of Education Classroom Achievement Tests	62	22	15	1	58	22	18	1
Subjective tests	14	22	58	7	9	23	58	10
Activity/experiment write-up	5	16	62	16	4	11	58	27
Individual work contracts	53	13	28	7	54	15	24	8
Reports on topics in science	6	15	68	11	6	17	64	14
Projects	4	9	70	17	4	14	64	19
Oral tests	35	28	33	5	47	31	20	2
Student self-reports	52	21	22	5	54	21	23	2
Attendance	67	13	14	6	67	17	9	6

[1] N = No emphasis, L = Little emphasis, S = Some emphasis, M = Much emphasis

ers indicated that Skills and Processes, Knowledge, and Critical Thinking should receive emphasis in the determination of a science student's final grade. The response modes were Skills and Processes, 30% emphasis; Knowledge, 40% emphasis; and Critical Thinking, 20% emphasis. In summary, science teachers regard a number of different student skills and characteristics to be of importance for evaluation purposes. The weighting applied to the skills and characteristics varied from one category to another with Knowledge receiving the heaviest weighting and Attitudes the least.

Science teachers were asked about the methods they used for evaluating student achievement. A number of common instruments and procedures were listed and the teachers were asked to indicate the emphasis they placed on each for student evaluation purposes. Table 3 lists the response frequencies for grades 4 and 7 teachers in relation to types of methods used to collect information about student achievement. Table 4 lists the response frequencies for grade 10 teachers.

Two trends emerge. First, teachers used a wide variety of methods to collect information related to student achievement: anecdotal records, sub-

Table 4 Assessment and Testing — Source of Assessment Data Grade 10			
Item	Percentage of Teachers		
How much importance do you place on each of the following in deriving final student evaluation?	Very Important	Important	Not Important
Anecdotal records			
– achievement	19	39	41
– general attitude	4	48	48
– work habits	8	63	29
Teacher-made objective tests	71	28	1
Standardized objective tests	14	43	43
Subjective tests	30	56	14
Laboratory write-ups	37	59	3
Individual work contracts	6	21	72
Reports on topics	17	64	20
Projects	17	61	22
Oral tests	4	26	70
Student self-reports	3	23	75
Attendance	17	50	33
Classroom behavior	15	43	42

jective tests, experiment write-ups, reports, and projects. Second, in all grades, teacher-made objective tests received the most emphasis (and presumably use) in the determination of student achievement. The Ministry of Education Classroom Tests, individual work contracts, oral tests, and student self-reports appear to be the least emphasized forms of assessing student achievement. The majority of grades 4 and 7 teachers (67%) did not use attendance for the determination of final grades. Yet most grade 10 teachers (67%) consider attendance to have at least some importance in the determination of a student's final grade.

In summary, teachers do not rely on a single source of data for evaluating student achievement. They use a variety of methods to measure stu-

Table 5 Assessment and Testing — Instrumentation for Student Grade Grade 10	
Item	Percentage of Teachers
Would you like to have student assessment based on ...	
schoolwide exam?	
No	21
Yes, about 10%	8
Yes, about 20%	50
Yes, about 30%	13
Yes, about 40%	4
Yes, about 50%	4
districtwide exam?	
No	75
Yes, about 10%	10
Yes, about 20%	12
Yes, about 30%	2
Yes, about 40%	0
Yes, about 50%	2
provincial exam?	
No	77
Yes, about 10%	6
Yes, about 20%	9
Yes, about 30%	5
Yes, about 40%	1
Yes, about 50%	3

dent performance with teacher-made objective tests receiving the most emphasis of those methods presented.

Grade 10 teachers were asked about their preferences for using school, district, or provincial examinations for evaluation of student achievement. The questions were asked in order to gauge teacher interest in and possible use of external sources of instrumentation. Teachers were asked the extent to which these various tests should "count" toward a student's final grade (Table 5). There was considerable support for the use of a schoolwide exam. A majority of teachers (79%) thought that student assessment should include the results of a schoolwide test counting for 20% or 30% of the final mark. However, 21% of teachers indicated that a schoolwide exam should not be used at all. In regard to the use of district or provincial exams, approximately 75% of grade 10 science teachers indicated that they would not like to base student assessment on districtwide or provincial exams. It appears that teachers did not favor the use of either district or provincial level tests for student evaluation purposes. It should be noted that a teacher would likely have direct involvement with the development of a school exam, whereas the opportunity for direct involvement is somewhat less for a district exam and almost nil for a provincial exam.

Teachers of grades 4 and 7 science were asked whether they had read any of the reports of the previous Provincial Science Assessment (Taylor, 1982) in order to estimate their interest in external sources of data related to student achievement in science (Table 6). Reports had been produced at the provincial and district levels; no school or class level reports were produced in this provincial assessment. Most teachers (approximately 70% or more) indicated that they had not read any of the reports produced.

Table 6
Assessment and Testing—
Utilization of 1982 Science Assessment Results
Grades 4 and 7

Item	Percentage of Teachers Responding *Yes*	
	Grade 4	Grade 7
Have you read the following publications of the 1982 Provincial Science Assessment?		
District Interpretation Report	25	32
Provincial Update flier	15	21
Provincial Summary Report	25	32
Provincial General Report	17	22

These results suggest that external sources of data, in this case from a provincewide assessment of student performance in the subject they are teaching, are not of great interest or importance to teachers.

In regard to the question of teacher use of external testing, the data presented here indicate that science teachers do not view positively the use of external testing for student evaluation. Nor do they have much interest in the data gathered from large-scale assessments.

Discussion

The results suggest that testing is a common classroom activity and that there is substantial variation in the methods and formats used to estimate student achievement. Teacher-made objective tests are the most common form of instrumentation in use, although many other formats for data generation and collection are used by science teachers in British Columbia. Teachers believe that student achievement should be evaluated in a number of different domains: attitudes, knowledge, and skills. Further, teachers are not interested in the use of external forms of testing, either as instrumentation or as the results of large-scale assessment, even in a subject they are currently teaching.

The results pertaining to teacher test use are not surprising. In an earlier study of a broad sample of Ontario teachers (Wahlstrom & Danley, 1976), it was found that teachers used a variety of methods in measuring student achievement and preferred to use instruments they developed themselves. However, Wahlstrom and Danley found that the preferred assessment technique of Ontario elementary teachers was observation of classroom work by the teacher, whereas secondary teachers prefer tests. These findings were similar to a recent American study (Stiggins & Bridgeford, 1985) which also found variation in preferences for student evaluation procedures by teachers across subject areas as well as across grade levels.

The pervasiveness of testing in the classroom coupled with the use of a wide variety of formats to measure different kinds of student achievement does raise a number of important issues in regard to the relationship between educational measurement and teacher practices in classroom assessment. To illustrate, consider one such issue: the combining of scores from different sources to arrive at a final grade. How do teachers combine the scores from a number of different testing formats when testing a number of different student abilities and characteristics collected over a period of time? Certainly the scores are combined, but how and with what effect? It is likely the task is conducted by simply summing up the numbers and assigning grades to these numbers. It would be of interest and utility to investigate the procedures actually employed in order to determine their consequences and the consistency of implementation within and between classrooms. Nagy, Traub, and MacRury (1986) have described methods for research into the procedures used by teachers in determining letter grades (standard setting). A description of these procedures and patterns of implementation would also illuminate some of the practices used by teachers, not only in the combining of scores to convert to grades, but also the attitudes of teachers toward achievement, and an estimate of the variability of achievement standards. A number of such studies are in progress (MacRury, 1988; Traub, 1988; Wilson & Rees, in press).

However, it is of concern that there is a widespread practice in student assessment that is not well addressed by educational measurement. It appears that there is a substantial practice of combining test data from various sources, but the issue is largely ignored in the literature. On the basis of an informal review of educational measurement textbooks and journals by the writer and as also noted by Stiggins et al. (1986), the literature focuses on single-test situations, that is, the development, administration, and analysis of a single test (or set of tests) as a discrete project. The most common manifestations of the single-test situation in schools are final examinations, assessment programs (such as the one from which the data of this study were derived), and standardized test programs—areas that are of importance educationally and lend themselves to systematic research and development, but are of little interest or use to the classroom teacher (Table 6). Yet it is likely that for most teachers the measurement practices employed in the classroom are derived from personal experience both as teachers and as students, and from techniques garnered from colleagues. These classroom practices would form the basis of "the craft of evaluation" (McLean, 1985), and would not necessarily coincide with practices derived from the science of measurement and its literature.

Assuming that most of the achievement testing being done in Canada is that done by teachers in classrooms, it appears that this practice could be better served by research. The apparent isolation of classroom testing practice from research activity is a problem that should be addressed to improve overall educational practice. The determination and description of the measurement practices in current use and the extent of variation in practice could lead to the development of better techniques for handling the data generated by classroom measurement practices and the generation of better data by classroom measurement. Because classroom derived technique predominates in testing and student evaluation practices, applied educational measurement should center its attention on the classroom.

References

Bateson, D.J., Anderson, J.O., Dale, T., McConnell, V., & Rutherford, C. (1986). *The 1986 British Columbia science assessment: General report.* Victoria, BC: British Columbia Ministry of Education.

Gullickson, A.R. (1986). Teacher education and teacher-perceived needs in educational measurement and evaluation. *Journal of Educational Measurement, 23*, 347-354.

MacRury, K. (1988). *Assigning course grades: Policies and practices*. Paper presented to the annual meeting of the National Council on Measurement in Education, New Orleans, LA.

McLean, L.D. (1985). *The craft of student evaluation in Canada*. Toronto, ON: Canadian Education Association.

McLean, L.D., & Goldstein, H. (1988). The U.S. national assessments in reading: Reading too much into the findings. *Phi Delta Kappan, 65*, 369-372.

Ministry of Education. (1981). *Elementary science curriculum guide: Grades 1-7*. Victoria, BC: British Columbia Ministry of Education.

Nagy, P. (1988). *The content basis of teaching and testing in mathematics*. Paper presented at the annual meeting of the National Council on Measurement in Education, New Orleans, LA.

Nagy, P., Traub, R.E., & MacRury, K. (1986). *Strategies for evaluating the impact of province wide testing*. Toronto, ON: Ontario Ministry of Education.

Rudman, H.C. (1987). The future of testing is now. *Educational Measurement: Issues and Practices, 6*(3), 5-11.

Stiggins, R.J. (1988). Revitalizing classroom assessment: The highest instructional priority. *Phi Delta Kappan, 65*, 363-368.

Stiggins, R.J., & Bridgeford, N.J. (1985). The ecology of classroom assessment. *Journal of Educational Measurement, 22*, 271-286.

Stiggins, R.J., Conklin, N.F., & Bridgeford, N.J. (1986). Classroom assessment: A key to effective education. *Educational Measurement: Issues and Practices 5*(2), 5-17.

Taylor, H. (1982). *The 1982 British Columbia science assessment: General report*. Victoria, BC: British Columbia Ministry of Education.

Traub, R.E. (1988). *A study of the marking process: Calculus teacher responses to a common marking task*. Paper presented to the annual meeting of the National Council on Measurement in Education, New Orleans, LA.

Wahlstrom, M.W., & Danley, R.R. (1976). *Assessment of student achievement*. Toronto, ON: Ontario Ministry of Education.

Wilson, R.J., & Rees, R. (in press). The ecology of evaluation: Measurement and evaluation within an administrative framework. *Canadian Journal of Education*.

Sources

Violato, C., & Travis, L.D. (1990). A national survey of education students: Some data on background, habits, and reasons for entering education. *Canadian Journal of Education, 15(3)*, 277-292. Reprinted by permission.

Murray, H.G., Rushton, J.P., & Paunonen, S.V. (1990). Teacher personality traits and student instructional ratings in six types of university courses. *Journal of Educational Psychology, 82(2)*, 250-261. Copyright © 1990 by the American Psychological Association. Reprinted by permission.

Byrne, B.M. (1991). Burnout: Investigating the impact of background variables for elementary, intermediate, secondary, and university teachers. *Teacher and Teacher Education, 7*, 197-209. Copyright © 1991 Pergamon Press Ltd. Reprinted by permission.

Markovits, H., Schleifer, M., & Fortier, L. (1989). Development of elementary deductive reasoning in young children. *Developmental Psychology, 25(5)*, 787-793. Copyright © 1989 by the American Psychological Association. Reprinted by permission.

Moore, C., Bryant, D., & Furrow, D. (1989). Mental terms and the development of certainty. *Child Development, 60*, 167-171. Reprinted by permission.

Gebotys, R.J., & Cupchik, G.C. (1989). Perception and production in children's art. *Visual Arts Research, 15(1)*, 55-67. Reprinted by permission.

Pancer, S.M., & Weinstein, S.M. (1987). The development of affective skills in school-aged children. *Journal of Applied Developmental Psychology, 8*, 165-181. Reprinted by permission od authors.

Serbin, L.A., & Sprafkin, C. (1986). The salience of gender and the process of sex-typing in three- to six-year-old children. *Child Development, 57*, 1188-1199. Reprinted by permission.

Andrews, L. & Kozma, A. (1990). Increasing teacher praise and altering its distribution to children of differing on-task levels. *Canadian Journal of Behavioural Science, 22(2)*, 110-120. Copyright © 1990 Canadian Psychological Association. Reprinted by permission.

Partridge, M.J., Gehlback, R.D., & Marx, R.W. (1987). Social Contingencies, physical environment, and prosocial behavior in children's play. *Journal of Research and Development in Education, 20(4)*, 25-29. Reprinted by permission.

Hope, J.A., & Sherrill, J.M. (1987). Characteristics of Skilled and Unskilled Mental Calculators. *Journal for Research in Mathematics Education, 18(2)*, 98-111.

Kobasigawa, A., Chouinard, M.A., & Dufresne, A. (1988). Characteristics of study notes prepared by elementary school children: Relevancy and efficiency. *Alberta Journal of Educational Research, 34(1)*, 18-29.

Pressley, M., & Brewster, M.E. (1990). Imaginal elaboration of illustrations to facilitate fact learning: Creating memories of Prince Edward Island. *Applied Cognitive Psychology, 4*, 359-369.

Kloster, A.M., & Winne, P.H. (1989). The effects of different types of organizers on students learning from text. *Journal of Educational Psychology, 81(1)*, 9-15. Copyright © 1989 by the American Psychological Association. Reprinted by permission.

Jamieson, D.W., Lydon, J.E., Stewart, G., & Zanna, M.P. (1987). Pygmalion revisited: New evidence for student expectancy effects in the classroom, *Journal of Educational Psychology, 79(4)*, 461-466. Copyright © 1987 by the American Psychological Association. Reprinted by permission.

Chambers, B., & Abrami, P.C. (1991). The relationship between student team learning outcomes and achievement, causal relations, and affect. *Journal of Educational Psychology, 83(1)*, 140-146. Copyright © 1991 by the American Psychological Association. Reprinted by permission.

Perry, R.P., & Penner, K.S. (1990). Enhancing academic achievement in college students through attributional retraining and instruction. *Journal of Educational Psychology, 82(2)*, 262-271. Copyright © 1990 by the American Psychological Association. Reprinted by permission.

Haggerty, S.M. (1991). Gender and school science: Achievement and participation in Canada. *Alberta Journal of Educational Research, 38(3)*, 195-208.

Staab, C.F. (1991). Teachers' practices with regard to oral language. *Alberta Journal of Educational Research, 38(1)*, 31-48.

Netten, J.E., & Spain, W.H. (1989). Student-teacher interaction patterns in the French immersion classroom: Implications for levels of achievement in French language proficiency. *Canadian Modern Language Review, 45(3)*, 485-501.

Crocker, R.K., & Brooker, G.M. (1986). Classroom control and student outcomes in grades 2 and 5. *American Educational Research Journal, 23(1)*, 1-11. Copyright © 1986 by the American Educational Research Association. Reprinted by permission of the publisher.

Barnes, M.J., & McCabe, A.E. (1986). The academic slipstream: Diversity within secondary school classrooms. *Teacher Education, 29*, 5-17. Reprinted by permission.

Spencer, F., Snart, F., & Das, J.P. (1989). A process-based approach to the remediation of spelling in students with reading disabilities. *Alberta Journal of Educational Research, 35(4)*, 269-282.

King, S.M., Rosenbaum, P., Armstrong, R.W., & Milner, R. (1989). An epidemiological study of children's attitudes toward disability. *Developmental Medicine and Child Neurology, 31*, 237-245. Copyright © 1989 MacKeith Press. Reprinted by permission.

Schneider, B.H., Clegg, M.R., Byrne, B.M., Ledingham, J.E., & Crombie, G. (1989). Social relations of gifted children as a function of age and school program. *Journal of Educational Psychology, 81(1)*, 48-56. Copyright © 1989 by the American Psychological Association. Reprinted by permission.

Day, E.M., & Shapson, S. (1988). A comparison study of early and late French immersion programs in British Columbia. *Canadian Journal of Education, 13(2)*, 290-305. Reprinted by permission.

Laing, D. (1988). A comparative study of the writing abilities of English-speaking grade 8 students in French-speaking schools. *Canadian Journal of Education, 13(2)*, 306-324. Reprinted by permission.

Swain, M., & Lapkin, S. (1991). Heritage language children in an English-French bilingual program. *Canadian Modern Language Review, 47(4)*, 635-641. Reprinted by permission.

Landry, R., Allard, R., & Théberge, R. (1991). School and family French ambience and the bilingual development of francophone western Canadians. *Canadian Modern Language Review, 47(5)*, 879-915. Reprinted by permission.

Braun, C., Rennie, B.J., & Gordon, C.J. (1987). An examination of contexts for reading assessment. *Journal of Educational Research, 80(5)*, 283-289. Reprinted by permission.

Common, R.W., & Frost, L.G. (1988). The implications of the mismeasurement of Native students' intelligence through the use of standardized intelligence tests. *Canadian Journal of Native Education, 15(1)*, 18-30.

Anderson, J.O. (1989). Evaluation and student achievement: Teacher practices and educational measurement. *Alberta Journal of Educational Research, 35(2)*, 123-133.

$2995

Printed in Canada